Exploring Intercultural Competence in Education

A Guide for Pre-Service Teachers

CUSTOM EDITION

Taken From:
*Understanding Human Differences: Multicultural Education
for a Diverse America,* Third Edition by
Kent L. Koppelman with R. Lee Goodhart

*Affirming Diversity: The Sociopolitical Context
of Multicultural Education*, Fifth Edition by
Sonia Nieto and Patty Bode

Foreword by Gregory P. Meyjes, Kennesaw State University

Learning Solutions

New York   Boston   San Francisco
London   Toronto   Sydney   Tokyo   Singapore   Madrid
Mexico City   Munich   Paris   Cape Town   Hong Kong   Montreal

Northwest State Community College

Cover Art: Courtesy of DigitalVision, Purestock, Stockbyte, Eyewire/Getty Images

Excerpts taken from:

Understanding Human Differences: Multicultural Education for a Diverse America, Third Edition
by Kent L. Koppelman with R. Lee Goodhart
Copyright © 2011, 2008, 2005 by Pearson Education, Inc.
Published by Allyn & Bacon
Upper Saddle River, New Jersey 07458

Affirming Diversity: The Sociopolitical Context of Multicultural Education, Fifth Edition
by Sonia Nieto and Patty Bode
Copyright © 2008, 2004, 2000, 1996, 1992 by Pearson Education, Inc.
Published by Allyn & Bacon
Upper Saddle River, New Jersey 07458

Pearson Learning Solutions, 501 Boylston Street, Suite 900, Boston, MA 02116
A Pearson Education Company
www.pearsoned.com

Printed in the United States of America

1 2 3 4 5 6 7 8 9 10 V3DZ 15 14 13 12 11 10

000200010270586715

BW

ISBN 10: 0-558-77742-2
ISBN 13: 978-0-558-77742-5

Contents

CHAPTER 6   Religion and Oppression: The Struggle for Religious Freedom   140

Taken from *Affirming Diversity: The Sociopolitical Context of Multicultural Education,* Fifth Edition by
Sonia Nieto and Patty Bode

CHAPTER 11

Taken from *Understanding Human Differences: Multicultural Education for a Diverse America,*
Third Edition by Kent L. Koppelman with R. Lee Goodhart

CHAPTER 14   **Pluralism in Schools: The Promise of Multicultural Education 392**

Foreword

Those aspiring to enter the teaching profession have been calling *"Exploring Sociocultural Perspectives on Diversity in Educational Contexts"* (EDUC 2120) one of the most significant courses of their college careers. This comes as no surprise to members of the Inclusive Education Department at Kennesaw State University. Participation in this course is liable to be as fascinating as it is mind-stretching. In large part, this is due to the considerable gap between, on the one hand, the sway culture holds over our lives and, on the other, the reality that even educated people tend to be unaware of the impact of culture on human affairs. Mandated by the State of Georgia, EDUC 2120 is designed to explore this very gap, however extensive. In order for course participants to become effective educators in today's highly intercultural society, it is essential that cultural matters be addressed, that cross-cultural dynamics be understood, and that intercultural skills be developed.

Regardless of the talent, caring, intelligence, interest, or worldview of teachers, they are first and foremost individuals, bound and limited by their own culturally-informed, largely subconscious perspectives. As professionals, however, they are called to inspire students from wide-ranging backgrounds, to guide discovery of our shrinking world, and to help those who will inherit it to develop the competencies of success in our heterogeneous local, regional, national, and global society. Given the largely hidden impact of culture, how can aspiring educators develop the necessary competencies without gaining awareness of their own cultural programming? How are they to develop appreciation for the diverse perspectives that confront them and that co-define the subject matter they desire to teach? If, as thinkers have long argued, "it is the viewpoint that determines the object" surely this notion applies all the more cogently to reality in cultural perspective. To gain competence, then, in meaningfully linking curricular content to children coming to school with an assortment of group-defined worldviews and values, it is imperative that aspirant educators explore socio-cultural difference and its pertinence to education. It is to future teachers, therefore, that EDUC 2120 is addressed.

Beyond our Comfort Zone

Though it can be uncomfortable at times, cultural difference is the norm in human societies. It is because the inner and outer workings of our *own* cultures – let alone those of others – tend to be ill understood that this course has so much to offer. However, the introduction of aspirant teachers to cultures their own worldviews have accustomed them to disregard, dislike, or discount is likely to result in discomfort. Dissonance is as probable as discovery; values will be uncovered, assumptions deconstructed, and beliefs contrasted. When fueling the engine of learning, however, such discomfort is productive. Thus, course participants are urged to take up the gauntlet of intercultural learning. Their viewpoints may be challenged but not devalued, regardless of their cultural background, their cross-cultural experience, or their initial skill level. The earnest engagement of all is appreciated. Success in this course is not a function of *what* participants feel or believe, but of the extent to which they review their pre-course perceptions in the light of new information and thus equip themselves to better consider various perspectives, including those formed in dissimilar cultures.

The instructors facilitate this discovery process. Adding their input, movies, texts, music, surveys, and the like, they present core course content in their own particular way. Guided by their personal insights and experiences, each instructor maps out a particular path. With relative freedom from bias, all instructors seek to connect content to the participants' values, perceptions, talents, and concerns. Recognizing that our worldviews are the very building blocks of learning, instructors aim to validate all heartfelt perspectives and to foster a safe environment for exploration. Motivated by professional – as opposed to personal or particular ideological – concerns, the goal is not to indoctrinate, but to educate, through guided co-discovery. The goal, more specifically, is to imbue prospective teachers with the awareness, level of comfort, and skills they need as facilitators of meaning and learning in and for today's society. In sum, instructors stimulate common investigation of the sensitive inter-group cultural differences that challenge and enrich our complex and dynamic society – and by extension our communities, schools, classrooms, curricula…and teachers.

A Cultural Education

Teachers embody and transmit socio-culturally-sanctioned knowledge, skills, and norms. To do so without training in cultural diversity is likely to limit their ability to know, represent, and transmit reality as educators. We live in a country where individual choices are highlighted and group characteristics downplayed. Indeed, to minimize group differences by focusing on individuals is one of the instruments of cultural mainstreaming. Another way to affirm the cultural status quo, to avoid inter-group issues, and/or to create implicit distance from one's own socio-cultural group is simply to deny the existence of group differences. This strategy can result in statements such as "we are all the same," "discrimination does not exist anymore," "I am 'color blind,'" or "all this talk of 'diversity' is nonsense." Minority group members tend to disagree and since all cultures by definition self-identify, it is they who have the final say on their own culture.

We often do not want to see what lies outside the reality to which we have grown accustomed. We are comfortable in our own group outlook and prefer not to question it. However natural, such cul-

tural myopia can easily cause us to stereotype, keep distant from, confirm prejudices about, and project our worldview onto the Other. Educators are prone to underestimate relevant group differences. They labor to transmit "the" curriculum to "the" students rather than to contemplate how competing worldviews and socio-cultural circumstance dictate or mitigate their efforts. The educational enterprise of which teachers are the prime deliverers is an eminently social one – whether seen from the perspective of sociology, public policy, organizational design, cultural theory, political ideology, or curriculum analysis.

Post-colonial societies – including our own – which make up most of the world today are culturally quite diverse. What, then, is culture? Of what does it consist? Is it truly significant to our personal and collective lives? Which group, if any, has all or most of it – and which does not? How relevant is it to educational practice and policies? What does culture really have to do with teaching students? Is cultural difference synonymous with diversity? Is intercultural competency desirable, or even achievable? Can one learn across cultures and, if so, how? Is multicultural education a good thing? Is it even "American?" Are intercultural skills relevant to ideals such as peace and/or prosperity? How would one teach with intercultural competence? How would one teach for intercultural competence? These are some of the key questions underlying this course.

While cultural anthropologists and cultural theorists debate these questions, some consensus about the meaning of "culture" emerges. Without denying personal ways of knowing, humans acquire much of their knowledge and identity through groups. Culture is that set of key defining attributes of groups, or "human aggregates," that however subliminally shape our experience of the world through a process called enculturation. With the possible exception of a very small handful of culturally homogeneous countries today, culture does not depend on statehood; cultural identity is often non-synonymous with citizenship. The roots of culture run deeper than those of the relatively recent 18th century concept of the "nation-state," the sovereign territory of a sole ethno-cultural group.

The most significant pillars of culture are language, religion, and/or race and ethnicity. For instance, it is largely through our native language or dialect (and to linguists all languages are dialects and all dialects languages) that we learn to understand, conceptualize, and verbalize the world around us. Culture, then, determines how we inwardly and outwardly represent the group that has molded us and whose manifold ways of life we have however intuitively adopted. As the essence of what makes each group different, culture is the particular set of behaviors, institutions, and attitudes that members of each group have learned to consider its social practices, institutions, and behaviors acceptable, respectable, important, professional, abnormal, offensive, prestigious, inappropriate and the like. As such, differences of culture are not a matter of personal choice. Rather than our lifestyle options as individuals, cultural differences reflect our common human need to make social meaning – i.e. our need, and thus our right, to encode our experience as members of distinct groups, or phrased differently to "classify, codify, and communicate" group identity through the use of outer and inner symbols.

How does all this relate to such concepts as "cross-cultural," "multicultural," and/or "intercultural" – and if these terms are not the same how do they differ? In a narrow sense, they constitute a continuum: while cross-cultural communication highlights the challenge of confronting cultural difference, multicultural education foregrounds the equality between cultures, and intercultural competency focuses on the tools of success in the marketplace of diverse cultures. Societies, however, often do not treat members of different cultural groups alike; most legitimize dominant group values as standard, while marginalizing others as non-standard or even sub-standard. Inter-group cultural dynamics are often fraught with tensions, the (ab)use of power, real and perceived issues of dominance, rights, and oppression. In societies present and past, this has led majorities to ignore, undervalue, distrust, disadvantage, scapegoat, imprison, displace, and annihilate non-mainstream groups. In some societies, mainstream dominance is not a function of numerical strength but of qualitative pressures such as economic or political rivalry, ethno-cultural politicking, silencing or restriction of movement – and even civil war or genocide.

Diversity

Unfortunately, the term "diversity" is as perplexing as it is pertinent. It covers a wide range of individuals and group realities from across the social and ideological spectrum. The term is used to refer to differences such as gender, class, sexual orientation, culture, marital status, physical and/or intellectual ability, socio-economic status, race, language, ethnicity, age, caste, faith and religion, political beliefs, or ideology. Given this multiplicity of meanings, there is little wonder that we may struggle with the term itself and that we wonder diversity is something we want, like, accept, need, or tolerate.

For the study of intercultural competence in education, the usefulness of the term diversity is, perhaps surprisingly, limited by its very elasticity. It can refer to differentiations stemming from personal choices as well as group distinctions. It may relate to institutional, partisan, geographic, or other non macro-cultural variances such as "school culture." That diversity is used to cover concerns ranging from minuscule to world-embracing means it could denote virtually every aspect of human life under the sun. Ironically, it can even be used as a smoke-screen for promoting a particular group's interests at the expense of others'. At times, it is also invoked to further an agenda too starry-eyed and uncritical to be effectual. In short, in order not to be so stretched to the point of vacuity, the term requires fine-tuning.

Despite the broad role of diversity in education, and however much personal choice may be valued in our society, EDUC 2120 focuses not on individual, but on collective forms of diversity. Not all diversity is cultural. The aim of this course is to explore the role of cultural diversity in education. In doing so, it zeroes in on the preeminent pillars of cultural self-definition – language and dialect, faith and religion, and race and ethnicity. Differences of individual psychology or personal choice are not the focus; nor are non-individual distinctions such as institutional culture, deaf culture, and such. Moreover, no meaningful attention will be paid to related forms of social interaction such as "ableism," sexism, heterosexism, and classism. The implication is not that other forms of diversity are irrelevant to education; gender and education, for instance, could make for very enlightening course content. Yet to avoid confusion with individual, family, lifestyle, institutional, and countless other distinctions, EDUC 2120 centers on cultural difference and education.

EDUC 2120

One of the trappings of culture is that it keeps us from recognizing that it acts as a prism on reality. Unaware of their own cultural biases, educators may mistake their reality, their students, and themselves as being a-cultural. Called to represent knowledge to students with a plethora of group-imbued perspectives, educators who do not appreciate the socio-cultural implications of their being, their role, their subject, their institutions, their society, and their calling may fall short of their professional goals. Education is a socio-politically embedded enterprise in which teachers act as the primary agents of delivery. Without a grasp of the socio-cultural dimensions of their craft, educators cannot truly serve the goals of either human or social betterment today.

To facilitate relevant learning, the course material of EDUC 2120 is organized into four sections. Part one explores "culture general" or "metacultural" perspectives, i.e. skills, issues, and attitudes that concern culture and intercultural dynamics in general. The goal is to help participants question their preparedness for intercultural study, consider the underlying issues, and familiarize themselves with some of the basic concepts. Section two presents significant areas of cross-cultural conflict that persist in our society today. It hones in on specific intercultural challenges: language and immigration, race and ethnicity, and religion and ideology. The third section focuses on schools through a cultural lens, i.e. issues such as school reform, language, and student achievement. The fourth and final part of the text broaches certain instructional, attitudinal, and social policy topics as they pertain to intercultural competence and the role of education in society.

We inhabit and inherit a country and a world replete with intercultural complexities and inequities where tensions seem to rise and fall erratically and marginalized populations sustain pressures so in-

tense they face extinction or at times commit self-defeating acts of violence and destruction. At the root of these costly problems are often differences of language, religion, and race/ethnicity, fundamental as they are to the construction of social meaning and identity. To many, education is the key to creating lasting change for the better. In today's world, teachers cannot fulfill this responsibility with cultural blindness. It is critically important that future educators engage in a safe and guided exploration of their own culture and that of others, to develop those pedagogies, reflexes, and abilities that allow to them appreciate divergent perspectives, serve distinct groups, and thus practice inclusion, intercultural competence, and global learning. It is our hope, therefore, that participants in EDUC 2120 will seize the opportunity offered and welcome, value, and take advantage of this ambitious, unique, and captivating course!

Gregory P. Meyjes, Ph.D.
Chair and Associate Professor of Linguistics
Department of Inclusive Education
Kennesaw State University

Further Reading

Althen, G., Ed. 1974. *Learning across cultures.* Washington, D.C.: NAFSA.

Aguirre, A., Jr. and D.V. Baker. 2008. *Structured inequality in the United States: Critical discussions on the continuing significance of race, ethnicity, and gender.* 2nd ed. Upper Saddle River, NJ: Prentice Hall.

Asante, M.K., and W.B. Gudykunst, Eds. 1989. *Handbook of international and intercultural communication.* Newbury Park, CA: Sage.

Bakanic, Von. 2009. *Prejudice: Attitudes about race, class, and gender.* Upper Saddle River, NJ: Prentice Hall.

Bennett, Milton J. 1998. *Basic concepts of intercultural communication.* Boston: Intercultural Press.

Bennett, J.M., Bennett, M.J., & Allen W. 1999. Developing intercultural competence in the language classroom. In R.M. Paige, D. Lange, & Y. Yershova, Eds. *Culture as the core: Integrating culture into the language curriculum* (pp. 13-45). CARLA Working Paper #15. Minneapolis, MN: University of Minnesota, CARLA.

Bennett, J.M. 1993. Cultural marginality: Identity issues in intercultural training. In M.R. Paige, Ed. *Education for the intercultural experience.* Yarmouth, ME: Intercultural Press.

Bucher, R. D. 2010. *Diversity consciousness: Opening our minds to people, cultures, and opportunities.* 3rd ed. Upper Saddle River, NJ: Prentice Hall.

--- (2008). *Building cultural intelligence (CQ): Nine megaskills.* 3rd ed. Upper Saddle River, NJ: Prentice Hall.

Bochner, S. 1977. The mediating man and cultural diversity. In R.W. Brislin, Ed. *Culture learning: Concepts, applications, and research.* Honolulu: University of Hawaii Press.

Brislin, R.W. 1987. *Cross-cultural encounter: Face to face interaction.* New York: Pergamon Press.

---- 1993. *Understanding culture's influence on behavior.* Fort Worth, TX: Harcourt Brace.

Brislin, R.W., S. Bochner, and W. Lonner, Eds. 1975. *Cross-cultural perspectives on learning.* New York: John Wiley.

Carr-Chellman, A. A., Ed. 2005. *Global perspectives on e-learning: Rhetoric and reality.* Thousand Oaks, CA: Sage Publications.

Dinges, N. 1984. Intercultural competence. In D. Landis and R.W. Brislin, Eds. *Handbook of intercultural training* (pp. 176-202). New York: Pergamon Press.

Farley, J. E. 2010. *Majority-minority relations.* 6th ed. Boston: Prentice Hall.

Fennes, H., and K. Hapgood, 1997. *Intercultural learning in the classroom.* London: Cassell.

Gudykunst, W.B., & Kim, Y.Y. 2003. *Communicating with strangers: An approach to intercultural communication.* 4th ed. New York: McGraw-Hill.

Hall, E.T. 1976. *Beyond culture.* New York: Anchor Books.

Hanvey, R. 1975. *Cross-cultural awareness: An attainable global perspective.* New York: Global Perspectives in Education.

Hess, J.D. 1994. *The whole world guide to culture learning.* Yarmouth, ME: Intercultural Press.

Kohls, L.R., and J.M. Knight.1994. *Developing intercultural awareness.* Yarmouth, ME: Intercultural Press.

Koppleman, K. L., with R. L. Goodhart. 2007. *Understanding human differences: Multicultural education for a diverse America.* Boston: Allyn Bacon,

LeMay, M. C. 2009. *The perennial struggle: Race, ethnicity, and minority group relations in the United States.* 3rd ed. Upper Saddle River, NJ: Prentice Hall.

Maxim, G. W. 2008. *Dynamic social studies for constructivist classrooms: Inspiring tomorrow's social scientists.* 8th ed. Upper Saddle River, NJ: Prentice Hall.

Nieto, S. and P. Bode. 2008. *Affirming diversity: the sociopolitical context of multicultural education.* 5th ed. Boston: Prentice Hall.

Paige, R.M., Ed. 1993. *Education for the intercultural experience.* Yarmouth, Maine: Intercultural Press, 1993.

Samovar, L.A., and R.E. Porter, Eds. 1993. *Intercultural communication: A reader.* Belmont, California: Wadsworth.

Schaefer, R. T. 2011. *Racial and ethnic groups: census update.* 12th ed. Boston: Prentice Hall.

Stewart, E.C., and Bennett, M.J. 1991. *American cultural patterns: A cross-cultural perspective.* Rev. ed. Yarmouth, ME: Intercultural Press.

Storti, C. 1994. *Cross-cultural dialogues: 74 brief encounters with cultural difference.* Yarmouth, ME: Intercultural Press.

PART ONE

Metacultural Perspectives

CHAPTER 1

Understanding Ourselves and Others: Clarifying Values and Language

❝I have striven not to laugh at human actions, not to weep at them, nor to hate them, but to understand them.❞

Baruch Spinoza (1632–1677)

"May you live in interesting times" is a Chinese curse. It implies that life is easier and more enjoyable when nothing out of the ordinary or controversial happens. As Americans living in a complex, multicultural society, we certainly live in interesting times. Is it the best of times or the worst of times? Like the question about whether the glass is half empty or half full, the answer is the same: It's a personal decision. We can choose to be engaged in the challenges and opportunities of diversity issues, or we can retreat and resign ourselves to an attitude of indifference or even despair. Because America is not only a diverse society but also a democratic one, we have the freedom to choose our perceptions, assumptions, and behaviors.

If we take Spinoza's quote seriously, we need to understand all kinds of diversity—including opinions, appearances, values, and beliefs—as well as the categories of race, ethnicity, social class, gender, sexual orientation, and disability. The study of human diversity obviously requires an examination of social groups that encounter discrimination. However, in addition to focusing on the sociocultural differences between groups, we must also acknowledge the importance of *individual* differences. Each of us wants to be recognized as an individual. Our experiences are affected by multiple factors, in-

cluding whether we are white or a person of color, female or male, from a low-, middle-, or upper-income family, or from a rural, suburban, or urban home. Each person's opinion offers a unique perspective that only the individual expressing it can fully understand. The task for us as listeners is to understand as best as we can the ideas, values, and beliefs articulated by the individuals we encounter.

What is the difference between beliefs and values?

Kniker (1977) suggests that **beliefs** are inferences about reality that take one of three forms: descriptive, evaluative, or prescriptive. A *descriptive belief* is exemplified by those who argued that the world was not flat but round because they observed boats sailing off to the horizon and recognized that the hulls disappear while sails are still visible. An *evaluative belief* is illustrated by Winston Churchill's conclusion about democracy based on his reading of history: He understood why some called democracy the worst form of government, but he found it to be better than all other forms of government that had been attempted thus far. An example of a *prescriptive belief* would be the recommendation that students take a role in creating classroom rules because research showed that students who help create rules are more likely to be cooperative and abide by them. All beliefs are predispositions to types of action. Rokeach asserts that a cluster of related beliefs creates an **attitude;** he defines **values** as "combinations of attitudes which generate action or deliberate choice to avoid action" (Kniker, 1977, p. 33).

The Role of Values in Human Differences

Rokeach is saying that values determine our choices: Values are the foundation for actions we choose to take—or to avoid (see Figure 1.1). What value do Americans place on wealth? For some, money and possessions are the primary measures of success. They admire others who are rich and successful, and they define their own worth by their income and wealth. For others, money is not a priority. Their main concern is to make enough money to support a comfortable lifestyle, however they choose to define it. There are also people who believe the biblical caution that love of money is "the root of all evil," and refuse to let wealth play an important role in their choices. Their behavior is a reflection of their values. While serving as vice president to John Adams, Thomas Jefferson was once turned away from a prominent hotel because his clothes were soiled and he had no servants with him. After the proprietor was told whom he had refused, he sent word to Jefferson, offering him any room in the hotel. Having been accepted into another hotel, Jefferson sent a reply politely refusing the offer of a room, noting that if the hotel proprietor did not have a room for a "dirty farmer," then he must not have a room for the vice president either (Botkin, 1957).

What is the relationship between a person's values and behaviors?

America has a history of social commentary on the role of values in people's lives, and scholars engage in research examining the relationship between expressed values and behavior. Searching for

FIGURE 1.1   The Relationship of Values, Beliefs, Attitudes, and Choices

From Charles R. Kniker *You and values education.* Published by Allyn & Bacon/Merrill Education, Boston, MA. Copyright © 1977 by Pearson Education. Reprinted by permission of the publisher.

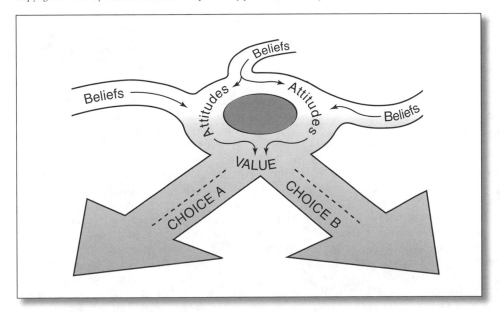

consistent patterns in values research is challenging. However, one theme from social critics has been repeatedly supported by research and case study: There is a *consistent inconsistency* between what we say we value and our actual behavior (Aronson, 2008; Lefkowitz, 1997; Myrdal, 1944; Terry, Hogg, & Duck, 1999).

The tendency for Americans to say we believe in a certain value and then engage in contradictory behavior is a curious and yet consistent pattern. Contradictory behavior by human beings has been criticized and even ridiculed by essayists, novelists, and observers of American society. In 1938, the Carnegie Foundation invited Swedish social economist Gunnar Myrdal to the United States to conduct a study on the "American Negro Problem." Myrdal (1944) went far beyond a study of racial relations: He attempted to identify and understand the core values of American society.

In his analysis of Myrdal's research, Risberg (1978) identified nine values that Americans perceived as defining their culture:

1. Worth and dignity of the individual
2. Equality
3. Inalienable rights to life, liberty, property, and the pursuit of happiness
4. Rights to freedom of speech, press, religion, assembly, and private association
5. Consent of the governed
6. Majority rule
7. Rule of law
8. Due process of law
9. Community and national welfare. (pp. 5–6)

These identified core values seem to be accurate, especially if we compare American culture to other cultures. For example, many nations around the world put great emphasis on the collective good, but in the United States we tend to focus on personal worth and to reward individual achievements. Expectations of equality and of having "inalienable rights" are expressed in founding documents such as the Declaration of Independence, and our various freedoms are guaranteed by the Bill of Rights to the U.S. Constitution. Our representative form of democracy is based on the assumption that local, state, and national governments will be elected by the majority, with an expectation that they will rule with the consent of the governed for

the welfare of the community, state, and nation. Finally, being ruled by laws and being given a chance to resolve issues by making our case in court (due process) was established to protect our citizens from the whims of the wealthy and powerful (a reaction to oppressive behavior from aristocrats and monarchs in the past). These values have historically defined America as a society, and they represent beliefs that all Americans share.

Despite the consensus about them, Myrdal observed that all of the values were regularly contradicted by American behavior. He provided examples from his observations, primarily based on race relations, to illustrate his conclusion.

What inconsistencies exist between American values and American behaviors?

Although Americans have always tended to emphasize individuality, American society quite consistently has demanded conformity. We Americans always seem to be uncomfortable with differences, often minimizing or ignoring them. In the turbulent era of the 1960s, many young people protested the Vietnam War, challenging authorities on college

> The primal principle of democracy is the worth and dignity of the individual.
>
> **Edward Bellamy (1850–1898)**

campuses and elsewhere in American society. Young men and women defied traditional gender roles in their choice of lifestyles and music, but most Americans did not celebrate this youth counterculture as an expression of individuality; instead, many denounced their behavior. Families were sundered and social critics predicted the downfall of American values. The protests passed, and expectations that Americans should conform have continued.

The influence of peers on individual behavior illustrates the seductive power of conformity. Social psychologists studying the influence of peer pressure have reported that people in groups engage in behaviors they would not undertake as individuals (Aronson, 2008; Haag, 2000; Terry, Hogg, & Duck,

1999). According to LeBon (1968), when individuals congregate, the group "presents new characteristics very different from those of the individuals composing it" (p. 27). In a study of young men who had assaulted homosexuals, Franklin (2000) found that many of the men she interviewed expressed tolerant attitudes toward homosexuality even though they admitted that when they were with friends, they participated in verbal or physical assaults on people perceived to be gay. When questioned, 35% said they were motivated by a desire to prove their "toughness" and to become closer to the friends who engaged in antigay behavior.

Contradictory behavior also is illustrated in the belief that Americans value equality. The Declaration of Independence proclaims that the United States is founded on the belief that "all men are created equal," and yet the man who wrote that statement owned slaves. During World War II, boxing champions Joe Louis and Sugar Ray Robinson signed up for military service. At a bus stop in Alabama, a military policeman insisted that the two "colored soldiers" move to the rear of the station. When they refused, they were arrested. After an officer had reprimanded them, Louis responded, "Sir, I'm a soldier like any other American soldier. I don't want to be pushed to the back because I'm a Negro" (Mead, 1985, p. 231). Although racial inequality has diminished to some degree in the United States, the gap between the wealthy and the poor has become greater than ever. A chairman of the board for the First National Bank of Chicago admitted that it was difficult to defend an economic system that permitted such a wide disparity of income as existed in the United States (Terkel, 1980, p. 23).

The United States also was founded on the rule of law and the belief in a justice system that would be fair to everyone, yet people with wealth and status are routinely able to circumvent our ideal. The view that our courts favor those who can afford the best lawyers is widely recognized and is often portrayed in films and on television. Despite the contradiction, Americans continue to believe that justice can prevail in a courtroom and they are resentful of cases where they believe it has not. For example, Claus von Bülow was a man of wealth and status who was tried and convicted for attempting to murder his wife. He subsequently hired the famous defense attorney Alan Dershowitz, who identified a legal technicality that necessitated a new trial for his client. At the retrial, the jury acquitted von Bülow of attempted murder (Wright, 1983). No one except von Bülow knows if he is guilty or innocent; however, there are poor people in prison today because they could not afford to hire a lawyer as skilled as Alan Dershowitz.

What Myrdal observed and reported in the 1940s continues to be true today: Americans behave inconsistently and engage in actions that contradict their expressed values. Myrdal's observations reinforced what American social critics had been saying for many years and what research and case studies have documented since the 1940s. These observations require some explanation, and it seems logical to begin by examining how people choose their values.

Are values individually chosen or are we taught to accept certain values?

The way American values are taught plays a major role in the values we hold. Individuals, subcultures, and institutions are involved in teaching values; parents, teachers, peers, clergy, relatives, and youth counselors are just a few examples. By studying how individuals and organizations in America teach values to children and youth, Raths, Harmin, and Simon (1978) identified seven traditional approaches.

A first way to teach values is to (1) *set an example.* Parents and teachers are supposed to be role models for children and youth. Young people are also told to emulate various individuals—from historical leaders to contemporary athletes whose achievements are attributed to practicing certain values. In similar fashion, schools and other organizations use (2) *rules and regulations* to promote certain behaviors in children and youth (and adults) that represent important values. Learning punctuality is considered important enough that teachers send children

> The law, in its majestic equality, forbids the rich as well as the poor to sleep under bridges, to beg in the streets, and to steal bread.
>
> **Anatole France (1844–1924)**

to the principal's office for a tardy pass if they are late for class. This example is especially interesting because the child securing the tardy pass from the principal is kept away from the classroom for additional time while the other children engage in some kind of learning activity, which is supposedly the primary purpose for requiring students to attend school.

Another approach is to (3) *persuade or convince* others to accept certain values. Respectful discussions with reasonable arguments can be an effective means of convincing someone that the values being espoused are appropriate for living a good life. Related to this is an (4) *appeal to conscience* in which a parent or teacher may challenge a child or youth who seems to advocate an inappropriate value or belief. This approach is illustrated when a teacher responds to a student making an inappropriate comment by saying, "You don't really believe that, do you?" The point of such questions is not to give the student a chance to explain or defend what he or she said, but to bring a subtle and insistent form of moral pressure intended to coerce the student into rejecting an unacceptable point of view.

Parents often teach values by offering (5) *limited choices.* By limiting choices, parents intend to manipulate children into making acceptable decisions. If a mother values cooperation and tells her children that family members should share in household duties, what can she do if one of her children refuses? She asks one child to wash dishes twice a week, but the child hates to wash dishes and refuses. The mother might say, "Either you agree to wash dishes twice a week or you will not be allowed to play with your friends after school." The child is restricted to two options in the hope that he or she will choose to do the dishes, reinforcing the mother's original objective of wanting her children to learn the value of sharing domestic responsibilities.

Organizations have employed the approach of (6) *inspiring* people to embrace certain values, often by sponsoring a "retreat" with inspirational or motivational speakers or a social function where the combination of speakers, films, and activities is designed to have emotional or spiritual impact. Although religious groups employ this approach, corporations sponsor such events to inspire employees to work harder to achieve personal or group goals, and in doing so, contribute to the achievement of organizational goals.

Some religious groups and secular organizations emphasize (7) *religious or cultural dogma* to teach values. To accept beliefs without questioning them is to be **dogmatic.** If a Christian with dogmatic beliefs were questioned, he or she might say "That's what the Bible says," or, similarly, a dogmatic Muslim might say "This is what it says in the Qu'ran," even though for centuries people have interpreted the teachings of Jesus and Muhammad in different ways. Even early Christians held widely divergent views on the meanings of the life and words of Jesus (Pagels, 2006). Dogmatic beliefs stifle debate by emphasizing tradition: "This is what we have always believed."

Dogmatic beliefs also can be found in a secular context. When someone questions a value based on cultural beliefs, a dogmatic response might be "We've always done it this way." The appeal to tradition in opposing change has been employed in such controversies as using Native American mas-

> When people are free to do as they please they usually imitate each other.
>
> **Eric Hoffer (1902–1983)**

cots for school sports teams and including the Confederate flag in the official flags of some southern states. Only in 2003 did Georgia change its state flag to remove the confederate symbol.

Understanding how values are taught provides some insight in answering the question about why people consistently behave in ways that contradict their expressed values. Each of the seven traditional approaches to teaching values seems to be based on a common assumption, and that assumption might explain the inconsistencies.

How does the way values are taught explain the inconsistency between values and behavior?

What do the seven traditional approaches to teaching values have in common? They are all based on an assumption that certain prescribed values are to be taught, and that the individuals being instructed should accept them. The person teaching values—the teacher, parent, scout leader, minister, priest, rabbi, imam, or employer—knows what values are appropriate. The goal is to persuade the student, child, parishioner, or worker to accept those values. In actuality, each approach is a form of **indoctrination,** where the intent is to dictate cultural values that must be accepted rather than assist people in deciding what is right and wrong (see Figure 1.2).

This assumption shared by all seven traditional approaches to teaching values in America caused Raths et al. (1978) to question whether all approaches were primarily successful in convincing people to *say* the right thing, yet not *do* the right thing. If this is true, there are important implications for how values should be taught. It is neither ethical nor prudent to teach values that are advocated but not practiced in our everyday lives. This does not teach values, but, rather, hypocrisy. If the goal of teaching is to help learners understand what they genuinely believe and choose values to incorporate into their behavior, those who teach must recognize the limitations of coercing children and youth to feign acceptance of prescribed values. For Americans to behave consistently with our expressed values, we must demonstrate authentic commitment to them.

FIGURE 1.2   Often found in public school textbooks, illustrations such as this one suggest that Native Americans and colonists had a peaceful, harmonious relationship, but the reality was one of consistent conflict as Indians were pushed off their lands and forced to move westward.

Source: "The First Thanksgiving," painting by Jean Leon Gerome Ferris (1863–1930). Library of Congress, Prints and Photographs Division (LC-D416-90423).

Why should anyone be concerned about inconsistencies between values and behavior?

If we understand our values and consistently act on them, it is more likely that our choices will reflect our highest ideals. We are constantly confronted with ethical dilemmas that challenge our values and require us to make moral choices. A *New York Times* reporter interviewed a national sales manager for Wachovia who was living in an upper-middle-class suburb of Atlanta—a homogeneous community where everyone was of the same race and social class, and even shared similar opinions on a variety of issues. At his corporate worksite, the manager said the importance of diversity was emphasized: "At work, diversity is one of the biggest things we work on." (Kilborn, 2007, p. 157) Yet in his private life, the manager admitted that he and his suburban neighbors were "never challenged" to learn about other groups, so they did not. The contrast between what happens at work and what takes place at home represents an inconsistency that could call into question the sincerity of the manager's commitment to diversity.

Another example of inconsistency that came up during the interview was when the sales manager said that his family attended church and Bible Study classes. Because they were secure in their own comforts, the manager admitted that he and his family didn't give much thought to other "economic groups," to families living in poverty. As a contrast, there is the example of Bono, lead singer for the rock group U2, who has used his position and wealth to lobby for human rights. Accepting an NAACP Image Award in 2007 for his work on poverty issues and the AIDS crisis in Africa, Bono identified Martin Luther King, Jr. as someone who inspired him, and he went on to say:

> The poor are where God lives. God is in the slums, in the cardboard boxes where the poor play house. God is where the opportunity is lost and lives are shattered. God is with the mother who has infected her child with a virus that will take both their lives. God is under the rubble in the cries we hear during wartime. God, my friends, is with the poor. God is with us if we are with them. This is not a burden. This is an adventure. (Gamber, 2007, p. 37)

Should parents rather than schools teach values to children?

The question of who should teach values is a rhetorical one. Both parents and schools in America are expected to contribute to the development of children's value systems. We constantly encounter people who reveal their values in everyday words and actions. Teachers model their values whether or not they consciously choose to do so. The question is not whether values should be taught, but how they should be taught.

Of the many approaches Kniker (1977) identified for teaching values, the most effective allow children and youth opportunity for discussion and debate, employing activities that stimulate them to think about their beliefs, hear other perspectives, and consider what effect different decisions could have for others as well as themselves. Discussing values, related behaviors, and possible consequences exposes young people to perspectives of others; evaluating arguments about values from their peers can help them decide which ones seem more attractive, compelling, and meaningful. In the process, they learn not only what values are important to them, but also to accept people with values different from their own.

As adults, we do not tend to make decisions about values at a particular point in time and then never change our minds. Our values are based on beliefs and attitudes that change frequently, resulting in an ongoing process in which decisions are made and reevaluated throughout our lives. Culture, geographical location, parents, and life experiences influence each person's decisions. Each individual

> Consciously we teach what we know; unconsciously we teach who we are.
>
> **Don Hamachek (Contemporary)**

must determine what he or she believes is best, and the cumulative decisions individuals make influence the evolution of our society (Bellah et al., 1991; Lappe, 1989; Zinn, 1990). School classrooms are part of this journey. Teachers must present students with moral dilemmas and trust that when our children and youth are given the freedom to choose, they will be capable of making ethical decisions.

What problems can interfere with making ethical decisions?

One of the main problems in making ethical decisions about human differences is confusion concerning the language employed to address those differences. Many essential words or phrases are either common terms with a history of misuse or unfamiliar terms. Confused language often reflects the discomfort people feel toward sensitive issues. For

> How often misused words generate misleading thoughts.
>
> **Herbert Spencer (1820–1903)**

example, the word *racism* did not appear in most English dictionaries until the 1960s. As the civil rights movement gained momentum and attracted considerable attention from the media and people across America, we could no longer avoid using the term. Similarly, the word *sexism* did not appear in dictionaries until the early 1970s, as the women's movement became increasingly successful at bringing issues concerning the treatment of women to public attention (Miller & Swift, 2000).

Using inaccurate or ambiguous language creates problems when we are addressing sensitive, uncomfortable issues. To be coherent and meaningful in our discussion of human differences, we must clarify our vocabulary and agree to specific appropriate meanings for significant words and concepts.

Defining Terms Related to Human Differences

One would expect that consultation with any scholarly authority would provide definitions for a term such as *prejudice*, but the scholarly world is not free

from confusion. Some textbooks have defined *prejudice* as a prejudgment that could be either positive or negative; this definition confuses prejudice with *bias*, a feeling in favor of—or opposed to—anything or anyone. *Stereotypes* always refer to people, and also can be positive or negative. As with stereotypes, prejudice always refers to people, but prejudice is always negative.

This chapter includes a series of definitions intended to clarify terms referring to human differences. Definitions throughout the text are based on the work of scholars from various fields in the behavioral sciences, including racial and ethnic studies, women's studies, education, sociology, and anthropology. Unless cited, definitions reflect a distillation of common themes identified in several scholarly sources (Andrzejewski, 1996; Feagin & Feagin, 2008; Herdt, 1997; Levin & Levin, 1982; Schaefer, 2008; Simpson & Yinger, 1985). The following series of definitions makes distinctions and indicates relationships between the terms.

Bias   A preference or inclination, favorable or unfavorable, which inhibits impartial judgment.

Stereotype   A positive or negative trait or traits ascribed to a certain group and to most members of that group.

Prejudice   A negative attitude toward a group and persons perceived to be members of that group; being predisposed to behave negatively toward members of a group.

Bigotry   Extreme negative attitudes leading to hatred of a group and persons regarded as members of the group.

Discrimination   Actions or practices carried out by a member or members of dominant groups, or their representatives, that have a differential and negative impact on a member or members of subordinate groups.

Notice that each of the first four terms just listed represents attitudes of greater intensity than the previous one. Regarding bias and stereotypes, attitudes can be either positive or negative and can influence a person's perceptions of a person or group. Having a *bias* related to a group creates an inclination to favor or dislike an individual from that group. (See Table 1.1.) *Stereotyping* a group indicates an expectation that most members of the group will

TABLE 1.1   Examples of Bias

The following selection comes from a list of 27 biases:

1. *Family Bias:* Believing information provided by family members without seeking evidence to support the accuracy of their information.
2. *Attractiveness Bias:* Believing information provided by attractive people.
3. *Confirmation Bias:* Believing information that reinforces beliefs already held and ignoring information that contradicts these beliefs.
4. *Self-Serving Bias:* Believing information that is beneficial to self-interest and goals.
5. *In-Group Bias:* Believing information from people who are members of our group (e.g., friends, co-workers, same racial or ethnic group, etc.).
6. *Expectancy Bias:* Pursuing information and drawing conclusions that reinforce our beliefs when looking for information (or even conducting research).
7. *Pleasure Bias:* Assuming that pleasant experiences offer greater insights for strengthening one's beliefs than unpleasant experiences do.
8. *Perceptual Bias:* Assuming that one's own perceptions and experience of reality reveal objective truths to confirm one's beliefs.
9. *Perseverance Bias:* Perpetuating one's beliefs even after encountering information that contradicts those beliefs.
10. *Uncertainty Bias:* Choosing to believe or disbelieve information rather than remain uncertain because of discomfort with ambiguity.

–Adapted from Newburg and Waldman (2006) *Why We Believe What We Believe*

behave in certain positive or negative ways. No positive option exists for prejudice or bigotry because of the greater intensity of these attitudes. *Prejudices* are negative attitudes based on a prejudgment of a group; *bigotry* involves hatred and represents a harsher form of prejudgment against a person or group. Note that whereas bias, stereotype, prejudice, and bigotry relate to attitudes, discrimination refers to actions taken that demonstrate negative attitudes. A person can have a bias, a stereotype, a prejudice, or even be a bigot and still not engage in any kind of negative or positive behavior. Unless an individual's attitudes are publicly expressed, others may not be aware of them. Discrimination can be seen and documented, and it can cause physical and emotional harm.

How do negative attitudes develop?

We learn various biases, stereotypes, and prejudices as we grow up. We can be biased in favor of or against certain kinds of foods, categories of books, styles of clothing, or types of personalities. Bias can affect decisions about what we eat, read, or wear; it can influence our choice of friends. A stereotype assumes that individuals possess certain human traits simply because they are members of a particular group. Although some traits are regarded as positive—such as blacks have rhythm, Asians are good in math—other traits are viewed as negative—certain groups are lazy, shiftless, dishonest, or violent. Although negative stereotypes are regarded as unacceptable, many people accept positive stereotypes. The problem with positive stereotypes is that they cause us to have specific expectations for individuals and groups even though we have little or no evidence for these assumptions. A positive stereotype may sabotage the process of forming a realistic and accurate perception of an individual.

During a coffee break at a midwestern university, three Asian American women employed by a student services office reminisced about their undergraduate days. They complained about how difficult math classes had been and laughed as they recalled some of their coping strategies. The student services director, an African American, walked into the room, overheard what they were saying, and interrupted their discussion to chastise them for "putting yourselves down." He said they should stop. He also said he was disappointed in them and departed.

After the director left, the three women initially were too surprised to speak. Once they started talking, they realized they were angry because his comments suggested that he assumed they all had good math skills and were not being honest when discussing their lack of math ability. The women thought the director viewed them as individuals; they were angry and hurt when they realized that he had allowed a stereotype to distort his perception of them. They were especially upset because they had not expected a person of color to believe in a stereotype—even a positive one about the math abilities of Asians—but apparently he did.

If negative stereotypes reinforce negative biases, prejudices can develop, and prejudices are always negative. Although prejudice is only an attitude, negative attitudes often lead to negative actions against an individual or a group. Taking negative action might strengthen the prejudices of a person until they become the intense hatred of bigotry, which is the basis for white supremacist groups such as the Ku Klux Klan, neo-Nazis, and the Aryan nation. Because hatred is such a strong emotion, bigots are more likely to express their hatred with *actions,* including violence. Negative behaviors are often directed against individuals from social groups based on such differences as race, ethnicity, or nationality.

What is the difference between race, ethnicity, and nationality?

Race is not a scientific concept but a social reality dictated by the color of one's skin, even though skin color as a basis for human categorization is absurd. African Americans are identified as black, yet the skin color for many African Americans is more accurately described as brown. Contrary to the racist term "redskin," the skin color for Native Americans is not red. Yellow is an inaccurate description of skin color for those of Asian heritage. At an elementary school in Minneapolis, young children created a poster with the title "The Human Rainbow."

The first band of their rainbow was colored with a light brown crayon, making a very pale brown band, and each band above it was a slightly darker shade of brown until the outer band, which was colored in such a dark brown color that it almost looked black. The children had created a realistic way of representing and understanding the effect of melanin on the color of human skin.

The concept of race is both easy and difficult to discuss. Most Americans believe they know the meaning of the term, yet we have no specific set of racial categories acceptable to the scientific community. In 1758, Carolus Linnaeus proposed the first racial classifications based largely on human geographical origins, but as Gould (2002) pointed out, J. F. Blumenbach has usually been credited as the originator of racial categories. It was Blumenbach who created the term *Caucasian,* and his taxonomy established a racial hierarchy with white people on top. This would be the foundation for much "scientific" theory and research in the eighteenth and early nineteenth centuries. In the 1930s, scientists such as anthropologist Franz Boas challenged theories describing a hierarchy of races (Gosset, 1997). In 1937, American historian Jacques Barzun bluntly denounced the spuriousness of race as a legitimate scientific concept:

> [Racial classifications] come and go and return, for the urge to divide mankind into fixed types and races is evidently endless. Each attempt only illustrates anew how race-groupings have been shaped not by nature but by the mode of thought or the stage of mechanical efficiency that mankind valued at the moment. The history of these attempts confirms . . . that race-theories occur in the minds of men for an ulterior purpose. (1965, p. 196)

The series of paintings on "Caste" from the Spanish colonial era (see Figure 1.3) supports Barzun's point about the historical effort to find ways to divide and label human beings. Current research on the human genome emphasizes human similarities

> In claiming the unity of the human race we resist the unsavory assumption of higher and lower races.
>
> **Alexander von Humboldt (1769–1859)**

FIGURE 1.3 Eighteenth-Century Paintings of "Castas"

A series of Mexican paintings from the eighteenth century identifies categories of people (such as Indian, Spanish, or African) and names the children of mixed marriages. For example, the child of a Spanish and African couple is a Mulatto, and the child of a Spanish and Mulatto couple is a Morisco. In these three paintings, the artist illustrates how descendants of a Spanish and Indian couple can regain status as a white person. The child of the Spanish and Indian couple is a Mestizo, the child of a Spanish and Mestizo couple is a Castiza, and the child of a Spanish and Castiza couple is considered Spanish.

Source: De Espanol, y India, na ce Mestiza (190.1996.1), De Espanol, y Mestiza, Castiza (190.1996.3), and De Espanol, y Castiza, Espanol (190.1996.2). c. 1775, Francisco Clapera, Frederick and Jan Mayer Collection, Denver Art Museum.

rather than differences. According to this research, every woman living today has the mitochondrial DNA of a single woman who lived approximately 150,000 years ago, and every man living today has the Y chromosome of a single man who lived approximately 59,000 years ago (Wade, 2006). Scientists involved in this research report that 85% of human genetic variation occurs *within* groups and only 15% of human genetic variation occurs *between* groups. And yet, as Olson (2002) acknowledges, "societies have built elaborate systems of privilege and control around these miniscule genetic differences" (p. 69).

Although race is based on perceptions of physical differences, **ethnicity** is based on cultural differences (Jones, 1997). Ethnicity refers to the historic origins of an individual's family. For immigrants to the United States, ethnicity identifies their country of origin or that from which their ancestors came: Poland, Mexico, China, Italy, Cuba, Ethiopia, Rus-

sia, or Iran. For those whose ancestors emigrated from different countries of origin, ethnicity can represent a choice about personal identity based on culture. As Dalton (2008) explains it,

> [Ethnicity] describes that aspect of our heritage that provides us with a mother tongue and that shapes our values, our worldview, our family structure, our rituals, the foods we eat, our mating behavior, our music—in short, much of our daily lives. (p. 16)

Most Americans identify more than one ethnic group as part of their heritage, and for that reason ethnicity may have little meaning because of a lack of strong cultural identification with one of those groups. Some of us with multiple ethnic heritages may claim a stronger cultural affinity with one of the groups. A person may be a mixture of Irish, German, and Swedish ancestry and yet, perhaps because her surname is Irish or because Irish traditions were more strongly promoted in her family, she identifies most strongly with being Irish (Banks, 1994).

For Native Americans, ethnicity generally refers to tribal affiliation: Apache, Kwakiutl, Cherokee, Seminole, Mohawk, Hopi, or Lakota. For most African Americans, ethnic identity was obliterated by the experience of slavery, making it practically impossible to trace one's heritage to a specific tribal group such as Hausa, Ibo, Tsutsi. The introduction of the term "African American" in the 1980s was intended to provide an "ethnic" label for black people as distinct from race (Dalton, 2008). Because of the unique preservation of his oral family history, Alex Haley (1976) was able to reconnect with his ethnic group as described in the book, *Roots.*

Nationality refers to the nation in which one has citizenship. To ask people about their nationality is to ask where they reside or what nation is identified on their passport. People curious about someone's ethnic heritage often ask, "What is your nationality?" instead of "What is your ethnic background?" Being asked about one's nationality may be considered quite insulting because it implies that the questioner does not perceive the other person as American but as belonging to another country (see Figure 1.4). What do the terms *race, ethnicity,* and *nationality* have in common? They each refer to people considered to represent minority groups in the United States.

What are minority groups and why are they called minority groups?

The term **minority group** does not necessarily imply anything about the number of people in the group; however, it does imply something about their power. Minority group members possess limited power compared to members of a dominant group. It is possible for a minority group to be larger than a dominant group because it is the group's lack of power that defines it. When the white minority held power in South Africa, black South Africans were the majority in terms of numbers, but they were considered a minority group because they lacked power under the racist system of apartheid. Women in the United States are included as a minority in affirmative action plans and equity proposals even though they are numerically the majority because historically they have not held as much power as have men.

A person in a minority group must overcome obstacles—handicapping conditions—related to her or his group identification based on such factors as race, ethnicity, gender, sexual orientation, socioeconomic status, religion, or disability. Some people refer to minority groups and diversity as if the two terms are synonymous, but **diversity** refers to the presence of human beings with perceived or actual differences based on a variety of human characteristics. Diversity exists both in classrooms having no minorities and in classrooms where all students are African American; too often, these differences can result in some children being stigmatized and marginalized by other children. The concept of diversity includes minority groups as well as groups identified according to differences based on age, marital status, parental status, educational status, geographic location, physical characteristics, and other factors that influence individual personality and behavior. As Banks (2006) has noted, it is imperative to recognize the interactions of all these variables in order to understand individual behavior.

How have minority groups been perceived by the majority?

The majority group has created derogatory names for members of minority groups. When a dominant group has the power to label a subordinate group, others will consistently associate that label with individuals from the subordinate group. The power to label results in the power to define the people in a group, not only for the dominant group, but sometimes for the members of the labeled group as well. In recognition of the power of such labels, many groups have engaged in efforts to label themselves in a positive way. In the 1960s, many in the group that the majority had labeled "colored people" or "Negroes" rejected the majority group's names and chose to call themselves "blacks." This was accompanied by calls for "black power" and claims that "Black is beautiful." Many black people continue to prefer that designation because they believe it makes a positive contribution to an individual's sense of identity. Since the 1960s, "African American" has also become a popular choice among black people and others as a positive label for this group.

When a majority group has the power to label and define those belonging to a minority group,

FIGURE 1.4
Nationalities of Ethnic Immigrants to America

Source: Schaefer, R.T. *Racial and ethnic groups, 10th Edition,* Copyright © 2006, p. 101. Reprinted by permission of Pearson Education, Inc., Upper Saddle River, NJ.

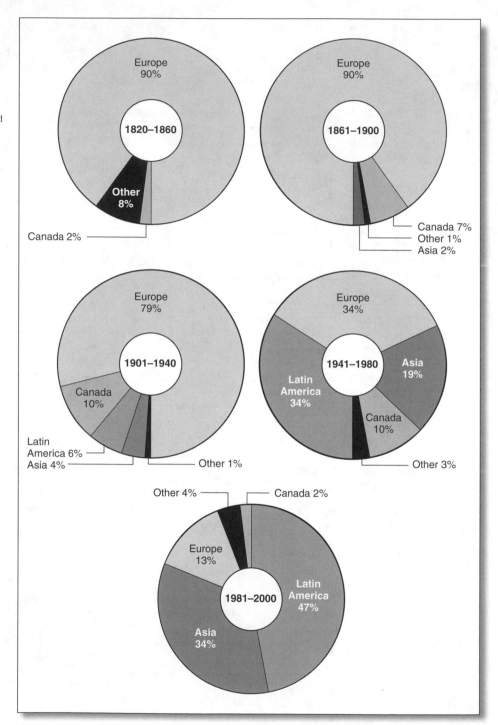

they also can control subordinate group members, obviously by limiting their opportunities, but sometimes in more subtle ways as well. Macedo and Bartoleme (2001) compare the term *migrant*, which most often labels Latinos seeking economic opportunity in the United States, with the term *settlers*, which is used to designate English and other Europeans immigrating to America to improve their economic opportunities. Reactions to the two terms are significantly different, even though both terms describe people engaged in a similar quest.

How have labels been used to define and control subordinate groups?

The idea that the power to label equals the power to define, which equals the power to control was illustrated by the 2007 media coverage of the incident at Virginia Polytechnic Institute in which South Korean student Seung-Chi Ho killed 32 students and wounded 25 others before taking his own life. The media reported Cho's history of mental illness and that he was hospitalized for a time, but the coverage never mentioned that Cho's violence was unusual for the 46% of American adults diagnosed with some form of mental illness at some point in their lives (Friedman, 2008). Perhaps the failure to report lack of violence from mentally ill people reflects the history of various forms of American media labeling and portraying mentally ill people as dangerous.

In American films, mentally ill characters are often presented as prone to violent acts, whether in classic films like Alfred Hitchcock's *Psycho* or in numerous low-budget "slasher" films. In addition, the news media tends to report incidents of violence when mentally ill people are responsible: A 2005 survey of 70 major U.S. newspapers found that almost 40% of the stories on mentally ill people emphasized how dangerous they are, and yet research indicates that mentally ill people are responsible for only 3–5% of the violence in the United States (Friedman, 2008). Since studies have found that drinking alcohol increases violent behavior, Friedman concludes: "You have far more to fear from an intoxicated businessman in a suit than from a homeless man muttering on the street corner" (2008, p. A3). This overemphasis on violent behavior and the lack of information on the reality of mental illness, including information about people who have achieved success despite having a mental disorder, has caused many Americans to accept the label and to stereotype mentally ill people as dangerous and violent. For this reason, many Americans believe that mentally ill people should not receive outpatient care, but be institutionalized for their own protection and for the protection of society.

Labels related to mental illness are official, formal, bureaucratic terms; others are informal and societal—terms used or heard by people in everyday life. The existence of **derisive labels**—terms reflecting a sense of contempt or ridicule based on factors such as race, class, disability, sexual orientation, and gender—and their variety suggest the extent to which prejudices exist. Words such as *nigger, spic, chink, buck,* and *squaw* represent only a few of the racist terms in English. Wessler (2001) described the observations of elementary educators who have heard children using such labels, especially during recess where children may feel they have more freedom to express themselves. Stephan (1999) insists that reducing prejudice requires that teachers help children become aware of the tendency to attach negative labels to others. After all, such words can be heard on the playgrounds of America, and some, for example, the word *squaw*, even show up in instructional materials such as maps, textbooks, or activities.

One theory of the origin of the word *squaw* is that it derives from a French word meaning vagina and was used by early French trappers to indicate that they wanted sex, usually followed by an offer to pay or barter something (Chavers, 1997). Other linguists claim that squaw has a more neutral origin, merely referring to a woman, but as Green (1975) demonstrated, its use has been consistently negative. The word *squaw* can still be found in elementary school materials and in names for lakes and other geographic sites around the United States.

Because they objected to the term, high school students in Minnesota successfully lobbied the state legislature to change the names of state geographical sites containing "squaw," yet at least one white community in Minnesota, Squaw Lake, refused to change. Chavers (1977) reports that students have lobbied other state legislatures to delete squaw in geographic sites or town names because the word is offensive and insulting to Native American women.

The power of labels was the focus of a study that asked subjects to supervise groups whose task was to make a collective decision on various issues (Zimbardo, 2007). The "supervisor" listened to the group's conversation from an adjacent room, and was asked to evaluate the group's decision-making process using criteria provided that was supposed to describe good decision-making. If the group made a bad decision, the supervisor was supposed to give them an electric shock ranging from a mild shock at level one to the maximum level of ten. No one was actually shocked, but supervisors heard a recording that simulated people being shocked.

The researcher was interested in how supervisors would be affected by overhearing labels ascribed to a group. The subjects "overheard" the researcher talking to his assistant over the intercom, describing the group that the subject was asked to supervise as an "animalistic, rotten bunch," or as a "perceptive, thoughtful group," another group was not labeled either positively or negatively. Supervisors tended to give minimal shocks to all groups after the first trial, but as the experiment went on and groups continued to make bad decisions, the "punishment" chosen for the groups began to diverge. Supervisors tended to shock the group labeled "animalistic" with more intensity and they increased the shock level on subsequent decision-making exercises, whereas those teams labeled positively were given the smallest amount of shock and the neutral group fell in between. The study suggested that labels can enhance or diminish the human qualities we ascribe to others, and when human qualities are diminished, our concerns for not harming an individual or group may also be diminished.

What is the impact of labels on individuals who are labeled?

Wright (1998) believes that young children are only minimally aware of skin color and often unaware of race. Asked what color she was, a three-year-old black girl wearing a pink and blue dress responded, "I'm pink and blue. What color are you?" At about the age of four, children begin to understand that skin color is permanent, yet they do not regard it as

negative. At five years of age, children are likely to become more interested in differences of skin color and may ask teachers many questions; they also begin to be aware of race and societal attitudes about racial differences. However, true racial awareness does not tend to become a significant issue until children are eight or nine years old. Because of children's growing awareness of skin color and racial attitudes, teachers must consciously confront name-calling and other forms of prejudice in their classrooms and on the playground.

Racist name-calling usually involves blatant, ugly words that carry harshly negative connotations: *coon, jungle bunny, gook, greaser, wetback, timber nigger.* What impact does it have on a child to hear such words? Sometimes members of a subordinate group believe and internalize myths, stereotypes, and prejudices expressed about their group by the dominant group. Even for those who do not internalize the negative messages, being called derisive names, especially by other children, has an impact on children and youth. Anthropologist Jamake Highwater, who was orphaned, Native American, and gay, commented on the many derisive terms he heard as a child:

> At first, the words had no meaning to me. Even when I was told their meaning, I couldn't easily grasp why they were supposed to be shameful . . . [They] were whispered in the classroom and remorselessly shouted when adults were not around. On the playground. In the locker room. In the darkness of the balcony at Saturday movie matinees. Those were the words that filled my childhood.
>
> They were words that aroused a sense of power and self-aggrandizement for those who shouted them; they brought shame and humiliation in those at whom they were shouted. Words were weapons, fired in rapid succession in order to hold back an intrusion of outsiders—the "them"—aliens, deviants, perverts, and barbarians. Words were a psychological Great Wall of China, staunchly guarding the frontiers of conformity and an unrelenting notion of the superiority of insiders. (2001, pp. 24–25)

Highwater believes that derisives, derogatory terms, damage individuals in the dominant group as well as those in subordinate or minority groups because derisive language creates boundaries. Derisive terms define the oppressor as superior and the oppressed as inferior. Herbst (1997) agrees that such terms create suspicion, fear, and contempt in members of dominant groups and arouse frustration and anger in individuals from subordinate groups. In his struggle for social justice, Martin Luther King, Jr. (1963) insisted that his followers not hate oppressors, but instead hate oppression. Some groups have tried to take over certain words, to "own" them and reshape them to make them less hurtful. African Americans, especially urban blacks, have taken the word *nigger* for their own purposes, as can be heard in their rap music (Kennedy, 2002). Gay men and lesbians, especially young people, are using the word *queer* as a generic term for the gay community, and courses in queer studies have sprung up on college campuses in an attempt to change formal, bureaucratic language (Jagose, 1996).

How are negative bureaucratic terms as harmful as social derisive terms?

When we think of derisive terms, we usually think of informal, social labels. Derisive terms for social class, such as *hillbilly* or *redneck,* often have a regional origin but may become widespread as in *white trash,* a term that evolved into a variety of forms including *trailer park trash.* Yet some argue that the most harmful derisive terms for low-income people come from formal sources such as government reports and scholarly studies; these terms include *culturally deprived, culturally disadvantaged, welfare households, inner-city residents.* What images do such terms conjure? Derisive bureaucratic terms are powerful purveyors of negative images primarily because they have the sanction of authority behind them.

In addition to negative images, derisive bureaucratic terms send a negative message. Being labeled culturally deprived represents a form of blaming the victim. What group are we talking about? What do they lack? The term *cultural deprivation* suggests that poor people lack an ability to appreciate arts and humanities; it does not acknowledge the reality that they are economically deprived and need financial assistance for such things as job training, employment, and better health care. Labeling poor people

culturally deprived implies that a deficiency in cultural qualities, perhaps certain values, is the cause of their problems.

People with disabilities are labeled with derisive social and bureaucratic terms. Around the world people have heard and told "moron jokes" as chil-

> One may no more live in the world without picking up the moral prejudices of the world than one will be able to go to Hell without perspiring.
>
> H. L. MENCKEN (1880–1956)

dren, and Linton (1998) argues that when children insult others by calling them *retard, dummy, cripple,* or *gimp,* they are asserting a claim to normalcy and rejecting those who are deviant and unacceptable because of disability. In a bureaucratic setting, the term *handicapped* labels people as deviant. Since the 1950s, people with disabilities have objected to the term *handicapped* and have lobbied with some success to have it removed from common bureaucratic usage. Derisive bureaucratic terms are also represented by such phrases as the retarded and the disabled. These terms isolate one adjective for a disabled person and make it a noun to label the group. According to Charlton (1998), people with disabilities persistently object to the practice of labeling them with such adjectives because "their humanity is stripped away and the person is obliterated, only to be left with the condition— disability" (p. 54).

To understand what Charlton means, imagine a person who is either active or acquiescent, bold or bashful, cynical or compassionate, devilish or devout, and now add disabled to the description. If the last adjective is singled out and made a noun, that word defines the person being imagined. Using a term like *the disabled* defines and diminishes people with a disability because it focuses on only one aspect of their existence. Historically, nondisabled people in America all too often have viewed people with disabilities as unable to care for themselves. *The retarded* and *the disabled* have been institutionalized and the action was justified by claims that it was "for their own good." The history of institutionalized people with disabilities illustrates the power of everyday language labels to define and ultimately control the quality of life for those who have been labeled.

How has our society responded to social problems experienced by minority groups?

Ryan (1976) described two radically different approaches involved in addressing social problems. The **exceptionalistic perspective** focuses on individuals; it perceives all problems as local, unique, and unpredictable. Because problems are viewed as a consequence of *individual* defect, accident, or unfortunate circumstance, proposed remedies must be tailored to fit each individual case that is an "exception" to the general situation. A criticism of this approach is that it treats only *symptoms* of problems and not causes; exceptionalistic remedies have been derided as "Band-Aid solutions" that alleviate but do not solve problems.

Ryan describes an alternative approach, a **universalistic perspective** that views social problems as systemic, beginning in fundamental social structures within a community or a society. Because social structures are inevitably imperfect and inequitable, the problems that emerge are predictable and preventable because they do not stem from a situation unique to one individual but rather from conditions common to many. The universalistic perspective emphasizes engaging in research to collect and analyze data and to identify patterns that predict certain outcomes. Once patterns and root causes are identified, appropriate solutions can be created and implemented through public action, institutional policy, or legislation. Research takes time, so the universalistic approach has been criticized because it does not address the immediate consequences of particular problems or assist people who are currently suffering.

To illustrate the difference between exceptionalistic and universalistic perspectives, Ryan describes two responses to the problem of smallpox. An exceptionalistic approach would be to provide smallpox victims with medical care to help them recover; a universalistic approach would first demand legislation to fund inoculation of the population to pre-

vent the disease from spreading. The contrast is similar to a metaphor from Kilbourne (1999) about bodies floating down a river and ambulances being called to rescue the drowning people. Although rescuing people from the river is important, it is also important to send someone upstream to investigate how people are falling in (p. 30).

The metaphors illustrate a need for both approaches. While people are engaged in studying problems, help must be provided to those who are suffering right now. If everyone goes upstream to discover how people are falling into the river, no one is left to save people who are drowning; if everyone stays downstream to rescue drowning people, the cause of the problem will never be found. Neither perspective can be neglected in the efforts employed to solve social problems.

AFTERWORD

The chapter began by discussing diversity and individuality. Holding differing values is part of both diversity and individuality. The values we choose are influenced by our membership in groups defined by such factors as race, ethnicity, gender, and social class; however, the ultimate decision to embrace certain values is up to the individual. Almost everyone

> Freedom is the right to choose: the right to create for yourself the alternatives of choice. Without the possibility of choice and the exercise of choice, human beings are not human but instruments, things.
>
> **Archibald MacLeish (1892–1982)**

holds some values similar to those of their parents, and almost everyone holds some values different from those of their parents. We share values with friends, yet we hold some values that are different from theirs. Values, and the attitudes and beliefs that determine them, are part of the landscape of human differences. But beliefs and attitudes change as we learn more information that helps us to understand

and appreciate diversity. For those interested in exploring their own attitudes concerning diversity issues, an Attitude Inventory is available on the MyEducationLab web site (www.myeducationlab.com). Respond to the statements now, and when you have finished reading this book, you may want to return to the Attitude Inventory and respond to the statements about these issues again.

Language is the primary tool we use to pursue understanding. When we use language that labels a group of people, we create misunderstanding. It is important to observe and evaluate the behaviors of others, but we will never understand them without interacting with them or reading what they have written. Confusing or ambiguous language is like a smudge on the lens of a microscope; it prevents us from having a clear understanding of our subject. This chapter has tried to clarify some confusing terms so that our view is not distorted as we begin our study of human differences.

When Jewish author Isaac Bashevis Singer was asked if he believed people had free will, he replied, "Of course we have free will, we have no choice." As citizens of a democracy, we have many choices. As human beings living in a diverse society surrounded by diverse global cultures, trying to understand human differences would seem to be a necessary choice. For every reader who has already made that choice, this book offers insights and information to enhance your understanding. For readers who have not made that choice, this book may help to create an understanding of why the choice is necessary. But it is still each person's choice to make; as Singer said, we have no choice about that.

TERMS AND DEFINITIONS

Attitude   A cluster of particular related beliefs, values, and opinions

Beliefs   Inferences a person makes about reality that take one of three forms: descriptive, evaluative, or prescriptive

Bias   A preference or inclination, favorable or unfavorable, that inhibits impartial judgment

Bigotry   Extreme negative attitudes leading to hatred of a group and persons regarded as members of the group

Derisive labels   Names that reflect attitudes of contempt or ridicule for individuals in the group being named

Discrimination   Actions or practices carried out by a member or members of dominant groups, or their representatives that have a differential and negative impact on a member or members of subordinate groups

Diversity   The presence of human beings with perceived or actual differences based on a variety of human characteristics

Dogmatic   To accept beliefs one has been taught without questioning them

Ethnicity   Identification of an individual according to his or her national origin and/or distinctive cultural patterns

Exceptionalistic perspective   Views social problems as private, local, unique, exclusive, and unpredictable, a consequence of individual defect, accident, or unfortunate circumstance, which requires that all proposed remedies be tailored to fit each individual case

Indoctrination   Instruction whose purpose is to force the learner to accept a set of values or beliefs, to adopt a particular ideology or perspective

Minority group   A subordinate group whose members have significantly less power to control their own lives than do members of a dominant, or majority group

Nationality   The nation in which an individual has citizenship status

Prejudice   A negative attitude toward a group and persons perceived to be members of that group; being predisposed to behave negatively toward members of a group

Race   A social concept with no scientific basis that categorizes people according to obvious physical differences such as skin color

Stereotype   A positive or negative trait or traits ascribed to a certain group and to most members of that group

Universalistic perspective   Views social problems as public, national, general, inclusive, and predictable; a consequence of imperfect and inequitable social arrangements which require research to identify their patterns and causes so that remedial institutional action can be taken to elimi-nate these problems and prevent them from reoc-curring

Values   Combinations of attitudes that generate action or the deliberate choice to avoid action

DISCUSSION EXERCISES

Discussion exercises are provided in which groups of three to five students can delve deeper into the content presented in the chapter.

Clarification Exercise—My Values: What I Believe

Directions: Create personal responses to each of the ten items below. Share your responses individually with several others and listen to their responses to those same items.

1. *Past and future:* Assume that you will have children. Why (or why not) will you treat your children the same way that your parents treated you?
2. *Success and achievement:* If you could wake up tomorrow morning having gained any one ability or quality, what would it be? Why would you choose that ability or quality?
3. *Friendship and personal life:* If you made up your mind to do something, but when your friends heard about it, they strongly advised you not to, why might you do it anyway?
4. *Possessions and priorities:* If you could have a wonderful new experience that you would remember for the rest of your life or be given something you have always wanted, which would you choose?
5. *Money and values:* Would you rather be given $100,000 for your own use or $1 million to give anonymously to strangers? If you prefer the former, what would you do with the money? If you prefer the latter, how would you arrange to contribute it?
6. *Living and dying:* Has your life ever changed dramatically as the result of some seemingly random event over which you had no control? To what degree, or in what ways, do you feel you have control over the course of your life?

7. *Physical well-being and disabling conditions:* Would you like to have a child much smarter than you? Much more handsome or beautiful than you? Would it bother you to have a child who had a disability or was physically unattractive?
8. *Leadership and responsibility:* If you were given full responsibility for creating a one-hour television show that millions of people would watch, about anything you wanted, what would it be about?
9. *Individuality and choices:* If you could be granted one magical power, what would you ask for?
10. *Social and personal responses:* When should it be illegal to help a terminally ill person to die? If someone is not dying but has chronic pain, should that person be assisted to commit suicide? What if the person is in emotional rather than physical pain?

Selected and adapted from Gregory Stock, *The Book of Questions* (1987) and *The Kid's Book of Questions* (1988) (New York: Workman Publishing).

Intergroup Exercise—A Mutual Support Dilemma

Directions: Examine the case situation explained below. Discuss it with those in your assigned group. Respond to each of the questions. Then, explain your group position to the class.

The Story of Mary and Luke: A Mutual Support Dilemma

Mary and Luke were married during their senior year in college. After their graduation, Mary took a secretarial job in the registrar's office of the university where Luke was attending graduate school. Mary worked for five years while Luke completed his doctoral degree. Their first and only child was born the second of the five years and Mary missed only two months of work at that time.

Luke has now been offered an assistant professorship at a prominent eastern school and is eager to accept it. Mary has applied and been accepted into graduate school at the University of Chicago. She is eager to accept the assistantship that she has been offered.

Mary argues that Luke should give her the chance for an education now that he has completed his. She also reminds him that he has been offered a job at the Chicago Junior College. Luke says that he intends to take the job in the east and that Mary can find someplace out there to go to school.

If Mary refuses to follow him, Luke promises to file for a divorce and seek custody of their three-year-old daughter.

Questions for discussion:

1. What would you do if you were Mary?
2. What advice do you have for Luke?
3. How could this situation be handled so that neither Mary nor Luke loses?
4. Does your group agree that either Mary or Luke loses?

REFERENCES

Andrzejewski, J. (Ed.). (1996). Definitions for understanding oppression and social justice. *Oppression and social justice: Critical frameworks*. Boston, MA: Pearson Custom Publishing.

Provides definitions for a variety of terms essential for discussing intergroup relations.

Aronson, E. (2008). *The social animal* (10th ed.). New York, NY: Worth Publishers.

Presents an overview of research in social psychology and describes people behaving inconsistently with their expressed attitudes in Chapter 2 on conformity.

Banks, J.A. (1994). The complex nature of ethnic groups in modern society. In *Multiethnic education: Theory and practice* (3rd ed.). Boston, MA: Allyn & Bacon.

Describes ethnic diversity in the United States, assimilation issues that have historically confronted ethnic groups, and how ethnicity influences individual identity in contemporary society.

Banks, J.A. (2006). Multicultural education: Characteristics and goals. In J.A. Banks & C.A. McGee Banks (Eds.), *Multicultural education: Issues and perspectives* (6th ed.). New York, NY: Wiley.

Describes the evolution of multicultural education, the importance of group identification, and how implementation of multicultural education meets the needs of diverse students.

Barzun, J. (1965). *Race: A study in superstition* (rev. ed.). New York, NY: Harper & Row.

Explains why race is a pseudoscientific concept with an appendix of racial (mostly racist) quotes from authors, scientists, and mystics.

Bellah, R., Madsen, R., Sullivan, W., Swidler, A., & Tipton, S. (1991). *The good society*. New York, NY: Vintage.

Presents quantitative and qualitative data from interviews with Americans talking about what values and behavior are necessary for creating a good society.

Botkin, B.A. (1957). *A treasury of American anecdotes*. New York, NY: Bonanza Books.

Includes over 300 anecdotes about famous, infamous, and ordinary Americans; the Jefferson anecdote originally appeared in a German Almanac published in Pennsylvania.

Charlton, J.I. (1998). *Nothing about us without us*. Berkeley: University of California Press.

Examines the status of people with a disability in various cultures.

Chavers, D. (1997). Doing away with the "S" word. *Indian Country Today, 16*(37), 5.

Describes efforts of high school students to force Minnesota to change the names of state geographic features that include the word *squaw.*

Dalton, H. (2008). Failing to see. In P. Rothenberg (Ed.), *White privilege: Essential readings on the other side of racism* (3rd ed.). New York, NY: Worth.

Discusses race and ethnicity and how white has been defined as the norm in the United States, making white people oblivious to the role of race in the formation of their identity.

Feagin, J., & Feagin, C. (2008). Basic concepts in the study of racial and ethnic relations. In *Racial and ethnic relations* (8th ed.). Upper Saddle River, NJ: Prentice Hall.

Explains major terms and concepts in intergroup relations and includes a glossary for all terms used in the book.

Franklin, K. (2000). Anti-gay behaviors among young adults. *Journal of Interpersonal Violence, 15*, 339–363.

A survey of 484 young adults concerning their participation in name-calling, physical violence, or threats against homosexuals.

Friedman, R.A. (2008, July/August). Media and madness. *The American Prospect, 19*(7), A2–A4.

Discusses media portrayals and descriptions of people with mental illness as violent and cites research refuting these stereotypes.

Gamber, F. (2007, March/April). Stars come out for NAACP Image Awards. *The Crisis, 114*(2), 36–37.

Identifies the recipients being honored at the 2007 NAACP Image Awards.

Gosset, T.F. (1997). *Race: The history of an idea in America.* Dallas, TX: Southern Methodist University Press.

Describes attitudes about race in colonial America, the evolution of this concept into a pseudo-scientific theory in the nineteenth century, and its debunking by scholars in the 1930s.

Gould, S.J. (2002). The geometer of race. In *I have landed: The end of a beginning in natural history* (pp. 356–366). New York, NY: Harmony Books.

Describes the origins and influence of J. F. Blumenbach's theory of racial classifications.

Green, R. (1975). The Pocohontas perplex: Images of Indian women in American cultures. *Massachusetts Review, 16,* 698–714.

Discusses the historic use of the term *squaw.*

Haag, P. (2000). *Voices of a generation: Teenage girls report about their lives today.* New York, NY: Marlow.

Examines responses of more than 2,000 females, ages 11 to 17, to six questions revealing a variety of explicit and implicit issues related to their public and privates lives.

Haley, A. (1976). *Roots.* Garden City, NY: Doubleday.

Describes the author's use of family stories to establish his ethnic background in Africa.

Herbst, P. (1997). Ethnic epithets in society. In *The color of words: An encyclopedic dictionary of ethnic bias in the United States* (pp. 255–259). Yarmouth, ME: Intercultural Press.

Describes the purpose of ethnic slurs and their effect on those who use them.

Herdt, G. (1997). *Same sex, different cultures: Exploring gay and lesbian lives.* Boulder, CO: Westview.

Reviews anthropological and cross-cultural evidence on attitudes toward sexual orientation and provides a glossary of essential terms.

Highwater, J. (1997). *The mythology of transgression: Homosexuality as metaphor.* New York, NY: Oxford University Press.

Describes the impact of derisive language directed against a child perceived by others as "different" in Chapter 2, "Inside the Walls" (pp. 23–30).

Jagose, A. (1996). *Queer theory: An introduction.* Washington Square, NY: New York University Press.

Explains why the term "queer" has evolved from derogatory slang to an umbrella term for people with diverse sexual self-identifications.

Jones, J. (1997). *Prejudice and racism* (2nd ed.). New York, NY: McGraw-Hill.

Integrates data from psychology, sociology, and history to explain the relationship between prejudice and racism in their appropriate sociocultural historical context.

Kennedy, R. (2002). *Nigger: The strange career of a troublesome word.* New York, NY: Pantheon Books.

Discusses the various historical uses of the term "nigger," including the more recent attempts by some African Americans to use the word in positive ways.

Kilborn, P.T. (2005). The five-bedroom, six-figure rootless life. In *Class matters* (correspondents of the *New York Times*) (pp. 146–165). New York, NY: Times Books.

Examines the increasing geographical isolation for middle/upper-middle class Americans as suburbs segregate not only by class but also by race, religion, and ethnic origin.

Kilbourne, J. (1999). *Deadly persuasion: Why women and girls must fight the addictive power of advertising.* New York, NY: The Free Press.

Argues that advertising is a pervasive cultural phenomenon that encourages people to objectify each other in a way that diminishes the quality of human relationships.

King, M.L., Jr. (1963). *Strength to love.* Philadelphia, PA: Fortress.

Contains many sermons addressing the idea of not hating oppressors, including "Loving Your Enemies."

Kniker, C.R. (1977). *You and values education.* Columbus, OH: Charles E. Merrill.

Summarizes theory and research concerning values and describes alternative approaches to teaching values in schools.

Lappe, F.M. (1989). *Rediscovering America's values.* New York, NY: Ballantine.

Presents a dialogue with one perspective emphasizing individualism and the other perspective emphasizing communitarianism and egalitarianism.

LeBon, G. (1968). The mind of crowds. In R. Evans (Ed.), *Readings in collective behavior.* Chicago: Rand McNally.

Examines the general characteristics of crowds and crowd behavior, especially the influence of emotional and moral factors on the behavior of crowds.

Lefkowitz, B. (1997). *Our guys: The Glen Ridge rape and the secret life of the perfect suburb.* Berkeley: University of California Press.

Explains the contradictions reflected in the upbringing and behavior of "All American" boys from the suburbs who gang rape a mentally retarded girl.

Levin, J., & Levin, W. (1982). *The functions of discrimination and prejudice* (2nd ed.). New York, NY: Harper & Row.

Describes the functions of prejudice for both the majority and minority groups; describes causes and effects of prejudice; and provides definitions of critical terms.

Linton, S. (1998). Reassigning meaning. In *Claiming disability: Knowledge and identity* (pp. 8–33). New York, NY: New York University Press.

Discusses "nice words" and "nasty words" for disabled people, and explains why some people with disabilities have begun to use the word *crip* in a positive way.

Macedo, D., & Bartolome, L.I. (2001). *Dancing with bigotry: Beyond the politics of tolerance.* New York, NY: Palgrave.

Examines issues concerning language, race, ethnicity, and limitations of teaching tolerance; the discussion of migrant versus settlers is in Chapter 1.

Mead, C. (1985). *Champion: Joe Louis—black hero in white America.* New York, NY: Charles Scribner.

Describes the life and boxing career of Joe Louis and his struggles with racism.

Miller, C., & Swift, K. (2000). *Words and women.* San Jose, CA: iUniverse

Analyzes sexism in the English language and provides many examples; discusses the inclusion of racism and sexism in dictionaries on page 141.

Myrdal, G. (1944). *An American dilemma: The Negro problem and modern democracy.* New York, NY: Harper & Row.

Describes values and contradictions in American culture and how they relate to the pervasive prejudice in American society.

Newberg, A., & Waldman, M.R. (2006). *Why we believe what we believe: Uncovering our biological needs for meaning, spirituality, and truth.* New York, NY: Free Press.

Proposes a new way of thinking about how convictions develop and influence individuals, based on recent research on how the brain perceives (and transforms) reality.

Olson, S. (2002). *Mapping human history: Discovering the past through our genes.* Boston, MA: Houghton Mifflin.

Describes human history as revealed by recent research on DNA that has concluded that human beings share a common African ancestor and do not consist of separate races.

Pagels, E. (2006). *The Gnostic gospels.* London, England: Phoenix.

Examines Gnostic beliefs as related to debates among early Christians regarding beliefs about Christ's resurrection and divinity, monotheism, and gender roles in the church.

Raths, L., Harmin, M., & Simon, S. (1978). *Values and teaching: Working with values in the classroom* (2nd ed.). Columbus, OH: Charles E. Merrill.

Addresses the issue of traditional approaches to teaching values as forms of indoctrination and describes these approaches.

Risberg, D.F. (1978, June 18). *Framework and foundations: Setting the stage and establishing norms.* Paper presented at the first annual National Conference on Human Relations, Minneapolis, MN.

Describes the development of human relations as an academic discipline incorporating knowledge from other disciplines but creating its own structure, paradigms, and language.

Ryan, W. (1976). *Blaming the victim* (2nd ed.). New York, NY: Vintage.

Explains exceptionalistic and universalistic perspectives on pages 17–20.

Schaefer, R.T. (2008). *Racial and ethnic groups* (11th ed.). Upper Saddle River, NJ: Pearson.

Provides information on racial and ethnic minorities, but also includes chapters on women, religious diversity, immigrants, and cross-cultural comparisons.

Simpson, G.E., & Yinger, J.M. (1985). *Racial and cultural minorities: An analysis of prejudice and discrimination* (5th ed.). New York, NY: Plenum.

Examines causes and consequences of prejudice and discrimination in the United States and includes definitions of important terms and concepts.

Stephan, W. (1999). *Reducing prejudice and stereotyping in schools.* New York, NY: Teachers College Press.

Reviews theories of prejudice and stereotyping, examines conditions to promote changes in negative attitudes, and describes techniques for improving race relations in schools.

Terkel, S. (1980). *American dreams: Lost and found*. New York, NY: Ballantine.

Interviews diverse people about their perceptions of America, including First National Bank board member Gaylord Freeman.

Terry, D., Hogg, M., & Duck, J. (1999). Group membership, social identity, and attitudes. In D. Abrams & M. Hogg (Eds.), *Social identity and social cognition* (pp. 280–314). Malden, MA: Blackwell.

Examines how attitude–behavior consistency is influenced by both congruence of individual attitudes with group norms and the significance to the individual of group membership.

Terry, R.W. (1993). *Authentic leadership: Courage in action*. San Francisco, CA: Jossey Bass.

Examines six leadership styles by defining leadership as the ability to frame issues correctly and to respond to issues by using power legitimately and ethically.

Wade, N. (2006). *Before the dawn: Recovering the lost history of our ancestors*. New York, NY: The Penguin Press.

Reviews recent scientific discoveries in biology and the social sciences and describes the increasingly detailed information now available on human evolution.

Wessler, S.L. (2001, January). Sticks and stones. *Educational Leadership, 58*(4), 28–33.

Describes the degrading and even violent language children use in schools and the impact of this language on its victims.

Wright, M.A. (1998). *I'm chocolate, you're vanilla: Raising healthy black and biracial children in a race-conscious world*. San Francisco, CA: Jossey-Bass.

Describes the changing awareness of skin color and social attitudes about race during child development and recommends strategies to preserve children's resilience and optimism.

Wright, W. (1983). *The Von Bulow affair*. New York, NY: Delacorte.

Provides a detailed review of the case; also of interest is the film "Reversal of Fortune" (based on Alan Dershowitz's book) available on videotape (Warner Brothers, 1990).

Zimbardo, P. (2007). *The Lucifer effect: Understanding how good people turn evil*. New York, NY: Random House.

Describes research in which college students role playing prison guards became abusive to those role playing prisoners and relates that study to the abuses at Abu Ghraib prison.

Zinn, H. (1990). *Declarations of independence: Cross-examining American ideology*. New York, NY: HarperCollins.

Examines American beliefs and inconsistencies between behavior and ideals.

CHAPTER 2

Understanding Prejudice and Its Causes

> ❝No one has ever been born a Negro hater, a Jew hater, or any other kind of hater. Nature refuses to be involved in such suicidal practices.❞
>
> **Harry Bridges (1900–1990)**

No credible studies have concluded that prejudice is part of human nature, an innate outcome of being human. Instead, as Bridges suggests, prejudice is learned. It is also important to remember that prejudice is an attitude, not an action. Whether you are looking at definitions in a dictionary or reading scholarly writing, you will inevitably encounter puzzling uses of the term *prejudice*. Some people believe that prejudice involves a hatred of others, but hatred is bigotry. Based on their study of world cultures, anthropologists have argued that people everywhere in the world have prejudices, yet they do not claim that hatred—or bigotry—is widespread.

Confusion—not clarification—is caused by a definition suggesting that prejudice is synonymous with bigotry. Such a definition may cause many of us to deny that we are prejudiced: A bigot hates, and we are certain we don't hate anyone. In addition, we deny the pervasiveness of prejudice because we don't observe widespread hatred in the world; thus confusing prejudice with bigotry creates misunderstanding about the nature and extent of prejudice.

Conceptions and Misconceptions of Prejudice

What are examples of misconceptions about prejudice?

We confuse prejudice with bias, stereotypes, and bigotry. As defined in Chapter 1, bias is a mildly positive or negative feeling about someone or something; and to stereotype is to associate positive or negative traits with a group of people. **Prejudice** is a stronger feeling, but it is always negative, and it always refers to a group of people. Prejudice predisposes us to behave negatively toward certain others because of a group to which they belong. And when prejudice reaches the intensity of hatred, it becomes bigotry.

Some dictionaries define *prejudice* as the process of forming opinions without looking at relevant facts, yet people with prejudices may examine relevant facts and simply interpret them to confirm their prejudices. Other definitions describe prejudice as being irrational, implying that those we acknowledge as rational could not possibly be prejudiced. The problem here is that rational people also hold prejudices; we know this from reading what they wrote. Aristotle claimed that a woman was an inferior man. Abraham Lincoln believed black people were intellectually inferior to white people. Carroll (2001) quoted Martin Luther warning German Christians, "do not doubt that next to the devil you have no enemy more cruel, more venomous and virulent, than a true Jew" (p. 368). However, their prejudices did not deter any of these men from achieving significant improvements in human rights.

It is easy to smile at ancient racist or sexist attitudes and to denounce past prejudices as absurd, yet often we do not acknowledge current widespread prejudices that future generations may find just as absurd. In fifty or one hundred years, what will people think about the programs for the poor in the United States today? Or how people with disabilities were so often isolated or ignored? Or how gay men and lesbians were condemned by so many people?

How widespread is prejudice?

Although this book focuses on attitudes in the United States, prejudices are not limited to one country or one race. People living in nations around the world possess negative attitudes toward others within their own borders or close to them. Preju-

> There are, in every age, new errors to be rectified, and new prejudices to be opposed.
>
> SAMUEL JOHNSON (1709–1784)

dices have been ignored, promoted, or tolerated, but rarely challenged. When prejudice has been challenged, the case often has become a *cause célèbre*, as when Emile Zola published "J'accuse," an essay denouncing anti-Semitism in France's prosecution of Alfred Dreyfus for treason (Bredin, 2008). Persistence of prejudice was illustrated by Jean-Paul Sartre's (1995) 1945 description of French anti-Semitic attitudes as Jews returned to France following World War II, even though French people were

aware of the existence of Nazi concentration camps and of the genocide against the Jews.

Today, nations around the world are being forced to confront historic prejudices because of economic globalization and population migrations that have created major demographic changes. Some responses to immigration have revealed the persistence of historic prejudices. In the opening paragraph of their book on prejudice and discrimination, Simpson and Yinger (1985) describe this phenomenon:

Western European nations discovered that "guest workers," whom they have employed by the millions, are something more than cogs in an economic machine.

And, for example,

England, with a steady migration of people from India, Pakistan, Bangladesh, Africa, and the West Indies, found herself faced with problems of a color bar and passed an unprecedented law limiting immigration. Pressures against persons of Indian descent in the new nations of East Africa not only reshaped intergroup relations in those lands but influenced Britain's restrictive immigration policy (p. 3).

As long as people lived in relative isolation from others, prejudice against those who were far away was not necessarily harmful. In a global economy requiring functional and respectful relationships between nations, prejudice can be a destructive force both in the world and in individual societies, especially diverse societies (Gioseffi, 1993). Language is an important source for understanding a culture because analyzing language reveals a culture's assumptions, beliefs, values, and priorities, as well as examples of prejudice. Some countries are now addressing their historic prejudices by changing or eliminating media images and language that have promoted negative attitudes, especially toward racial or ethnic groups.

How are prejudices reflected in American media?

To understand how prejudices are transmitted in our culture, we need only observe some of the prevalent images of racial or cultural groups in society. As Giroux (1998) said,

My concern with such representations . . . lies not in deciding whether they are "good" or "bad" but in analyzing them in relation to the pedagogical work they are doing. That is, what knowledge, values, and pleasures do such representations invite or exclude? (p. 27)

Look for magazine advertisements that depict Native Americans, Asian Americans, or Hispanic Americans. Why is it that most advertisements seem to use African American models to reflect diversity? If people of color are included in advertisements, why are they often featured in ways that reflect historic stereotypes? Native Americans are almost never portrayed as contemporary people but as nineteenth-century warriors; Asian Americans are often shown working at computers or in math-related professions; Mexican Americans are presented as gardeners or servants. Problems of omission and stereotyping affect other groups as well: People with disabilities are invisible, blue-collar workers are usually stereotyped, if they appear at all, and women appear frequently in advertisements as sex objects to sell products. Still, we typically don't recognize these advertisements as stereotypes because these images are so familiar that they seem not to be stereotypes at all, but rather to portray reality. This is one reason so many white Americans do not understand why Native Americans find offensive the use of Indian mascots for sports teams. (See Figure 2.1.)

Media portrayals of Muslim Americans represent the most recent example of pervasive stereotyping. Although anti-Muslim attitudes in the United States have a long history, Ansari (2004) insists that ever since the 1979 Iranian hostage crisis, the media has focused on activities of militant Muslims. Since then, media portrayals have often presented Muslims as "irrational, undemocratic (and) opposed to equality, freedom, and peace" (Khan, 2004, p. 100). According to McCloud (2006), the stereotype of Muslims as evil terrorists existed prior to 9/11, but such representations in the media have increased, and these portrayals have most likely contributed to the results reported in a 2004 opinion poll, where 25% of Americans said they had negative attitudes about Muslims and 50% supported the federal government restricting the civil liberties of Muslim Americans (Barrett, 2007). McCloud (2004) concluded that American media "have declared Islam and Muslims as violent, irrational, and anti-modern" (p. 79).

FIGURE 2.1

Source: John Branch, *San Antonio Express-News.*

Although the media bears some responsibility for reinforcing a variety of stereotypes, there are other sources that foster negative attitudes. One reason why many Americans may not even recognize portrayals of certain groups as stereotypical is because of the prejudices embedded in our language.

What examples of prejudice exist in our language?

One pattern observed in the English language has been called the **black/white syndrome**. Scholars report that this language pattern emerged in English long before the British knew that people described as black were living in Africa (Moore, 2006). Although the pattern likely originated in biblical language referring to Satan, evil, and hell as black or dark, it has been argued that a consistently negative pattern for references to black affected British perceptions of Africans and that negative connotations for blackness were readily applied to all dark-skinned people they encountered. A negative pattern for black has persisted in the English language, as can be seen in familiar phrases: black deed, black day, black hearted, black mass, black magic, the Black Death, black thoughts, black looks, and blacklist. Such words and phrases illustrate the point made by linguist Skuttnab-Kangas (2000), "Dominant groups keep a monopoly of defining others, and it is their labels we see in dictionaries" (p. 154).

Skuttnab-Kangas also argues that labeling others includes "the power to define oneself" by not having to accept the definitions others have for your group. It should not be surprising that references to "white" in the English language follow a consistently positive pattern: telling little white lies, having a white wedding, cheering white knights (in shining armor), indicating approval by saying "that's really white of you," and even engaging in white-collar crime (perceived as less harmful than other crimes). Some authors have exploited the pervasive black/white pattern by deliberately using white as a negative term, invoking images of sterility, death, or evil to shock readers with unexpected associations. Robert Frost employed this reversal in some of his poems, and it was no accident that Herman Melville chose to make Moby Dick, the symbol of evil in Ahab's obsession, a white whale.

Sometimes prejudice is not obvious, as in the expression, "Where there's a will there's a way." At first glance, this expression seems nothing more than an attempt to encourage children and youth to try hard, but it has another meaning: If all that it takes to be successful is to have the will to succeed, then those people who are not successful are at fault for their failure because they just didn't "try" hard enough. This belief leads to blaming the victim, providing an ethical escape for middle-class people. After all, if they were successful because they worked hard, then someone who is poor must not have worked hard enough, perhaps because they are lazy or incompetent.

Such stereotypes for "the poor" reinforces the conclusion that poor people are responsible for their poverty, and the rest of us are under no obligation to help them. Other stereotypes may be revealed in expressions. When people negotiate with the seller on the price of a product they might say, "I Jewed him down," alluding to an old stereotype. Parents and teachers have been overheard telling children to stop behaving "like a bunch of wild Indians."

> You can tell the ideals of a nation by its advertisements.
>
> NORMAN DOUGLAS (1868–1952)

Teenagers who say, "That's so gay" do not intend it as a compliment. Boys are still ridiculed by comments such as "he throws like a girl" or "he's a sissy." Children are no longer limited to the term *sissy*. Today, even elementary children can be heard calling one another a *faggot*. They may not be certain what the word means, but they know it is a negative term (Wessler, 2001).

And then there are jokes, based on racial, ethnic, gender, or other prejudices. When we complain that these jokes aren't funny, we are likely to be told we don't have a sense of humor: "It was a joke!" Just a joke. Although people are more careful today about telling racist jokes, sexist jokes are frequently told at work and in school. Perhaps the numerous examples of sexist words and phrases in our language make it easier to express sexist attitudes publicly.

How does gender prejudice in our language promote sexist attitudes?

Unlike many other languages, English does not have a neutral pronoun that includes both men and women, so the word *he* is used to refer to someone of indeterminate gender. *Man* has traditionally been used in words or phrases where the referent could be female (even though there are neutral nouns such as *human* and *people*). Some people continue to insist that *man* is generic when used in words such as *businessman, chairman, congressman, fireman, layman, mailman, policeman, salesman, spokesman*, and *statesman*, but studies do not support the claim. Arliss (1991) described studies using subjects ranging from elementary children to adults; all concluded that generic language invoked mental images of males.

In a study reported by Miller and Swift (2000) involving 500 junior high students, one group of students received instructions to draw pictures of "early man" engaged in various activities and to give each person drawn a name (so researchers could be certain that a man or woman was the subject of the drawing). The majority of students of both sexes tended to draw only males for every activity identified except the one representing infant care, and even for that activity, 49% of boys drew a male image. A second group of students was instructed to draw pictures of "early people" engaged in the same activities and to give each human figure drawn a name; once again, the majority of the humans drawn by both sexes were male. It is possible

> I am, in plainer words, a bundle of prejudices—made up of likings and dislikings.
>
> **Charles Lamb (1775–1834)**

that the phrase *early people* sounded strange and that many students translated it as "cave men" and drew male pictures. The third group of students was asked to draw pictures of "early men and early women," once again giving names to human figures. Only in this group did the figures drawn by students include a significant number of female images, but even with these instructions, some students of both sexes drew only male figures.

What sexist terms for men could be considered derisive?

Although a plethora of derisive terms exist for women, derisive language directed at men often sends a mixed message. It may be intended as an insult to call a man a *prick* or a *bastard*, but it can also be interpreted as the speaker being envious of the man's power or position. Men may feel that they have to be tough, ruthless, and relentless if they are going to be successful in a "dog eat dog world"; such language could be regarded as a compliment to a man's prowess, his masculinity.

In American English, unambiguously derisive terms for men often accuse a man of being feminine. No little boy wants to be called a *sissy;* no man wants to be called a *wimp* or a *pussy*. Although a man may not like being called a name that implies he acts like a woman, according to Baker (1981), it is even more insulting to be called a name suggesting that a woman controls him, that he's *pussy whipped*. Men often use such language in a joking manner, but the message is serious.

That it is an insult for a man to be compared to a woman was illustrated at a recent summer festival. The dunking booth was not open yet, but a man and his son were getting it ready. Three young men came up to the booth and volunteered to be dunked. The man thanked them but said he had all the volunteers he needed. Animated by the alcohol they had consumed, the three of them badgered the man for several minutes before they gave up. As they walked away, the man at the booth said, "Good-bye, girls!" One of the young men turned around quickly and shouted, "What the fuck did you call me?" The vehemence of the young man's response was both surprising and disturbing as he came storming back. Even though the father had his son next to him, the young man was prepared to use violence to defend his manhood against such a degrading insult.

A mother and daughter were standing nearby in a line for face painting. Having observed this confrontation, the mother shouted sarcastically to the young man, "Oh, what a terrible thing to be called!" He looked over at the face-painting line, and other mothers standing with their daughters shouted similar comments. As the young man looked at them, his face betrayed his confusion. His body had swelled up with anger, but now it seemed to deflate.

His shoulders drooped and his expression became almost sheepish. As he approached the man at the dunking booth, he was still angry but not to the point of engaging in violence. After a brief conversation, a security officer appeared to escort the young man away. Considering the hostility aroused by such a flippant remark, one has to wonder about the attitudes males are being taught concerning women. Is it possible for a man to hate the idea of being called a female and not subconsciously hate women as well?

Aren't some prejudices positive?

Some people misuse the term *prejudice* by saying they are prejudiced *for* something, but a prejudice is always a negative attitude. A milder attitude of liking or disliking anything or anyone is a bias; however, the concept of prejudice involves learning to fear, mistrust, and strengthen stereotypes we have been taught about other groups of people. Once we learn to be prejudiced against a certain group, we tend to *behave* in negative ways toward others who appear to be members of that group. Negative behavior is discrimination: We no longer merely hold a negative attitude—we have acted on that attitude.

Consequences and Causes of Prejudice

With regard to discriminatory actions, Allport (1979) identified five negative behaviors caused by prejudice: (1) *verbal abuse* against others that occurs among friends or results in name-calling directed at others from a particular group. Name-calling can escalate into (2) *physical assaults.* The victim doesn't even have to be a member of the despised group to be assaulted; anyone could be a victim by being perceived as one of "them." When a large group of ethnic Hmong from Southeast Asia settled in a Wisconsin community of 50,000 people, some local citizens did not accept them. A Japanese foreign exchange student who attended a college in that community was severely beaten by a white man in the mistaken belief that his victim was Hmong. Another

common example of violence based on misperceptions is that heterosexual men have been physically assaulted because they were perceived to be gay.

If prejudice evolves into bigotry, one's hatred can lead to (3) *extreme violence,* including the desire to commit murder. Such behavior is now called a "hate crime." In 1982, two Detroit men lost their jobs at an automobile factory and believed it was related to the popularity of imported Japanese cars. When they encountered Vincent Chin, a Chinese American, they mistakenly thought he was Japanese. Motivated by hatred and rage, they brutally murdered him. If homicidal rage spreads, it might lead to the extreme form of violence called **genocide**—the systematic and deliberate extermination of a nationality or a racial or ethnic group (Feagin & Feagin, 2008). A person can play a passive role that still supports genocide. After World War II, most Germans (also Poles, Austrians, and others) claimed they didn't know that six million Jews were killed in concentration camps; persuasive evidence has been gathered to argue that they knew but were not concerned enough to do anything about it (Goldhagen, 2002).

In contrast to confrontational negative behavior stemming from prejudice and bigotry, a more passive negative response to prejudice is to avoid members of other groups. We do this by (4) *limiting our interactions* with people from racial or ethnic groups other than our own. Measuring attitudes about avoiding others was the focus of research by Bogardus; this study used a Social Distance Scale in which people encounter a list of racial, ethnic, and religious groups and are asked to rank them in order of preference (Schaefer, 2008). People consistently reveal a preference for those groups most like their own, and they have less regard for people from groups they perceive as least like themselves.

Another way to avoid certain groups is (5) to *engage in or condone discrimination* in such areas as education, employment, and housing. To illustrate this behavior, consider how people choose what sort of neighborhood they want to live in. In the 1960s, when courts ordered urban school districts to desegregate, many school administrators responded by busing students to different schools, a controversial solution that caused massive movement of white families from urban neighborhoods to racially segregated suburbs, the **white flight** phenomenon (see Figure 2.2). Despite the passage of the 1968 National Fair Housing Act, studies have documented the preference of most white Americans to live in racially segregated neighborhoods (Farley, 2005; Massey, 2001). As Massey noted, the Fair Housing Act "theoretically put an end to housing discrimination; however, residential segregation proved to be remarkably persistent" (p. 424).

FIGURE 2.2

Neighborhood Preference of White Respondents

In a study cited by Farley (2005), subjects were shown diagrams of neighborhoods consisting of 15 homes with an X on the home in the center of the neighborhood indicating the subject's home. Each shaded home represented an African American family. White respondents were asked: How comfortable would they feel in each neighborhood? If they were uncomfortable, would they leave? Would they move into such a neighborhood? The percentage not willing to live in those neighborhoods where only a fifth or a third of homeowners were African Americans illustrates attitudes that produced white flight.

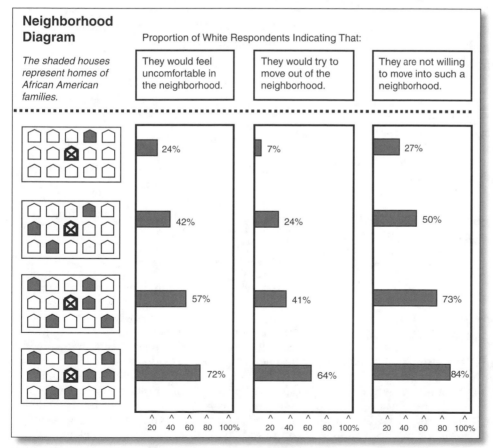

Is prejudice the main cause of discrimination in society?

For years we believed that discrimination was caused by prejudice; therefore, the way to reduce discrimination was to reduce prejudice. Efforts were made in schools and in popular culture to address and reduce prejudice, and they produced positive results. In recent years, research has shown a significant decrease in prejudice; however, studies have reported little decrease in discrimination (Astor, 1997). Based on efforts by scholars seeking alternative explanations, Feagin and Feagin (1986) described three theories of discrimination: the interest theory, the internal colonialism theory, and the institutionalized discrimination theory, all of which identify historic and contemporary forces responsible for inequities being perpetuated without the involvement of prejudice.

How does the interest theory explain discrimination?

The **interest theory** describes discrimination resulting from people protecting their power and privilege. Instead of being motivated by prejudice, people discriminate against individuals from subordinate groups because of self-interest. For example, white men may object to affirmative action programs not because of their prejudice but from fear of policies that might reduce their opportunities to be hired, retained, or promoted. Homeowners might persuade neighbors not to sell their home to a family of color because they are worried about what will happen to property values. Discrimination is a function of protecting one's interests; this is similar to the internal colonialism theory.

How is self-interest involved in the internal colonialism theory?

The **internal colonialism theory** of discrimination is an analysis of how privilege was created in the United States when the dominant group—white male Europeans—exploited subordinate groups to assume control of America's resources: land from American Indians, unpaid labor by African slaves, and wages and property of wives. Furthermore, by gaining control over resources and exploiting them to their advantage, certain white male Europeans achieved positions that provided them access to technological developments and control of industrial developments in the United States, including military technology. Once they are in a position of power, people will do what they can to maintain their advantage and stay in power.

Although initially established by force, unequal distribution and control of economic and political resources eventually became institutionalized. The theory of internal colonialism asserts that continued domination of nonwhites and women by white men is maintained by the way that institutions function in the United States. Internal colonialism theory creates the foundation on which the theory of institutionalized discrimination was built.

How is discrimination explained by the institutionalized discrimination theory?

The **institutionalized discrimination theory** accepts the history of internal colonialism but focuses on contemporary discrimination. This theory describes institutional policies and practices that have different and negative effects on subordinate groups. It examines how privilege and advantage are embedded in an organization's norms, its regulations, informal rules, and roles—social positions with their attendant duties and rights. An analysis based on this theory seeks to understand mechanisms and methods that lead to discrimination in institutional policies and practices. Similar to the other two theories, institutionalized discrimination theory is not concerned with prejudice (what U.S. courts have called "evil intent") but is based on the assumption that much discrimination today is unintentional.

When a number of women in city government in an urban area were interviewed for a research project, one department head explained how a group of female department heads had solved a problem. At the end of a workday, the women tended to leave immediately because of family responsibilities such as picking up children and preparing meals. Male department heads tended to meet for a drink after work once or twice a week, and to play golf together on weekends while women department heads spent that time with their families. At meetings where they had to make decisions about funding for programs, female department heads were frustrated by their inability to be as effective as their male counterparts in supporting each other.

The women understood why the men had an advantage. Because of their social activities, male department heads knew more about each other's departments, so they could make informed arguments in support of each other's programs. To create a similar advantage for themselves, the women started meeting together one evening every month (child care provided) to talk about their programs and needs, and to prepare for debates on funding priorities. As a result of their efforts, a greater amount of funding was distributed to departments headed by women (Koppelman, 1994).

The institutionalized discrimination theory provides a realistic basis for understanding discrimination: The actions of the male department heads were not based on a prejudice against women; rather, they were doing their job in accordance with historic practices that benefited their departments. The women understood that the solution was not to berate the men but rather to devise a strategy to offset advantages already established for male department heads. Even though informal institutional procedures favored the men, the women found a way to "play the game" more effectively. Discriminatory actions can still be a direct result of prejudice on the part of people making decisions, but it is more likely that causes for discrimination stem from reasons far more subtle and complex. Although prejudice may not be the main cause of discrimination, we should continue with research to understand what causes prejudice and do what we can to reduce it.

What factors promote the development of prejudice?

Considerable research has been conducted addressing the question of how individuals become prejudiced. Some studies suggest that elitist attitudes foster prejudice. **Elitism** is the belief that the most able people succeed in society and form a natural aristocracy while the least able enjoy the least success because they are flawed in some way or lack

the necessary qualities to be successful. This condescending attitude promotes the belief that those in the lower levels of society deserve to be where they are and that successful people have earned their place in society. Unsuccessful people are often held responsible for their failure. Elitist attitudes are a major factor in studies based on social dominance theory (Howard, 2006; Stephan, 1999).

The eugenics movement beginning in the late 1800s argued that an individual's genetic inheritance determined his or her fate and that environment played little or no role in human development (Selden, 2006). Based on this argument, proponents of the eugenics movement in the United States were promoting elitist attitudes. Selden quotes American biologist George W. Hunter, author of several biology textbooks widely used in schools between 1914 and 1941, who expressed this elitist attitude clearly:

> Those of low grade intelligence would do little better under the most favorable conditions possible, while those of superior intelligence will make good no matter what handicaps they are given. (p. 75)

Other studies suggest a link between prejudice and attitudes about power. Some people express a **zero-sum** attitude, a highly competitive orientation toward power based on the assumption that

> Everyone is a prisoner of his own experiences. No one can eliminate prejudices—just recognize them.
>
> **Edward R. Murrow (1908–1965)**

the personal gains of one individual mean a loss for someone else; therefore, to share power is regarded as having less power. According to Levin and Levin (1982), an individual with a zero-sum orientation toward power tends to be a person with strong prejudices. Thurow (2001) has described the adverse consequences for society when a zero-sum orientation is prevalent. Studies also suggest that people with authoritarian personalities tend to be more prejudiced, although other studies refute the idea

(Farley, 2005). Some have even proposed that prejudice is innate, but there are no scientific studies to support that claim.

To be as pervasive and persistent as it has been, prejudice must serve some purpose and offer some benefit to individuals or to society. Having reviewed research concerning causes of prejudice, Levin and Levin (1982) identified four primary causes, and within these causes, functions of prejudice that sustain it. The four causes include (1) personal frustration, (2) uncertainty about a person based on lack of knowledge or experience with the group to which they belong, (3) threat to one's self-esteem, and (4) competition among individuals in our society to achieve their goals in relation to status, wealth, and power.

How does frustration cause prejudice?

The frustration-aggression hypothesis maintains that as frustration builds, it leads to aggressive action. Frustration causes tension to increase until a person chooses to act on the frustration to alleviate the tension. Jones (1997) and others have called this the "scapegoat phenomenon." The word **scapegoat** derives from an ancient Hebrew custom described in Leviticus 16: 20–22, where each year the Hebrew people reflected on their sins during days of atonement. At the end of that time, a spiritual leader would stand before them with a goat, lay his hands on the goat's head, and recite a list of the people's sins, transferring the sins of the people to the goat—which was then set free. In modern America, the term generally refers to blaming a person or group for problems they did not cause.

When we take aggressive action—from verbal abuse to physical violence—we inevitably cause harm to others. Because most individuals define themselves as "good" according to some criteria, they will usually find a way to rationalize their actions as being good or at least justified. When southerners lynched black people in the late nineteenth and early twentieth centuries, they justified their actions by insisting that all blacks were lazy, lustful, or liars. Using the Kafkaesque reasoning that all blacks were guilty and therefore it didn't matter what crime a black person was accused of committing, they executed victims with no regard for whether that specific black person was guilty of a crime.

Ironically, data from some studies have shown that aggressive action may not alleviate frustration, but instead may exacerbate it. In one study, two groups of subjects were asked to allow medical technicians to take physical measurements of their bodies. After taking the measurements, the technicians made derogatory comments intended to make the subjects angry. One group was taken to the technician's "supervisor" if they wanted to complain; the other group was not. The researchers thought that members of the group being allowed to "vent" their anger would feel less hostile toward the technician afterward, yet those who complained reported stronger feelings of hostility than the subjects who were not allowed to complain (Aronson, 2008). The findings suggest that identifying a scapegoat on which to vent one's frustration does not solve a person's problems, and it may make matters worse.

The implication that finding a scapegoat does not solve problems is illustrated in domestic abuse cases. When a man takes out his frustrations by abusing his partner, he has to justify his actions. It is common for men arrested for domestic abuse to explain their behavior by saying, "She made me do it," or "She kept nagging and wouldn't shut up." This not only depicts the man as a victim (the suffering husband), but also it reinforces the stereotype of nagging wives, providing the husband with an excuse for assaulting the woman he once claimed to love. Because violence escalates with each domestic abuse complaint from the same home, it is obvious that blaming one's spouse or partner doesn't solve the problem; it may possibly cause the abuser to become more violent toward those interfering with his actions.

Because of the high rates of injury and death to police officers responding to domestic abuse cases, many American cities, counties, and states require officers to file abuse charges directly, even over the objections of the one abused. Courts often mandate counseling for abusers to address and understand how gender prejudices and stereotypes created negative attitudes leading to abuse, and to teach abusive men effective, nonviolent strategies for managing anger. The role of gender stereotypes in contributing to domestic abuse illustrates another major cause of prejudice—uncertainty.

What do stereotypes have to do with uncertainty and how do they cause prejudice?

Most of us only have knowledge of the groups to which we belong; often we do not know much about other groups. In the United States, schools have historically implemented curricula reflecting perspectives, contributions, and experiences of the dominant (white) group; many of our neighborhoods still tend to be segregated by race or social class. The result is that people from different racial and ethnic groups have few opportunities to learn about one another. Because of our lack of accurate information, we may believe in stereotypes as a way to convince ourselves that we know about certain groups. (See Figure 2.3.) Our stereotypes can be reinforced by images or information contained in such media as advertisements, textbooks, and films.

For an example of ignorance promoting prejudice, how many Americans know that Muslims have been in the United States from colonial times because many slaves brought to America from West Africa were Muslim? The evidence is in the names that "read like a Who's Who of traditional Muslim names"—Bullaly (Bilali), Mahomet (Muhammad), Walley (Wali), and Sambo meant "second son" to Muslim Fulbe people (Abdo, 2006, p. 66). While Americans tend to stereotype all Arabs as Muslims, the majority of Arabs immigrating to the United

FIGURE 2.3

This drawing has been used for research and in classrooms. One person is shown this picture and whispers a description of the entire scene to another person, who then whispers the description to another person until each person in the room has heard it. The last person is asked to describe the scene to everyone. Typically, the person describes a poorly dressed black man with a weapon preparing to attack a well-dressed white man, thus illustrating the power of racial stereotypes.

States in the late nineteenth century were Christians. How many Americans know that in the 1920s a small group of Muslims settled in Ross, South Dakota, and built the first mosque in the United States, or that the oldest continuously functioning mosque is in Cedar Rapids, Iowa (Abdo, 2006)?

Even if they don't know this history, how many Americans know that Muslim Americans today own over 200,000 businesses and that there are over 2,000 mosques in the United States (Ansari, 2004)? How many Americans know that Muslim American adults are better educated than the average American (59% have college degrees compared to 27% of other Americans) and wealthier (a median annual income of $60,000 compared to the national median annual income of $50,000) (Barrett, 2007)? Muslims have done what America expects of immigrants. But unaware of this information, and surrounded by stereotypes and media's focus on Islamic terrorists, how many Americans harbor negative views of both the Islamic faith and Muslims? According to a 2004 survey by the Pew Forum on Religion and Public Life, nearly 50% of Americans perceived the Islamic faith as more likely to promote violence than other religions (a percentage that doubled compared to the results of a similar survey conducted two years earlier) and nearly 40% expressed a negative view of Muslims (Abdo, 2006).

When a person actually encounters individuals of a different race, ethnicity, or social class, selective perception of the behaviors of those individuals often reinforces his or her stereotypes. Stephan (1999) reported on one study where subjects were presented with equal amounts of positive and negative information about a group to which they belonged (in-group) and a group to which they did not belong (out-group). Subjects tended to recall more positive information about the in-group and more negative information about the out-group. According to Stephan, negative attitudes in our memory tend to increase over time.

Selective perception was illustrated in another study where two groups of subjects viewed consecutive videotapes: The first videotape was of a fourth-grade girl playing with friends, and the second videotape was of the same girl taking an oral test in school where she answered some difficult questions correctly but missed some easy questions.

Although the second videotape was the same for both groups, the first videotape shown to one group was the girl playing in a low-income neighborhood, and first videotape shown to the other group was the girl playing in a high-income neighborhood. After watching both videotapes, subjects were asked to judge the girl's academic abilities. Those who saw her playing in the low-income neighborhood rated her academic ability lower than those who saw her playing in the more affluent neighborhood. Whether the subjects focused more on the girl's correct or incorrect answers appeared to have been influenced by the neighborhood where they believed she lived and stereotypes associated with affluence and poverty (Aronson, 2008).

Researchers have also shown that becoming more knowledgeable about others helps people overcome stereotypical perceptions. In a psychiatric hospital with an all-white staff, patients acting violently were either taken to a "time-out room" or

> Sometimes (prejudice) is like a hair across your cheek. You can't see it, you can't find it with your fingers, but you keep brushing at it because the feel of it is irritating.
>
> **MARIAN ANDERSON (1897–1993)**

subjected to the harsher penalty of being put in a straitjacket and sedated. In the first month of a research study, both black and white patients were admitted. Although the black patients admitted were diagnosed as being less violent than the whites, they were four times more likely to be put in a straitjacket and sedated by the staff if they became violent. The discrepancy in the white staff's use of restraints suggests that they believed in the stereotype that black people were more prone to violence. As they became better acquainted with the patients, the staff responded to violent incidents with more equal use of restraints for both black and white patients (Aronson, 2008). Stereotypes that portray a group as being prone to violence, lazy, or less intelligent can influence a person's behavior; stereotypes can also play a part in a person's self-esteem being threatened, which is another major cause of prejudice identified in research.

How does threat to self-esteem cause prejudice?

In the United States, people are encouraged to develop self-esteem by comparing themselves with others. We do so by grades in school, music contests, debates in speech, and athletic competitions. But what happens when positive self-esteem is achieved by developing feelings of superiority to someone else? Or when we achieve our sense of superiority by projecting our feelings of inferiority onto another person or group? If we believe in the innate superiority of our group compared to other groups, then we believe we are better than anyone who is a member of the inferior group. If members of an inferior group become successful, their achievements threaten those whose self-esteem was based on feelings of group superiority and unconsciously transforms a condescending attitude into prejudice.

People of color confront the issue of self-esteem based on race as a cause of prejudice when they encounter white people whose self-esteem is threatened by their achievements or success. The first African American to teach at Harvard University Law School commented,

> You have to simultaneously function on a high level and try not to upset those whose racial equilibrium is thrown off when they recognize that you are not incompetent, not mediocre, and don't fit the long accepted notions about persons of color that serve as unrecognized but important components of their self-esteem. (Bell, 2002, pp. 66–67)

When we possess this kind of self-esteem, we are insecure and easily threatened. Coleman (2007) argued that people perceiving others as inferior "are more likely to identify and maintain negative stereotypes about members of stigmatized groups" (p. 222).

Studies suggest that part of the self-esteem for many men derives just from being male. In Michigan, over a thousand children wrote essays about what their lives would be like if they were the opposite gender. Although almost half the girls found many positive things to say about being male, 95% of the boys could find nothing positive to say about being female (Sadker & Sadker, 1994). Similar attitudes appear among adults. In their research on self-esteem, Martinez and Dukes (1991) reported that males displayed higher self-esteem than did females, and that white males had the highest self-esteem of all groups.

When male self-esteem derives from perceiving one's gender as superior, it is easily threatened by women's achievements. American men often rationalize female achievements by attributing women's success to reasons other than competence. Their rationalizations may be characterized by resentment or anger, which intensifies the prejudice that created the initial illusion of superiority. If a woman receives the promotion a man wanted, he might complain that she is "sleeping her way to the top." Because self-esteem based on a belief in gender superiority is an illusion, it is ultimately inadequate because the individual has done nothing to earn it. Fearing that an "inferior" person might receive rewards the "superior" individual desires is related to the fourth primary cause of prejudice: competition for status, wealth, and power.

How does competition for status, wealth, and power cause prejudice?

There is evidence that competition fosters prejudicial attitudes. Jones (1997) described a study at a summer camp where Boy Scouts were given time to become acquainted and to develop friendships before being divided into two groups and housed in separate bunkhouses. The groups were divided so that approximately two thirds of each boy's friends were in the other bunkhouse. The two groups were encouraged to play a series of competitive games such as tug-of-war, football, and baseball. Boys who had liked each other began to intensely dislike each other and to engage in name-calling. Although there was solidarity within groups, friendships that had been established with boys from the other group no longer existed. After competitive games were concluded, researchers brought the boys together, but animosity remained until the boys were given tasks that required them to cooperate with each other. Working together to achieve a common goal reduced the hostility and resulted in the boys again making friendships with individuals from the other group.

The Perpetuation of Prejudice

People want to be successful and will try to promote their own self-interests. When members of one group believe that individuals from another group are becoming more successful than they are, they may become angry at those individuals—even hostile toward the entire group—by rationalizing an advantage other than talent or skill that is responsible for their success. White American men sometimes resent affirmative action because they believe it provides women and racial or ethnic minorities with an advantage in being hired and promoted. Resentment from economic competition for good jobs with high salaries and status fosters prejudice. Because humans are intelligent enough to identify these various causes of prejudice, it seems logical to assume that people should be able to recognize that they have prejudices and attempt to eliminate them.

How are prejudices perpetuated?

A major factor in the perpetuation of prejudice is the tendency to rationalize prejudices and the negative behaviors prejudices promote. As Gioseffi (1993) has noted, "Just as individuals will rationalize their hostile behaviors . . . so nations do also" (p. xvii). Vega (1978) described rationalizations taking three forms: denial, victim-blaming, and avoidance. To unlearn our prejudices and develop effective ways of confronting prejudices expressed by others, we need to recognize these rationalizations so we can make an appropriate response when they are expressed.

Denial rationalizations

In making **denial rationalizations,** we refuse to recognize that there are problems in our society resulting from prejudices and discrimination. Such claims are astonishing in their ignorance, yet they continue to be made. In response to assertions of racism, the most common denial rationalization is the reverse discrimination argument that claims that women and minorities receive the best jobs because of affirmative action programs. Is there any truth to this claim?

According to population demographics, women now comprise almost half of the workforce; another 10% consists of men of color, which means that white men constitute about 40% of the workforce (Daft, 2003). A job paying an annual salary of $50,000 or more is a criterion to identify which jobs involve some degree of authority, status, and decision-making power. How many of these jobs are in the hands of white men? It would be consistent with their proportion of the workforce if white men had slightly less than half of these jobs, yet according to the Bureau of Labor Statistics (2001), white men hold over three fourths of these positions, about twice as many as the percentage of white men in the workforce. Claims that white men are unfairly discriminated against as a result of affirmative action policies would appear to be dubious (see Table 2.1).

The most common denial rationalization related to sexism is the "natural" argument, which denies gender discrimination, claiming that it is natural for women to do some things better than men, and for men to do some things better than women. This denial rationalization is offered as an explanation for why men and women have historically held certain types of jobs. The argument does not explain the difference between the skills of a tailor (predominantly men) compared to a seamstress (predominantly women) to justify the differences in their compensations. Nor does it explain why construction workers (mostly men) should be compensated at a greater rate than college-educated social workers (mostly women). Historically, women have been paid less than men for doing the same work, and occupations dominated by women still receive lower wages than occupations dominated by men (Bureau of Labor Statistics, 2001). This is the reality, but denial rationalizations have little to do with reality.

The most subtle denial rationalization is personal denial illustrated by the man who says, "How can I be sexist? I love women! I married a woman. I have daughters." This seems a reasonable statement: Someone denying he has gender prejudices does not appear to deny the existence of widespread prejudice against women—but the statement actually does imply a more sweeping denial. Psycholog-

TABLE 2.1 Annual Incomes of Full-Time Workers in the United States

Race/Gender	Median Weekly Earnings	
	1994	2004
White males	$690 (100%)	$732 (100%)
Black males	$505 (73.2%)	$569 (77.7%)
Hispanic males	$433 (62.8%)	$480 (65.6%)
White females	$514 (74.5%)	$584 (79.8%)
Black females	$437 (63.3%)	$505 (69.9%)
Hispanic females	$384 (55.7%)	$419 (57.2%)

Source: U.S. Census Bureau (2004). *Statistical abstract of the United States.*

ically, most people feel they are normal, average people. If a person denies being prejudiced, he or

> Prejudice blinds, ignorance retards, indifference deafens, hate amputates. In this way do some people disable their souls.
>
> MARY ROBINSON (1944–)

she is actually denying that most other normal, average people are prejudiced as well. The real meaning of such a statement is that the speaker does not believe prejudice and discrimination are serious problems in society. If someone argues this point, the person making this denial rationalization might resort to victim-blaming responses because the two are closely related.

Victim-blaming rationalizations

People employing **victim-blaming rationalizations** reject the notion that prejudice and discrimination are problems in society, even though they admit that problems exist. The problems they identify, however, are typically deficiencies or flaws in members of minority groups (Ryan, 1976). Victim-blamers focus on the group being harmed by soci-

etal prejudices and insist that society doesn't need to change: The group needs to change. Victim-blamers urge individuals to stop being so sensitive or so pushy, to work harder, and to quit complaining. Group members are told they are responsible for whatever problems they must overcome.

Victim-blaming often occurs among people who want to believe in a just world. In one study, subjects observed two people working equally hard at a task. By a random decision, researchers gave one of the workers a significant reward when the task was completed; the other worker received nothing. When asked to rate how hard the two people had worked, the subjects tended to describe the person who received nothing as not working as hard as the person receiving the reward. Aronson (2008) concluded his analysis of this study by suggesting that "we find it frightening to think about living in a world where people, through no fault of their own, can be deprived of what they deserve or need" (p. 323).

People who engage in victim-blaming rationalizations often go beyond blame to propose solutions. By defining the problem as a deficiency existing in the victimized group, every solution proposed by a victim-blamer involves what *they* need to do because *they* are the problem. The rest of us need do nothing. Rape is increasing on college campuses? That's a woman's problem, so what they need to do is to wear less provocative clothing, avoid going out late at night, and learn to defend themselves by taking martial arts classes or carrying pepper spray. What to do about the men who rape isn't addressed. Because victim-blamers offer solutions, it is easy to confuse victim-blaming with some avoidance rationalizations.

Avoidance rationalizations

Unlike people who employ denial and victim-blaming, those who promote **avoidance rationalizations** recognize the problems in society as stemming from prejudice and discrimination. This is a significant difference from the previous rationalizations. Even though a person making avoidance rationalizations admits there are problems, he or she will not address them and will rationalize a reason to avoid them. Ways to avoid confronting issues include offering a solution that addresses only part of a problem, or suggesting a false solution that does not address the problem at all.

If college administrators decide to confront prejudice by requiring students to take an ethnic studies course, that requirement will address a small part of the problems caused by racial prejudice and discrimination. Learning more about ethnic groups is a good idea, but if colleges are serious about actively opposing racism and improving race relations, administration and faculty must recruit diverse students, hire diverse faculty, and promote cultural diversity through workshops and seminars both on campus and in the community.

A false solution that does not address the problems of sexism whatsoever is the proposal that "sexism would just disappear if we didn't pay so much attention to it." Problems created by sexism did not suddenly appear and they won't disappear unless people engage in actions to confront, challenge, and change sexist attitudes, policies, and laws. The only way any society can solve problems and improve conditions is to analyze a problem, create appropriate solutions, implement the solutions that seem most likely to be effective, and, after time passes, assess the impact of these solutions.

Another form of avoidance rationalization involves making an argument that distracts attention from the issue or question being discussed. Imagine a group of people discussing efforts that could be made to increase social justice in our society. Suddenly someone says, "You're being too idealistic.

We are never going to solve this problem because we're never going to have a utopia." The speaker was not arguing for the creation of a utopia, a perfect society, but for ways to improve society. By making the reasonable statement that utopias are not possible, the speaker has shifted the focus of the conversation to a different topic that avoids the issue. It is not realistic to believe that it is possible to create a perfect society, but it is possible—in fact, essential—to believe that any society can be improved.

In a discussion about the need for child-care centers at work sites, someone might say, "I support the idea, but it takes time; it's not going to happen overnight." A reasonable response, except if the discussion ends with that comment, what has been achieved? To implement any solution successfully, it is necessary to clarify what is entailed: What needs to be done? Who will do what? Which actions should be taken next month? What can we expect in the next six months? Who will determine whether the solution is working, and how will that be determined? Saying a solution takes time may be true, but it is still necessary to discuss what must be done to implement it. To avoid that discussion is to avoid the problem. Problems are not solved by talk or the passage of time but by taking some kind of action.

Conservatives are often accused of engaging in denial and especially victim-blaming rationalizations. Their solutions tend to concentrate on perceived flaws in victims of prejudice rather than addressing the prejudice and discrimination that create many of these difficult circumstances. On the other hand, liberals are more likely to be criticized for engaging in avoidance rationalizations in which they acknowledge and express sympathy for the problems faced by oppressed groups, but never do anything to address the causes of these problems. As long as significant numbers of individuals continue to employ such rationalizations, Americans are not likely to perceive or confront persistent structural causes of inequities based on race, gender, and other human differences.

AFTERWORD

If prejudice were part of human nature, people would be justified in feeling despair because the implication would be that human beings eventually will destroy each other. But no evidence supports the idea that prejudice is innate. Instead, studies have consistently concluded that prejudice is learned. The fact that prejudice is learned offers hope because anything that can be learned can be unlearned. Education can confront negative attitudes both in the media and in our language to help students unlearn prejudices they have been taught,

> [There is a] strangely irrational notion that there is something in the very flow of time that will inevitably cure all ills. Actually time is neutral. It can be used either destructively or constructively.
>
> **Martin Luther King, Jr. (1929–1968)**

and also understand why it is in everyone's best interest not to act on prejudices.

In their study of brain research, Newberg and Waldman (2006) found that people could "interrupt" prejudicial beliefs and stereotypes and generate new ideas, and that these new ideas "can alter the neural circuitry that governs how we behave and what we believe. Our beliefs . . . aren't necessarily static. They can change; we can change them" (p. 9).

Prejudice can be reduced by accurate information, by formal and informal learning, and by establishing equitable workplace policies and practices. Prejudices can also be unlearned by friends challenging one another's negative attitudes. Even though some people may not be able to give up their prejudices, they do not have to act on them. It is not inevitable that our prejudices control us. When we can identify our prejudices and understand how we learned them, we can choose to limit their influence on our behavior. We can control them instead of letting them control us.

When we make positive choices, we affirm the basis for having hope for the future. Positive choices that individuals have made throughout history have resulted in genuine human progress. If our society is to benefit from its diversity, it will be because enough Americans have chosen to regard diversity as an asset and to confront their preju-dices. Those who make such positive choices today will shape the nature of the society in which our children and their children must live.

TERMS AND DEFINITIONS

Avoidance rationalization   A response to a social problem—such as injustice toward a minority group—that acknowledges the existence of a problem but avoids confronting the problem by offering partial or false solutions or by using arguments that do not address the situation as in "Yes, but you should have seen how bad it was last year."

Black/white syndrome   A pattern in the English language consisting of negative meanings for phrases including the word *black* and positive meanings for phrases including the word *white*

Denial rationalization   A response to a social problem—such as injustice toward a minority group—that does not acknowledge the existence of a problem but insists instead that no injustice has occurred as in "That's not discrimination, men have always been the boss; it's just the way things are meant to be."

Elitism   The belief that the best people ascend to a place of superiority in society and represent a natural aristocracy, whereas those who are not successful are viewed as lacking the necessary qualities to be successful within society

Genocide   The deliberate and systematic extermination of a particular nationality, or racial, ethnic, or minority group

Institutionalized discrimination theory Institutional policies and practices that have differential and negative effects on subordinate groups in a society

Interest theory   People engaging or acquiescing in discriminatory actions based on a desire to protect their power or privilege

Internal colonialism theory   Explains contemporary discrimination as the maintenance of inequities resulting from historic exploitation of subordinate groups by the dominant group

Prejudice   A negative attitude toward a group and anyone perceived to be a member of that group; a predisposition to negative behavior toward members of a group

Scapegoat An individual or a group of people blamed for another person's problems or difficulties; identifying a scapegoat is often employed to justify one's taking a negative action against that individual or group

Victim-blaming rationalization A response to a social problem—such as injustice toward a minority group—that identifies the problem as a deficiency in the minority group and not a societal problem, as in "If poor people want to escape poverty they just have to be willing to work harder."

White flight The migration of white families from an urban to a suburban location because of court rulings to desegregate urban schools

Zero sum An orientation toward power and resources based on assumptions of scarcity, as when struggling to achieve goals, one person gains at the expense of another. The belief that sharing power means a reduction of power

DISCUSSION EXERCISES

Clarification Exercise—Rationalizations: Victim-Blame, Denial, and Avoidance

Directions: This exercise provides everyday statements we might hear; each one is a specific kind of rationalization. Based on the text and on your group discussion, identify the statements below according to one of the three types of rationalizations. First, select which passages would most likely represent an **avoidance** of a problem. Then select those in which the speaker employs a **denial** rationalization—that the problem either does not exist or that the speaker is suggesting "That's just the way things are." Finally, locate **victim-blame** statements where a specific person or group is being charged with its own downfall or problem.

Rationalizations for Our Prejudices

Directions: Decide whether the following statements represent a **denial** of the problem (D), a **victim-blame** that it is the speaker's problem (D/VB), or an **avoidance** of the problem (A).

_____ 1. Women and minorities are getting everything their way. They are taking away our jobs and pretty soon they are going to take over everything.

_____ 2. What we have here, basically, is a failure to communicate. We must develop better programs in interpersonal communications to address this issue.

_____ 3. This is the way these people want to live. You can't change poor people; they can't help the way they are.

_____ 4. We must move with deliberation on these issues. Real change takes time. We have to educate people.

_____ 5. All those women on welfare have it made. All they do is stay home and make babies while the rest of us have to work and pay taxes to support them.

_____ 6. I can't figure out what to call all these people. Why can't we all just be human instead of black, Chicano, Latino, Native American, or Asian American?

_____ 7. Indians are their own worst enemy. They should stop fighting among themselves and get together on whatever it is they really want.

_____ 8. If blacks want to make it in our society, they are going to have to get rid of those dreadlocks and other weird hairstyles, the baggy clothes, funny handshakes, and they better start speaking better English.

_____ 9. Yes, but in the old days, race and sex discrimination were much worse. And even today, women and minorities are much better off in this country than anywhere else in the world.

_____ 10. Women are just too sensitive about sexism. They need to look at these things less emotionally and much more rationally.

_____ 11. We need more programs in African American studies, Latino studies, Native American studies, and Asian American studies to learn about all the contributions these groups have made to our society.

_____ 12. Feminists are pushing too hard for the changes that they demand. They are hurting themselves more than they are helping.

_____ 13. I understand that some people face more difficulties than others, but this is a free country and I believe that anybody who is willing to work hard enough can be successful.

Follow-Up: Select any two from each of the three categories—D, VB, and A—and rewrite them to be the fourth kind of statement—those *without* rationalization. Explain why you chose to rewrite them as you did.

Exercise—The Liver Transplant Problem

Background: Today, the only medical procedure available to save the lives of persons suffering from diseases of the liver is an organ transplant. Unfortunately, there are not enough livers to take care of all cases now, and there will not be enough in the near future to save the lives of all those in need.

Your Role: The decision about which people can be saved must be made on criteria other than medical criteria. Your hospital has decided that the best way to select persons for a transplant is by setting up a volunteer citizens panel to make the decisions. You are on the panel and receive a Profile Sheet of applicants for transplants (see the table). Doctors have screened all patients, and all have equal prognosis for medical success.

Problem: There is a liver available for one person on the list. All those not served will die. The availability of other livers cannot be anticipated, although if other livers become available, additional persons on the list could receive transplants.

Directions: Your panel must make a *unanimous* decision regarding the person to be the liver recipient. A lottery violates institutional ethics and is not an acceptable strategy. As you deliberate, discuss your values and consider those of others related to the process being utilized and the criteria that you propose:

1. The criteria you develop for choosing the recipient.
2. Why you believe that the person you chose best fits your criteria.
3. How your panel arrives at a single selection of a recipient.

Please see the next page for more detailed notes about the recipients.

Liver Transplant Recipient Profile Sheet

Code	Age	Race	Sex	Marital Status	Religious Affiliation	Children	Occupation
A	24	Black	M	Married	Muslim	None	Postal worker
B	45	White	M	Married	Atheist	2	Executive
C	39	Asian American	F	Divorced	Buddhist	None	Medical doctor
D	40	White	F	Married	Jew	3	Housewife
E	23	White	M	Unmarried	Episcopal	None	PhD student
F	40	White	F	Unmarried	Pentecostal	9	Welfare mother
G	28	Native American	M	Unmarried	Native	3	Seasonal worker
H	30	Latina	F	Married	Catholic	7	Housewife
I	19	White	M	Unmarried	Baptist	None	Special student

Notes about Recipients:

A. Devotes time to volunteer work for black organizations
B. Possible candidate for U.S. Senate
C. College physician and feminist speaker
D. Active in local synagogue and charitable activities
E. Middle states chair of a gay rights task force
F. Advocate and organizer of welfare mothers
G. State chair, Indian Treaty Rights Organization
H. Blind and physically disabled
I. Cognitively disabled

REFERENCES

Abdo, G. (2006). *Mecca and main Street: Muslim life in America after 9/11.* Oxford, England: Oxford University Press.

Describes the efforts of a variety of Muslim Americans to live in the United States and to maintain their faith while being confronted by stereotypes, prejudice, and discrimination.

Allport, G. (1979). *The nature of prejudice.* Reading, MA: Addison-Wesley.

Examines prejudice and its consequences for individuals who act on prejudice as well as those victimized by prejudice.

Ansari, Z.I. (2004). *Islam among African Americans: An overview.* In Z.H. Buhhari, S.S. Nyang, M. Ahmad, & J.C. Esposito (Eds.), *Muslims' place in the American public square* (pp. 222–267). Walnut Creek, CA: Altamira Press.

Provides a history of Islam in African American communities and examines the recent revival of interest in Islam represented by increasing numbers of African American converts.

Arliss, L.P. (1991). *Gender communication.* Englewood Cliffs, NJ: Prentice Hall.

Analyzes sexist language in Chapter 3, "Debates About Language and Sexism."

Aronson, E. (2008). *The social animal* (10th ed.). New York, NY: Worth Publishers.

Presents an overview of research in social psychology and describes patterns and motives revealed in these studies concerning human behavior.

Astor, C. (1997, August). Gallup poll: Progress in black/white relations, but race is still an issue. USIA electronic journal, *U.S. Society & Values, 2*(3), 19–212.

Highlights information from a Gallup Poll Special Report on "Black/White Relations in the United States"; access the complete poll at http://www.gallup.com

Baker, R. (1981). "Pricks" and "chicks": A plea for persons. In M. Vetterling-Braggin (Ed.), *Sexist language: A modern philosophical analysis* (pp. 161–182). Lanham, MD: Littlefield, Adams.

Explores sexist attitudes in our society as expressed in sexual slang.

Barrett, P.M. (2007). *American Islam: The struggle for the soul of a religion.* New York, NY: Farrar, Straus and Giroux.

Describes the perceptions and experiences of a variety of Muslim Americans based on interviews conducted after the terrorist attacks on 9/11.

Bell, D. (2002). *Ethical ambition: Living a life of meaning and worth.* New York, NY: Bloomsbury.

Discusses six factors that are critical in determining the quality and meaningfulness of one's life: passion, courage, faith, relationships, role models, and humility.

Bredin, J. (2008). *The affair: The case of Alfred Dreyfus.* Bethesda, MD: Gryphon Editions.

Describes the historical background and the ensuing controversy surrounding this notorious example of anti-Semitism.

Bureau of Labor Statistics. (2001). Chapter 1: Counting Minorities: A brief history and a look at the future. *Report on the American workforce.* Washington DC: U.S. Department of Labor. Retrieved December 20, 2008, from http://ww.bls.gov/opub

Analyzes statistics pertaining to the American workforce and the role and nature of the participation in that workforce by women and minorities.

Carroll, J. (2001). *Constantine's sword: The church and the Jews, a history.* Boston, MA: Houghton Mifflin.

Examines the history of relations between the Catholic Church and the Jews and explains the basis for the historic pattern of anti-Semitism that still exists in the church.

Coleman, L.M. (2007). Stigma. In L. Davis (Ed.), *The disability studies reader* (2nd ed., pp. 216–233). New York, NY: Routledge.

Discusses the origin of the concept of stigma and analyzes the reasons why some differences in human beings are valued and others are stigmatized.

Daft, R.L. (2003). Managing diverse employees. *Management* (6th ed., pp. 436–468). Versailles, KY: Thompson Southwestern.

Discusses diversity in the workforce and how corporate culture is accommodating diversity.

Evans, S. (1989). *Born for liberty: A history of women in America.* New York, NY: The Free Press.

Provides evidence of the influence of women on the colonies and in the nation that emerged.

Farley, J. (2005). *Majority-minority relations* (5th ed.). Upper Saddle River, NJ: Prentice Hall.

Discusses the research on authoritarian personalities in Chapter 2 and racial segregation in U.S. neighborhoods in Chapter 10.

Feagin, J., & Feagin, C. (1986). *Discrimination American style* (2nd ed.). Malabar, FL: Krieger.

Describes the three alternative theories of discrimination on pages 7–12.

Feagin, J., & Feagin, C.B. (2008). Glossary. *Racial and ethnic relations* (8th ed.). Upper Saddle River, NJ: Prentice Hall.

Provides definitions of major terms and concepts in intergroup relations.

Gioseffi, D. (Ed.). (1993). *On prejudice: A global perspective.* New York, NY: Anchor.

Contains excerpts from historic and contemporary authors from around the world describing the existence and consequences of human prejudice.

Giroux, H. (1998). *Channel surfing: Racism, the media, and the destruction of today's youth.* New York, NY: St. Martin's.

Analyzes media images, especially films, and their impact on children and youth.

Goldhagen, D.J. (2002). *Hitler's willing executioners: Ordinary Germans and the Holocaust* (2nd ed.) New York, NY: Knopf.

Presents evidence for the controversial thesis that Germans readily collaborated in the Nazi Holocaust.

Howard, G.R. (2006). *We can't teach what we don't know: White teachers, multiracial schools* (2nd ed.) New York, NY: Teachers College Press.

Integrates theory, research, and personal experiences to describe problems created by racism and white privilege and discusses actions to bring about positive changes.

Jones, J. (1997). *Prejudice and racism* (2nd ed.). New York, NY: McGraw Hill.

Integrates data from psychology, sociology, anthropology, biology, political science, and history to explain prejudice and racism and the relationship between them.

Khan, M.A.M. (2004). Living on borderlines: Islam beyond the clash and dialogue of civilization. In Z.H. Buhhari, S.S. Nyang, M. Ahmad, & J.C. Esposito (Eds.), *Muslims' place in the American public square* (pp. 84–113). Walnut Creek, CA: Altamira Press.

Addresses conceptual and practical issues facing American Muslims and describes the influence of two groups—idealists and realists—on Muslims in the United States and worldwide.

Koppelman, K. (1994). *Race and gender equity in urban America: The efforts of six cities to define the issues and provide solutions.* Paper presented at the national conference of the Renaissance Group in San Antonio on October 15, 1994.

Describes policies and programs of public and private agencies in six urban areas to address racial and gender inequities.

Levin, J., & Levin, W. (1982). *The functions of discrimination and prejudice* (2nd ed., p. 202). New York, NY: Harper & Row.

Examines the causes and effects of prejudice summarized on two flow charts.

Martinez, R., & Dukes, R.L. (1991, March). Ethnic and gender differences in self-esteem. *Youth & Society, 22*(3), 318–339.

Presents findings from a study of self-esteem in a multiracial population of students in grades 7–12 who attended the largest school district in Colorado Springs, Colorado.

Massey, D.S. (2001, January). Residential segregation and neighborhood conditions in U.S. metropolitan areas. In N. Smelser, W. Wilson, & F. Mitchell (Eds.), *America becoming: Racial trends and their consequences.* (ERIC Document Reproduction Service No. ED449286)

Describes how segregation has increased in recent years, especially for blacks, as well as the nature of segregation for Hispanics and Asian Americans.

McCloud, A.B. (2004). Conceptual discourse: Living as a Muslim in a pluralistic society. In Z.H. Buhhari, S.S. Nyang, M. Ahmad, & J.C. Esposito (Eds.), *Muslims' place in the American public square* (pp. 73–83). Walnut Creek, CA: Altamira Press.

Examines the role of the media in creating negative images of Muslims and discusses the inconsistency between American responses to Muslims and American values.

McCloud, A.B. (2006). *Transnational Muslims in American society.* Gainesville, FL: University of Florida Press.

Examines the experiences of Muslims who have recently become citizens of the United States and explores the success of their various strategies for adapting to American culture.

Miller, C., & Swift, K. (2000). *Words and women.* San Jose, CA: iUniverse.

Explains the study of junior high students' drawings of "early man" along with other studies concerning the sexism of generic terms in Chapter 2, "Who Is Man?"

Moore, R.B. (2006). Racism in the English language. In K. Rosenblum & T. Travis (Eds.), *The meaning of difference: American constructions of race, sex and gender, social class, and sexual orientation* (4th ed., pp. 451–459). Boston, MA: McGraw-Hill.

Examines the origins and implications of many racist words and phrases.

Newberg, A., & Waldman, M.R. (2006). *Why we believe what we believe: Uncovering our biological needs for meaning, spirituality, and truth.* New York, NY: Free Press.

Proposes a new way of thinking about how convictions develop and influence individuals based on recent research about how the brain perceives (and transforms) reality.

Ryan, W. (1976). *Blaming the victim* (2nd ed.). New York, NY: Vintage Books.

Describes and analyzes victim-blaming attitudes toward blacks in the inner cities.

Sadker, D., & Sadker, M. (1994). *Failing at fairness: How America's schools cheat girls.* New York, NY: Charles Scribner.

Discusses how boys are favored and girls are discriminated against in schools; describes the Michigan study in Chapter 3, "The Self-Esteem Slide," on pp. 83–85.

Sartre, J.P. (1995). *Anti-Semite and Jew.* New York, NY: Schocken.

Describes French anti-Semitism expressed after World War II despite French people's awareness of the Nazi Holocaust.

Schaefer, R.T. (2008). *Racial and ethnic groups* (11th ed.). Upper Saddle River, NJ: Pearson.

Reviews changes in the composition of U.S. immigrants and anti-immigrant sentiments in Chapter 4, "Immigration and the United States"; discusses findings of research using the Social Distance Scale in Chapter 2, "Prejudice."

Selden, S. (2006). *Inheriting shame: The story of eugenics and racism in America.* New York, NY: Teachers College Press.

Examines the development of the eugenics movement in the United States and what lessons should be learned from it.

Simpson, G.E., & Yinger, J.M. (1985). *Racial and cultural minorities: An analysis of prejudice and discrimination* (5th ed.). New York, NY: Plenum.

Provides an in-depth examination of prejudice and discrimination, including studies that used the Social Distance Scale.

Skuttnab-Kangas, T. (2000). *Linguistic genocide in education—or worldwide diversity and human rights?* Mahwah, NJ: Lawrence Erlbaum Associates.

Uses contemporary theory and research to examine the impact of linguistic imperialism on human rights in general and the assault on linguistic diversity in particular.

Stephan, W. (1999). *Reducing prejudice and stereotyping in schools.* New York, NY: Teachers College Press.

Reviews theories of prejudice and stereotyping, examines conditions to promote changes in negative attitudes, and describes techniques for improving race relations in schools.

Thurow, L. (2001). *The zero-sum society.* New York, NY: Penguin.

Describes economic implications when a society accepts and acts on zero-sum thinking.

United States Bureau of the Census. (2008). *Statistical abstract of the United States.* Retrieved October 15, 2008 from http://www.census.gov/compendia/statab.

Provides historic and current statistical data on the demographics of the U.S. workforce.

Vega, F. (1978). *The effect of human and intergroup relations education on the race/sex attitudes of education majors.* Unpublished doctoral dissertation, University of Minnesota, Minneapolis.

Discusses the development of individual racist and sexist attitudes from cultural and institutional influences and measures the impact of a course on those attitudes.

Wessler, S. L. (2001). Sticks and stones. *Educational Leadership, 58*(4), 28–33.

Describes the degrading and even violent language children use in schools and the impact of this language on its victims.

CHAPTER 3

Communication, Conflict, and Conflict Resolution

❝ If I were to summarize the single most important principle I have learned in the field of interpersonal relations it would be this: Seek first to understand, then to be understood. ❞

Stephen Covey (1932–)

Communication seems simple. One person talks, and other people listen to understand what the speaker is saying; when the first person stops talking, another person responds, perhaps to agree or disagree with the first speaker. Nothing seems complicated here, so why are there misunderstandings that so often lead to conflicts among individuals, groups, organizations, and nations? One answer was suggested in the 1960s film *Cool Hand Luke,* in which Paul Newman as Luke, an inmate, keeps breaking the warden's rules. As he prepares to punish Luke once again, the warden says, "What we have here is a failure to communicate." Actually it's not that Luke doesn't understand the rules; the problem is he doesn't *respect* the rules, so he violates them. By referring to a failure in *communication,* the warden means that Luke has not demonstrated his understanding that he must conform to the rules.

Communication and Conflict

In communication, more is going on than speaking, listening, and comprehending one another's words. Understanding communication requires some knowledge of the purpose served by that communication and what attitudes support it. Spitzberg (2008) reported that we interact with other people 70% of the time we are awake. Communicating effectively is an asset in one's personal and professional life, especially when conflicts occur. And conflicts are likely to be resolved only if those people involved communicate effectively.

What is an appropriate definition of communication?

Most people assume that the term *communicate* refers to interpersonal communication, but mass media represent another form of communication. Kougl (1997) offers a practical definition of **interpersonal communication:** "A dynamic process of interaction between people in which they assign meaning to each other's verbal and nonverbal behavior" (p. 7). Two features of this definition provide clues about how communication can lead to conflict: *assign meaning* and *nonverbal behavior.*

How does assigning meaning lead to conflict?

We not only listen to words; we also make assumptions about what the other person means. If our assumptions are accurate, there is no problem, but if they are not, the result is likely to be a misinterpretation of the message.

When interaction occurs between members of different groups, individuals may interpret the meaning of a statement in terms of the perceived influence of stereotypes or prejudices. During the second presidential debate in 2008 between John McCain and Barack Obama, McCain referred to an energy bill endorsed by President George W. Bush and Vice President Dick Cheney that came before the Senate. McCain claimed that the bill included significant funding for oil companies and stated, "You know who voted for it? You might never know. That one (pointing to Obama). You know who voted against it? Me."

The interpretation of Senator McCain's use of the phrase "That one" to refer to his Senate colleague was immediate, and overwhelmingly negative. The web site for CNN News soon posted a number of responses suggesting that the phrase was considered rude at the very least, if not racist: "Next he'll probably call (Obama) boy." An Executive Director of the Republican Party defended the party's candidate by saying: "I think McCain didn't mean anything negative. I think he was in the middle of his speech and was just getting passionate." But most of the respondents appeared to share the view of a woman from Chicago who wrote: "As soon as McCain referred to Obama as 'that one' my husband and I looked at each other in astonishment. John McCain's disdain for Obama is palpable . . . and incredibly ugly." According to some pundits, McCain may have appeared to show disdain for Obama to reinforce the campaign theme that Obama was inexperienced and not ready to be President, but his attitude was not well received by many viewers.

Another example of assigning meanings to statements occurred during a college ethnic studies class discussion of offensive words, phrases, and images based on ethnic and racial differences. An Asian American college student described his visit to a local middle school. As soon as he entered the building, he saw a few white male students put their fingers next to their eyes and pull their skin to create a "slant-eyed" look, and they began talking with a stereotypical Asian accent. The Asian American college student was appalled that these middle school students would taunt a visitor to their school with such blatant stereotypes, but another college student said this did not necessarily reflect their prejudice, just their immaturity. He argued that stu-

dents at that age, especially boys, tend to be very insecure and they make fun of everyone and everything to get attention.

An American Indian student disagreed, saying that when he was in middle school and high school he heard a lot of students talking in terms of stereotypes. That was one of the reasons he was opposed to using Indians as mascots for sports teams because such images reinforced stereotypes for American Indians. A white woman in the class who was a nontraditional student said she didn't think there was anything wrong with Indian mascots because they had an Indian mascot at her high school and she felt that it was used to honor Indian people. That led to the following dialogue among the white female (WF), American Indian (AI), and Asian American (AA) students:

AI: How am I supposed to be honored by an image like the Cleveland Indians mascot? These things are caricatures, cartoon figures! Even images that try to be respectable are just "noble savage" stereotypes that do not realistically depict real Indian people today . . . or at any time actually.

WF: Well, I suppose if you look at something long enough you can always find something to be offended about.

AA: Hold on, wait a minute! Are you saying that the problem is just in his head? That some people just make up stuff to be offended about but there's really nothing offensive there, nothing going on?

WF: No, no, I'm not saying that. I just meant that . . . like with the Indian mascots . . . I don't think anyone intends to offend anyone, but some people are offended.

AA: But you seem to be saying that the problem isn't real; that it's only a problem because of the way some Indian people look at this issue.

AI: Yeah, it sounds like you don't think Indian mascots are stereotypes, and if we would just stop saying they were, then there'd be no problem.

AA: Isn't that just another example of what we've talked about before? . . . You know, blaming the victim?

WF: But that's not what I'm saying!

AA: Maybe not, but that's what it sounds like, and if we keep talking like that, then no one will ever confront the stereotypes that kids have learned about Asians or Indians or Blacks or any other group. It's not about immaturity or good intentions. It's about what people are doing, you know, it's about certain behaviors that should be confronted, especially in schools, and how to go about doing that.

The white woman continued to defend her position, but she was frustrated that she could not seem to get the other students to understand what she was saying—yet they felt they understood her meaning all too well. They perceived that she was denying the problem of stereotypes affecting white people's perceptions of people of color; they also believed that she blamed people of color for being offended about things that were never meant to be

> The meanings of words are not in the words; they are in us.
>
> **S. I. Hayakawa (1906–1992)**

offensive. The white woman wanted to emphasize intent, but the other two students were focused on the consequences for people of color no matter what was intended. In both of the examples just given, the conflicts resulted from the meanings assigned to verbal statements. People make assumptions and interpretations about the meaning of another person's statements, regardless of whether it was what the other person intended. When the meaning assigned to a speaker's words becomes significantly different from what was intended, a conflict is likely to occur. Similarly, nonverbal communication can also lead to conflict based on someone's interpretation of the meaning of a nonverbal message.

How does nonverbal communication lead to conflict?

Hecht and DeVito (2008) define **nonverbal communication** as "all the messages other than words

that people exchange" (p. 4). Estimates of how much meaning is taken from interpretations of nonverbal communication have been as high as 93%, although Burgoon (2002) estimated that 60% to 65% is more realistic. Children don't tend to find as much meaning from nonverbal behavior as do adults; still, parents and teachers must be conscious of their nonverbal cues, especially when they express disapproval or take disciplinary action. For a child to understand what adults mean, messages must not be contradicted or confused by nonverbal messages (Kougl, 1997).

Disciplinary action may be required in response to a child's unacceptable behavior—perhaps the child is teasing or taunting other children. The adult says, "Teasing is bad. It hurts people's feelings. It may make them angry and it certainly makes me angry. You must stop doing this or no one will like you and no one will want to play with you." The message is clear and provides good reasons, including self-interest, for the child to change his or her behavior. However, if this message is accompanied by angry looks, a loud voice, and gestures such as the adult pointing or jabbing a finger at the child, the good advice may get lost. The message the child gets is not that the behavior is bad but that "I'm bad" or "She hates me." (See Figure 3.1.)

Children receiving this message are not likely to change their behavior, but to persist in it, either as a way of rebelling against the adult who has made this negative comment about them or as a self-fulfilling prophecy: "She says I'm bad so I might as well be bad." Being told that certain *behavior* is unacceptable implicitly offers a child the power to choose. Children may not think they can change who they are, but they know they can change their behavior. If they hear an adult make a negative judgment about who they are, they can do nothing about that. Conflicts arising from such misinterpretations of nonverbal messages also occur among adults.

The need to assign meaning and the influence of nonverbal messages address two misconceptions about communication: (1) that communication simply means telling people something and (2) that communication is a verbal process to transmit messages using only words. Teachers who are committed to being good communicators understand the need to seek constant feedback from students to ensure that the knowledge they impart is being under-

FIGURE 3.1 According to Ekman (2003), expressions of contempt and disgust are often used to indicate hatred of another. Prior studies have indicated that expressions of hatred and anger are often confused. In these two photographs from Ekman's research, one expression represents contempt and the other is anger. Try to identify the emotion represented in each facial expression. (For the answer, see the Ekman annotation in the References at the end of the chapter.)

Source: Used by permission of Paul Ekman.

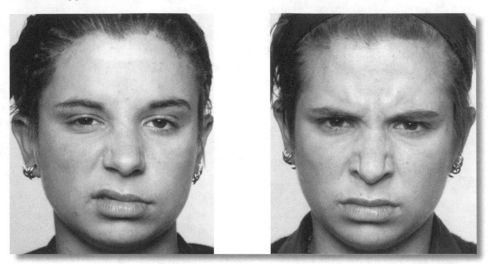

stood. Postman and Weingartner (1987) criticized educators for taking an "inoculation approach" in which teachers communicate information to students as if inoculating them against ignorance. When grades on tests reveal that students didn't re-

> Communication is something so simple and so difficult that we can never put it into simple words.
>
> **T.S. Matthews (1901–1991)**

tain much information, often the teacher's reaction is similar to that of a physician who doesn't understand why a vaccine had no effect when she knows she injected it. In discussing classroom communication, Kougl (1997) emphasized that teaching is not just talking; it involves more than words, as is true of all communication.

What are other misconceptions about communication?

Of the many misconceptions about communication identified by Stone, Singletary, and Richmond (1999), the following five examples are especially important to recognize:

Communication is a natural human ability.
Communication is a good thing and should be encouraged.
Communication will solve all our problems.
Communications can break down.
Communication competence is equal to communication effectiveness. (pp. 56–61)

Communication is a natural human ability. In a longitudinal study of three communities in the Piedmont Plateau region of the Carolinas, Heath (2006) described the way children learned communication skills and how skills varied depending on how the children had been taught. Heath found that low-income white parents taught language to children by reading storybooks with a moral for each tale. Parental communication style was didactic and authoritarian; their children memorized Bible verses, learned strict rules for right and wrong, and were severely punished for lying. When the children went to school, they did well initially because learning activities and communication styles of teachers were similar to what they had experienced at home. The children obeyed teachers, looked for a single meaning—the moral—of a story, and memorized material as required.

As the children from low-income white families progressed through elementary school, however, they encountered activities requiring critical thinking and creativity. They had trouble making up stories because it seemed like lying. They struggled to make sense of stories with multiple meanings and to identify and analyze different perspectives for strengths and weaknesses. Their life experiences had not prepared them for reading, thinking, and communicating at any level of complexity. As they approached middle school their grades declined, as did their confidence. The majority never achieved academic competence in school, and some dropped out before finishing high school.

Heath described the language learning of black children from low-income homes as a more creative process where children listened to adults tell stories that often had no particular moral point; these stories related what happened at work or in the neighborhood or gossip about "crooked politicians . . . or wayward choir leaders" (p. 168). Adults often told stories with a basis in fact, but with embellishment. When the stories got too far removed from reality, the teller was accused of "talkin' junk." In addition to hearing stories, boys developed language skills to respond to teasing based on "feigned hostility, disrespect and aggressive behavior" while girls became proficient in language by making up songs when skipping rope (p. 85). Both boys and girls practiced telling stories and, like adults, learned to embellish their stories with fictional details.

Black children from low-income homes came to school with highly creative communication skills, but they did not do well in the early elementary classes because they were not as adept at memorization or sticking to the facts. They saw many meanings to a story other than the simple moral the teacher wanted. As the students struggled with their assignments and growing feelings of inadequacy, they lost confidence in themselves as learners. When they finally encountered the more creative and complex learning activities later in elementary school, they were not successful because they had given up the possibility of success.

Heath noted that the children who succeeded in school at all levels were from middle-class homes, black as well as white, where their parents had read to them and had asked for didactic meanings of stories but also encouraged engagement in creative and analytical activity. A parent might read a story and then ask, "Would you have liked to go fishing with Little Bear? What do you think you would have caught?" (p. 250). Middle-class children came to school with a range of communication and language skills: They were successful at memorization and didactic activities during early elementary years; they were also able to adjust to activities emphasizing creativity or critical thinking in later years. Heath's research demonstrated that learning to communicate is not a natural human ability but rather is a product of the cultural and social context one experiences as a child.

Communication is a good thing and should be encouraged. Communication is a tool, and tools can be employed for good or bad purposes. Hitler used oratorical skills to arouse feelings of Aryan superiority and to deepen the anti-Semitic prejudices of Germans into a hatred that condoned persecution and execution. Martin Luther King, Jr., employed his oratorical skills to urge nonvio-

> Think like an active person; act like a thoughtful person.
>
> **Henri Bergson (1859–1941)**

lent resistance to oppression, warning his followers not to hate oppressors but to focus on the cause of justice. With any communication it is essential to ascertain the speaker's purpose and then determine whether that purpose is a good one. As Skuttnab-Kangas (2000) says, language is "a tool for domination (or) a tool for change and self-determination" (p. 134).

It is also important to recognize when additional communication is not necessary—when the time has come to take action. Martin Luther King, Jr., deplored the "paralysis of analysis" as when people continue to talk about problems without ever doing anything. Of course it is essential to be thoughtful before acting, taking time to consider alternatives and consequences before deciding on a course of action, but there comes a time when one must stop analyzing every possible outcome and take action. After taking action, it is important to consider the consequences to determine whether to continue or choose another tactic. It is what Freire (2004) meant by the term **praxis**—taking action to address injustice and then reflecting on the effectiveness of the actions taken as the person or group continues their activities.

Communication will solve all our problems. Communication has the potential to solve problems, but it also has the potential to create them. In a speech to college students, poet Maya Angelou noted that whenever anyone asks, "Can I be brutally honest?" she always says "No" because she does not want to encourage anyone to do anything brutally. Whether information is accurate or inaccurate, truthful or distorted, if communication is delivered brutally it will be hurtful, and hurting people will create problems rather than solve them. We can communicate honestly without being brutal; we can show respect and sensitivity to the feelings of any person or group we encounter.

Ironically, some communication addresses problems with no *intent* of solving them. Berne (2004) described such interaction as playing "games." In the "Ain't It Awful" game, two people talk about a problem, not to solve it but to affirm each other's perceptions, sometimes at the expense of another. Imagine two teachers discussing a student. One describes Danny's misbehavior; the other responds with a similar story about something Danny did in her class, and they continue to exchange stories. The teachers are not trying to understand the boy's behavior to help him; instead, each is telling the other, "You and I are all right. Danny is the problem." When their conversation ends, both teachers walk away believing they are not to blame or obligated to do anything. Their communication has not solved Danny's problem, but it has made them feel better.

Another game Berne has described is "Yes, but . . . ," where one person comes to another asking for advice but actually wanting something else. For example, Luis is a teenager who is having problems with his parents. He goes to his best friend for advice. His friend suggests several strategies, and each time Luis says either (a) he tried that (or something similar) and it didn't work, or (b) he thought about doing that but explains why the suggestion wouldn't work. After the friend has exhausted all possible strategies he can think of, he may say something like, "Well I don't know what else to tell you. I don't know what else you can do." At this point, Luis walks away saying, "That's okay." The friend may be frustrated that he could not help solve the problem, but for Luis, the point of the conversation was to hear that he had done everything he could and there was nothing more for him to do. Now he can say the problem is not his responsibility; it is up to his parents. Both "Ain't It Awful" and "Yes, but . . ." involve a "solution" only in the sense that someone gets what he or she wants from the interaction, but the communication is not intended to solve the problem.

Communications can break down. Most of us have used this particular misconception about communication to justify ongoing conflicts. Rebellious teenagers say their parents don't understand them; husbands and wives complain that their partners don't appreciate them; workers may go on strike

> Information voids will be filled by rumors and speculation unless they are preempted by open, credible, and trustworthy communication.
>
> **Jean Keffeler (Contemporary)**

claiming that management isn't bargaining in good faith. In such cases, we may rationalize that our conflict cannot be resolved because communication has broken down. When machines break, they stop; however, communication cannot break down because it never stops, even if people stop talking to each other. Their communication could be hearsay or it could be nonverbal; it could consist of interpretations by one person about perceived decisions and actions of another.

Communication occurs because one person wants or needs to know what the other is thinking about or doing; a person may make decisions to do (or not to do) something based on assumptions about someone else. One person may decide not to attend a Christmas party so that a co-worker will know he is still angry with her, or he may decide to attend the party but not speak to the co-worker or make eye contact. In an extreme example, Dylan Klebold and Eric Harris had stopped responding to the taunts of some classmates and endured the verbal abuse at Columbine High School in silence, but when they went home, they left written and videotaped records of their repressed rage and their plans for revenge (Brown & Merritt, 2006). Communication can be ineffective or effective, but communication does not stop. If *verbal* exchange ceases, communication in some other form—whether words or actions—will replace it.

Communication competence is equal to communication effectiveness. This is a misconception few college students should believe because almost every college student is familiar with professors who are knowledgeable about their subject matter but ineffective at communicating that knowledge. We are competent to communicate on a topic if we have sufficient knowledge of it; however, possessing knowledge does not mean that we can communicate in a way that is easily comprehended.

A major function of teacher education programs consists of preparing people to be effective at organizing and communicating information. Whether they are lecturing or using alternative means of delivering information, teachers must understand what studies have concluded about effective ways of helping people learn. To assess how effectively they deliver information, teachers must also evaluate how well students learn. Tests and other forms of assessment may measure student learning; more importantly, they reveal how effectively the teacher communicated.

Except for those in teacher education, most college professors learn how to communicate from mentors or self-study. Many professors have acquired the skills to become good teachers, yet the misconception that communication competence

equals communication effectiveness is often the basis for student complaints that they aren't learning because a professor is incompetent. Professors may have **communication competence** because they have the knowledge needed for communication and may even have published articles and books on their specialty, yet they may not display **communication effectiveness** because they lack the appropriate skills to communicate effectively in a classroom.

How does effective communication occur?

Numerous excellent models have been developed that examine the communication process and analyze communication to ascertain why misunderstandings occur (Narula, 2006; Stone et al., 1999). The following model describes four factors involved in interpersonal communication. Each instance of a person interacting with another is influenced by these four cumulative factors (see Figure 3.2).

A Circular Model of Communication

1. Attitudes toward people or groups
2. Observations and assumptions
3. Conclusions and judgments
4. Verbal and nonverbal action

First, the communication process is grounded in an individual's *attitudes toward people or groups*. All people develop a general attitude about their interactions with others. Some of us are trusting, others are suspicious; some are willing to share ideas, others are reserved; some are motivated by dominance and control, others function with an egalitarian view. Our attitudes may change because of those involved in our interactions. Our interactions with family are different than they are with strangers. We communicate differently within same-gender groups than in mixed groups or with people of the opposite gender. Our behavior is different with others of our own race or ethnic group as opposed to being in mixed groups or with individuals from another race or ethnic group. Having prejudices or stereotypes about a particular minority group will certainly influence our interactions with a member of that group.

Second, our *observations and assumptions* about another person shape the communication between us before anything is said. Our initial reaction may be friendly and accepting, aloof and suspicious, or even hostile and rejecting, depending on the appearance

FIGURE 3.2

The Circular Model of Communication

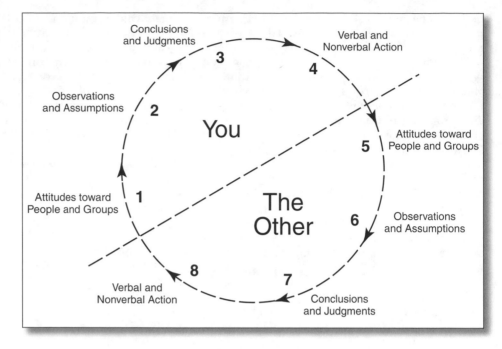

of the other person and sometimes on which behaviors we choose to observe—a phenomenon known as **selective perception.** If an individual believes a stereotype about someone from a certain group, that stereotype is likely to be reinforced by selective perceptions.

How do our observations influence our assumptions? What if a person were introduced to a long-haired young white male who was dressed in torn overalls and wore a red bandana around his head? Based on observation, one might assume that the young man has rejected our materialistic society by imitating college students from the 1960s who questioned authority figures and rebelled against middle-class values, conformity, and the Vietnam War. These observations and assumptions are now taken to the next level.

The third step, *conclusions and judgments,* refers to the values and beliefs we employ to draw conclusions or to judge others. In the example of the young man with long hair, various people observing him and making reasonable assumptions could come to different conclusions. One person may have been in college in the 1960s and remember it as an exciting time that had a profound influence on his life. His initial reaction may be a positive conclusion: "That

young man reminds me of myself when I was his age." Conversely, someone who was taught to respect authority and appreciate the material comforts of our society and whose goal is to acquire those material comforts may make a negative judgment, perhaps generating additional assumptions about the young man smoking marijuana or using other illegal drugs. Prejudice and negative stereotypes lead to negative assumptions, which result in a negative judgment of another person.

The fourth and final step in the process is *verbal and nonverbal action.* When individuals meet, one person will say or do something to initiate interaction. Doing something might be as simple as smiling or frowning, making eye contact with the other or looking away. Nonverbal behavior employing such body language can initiate communication as much as words, often just as powerfully.

What does this communication model suggest about conflict resolution?

If conflict occurs during interaction, how can we resolve it? Our most common response is to focus on the action taken, on the words or behavior that initiated the conflict. For example, elementary teachers often witness conflict during recess where one child insults or hurts another. Some teachers respond by making the perpetrator apologize: The problem was the child's action, so the teacher forces the child to take another action to offset the first. This response focuses on the symptoms of the conflict and not the cause, so it is not likely to result in a resolution. Because the child may not feel genuinely sorry, what is learned from such an apology is a lesson in hypocrisy—being forced to say something that is not true.

Effective conflict resolution rejects superficial attention to actions and analyzes other factors to identify probable causes of the conflict. As Schramm (1973) stated, "The full significance of acts of communication is seldom on the surface" (p. 23). For this reason, most strategies for resolving conflicts are intended to get past surface meanings: Expressing "I" messages (Gordon, 2000); engaging in transactional analysis (Harris, 2004); using empathy to promote understanding (Rogers, 1995); and negotiating "Win/Win" strategies (Jandt, 1985). Still, even a proven approach may be ineffective if the people involved do not accept the value of the techniques employed.

The table on page 56 offers an analysis that employs the four factors of communication that preceded the conflict to understand the cause of a father/ daughter conflict. The situation concerns a father and Abby, his daughter. Abby is talking on the telephone and making plans to meet with some friends whom her father doesn't like.

If Abby and her father were to resolve their conflict by focusing on what each one said and did, resolution would be unlikely, but resumption of the quarrel would be quite likely. Instead, they could analyze factors involved prior to their argument to determine common ground on which to create a resolution. The cause of their quarrel stems from the father exercising his authority as a parent in conflict with Abby's desire for greater independence. They will need to discuss their conflicting assumptions and desires. The father must understand that adolescents typically resent parental authority and not take her rebelliousness personally. Abby must recognize her father's authority as legitimate. A resolution is likely to come from agreements about the father supporting Abby's desire to be more independent and Abby recognizing his con-

cern to protect her from the consequences of what he perceives as bad decisions. The causes of an interpersonal conflict will rarely be found in an analysis or discussion of individual behaviors; they are more likely found in observations, assumptions, conclusions, or judgments made about each other, and sometimes in contrasting attitudes toward people and groups.

How can attitudes toward people or groups create conflict?

When people involved in interpersonal communication identify themselves—or are identified by others—as part of a specific group (such as by race or ethnicity), individual attitudes can be significantly influenced. In a multicultural society such as the United States, it is probable that people, especially in urban areas, will interact with others who are different by race, ethnicity, nationality, or religion (see Figure 3.3.). How much the cultures of different nationalities or people of different racial or ethnic groups affect communication will depend on the level of cultural awareness that the person has.

What are the levels of cultural awareness?

Kimmel (2006) identified levels of cultural awareness:

Cultural chauvinism Belief that one's culture is the best, superior to all other cultures; feeling no need to learn about other cultures.

Tolerance Awareness of cultural differences, recognition that differences stem from the country of origin for that person (or his or her ancestors); no judgment of cultural differences as inferior, simply as different ways of thinking or behaving.

Minimalization Minimizing cultural differences by emphasizing a universality of human needs and behaviors as a means of creating a stronger sense of relationship or connectedness with culturally different people.

Understanding Recognizing that reality is shaped by culture and that each person's reality is different from that of a person from a different culture; having no judgment of different

	Father	Abby
Interpersonal and Intergroup Attitudes:	Loves his daughter and wants her to be happy.	Loves her father but resents the authority he has over her.
Observations and Assumptions:	Remembers Abby as an obedient child, but she has been rebellious since becoming a teenager; she has been challenging his authority and questioning his decisions rather than giving him the respect he deserves.	Perceives her father as using his authority to control her and not being fair to her; expects him to interfere with decisions that she believes she has the right to make by herself.
Conclusions and Judgments:	Believes that Abby's behavior is a personal rejection of him; he has also concluded that Abby's friends have encouraged her to reject him by disobeying him.	Values independence and wants more freedom; regards her father as hypocritical for denying her what he values; ready to rebel against attempts to control her.
Nonverbal and Verbal Action:		Hangs up the phone and says, "I'm bored so I'm going out to meet my friends."
	Questions her choice of friends— "Why are you always hanging out with that bunch? Can't you find any other friends?"	
		"You are always criticizing my friends! You have no right to tell me who to be friends with!"
Conflict:	Becomes angry at her disrespectful tone of voice (which he expected to hear); tells her she cannot leave the house and orders her to her room.	Becomes angry about his attempt to control her (which she expected), shouts "Just leave me alone!" and runs out of the house, slamming the door behind her.

cultural realities; accepting and respecting cultural differences (cultural relativism).

Communication conflicts occur readily between people at the cultural chauvinism level, and they also may occur at the tolerance and minimalization levels. Only when people understand cultural differences and practice cultural relativism is it likely that conflicts between people from different cultures can be avoided or resolved.

Culture, Communication Style, and Conflict

Differences in cultural norms can cause misunderstanding and conflict. In the United States, business executives usually engage in minimal personal conversation before discussing a proposal at a group meeting. In some other cultures, communication is commonly expected to focus first on personal mat-

FIGURE 3.3 United States: Present and Future

As ethnic diversity increases in the United States, being aware of cultural differences will become increasingly important.

Source: Uncle Sam image, courtesy Library of Congress. Data from U.S. Census.

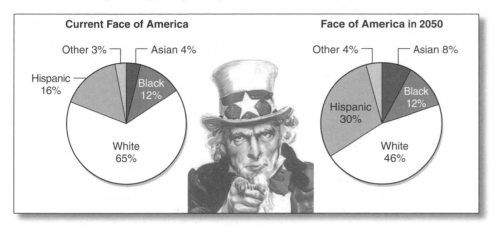

ters—questions about the person's health, family, or interests—before business is discussed. Ismail (2001) stressed how the global marketplace requires business executives to be knowledgeable about and employ appropriate communication strategies concerning use of direct speech, accept-

> The test of a first rate intelligence is the ability to hold two opposed ideas in the mind at the same time, and still retain the ability to function.
>
> **F. Scott Fitzgerald (1896–1940)**

able levels of informality, attitudes about time, and expressions of emotion to negotiate successfully with people from other cultures.

What are some communication style differences that are based on culture?

In the United States, it has become acceptable to take a direct approach to conflict resolution, with

each party openly expressing their concerns. In other cultures, people are expected to show sensitivity to the feelings of others by taking an indirect approach to resolving conflicts. In some cultures, people tend to speak in a linear progression, going from one idea to the next, but in other cultures, people digress, often telling stories or anecdotes to illustrate their point. Cultures also reflect differences in nonverbal behavior. In Arab cultures, people tend to stand much closer in conversation than do Americans. In the United States, men greet one another with a firm handshake; in France, anything other than a quick handshake is considered rude; in Ecuador, greeting a person without offering one's hand is a sign of special respect. In the United States, the forefinger to thumb gesture means "okay"; in France, it signifies that something is worthless; and in Brazil, the gesture is considered obscene (Jandt, 2003).

Differences in communication styles have also been identified in subcultures in the United States. Kochman (1981) described how black and white children learn to express aggression. For most middle-class white people, aggressive language is viewed as a harbinger of aggressive behavior. "Fighting words" are words that may provoke a physical confrontation. (Meltzoff, 2007). Most white children learn to repress aggressive feelings and maintain a calm demeanor even though they may be furious. If they begin using language aggressively, it is likely that a fight is imminent. For some black males, however, words can be used aggressively without a conflict. Foster (1986) described how urban black male children may taunt one another in a playground game known by different names including "sounding" or "playing the dozens." Situations may become intense and emotional; however, a fight will only occur if a child gives an obvious signal such as making a fist to indicate that he is angry.

The contrast between the reactions of black and white people to aggressive language can lead to misunderstanding. Imagine two black children still playing the insult game as they come back to their classroom after recess. The teacher tries to intervene, but the boys continue to insult each other. A black teacher may recognize the childhood game and firmly tell them to stop, but a white teacher may perceive the boys as engaged in a hostile quarrel and order them to the principal's office. If the principal asks them why they were sent, they are likely to say they don't know. When the principal says their teacher saw them fighting, they will vigorously deny it, insisting that they were just teasing each other. Because the teacher has made this "false accusation," they might think she doesn't like them and become hostile to her in return.

Kochman (1981) describes another difference in communication styles concerning the conduct of arguments. White people are encouraged to present

> Misunderstandings and inertia cause perhaps more to go wrong in this world than slyness and evil intent.
>
> **Johann Wolfgang von Goethe (1749–1832)**

unbiased, objective arguments, but black people tend to accept the existence of bias and are skeptical of claims of objectivity. Although white people have been taught to argue in a calm, dispassionate manner, people in many black communities defend their beliefs passionately. In debates, black people do not expect impersonal or dispassionate argu-

ments and may distrust people who are not passionate. Expressing ideas passionately during an argument is regarded as a measure of sincerity. In white society, the norm in debating issues is to repress emotions because they are believed to interfere with keeping an open mind. For many white Americans, arguing passionately seems confrontational; they think it exacerbates conflict and makes consensus less likely.

The potential for misunderstanding about how arguments are conducted was revealed in a televised program showing academics discussing racial issues in which a white professor misperceived a black professor based on his communication style. The black professor was making an eloquent and passionate argument. The white professor sitting beside him appeared uncomfortable, yet displayed no emotion. As the black professor paused before concluding, the white professor remarked in a defensive tone of voice but without facial expression, "Well you don't have to be so angry." Startled by the interruption, the black professor looked over at his white colleague and said, "Excuse me, you are mistaking intensity for anger."

In describing communication style differences, the intent is not to find fault with any group or person, nor is it to say that one communication style is better than the other. What is important is to understand that communication styles are influenced by cultural heritage; we should not make assumptions about others based on their communication style. If a conflict occurs in a group whose members are different races or cultures, individuals in the group must articulate their perceptions about the cause of the conflict to see if everyone has a similar perception. Understanding our perceptions of others provides a basis for resolving cultural misunderstandings and conflicts. Meanwhile, research suggests that differences in communication styles create misunderstandings between men and women as well.

How does gender influence communication styles?

Communication differences based on gender are said to originate in differences in the way boys and girls are socialized. Traditionally, Americans have encouraged boys to be aggressive and girls to be nice; this has been documented in studies of children's play activities. American boys tend to play outdoors, typically in competitive games that require groups and involve aggressive behavior; they resolve disputes by engaging in debates in which everyone participates. In contrast, girls tend to play indoor types of games in small groups or with a friend; these games involve conversation and collaboration, and a quarrel will usually disrupt the game (Dow & Wood, 2006; Honig, 2006).

Gender differences persist even as children leave childhood behind. Some scholars believe that male aggressiveness in conversation is revealed in studies where men interrupt women more than women interrupt men (Dow & Wood, 2006), but Tannen (1994) argued that it is simplistic to say such behavior is always a dominance issue. Reviewing communication research on gender differences, Burgoon (2002) reported that women are more competent than men at giving and understanding nonverbal messages. Grumet (2008) found that women tend to have more eye contact than men and to pay more attention to their conversational partner.

Differences in degree of eye contact and face-to-face interaction often reflect differences in how women and men express intimacy. Tannen (2007) described differences in male and female communication styles originating in childhood and continuing into adult years. In one study with subjects ranging from children to young adults, two people of the same age and gender were taken to a room, seated in chairs placed side by side, and asked to talk about a serious topic. The younger boys had trouble with the task; they didn't move the chairs, did not make eye contact, and spent much of their time shifting restlessly and talking about not wanting to talk. Males of all ages would sit in the chairs in their original position with minimal face-to-face interaction. At all age levels, female partners either moved the chairs or positioned themselves to face each other; they began talking immediately on a serious topic as requested.

High school boys express intimacy through aggressive behavior. Pushing, shoving, even punching each other is an indication of a close friendship. As adults, men transform aggressive physical behavior into aggressive verbal behavior. For example, American men are careful about expressing disagreement with someone they don't know very well, but they bluntly disagree with and even use sarcasm with a close friend. It is a sign of intimacy and trust when men don't have to "pull their punches" with each other.

From childhood through adulthood, American women tend to express intimacy by engaging in face-to-face interactions and expressing concern for the other person's feelings. For most, outright disagreement is regarded as a threat to intimacy, a lack of sensitivity or respect. When a woman disagrees with another woman, she will often begin by saying something positive or something they agree on, and then address the issue about which they disagree. The difference in male and female communication styles creates opportunities for misunderstanding. If a man and a woman have an intimate relationship and discuss an issue on which they disagree, he may make direct, honest comments because he feels so close to her, but she may interpret his harsh comments as insensitive, disrespectful, and even contemptuous of her opinions.

With such an emphasis on competition and aggression, boys become men who directly express wants, needs, or demands. With such an emphasis on cooperation, being nice, and caring about how others might feel, girls become women who are concerned about not imposing their wants or demands, preferring consensus. A man might attempt to convince someone to do what he wants, but a woman is more likely to ascertain whether the other person is interested in doing what she wants to do. Tannen (2007) argues that this difference may be a basis for historic gender stereotypes that have contributed to misunderstandings and conflict: men perceiving women as devious and cunning, and women perceiving men as arrogant and intimidating.

How do gender differences in communication styles lead to misunderstanding and conflict?

Imagine a woman coming home from work, greeting her husband, and then remembering, "Oh John, I meant to stop at the store and pick up a few things, but I am so tired I forgot to do it. This has been such a rotten day." She is indirectly asking him to go to the store for her, yet he may not get the message. Even if he tries to be sympathetic—"I'm sorry to hear that"—she will be upset if he doesn't offer to go to the store. If he wanted her to go to the store he would ask her directly; he needs to understand that her socialization and her communication style does not allow her to make demands as he would.

In a similar example, after leaving early for a long trip, a couple has been driving all morning on the interstate and it's almost noon. She sees a sign advertising a restaurant she likes at the next exit, points it out to him, and says, "Would you like to stop there and get something to eat?" He hears her comment not as an indirect request, but as a genuine question. He wants to drive for another hour before stopping to eat, so he says "No" and drives on. When he realizes that she is upset, they discuss the reason, and he criticizes her for not stating explicitly what she wanted. She thinks he should be able to understand that she did tell him in a manner that took account of his feelings. She believes that she has been sensitive and he has not. He believes she was being dishonest while he was being straightforward with her.

The reason for identifying gender differences is not to blame men or women, nor to say that one communication style is better than another. It is important to recognize the diverse ways people communicate so that differences in communication styles do not result in conflict. Knowing the influence on communication style of such factors as gender or culture provides a basis to prevent misunderstandings. If people recognize problems as possibly stemming from a difference in communication styles, they can modify their interaction to communicate more effectively (Jandt, 2003; Prince, 2004).

Conflict Resolution

Sometimes resolving conflicts seems hopeless. Groups have been in conflict for centuries; individuals take unresolved conflicts to their graves. Obviously, conflict resolution is not easy, and most people approach conflict with apprehension. In a study by McCorkle and Mills (1992), every metaphor chosen by participants to describe conflict was negative, often involving feelings of helplessness and of being an innocent victim.

Because K–12 schools are an environment for children and youth with adult supervision, we would expect to find less conflict, and yet studies find that considerable conflict occurs there. According to Wessler (2003), these conflicts usually stem from human differences such as race, mental disability, sexual orientation, and gender. Sexual orientation alone appears to result in many instances of harassment and conflict. According to an NMHA survey, students who were both gay and straight reported 20 or more incidences a day of hearing slurs and insults that were directed at their peers who were openly gay or simply perceived as gay. One third of the gay students in that survey had been threatened or actually injured at school in the previous 12 months (Roberts Jr., 2006). Garrett (2003) cites research documenting the consequences of harassment and conflicts between students:

10% of students drop out of school
20% of students avoid going to restrooms during the school day
54% of students say it would be easy for them to get a gun
30% of students have heard a peer threaten to kill someone
25% of students know a peer who has brought a gun to school (p. 12)

With so much conflict occurring, how are conflicts resolved?

Conflict offers opportunity for constructive change, if all parties are prepared to make concessions and to establish a context conducive to resolution. Deutsch (2006) identified values that participants must share if they want to resolve conflict: fallibility, equality, reciprocity, and nonviolence.

Fallibility refers to accepting the possibility of being wrong. In conflict, people are customarily presented with evidence and arguments. However, presenting evidence will not help resolve a conflict if participants refuse to acknowledge that their position could be wrong. During deliberations in a jury room, the foreman of a jury said he believed the defendant was guilty and that he would not change his mind. Another jury member pointed out that such an attitude violated the jury process that requires discussing and debating evidence, listening to arguments with an open mind, and changing one's mind if justified by the weight of evidence or arguments. Although still believing the defendant guilty, the foreman admitted the jury member was right, and he agreed to listen with an open mind. Ultimately he changed his mind.

Equality refers to the belief that every human being, regardless of status, occupation, or wealth, deserves to be treated respectfully, with consideration for his or her values, beliefs, and behavior. It is an acknowledgment that every human life has value and that no one should be treated unjustly. In another jury trial, some members of the jury began to criticize testimony of two overweight and casually dressed female witnesses, based on their appearance rather than on what they said. Another juror chastised them for their negative attitudes and argued that if the jury was to render a just verdict, they should focus on the evidence the women presented, not on how they looked. Other jurors agreed.

Reciprocity means that participants in a conflict must behave toward others with the same sense of fairness and attentiveness that they would want for themselves—a restatement of the golden rule that appears as an ethical principle in practically all cultures, or as modified by Confucius: "Do not do to others what you would not like yourself" (Waley, 1938, p. 162). Apparently Confucius believed one did not have to be good to others as long as no harm was done to them. Either way, the feeling of reciprocity is essential for participants in a conflict if they hope to negotiate a resolution to it.

To value *nonviolence* is to believe that the only genuine solutions are peaceful ones. As Deutsch ex-

> The man who strikes first admits that his ideas have given out.
>
> **Chinese Proverb**

plained in his fourth shared value, coercing others into accepting an imposed solution winds a long and tragic path through human history marked by brutality and blood, civil and global wars, leaving little evidence that solutions imposed by the strong on the weak are effective—or lasting—solutions.

In the context of the four shared values proposed by Deutsch, conflict need not be a destructive event; it can be a constructive opportunity. Appleton (1983, p. 185) quotes educational philosopher John Dewey: "Conflict is the gadfly of thought. It steers us to observation and memory. It instigates to invention. It shocks us out of sheep-like passivity." If participants use effective negotiation strategies, they may be able to identify sources of conflict and determine appropriate solutions leading to improved relations between people.

Johnson, Johnson, and Tjosvold (2006) identified effective negotiation strategies to engage in what they termed **skilled disagreement.** Their first strategy for engaging in skilled disagreement is similar to what the jury member described in the fallibility anecdote: that all parties (1) agree to emphasize rationality, seek the best possible answer based on the available evidence and arguments, and be willing to change their position when justified by the evidence. Another strategy is that participants (2) agree that criticizing an idea is not criticizing those who propose the idea—that their worth as human beings is separate from their ideas.

It is also important that participants (3) make a conscious commitment to encourage others to contribute to discussion and to listen thoughtfully to the contributions they make. To ensure the process is effective, it is helpful when participants (4) restate ideas if they're not clear on what was said so that everyone understands the issue from all perspectives being presented. Finally, it is essential that participants (5) remember that the problem and any recommended solution will affect everyone; they must not be focused on winning a debate but upon arriving at a collaborative solution everyone can support. These conflict resolution skills are not difficult to learn, and many educators say they can and should be taught in schools, even to young children. Based on her review of research, Garrett (2003) argues that "Conflict resolution skills . . . learned by all students will help to change a school's atmosphere" (p. 135). By teaching these skills, educators may foster the development of not only cognitive abilities but also moral reasoning abilities.

How do people develop moral reasoning abilities?

Different theories of moral reasoning have been described, but some have not been carefully researched; others do not seem widely applicable to different cultures or genders. Perry (1999) has described a theory of moral reasoning that develops along a continuum, providing an accurate description of moral reasoning engaged in by people of different ages, from different cultures or subcultures, and from both genders (Belenky et al., 1997; King & Kitchener, 1994). Using this theory, teachers can provide students with moral dilemmas and controversial issues, then analyze student discussions and engage students with questions intended to challenge and improve the quality of their moral reasoning. What is this theory of moral reasoning that Perry has developed?

Perry's theory is based on the assumption that changes in moral reasoning are related to cognitive development: Increased cognitive ability allows individuals the possibility of increasing the complexity of their moral reasoning. Although there are nine developmental positions in Perry's continuum, as an introduction to the theory, it is sufficient to understand two major areas Perry has identified—dualism and relativism—and the mental shift that occurs within each: A dualistic thinker transitions into multiplicity, a relativistic thinker transitions into making commitments (see Figure 3.4).

Dualism   All human beings begin as dualistic thinkers when confronted with moral decisions; children tend to operate simplistically with absolute categories of right and wrong. In **dualism,** every moral issue is a question of either/or: Either it's right or it's wrong, it's true or it's false, it's good or it's bad. This is also called "black and white" thinking because there are no "shades of gray" for dualistic thinkers. To be dualistic is to believe that what is true must be regarded as an absolute truth: It has always been and will always be true. Newberg and Waldman (2006) say that brain research offers a biological explanation for dualistic thinking: "The brain tends to reduce cause-and-effect cognition into dualistic scenarios because they are an easy, neurologically efficient way to make sense of the world" (p. 88).

Believing in absolutes is challenged when a person is confronted with problems that don't lend themselves to the either/or style of thinking. A popular moral dilemma exercise is to ask people what they would have done if they were hiding Jews in the early 1940s and Gestapo officers came to their home to ask if they knew where there were any Jews. For the person who believes "honesty is the best policy," this is a difficult question to answer. Another problem with dualistic thinking is that the cognitive process of simplification and generalization inevitably leads to stereotyping others because the process does not consider individual differences. As studies have reported, the "'us-versus-them' mentality can be easily converted into racism" (Newberg & Waldman, 2006, p. 89). Complex issues that challenge dualistic thinking may not occur until a student enters high school or college, but when students confront such issues, they often feel

FIGURE 3.4 A Continuum of Moral Reasoning

Source: Perry, W. (1970). *Forms of Intellectual and Ethical Development in the College Years: A Scheme.* New York: Holt, Rinehart & Winston.

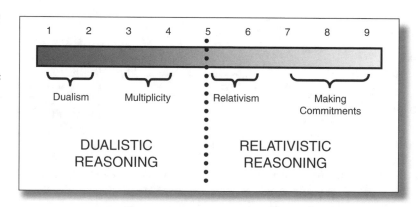

compelled to move away from rigid dualistic thinking and engage in the kind of moral reasoning called multiplicity.

Multiplicity The perspective of **multiplicity** recognizes the difficulty of knowing "the right answer" in every situation. When the right answer is not obvious, the only recourse is for the individual to examine various opinions or multiple perspec-

> The question should never be who is right, but what is right.
>
> **Glenn Gardiner (Contemporary)**

tives without being certain which one is right. Each person must consider the different perspectives and decide which one seems best. This is not satisfying for people at the multiplicity position because they are still influenced by dualistic thinking. They would prefer to know the answer or the truth in a given situation, and often complain that all we have are opinions. Because of the influence of dualistic thinking, people at a multiplicity position still believe the truth can be known and will be known some day, but for the moment, they reluctantly accept that they do not know the answer for a number of issues.

Relativism When people move beyond multiplicity to relativism, they tend to exhibit a change in attitude from reluctantly accepting the existence of multiple perspectives to becoming intrigued by the idea that each person must decide what is right. **Relativism** is based on the assumption that there are no absolute truths, and truth is relative, a concept reflected in the familiar phrases: "One man's meat is another man's poison" and "One person's treasure is another person's junk." The relativist is stimulated by differences of opinions, is interested in debates, and may enjoy playing the devil's advocate in a discussion by articulating arguments and ideas to defend a particular perspective without really believing in it.

Relativism requires an individual to be comfortable with ambiguity and not demand specific answers that are right for everyone. Many people are uncomfortable living in a world where they have to accept many points of view without regarding any of them as the right one. The difficulty of accepting such ambiguity causes some people to "retreat" (as Perry calls it) by resuming a dualistic thinking process. Other people who never progress beyond relativistic thinking sometimes adopt a cynical attitude toward life because relativistic thinking does not often result in becoming passionate about or personally invested in any issue or cause. However, some people who have also felt a sense of dissatisfaction with relativism's moral ambiguity have identified questions they wanted answered and are engaged deliberately in efforts to find their own answers.

Commitment Relativistic thinkers who continue to develop their moral reasoning are attracted to the idea of making **commitments** to certain personal truths, ideals, or causes that seem to give meaning to their lives. Most people need to believe in something and to feel a sense of satisfaction that their belief enhances the quality of their lives. Commitments may include being active in a political party or joining a church, an advocacy group, or some other organization. A commitment may result in volunteer work or influence a person's career decision. Whatever the choice, it is made from among many alternatives and the individual makes the commitment because it reflects his or her values.

Once people make commitments, they often become advocates for that particular cause or perspective. Because commitment is made in the context of relativistic thinking, people who reflect this perspective do not advocate like dualistic thinkers whose arguments are based on a sense of certainty. Relativistic thinkers may emphasize the sense of satisfaction they feel that their commitment provides a stronger sense of meaning and purpose in their lives, and they invite others to join them. In contrast, when dualistic thinkers advocate for truths they believe are absolute, they tend to view those who agree with them as right and those who disagree as wrong. There is no other option. When people at the commitment level argue on behalf of their commitments, they do not tend to judge those who agree or disagree. They recognize that it is an individual's obligation to make his or her own choices, and they respect the person's right to choose. Someone at the commitment level does not reject relativism and its view of reality as ambiguous, but this person does recognize the satisfaction that may be gained by making commitments to provide a sense of meaning and purpose to his or her life. Being able to respect individual choice is not only important for moral reasoning, it is also essential for engaging in successful conflict resolution.

AFTERWORD

Even if we say exactly what we want to say, we can never assume that the meaning is heard and understood in the way we intend. Miscommunication happens when people do not check with others to

> Wrongdoing can only be avoided if those who are not wronged feel the same indignation at it as those who are.
>
> **Solon (640–558 bce)**

ensure that they were understood. When misunderstandings are not clarified at the time they occur, they can cause people to become antagonistic toward others, thereby laying the foundation for an eventual conflict.

Some efforts to reduce conflict in schools have been successful, and there is much to be learned from them. In elementary classrooms, teachers must emphasize respect and nonviolence in their work with students. At the middle and high school levels, schools can empower students to intervene in conflicts by sponsoring workshops and providing other opportunities to develop mediation skills. At all levels it is important for students to work in groups and to have other experiences (e.g., peer tutoring) where they become better acquainted. According to Garrett (2003), studies have reported a reduction of conflict in schools when children and youth have more opportunities to get to know each other.

Conflict resolution is not easy, yet it's better than coping with unresolved conflict. It is in everyone's interest to embrace the values that make conflict resolution possible and to practice communication strategies necessary for engaging in skilled disagreement. Conflict—from intimate disagreements between husbands and wives to global disputes among nations—is inevitable. The resolution of conflicts, however, is not inevitable. Teachers must challenge and enhance the moral reasoning abilities of our children and youth, and all of us must choose to engage in and be committed to the process of conflict resolution. The quality of individual lives and the quality of life for communities and for countries depends on the willingness of people to choose to resolve conflicts rather than hopelessly perpetuate them.

TERMS AND DEFINITIONS

Commitment   Moral reasoning in a relativist context that recognizes the importance of becoming actively committed to certain personal truths to strengthen and deepen the meaningfulness of one's life experiences

Communication competence   Having sufficient knowledge of a subject to communicate accurate information about that subject

Communication effectiveness   Having the skills to communicate information in order to be easily understood

Cultural chauvinism   An attitude that one's culture is the best, superior to other cultures

Dualism   Moral reasoning involving a belief in absolute truths and unambiguous categories of right and wrong behavior; also called "either/or reasoning"

Interpersonal communication   A dynamic process of interaction between people in which they assign meaning to each other's verbal and nonverbal behavior (Kougl, 1997)

Minimalization   An attitude about other cultures that reduces importance of cultural differences and emphasizes the universality of human needs and behaviors to create a stronger sense of relationship with all people

Multiplicity   Moral reasoning in a dualistic context recognizing that it isn't possible to know what is the right behavior in certain situations, in which case opinions from multiple perspectives must be examined; a person can't be confident of the final decision in such instances because he or she can't be certain of having made the right choice

Nonverbal communication Those messages other than words that people exchange, also called "nonverbal behavior" or "nonverbal messaging"

Praxis Taking action to address injustice and then reflecting on the effectiveness of the actions taken as the person or group continues their activities

Relativism Moral reasoning that rejects absolute truth and is based on the assumption that all truth is relative and determining the right behavior depends on the individual and the situation

Selective perception Paying attention to behaviors of another person that reinforce our expectations for that person

Skilled disagreement Strategies that have been proven effective in achieving a successful resolution to conflicts

Tolerance Aware of cultural differences without judging cultures as superior or inferior

Understanding Recognizing that culture shapes individual reality including acceptance of and respect for cultural differences

DISCUSSION EXERCISES

Exercise 1: Statements Illustrating Perry's Continuum

Directions: Conversations can be categorized according to Perry's concepts. Identify each of the following statements according to the four broad areas in Perry's continuum of moral development. You will find three examples from each area. Record your answers as (a) dualism, (b) multiplicity, (c) relativism, or (d) commitment.

Statements Illustrating Perry's Continuum

_____ 1. In areas where even the experts disagree, everyone has a right to his own opinion. I mean, if answers aren't given, like in lots of things, then it has to be just anyone's opinion.

_____ 2. Understanding another point of view, especially a contrary one, helps me understand my own point of view. So trying to see through the other person's eyes helps my own understanding of the issue.

_____ 3. I came here from a small town in the Midwest where everyone believed the same things and everyone is, like, Methodist and Republican. But here, there is a variety of Protestants and Catholics and a Chinese boy who follows the teaching of Confucius. . . . Some people are quite disturbing; they say they're atheists, but I don't think they are.

_____ 4. I'm not sure how to make any decision at all. When you are here and having the issues thrust at you and reading about the people who pushed their thought to the absolute limit and seeing how that did not result in an all-encompassing answer . . . , you begin to have respect for how great their thought could be even though it did fall short.

_____ 5. The science lectures are all right. They sort of say the facts, but when you get to a humanities course, they are awful! The lecturer is just reading things into the book that were never meant to be there.

_____ 6. This place is full of bull. If you turn in a speech or a paper that is well written, whether it has one single fact in it or not is beside the point. . . . So you sit down and write a paper in an hour, just because you know that whatever it is isn't going to make any difference to anyone.

_____ 7. I get frustrated in class when the teacher only looks at things from her point of view. There are other ideas to consider. What is important to me is trying to understand and evaluate ideas and to come up with my own. I dislike discussions in which everyone just voices an opinion without backing it up. What good are opinions unless you put them to the test?

_____ 8. When I have an idea about something and it differs from the way another person is thinking about it, I will usually try to look at it from that person's point of view, see how they could say that, why they think they are right, why it makes sense.

_____ 9. In science you don't really want to say that something is true. We're dealing with a model and models are always simpler than the real world, which is more complex than anything we can create. We simplify so we can work with it. When we try to describe things, we leave out the truth because we are oversimplifying.

_____ 10. About the only thing I guess I would say to a prospective student is that if you come to this college, you had better do everything you are supposed to do and then you will be all right. That's just about all.

_____ 11. As soon as someone tells me his point of view, I immediately start arguing in my head the opposite point of view. When someone is saying something, I can't help turning it upside down.

_____ 12. I can't really say that one opinion is better than another. It depends on your beliefs. I am the type of person who would never tell someone that their opinion is wrong. If they have searched, well, even if they haven't searched, if they just believe it, that's cool for them.

Exercise 2: Words and Phrases That Hurt

Directions: Our conversations carry implications that reflect personal understanding, values, or beliefs. The 10 statements here contain implications that can offend others. Considering who the communicants are, why might the statements have been made in the first place? What are the implications in each? How does the context in which each is spoken make it offensive or hurtful?

1. A white person to a black person: "We must have law and order."

2. In a discussion of inequitable school funding, a suburban parent to an inner city parent: "You can make your schools as good as ours."

3. A Korean American to a black acquaintance: "You're different from most blacks."

4. A white employer announcing the intention of integrating the workplace: "Of course, we will make sure we only hire a _qualified_ minority applicant."

5. In a discussion of racial discrimination in America, a black person to a Japanese American: "Asians have done well in America; you shouldn't have anything to complain about."

6. A white person to a Chicano: "I don't understand what you people want."

7. A white person to a black person: "Our old neighborhood used to be good when I was a kid, but it's gone downhill since it was integrated."

8. A Chinese American to a black person: "The death of Martin Luther King was a terrible loss to your race."

9. A black Christian to a Jew: "Oh, you're Jewish? I didn't realize you were Jewish—you sure don't act like one."

10. A white person to a Native American: "I think your people have made great progress."

REFERENCES

Appleton, N. (1983). _Cultural pluralism in education: Theoretical foundations._ New York, NY: Longman.

Examines how the United States has become pluralistic, how American education has responded to pluralism, and what our pluralistic society might look like in the future.

Belenky, M.F., Clinchy, B.M., Goldberger, N.R., & Tarulle, J.M. (1997). _Women's ways of knowing: The development of self, voice, and mind._ New York, NY: Basic Books.

Describes the ways of gaining knowledge that women have developed and the obstacles women must overcome in developing their intellectual abilities.

Berne, E. (2004). *Games people play: The psychology of human relationships.* New York, NY: Ballantine. (Originally published in 1964)

Examines the purposes behind conversational "games" and analyzes a number of them, then provides suggestions to promote more honest interactions.

Brown, B., & Merritt, R. (2002). *No easy answers: The truth behind death at Columbine.* New York, NY: Lantern Books.

Describes the bullying and taunting of Dylan Klebold and Eric Harris by other students that resulted in their murder spree and suicides at Columbine High School.

Burgoon, J.K. (2002). Nonverbal signals. In M. Knapp & G. Miller (Eds.), *Handbook of interpersonal communication* (3rd ed., pp. 344–390). Beverly Hills, CA: Sage.

Reviews research to describe the nature, structure, and social functions of nonverbal communication including the impact of cultural norms, gender, and social status.

Deutsch, M. (2006). Cooperation and competition. In M. Deutsch, P. Coleman & E.C. Marcus (Eds.), *The handbook of conflict resolution* (2nd ed., pp. 21–40). San Francisco, CA: Jossey-Bass.

Describes constructive and destructive forms of competition and the implications of a cooperative orientation for more effectively resolving conflicts.

Dow, B.J., & Wood, J.T. (2006). *The SAGE handbook of gender and communication.* Thousand Oaks, CA: Sage Publications.

Reviews gender research on a range of communication issues such as perception, self-image, sex roles, language, and media images.

Ekman, P. (2003). *Emotions revealed: Recognizing faces and feelings to improve communication and emotional life.* New York, NY: Times Books.

This cross-cultural study of nonverbal communication reveals the effectiveness of facial expressions in communicating meaning. [The picture on the left was anger; on the right, contempt.]

Foster, H.L. (1986). *Ribbin', jivin', and playin' the dozens* (2nd ed.). Cambridge, MA: Ballinger.

Describes verbal and nonverbal communication of urban black youth to prevent misunderstandings and to provide teachers with effective interaction strategies.

Freire, P. (2000). *Pedagogy of the oppressed.* New York, NY: Continuum. (Originally published in 1970)

Analyzes the dynamics of oppression including the role of the oppressor, the responses of the oppressed, and the consequences of oppression for both.

Garrett, A.G. (2003). *Bullying in American schools: Causes, preventions, interventions.* Jefferson, NC: McFarland & Company, Inc.

Defines and discusses characteristics of bullies, identifies myths about bullies while reviewing research that refutes those myths, and describes successful interventions.

Gordon, T. (2000). *Parent effectiveness training: The proven program for raising responsible children.* New York, NY: Crown.

Describes a variety of strategies for parents to use not only to resolve conflicts with their children but also to teach children how to make responsible choices.

Grumet, G.W. (2008). Eye contact: The core of interpersonal relatedness. In J. DeVito & M. Hecht (Eds.), *The nonverbal communication reader* (3rd ed., pp. 126–139). Long Grove, IL: Waveland.

Presents an overview of research related to the significance of eye contact on relationships and the function of eye contact in interpersonal communication.

Harris, T. (2004). *I'm OK—you're OK.* New York, NY: Morrow/Avon.

Uses Berne's theory of transactional analysis (TA) to explain how TA can become an analytical tool to understand interactions with others and resolve conflicts.

Heath, S.B. (2006). *Ways with words.* Cambridge, UK: Cambridge University Press.

Describes how children learn language in three distinct communities and the consequences of the way they have learned language with regard to their ability to be successful in school.

Hecht, M.L., & DeVito, J.A. (Eds.). (2008). Perspectives on defining and understanding nonverbal communication: Classic and contemporary readings. In *The nonverbal communication reader* (3rd ed., pp. 3–17). Long Grove, IL: Waveland.

Reviews research to describe the characteristics of nonverbal communication and to explain the relationship between verbal and nonverbal communication.

Honig, A.S. (2006). Socio-cultural influences on gender-role behaviors in children's play. In D.P. Fromberg & D. Bergen (Eds.), *Play from birth to twelve and beyond: Contexts, perspectives, and meanings* (2nd ed., pp. 328–347). New York, NY: Routledge.

Describes gender differences in play activities, stereotyping in toy preference, and the influence of parents, peers, and television on children's play.

Ismail, N. (2001, September). Communicating across cultures. Victoria, BC: Pertinent Information. Available at http://pertinent.com/pertinfo/business/yaticom.html

Examines factors that affect communication between people from different cultures and offers suggestions for improving such cross-cultural interactions.

Jandt, F.E. (1985). *Win-win negotiating: Turning conflict into agreement.* New York, NY: Wiley.

Provides examples of conflicts that failed to reach a satisfying conclusion and describes alternative strategies that have proven to be more successful in resolving conflicts.

Jandt, F.E. (2003). *Intercultural communication: An introduction* (3rd ed.). Thousand Oaks, CA: Sage.

Describes how cultural norms and values create a context for communication and how understanding different cultures is necessary for successful intercultural communication.

Johnson, D.W., Johnson, R.T., & Tjosvold, D. (2006). Constructive controversy: The value of intellectual opposition. In M. Deutsch, P. Coleman & E.C. Marcus (Eds.), *The handbook of conflict resolution* (2nd ed., pp. 65–85). San Francisco, CA: Jossey-Bass.

Explains how conflict can be constructive and reports on the positive results of research involving people who were taught to use the strategies for "skilled disagreement."

Kimmel, P.R. (2006). Culture and conflict. In M. Deutsch, P. Coleman & E.C. Marcus (Eds.), *The handbook of conflict resolution* (2nd ed., pp. 453–474). San Francisco, CA: Jossey-Bass.

Describes the influence of culture on individual communication and the need to practice cultural relativism to avoid conflict in intercultural communication.

King, P.M., & Kitchener, K.S. (1994). *Developing reflective judgment: Understanding and promoting intellectual growth and critical thinking in adolescents and adults.* San Francisco, CA: Jossey-Bass.

Reviews research on the development of reflective judgment from childhood through adult years and includes cross-cultural and gender comparisons.

Kochman, T. (1981). *Black and white: Styles in conflict.* Chicago, IL: University of Chicago Press.

Explains differences in communication styles commonly used by black and white people in urban America and how those differences can lead to conflict.

Kougl, K. (1997). *Communicating in the classroom.* Prospect Heights, IL: Waveland.

Analyzes the dynamics of communicating in a classroom, including communication problems that often occur, and describes optional strategies for responding to those problems.

McCorkle, S., & Mills, J.L. (1992). Rowboat in a hurricane: Metaphors of interpersonal conflict management. *Communication Reports 5*(2), 57–67.

Examines the relationship between the metaphor selected by an individual to describe conflict and how that individual addressed conflict situations.

Meltzoff, N. (2007, Spring). Use another word. *Rethinking Schools. 21*(3), 46–48.

Reports on the success of a student initiative to reduce name-calling at school and references the U.S. Supreme Court's ruling concerning "fighting words."

Narula, U. (2006). *Handbook of communication models, perspectives and strategies.* New Delhi, India: Atlantic.

Provides an overview of communication research, describes various communication models, and analyzes the functions of contemporary communication.

Newberg, A., & Waldman, M.R. (2006). *Why we believe what we believe: Uncovering our biological needs for meaning, spirituality, and truth.* New York, NY: Free Press.

Proposes a new way of thinking about how convictions develop and influence individuals, based on recent research on how the brain perceives (and transforms) reality.

Perry, W.G., Jr. (1999). *Forms of intellectual and ethical development in the college years: A scheme.* San Francisco CA: Jossey-Bass, Inc.

Describes nine positions in the development of moral reasoning based on interviews with Harvard students and including interview excerpts illustrating developmental positions.

Postman, N., & Weingartner, C. (1987). *Teaching as a subversive activity.* New York, NY: Dell Publishing. (Originally published in 1969)

Advocates that teachers use the inquiry method in their teaching and provide a relevant curriculum so that students become critical thinkers who are interested in their learning.

Prince, D. W. (2004). *Communicating across cultures.* Greensboro, NC: Center for Creative Leadership.

Examines factors that affect communication between people from different cultures and offers suggestions for improving cross-cultural interactions.

Roberts, Jr., W. B. (2006). *Bullying from both sides: Strategic interventions for working with bullies and victims.* Thousand Oaks, CA: Corwin Press.

Describes characteristics of bullies and victims and successful intervention strategies.

Rogers, C. (1995). *A way of being.* New York, NY: Mariner Books. (Originally published in 1980)

Describes the philosophical basis for his professional practice and provides examples from his person-centered approach to therapy; Chapter 7 focuses on the value of empathy.

Schramm, W. (1973). *Men, messages, and media: A look at human communication.* New York, NY: Harper & Row.

Provides a historical overview of communication and uses research to analyze the functions of contemporary communication; communication models are explained in the appendix.

Skuttnab-Kangas, T. (2000). *Linguistic genocide in education—or worldwide diversity and human rights*? Mahwah, NJ: Lawrence Erlbaum Associates.

Uses contemporary theory and research to examine the impact of linguistic imperialism on human rights in general and the assault on linguistic diversity in particular.

Spitzberg, B.H. (2008). Perspectives on nonverbal communication skills. In J. DeVito & M. Hecht (Eds.), *The nonverbal communication reader* (3rd ed., pp. 18–22). Prospect Heights, IL: Waveland.

Describes how nonverbal communication contributes to communicating effectively and provides a rating scale to measure nonverbal communication skills.

Stone, G., Singletary, M., & Richmond, V.P. (1999). *Clarifying communication theories: A hands-on approach.* Ames: Iowa State University Press.

Explains the theoretical foundations for communication, examines aspects of interpersonal communication and mass communication, and describes communication research methods.

Tannen, D. (1994). *Gender and discourse.* New York, NY: Oxford University Press.

Six essays on language and gender including such topics as conversational strategies, issues of power, and the impact of culture and status on linguistic strategies.

Tannen, D. (2007). *You just don't understand: Women and men in conversation.* New York, NY: Harper Collins (Originally published in 1990)

Discusses how gender influences communication styles and explains how conflicts between men and women can result from these communication style differences.

Waley, A. (Ed.). (1938). *The analects of Confucius.* New York, NY: Vintage.

Provides the social and political background for the philosophy of Kongfuzi (Confucius) and an annotated translation with explanations of references to events and individuals.

Wessler, S. L. (with W. Preble). (2003). *The respectful school: How educators and students can conquer hate and harassment.* Alexandria, VA: Association for Supervision and Curriculum Development.

Describes the impact of degrading language and the pattern (and escalation) of abuse, and discusses strategies for reducing harassment and promoting positive student interaction.

PART TWO

Cross-Cultural Concerns

CHAPTER 4

Immigration and Oppression: The Assault on Cultural and Language Diversity

> ❝We are all citizens of one world; we are all of one blood. To hate someone because he was born in another country, because he speaks a different language or because he takes a different view on a subject, is a great folly.❞
>
> John Comenius (1592–1670)

As British colonists settled in America, they struggled with the issue of ethnic diversity because the need for more people to settle this new land conflicted with their **xenophobia**—the fear of or prejudice against people from other nations. There was no such struggle with racial diversity. As Kammen (1972) noted, European colonists came to America with racist notions of primitive Africans and savage Indians that justified enslaving them; seeds of white supremacy were sustained—and nurtured—on American soil. Ethnic diversity, however, was different. As the dominant ethnic group, British immigrants witnessed people from other European nations coming to the colonies, creating the difficult task of coexistence in a diverse community of immigrants. The challenge of devising an appropriate response to diversity has never been fully resolved. Instead, America has been enmeshed in an ongoing paradox of established immigrants fearing each wave of newcomers.

As the dominant ethnic group, how did British colonists react to diversity?

Part of the dilemma of ethnic diversity was the determination of British colonists to retain their identity. The French who settled to the north in Canada had readily adapted to Indian ways, especially with regard to economic practices such as trapping and through intermarriage with Native American women. The Spanish came as conquerors, but after their conquest, they still required Indian labor to sustain their control of conquered territory. Like the French, the Spanish borrowed cultural elements from conquered peoples, and intermarriages produced what would eventually be termed a new race: "La Raza."

Those who settled the English-speaking colonies tended to emigrate in family groups. Although some immigrants came to seek their fortune and return home, most came to establish permanent settlements. The British came as subjects of the English king, prepared to create an English colony as an extension of Britain. Although settlers occasionally used information gained from Indians about such things as edible plants and food preparation, their goal was to recreate as much of the Old World as was possible in the New World.

The problem with recreating the Old World was that it was not possible to make the colonies into a *New England.* In addition to British colonists (English, Scottish, and Irish), significant numbers of

Dutch, German, and French colonists arrived, as well as small groups from other European countries and adventurers from parts of the world other than Europe. Germans in particular were as adamant as the English about maintaining their cultural heritage. They lived together in communities, spoke to each other in German, posted signs in German, imported books from Germany, and founded schools where their children were taught in German.

By the beginning of the eighteenth century, British colonial leaders became so alarmed by German behavior that some called for restricting or excluding Germans from further immigration. Benjamin Franklin believed it was necessary to Anglicize the Germans because of the size of their population. As their numbers continued to grow, he feared that the Germans would "shortly be so numerous as to Germanize us instead of us Anglifying them" (Feagin, 1997, p. 18). Although Franklin obviously shared the desire of British colonists to Anglicize the colonies, he also recognized positive attributes of German immigrants and the contributions they were making to colonial development: "All that seems necessary is to distribute them more equally, mix them with the English, and establish English schools where they are now too thick settled" (Brands, 2000, p. 219).

Franklin was concerned with Anglicizing Germans and all immigrants who were not from Britain and, therefore, unfamiliar with British customs and language. In 1749, he sponsored the establishment of a school that included no foreign language instruction. His desire to Anglicize foreign colonists was also reflected in the views of President George Washington: "The more homogeneous our citizens can be made . . . the greater will be our prospect of permanent union" (Kammen, 1972, p. 74). Perhaps the desire for a more homogeneous citizenry was the reason the New American Congress passed a law in 1790 that limited citizenship in the United States to immigrants who were

> Law is a reflection and source of prejudice. It both enforces and suggests forms of bias.
>
> **Diane Schulder (1937–)**

"white" persons. This early expression of xenophobia would lead to the growth of nativism in the United States.

Causes of Xenophobia and Nativism in the United States

Assimilation refers to a process in which immigrants adopt cultural traits from their host country and are absorbed into society (note Figure 4.2 on page 77). British colonists preferred a homogeneous population of immigrants who could be assimilated into a dominant Anglo culture, but immigrants from other countries often demonstrated a persistent wish to maintain their own ethnic heritages. Their desires contributed to the development of xenophobia in response to the constant infusion of ethnicities among immigrants to America. When established immigrants, who considered themselves "natives," felt threatened by the many non-British immigrants in their midst, organizations based on nativist concerns would appear. Feagin and Feagin (1996) define **nativism** as "an anti-immigrant ideology that advocates the protection of native inhabitants of a country from [new or potential] immigrants who are seen as threatening or dangerous" (p. 503). Nativists have been the primary group engaging in the oppression of immigrants consistent with the definition of *oppression* (Andrzejewski, 1996) quoted in the section introduction.

Franklin's desire to Anglicize non-British immigrants and Washington's desire for a homogeneous population can be described as a benign form of nativism based on nationalistic concerns. Although nationalism represents one of the primary themes of nativist activities in the United States, two additional themes have characterized many nativist attitudes and actions: anti-Catholicism and anti-radicalism.

Nativism as anti-Catholicism

Although the religious beliefs of Benjamin Franklin, Thomas Jefferson, and other founders of the American republic were quite different from those of most Christians today, at its birth the United States was a nation strongly influenced by Protestant Christianity. The presence of Catholics had been tolerated throughout the colonial period, but by 1820, the 200,000 Catholics in the United States stimulated anti-Catholic sentiment, especially in urban areas. (See Figure 4.1.) By 1850, there were almost two million Catholics in the United States; the Irish alone constituted 42% of that foreign-born population (Fuchs, 1990).

During George Washington's presidency, immigrants had to be U.S. residents for a minimum of five years to be eligible for citizenship. The Nationalization Act signed by President John Adams changed the requirement to fourteen years of residency, but it was returned to five years after Thomas Jefferson became president. A nativist group calling itself "Native Americans" began forming in some of the larger cities; the party lobbied vigorously against immigrants becoming eligible for citizenship after five years. The Native American party insisted on a residency of twenty-one years before an immigrant was eligible for citizenship. Their main concern was voting, arguing that immigrants coming from nations governed by monarchs were not prepared to be self-governing. Since an immigrant came with:

> all his foreign habits, prejudices and predilections . . . can it be believed that he can disburden himself so completely of these, and have so learned to fulfill the duties of a citizen of the United States, in the very short term of five years? (Myers, 1960, p. 111)

At first, the Native American party encouraged people to welcome immigrants and only opposed their eligibility for citizenship after five years; however, by 1843, the movement had become hostile to continued immigration of both Irish and Catholics. In Philadelphia, the Native American party held a meeting in an Irish district of the city, initiating a confrontation between Protestants and Catholics; the violence that followed culminated in an angry mob setting fire to many buildings, reported in newspapers around the country. Federal troops were called in to restore order, which was no easy task, and peace prevailed for a little more than a

FIGURE 4.1

A major factor in the anti-Catholic sentiment was the fear that Catholics would try to convert Protestants, especially children. The cartoonist, Thomas Nast, made Catholic bishops into alligators coming to U.S. shores, reflecting such fears.

Source: 1876 cartoon from Harper's Weekly Magazine, by Thomas Nast.

month before mobs attacked a Catholic church and troops fired at the crowd to force them to disperse. Two more days of violence resulted in two soldiers being killed and twenty-six soldiers wounded.

Being confronted with such extreme violence was unusual, but American Catholics employed a number of strategies in response to anti-Catholic activities. To avoid having their children subjected to anti-Catholic sentiments in public schools, Catholics created their own privately funded K–12 schools nationwide, eventually establishing Catholic colleges and universities as well. To counter anti-Catholic rhetoric in mainstream and Protestant newspapers, Catholics published their own newspapers. Hennesey (1985) described how Bishop John Hughes submitted several anti-Catholic articles to a Protestant newspaper under the name of "Cranmer," then publicly announced that he was the author and that the articles included lies and distortions that the editors had not bothered to question or confirm. In addition, several Catholic organizations were founded in the 1800s, including the Knights of Columbus, which engaged in political activism but also provided centers for recreational activities and chapels for meditation and prayer. By the 1920s, church leaders adopted a different strategy, encouraging Catholics to become involved with "general reform groups in society and not limit their exertions to narrowly conceived partisan issues" (Hennesey, 1985, p. 247).

Nativism as anti-radicalism

Both anti-Catholicism and prejudice against the Irish fueled the nativism movement that flourished briefly in the 1850s, but the other negative sentiment contributing to the success of nativism was anti-radicalism. Most immigrants admitted to the United States in the first decades of the nineteenth century were overwhelmingly impoverished European laborers with minimal skills and little education. Some were sponsored by American capitalists to be contract laborers paid less than the wage native workers would accept. As new immigrant workers adapted to life in the United States, they came to realize how they were being exploited; many joined or helped create unions to demand better wages and benefits by engaging in strikes, marches, and protests. Nativists saw union actions

as un-American, especially when the "foreigners" expressed socialist, anarchist, or other radical ideas. The antagonism toward what was regarded as radical activities by recent immigrants was clearly and frequently expressed on the editorial pages of urban newspapers (Higham, 1955):

> "Our National existence and . . . our National and social institutions are at stake."
> "These people are not Americans, but the very scum and offal of Europe."
> "There is no such thing as an American anarchist."
> "Europe's human and inhuman rubbish." (p. 55)

The first quotation illustrates the nationalism often expressed in nativist sentiments; the other quotations reveal hostility and a dehumanized view of the perceived "radicals." The un-American implication in each statement is central to the nativist perspective. Nativist concerns at that time also had to do with the decreasing amount of land available for immigrants in the Midwest and West; as a result, immigrants increasingly settled in urban areas. Because many immigrants were moving from southern and eastern Europe, land reformer Henry George commented, "What, in a few years more, are we to do for a dumping ground? Will it make our difficulty the less that our human garbage can vote?" (Higham, 1955, p. 42). The issue of immigrants becoming eligible for citizenship and voting continued to fuel individual xenophobia, and nativist political actions document a fear of the potential political power of incoming immigrants.

Nativism, Politics, and Social Change

The Native American party never gained political dominance, yet by the 1850s it had prepared the way for the rise of the "Know-Nothings," a somewhat secret movement whose members were told to respond to any question about the organization by saying that they knew nothing about it. Staunchly anti-immigrant and anti-Catholic, Know-Nothings were concerned with what they perceived as the growing political influence of Catholics; these fears were confirmed by President Franklin Pierce's appointment of a Catholic, James Campbell, to be the nation's attorney general.

How successful were the nativists in their political activities?

The Know-Nothings fielded candidates for the American Party, and in 1854 elected 9 governors, 8 (of 62) senators, and 104 (of 234) members of the House of Representatives (Myers, 1960). In the 1856 elections, Know-Nothing members used force and threats to keep immigrants from voting and encouraged election-day riots in Louisville, Kentucky, and St. Louis, Missouri. When the Whig Party refused to nominate Millard Fillmore for a second term as president, the American Party nominated him as their candidate. Despite the success of other American Party candidates, Fillmore received only eight electoral votes.

Reaction to the political success of the Know-Nothings was swift. In Congress a resolution was submitted, then voted down, condemning secret organizations and citing the Know-Nothings as a specific example. Political and religious leaders across the nation denounced the activities of the Know-Nothings, including the young political aspirant Abraham Lincoln, who wrote in a letter to a friend,

> As a nation we began by declaring that "all men are created equal." We now practically read it, "all men are created equal except Negroes." When the Know-Nothings obtain control, it will read: "All men are created equal except Negroes, foreigners, and Catholics." (Myers, 1960, p. 146)

Why did nativists fail to form a major political party?

The political success of nativism in the 1850s was brief because the issue of slavery began to take precedence over anti-Catholic prejudice and fears, and it divided the Know-Nothings. By the end of the Civil War, the Know-Nothings and the American Party were no longer a political force, although the nativist fears that fueled their activity persisted as a major influence in the United States. As the American people debated the issue of slavery, American capitalists continued to sponsor importation of labor from overseas to keep wages low and profits high.

Throughout U.S. history, a significant percentage of Americans consisted of recent immigrants or children of immigrants who appreciated the opportunities in America and vigorously opposed attempts by nativists to restrict immigration. Meanwhile, there was constant pressure from society to promote the **Americanization** of immigrants, and public schools carried out societal expectations by encouraging immigrants to abandon their heritage and conform to American ways (Pai & Adler, 2006). Nativist attitudes in the United States continued to wax and wane, with xenophobia historically balanced by those who believed in America as a place for oppressed people to achieve freedom and fortune.

The demand for Americanization of immigrants intensified in the late 1800s as the majority of immigrants were not northern Europeans—Greeks, Italians, Slavs, and Jews—people who did not con-

> There is no room in this country for hyphenated Americans.
>
> **Theodore Roosevelt (1858–1919)**

form to the Anglo ideal. Because of an economic downturn in the 1890s, nativism experienced a renewed popularity with American people; then in the ebb and flow of xenophobia, nativist fears succumbed to a confidence inspired by the U.S. triumph in the Spanish-American War and by heroes such as Teddy Roosevelt. Although nativists never again succeeded in sponsoring an independent political party, events in the early twentieth century would establish the foundation for their greatest political triumphs.

What influenced twentieth-century nativist attitudes in America?

It seemed certain to most Americans that if the United States was going to become a dominant political and economic power in the world, immigrants were needed in the labor market of its dynamic economy. But when World War I began, attitudes changed. Nativism surged again, driven by feelings of nationalism and anti-radicalism. German Americans were singled out for especially opprobrious treatment, and their loyalty to the United States was questioned. Rumors abounded that German Americans were spying for Germany.

Because German Americans insisted on maintaining their dual identity as Americans of German descent, people of influence such as Teddy Roosevelt admonished them by denouncing all immigrants who claimed a dual identity. German Americans were surprised by such criticisms. From colonial times they had maintained their culture, language, and traditions through separate schools, organizations, and newspapers. Because of their industriousness, efforts to preserve their German heritage had been tolerated by American society until World War I, when nativist individuals and organizations attacked German Americans for keeping themselves separate and not assimilating to an Anglo ideal.

During World War I, surging patriotism intensified the demand that immigrants be Americanized quickly. Although this nationalism was a less abrasive form of nativism, it became more virulent when reinforced by anti-radical attitudes. Radical organizations were attacked as un-American, especially radical unions like the International Workers of the World, the "Wobblies." Nativists accused certain immigrants of espousing ideas that were disloyal to the country and demanded their deportation.

German Americans were not the only targets of anti-American accusations. **Anti-Semitism**—having prejudices, stereotypes, or engaging in discrimination against Jews—increased with the success of the Russian Revolution in 1917. Jews were associated not only with communism, but also with international financiers who profited from the war. After World War I, nativists continued to complain that the Anglo ideal for America would disappear if diverse European ethnic groups continued to emigrate; however most Americans seemed to believe that those who came eventually would assimilate into the dominant culture.

By the 1920s, a revised perspective was being expressed. In settlement houses such as Hull House in Chicago, people providing social services began to appreciate the diversity of the immigrants. Social activist Jane Addams, cofounder of Hull House, and University of Chicago philosopher John Dewey described the advantages of diverse cultures and the value of people maintaining their heritages while

FIGURE 4.2
Assimilation Issues?

still learning, as Benjamin Franklin had recommended, the language and customs of American culture. Although resentment toward Germans slowly dissipated after the war, anti-Semitism persisted as part of a new development in xenophobic attitudes in the United States.

What new development affected xenophobic attitudes in the United States?

In 1899, William Z. Ripley, an economist from the Massachusetts Institute of Technology, published a so-called scientific study identifying and describing three European races: Teutonic, Alpine, and Mediterranean (Higham, 1955). Based on emerging theories about race, Nativists argued that for U.S. citizenry to achieve unity, immigrants of the blue-eyed, blond-haired Teutonic type (also called "Nordic" or "Anglo Saxon") should be given preference. Senator Henry Cabot Lodge of Massachusetts called for an end to all further immigration to the United States, and Teddy Roosevelt chastised Anglo Saxon women in America for contributing to the possibility of "race suicide" by not producing as many children as immigrant women (Brodkin, 2002). In the aftermath of World War I, pessimism about diverse groups being able to assimilate into an Anglo Saxon American culture fueled

racist sentiments expressed in widely read books such as Lothrop Stoddard's *The Rising Tide of Color.* (See Figure 4.3.)

Madison Grant (1916/1970) provided the most influential expression of this pessimism in *The Passing of the Great Race, or the Racial Bias of European History.* Grant rejected the idea that immigrants from other than Nordic heritage could achieve the Anglo Saxon ideal; thus the "Great Race" of Anglo Saxons was doomed to disappear in America. Claiming that his ideas were grounded in the emerging science of genetics, Grant concluded that intermarriage between races produced degraded offspring who would revert to lower qualities contained in their parents' genes. Referring to Ripley's three European races, Grant stated, "The cross between any of the European races and a Jew is a Jew" (p. 16). Confirming Grant's assertion, the eugenics movement provided "scientific" evidence of the human degradation caused by miscegenation, and 30 states passed laws banning interracial marriage (Stubblefield, 2007). Many well-known and respected Americans such as automaker Henry Ford expressed beliefs consistent with Madison Grant's theories and the findings of eugenics, and racism—including anti-Semitism—was incorporated into traditional xenophobic attitudes.

FIGURE 4.3

This advertisement from a 1923 *Time* magazine warns its readers that the days of white supremacy may be numbered and urges white people who want to do something about it to read Stoddard's book, *The Rising Tide of Color.*

Three books by LOTHROP STODDARD

The Revolt Against Civilization

"The reason why this book has attracted such an extraordinary amount of attention is not far to seek. It is, so far as we know, the first successful attempt to present a scientific explanation of the world-wide epidemic of unrest that broke out during the Great War and still rages in both hemispheres."—*Saturday Evening Post.* $2.50

The New World of Islam

This book is *true*—current events are bearing it out in startling fashion. "He has presented, in compact and readable form, what did not exist before in any language: a short, concise account of the modern Mohammedan world and its reaction to the invasion of the West."—*Atlantic Monthly.* With maps. $3.00

The Rising Tide of Color

White world supremacy is in danger. The world-wide ascendancy of the white race, apparently so unshakable, is in reality threatened by the colored races. This is a startling book, one for the reader who is able to stand up against the impact of new ideas. It is a clear, sharp warning to the whites, and an appeal for white solidarity. With maps. $3.00

© *Bachrach*
LOTHROP STODDARD

From early manhood he has prepared himself, by wide travel and extensive study, to qualify as a true expert on world affairs. His is the mind of a trained observer who has received the soundest scientific training.

How did racism affect nativist attitudes and actions?

Nativists used the new racist concern for preserving the nation's Anglo Saxon heritage to sound the alarm about the numbers of immigrants from southern and eastern Europe—80% of all U.S. immigrants from 1900 to 1910. Stanford University's Ellwood P. Cubberley echoed their concerns in his history of education textbook (1919):

> These Southern and Eastern Europeans were of a very different type from the North and West Europeans who preceded them. Largely illiterate, docile, lacking in initiative, and almost wholly without the Anglo-Saxon conceptions of righteousness, liberty, law, order, public decency, and government, their coming has served to dilute tremendously our national stock . . . our national life, for the past quarter of a century, has been afflicted with a serious case of racial indigestion. (p. 338)

Nativists triumphed in 1924 with the passage of an immigration law establishing quotas for immi-

> [America can have] a unity created by drawing out and composing into a harmonious whole the best, the most characteristic, which each contributing race and people has to offer.
>
> **JOHN DEWEY (1859–1952)**

grants based on country of origin. The quotas ensured that immigrants from northern Europe (the so-called Nordic type) would constitute the majority of U.S. immigrants, guidelines that remained largely unchanged for the next four decades. Although people of color were the primary targets of nativists, other groups were also affected by racist attitudes.

What groups were affected by the addition of racism to xenophobia?

This new racist form of nativism was directed not only against people of color, but also against white people perceived as not being white enough, which often meant not sharing the common prejudices of the white majority. This was especially observed in

> We gave [immigrants] disparaging names: Micks, Sheenies, Krauts, Dagos, Wops . . . until [each group] became sound, solvent . . . whereupon each group joined the older boys and charged down on the newest ones. . . . Having suffered, one would have thought they might have pity on the newcomer, but they did not.
>
> **JOHN STEINBECK (1900–1969)**

southern states. In 1898, debates at Louisiana's state constitutional convention focused on who would be denied the right to vote. Although blacks were the main targets, Italians were considered "as black as the blackest negro in existence" (Barrett & Roediger, 2002, p. 32). Because of such perceptions, some Italians were victims of southern violence in the nineteenth century. In Tallulah, Louisiana, five Sicilian immigrants owned businesses that served primarily black customers. Local whites resented the immigrant storekeepers because they treated black people as equals. Before long, the locals fabricated a quarrel over a goat and lynched the five Sicilians (Higham, 1955).

The idea of perceiving Italians, Irish, or others as separate races based on their national origins seems strange today; yet most Americans, including members of identified "races," accepted this designation. In the 1930s, an Irish campaign manager representing an Irish politician made the following speech at an Italian neighborhood meeting to ask the Italian men to vote for his candidate in the upcoming election:

> Maybe I'm the only Irishman here, but this is not a racial contest. You don't select your man because of his race. There are too many who cry him down because of that. But these people that sit behind closed doors and discriminate against a man because of his race have no place in American life. . .

FIGURE 4.4

Source: David Horsey
© 2007. Tribune Media
Services. Reprinted by
permission.

This district don't house men and women that vote only because of their racial strain. For the immigrants of your race and my race, I have no apology. In the time of need, we answered the call of our country. One of the largest quotas of men was sent out from this district. At that time there was no discrimination because of a man's race, there was no turning men back for that reason. We sent out boys by the thousands in order that we might enjoy the blessings of free government. Here we never turn down a man because of his race or creed. (Whyte, 1955, p. 227)

The idea of national origin defining separate races declined as skin color became the primary determinant of racial identity, and racism would prolong the oppression of people of color beyond the time normally experienced by white ethnic groups.

The experiences of the four major racial groups are the focus of Chapter 5.

As the civil rights movement gained momentum, allegations of racism were made in many areas. President John Kennedy admitted to inequities in immigration policies based on the 1924 law. Attorney General Robert Kennedy characteristically stated the issue more bluntly, "As we are working to remove the vestiges of racism from our public life, we cannot maintain racism as the cornerstone of our immigration laws" (Eck, 2001, p. 7). In 1965, Congress amended immigration laws to eliminate the racially biased National Origins Quotas. From 1968 to 1993, 80% of the people immigrating to the United States came from Central or South America, the Caribbean, and Asia (Roberts, 1997). The influx of Latino immigrants spawned a renewed xenophobia, especially in California (see Figure 4.4).

The Paradox of Xenophobia and Nativism in a Nation of Immigrants

Daniels (2002) noted the absurdity among Americans to regard the people who first came to the United States as "colonists" or "settlers" and then to identify the people who came later as "immigrants." Social observers such as author John Steinbeck (1966) have described how immigrants were initially reviled only to be accepted later: "the surges of the new restless, needy, and strong . . . were resisted, resented, and accepted only when a new and different wave came in" (p. 14). Part of being accepted involved the former immigrants expressing xenophobic sentiments against current immigrants. In fairness, Americans have not consistently expressed such sentiments; instead, Daniels (2002) has observed the following pattern:

> When most Americans are generally united and feel confident about their future, they seem to be more willing to share that future with foreigners; conversely, when they are divided and lack confidence in the future, nativism is more likely to triumph. (pp. 265–266)

As previously mentioned, nativists used the work of scholars and scientists within the growing ranks of the eugenics movement in support of their efforts to limit immigration. British scientist Francis Galton coined the term **eugenics** as "the study of agencies under social control that may improve or repair the racial qualities of future generations, either physically or mentally" (Lynn, 2001, p. 4). American scholars endorsing the eugenics movement were concerned about the perceived degeneration of mental abilities among Americans. Many believed there was a racial component to the problem represented by immigrants whom they regarded as the primary cause of this decline of intelligence in America. As Stubblefield (2007) noted, many scholars believed that "White people were 'civilization builders,' while members of other races supposedly lacked the ability to produce civilization" (p. 163). Scholarly support for the eugenics movement would decline precipitously after the Nazis tainted it with their emphasis on race purification and their implementation of genocidal practices.

Although the eugenics movement in the United States never attracted a majority of academics, some in the eugenics camp were influential scholars: Robert Yerkes of Harvard (president of the American Psychological Association), Lewis Terman of Stanford, and Edward Thorndike from Teachers College, Columbia University (Selden, 2006). Because of their academic interests, Yerkes, Terman, and Thorndike were responsible for developing early intelligence tests (see Table 4.1). When Henry Goddard implemented intelligence tests with the immigrants at Ellis Island, he reported that 80% were "feeble minded" (Brodkin, 2002).

Because some respected scholars supported it, the eugenics movement flourished from 1910 to 1940, shaping the content of biology textbooks, reinforcing popular views concerning white supremacy, and contributing to the growth of anti-immigrant attitudes. One legacy of the eugenics movement is the standardized testing used to measure academic achievement that students still take today—but testing is not the only legacy of the eugenics movement.

Established in 1937 to promote eugenics policies, the Pioneer Fund advocated the forcible removal of "American Negroes" to Africa. The first Pioneer Fund President, Harry Laughlin, wrote the Model Eugenical Sterilization Law, adopted by thirty states in the United States and Nazi Germany. Laughlin proposed that Adolf Hitler be given honorary membership in the American Eugenics Society. The Pioneer Fund continues to support scholars working on race-based IQ theories, including work employed in support of the controversial comments about race made in *The Bell Curve* (Herrnstein & Murray, 1994). The Pioneer Fund also supported a recent book by Lynn (2001) arguing in favor of eugenic principles, and has continued to be a major funding source for the English Only movement (Tatalovich, 1997).

How is the English Only movement an example of xenophobic behavior?

Nativists have always been critical of immigrants who maintain their native language. They lobbied for literacy tests primarily as a strategy to reduce immigration, but for almost two decades Congress

TABLE 4.1 Sample Questions from the World War I Army Mental Tests

Alpha and Beta Tests developed by psychologists Robert Yerkes, Lewis Terman, and Henry Goddard assisted by Carl Campbell Brigham, founder of Educational Testing Service (ETS)

These sample questions reveal how culturally biased and inappropriate the early tests of "intelligence" could be; yet such tests were used with immigrants to determine which ones were of acceptable intelligence and which were "feeble minded."

From Alpha Test 8:

2. Five hundred is played with: rackets   pins   cards   dice

3. The Percheron is a kind of: goat   horse   cow   sheep

7. Christy Mathewson is famous as a: writer   artist   baseball player   comedian

10. "There's a reason" is an "ad" for a: drink   revolver   flour   cleanser

19. Crisco is a: patent medicine   disinfectant   tooth-paste   food

29. The Brooklyn Nationals are called the: Giants   Orioles   Superbas   Indians

32. The number of a Kaffir's legs is: two   four   six   eight

35. The forward pass is used in: tennis   hockey   football   golf

38. The Pierce Arrow car is made in: Buffalo   Detroit   Toledo   Flint

Source: Owen, David. *None of the above: The truth behind the SATs,* 1999, p. 176.

rejected the idea. When Congress finally passed such legislation, both Democratic and Republican presidents vetoed these laws until 1917, when Congress passed this requirement over President Wilson's veto (Delgado, 1997). Nativist opposition to immigrants maintaining their native language was evident in their criticisms of German immigrants, and culminated during World War I with state and local laws that forbade public displays of signs with German words and banned the teaching of German in public schools. In some communities German textbooks were burned as an act of patriotism (Crawford, 2000). The percentage of students taking German in U.S. high schools went from 25% in 1915 to 0.6% by 1922 (Baron, 2000). Today, **English Only** advocates demand that English be declared the "official language" of the United States, and they are working toward that goal on a state-by-state basis. English Only supporters claim that their desire to establish English as the official language of the United States is simply a response to the large number of immigrants who refuse to learn how to speak English.

The problem with this claim is the lack of supporting evidence. English Only proponents point to the existence of dual language street signs, billboards and government brochures and to bilingual instruction in schools. They believe that the use of non-English languages, especially in bilingual instruction, legitimizes these languages and elevates their status as well as the status of those who speak these alternate languages. Yet studies do not indicate a threat to the widespread use of English, reporting that well over 90% of U.S. residents speak English fluently (Crawford, 2000; Wiley, 2005). Critics of English Only activities argue that it is no coincidence that the current movement was initiated just 15 years after the 1965 immigration reform that resulted in the majority of U.S. immigrants becoming people of color, and there is some evidence of a xenophobic motivation behind English Only organizations. For example, Crawford (2000) reports on an investigation of US English, a major English Only organization, that found evidence of their real agenda: "determination to resist racial and cultural diversity in the United States" (p. 23). Baron (2000) argues that the history of such organizations "often masks racism and certainly fails to appreciate cultural difference" (p. 447). Latino immigrants appear to be the main targets; in a survey asking financial supporters of US English why they contributed to the organization, 42% of respondents agreed with the statement: "I wanted America to stand strong and not cave in to Hispanics who shouldn't be here" (Crawford, 2000, p. 24). Such attitudes support criticism that English Only activities disguise xenophobic attitudes by insisting that their goal is to promote assimilation by encouraging immigrants to learn English. Reviewing historic and current efforts to pass English Only legislation, Baron (2000) concludes: "no matter how idealistic or patriotic its claims . . . (it has) a long history of nativism, racism, and religious bigotry" (p. 451).

Immigrants have always tended to learn English out of necessity for economic and social well-being. Today, fewer than 14% of Americans speak a language other than English: Less than 6% of Americans speak no English (Wiley, 2005). Despite these facts, the English Only movement has been successful in promoting state legislation to establish English as the official language. Almost half the states have existing laws declaring English as the official language. Some laws are largely symbolic, no penalties are enforced, and there is no prohibition against teaching foreign languages or implementing and supporting bilingual programs. However, some state laws prohibit their governments from printing materials in other languages.

Because Spanish is the first language of a significant percentage of immigrants, English Only laws prevent recent immigrants who are trying to learn English from having access to useful information. Such laws may also prevent legally eligible people from voting (Tatalovich, 1997). Whether symbolic or harmful, English Only laws reflect the xenophobic reaction of a great many people in the United States against many of our recent immigrants, primarily people of color whose first language is not English and who may not yet be literate in English. English Only laws justify the antagonism some individuals feel toward people speaking a different language; at times this antagonism even results in violence.

How have xenophobic attitudes promoted violent behavior?

Today, immigrants or people who appear to be immigrants have been victims of violence. Recent Cambodian, Vietnamese, and Hmong immigrants can attest to this. White shrimp fishermen in Texas threatened Vietnamese fishermen when shrimp became scarce. In Wisconsin, a young white man attacked a Japanese exchange student whom he mistakenly believed was a Hmong immigrant. Xenophobia encourages individuals to see recent immigrants as "foreign"; instead of applauding their hard work and success, xenophobia causes people

> We must get rid of fear; we cannot act at all till then. A man's acts are slavish, not true but specious; his very thoughts are false, he thinks as a slave and coward, till he have got fear under his feet.
>
> THOMAS CARLYLE (1795–1881)

to criticize immigrants for taking "our" jobs. This kind of prejudice against foreigners and the stereotypes that accompany it can foster animosity and even violent behavior.

Such violence has occurred many times, but an especially outrageous example occurred in 1997 in Rohnert Park, California. What made this incident especially deplorable was that police officers were responsible for the violence that resulted in the death of an Asian immigrant. An engineer of Chinese descent had gone to a bar with co-workers to celebrate his new job. At the bar, some patrons taunted him with racist slurs and insults. When he arrived home, he was still angry and still under the influence of alcohol as he raged about the bar incidents. Neighbors heard his shouts and called the police. When police officers arrived, the father of three young children walked out of his garage holding a long stick approximately one-eighth of an inch thick. When he waved the stick at the police, they shot him. Although the man's wife was a nurse, the police officers wouldn't let her help her husband; instead, they handcuffed the wounded man as he lay in a pool of blood in his driveway and bled to death. According to Martinez (2000), the police officers justified the shooting by saying that because he held a stick, they anticipated that: "the man would use 'martial arts' against them" (p. 95). Even the "model minority" stereotype was not enough to overcome prejudice and negative stereotypes.

What American nativist attitudes are evident today?

By the early 1990s, 73% of Americans surveyed believed the United States needed to strictly limit immigration, and surveys since then find that this sentiment continues to be widely supported (Ramos, 2002). The brunt of anti-immigrant backlash is largely directed at Latinos, especially Mexicans in areas such as Southern California where the Mexican population is expected to increase by two thirds from 2000 to 2020. Scherer (2005) quotes one Southern Californian's reaction: "Migration from Mexico is the catalyst that's starting the demise of America" (p. 57). This is not an isolated opinion. According to a 2005 NBC News/Wall Street Journal poll, almost half of Americans polled agreed with the statement: "Immigration detracts from our character and weakens the United States" (Scherer, 2005, p. 53).

Since the 1990s, anti-immigrant activity in America against Spanish-speaking immigrants has steadily increased, especially against illegal immigrants. Because immigrants from Spanish-speaking ethnic groups, referred to as Hispanics or Latinos, have constituted more than 50% of all U.S. immigrants, it is not surprising that they are the primary targets of anti-immigrant activity (Lee, 2004). Today nearly 40 million Latinos live in the United States, with perhaps one out of six arriving illegally as undocumented workers. Latinos are currently 12% of America's workforce, a figure expected to double in just two generations, in part because today one of every five babies born in the United States is Latino (Grow, 2004).

Still, many Americans accept immigrants coming to the United States. The NBC News/Wall Street Journal poll reported that 41% of those surveyed felt that immigrants made America a better place. Some Americans argue that racism is behind much of the anti-immigrant sentiment today, just as in the past. Buchanan and Kim (2005) profiled twenty-one leaders of anti-immigrant groups and described evidence of overt racist behavior for many of them: One was a member of the Council of Conservative Citizens, a white pride group that opposes "race-mixing"; one had published numerous articles reflecting a white supremacist perspective; the Web site of another claimed that the Mexican government was plotting to take over the southwestern United States; and a group founded by one leader was identified as a hate group by the Southern Poverty Law Center, an organization that tracks activities of hate groups in the United States.

Some of the harshest comments are directed at "illegal aliens." Scherer (2005) quoted the leader of an Arizona anti-immigrant group who said America "was being flooded with illegals, people that are substandard humans" (p. 57). Jim Gilchrist, one of the founders of the Minuteman Civil Defense Corps, a vigilante group sponsoring "border patrols" of armed citizens to prevent illegal entry into the United States, helped found his group because "Illegal immigrants will destroy this country" (p. 32). Gilchrist has not expressed concern about the increasing involvement by white supremacist groups to recruit people for the Minuteman organization. In the wake of this hostility toward illegal immigrants, which is constantly reinforced by some talk show hosts on radio and cable television, it should not be surprising to learn that the FBI reported a 40% increase in hate crimes against Latinos from 2003–2007 (O'Grady, 2009).

In response to anti-immigrant hostility, Shorris (2001) argues that illegal immigrants make an important contribution to the U.S. economy by taking "the worst of jobs, the ugly work, the dangerous work, the backbreaking debilitating work, the jobs that even the jobless reject" (p. 272). Some of these jobs are extracting innards from slaughtered chickens on a conveyor belt; cultivating and harvesting mushrooms in damp caves; doing fieldwork as contract laborers (digging onions, picking beans, or harvesting other fruits and vegetables); skinning, gutting, and butchering animals at meatpacking plants; and working in manufacturing sweatshops for Third World wages. Despite complaints about illegal immigrants, it is not clear that Americans would be willing to pay the price, literally, if they were absent. (See Figure 4.4.) Scherer (2005) quotes one Arizona resident: "I don't want to pay five bucks for a can of string beans" (p. 56).

At the University of California, Los Angeles, the North American Integration and Development Center analyzed the work performed by 3 to 4 million undocumented workers in the United States. Their report stated that undocumented workers generated $154 billion toward America's gross domestic product, including $77 billion toward the state domestic product of California alone. Anti-immigrant leaders insist that illegal immigrants are receiving services such as welfare and health care that deplete limited resources of state and local governments. According to a University of California, Davis study, however, the vast majority of undocumented workers do not enroll in government assistance programs because (1) many are not adequately fluent in English, (2) many are not aware of such programs, and (3) many are reluctant to ask for help for fear of being detained by authorities and deported (Ramos, 2002).

Another criticism directed at Spanish-speaking immigrants is that they aren't learning English fast enough and are changing American culture from Anglo to Spanish. Scherer (2005) quotes a Southern Californian arguing that where he lives has changed "literally overnight into a foreign country. The Fourth of July was not being celebrated but Cinco de Mayo was. All the billboards [were] in a foreign language" (p. 55). Although the Census Bureau reports that 78% of U.S. Latinos tend to speak in Spanish even if they can speak English, a study by HispanTelligence found that the number of Latinos fluent in both English and Spanish had increased to 63% (Grow, 2004). Ramos (2002) cites a University of Southern California research project reporting that 7 of 10 Latino children write and speak English fluently.

It is true that Latino children are more likely to maintain their native language than are other immigrant children, but that is consistent with past practices of immigrating groups. Germans, Italians, Norwegians, Chinese, Jews, and Japanese immigrants established schools, which children usually attend after public school, to maintain their native language and culture. It is also true that Latinos have changed U.S. society. It is easy to identify Latino influences on American music, entertainment, literature, business, scholarly activity, and even on the English language (see nearby box). Mexican cuisine can be found almost everywhere from fine restaurants to fast food; salsa recently surpassed ketchup as the most popular American condiment. Addressing Latino influences, Shorris (2001) insists that they are not "signs of conquest. . . . Civilization need not be a zero sum game. The victories of Latino culture are victories of pluralism, additions" (p. 47). They are also victories for the American economy, even though anti-immigrant critics don't seem to understand the significance of their contribution.

> **Spanglish?**
>
> Many commonly used words in American English are direct or slightly modified borrowings from the Spanish language. There are many place names, including cities such as San Diego, Los Angeles, San Francisco, and Santa Fe, and states such as Arizona, California, Colorado, Florida, Montana, and Nevada. This list includes just a few of the many Spanish contributions to American English:
>
> adios, adobe, amigo, bronco, burro, canyon, chili, cigar, coca, cola, coyote, guerrilla, hacienda, hombre, hurricane, lasso, loco, macho, mesquite, mosquito, padre, peon, pinto, plaza, poncho, ranch, rodeo, savvy, sombrero, vista

How do immigrants contribute to the American economy?

The anti-immigrant argument, directed primarily against Mexican Americans, is that they don't contribute to our economy but to the Mexican economy, because they tend to send much of their money home to families and relatives in Mexico. Ramos (2002) cites a study by the National Academy of Science finding that legal and illegal immigrants spend more than $10 billion each year within the U.S. economy. As they were becoming the largest minority group in the United States with almost 40 million people, Latinos' disposable income increased from 2001 to 2003 by about 30% to a total of $652 billion (Grow, 2004). As this population continues to increase, so will their purchasing power, estimated to exceed $1 trillion by 2010. Latinos are currently about 13% of the U.S. population, and demographers predict that they will constitute 18% by 2030 and 22% by 2050 (Ramos, 2002).

Private sector businesses have started courting Latino consumers. Surveys report that Latinos tend to purchase high-quality brand-name products and maintain loyalty to those brands. Procter & Gamble spent $90 million in one year, 10% of its budget, on an advertising campaign targeting Latinos. Kroger Company, the nation's leading grocery store chain, spent almost $2 million creating a *supermercado* in a Houston neighborhood that had become 85% Latino. In addition, more Latinos are becoming entrepreneurs. According to the Internal Revenue Service, from 1988 to 2003, Latino entrepreneurs increased by 30% (Grow, 2004). Perhaps inspired by Cuban success, entrepreneurs from other Latino groups have discovered that their fluency in Spanish gives them an advantage in working with their counterparts in Central and South America. Despite this commercial success, most Americans still don't seem to appreciate the potential and immediate benefits of having a linguistically diverse citizenry.

The Value of Cultural and Linguistic Diversity

Cultural and linguistic diversity have evolved in human societies around the world, and each manifestation of a distinctive culture and language illustrates the complexity and richness of human creativity. Although human beings occupy the same planet, each language demonstrates how diverse

groups interpreted and understood their world, and the differences between languages reveal that despite our similarities, human beings tend to see that world in distinctive ways. The four languages spoken by the most people in our global population are Mandarin Chinese (16%), English (8%), Spanish (5%), and Arabic (4%), but over 200 languages today are spoken by more than a million people (Skutnabb-Kangas, 2000). Taken together, these different worldviews provide a dynamic perspective on human beings accommodating to diverse environments.

Skutnabb-Kangas (2000) defines **linguistic diversity** as "the range of variation exhibited by human language" (p. 70), and she reports that there are between 6500 and 10,000 languages throughout the world, as well as a number of different sign language systems. A more precise estimate is impossible because so many languages are disappearing. In the United States alone there used to be more than 300 indigenous languages, but only 175 still remain and many are becoming extinct. Linguists have identified 43 indigenous languages that are on the verge of extinction, and as for the rest, they are only confident that three indigenous languages will survive: Cree, Ojibway, and Inuktitut (Crawford, 2000). When 93-year-old Helen Sater died in a Canadian hospital in 1996, she was the last living person who was fluent in her native Tuscarora language (Skutnabb-Kangas, 2000). The Tuscarora were once part of the powerful alliance known as the Six Nations of the Iroquois Confederacy. With over 300 indigenous languages already present and with the arrival of people speaking diverse European languages, the history of North America should be regarded as an ongoing chronicle of communities that were multilingual as well as multicultural; yet Americans continue to be ambivalent about linguistic and cultural diversity. The reality of linguistic diversity in the United States today can best be appreciated by visiting our urban classrooms.

Do Americans support or oppose linguistic diversity?

According to Gort (2005), 25% of all K–12 students in the United States currently come from a home where a language other than English is spoken. Although more than three fourths of these students are Spanish-speaking, the following list includes other languages spoken by children in U.S. schools:

Southeast Asia:	Hmong, Khmer, Lao, and Vietnamese
South Asia:	Hindi, Punjabi, and Urdu
Asia:	Cantonese, Japanese, Korean, Mandarin, and Russian
Europe:	Armenian, French, Polish, Portuguese, and Serbo-Croatian
Other:	Arabic, Haitian Creole, Tagalog, and Navajo

Continuing the pattern of using nationalistic justifications for nativist attitudes, some Americans argue that immigrants and their children should not be encouraged to maintain fluency in their native languages, but should instead focus on learning English and assimilating into American society. They often cite other countries such as Canada, the former Yugoslavia, India, or the former Soviet Union to illustrate their concern that social disruptions can occur when groups within a nation maintain their cultural and linguistic heritage, but as Baron (2000) has written, "where multilingualism has produced civil strife . . . (it) invariably occurs when minority-language rights are suppressed" (p. 451). Another argument against promoting bilingualism or multilingualism is based on the perception that it is normal for a nation's citizens to be monolingual, yet most individuals in the world today are either bilingual or multilingual. As Skutnabb-Kangas (2000) has noted, those of us who are monolingual are the abnormal ones.

A primary motivation for maintaining one's native language is to preserve one's sense of identity and ability to function within a linguistic community. The Latino parents that Villanueva (1997) interviewed were committed to helping their children become bilingual and bicultural so that the children could communicate with their grandparents and participate meaningfully in cultural celebrations in their community. In addition, an individual's identity is often grounded in his or her religious faith, and Skutnabb-Kangas (2000) has described the in-

timate relationship between language and religion. She reports that people who have learned to pray in their native language have established their sense of connection to their God in a way that often makes it difficult for them to pray in their second language. Despite these and many other reasons for maintaining one's native language, most immigrant families in the United States tend to learn English and eventually cease to be fluent in their native language.

Why do immigrant families tend to lose their native language?

In contrast to American fears concerning the failure of immigrants to learn English and assimilate into American culture, studies document a pattern of the loss of linguistic diversity in subsequent generations of immigrant families. In her review of this research, Gort (2005) concludes that fluency in the native language is usually lost by the third generation and cites some studies suggesting that the loss of language among U.S. immigrant families is accelerating rather than diminishing. Tse (2001) provides the following description to illustrate the typical pattern among immigrant families. Adult immigrants with or without children come to the United States and learn enough English to function in their daily lives while retaining fluency in their native language. They teach the native language to their children, but once these children begin attending K–12 schools, they learn English, speak English with their peers not only at school but in their community, and tend to prefer using English by the time they leave elementary school. When these children become adults and have children of their own, English is usually the only language spoken at home, resulting in grandchildren who are only able to talk to their grandparents in English.

Some Americans insist that this pattern does not accurately describe what is happening in the families of recent Latino immigrants, but Portes (2007) has reviewed studies of second generation Latino families in the United States reporting that 98% of the members of these families are fluent in English, whereas only 35% retain their fluency in Spanish. This loss of language is consistent across Western nations in which the dominant group (speaking English or French or German) demands that immigrants abandon their own language and heritage and adopt the language and cultural traditions of the dominant group. This can be most clearly seen in the education of immigrant children. After describing this form of assimilation that demands cultural and language conformity, Skutnabb-Kangas (2000) concludes: "This is the preferred Western strategy in the education of ethnic minority children. It amounts to linguistic genocide" (p. 174). Some educators in the United States and elsewhere have been sensitive to this issue and have advocated a different approach.

What alternative pedagogical strategy have American educators proposed?

American educators have advocated for bilingual education in an effort to preserve linguistic diversity in the United States; after some initial success, they have been losing ground over the past three decades. As part of the reform efforts of the 1960s, Congress overwhelmingly passed the Bilingual Education Act in 1968. To understand why bilingual education soon attracted critics, it is important to understand the rationale for the passage of this Act. The bill's chief sponsor offered the following argument to his Senate colleagues:

> It is not the purpose of this bill to create pockets of different languages throughout the country. It is the main purpose of the bill to bring millions of school children into the mainstream of American life and make them literate in the national language of the country in which they live: namely, English (Crawford, 2000, p. 88).

Ralph Yarborough (D-Texas) made this argument to convince his Senate colleagues that this bill would serve the needs of Mexican Americans like those in his district where adults with limited English skills were trying to find jobs while their children struggled to learn English. He portrayed the Bilingual Education Act as an anti-poverty program for a constituency he believed had largely been overlooked in other "Great Society" programs. This means that from the beginning, most politicians and Americans viewed bilingual education not as a way to achieve bilingualism but as a more effective means of encouraging assimilation. If students learned better by teaching them in Spanish, then some instruction could be delivered in Spanish so

that students would not fall behind in their content learning. The assumption was that bilingual education was a transitional program that would temporarily maintain fluency in a native language until the student's English skills were sufficient to allow all of his or her instruction to be in English.

Many advocates for bilingual education disagreed with this interpretation, arguing that students had a right to maintain not only their native language but also their cultural heritage while they learned English and adapted to their new culture. These advocates were not opposed to assimilation, but they believed that it should be done in a more culturally pluralistic fashion. In the early 1970s, Massachusetts and several other states had to repeal their English Only laws to establish "transitional bilingual education," but these states and Americans across the country were disturbed when a nationwide study in the late 1970s reported that 86% of bilingual programs retained Spanish-speaking students after they had become fluent in English. This caused considerable consternation among state and federal lawmakers who had believed that bilingual education programs would take a transitional approach (Crawford, 2000). In 1978, Congress voted to allow federal funds to be used only for "transitional" bilingual education programs. Lost in this controversy was another finding from the same study that half of all bilingual teachers were not proficient in the students' native languages, raising doubts about whether bilingual education programs could produce students who were genuinely fluent in their native language as well as English. In 1980, a report by the President's Commission on Foreign Language and International Studies encouraged advocates for bilingual education by stating: "The melting pot tradition that denigrates immigrants' maintenance of their skills to speak their native tongue still lingers, and unfortunately causes linguistic minorities (in the U.S.) to be ignored as a potential asset" (Tse, 2001, p. 51).

Even so, the nationwide study raised doubts that would continue to plague bilingual education programs, and early research did not diminish these doubts. Shorris (1992) described numerous conflicting studies that reported findings that were both supportive and critical of bilingual education. Increasingly, critics of bilingual education portrayed it as a language-maintenance program rather than as a way for children of immigrants to learn English and academic content more effectively. In the midst of this debate, the Reagan administration chose to promote and fund the implementation of English-only approaches to teaching students learning English as a second language (Crawford, 2000).

As the controversy continued, it became obvious that this was not simply an educational debate, but that there were social and political aspects as well. Advocates for bilingual education were interested in more than language learning; they argued for the value of teaching diverse "viewpoints, histories, sociopolitical realities and languages, and to promote the intrinsic worth of diversity in general" (Gort, 2005, p. 34). Opponents were adamant that such goals went beyond the original mandate of helping non-English speaking students to learn English, and they also criticized bilingual programs for separating their students from students in the regular classes, isolating them from the kinds of interaction with their American peers that might enable their assimilation into American society. Critics of bilingual education were more successful in their efforts to persuade Americans that bilingual education programs were not working.

By the 1990s, many Americans perceived bilingual education as being more likely to promote students' maintenance of their native language and culture rather than their learning English and assimilating into American society, even though ongoing research began to make a stronger case for the efficacy of bilingual education programs. Salas (2005) cites a number of studies finding that students whose first language was not English achieved more academic progress in English when they also had instruction in their first language. Salas also referred to a review of research on bilingual education programs concluding that students in these programs "do as well as or better on standardized tests than students in comparison groups of English-learners in English-only programs" (p. 34). Still, the five million English language learners (ELLs) in K–12 public schools today are unlikely to be enrolled in bilingual programs because the federal Bilingual Education Act was not renewed in 2002, and, despite research supporting bilingual education, federal policies continue to emphasize English-only educational programs for ELLs.

Have research studies identified effective approaches to ELL instruction?

English-only programs have often involved a total immersion approach in which only English is spoken in the classroom, yet advocates for this approach can produce no credible studies to support it; instead, they usually offer anecdotal evidence. By contrast, there are numerous studies documenting the diverse outcomes achieved in bilingual education programs. Gort (2005) reviewed these studies and reported: ". . . a growing body of research points to the educational, social, and psychological benefits associated with educating bilingual learners in their native language as they develop skills in English" (p. 25). In 2006, the National Literacy Panel published its review of research on programs educating ELLs, and in that same year the Center for Research on Education, Diversity and Excellence published its review of these programs. Literacy expert Claude Goldenberg of Stanford University engaged in a meta-analysis of these two major reviews of literacy studies to determine what conclusions could be reached.

Goldenberg (2008) began by providing some demographic data: Of the five million ELLs in U.S. schools, 80% are Spanish-speaking. Approximately 60% of ELLs are receiving some form of English-only instruction. Test results reveal that ELLs tend to have low scores on measures of academic achievement, but there is no way of knowing if these low scores reflect poor content knowledge or the limitations of the students' proficiency in English because the tests taken by ELLs were in English. Although that question cannot be answered, Goldenberg (2008) reports that one of the major findings emerging from both studies was that "Teaching students to read in their first language promotes higher levels of reading achievement in English" (p. 14). Goldenberg also noted that this finding was consistent with four previous meta-analyses of research on ELLs. He emphasized the significance of this finding: "No other area in educational research with which I am familiar can claim five independent meta-analyses based on experimental studies, much less five that converge on the same finding" (p. 15). Further, both research reviews that Goldenberg analyzed reported that ELLs in bilingual education programs tended to develop sufficient literacy skills to be not only fluent in speaking two languages, but also fluent in reading and writing in both languages (i.e., not only bilingual but biliterate).

Why should educators be advocates for bilingual programs?

Tse (2001) suggests that American educators should refer to the report from the 1980 President's Commission on Foreign Language and International Studies, which stated: "Our vital interests are impaired by the fatuous notion that our competence in other languages is irrelevant" (p. 50). In addition, Gort (2005) argued that there is support for bilingual education in the No Child Left Behind Act of 2002 because it identified learning a foreign language as a "core academic subject" (p. 33). As the global economy becomes an increasingly important factor for our national economy, it is advantageous for the United States and any nation today to have citizens fluent in one or more languages other than their native language. There is evidence that this advantage has been apparent at the federal level for decades. Since 1946, when it was first established, the largest foreign language school in the United States has been the Defense Language Institute for military and government personnel.

Tse (2001) addresses the reason for establishing the Defense Language Institute in the first of her three arguments describing the advantages of increasing the number of bilingual or multilingual Americans. The first advantage is for *diplomacy/security*—having fluent speakers of the world's languages enables the United States to play a major role in global affairs and negotiate peaceful solutions to political conflicts. Bilingual Americans also strengthen our ability to gather credible intelligence with regard to issues affecting our national security. The second advantage is *economic*—because of globalization, businesses increasingly need employees who can not only speak another language, but also understand the culture where the language is spoken. Businesses that are able to navigate the linguistic and cultural terrain will be able to establish better relations with trading partners around the world. The third advantage is *educational*—promoting bilingualism in our children and youth will inevitably increase the numbers of college students majoring in a language, and that will likely result in

increasing the numbers of bilingual students choosing to enroll in teacher training courses. For many years now, it has often been difficult for our K–12 schools to find teacher candidates who are both fluent in a language and have teaching certification.

For all of these reasons, educators who are advocates for bilingualism may be more successful today if they renew their efforts to implement bilingual education programs in our K–12 schools. There are also various forms of bilingual education approaches such as dual language (also known as two-way immersion) that have experienced great success with students and parents. Dual language programs pair ELLs with students who want to learn another language in the same classroom. A bilingual teacher may provide instruction in two languages and the students serve as resources for each other. In a program with Spanish-speaking students, the students learning Spanish use their ELL peers as language tutors, and ELLs use their partners to tutor them in English. The growing need in the United States and in the world for linguistic diversity and cultural competence should be a catalyst for a more pluralistic attitude toward diverse languages and cultures. If Americans develop greater respect for the linguistic and cultural diversity of immigrants to the United States, it could dispel some of the myths about immigrants that too many Americans still believe.

What myths about immigrants do many Americans believe?

Myths about "foreigners" who legally or illegally enter the United States have long fueled negative attitudes toward immigrants. Many Americans have expressed anti-immigrant sentiments openly, and immigrants and their children cannot help but hear them. As part of a longitudinal study, immigrant youth in high schools were asked what most Americans think about "people from my country"; 65% of their responses were negative—being stupid, lazy, thieves, and gangsters (Suarez-Orozco & Suarez-Orozco, 2001).

Although most myths about immigration refer to all immigrants, some refer specifically to immigrants with refugee status. According to the United Nations, a *refugee* is a person "unable or unwilling to return to his or her country because of a well-founded fear of persecution . . . based on race, religion, nationality, or membership in a particular social group or political party" (Pipher, 2002, p. 18). The myths highlighted in this chapter reveal current nativist attitudes about immigrants and refugees.

> **MYTH #1:** Immigrants arrive ignorant, penniless, with very little formal education and immediately have to go on welfare.

Macedo and Bartolome (2001) record an example of this myth being expressed by a former president of Boston University complaining about the number of Cambodians in Massachusetts: "There has to be a welfare magnet going on here. . . . Why should Lowell be the Cambodian capital of America?" (p. 11). In fact, immigrants often have been professionals in their country of origin—doctors, professors, and engineers. Although the figure varies each year, in 2007, 28% of U.S. immigrants had a college degree (Just the Facts, 2008). Still, even those arriving with college educations may take minimum wage jobs because institutions or professional organizations in the United States may not recognize their practices, skills, or degrees, forcing them to return to school to be certified in their profession or retrained in related fields. Despite obstacles of language and culture, the percentage of immigrants, including refugees, receiving welfare is approximately the same as native residents (Levinson, 2002). The statistics about modern immigrants to the United States document that they rarely become permanent recipients of public assistance.

Immigrants are consumers who pay rent and buy groceries and other products that help strengthen the economy. Most studies of the economic impact of immigrants report that they ultimately benefit local economies, even taking into account the services that may be required to assist them during their first few years in the country. With regard to undocumented immigrants, they are not eligible to receive most forms of public assistance beyond admitting their children to public schools or to the emergency room of a hospital, but they do pay taxes. The *New York Times* reported that

illegal undocumented immigrants contribute approximately $7 billion each year to Social Security, and since they can never claim this money, it will be used to fund the benefits of other workers in the Social Security system (Scherr, 2008). Despite such contributions, many Americans express negative attitudes toward recent immigrants, especially the majority who are Spanish-speaking. Baron (2000) observes that some Americans appear to equate bilingualism with a lack of patriotism. Perhaps this was the basis for the animosity expressed by one caller to a Massachusetts radio talk show who re-

> All the people like us are We.
> And every one else is They,
>
> **Rudyard Kipling (1865–1936)**

ferred to Spanish-speaking immigrants as "bilinguals" in a clearly derisive manner (Macedo & Bartolomé, 2001). It is ironic to see the ability to speak fluently in more than one language transformed into a racial slur.

> **MYTH #2:** Immigrants cling to their culture, language, and traditions, and refuse to assimilate into the American "melting pot."

New immigrants have always maintained their cultural heritage, in part because their identity has been profoundly shaped by the native culture. When immigrant children become adults, they typically integrate their cultural heritage with American culture, producing a hybrid of traditions and values taken from both. As for learning English, it is not unusual to find that immigrants are multilingual when they arrive; often English is one of the languages they know.

Immigrants pay taxes, send children to schools, serve in the military, and are affected by local political decisions. Recent immigrants have demonstrated their desire to be actively engaged in our democratic society by participating in voter registration efforts and transporting voters to the polls for elections. Because the Constitution leaves the issue of voting qualifications up to the local government, some cities have responded by giving voting rights to immigrants who are not yet citizens. The assimilation of immigrants is further complicated by a backlog of those pursuing naturalization, a process that can take years if not decades before they are granted legal permanent resident status, and the process has been delayed even further since the 9/11 tragedy (Wucker, 2003).

> **MYTH #3:** The United States is taking more than its fair share of immigrants; other countries need to take more.

In many European countries, immigrants represent over 10% of the population. In Germany, this percentage is predicted to rise to 30% by 2030. The countries accepting more immigrants than the United States include Canada, Australia, Germany, and Switzerland (Ramos, 2002). The main difference between U.S. immigration and that of other countries is that more diverse groups are admitted to the United States than are accepted by other countries. Between 70% and 80% of immigrants around the world are refugees. The United States accepts less than 1% of the refugees; several other countries admit a higher percentage. According to the 2000 Census, immigrants constituted 10% of the U.S. population, whereas in 1900, they constituted 15% (Passel & Edmonston, 1994; Pipher, 2002).

People who express concerns about excessive admission of immigrants to the United States often refer specifically to Mexicans, who constituted 25% of all legal immigrants in the 1990s, and an undetermined number of illegal immigrants. Current xenophobic attitudes have demanded restrictions on Mexican immigration and more money for border patrols to keep out illegal immigrants. Mexican immigration has not diminished, but increased border scrutiny has caused legal Mexican immigrants to stay in the United States rather than return home for fear they might not be allowed reentry: The number of those returning to Mexico plummeted in the 1990s. Although stricter border enforcement has not kept illegal immigrants from coming, it has resulted in three times as many deaths of those attempting to enter the United States (Massey, 2003).

> **MYTH #4:** The main problem with U.S. immigration is the large number of illegal immigrants getting into the country.

Illegal immigrants make up 20% of the immigrant population and about 2% of the U.S. population. According to the U.S. Citizenship and Immigration Service, the number of illegal immigrants in the United States is relatively stable, increasing slightly since 1996 (USCIS, 2005). The popular image of illegal immigrants is that of Mexicans illegally crossing the border into the United States. In fact, over 41% of illegal immigrants in the United States entered legally, often recruited by employers, and only become illegal by remaining after their work visas expire.

The United States has a visa waiver program for residents of twenty-two selected countries, mostly in Western Europe, whose citizens can come to America for up to 90 days simply by purchasing a round-trip travel ticket. The Immigration and Naturalization Service (INS) reports that many people who come with such visas stay well beyond the 90-day limit, also becoming illegal aliens. According to the INS data, major abusers of the privilege come from France, Sweden, and Italy (Hernandez-Truyol, 1997). So why is it that only Mexicans are viewed as "illegals"? The stereotype of Mexicans sneaking across the U.S. border illustrates not only xenophobia, but racism.

> **MYTH #5:** Illegal immigrants are responsible for increased crime, disease, and terrorism in the United States.

This allegation appeared in a 34-page booklet on illegal immigration published by the American Legion and disseminated to its nearly three million members. It included the false assertion that illegal immigrants infected more than 7,000 Americans with leprosy, even though this myth had already been proven false through investigations by many sources, including the news program *60 Minutes* (Scherr, 2008). Further, the source for the claim that immigrants were bringing various diseases into the United States came from an article written by a lawyer with a history of anti-immigrant attitudes and no medical expertise. According to Scherr (2008), there is no medical research reporting an increase in the numbers of Americans with diseases stemming from the presence of immigrants.

Unlike the disease myth, the myth about immigrants engaging in criminal acts seemed to be supported by a *New York Times* article claiming that 21% of all crime in the United States was committed by undocumented workers; however, after the researcher making the claim was confronted with evidence of errors in his interpretation of the data, he corrected his calculations and reduced his estimate to 6.1% (Wilson, 2008). In addition, estimates of criminal behavior often come from data about people in prisons, and many immigrants are in prison for violating immigration laws, not for violent crimes. As Wilson (2008) reported, research on criminal activities over several decades has consistently concluded that: "Immigrants aren't a crime problem" (p. 21). Finally, with regard to the terrorism aspect of this myth, Scherr (2008) cites a 2005 study by the Nixon Center reporting that this allegation was patently false, concluding that ". . . not a single (terrorist) entered from Mexico" (p. 34).

MYTH #6: Immigrants are taking jobs away from Americans.

For as long as there has been immigration, business owners have insisted and continue to insist that immigration is necessary to sustain U.S. economic growth. According to a Cato Institute study, immigrants do not increase joblessness, even in lowest-paid worker categories. A 2006 study found that states with large increases in immigration did not experience more unemployment for native-born workers (Scherr, 2008). Studies have also found that an influx of immigrant labor may create new jobs: One Los Angeles County study of a decade of immigration reported that Mexican immigrants created 78,000 new jobs (Cole, 1996). A 2005 study by the Kenan-Flagler Business School found that Hispanics accounted for 35% of the increase in the North Carolina workforce, and the increased number of Hispanic workers created 89,000 new jobs in the state (Wiggins, 2006).

As in the past, it is employers who are demanding immigrant labor for available jobs. In 1986, the U.S. government made it a crime for an employer to hire undocumented workers; now, many employers hire subcontractors to supply them with workers, thus placing the risk of arrest on the subcontractors for hiring undocumented workers. Unions have begun to accept the reality of immigrant labor and have been attempting to organize workers—especially laundry workers, janitors, hotel housekeepers, and waiters. These unions have become the main voice representing immigrant concerns (Massey, 2003).

A new and possibly growing problem may be the fault of businesses that urge opening immigration to more workers: the use of H1(b) visas and professional visas for entry into the United States. During the labor shortage of the 1990s, American companies increased their use of H1(b) visas to recruit qualified workers for vacant jobs, and there have been allegations of abuse concerning the use of these visas. Trade pacts signed by the Bush administration relax H1(b) rules to allow into the United States additional thousands of workers from countries with whom the United States has free trade agreements. If this problem continues, immigration laws in the United States will likely be revised once again. Maintaining fairness in addressing the diversity and complexity of immigration issues in the American economy is an ongoing challenge, but the goal should be to provide opportunity to immigrants, no matter when they came to the United States.

AFTERWORD

This history of immigration demonstrates that there have been and still are diverse but clearly defined attitudes toward immigration on the part of American citizens, political leaders, and representatives of business and industry. Although entrenched workers sometimes resent the economic competition, our society has always benefited from the willing labor of immigrant workers. We have also benefited from the cultural diversity represented by immigrants from so many different nations. Although some have complained that immigrants do not assimilate and have repeatedly insisted that immigrants should rid themselves of their old culture, history teaches us that there is no royal road for

America, it would seem, is miraculously both singular and plural, organized and scattered, united and diffused.

Henry Kariel (1924–)

immigrants trying to adjust or adapt to a new culture; in reality, there are diverse pathways. Each immigrant may take a different route, but each will end at the same destination—becoming an American.

myeducationlab

Now go to Topics #1, 4, and 10: **Ethnicity/Cultural Diversity, Language,** and **Immigration** in the MyEducationLab (www.myeducationlab.com) for your course, where you can:

- Find learning outcomes for these topics along with the national standards that connect to these outcomes.
- Complete Assignments and Activities that can help you more deeply understand the chapter content by viewing classroom video and ABC News footage.
- Apply and practice your understanding of the core teaching skills identified in the chapter with the Building Teaching Skills and Dispositions learning units.

TERMS AND DEFINITIONS

Americanization   The demand that immigrants to the United States reject their ethnic or cultural heritage and conform to American ways as defined by the dominant group

Anti-Semitism   Having anti-Jewish prejudices or stereotypes, or engaging in discrimination against Jews

Assimilation   A process whereby immigrants adopt cultural traits of the host country in order to be identified with that country and integrated into the immediate society

English Only   A movement in various states demanding that legislatures make English the official language of the state, with the eventual goal of having the federal government make English the official language of the United States

Eugenics   The study of agencies under social control that may improve or repair the racial qualities of future generations, either physically or mentally

Linguistic diversity   The range of variation exhibited by human language (Skutnabb-Kangas, 2000)

Nativism   An anti-immigrant ideology advocating the protection of "native" inhabitants of a country from new or potential immigrants who are viewed as threatening or dangerous (Feagin & Feagin, 1996)

Oppression   When any entity (society, organization, group, or individual) intentionally or unintentionally distributes resources inequitably, refuses to share power, imposes ethnocentric culture, and/or maintains unresponsive and inflexible institutions toward another entity for its supposed benefit and rationalizes its actions by blaming or ignoring the victim (Andrzejewski, 1996)

Xenophobia   Fear of or prejudice against people from nations other than one's own

DISCUSSION EXERCISES

Exercise #1 What I Know Is . . . What Do We Know about Hyphenated Americans?

Directions: In a society as diverse as that in many parts of the United States today, immigrant cultures are sometimes strongly demonstrated, as in those described here. After reading each item, explain what you know and how you tend to feel about the subcultural diversity illustrated within each category. If possible, explain what knowledge you have and/or the feelings you hold about those differences. Finally, attempt to explain any animosity or frustration that could result from experiencing those cultural differences.

1. Differences in social interaction:
    A. How loudly some racial or ethnic groups seem to talk in conversation.
    B. Direct eye contact between conversants is prohibited in some cultures.
    C. Some family sizes are large and seem to be happy living together, even in smaller spaces than actually needed.
    D. Physical contact in public between men and women is forbidden, and neither is walking together allowed.
2. Differences in dress:
    A. Women from a number of countries wear a traditional sari, many of them of exquisitely beautiful fabrics.
    B. The Sikh male turban is part of culture and religion.
    C. The burqua for Muslim women may be required by cultural and religious policy.
    D. Male Hasidic Jews wear black suits, hats, and payess (uncut sideburns).
3. Differences in cultural traditions:
    A. Preparing foods from many countries involves ingredients that are not familiar to

many of us whose parents and grandparents have more thoroughly integrated customs and foods into a standard American fare.
    B. National celebrations such as Cinco de Mayo and Syttende Mai are often unknown to a majority of Americans, even though American citizens with heritages from different countries work to keep their homeland traditions alive.
    C. The significant events of a culture can be observed through seasonal rituals, religious occasions, wedding ceremonies, and family activities and vary according to ethnicity, religion, and country, such as gathering for H'mong New Year and for funeral rites.

Exercise #2 The Immigration Letter to the Editor

Directions: This letter appeared in newspapers across the United States, each signed as if written locally. Discuss your understanding of its message, and then move to the Questions for Discussion. As you read, consider which of the four ethnic perspectives presented in this chapter is illustrated.

I am tired of this nation worrying about whether we are offending some individual or their culture. . . . I am not against immigration, nor do I hold a grudge against anyone who is seeking a better life by coming to America. Our population is almost entirely made up of descendants of immigrants. However, there are a few things that those who have recently come to our country, and apparently some born here, need to understand.

This idea of America being a multicultural community has served only to dilute our sovereignty and our national identity. As Americans, we have our own culture, our own society, our own language and our own lifestyle. This culture has been developed over centuries of struggles, trials, and victories by millions of men and women who have sought freedom.

We speak ENGLISH, not Spanish, Portuguese, Arabic, Chinese, Japanese, Russian or any other language. If you wish to become part of our society, learn the language! "In God We Trust" is our national motto. This is not some Christian, right wing, and political slogan. We adopted this motto because Christian men and women, based on Christian principles, founded this nation, and this is clearly documented. It is certainly appropriate to display it on the walls of our schools. If God offends you, then I suggest you consider another part of the world as your new home, because God is part of our culture.

We are happy with our culture and have no desire to change, and we really don't care how you did things where you came from. This is OUR COUNTRY, our land, and our lifestyle. Our First Amendment gives every citizen the right to express opinions and we will allow you every opportunity to do so. But once you are done complaining, whining, and griping about our pledge, our national motto, or our way of life, I highly encourage you to take advantage of one other great American freedom, THE RIGHT TO LEAVE.

God Bless America

Questions for Discussion

1. What do you think the writer means in saying that the view of America as a multicultural community "has served only to dilute our sovereignty and our national identity"?
2. Are large numbers of immigrants not learning English?
3. Should Spanish-speaking immigrants who are learning English be criticized for trying to maintain fluency in Spanish or other native languages spoken by other immigrants?
4. Are immigrants complaining about the use of "God" in the Pledge of Allegiance?
5. If "God is part of our culture," do you have to believe in God to be an American?
6. Who is intended to be included in the "We" of the last paragraph?
7. How could the letter be written to reflect any of the other ethnic perspectives?

REFERENCES

Andrzejewski, J. (1996). Definitions for understanding oppression and social justice. In J. Andrewski (Ed.), *Oppression and social justice: Critical frameworks* (5th ed., pp. 52–59). Needham, MA: Simon & Schuster.

Provides definitions for a variety of terms essential for discussing intergroup relations.

Baron, D. (2000). English in a multicultural America. In K.E. Rosenblum & T.C. Travis (Eds.), *The meaning of difference: American constructions of race, sex and gender, social class, and sexual orientation* (pp. 445–451). Boston, MA: McGraw-Hill.

Reviews the history of linguistic diversity in the United States and its implications for concerns expressed by people in the English-Only movement.

Barrett, J.R., & Roediger, D. (2002). How white people became white. In P. Rothenberg (Ed.), *White privilege: Essential readings on the other side of racism* (pp. 29–34). New York, NY: Worth.

Discusses the process of Americanization of immigrants to the United States with attention to the use of white privilege as an inducement for immigrants to conform to the majority.

Brands, H.W. (2000). *The first American: The life and times of Benjamin Franklin*. New York, NY: Doubleday.

Describes Franklin's development as a scholar, entrepreneur, political leader, and the influence he had on the emerging nation.

Brodkin, K. (2002). How Jews became white folks. In P. Rothenberg (Ed.), *White privilege: Essential readings on the other side of racism* (pp. 35–48). New York, NY: Worth.

Discusses the racism and anti-Semitism that has characterized anti-immigrant sentiment and the factors that resulted in the ultimate acceptance of white ethnic immigrants.

Buchanan, S., & Kim, T. (2005, Winter). The nativists. *Intelligence Report, 120*, 25–42.

Profiles twenty-one leaders of anti-immigrant groups in the United States and describes their attitudes and the actions they and their groups have taken.

Cole, D. (1996). The new Know-Nothingism: Five myths about immigration. In J. Andrzejewski (Ed.), *Oppression and social justice: Critical frameworks* (5th ed., pp. 152–154). Needham, MA: Simon & Schuster.

Describes some popular myths about immigration and provides information disproving each of these myths.

Crawford, J. (2000). *At war with diversity: US language policy in an age of anxiety.* Clevedon, England: Multilingual Matters LTD.

Discusses reasons for decreased linguistic diversity in the United States, especially the demise of indigenous languages, the growth of the English-only movement, and bilingual education.

Cubberley, E.P. (1919). *Public education in the United States.* Boston, MA: Houghton Mifflin.

Describes how schools were established in the United States and the influences that shaped the development of American public schools.

Daniels, Roger. (2002). *Coming to America: A history of immigration and ethnicity in American life* (2nd ed.) New York, NY: Perennial (HarperCollins).

Describes U.S. immigration patterns from the colonial period to the present, paying particular attention to the ethnic minorities who immigrated.

Delgado, R. (1997). Citizenship. In J.F. Perea (Ed.), *Immigrants out!: The new nativism and the anti-immigrant impulse in the United States* (pp. 318–323). New York, NY: New York University Press.

Discusses recent proposals directed toward making U.S. citizenship more difficult to obtain.

Eck, D.L. (2001). *A new religious America: How a "Christian Country" has become the world's most religiously diverse nation.* New York, NY: HarperCollins.

Examines the growth of diverse religions in the United States, especially with regard to immigration patterns since 1965, and describes its impact and potential.

Feagin, J. (1997). Old poison in new bottles: The deep roots of modern nativism. In J.F. Perea (Ed.), *Immigrants out!: The new nativism and the anti-immigrant impulse in the United States* (pp. 13–43). New York, NY: New York University Press.

Presents an overview of the development of nativist sentiment in the United States from the early 1800s to the present.

Feagin, J., & Feagin, C. (1996). Basic concepts in the study of racial and ethnic relations. In *Racial and ethnic relations* (5th ed., pp. 6–26). Upper Saddle River, NJ: Prentice Hall.

Provides definitions of essential terms and concepts for intergroup relations.

Fuchs, L.H. (1990). *The American kaleidoscope: Race, ethnicity and the civic culture.* Hanover, NH: University Press of New England.

Argues that immigrant groups have been successful in embracing and practicing basic social and political principles of U.S. society.

Goldenberg, C. (2008, Summer). Teaching English Language Learners. *American Educator 32*(1), 8–23, 42–43.

Provides a meta-analysis of two major reviews of research on English Language Learners.

Gort, M. (2005). Bilingual education: Good for U.S.? In T. Osborn (Ed.), *Language and cultural diversity in U.S. schools: Democratic principles in action* (pp. 25–37). Westport, CT: Praeger.

Discusses misconceptions about bilingual education, describes quality bilingual programs, and explains why bilingual education is necessary for educational equity.

Grant, M. (1970). *The passing of the great race, Or the racial basis of European history* (Rev. ed.). New York, NY: Arno Press. (Original work published 1916)

Expresses fears that the white race may be losing its position of supremacy in the world.

Grow, B. (2004, March 15). Is America ready? *Business Week,* pp. 58–70.

Describes current Latino population and its projected growth and the economic implications currently and in the future.

Hennesey, J. (1985). *American Catholics: A history of the Roman Catholic community in the United States.* New York, NY: Oxford University Press.

Provides a comprehensive description of the experience of Catholics in America from the colonial period to the present.

Hernandez-Truyol, B.E. (1997). Reconciling rights in collision: An international human rights strategy. In J.F. Perea (Ed.), *Immigrants out!: The new nativism and the anti-immigrant impulse in the United States* (pp. 254–276). New York, NY: New York University Press.

Discusses the basis for advocacy of human rights globally and in the United States.

Herrnstein, R.J., & Murray, C. (1994). *The bell curve: Intelligence and class structure in American life.* New York, NY: Free Press.

Analyzes research to argue that differences in intelligence stem from race/ethnicity and are genetically determined and that economic success or failure is determined by intelligence.

Higham, J. (1955). *Strangers in the land: Patterns of American nativism, 1865–1925.* New Brunswick, NJ: Rutgers University Press.

Describes the growth of anti-immigrant sentiment in the United States, culminating in significant anti-immigrant policies and legislation of the 1920s.

Just the Facts. (2008, June). Immigrants and education. Retrieved on June 14, 2009, from the Public Policy Institute of California at www.ppic.org (Publications).

Provides data on educational attainment of recent immigrants.

Kammen, M. (1972). *People of paradox: An inquiry concerning the origins of American civilization.* New York: Vintage.

Analyzes and attempts to reconcile contradictory aspects of American culture as revealed in the history of the colonial experience and in the emerging nation.

Lee, E. (2004). American gate keeping: Race and immigration law in the twentieth century. In N. Foner & G.M. Frederickson (Eds.), *Not just black and white: Historical and contemporary perspectives on immigration, race and ethnicity in the United States* (pp. 119–144). New York, NY: Russell Sage Foundation.

Examines changes in racial composition of immigrants since 1965.

Levinson, A. (2002). Immigrants and welfare use. Retrieved on May 15, 2009, from the Migration Policy Institute at www.migrationinformation.org/US-Focus.

Describes the extent and nature of immigrants using welfare services.

Lynn, R. (2001). *Eugenics: A reassessment.* Westport, CT: Prager.

Provides background on the historical formulations of eugenics, gives examples of how eugenics has been implemented, and discusses the role that eugenics could play in the future.

Macedo, D., & Bartolome, L.I. (2001). *Dancing with bigotry: Beyond the politics of tolerance.* New York, NY: Palgrave.

Examines issues of language and limitations in multicultural education; the first quote is from John Silber, who was chair of the Massachusetts State Board of Education at the time.

Martinez, E. (2000). Seeing more than black and white. In M. Adams, W.J. Blumenfeld, R. Castañeda, H.W. Hackman, M.L. Peters, & X. Zuñiga (Eds.), *Readings for diversity and social justice* (pp. 93–98). New York, NY: Routledge.

Discusses the need to go beyond the focus on black people and white people in addressing problems of racism in the United States.

Massey, D.S. (2003). Closed-door policy. *American Prospect 14*(7), 26–28.

Analyzes recent trends in Mexican immigration to the United States and the impact of U.S. government reactions taken in response to these trends.

Myers, G. (1960). *History of bigotry in the United States.* New York: Capricorn.

Describes the historic targets of bigotry since colonial days, with emphasis on Catholics, Jews, and immigrants, and the actions taken against these minorities by the majority.

O'Grady, C. (2009, May). Hate speech, media activism and the first amendment. *Extra! 22*(5), 8–9.

Reviews racist rhetoric against illegal immigrants in the media and the efforts of activists to challenge such hate speech.

Pai, Y., & Adler, S. (2006). Schooling as Americanization: 1600s–1970s. In *Cultural foundations of education* (4th ed., pp. 55–91). Upper Saddle River, NJ: Merrill Prentice Hall.

Describes the evolution of the Americanization concept and its implementation in schools.

Passel, J., & Edmonston, B. (1994). Immigration and race: Recent trends in immigration to the U.S. In B. Edmonston & J. Passel (Eds.), *Immigration and ethnicity: The integration of America's newest arrivals* (pp. 31–71). Washington DC: Urban Institute Press.

Examines 1980s immigration and compares it to immigration trends from 1880 to 1920.

Pipher, M. (2002). *The middle of everywhere: The world's refugees come to our town.* New York, NY: Harcourt.

Presents stories about a variety of recent immigrants, including the conditions that forced them to immigrate and the difficulties they encounter trying to adjust to American culture.

Portes, A. (2007, October). The fence to nowhere. *The American Prospect 18*(10), 26–29.

Discusses historic cyclic migration of Latino workers into the United States and confronts various misconceptions about recent Latino immigrants.

Ramos, J. (2002). *The other face of America.* New York, NY: Rayo.

Provides statistics and describes studies on U.S. immigrants, focusing on the contributions of Latinos and the implications of Latino immigration.

Roberts, D. (1997). Who may give birth to citizens: Reproduction, eugenics, and immigration. In J.F. Perea (Ed.), *Immigrants out!: The new nativism and the anti-immigrant impulse in the United States* (pp. 205–219). New York, NY: New York University Press.

Discusses proposals to deny citizenship to children of undocumented immigrants, relating this to the eugenics movement and other historical examples of racism.

Salas, K.D. (2006). Defending bilingual education. *Rethinking Schools, 20*(3), 33–37.

Discusses criticisms of bilingual education, implications of NCLB for bilingual programs, and studies documenting the effectiveness of bilingual programs.

Scherer, M. (2005). Scrimmage on the border. *Mother Jones, 30*(2), 50–57.

Describes current anti-immigrant controversy, especially in Southern California, with comments from immigration critics and supporters.

Scherr, S. (2008, Fall). Legionnaires' Disease. *Intelligence Report,* 131, 28–35.

Reviews several anti-immigrant myths reported in a publication by the American Legion and debunks all of them.

Selden, S. (1999). *Inheriting shame: The story of eugenics and racism in America.* New York, NY: Teachers College Press.

Analyzes the development of the eugenics movement in the United States in the early twentieth century and what lessons should be learned from this development.

Shorris, E. (2001). *Latinos: A biography of the people.* New York, NY: W.W. Norton.

Provides a personal narrative of the diverse Latino groups in the United States using many personal stories told within a historical context.

Skutnabb-Kangas, T. (2000). *Linguistic genocide in education—or Worldwide diversity and human rights?* Mahwah, NJ: Lawrence Erlbaum Associates.

Describes how the education of indigenous and ethnic minority children contributes to the loss of linguistic diversity in Western societies including the United States.

Smedley, A. (2007). The arrival of Africans and descent into slavery. *Race in North America: Origin and evolution of a world view* 3rd ed. Boulder, CO: Westview.

Describes the arrival of Africans to America and how they lost their equal status with other immigrants.

Sorenson, E., & Enchautegui, M.E. (1994). Immigrant male earnings in the 1980s: Divergent patterns by race and ethnicity. In B. Edmonston & J. Passel (Eds.), *Immigration and ethnicity: The integration of America's newest arrivals* (pp. 139–161). Washington DC: Urban Institute Press.

Examines how the earnings of immigrants are affected by trends in skill composition and the length of time immigrants have lived in the United States.

Steinbeck, J. (1966). *America and Americans.* New York, NY: Viking Press.

Includes observations of America with regard to politics, democracy, values, contradictions, consumerism, diversity, environment, global perceptions, and the future.

Stubblefield, A. (2007, Spring). "Beyond the pale": Tainted whiteness, cognitive disability, and eugenic sterilization. *Hypatia 22*(2), 162–180.

Explains how eugenicists manipulated the concept of "feeble-mindedness" at the start of the 20th century to label people of color, poor people, and women as inferior.

Suarez-Orozco, C., & Suarez-Orozco, M. (2001). *Children of immigration.* Cambridge, MA: Harvard University Press.

Describes the lives of recent immigrants based on the authors' longitudinal study and other studies, and examines the difficulties they face as they try to assimilate.

Takaki, R. (2000). *A different mirror: A history of multicultural America.* Boston, MA: Little Brown.

Describes the experience of diverse racial and ethnic groups in the United States.

Tatalovich, R. (1997). Official English as nativist backlash. In J.F. Perea (Ed.), *Immigrants out!: The new nativism and the anti-immigrant impulse in the United States* (pp. 78–102). New York, NY: New York University Press.

Examines the English Only movement as an example of the new nativism.

Tse, Lucy. (2001). *"Why Don't They Learn English?": Separating fact from fallacy in the U.S. language debate.* New York, NY: Teachers College Press.

Explains causes and consequences of language loss in the United States and debunks myths about English language learning among immigrant children.

United States Citizenship and Immigration Services (USCIS). (2005). *Illegal Alien Resident Population.* Retrieved July 5, 2006, from http://www.uscis.gov

Provides data on illegal residents in the United States, formerly the Immigration and Naturalization Service (INS) until merged with Homeland Security.

Villanueva, I. (1997). The voices of Chicano families: Life stories, maintaining bilingualism and cultural awareness. In M. Seller & L. Weis (Eds.), *Beyond Black and White: New faces and voices in U.S. schools* (pp. 61–79). Albany, NY: SUNY Press.

Describes the efforts of several Latino families who believe in the importance of being bilingual and bicultural, and how they are helping their children achieve both goals.

Whyte, W.F. (1955). *Street corner society: The social structure of an Italian slum.* Chicago, IL: The University of Chicago Press.

Presents an ethnographic study of an urban Italian neighborhood in the 1930s.

Wiggins, L.D.R. (2006). Will the immigration debate impact black employment? *The Crisis, 113*(3), 6–7.

Discusses African American attitudes concerning the current immigration debate, especially with regard to employment opportunities.

Wiley, T.G. (2005). Literacy and language diversity in the United States (2nd ed.). Washington DC & McKinney, IL: Center for Applied Linguistics & Delta Systems.

Provides statistics and commentary concerning language diversity in the United States.

Wilson, D.L. (2008, October). The illusion of immigrant criminality. *Extra! 21*(5), 21–22.

Reviews allegations of criminal behavior by immigrants and evidence used in support of such claims to refute the claims and show how data has been misused or misinterpreted.

Wucker, M. (2003). Civics lessons from immigrants. *American Prospect 14*(7), 45–46.

Examines efforts of recent immigrants to express political concerns and play an active role in addressing local issues.

CHAPTER 5

Race and Oppression: The Experiences of People of Color in America

> ❝Everyone likes to give as well as to receive. No one wishes only to receive all the time. We have taken much from your culture. I wish you had taken something from our culture for there were some good and beautiful things in it.❞
>
> Chief Dan George (1899–1991)

The categorizing of human beings into racial groups has resulted in a history of racial oppression in America, beginning with the colonial period and continuing as rebellion against England created a new nation. Although all immigrants to the United States encountered obstacles and opposition, being perceived as white initially or eventually proved an enormous benefit. Whether they came voluntarily as immigrants or were brought involuntarily as slaves, people of color had to contend with blatant forms of oppression. Some of these experiences were similar for all groups, but other forms of oppression were unique to a particular group.

The quotation from Chief Dan George describes a problem for **indigenous people,** those who were established in the New World, in their encounter with European colonists. All immigrants of color would experience some version of this problem. Although perceived as different because of "race," the real difference that defined people of color was the different culture of each particular ethnic group. In rejecting them because of race, the majority also rejected the cultural gifts each group could have shared. The diversity created by people of color in the United States began with the American Indians, whose culture and knowledge were ignored first by the colonial settlers, and later by the citizens of the new nation called the United States.

Native Americans

The Arawaks were one of more than 500 nations of indigenous people in the Americas when Columbus "discovered" a Caribbean island he called Hispaniola. Columbus created the pattern of oppression repeated by those who followed. After a brief period of peaceful relations, the Columbus party exploited the Arawaks and their natural resources. Columbus kidnapped a number of Arawaks to auction as slaves in Spain. When most of them died on the voyage back to Spain, Columbus looked for other ways to profit when he returned.

Columbus noticed gold jewelry worn by Arawaks, so he told them to bring him gold. They insisted that there was only a little gold on the island, but Columbus did not believe them. He demanded gold and warned them not to return without it. If any Arawaks came back empty-handed, Columbus had his men cut off their hands as punishment to intimidate the rest into complying (Zinn, 2003). By such brutal behavior, Columbus and his followers almost eradicated the Arawaks. Europeans eventually exterminated nearly half of the 500 nations of indigenous people in the Americas, and they almost eradicated the cultures of many of the nations that still remain today (Josephy, 2005).

What did Europeans learn from Native Americans?

English settlers in America tended to build on existing Indian settlements and walked on Indian paths, many of which eventually became the roads of the new nation. Benjamin Franklin studied the governance structure of the Iroquois League and borrowed heavily from it to create his "Albany Plan," the basis for the Articles of Confederation that was the first form of government implemented in the United States (Weatherford, 1988). Although he borrowed ideas from the Iroquois League, Franklin's prejudice against Indians appears in a letter to James Parker:

> It would be a very strange Thing, if six Nations of ignorant Savages should be capable of forming a Scheme for such an Union and be able to execute it in such a Manner, as that it has subsisted for Ages, and appears indissoluble; and yet that a like Union should be impracticable for ten or a Dozen English Colonies, to whom it is more necessary. (Le May, 1987, p. 444)

Unlike Franklin, most colonists did not care to learn from Indians. Their ethnocentric goal was to establish the culture and traditions of their own European heritage in America. **Ethnocentrism** is the belief that one's own race, nation, or culture is superior to all others, illustrated by colonial choices for settlement names. Dutch settlers called their town New Amsterdam until the English captured it and renamed it New York. Many settlements were named without even adding the term *new*, which can be seen by comparing city names on current maps of New England states with city names on maps of England. Williams (1954) described an example of ethnocentrism when English colonists

What's in a Name

Although the term *Native American* has become widely used, there is still not a consensus among native peoples about the generic term they prefer. Popular author Sherman Alexei is adamantly against the term, preferring to be called an American Indian. Some prefer to be called "indigenous people"; others are content with the traditional label of "Indian." In this chapter, all of the terms are used to reflect this diversity of preferences. The only consensus among all of the indigenous people is their preference to be identified by their tribal affiliation such as Hopi, Apache, Sioux, Mohican, Kwakiutl, or Inuit. In conversations with individual American Indians, one would do well to follow Beverley Tatum's advice—ask the individual what his or her preference is, then use that term.

called a bird a robin because it reminded them of an English robin. We still call this bird a robin today, but it's not an English robin, nor is it related to the English robin.

What did European settlers fail to learn from Native Americans?

If Europeans had been willing to listen, they could have learned much from Native Americans. The following five areas provide a few examples.

Foods and Medicines.   European settlers did not want to eat food initially unfamiliar to them such as potatoes, peanuts, corn, squash, tomatoes, peppers, and pumpkins. Later, these foods came to be exported around the world and had a major influence within countless nations. As Weatherford (1988)

> God teaches the birds to make nests, yet the nests of all birds are not alike.
>
> **Duwamish Proverb**

wrote, "It is difficult to imagine what Ireland would be today without the potato" (p. 64). Similarly, it is difficult to imagine what Italian food was like before the American tomato became part of its cuisine.

Europeans did not try to learn the indigenous people's knowledge of medicinal properties of plants. (See Figure 5.1.) For example, scurvy is a disease resulting from vitamin C deficiency, causing bleeding gums and fatigue; it often afflicted people voyaging on ships because fruit didn't last long at sea. Native Americans knew how to cure scurvy long before Europeans found a cure by noticing that German sailors on boats stocked with sauerkraut did not tend to get this illness (Weatherford, 1988). Suzuki and Knudtson (1992) estimate that 75% of prescription drugs derived from plants were discovered based on clues stemming from the healing practices of the indigenous peoples of the world. According to Harvard botanist Richard Schultes, every time a shaman dies, "it is as if a library had burned down" (Gell-Mann, 1994, p. 339).

Hygiene. According to Spring (2001), European descriptions of Indians as "filthy savages" had nothing to do with hygiene but with their "seemingly unrepressed sexuality" (p. 10). American Indians practiced frequent bathing while Europeans did not. Europeans believed that exposing one's body to the air could cause colds and other health problems. Christian church leaders also disapproved of public bathing, fearing that nude people mingling in a public bath might inspire lust. Instead, throughout Europe, many, including the aristocracy, would dry-rub themselves with sand, ashes, or pumice stone. For the rich or royal, perfume disguised body odor. According to Smith (2001), England's Queen Elizabeth I took a bath once a month, and Spain's Queen Isabella proudly claimed that she had only taken two baths in her life: when she was born and when she was married. No wonder perfume was so expensive and so highly valued!

Governance and Gender Equality. In 1642, Virginians met with a Cherokee delegation led by Cherokee leader Outacite to negotiate for a peaceful resolution of their recent conflicts. As he approached the colonial delegation, Outacite asked why he saw no women. Hearing that the colonists had brought no women, Outacite returned to his people saying he could not negotiate because the colonists did not have half of their people. Perdue (1998) also described a 1757 meeting of the South

FIGURE 5.1 The use of Indian images on medicine bottles in the 1800s suggests that Americans were aware that Indians understood the medicinal value of plants. Instead of acquiring that knowledge, entrepreneurs created concoctions (usually including alcohol), put an image of an Indian on the bottle, and sold the bogus medicine to naïve customers.

Source: Pictures of Record, Inc.

> Take only what you need and leave the land as you found it.
>
> **Arapaho Proverb**

Carolina Governor's Council to which the noted Cherokee leader Attakullakulla had been invited. His first comment was to ask why no women were on the council. If Indian women owned property, it remained in their control regardless of marital status (White, 2001). Indian women belonging to the Iroquois League did not serve on the governing tribal council, but they selected the men who served (Woodward, 1988).

Childcare. Europeans might also have benefited from learning childcare practices from American Indians. Children of European immigrants, like children in Europe, were expected to work on domestic chores at an early age. If they misbehaved, they were punished severely with beatings and whippings to teach them obedience to parental authority, just as parents had to be obedient to their superiors. Children were rarely shown overt affection and were allowed little freedom. By contrast, European observers of American Indian societies were surprised by the amount of freedom given to Indian boys and girls. Young children were not expected to assist their parents with farming, hunting, or household tasks. There were few restrictions on their activities as they became intimately familiar with their surroundings. Instead of punishing with straps or rods, Indian children were scolded and made to feel a sense of shame about misbehaving. The parents' goal was to promote a sense of personal pride and an independent, courageous spirit. They believed that threats and physical punishment would cause children to become passive and fearful (Mintz, 2004). European children who were captured and raised by Indians were called "white Indians." Even if offered a chance to return to their families, many of these children refused to leave. When "white Indian" children were returned to colonial society, most preferred to return to their Indian families. Benjamin Franklin addressed this phenomenon in 1753 (Mintz, 2004):

When white persons of either sex have been taken prisoners young by the Indians, and lived awhile among them, tho' ransomed by their Friends, and treated with all imaginable tenderness to prevail with them to stay among the English, yet in a Short time they become disgusted with our manner of life . . . and take the first good Opportunity of escaping again into the woods, from whence there is no reclaiming them. (p. 8)

Ecology. Native Americans have expressed the belief that human beings share a spiritual kinship with the natural world and are obligated to live in harmony with it. Suzuki and Knudtson (1992) cite a declaration by the Iroquois Confederacy deploring the destruction of forests by entrepreneurs, the depletion of wildlife by sports hunters and pesticides, the pollution of the air by factories, the pollution of water and poisoning of fish by industry and agribusiness, and toxic wastes deposited in chemical dumps across the country. The Iroquois declaration calls on people to preserve life around us, to "carry out our function as caretakers of the land" (pp. 240–241).

What relationships did colonists have with native people?

Instead of learning lessons from Native Americans, colonists practiced lessons already learned about conflict, conquest, and survival. Europeans usually began by being friendly toward Indians until they no longer needed them. For example, colonists at an early Connecticut settlement had good relations with the Pequot and Narragansett Indians until Fort Saybrook was built and stocked with munitions. The Pequots and Narragansetts did not understand why the fort was built. They had helped the settlers and signed treaties with them. Fortunes changed, however, when Narragansetts killed a colonist, John Oldham, in revenge for an unnamed outrage, probably holding him responsible for the outbreak of smallpox that took the lives of 700 of their people. With military might sufficient to ensure victory and Oldham's death as an excuse, General John Endecott was sent to Fort Saybrook to attack not only Narragansetts but also innocent

Pequots. After initial skirmishes, some Pequots met with Lieutenant Lion Gardiner to determine if they could resume peaceful relations, but Gardiner was not willing to stop fighting. Having heard of Dutch brutality, the Pequots asked Gardiner if it was true that Europeans did not just kill warriors, but women and children. They expected him to deny such a harsh accusation; Gardiner replied, "they should see that hereafter" (Jennings, 1976, p. 212). They understood his meaning and returned to tell their people of this threat from their formerly friendly neighbors.

What was the main source of conflict between Europeans and Indians?

The primary contention between European colonists and Indians was land ownership. In school, children are often taught that Columbus planted Spain's flag in the New World to claim the land for Spain, implying that Spanish and Indian representatives would resolve the competing claims by negotiating a treaty or by warfare. Engaging in war based on claims to land was common in European history. Nations gained or lost inhabited land through conquest because only uninhabited land could be claimed, a principle identified as *vacuum domicilium* (Berkhofer, 2004). Even in 1492, international law recognized the rights of indigenous people to own the land where they lived. Explorers were given charters to allow them to claim land under the legal principle of *terra nullius,* an ambiguous term suggesting lands without people, but interpreted as including land inhabited by a people not possessing religions and customs equal to that of Europeans.

When Columbus planted the Spanish flag, he was establishing the legal right for Spain to possess uninhabited land or to purchase the land if indigenous people had a legitimate claim to it. But most legal claims for land inhabited by Native Americans were not made under the principle of *vacuum domicilium* because natives made it clear that the land where they lived belonged to them collectively, and they belonged to the land. To resolve the ambiguity of making a *terra nullius* claim, European nations wanting to take possession of Indian land created a new concept called *occupatio bellica,* referring to peaceful seizure of land underutilized by the indige-

> They made many promises, so many I can't remember, but they only kept one. They promised to take our land, and they took it.
>
> **Red Cloud (1822–1909)**

nous people. Although indigenous people might not agree with what was viewed as "underutilized," the principle allowed Europeans to take possession of land by peaceful means, such as by erecting crosses throughout the land marked with the royal seal or by bribing a few indigenous individuals to sign an agreement conceding the land.

Nomads were the exception. Defined as "pastoral people" wandering on the land and never staying in one place, **nomads** were not granted legal claim to land. In making land claims, colonists described indigenous people as "nomadic" because they would move their villages every few years because of soil depletion and decreasing crop productivity. After many years at another site, they might move again, eventually returning to a site abandoned decades before where the soil would now be replenished (Berkhofer, 2004). Such a pattern does not fit the definition of nomadic. Although Plains Indians, such as the Sioux or Cheyenne, were nomadic and followed historic migratory patterns, most indigenous people lived in villages. If villagers resisted encroachment on their land, the result was often armed conflict ending with a treaty mandating the loss of land and Indian resettlement.

Why are Indian treaties still important today?

A **treaty** is a legal document negotiated between two (or more) sovereign nations involving terms of peace, trade, and other matters. Indian treaties document the cession of Indian lands to the U.S. government that were then made available for settlement. Land was also confiscated for resources. As described in Gedicks (1993), historian David Wrone has calculated that 19.5 million acres of land taken from one indigenous group alone, the Chippewa, resulted in the United States gaining significant wealth. Besides taking possession of the land, the resources from the land included "100 billion board feet of timber; 150 billion tons of iron ore; 13.5 billion pounds of copper" (p. 51). Other resources taken from Indian land included water, ports, fish, fowl, and game, all contributing to a profitable tourism industry that has yielded considerable wealth to members of the dominant society who gained access as a result of treaties.

A treaty signed by an Indian nation and the United States was an agreement between sovereign nations. Treaties were written with provisions to be maintained in perpetuity, yet the U.S. government has violated virtually every treaty made with indigenous peoples, often during the lifetimes of those who signed the treaty (Josephy, 2005; Wilson, 1998). Yet treaties continue to be important documents because they affirm the status of Indian Sovereignty. Deloria (2001) described **Indian Sovereignty** as a principle affirming the legal right of Indian nations to define themselves on their own terms and to behave as unique cultural and legal entities.

Why were Native American treaties consistently violated?

When Indian treaties were signed, the land designated for indigenous people was often regarded as expendable, yet if the land became desirable, Indians were forced to surrender it. When settlers migrated to Wisconsin, Winnebago Indians were removed to Nebraska and Kansas. Many refused to leave and hid from authorities; others left but eventually returned (Bieder, 1995). As colonists and settlers demanded land, treaties with Indian nations were renegotiated, often forcefully.

The Cherokee possessed legal deeds to Georgia land where they had built homes and businesses. When ordered to go to Oklahoma territory, they took their case to the U.S. Supreme Court, which ruled in their favor; however, President Andrew Jackson refused to enforce the ruling. In 1838, he ordered federal troops to march the Cherokee to Oklahoma, a journey now called the Trail of Tears because of numerous deaths that occurred on the way (Wallace, 1993).

Because of treaties, several Indian nations were forced to occupy Oklahoma territory until white demands for cheap land led the United States to renegotiate the treaties, restricting Indians in Oklahoma to the least desirable land and allowing settlers to claim the rest. Americans had little interest in Indian land in Oklahoma—until oil was discovered. The treaty was renegotiated. Similarly, an 1868 Treaty of Fort Laramie declared that the Sioux would permanently retain lands sacred to them in the Black Hills—until gold was discovered. The treaty was renegotiated (Josephy, 2005; Wilson, 1998). This pattern has continued.

Many treaties signed over a century ago relegated Indians to small reservations but affirmed their right to hunt and fish on tribal lands beyond reservation boundaries. For native people, being able to hunt and fish on former tribal land was a critical concession that may have seemed an innocuous benefit to the other side when the treaty was signed. As hunting and fishing became profitable tourism activities, complaints that the treaties should be abrogated or renegotiated have increased. People promoting outdoor recreational activities have protested Indian hunting and fishing privileges, even though treaties guarantee such privileges. Indigenous people have responded by insisting on maintaining the treaties and respecting their rights as sovereign nations.

What are other contemporary issues affecting indigenous people?

Regarding the origin of indigenous peoples in the Americas, anthropologists have called Indians the first immigrants, claiming that they crossed a land bridge along the Bering Straits 15,000 years ago, but American Indians insist that they have always been here. Increasing archaeological evidence makes it difficult to ignore the conclusion that indigenous people appear to have been living in both North and South America for more than 30,000 years, long before the land bridge (Chatters, 2001; Parfit & Garrett, 2000).

Many schoolchildren are not taught about the multiplicity of Indian cultures that existed in early America. The diversity that existed among more than 500 Indian nations encompassed political governance, economic structures, and cultural patterns. For example, diversity was apparent in Indian homes: the long houses of Northeastern woodland

Indians such as the Wampanoag, Pawnee earth homes later copied by Midwest pioneers as sod houses, grass houses of the Wichita, adobe houses of the Navajo, log houses of Kwakiutl and other Northwestern Indians. Ask American children about Indian homes, and they will likely say Indians lived in "tepees." Instead of educating youth about Indian diversity, teachers have tended to promote a stereotype based on the Plains Indians, which is reinforced by the use of Indian mascots.

Many Native Americans and tribal councils have spoken out against Indian logos and mascots for sports teams, saying they are racist and offensive (Connolly, 2000). They have asked schools and colleges displaying such images to discontinue this practice! (See Figure 5.2.) Most sports fans say they don't see what is so offensive, insisting that mascots are meant to honor and show respect for Native Americans. But how can we "honor" a people in a

> All wars are civil wars because all men are brothers. . . . Each one owes infinitely more to the human race than to the particular country in which he was born.
>
> **Francois Fenelon (1651–1715)**

manner that they find objectionable? We argue that Indian mascots honor a proud, fighting spirit; meanwhile we criticize or ignore Indians who proudly fight to eliminate the use of Indian mascots.

The response of non-Indians to Indian mascots illustrates how contemporary Indians are perceived. According to Berkhofer (2004), Americans tend to hold one of the following two images of Indians: the noble savages who lived long ago and were exterminated, or contemporary Indians who have lost their culture and been degraded by white people's ways. Many school textbooks reinforce the former by presenting information about Native Americans only up to the nineteenth century; twentieth-century Indians don't appear. Students are left to assume that Native Americans lived long ago and then ceased to exist, except perhaps for a few living on reservations (Hawkins, 2005). Critics of American education charge that children and youth are not regularly taught about Indians living in urban areas or about current issues such as resistance by reservation Indians to the use of their land as sites for dumping toxic wastes or other forms of environmental exploitation (Hendry, 2003).

One of the few facts about contemporary Indians that seems to be widely known is that they operate casinos, even though less than 1% of the total Native American population makes substantial revenue from gambling profits. If a state sanctions gambling activity, then by federal law it is legal for Native Americans living on reservations in that state to have gambling facilities. Although American Indians have been criticized for operating casinos, profits often have been employed to purchase land, build or improve schools, offer academic scholarships, support job-training programs, create jobs, and fund an array of projects intended to improve opportunities for Indian people and to perpetuate their culture.

FIGURE 5.2

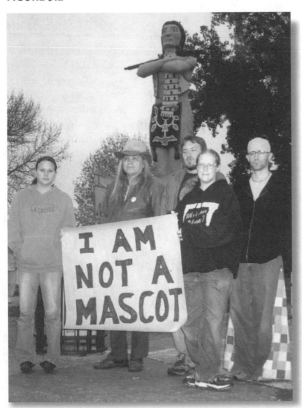

Despite the financial gains from casinos on a few reservations, many living on reservations still confront consequences of their forced assimilation into the dominant society, including extremely high unemployment rates, low school completion rates, widespread domestic abuse, and considerable alcoholism. Tribal elders have witnessed the deterioration of cultural traditions and ancient beliefs, and they fear the survival of their people is in jeopardy. Despite the need for economic resources on reservations, many American Indians oppose corporate enterprises that have identified resources on reservation land and tried to purchase mineral or water rights (Gedicks, 1993; Matthiessen, 1993).

Legal action is a critical part of the ongoing struggle of indigenous people with the U.S. government. A recent class action suit accuses the Department of the Interior of mismanaging Indian lands and funds, denying Indian tribes an estimated $176 billion. The judge has delivered several rulings in favor of the Indian tribes. According to Whitty (2005), the U.S. government is continuing to appeal the case using resources at its disposal including "35 of the country's most expensive private law firms" (p. 58). This largest class action suit ever filed may eventually provide Native Americans with needed economic resources.

African Americans

The first Africans in the New World came not as slaves but as soldiers and explorers. Although we do not have individual names, records indicate that Africans came with Cortez and Pizarro in the early 1500s, that 30 Africans sailed with Balboa, and 200 accompanied Alvarado to Quito. The names of a few black adventurers have survived. In the early sixteenth century, Estevanico (from Morocco) explored the American Southwest, preparing the way for later Spanish conquest. In the late eighteenth century, Jean Baptist Point du Sable (from Haiti) came with French explorers and founded a permanent trading post in a settlement called Chicago (Painter, 2005).

The first Africans in the American colonies arrived in 1619. A Dutch ship traded twenty Africans to Jamestown settlers for food and water (Reiss, 1997). The seventeen men and three women were not slaves but indentured servants, able to gain their freedom after specified years of servitude. During the seventeenth century, 75% of American colonists came as servants, many of them indentured servants (Takaki, 1993), but Zinn (2003) argues that English colonists regarded African indentured servants as inferior to white servants and treated them accordingly.

How were the black indentured servants treated differently?

A few Africans were able to earn their freedom, and some had to resort to courts to free them from unwilling owners, but most were never free. A few free blacks bought property, including slaves, but by the mid-1800s, the colonies were establishing different rules for white and black servants. Based on assumptions of black inferiority, Africans were often forced to accept permanent servitude status. A 1662 Virginia statute decreed that children born to a woman who was a permanent indentured servant must take her status (Reiss, 1997). Not surprisingly, 70% of Africans in Virginia at this time were permanent indentured servants (Takaki, 1993).

As southern agriculture gravitated toward large plantations for the export of crops, the use of slaves became increasingly attractive. Indian workers knew the area and easily escaped, and white indentured servants escaped and passed as free whites. Blacks could be easily identified, captured, and returned to their owners. Because England was already invested in the slave trade, exporting Africans to America was simply an expansion of an existing business. From the late 1500s to the early 1800s, more than 10 million Africans were brought to America.

Where and how did the British procure Africans?

In the sixteenth century, European traders had marveled at West African civilizations in Mali, Timbuctu, and Ghana. By the seventeenth century, British merchants had established strong trade relations in West Africa, including the export of slaves (Smedley, 2007). Spivey (2003) says that 90% of all African Americans are descended from West African ancestors.

> Until lions have their historians, tales of the hunt will always glorify the hunter.
>
> **African Proverb**

Historically, slaves have been victims of conquest. African slaves tended to be prisoners of war, and some were sentenced to slavery for crime or debt, but the removal of 15 to 18 million Africans to America, as Franklin and Moss (2000) have stated, was "one of the most far-reaching and drastic social revolutions in the annals of history" (p. 49). Not all Africans sent to the New World arrived; a third are believed to have died during what is called the **Middle Passage.**

Why did so many Africans die during the Middle Passage?

Conditions on slave ships were horrendous. According to Reiss (1997), a full-grown man was allotted a space 6 feet long and 18 inches wide in the hold. Women and children were given even less. There was no room to sit up. Slaves were chained together and packed into the hold in a "spoon" position to maintain maximum space. Reiss quoted Lord Palmerston, "They had less room than a corpse in a coffin" (p. 34).

Enroute, slaves were fed twice a day and given buckets to relieve themselves; the buckets were seldom emptied and frequently overflowed. Many were unable to get to the buckets and soiled themselves where they lay. Not surprisingly, disease was a major cause of death, including typhoid, smallpox, yellow fever, and malaria (Painter, 2005).

Because bodies of the dead were tossed overboard, sharks routinely accompanied slave ships. As slaves were brought up on deck during the day, some took the opportunity to escape by leaping into the shark-infested waters. Scholars estimate that from 5 to 6 million Africans died during Middle Passage, and some who survived the voyage were left permanently disabled (Reiss, 1997). As bad as conditions were on slave ships, slavery was even more brutal.

What was it like to be a slave?

Although slavery existed throughout all the colonies, it never led to the economic advantage in the North that it did on southern plantations where work was backbreaking and punishments severe. Working days were as long as 18 hours during harvest, with brief rest periods to eat. Overseers punished those who didn't appear to be working hard enough, usually by whipping. Other tasks included clearing land for planting, chopping wood, digging drains, or improving roads. At night, seven or eight slaves might be crowded into dirt-floor one-room cabins. Women worked with men, performed domestic chores, and often suffered sexual assault from masters and overseers. As former slave Harriet Jacobs (1861/1987) said, "Slavery is terrible for men, but it is far more terrible for women" (p. 77). But slavery enriched slave owners. A British visitor once asked future president James Madison how much profit he made from slaves. Madison replied that he only had to spend $12 to $13 annually for one slave who could produce almost $260 of profit each year (Zinn, 2003). Despite these huge profits, many people opposed slavery.

How did Africans resist the oppression of slavery?

African captives engaged in a range of activities in their resistance to slavery. Some cut off their toes or mutilated themselves in other ways so they would be less useful workers for their masters. In addition, some slaves murdered their masters; many slave owners lived in fear of being poisoned by their slave servants (Franklin & Moss, 2005). Some slaves learned to read and write either by tricking their masters into teaching them or by converting to Christianity and persuading their master to give them the literacy skills needed to read the Bible (Cornelius, 2000). They perceived competent literacy skills as a useful tool to assist themselves and other slaves, and as an important asset if they managed to escape from slavery.

When slaves converted to Christianity, their owners tried to use aspects of the faith to manipulate them into being more docile and obedient, but slaves usually resisted. For example, although white owners exhorted slaves to obey the commandment against stealing, slaves continued to steal. They justified their thefts by regarding their owners as hypocrites with no moral authority on this issue: White people were responsible for stealing Africans from their homeland and their families, and slave owners continued the offense by maintaining possession of this stolen property. The captive Africans also rejected many "moral" precepts emphasized by white ministers. Raboteau (2000) described a service for slave converts in which a white clergyman used a passage from the Apostle Paul in a sermon condemning slaves who ran away. During the sermon, the clergyman reported that, "one half of my audience deliberately rose up and walked off" (p. 31).

Who opposed slavery and what did they do?

Africans, enslaved or free, adamantly opposed slavery. Thousands of slaves ran away and many successfully escaped. Former slaves Harriet Jacobs and Frederick Douglass gave speeches and wrote books denouncing slavery. In addition, from 1750 to 1860, there were an estimated 250 slave rebellions, each involving ten or more slaves (Zinn, 1999), and numerous smaller rebellions. Perhaps the best-known rebellion was inspired by a solar eclipse in February 1831, that Nat Turner interpreted as an omen (Franklin & Moss, 2005). Six months later he led a slave rebellion that began with the killing of Turner's owner and family, and went on to result in the deaths of 60 other slave owners before the slaves were overpowered by federal troops.

As early as the 1770s, free blacks petitioned colonial legislatures to emancipate slaves. Using the words of revolutionary leaders, they challenged whites to live up to their ideals of democracy and equality by making them a reality for all (Painter, 2005). As colonial leaders considered issues related to self-government, they recognized "a marked inconsistency in their position as oppressed colonists and slaveholders" (Franklin & Moss, 2000, p. 80). The Declaration of Independence denounced slavery as an "execrable" practice until the Continental Congress deleted that particular passage at the insistence of southern slaveholders. Even the participation of blacks in the Revolutionary War did not resolve conflicting opinions about slavery.

Why did blacks fight on the American side during the Revolutionary War?

When the war began, George Washington and his aides agreed that the Continental Army would not recruit blacks. Alexander Hamilton warned that if they did not, the British would (Chernow, 2004). In November 1775, Washington issued his policy against recruiting blacks, and British supporters quickly recruited slaves by promising emancipation for military service. Washington issued a new policy in December, permitting free blacks to serve in the Continental Army. Meanwhile, colonial militias were already recruiting slaves as well as free blacks. According to Franklin and Moss (2000), 5,000 of the 300,000 colonial troops were Africans, primarily free blacks from northern colonies. The bravery of black soldiers refuted the pervasive stereotypes, but their achievements were betrayed when the U.S. Constitution was drafted.

How did the U.S. Constitution address the issue of slavery?

Although slaves represented 20% of all Americans at this time, the word *slave* does not appear in the Constitution of the United States (Painter, 2005); instead, it refers to "unfree persons." Article II, section 9, states that "importation of such persons as any of the States now-existing shall think proper to admit, shall not be prohibited by Congress prior to the year 1808." In other words, in deference to southern plantation owners and businesses, the new nation had agreed to ignore the slave trade for twenty years; however, taxes were to be collected on imported slaves. Even northern states that had abolished slavery profited from the continued importation of slaves.

Another issue in drafting the Constitution concerned the question of whether slaves should count in determining political representation. With 300,000 slaves representing 40% of its population, Virginia wanted slaves counted, as did North and South Carolina with over 100,000 slaves in each state (Painter, 2005). The constitutional compromise was to count each slave as three fifths of a person, giving significant political power to southern states: Ten of the first fifteen American presidents were slavcholders. Nevertheless, anti-slavery organizations became increasingly influential.

Were these anti-slavery organizations widely supported and effective?

In 1775, Quakers organized the first anti-slavery society in Philadelphia; ten years later another was formed in New York. Anti-slavery societies soon formed throughout New England (Chernow, 2004). In 1777, Vermont abolished slavery in its state constitution, and in 1783, New Hampshire and Massachusetts did the same. In two decades, all northern states had abolished slavery or legislated a timeline for its extinction. Some organizations lobbied to end the slave trade and others wanted to deport slaves, but all agreed on the principle of abolishing slavery. When the twenty-year constitutional hiatus ended, anti-slavery groups successfully lobbied Congress to pass a law that prohibited importation of slaves to the United States. The law was primarily a moral victory because the American coast was too long and the U.S. Navy too small to stop the smuggling of slaves. Meanwhile, slaves continued to rebel against slavery, and many were able to escape by using the Underground Railroad.

What was the Underground Railroad?

Named in the 1800s because of the popularity of steam railroads, the **Underground Railroad** existed as early as the late 1700s as a network of people helping slaves escape. Franklin and Moss (2000) quote a 1786 letter from George Washington complaining that one of his slaves escaped and went to Philadelphia where "a society of Quakers, formed for such purposes, have attempted to liberate (him)" (p. 205). By 1804, this informal network had become more organized and had established "stations" 10 to 20 miles apart for runaways to rest and eat after traveling all night. In the 1830s, the steam railroad's popularity was responsible for the name of the Underground Railroad. The organization eventually included over 3,000 people of all races (Painter, 2005). They had to be careful because helping slaves escape was a criminal activity, violating federal fugitive slave laws that compelled the return of any runaway slave.

Some slaves had a "conductor" to help them escape; one of the best known was Harriet Tubman who made 19 trips and freed over 300 slaves. Plantation owners offered $40,000 to anyone who caught her, but they never did (Painter, 2005). Although it is impossible to determine how many slaves escaped using the Underground Railroad, one southern governor estimated that from 1810 to 1850 the South had lost 100,000 slaves worth $30 million (Franklin & Moss, 2000). Still, all enslaved Africans in America would not gain their freedom until the end of the Civil War.

Did slaves and free blacks fight for the Union during the Civil War?

Slaves supported the North during the Civil War by disrupting southern productivity. Many refused to work even though they were severely punished; others engaged in subversive tactics such as supplying information to approaching Union troops. When Union soldiers came near a plantation, slaves would abandon it. Early Union victories in western states liberated slaves, but the federal government had not allocated resources to assist them. In northern cities, relief societies formed to raise money for food, clothing, and shelter and provided some education and job training for newly freed blacks.

When the war began, free blacks offered to enlist, but once again they were rejected. Few people believed the conflict would last long, but when it did, the need for more soldiers intensified. In September of 1862, the **Emancipation Proclamation** freed blacks in rebellious states, but slave owners in Delaware and Kentucky kept slaves until the 13th Amendment was ratified. Issued in January 1863, the final version of the Emancipation Proclamation allowed free blacks to enlist in the army. Over 200,000 blacks enlisted. By August, 14 black regiments were trained and ready for service, with 20 more regiments in preparation (Franklin & Moss, 2000).

Black soldiers protested the Congressional Enlistment Act that established lower compensation for them. Two black regiments from Massachusetts refused their wages rather than be paid less than white soldiers. When the Massachusetts legislature offered them money to make up for the difference, the black soldiers refused that offer. They were fighting for the Union, and they insisted that the Union pay them fairly. In 1865, the War Department finally approved equal pay for black and white soldiers (Painter, 2005), even though it came too late for the 38,000 black soldiers who had died. For those who survived the war, the next task was to create a new society in the South that would include a significant number of free blacks.

Did blacks play a role in shaping the new South?

Black males (but not females) could vote and run for office, and over 600 were elected to state legislatures. Although black legislators never became a majority, free black people participated in drafting new state constitutions. In response, angry southern whites formed secret societies such as the Knights of the Ku Klux Klan to bribe or intimidate blacks and ostracize those whites who seemed to support the developing new social order. Many racist groups began to use violence to reestablish white supremacy in the South, usually engaging in activities at night.

Blacks who registered to vote were harassed; some were forced to leave their communities and some were lynched. In 1871, blacks elected to the South Carolina legislature were given fifteen days to resign. State laws prohibited such harassment, but even Union troops stationed throughout the South were ineffective to stop it. The U.S. Congress passed laws giving the president broad powers to punish anyone interfering with a citizen trying to vote. Hundreds were imprisoned, but violence persisted.

Throughout the 1870s, the Democratic Party, led by white southerners, elected majorities to state legislatures. Congress no longer required federal troops at all southern polling places during elections, and even the U.S. Supreme Court refused to rule on cases involving protection of black voting rights

(Franklin & Moss, 2000). By 1877 when President Harrison withdrew federal troops, the transformation to white control in the South was almost complete.

How did black citizens in the South respond to this transformation?

Southern blacks did not accept the threats and harassment passively, yet without support from the federal government or northern organizations, they did not have the resources to combat white supremacists. They regarded education as the best way to acquire resources and power on their own, but with minimal state funding for schools, educational opportunities were limited. As late as the 1890s, southern states supported segregated private schools, spending an average of less than $2 annually per student in public schools compared to $20 per student provided in northern states (Lewis, 1993).

In 1881, Booker T. Washington came to Tuskegee Institute and created an educational approach that appealed to whites and many blacks. Washington wanted blacks to carve out a niche in the southern economy, and he knew that white people could accept black people doing agricultural, domestic, and factory work. Washington cultivated good relations with local leaders by having his students provide food and services to the community, and he promoted his school as a model for black education in the South. Eventually Washington attracted interest and funding from northern whites, many of them industrialists who wanted a better trained workforce in the South.

At the Atlanta Cotton Exposition of 1895, Washington declared that he believed black people would be willing to accept social inequality in exchange for economic opportunity. White politicians, business leaders, and the press claimed that Washington spoke for black Americans, but some blacks, notably W. E. B. Du Bois, believed black Americans deserved more.

What did Du Bois want for black Americans?

Based on his own experience as the first black graduate from Harvard, Du Bois felt that blacks could demonstrate academic ability if given an opportu-

> The basic race hatred in the United States is a matter of the educated and distinguished leaders of white civilization.
>
> **W. E. B. Du Bois (1868–1963)**

nity. Du Bois rejected the idea that social inequality for blacks was acceptable under any conditions. He supported vocational training for black students but not for those who demonstrated academic ability. Du Bois's approach was overt and confrontational. Although Washington worked within the status quo, secretly donating money in support of legal efforts opposing racial segregation, Du Bois challenged the status quo, publicly denouncing all racial discrimination, as in the following statement (Lewis, 1993):

> Such discrimination is morally wrong, politically dangerous, and industrially wasteful and socially silly. It is the duty of whites to stop it, and to do so primarily for their own sakes (p. 208).

In 1910, Du Bois helped found the **National Association for the Advancement of Colored People (NAACP)** and for twenty-five years he served as editor of its main publication, *The Crisis*. For eighteen years he hosted a conference on race problems at Atlanta University, and he helped found the American Negro Academy for black intellectuals. Throughout his life, Du Bois attacked racism and promoted racial equality in his research, reports, essays, and even fiction (Lewis, 2000).

What were black Americans doing to cope with race problems?

In the late 1800s, southern blacks began to migrate to northern cities, driven by economic need and persistent violence in the South, especially lynching. (See Figure 5.3.) For more than thirty years, Ida Wells-Barnett ignored death threats to take a public stand against lynching. In 1914, *The Crisis* published the names of 2,732 blacks lynched between 1885 and 1914, and the NAACP challenged Congress to pass anti-lynching laws (Lewis, 1993). According to Feagin and Feagin (2008), at least half of all lynchings were not recorded, so the total number is estimated to be over 6,000. The House of Representatives passed anti-lynching bills in 1922, 1937, and 1940, but southern senators blocked them. It was not until June 2005 that the Senate finally took a stand, voting to issue a public apology for its failure to pass an anti-lynching law.

Southern migration to the north was not dramatic until the twentieth century. According to Feagan and Feagin (2008), 90% of all black Americans

FIGURE 5.3 Cartoonist Albert Smith illustrated "The Reason" for blacks to migrate north in the 1920s.

still lived in the South in 1900. Migration increased significantly between 1914 and 1918 when World War I created labor shortages because so few Europeans immigrated. By the time the war ended, a million southern blacks had moved to northern cities. In addition, over 360,000 out of more than 2 million registered blacks served in World War I, and many returning southern black soldiers settled in northern cities (Franklin & Moss, 2000). In 1900, Chicago had 30,000 blacks; by 1920, it had over 109,000. By 1930, 2 million southern blacks had migrated to northern cities (Takaki, 1993).

As Americans welcomed war heroes from World War I, buried the dead, and cared for maimed and suffering veterans, they were ready for a new era. As F. Scott Fitzgerald said, "The uncertainties of 1919 were over—there seemed little doubt about what was going to happen—America was going on the greatest, gaudiest spree in history" (2005, p. 188). Prohibition drove drinking into the shadows of speakeasies. Jack Dempsey drew the first million-dollar gate in boxing. Babe Ruth became the highest paid baseball player in history. And in New York City, black people began a cultural and literary development called "the Harlem Renaissance."

What was the Harlem Renaissance?

Whites came to Harlem in the 1920s to enjoy the clubs, the dancing, and the jazz, creating an open community where people from all races would dance to Duke Ellington at the Cotton Club or listen to Louis Armstrong at the Savoy. As Americans enjoyed a variety of new music, new dances, new artists and new writers, Harlem contributed the novels of Jean Toomer, the poetry of Langston Hughes, and many others who expressed the uniqueness of the black experience in America. Although it was a racially segregated community, Harlem was home to diverse black peoples including newly arrived southern blacks, Africans, and

> Had it not been for our art and our culture, when all else was ripped from us, we would never have been able to survive as a people.
>
> **Harry Belafonte (1927–)**

West Indians. Spivey (2003) notes that this mix of people produced a new kind of black individual, quoting Alain Locke's description of how this "New Negro" emerged: "Each group has come with its own separate motives and its own special ends . . . but their greatest experience has been the finding of one another" (p. 165).

Was there a decrease in discrimination against blacks after World War I?

Many African Americans were upset that the U.S. military did not recognize the achievements of black soldiers during World War I. For more than six months, the black first battalion of the 369th infantry endured continuous fire while fighting in France. The French awarded the Croix de Guerre to

the battalion, but the U.S. Army did not invite the first battalion (or any black units) to Paris for the victory parade in August 1918 (Lewis, 1993). Many black mothers received Gold Stars symbolizing the loss of a son, but when the French government invited American Gold Star mothers to France to honor them, the army only paid for the white mothers. Black mothers who attended had to pay their own way (Painter, 2005).

The 1920s saw the rebirth of the Ku Klux Klan, reaching a peak of 5 million members in 1925. In 1921, a white mob in Tulsa, Oklahoma, set fire to all of the buildings in the black community and burned them to the ground. In 1923, whites also destroyed the black community of Rosewood, Florida. It is not surprising that the NAACP experienced dramatic growth at this time, expanding from 50 chapters to more than 500 between the two world wars (Woodward, 1966).

The 1920s were not "good times" for American farmers, especially black farmers in the South because two thirds of them did not own their own land (Painter, 2005). During the Great Depression, black farmers suffered even more than white farmers, with many being ejected from their land. As for black workers in northern cities, over twenty-six unions did not accept black members in 1930, and black unemployment was three to four times higher than that of whites (Feagin & Feagin, 2008).

In October 1933, 18% of blacks were receiving government assistance ("relief") compared to 10% for whites, and relief programs often provided black families less than was given to whites (Takaki, 1993). In urban areas, some civic and religious organizations refused to serve black people in their soup kitchens. The best hope for black people seemed to be the nominee of the Democratic Party, Franklin Delano Roosevelt, but many black Republicans were still loyal to "the party of Lincoln." The "New Deal" would eventually convert most into Democrats.

Did the New Deal programs help black Americans?

Millions of black people benefited from New Deal programs, yet millions did not. The Social Security Act provided financial security for older Americans and the Fair Labor Standards Act established a minimum wage, but both excluded agricultural and domestic work, jobs largely held by blacks (Lui, 2004). Black union leader A. Philip Randolph threatened to organize a march on Washington until President Roosevelt issued Executive Order 8802 banning racial discrimination in defense industries and creating a Federal Employment Practice Commission. He was criticized, however, for appointing a white Mississippian to head the commission (Lewis, 2000).

Despite the president's mixed record, blacks appreciated the social activism of Eleanor Roosevelt and her close relationship with black activist Mary McLeod Bethune. In 1936, while heading the Division of Negro Affairs, Bethune helped create the Federal Council on Negro Affairs, an advisory group to the president consisting of thirty black professionals. Media soon referred to them as FDR's **Black Cabinet.** FDR appointed blacks to serve in the Federal Housing Authority, Department of the Interior, and other federal agencies, and black Americans were increasingly changing their allegiance to the Democratic Party, but their participation in the nation's economic recovery was not meaningful until World War II began.

What gains did black Americans make during World War II?

With so many men enlisting in the military, including more than a million who were black, jobs were available for black men and women, especially in defense industries. Blacks in the military were selected for programs that had not been permitted before, such as the engineer corps, pilot training, and officer training. For the first time in its history, the Marine Corps recruited African Americans. When the navy restricted blacks to mess hall duties, they

> There is nothing quite so effective as a refusal to cooperate economically with the forces and institutions which perpetuate evil in our communities.
>
> **Martin Luther King, Jr. (1929–1968)**

protested, and within a year they were given general assignments and included in officer training programs (Franklin & Moss, 2000). In 1948, President Truman issued Executive Order 9981, officially desegregating the U.S. Armed Forces.

What happened to African Americans after the war?

Americans seemed to regard the defeat of Nazi Germany as a victory over Nazi beliefs of racial superiority. By the war's end, half of the major unions had accepted black members (Feagin & Feagin, 2008). In business and industry however, the percentage of black men and women laid off during the postwar period was considerably higher than that for whites, suggesting a possible return to "business as usual" attitudes with regard to racial discrimination.

As the United Nations was being formed, W. E. B. Du Bois objected to its lack of representation for "750 million people, a third of mankind, [who] live in colonies" (Lewis, 2000, p. 504). People of color were engaged in a global struggle to free themselves from European domination. In 1947, Mahatma Gandhi's success in gaining India's independence from Britain encouraged African Americans who demanded their rights as citizens of the United States. Court cases involving transportation and education ruled against racial segregation, and in 1954, the **Brown v. Board of Education** decision overturned decades of legal discrimination based on race. It was a victory more in principle than in practice as segregation in America persisted; nevertheless, in the context of these national and global events, the civil rights movement was born, and Americans were challenged to recognize their prejudices and stereotypes. (See Figure 5.4.)

With more black people demanding their rights as American citizens, the response from southerners became more violent. In August 1955, a 14-year-old black youth from Chicago came to Mississippi to visit relatives. After Emmett Till showed a group of black friends a picture of a white girl he knew in Chicago, one of the boys dared him to go into the nearby store and talk to the white woman working there. After buying candy in the store, Emmett turned before leaving and said, "Bye, Baby." The woman's husband was out of town, but soon

FIGURE 5.4 Despite the commercial advantage of maintaining a familiar face on one's product, Quaker Oats felt that the old image (B) of Aunt Jemima was too much of a stereotype and updated her image in the 1960s. (A)

(A)

(B)

Emmett's mother demanded an open casket at his funeral so that mourners could see what had been done to her son. Americans were shocked and revolted by the photographs of the boy's mangled face that appeared in newspapers across the nation. The three men responsible were arrested and brought to trial. Despite the courageous testimony of Mose Wright, who identified the accused men as the ones who took Emmett Till from his house, the all-white jury acquitted all three men of kidnapping and murder. People of all races across the nation expressed outrage at the violence and the injustice, and the civil rights movement grew in number and increased in resources as more people rose up to challenge racist attitudes and practices in America (Williams, 1987).

What did the civil rights movement achieve for African Americans?

In Montgomery, Alabama, Rosa Parks and Martin Luther King, Jr., inspired African Americans to conduct a boycott of city bus services to end racial segregation. The boycott lasted over a year; then in 1957, the U.S. Supreme Court upheld a federal court ruling to desegregate public bus transportation systems. Although Congress passed civil rights laws in 1957 and 1960, they were ineffective in addressing problems of segregation and racial discrimination.

In February 1960, as a practical demonstration of civil rights, four black college freshmen in Greensboro, North Carolina, entered a Woolworth store and deliberately sat at a lunch counter that served only whites. When refused service, the black students opened their textbooks and read. They eventually left, but they returned, and other students came with them. The idea spread across the nation as 70,000 students, mostly black but some white, staged more than 800 sit-ins in over 100 southern cities. As more than 4,000 students were arrested, whites stayed away from lunch counters, and many would not shop in stores where sit-ins were occurring. The economic losses forced many businesses to begin offering services to blacks (Lomax, 1963).

Although Martin Luther King, Jr., encouraged nonviolent tactics, younger, radical black leaders encouraged black Americans to return violence for violence. The passionate oratory of Malcolm X may

returned. It was shortly after midnight when he and two friends came to the home of Mose Wright where Till was staying and dragged the boy out of bed. They brutally murdered him and threw his body in the Tallahatchie River. When his corpse was found three days later, it was so badly mutilated that Mose Wright could only identify the boy by a ring on Emmett's finger (Williams, 1987).

have predisposed some whites to be more comfortable listening to the peaceful rhetoric of change expressed by King and his followers. Even after Malcolm X ended his association with the extremist Nation of Islam to pursue a more authentic Islamic faith, he still insisted that black people should demand the same rights that white Americans enjoyed—not just civil rights but their human rights (Malcolm X, 2000):

> When you expand the civil-rights struggle to the level of human rights, you can then take the case of the black man in this country before the nation in the U.N. . . . You can take Uncle Sam before a world court. . . . Civil rights keeps you in his pocket. Civil rights means you're asking Uncle Sam to treat you right. Human rights are something you were born with. Human rights are your God-given rights. (p. 596)

Another militant voice came from the Black Panther Party founded in 1966 by Huey Newton and Bobby Seale. The Black Panthers attracted black youth, especially in urban areas. Despite the Panthers' sponsoring community service activities such as a free breakfast program for black children, they were viewed by white authorities as a paramilitary organization. The FBI Counterintelligence program targeted its leaders for surveillance, and Panther members were subjected to police raids. Newton's 1967 arrest and imprisonment on murder charges weakened the Panthers, as did the violent assaults on party members that left 28 dead (Carson & Carson, 2000). By the mid-1970s, most of the Panther leaders either had been expelled from or had voluntarily left the organization.

Throughout the 1960s, the South was the primary scene for marches, protests, and demonstrations. In 1963 alone, the Department of Justice recorded over 1,400 events in three months (Zinn, 2003). As usual, the white response was immediate and violent, but now some of the violence was recorded by a national press and witnessed by a national audience. The images of law enforcement officers using dogs, fire hoses, and clubs to assault unarmed black people left many white viewers appalled, yet even more violence took place. Mississippi civil rights leader Medgar Evers was shot and killed on his front porch. Four black children were killed by a secretly planted bomb in the basement of their Birmingham church, and Martin Luther King, Jr., was assassinated in Memphis.

Being white did not protect protestors from southern wrath. When Freedom Riders rode integrated buses to test southern compliance with desegregation laws, mobs attacked the buses, assaulting whites and blacks as local law enforcement and the FBI observed the violence but did nothing (Zinn, 2003). In Mississippi, authorities found the bodies of three young civil rights workers who had been murdered. During a Selma-to-Montgomery march in Alabama, a white minister was beaten to death, and a white housewife transporting marchers to Selma was shot and killed (Painter, 2005).

Amid this turmoil, Congress passed the Civil Rights Act of 1964 and the Voting Rights Act of 1965, forbidding discrimination in public accommodations, federally assisted programs, public facilities, education, and voting. In 1952, 20% of eligible southern blacks were registered to vote, but because of this legislation, 40% of eligible southern black voters were registered in 1964, and by 1968, 60% of blacks were registered, the same percentage as for whites (Zinn, 2003). Although some problems in the South were being addressed, 1960s race riots in urban areas demonstrated that racial problems also existed in northern cities. The Kerner Commission's investigation of this outbreak of urban violence concluded that the major cause of the riots was the persistence of white racism. Naming the problem did not solve it, and discrimination against African Americans in the United States has persisted and continues to contradict our American ideals.

Asian Americans

The first Asian immigrants to the United States were from four villages in the Canton province of China. Arriving in 1850, they set the Chinese pattern of predominantly male migration to America with a ratio of 10 men for every 1 woman (Lowe, 2000). Chinese immigrants tended to be young and married, lured to California by the thought of finding gold and returning to China. San Francisco welcomed the new arrivals by inviting them to participate in California's statehood ceremonies, but by 1870, 63,000 Chinese immigrants had arrived, with more than 75% in California, representing 25% of the state's workforce (Fong, 2000). Chinese immigrants quickly became the targets of Nativist sentiments expressed in slogans such as "California for Americans."

What actions did Nativists initially take against the Chinese in America?

Nativists lobbied the California legislature for a tax on people mining for gold who were not U.S. citizens (Takaki, 1993). Although the tax penalized any immigrant, the passage of the "foreign miners" act was a major setback for the Chinese. Most had borrowed money and were expected to repay their debts on arriving in America. In addition to paying for their passage, they were expected to send money home to support their wives and families, and two thirds of them managed to earn enough money to take care of their financial obligations and return to China (Glenn & Yap, 2000). Because of the 1790 law restricting U.S. citizenship to "whites only," there was little incentive to remain in the United States.

Why didn't Chinese men bring their wives and families?

In places like Singapore and Hawaii, Chinese men who chose to remain either married local women or sent for their wives, but neither option was possible in America. California law forbade interracial marriage, and entrepreneurs imported Chinese women to work as prostitutes. In 1870, the California legislature passed the Page Law to stop the immigration of Chinese prostitutes, but this resulted in the exclusion of almost all Chinese women. By 1890, the ratio of Chinese men to women was 26 to 1 (Fong, 2000).

Who employed Chinese immigrants?

Unable to mine for gold, many Chinese men found work as laborers on the western portion of the transcontinental railroad. Railroad owners paid the Chinese less than other workers and forced them to work during the winter of 1866, despite snowdrifts

as high as 60 feet. They had to tunnel under the snow, digging shafts to allow for air so they could work. After that winter, Chinese workers went on strike for higher wages, only to be denounced by local newspapers and literally starved into submission when railroad owners cut off food supplies (Takaki, 1993). After the railroad was completed, most Chinese laborers returned to China, but some chose to stay, particularly in the area of San Francisco.

Wherever they settled, Chinese men continued to be paid low wages. In addition to agricultural jobs, they worked in factories or were employed as houseboys, gardeners, and cooks, and a few started small businesses. Starting a laundry was especially tempting because it required minimal investment for equipment and minimal English skills. Being self-employed enabled them to avoid exploitation by employers as well as competition with hostile white laborers.

What kind of hostile actions did the Chinese encounter?

The resentment of white laborers was not the only source of hostility; the white population in general tended to perceive the Chinese as refusing to give up their "foreign" identity and become "Americanized." Some white men would occasionally target Chinese men who maintained traditions such as the "queue," a long single braid of hair worn down their back. (See Figure 5.5.) Chinese laborers complained of white men grabbing or even cutting off their queue. It wasn't long before such hostility escalated to violent confrontation.

The U.S. economy experienced a depression in the 1870s, yet the numbers of Chinese increased, and many were becoming visibly prosperous. Looking for a scapegoat, white politicians and labor leaders blamed economic problems on the Chinese, and newspapers published and disseminated their views. In 1871, mob violence resulted in the deaths of 21 Chinese men in Los Angeles; in 1885, 28 Chinese railroad workers were killed in Rock Springs, Wyoming (Fong, 2000; Wu, 1972). Although Chinese immigrants constituted less than 1% of the U.S. population in 1882, Congress passed the **Chinese Exclusion Act** to prohibit Chinese immigra-

FIGURE 5.5 Newspapers often expressed their hostility to Chinese immigrants in cartoons.

PACIFIC CHIVALRY.

Encouragement to Chinese Immigration.

c 1999 HARPWEEK®

tion for the next ten years; it was renewed for another ten years in 1892, and renewed indefinitely in 1902. The door to the "Gold Mountain" closed.

During another economic recession in the 1890s, unemployed white workers rioted, beating and shooting Chinese workers. Such violence often discouraged the Chinese from continuing to work as laborers except for Chinese employers. The Chinese created their own communities in urban areas—Chinatowns—where they felt safe establishing businesses and homes, and less vulnerable to white discrimination and violence. Chinese entrepreneurs often pooled their resources to start a business, and they would employ other Chinese. By 1890, 6,400 Chinese workers employed in California laundries constituted 69% of all laundry employees in the state (Takaki, 1993).

Although they were willing to live in separate communities, most Chinese who remained in America were unwilling to be perceived as foreigners in the land. By 1924, Andrew Kan had lived and worked in the United States for over forty years, and he took his case to court to insist on his right to be an American citizen; the courts disagreed. Anti-Asian sentiment would intensify during World War II as the United States fought a Japanese enemy portrayed as treacherous and brutal.

> If we believe absurdities we shall commit atrocities.
>
> **Voltaire (1694–1778)**

How did Americans view the Japanese before World War II?

Initially Japanese immigrants settled in Hawaii to work on plantations. By 1880, only 148 Japanese lived in the United States (Fong, 2000); however, 150,000 Japanese immigrated to the mainland between 1880 and 1908. By the 1920s, the Japanese population in America was twice as large as the Chinese (Zia, 2000). Unlike the Chinese, Japanese immigrants tended to include women. By 1920, women constituted 46% of the Japanese in Hawaii and 35% in California (Takaki, 1993). Based on their awareness of the hostility toward the male Chinese immigrants; Japanese government officials screened immigration applications to ensure that those approved included married couples and to eliminate anyone who might engage in prostitution, gambling, or other vices that had been used to justify American anti-Chinese attitudes.

Despite these efforts, in 1905, California newspapers initiated a campaign against the **Yellow Peril** based on the belief that the Japanese, like the Chinese, could not or would not adopt the American culture (Feagin & Feagin, 2008). In reality, many Japanese immigrants had assimilated and desired to become American citizens. In 1922, Takao Ozawa challenged the 1790 law restricting U.S. citizenship to white people. Ozawa had been educated in American schools, belonged to a Christian church, and spoke only English at home. Ozawa's argument to the U.S. Supreme Court was that he had done everything that any immigrant could be asked to do to assimilate into the culture, and the only thing that prevented his citizenship was his race. The Supreme Court said that was all that mattered, and rejected his appeal.

Before the Supreme Court made their decision, California legislators in both houses passed a resolution calling for the prohibition of further Japanese immigration. Responding to such nativist sentiment, President Theodore Roosevelt met with Japanese officials in 1908 and reached the **Gentleman's Agreement** that Japan would prohibit further immigration except for the close relatives of those already in the United States. Japanese immigrants could use this loophole until 1920 to bring family members—including "picture brides"—to join them in America.

What was a picture bride?

Japanese culture regarded marriage as an affair negotiated between families. In the **picture bride** system, matchmaking resulted from an exchange of photographs. Combining those who came with their husbands and those who came as picture brides, 60,000 Japanese women immigrated to America (including Hawaii) and gave birth to almost 30,000 children. These children, **Nisei,** were Americans by right of birth. Most Japanese immigrants still lived in Hawaii, constituting 40% of the population; they were less than 2% of California residents (Zia, 2000).

Where were Japanese immigrants employed?

The Japanese often worked in canneries and took a variety of jobs, but many became agricultural laborers as they had been in Japan. Some began to contract for land, negotiating a share of the profits with the owner or guaranteeing a set price after the crop was sold. The owner provided seed and equipment, so with minimal investment and intense labor, Japanese farmers were able to be quite successful. Some saved enough money to secure a loan and lease or purchase land, giving them the opportunity for higher profits. By 1910, Japanese farmers in California owned or leased about 200,000 acres of land, producing almost all of the state's celery and snap beans, three quarters of the strawberries, and almost half of the onions and green peas (Takaki, 1993).

In 1913, California legislators passed the Alien Land Law to prohibit any immigrant ineligible for citizenship from owning land or leasing land for more than three years. Because their children, the Nisei, were American citizens, the Japanese leased or purchased land in their children's names; those who had no children paid other families for the right to use their children's names as their "landlords" (Zia, 2000). This prompted the California legislature to pass a new Alien Land Law in 1920, prohibiting the use of children's names to lease or purchase land.

Japanese immigrants were disappointed that their success, their efforts to assimilate, and their children's citizenship status did not reduce hostility against them. Even when possessing a college diploma, their children were not likely to find work.

Many returned to the family business, and those who were doctors or dentists tended to work in the Japanese communities (Takaki, 1993). Then World War II began, and Japan became America's enemy.

How did the war affect American attitudes toward Japanese families living in the United States?

Given the history of anti-Japanese sentiment, it is not surprising that rumors of spying and sabotage began circulating immediately. Japanese farmers were accused of planting flowers in a particular pattern to guide airplanes carrying bombs to their target (Feagin & Feagin, 2008). Fearing a broad anti-Asian backlash, many Asian-owned businesses posted signs saying that the owners were Asian but not Japanese. Some shops sold buttons that said, "I am Korean" or "I am Chinese" so Americans would not confuse them with Japanese (Koppelman, 2001).

What actions were taken against the Japanese during World War II?

Barely two months into the war, President Roosevelt issued Executive Order No. 9066 that was the basis for taking Japanese Americans from their communities and relocating them in federal "camps." Japanese families were given a week or less to sell property and possessions, packing what remained into their suitcases. More than 100,000 people, two thirds of them American citizens, lost almost everything as they were evacuated to ten federal camps. The path to these relocation camps was paved with widespread prejudices that were affirmed by political leaders at all levels of state and national government. (See Figure 5.6.)

Once at the camps, Japanese families were informed that the U.S. government required them to take a loyalty oath renouncing their allegiance to Japan. The Nisei were already American citizens, so this was not an issue for them, but for their parents, renouncing Japanese citizenship with no chance of becoming an American citizen meant that they would become a people without a country. When 4,600 of them refused to sign the oath, they were sent to federal prisons (Zia, 2000). Despite such treatment, 23,000 Japanese men joined the army to

FIGURE 5.6 The Japanese American relocation camps of World War II illustrate the perception of these American citizens as "foreign." Rumors that there were spies from Japan circulating among them were enough to justify confiscating their property and keeping them behind barbed wire for the duration of the war.

Source: The Japanese American Citizens League.

prove their loyalty. The army segregated its troops by race, and a Japanese American regiment, the 442nd, became the most highly decorated unit of the war. Yet, until the war's end, Japanese families continued to be kept in camps with barbed wire and armed soldiers. It is a tribute to the tenacity of Japanese Americans that so many were able to rebuild their lives and their finances after the war.

What other Asian immigrants faced anti-Asian attitudes?

Between 1907 and 1910, large numbers of Filipinos immigrated primarily to Hawaii as agricultural laborers. When the 1924 immigration law prohibited Asian entry into the United States, Filipinos immigrated, not as Asians but as "nationals" because the Philippines had become American territory after the Spanish-American War. Of the 45,000 who had entered the United States by 1930, most were young men who worked as agricultural workers or domestic servants. Filipinos tended to be active in labor unions, causing resentment among both white landowners and other laborers (Fong, 2000).

In 1934, Congress passed legislation restricting Filipino immigration to 50 people annually. Filipinos were prohibited from entering many profes-

> Almost all people have this potential for evil, which would be unleashed only under certain . . . social circumstances.
>
> **Iris Chang (1968–2004)**

sions and were declared ineligible for federal aid during the Great Depression. Yet, during World War II, the army recruited 30,000 Filipinos to fight the Japanese in the Philippines. Although Filipino soldiers were promised full citizenship, the promise was not kept until 1990, long after many had died (Feagin & Feagin, 2008).

Koreans first began immigrating to the United States in the early 1900s to work in agriculture or as domestic servants. Like other Asian immigrants, they encountered oppression. They were refused entrance into some restaurants, not allowed access to some public places, and restricted to racially segregated neighborhoods. Because Japan had conquered Korea in the late 1930s, Koreans hoped that the allies would defeat their historic enemy during World War II; instead, the U.S. government classified Koreans as "Japanese" during the war because Japan governed Korea (Feagin & Feagin, 2008).

After the war, the total ban on Asian immigration was slightly modified, but the number of Korean immigrants was minimal until the Korean War. Because the U.S. army maintained a presence in South Korea, many American soldiers returned with Korean wives who were exempt from Asian immigration quotas. As with other Asian groups, the number of Koreans in America has increased

dramatically since the Immigration Reform Act of 1965. There have also been significant increases in the numbers of other Southeast Asian immigrants such as Vietnamese, Cambodians, Laotians, and Hmong. Even though they have encountered prejudice, most refugees emigrated to escape violence in their native countries. Living safely with their families, they tend to be more optimistic about overcoming difficulties here (Pipher, 2002).

In the early 1900s, Sikh farmers were the first Asian Indian immigrants to America. Landowners employed them instead of Asians who had been targets of nativist outrage. In 1923, a Punjabi immigrant named Bhagat Singh Thind applied for U.S. citizenship using "scientific" race theories to prove he was white. Having cited race theories to deny citizenship to previous nonwhite applicants, the U.S. Supreme Court nevertheless chose to ignore "science" in this case, asserting that Thind was not white because they did not believe him to be white (Zia, 2000).

Most Asian Indian immigration has occurred since 1965, with 80% of Indo-Americans being the first generation of immigrants. Yet Asian Indian immigration has involved significant numbers of people, producing an Indo-American population that is the fourth largest among all Asian groups (after Chinese, Japanese, and Filipinos). Asian Indians are notable for linguistic and religious diversity, and they are culturally diverse, more likely to identify with a province such as Bengal or Punjab than with

> America has traveled and is still traveling a long, hard road . . . littered with persistent intolerance and bigotry. However, our progress as a nation has been marked by a succession of civil rights laws . . . (but) without proper enforcement, these laws are merely empty promises.
>
> **Bill Lann Lee (1949–)**

India. Migrating Asian Indians often have academic qualifications in fields such as engineering, medicine, mathematics, and computer management. In one study of Asian immigrants employed as physicians, over half were Asian Indians (Kar et al., 2000). Their success has contributed to the "model minority" myth that has been used to counter claims of discrimination by other minority groups.

What is the model minority myth?

Beginning in the 1960s, white Americans praised Asian Americans as a **model minority** because they had overcome all obstacles and achieved success. People of color were told that if they were willing to work as hard as Asian Americans, they could be just as successful, and if they failed it was their own fault. The model minority myth has created resentment among people of color, particularly African Americans, toward Asian Americans. Takaki (1993) suggests that this was the intent of those promoting the model minority myth: "Our society needs an Asian American 'model minority' in an era anxious about a growing black underclass" (p. 416). The model minority myth has often been criticized as a distraction that avoids the reality of ongoing discrimination against Asian Americans.

How does the model minority myth distort reality?

As a group, Asian Americans exist on both extremes of social status, but the model minority myth focuses on the upper extreme. Data that seems to document their financial success needs to be put in context. Asian Americans tend to live in urban areas of states where cost of living is high, inflating salary data. One study said 60% of all Asian Americans lived in three states—Hawaii, California, and New York (Woo, 2000). Asian American incomes are also inflated because they are reported as household incomes. Although most American households consist of dual wage earners, Asian American households often have additional earners.

At the other extreme are Asian Americans working for low wages. In San Francisco, Asian American women constitute 80% of all garment workers averaging 10 to 12 hours a day, 6 to 7 days a week (Louie, 2000). Their wages are low because they are competing against Third World workers who are hired by companies outsourcing jobs or establishing factories in other countries, making multiple incomes a necessity for many Asian American households. Although it is appropriate to celebrate the

success of those who overcome oppression, the model minority myth actually harms Asian Americans, as Fong and Shinagawa (2000) have explained:

> [It] diverts attention away from serious social and economic problems that affect many segments of the Asian American population, detracts from both the subtle and overt racial discrimination encountered by Asian Americans, places undue pressure on young Asian Americans to succeed educationally and professionally, and fuels competition and resentment between Asian Americans and other groups. (p. 191)

Hispanic Americans/ Latinos/as

There is no clear consensus on an appropriate term that includes all diverse Spanish-speaking ethnic groups in the United States, but the immigration of Mexicans, Puerto Ricans, Cubans, Central Americans, and South Americans has created a need for an inclusive generic term. In 1980, the U.S. Census Bureau suggested *Latino* as the generic term; however, some critics said that sounded like "Ladino," an ancient form of Castilian Spanish spoken by Spanish Jews. The Bureau chose *Hispanic,* a label rejected by many Spanish-speaking people as a contrived, bureaucratic term (Shorris, 2001). Although *Hispanic* seems to be the preferred term in the southeastern United States and Texas, it is rejected in many other places, including most of California and much of the Midwest. Given this lack of consensus, both *Hispanic* and *Latinos* are used in this final section.

What was the first Spanish-speaking group to come to the United States?

The Spanish established the first permanent U.S. settlements in 1565 at St. Augustine, Florida, and in 1598 at Santa Fe, New Mexico, yet rarely do American history books mention this. Historically, school textbooks have focused on the English settlements in 1607 at Jamestown, and in 1620 at Plymouth (Loewen, 2008). When the U.S. annexed Texas, Mexicans living there (Tejanos) found themselves in America; as the Tejanos like to say, "We didn't cross the border; the border crossed us" (Shorris, 2001, p. 37). After the Mexican-American War, Mexico signed the Treaty of Guadelupe Hidalgo, giving up a million square miles of land, half of its territory. Mexicans living there were given six months to decide either to stay and become U.S. citizens or to return to Mexico. Of the more than

> Poor Mexico, so far from God, so near to the United States.
>
> **Porfirio Diaz (1830–1915)**

82,000 Mexicans who had to choose, about 80,000 chose to stay (Duignan & Gann, 1998).

Article X of the treaty promised to honor the land claims of Mexicans who became citizens, but when the American Congress ratified the treaty, they rejected Article X. To reassure Mexico that land titles and civil rights of Mexicans would be respected, American representatives presented a "Statement of Protocol" to the Mexican government with assurances that the U.S. government would not annul Mexican land grants and that these claims would be considered legitimate in American courts (Vento, 1998). That promise proved to be false.

Only a few **Anglos,** as Mexicans called white settlers, came to the new territory at first, but after gold was discovered in California, they flooded the land. Anglos settled on Mexican American land, refusing to move, and authorities took no action against the "squatters." When Anglos made legal claims to the land, Mexican Americans were forced to retain white lawyers to represent them because court proceedings were conducted in English. Although courts confirmed land grants for more than 2 million acres owned by Mexican Americans, they rejected Mexican American claims for almost 34 million acres (Vento, 1998). Even when the courts affirmed their claims, landowners often had to sell portions of their land to pay legal fees. Aggressive Anglo efforts soon created a society in former Mexican territory consisting of Anglo landowners and entrepreneurs and a pool of primarily Mexican laborers. What Shorris (2001) said of California was true for all of the former Mexican territory: "In less

than a quarter of a century California changed from Spanish to Anglo" (p. 31); it was an enormous transfer of wealth and culture.

What was the experience like for Mexicans immigrating to the United States?

In the 1880s, Mexicans began crossing the border into the United States, recruited by American employers after the Chinese Exclusion Act was passed in 1882. Mexican immigrants tended to take jobs in agriculture, mining, and construction; they constituted 70% of workers laying track for Southern Pacific and Santa Fe railroads. Although American businesses actively recruited them, many Anglos perceived Mexicans as inferior. Mexicans were refused admission to public places such as beaches and restaurants. Takaki (1993) quotes the wife of an Anglo rancher arguing that a Mexican "is not as good as a white man. God did not intend him to be; He would have made him white if He had" (p. 327). All members of Mexican families participated in agricultural work; child labor laws were not enforced. Experienced workers might make up to $1.50 per day compared to $4 to $5 a day earned by miners (Duignan & Gann, 1998).

Mexicans did not passively accept such exploitation. In 1903, Mexican and Japanese farm workers formed the Japanese-Mexican Labor Association (JMLA) and engaged in a strike to increase hourly wages. They were successful, but they couldn't survive without support from national labor organizations. They petitioned the American Federation of Labor (AFL) to accept JMLA members, but AFL president Samuel Gompers insisted that the JMLA would be granted a membership charter only if it excluded Asian members. The Mexicans refused to betray their Japanese co-workers, so the charter was not granted (Takaki, 1993). Although the JMLA did not survive, Mexican farm workers continued to strike and protest against low wages.

Because of the Gentleman's Agreement of 1908 and the restrictive 1924 immigration law, Mexico was regarded as an excellent source of cheap labor. By 1910, 222,000 Mexicans lived in the United States, some as far north as Montana. Many migrated to escape the violence of the Mexican Revolution from 1910 to about 1920. When the revolution was over, only 10% of Mexico's citizens were landowners, and the northern migration continued (Vento, 1998). By 1930, 90,000 Mexicans lived in Los Angeles, representing about 10% of the city's population. Smaller numbers settled in Denver, Pittsburgh, and St. Louis, and over 20,000 Mexicans lived in Chicago (Duignan & Gann, 1998). Only a small number of these immigrants applied for citizenship, perhaps because the proximity of Mexico made it easier to consider returning.

To promote Latino immigrants applying for citizenship, the **League of United Latin American Citizens (LULAC)** was formed in the 1920s. In addition to being American citizens, members promoted assimilation by encouraging the use of English and affirming the virtues of citizenship. Although criticized for its middle-class bias, for many years LULAC was the only Latino organization to have a national presence. LULAC worked to improve education for Latino students, to protest discrimination, and to promote civil rights for Hispanic Americans (Vento, 1998). LULAC also encouraged Latinos to become citizens so they would be less vulnerable to Nativist activities.

What did Nativists do to keep Mexicans from immigrating?

Nativists were upset that no quotas were established for Mexicans in the 1924 immigration law. During the widespread unemployment of the 1930s, Nativists persuaded Congress to pass legislation restricting Mexican immigration, and the Immigration and Naturalization Service (INS) pursued Mexicans not living in the country legally. By 1935, almost 500,000 Mexicans had been deported, including some who were U.S. citizens (Duignan & Gann, 1998). When World War II began, however, attitudes about recruiting Mexican workers changed.

Why did attitudes toward Mexicans change during World War II?

When the United States entered the war, the government began negotiations for Mexicans to replace the workers who had joined the military and the Japanese workers who had been taken to relocation camps. The U.S. proposed a **Bracero Program,** *braceros* referring to contract laborers. The U.S. government offered transportation and jobs, and the

Mexican government felt that this program would also provide Mexicans with an opportunity to learn about American agricultural practices. In 1942, the Bracero Program was implemented.

The U.S. government had guaranteed that Mexican workers would be paid the "prevailing wage" for their labor, but supervision of the program was inadequately funded, and many growers abused it by failing to pay the promised wages. In Texas, growers with a history of employing illegal immigrants continued to use them because they were less costly to hire. Although the Bracero Program was criticized on both sides of the border, it lasted well beyond World War II. When it ended in 1964, the program had issued almost 5 million contracts to Mexican workers (Vargas, 2000). In addition to the contribution of Mexican workers, more than 500,000 Spanish-speaking soldiers, primarily Mexican Americans, joined the American armed forces, the highest percentage of soldiers from any ethnic community (Takaki, 1993). Despite their willingness to fight for the country, Latino soldiers encountered prejudice from fellow soldiers and in communities where they were stationed. One of the most publicized examples was the **Zoot Suit Riots.**

What were the Zoot Suit Riots?

On June 3, 1943, eleven sailors on shore leave in Los Angeles claimed to have been attacked by a gang of Mexican youth. Local media often stereotyped young Mexicans in flamboyant "zoot suits" as

> I believe cruelty is the inability to assign the same feelings and values to another person that you harbor in yourself.
>
> **Carlos Fuentes (1928–1999)**

criminals and gangsters. (See Figure 5.7.) On June 4, soldiers and sailors rented twenty taxicabs and cruised the barrio, attacking those who looked Latino, especially anyone wearing a zoot suit. At the Carmen Theater, sailors charged in and grabbed youth wearing zoot suits, ripping off their clothes

FIGURE 5.7 After the Zoot Suit Riots, servicemen justified attacking Mexican youth by claiming that it was unpatriotic to wear zoot suits requiring so much cloth when cloth was being rationed because of the war.

Courtesy: J.S. Koppelman.

Mexican American youth. Eleanor Roosevelt declared in her newspaper column that the riots were the result of "long standing discrimination against Mexicans" (Vento, 1998, p. 187). Los Angeles police and city government denied the accusation, but as they followed the events in the newspapers, Latinos, especially Latino soldiers, were angry that they were still not accepted in their adopted land.

Was it better for Latinos after the war?

Latino communities felt a great deal of pride in their returning veterans. Latino soldiers earned numerous bronze and silver stars given for bravery in battle, and seventeen Latino soldiers received the nation's highest military award—the Congressional Medal of Honor (Duignan & Gann, 1998). Because Latino soldiers had not been segregated, they not only served with white soldiers, some also rose to positions of command. As Shorris (2001) stated, "Men who had commanded Anglo troops in battle did not cringe before them in civilian life" (p. 97).

Although they had encountered difficulty getting home loans before the war, Latino soldiers now had their loan applications approved. The G.I. Bill allowed many to pursue college educations. These soldiers represented only a small portion of Latinos, but their experiences demonstrated that Latinos could receive equitable treatment. Yet the majority of Latinos still encountered prejudice and discrimination, even those who had served in the military. At Three Rivers, Texas, a funeral home director refused to bury Felix Longoria, a Mexican American who had been decorated for heroism in World War II. After Mexican Americans protested, Longoria was finally buried with military honors at Arlington National Cemetery (Shorris, 2001).

How did Mexican Americans respond to discrimination after the war?

and beating them severely. The police arrested several Mexican American youth, and the local media portrayed the sailors as heroes (Banks, 2003; Vento, 1998).

The following night sailors and soldiers marched into the barrio invading bars and businesses, destroying property and attacking patrons. Local police refused to charge them with destruction of private property or assault. On June 7, civilians and serviceman formed a mob of thousands, attacking anyone who looked Latino, including several Filipinos and blacks. Some were left naked and bleeding on the streets. Los Angeles police arrested 600

Challenging racially segregated schools, Mexican Americans brought *Mendez v. Westminster School District* to California courts in 1946; the judge ruled it was unconstitutional to segregate Mexican American children. This case and others would create a legal context that helped the NAACP to bring *Brown v. Board of Education* to the Supreme Court in 1954. Recognizing the need for a legal organization similar to the NAACP, an attorney in San Antonio named Pete Tijerina persuaded the Ford Foundation to provide $2.2 million to establish the **Mexican American Legal Defense and Educational Fund (MALDEF).** MALDEF continues to be involved in confronting discrimination and addressing civil rights issues affecting Mexican Americans.

To establish a fair wage for agricultural workers in California, Cesar Chavez assisted farm workers in creating a union. Chavez led a strike lasting from 1965 until 1970, resulting in a contract with one of the major growers. After another seven years of activism, the remaining growers agreed to pay farm workers standardized wages and benefits. Also in the 1960s, Reies Tijerina came to New Mexico in his quixotic pursuit of restitution for descendants of Mexicans who lost millions of acres of land they owned prior to the Treaty of Guadalupe Hidalgo (Tijerina, 1971). In Crystal City, Texas, Mexican Americans who were a large majority of the residents formed a third party called La Raza Unida and won control of the city council and the school board. They instituted bilingual education programs and hired numerous Mexican American administrators and teachers.

In 1957, El Paso citizens elected Raymond Telles to be the first Mexican American mayor in the United States. In 2005, Antonio Villaraigosa was the first Mexican American elected as mayor of Los Angeles. Political candidates in the Southwest, in urban areas, and in California eagerly court Mexican American voters. Mexican Americans have been elected to local, state, and national offices. Today, Mexican Americans are two thirds of all Latinos, the largest Spanish-speaking ethnic group in the United States followed by Puerto Ricans and Cubans (Shorris, 2001). Unlike other Latino immigrants, Puerto Ricans came to America already claiming U.S. citizenship.

How did Puerto Ricans become citizens of the United States?

When Spanish ships arrived in 1493, they called the island San Juan Batista and the harbor Puerto Rico; over time the names reversed and the "rich port" of San Juan became the capital of the island of Puerto Rico (Fitzpatrick, 1971). The 70,000 Tainos inhabiting the island were almost exterminated, so Africans were imported to work as slaves. Because

Spain mainly sent soldiers, marriages and relationships took place between Spaniards, Tainos, and Africans, producing the range of skin colors from light to dark that can be found among Puerto Ricans today. In 1897, the Spanish government agreed to give Puerto Rico more autonomy, but the Spanish-American war made Puerto Rico a U.S. possession.

After almost twenty years of autocratic rule by the United States, Congress responded to Puerto Rican demands for more autonomy by passing the Jones Act in 1917. Puerto Ricans elected representatives to their two legislative bodies as well as a resident commissioner, but the U.S. president still appointed the governor and maintained veto power

> Come from where it may, racism divides.
>
> **Jose Marti (1853–1895)**

(Fitzpatrick, 1971). The Jones Act also provided the opportunity for Puerto Ricans to become U.S. citizens, giving them six months to decide. Although it made them eligible for military service, only 287 out of more than a million people rejected U.S. citizenship (Perez y Gonzalez, 2000).

What effect did becoming part of the United States have on Puerto Rico?

When the United States assumed control, Puerto Rican farmers owned 93% of the farmland. By 1930, 60% of sugar beet production and almost all tobacco production came from farms with absentee owners, primarily American corporations. Although the United States built more roads and schools, the basis of the economy was transformed from small farms producing food to meet the local need to large farms hiring low-wage workers and exporting their products (Feagin & Feagin, 2008). Soon the island was not producing enough food for its own people, and malnutrition became common. Because of improved health care, Puerto Rico's population doubled by 1940, but jobs did not. Agriculture jobs paid as little as six cents an hour. By 1910, about 1,500 Puerto Ricans had come to America because of economic hardship, with a third of them living in Spanish Harlem in New York City (Duignan & Gann, 1998).

In the 1930s, Luis Marin formed the Popular Democratic Party (or "Populares") to address Puerto Rico's economic problems. They sponsored legislation to limit land that absentee owners could control; land returned to the government was redistributed to small farmers, but two thirds of American corporations refused to cooperate with the law (Perez y Gonzalez, 2000). Puerto Ricans expressed their frustration by demanding more autonomy from the United States.

In 1949, the United States allowed Puerto Ricans to elect their own governor, and they elected Luis Marin. Three years later, Congress approved the proposed Puerto Rican Constitution, giving the island the status of a commonwealth. Although it now had more autonomy, Puerto Rico also had significant economic problems. After sixty years of American rule, more than 50% of the total national income went to 20% of the people, and there was persistent unemployment and underemployment (Duignan & Gann, 1998).

Governor Marin proposed an ambitious economic plan called **Operation Bootstrap** that offered incentives such as a large supply of cheap labor and tax exemptions for businesses moving to Puerto Rico. Many corporations took advantage of this offer. Throughout the 1950s and 1960s, Operation Bootstrap expanded the island's industrial base and created 140,000 manufacturing jobs. Personal income rose from an annual average of $118 in 1940 to $1,200 by 1970 (Perez y Gonzalez, 2000). Tourism increased, and Puerto Rico was called the "Showcase of the Americas," but economic problems persisted. With so much land being used for industry, the number of agricultural jobs decreased, resulting in unemployment rates as high as 10%. So much land was given over for industrial use that Puerto Rico had to import food. Corporate tax exemptions required Puerto Ricans to pay higher taxes to fund the necessary improvements in sewers, roads, electricity, and water (Feagin & Feagin, 2003).

For many Puerto Ricans, the primary economic benefit was the opportunity to earn enough money to migrate to the United States. By the 1980s, more than 900,000 were living in New York City alone, comprising about 12% of the city's population, and the 3 million Puerto Ricans living in the United States represented 11% of all Latinos. Approximately 60% of Puerto Ricans lived in either New York or New Jersey, but with unemployment rates as high as 23%, nearly 60% of these Puerto Rican families lived in poverty (Banks, 2009; Duignan & Gann, 1998).

How do the experiences of Puerto Ricans in the United States compare to other Latino groups?

Puerto Ricans have encountered many obstacles in the United States. The percentages of Puerto Ricans unemployed or on welfare have been higher than for other Latino groups. In part, the high unemployment rate is the result of a decline in unskilled and semiskilled jobs in urban areas where they have settled. Puerto Rican children living in poverty have attended racially segregated urban schools without resources to provide the quality of education necessary for their students to compete for better paying jobs. One consequence of these economic and social problems is that Puerto Ricans have higher rates of drug use, drug addiction, and crime than other Latino groups. Single-parent families headed by women constitute a third of all Puerto Rican families, more than for any Latino group except Dominicans (Perez y Gonzalez, 2000). Shorris (2001) described the typical situation for many Puerto Ricans in New York City:

> Puerto Ricans work in marginal businesses; they have no unions, no benefits, nothing but the weekly paycheck, from which social security may or may not have been deducted and paid; when the marginal business goes broke after a few or even many years, . . . the loyal Puerto Rican employee is left with nothing. (p. 87)

Yet Puerto Ricans have succeeded in a variety of fields including literature, sports, politics, the arts, music, medicine, and more. For over forty years the Puerto Rican organization called Aspira has supported high school clubs to encourage Puerto Rican youth to graduate and go to college. Regardless of their success or failure, Puerto Ricans resent other Americans perceiving them as foreigners rather than regarding them as the fellow citizens that they are. If they migrate from Puerto Rico to a state, or from one state to another, Puerto Ricans should be viewed the same as a Minnesotan who moves to New York.

Today, the majority of Puerto Ricans living in the United States were born here. Puerto Ricans tend to be bilingual and bicultural, identifying themselves as Puerto Ricans but proud of their status as American citizens. Like other Latinos, they often speak Spanish at home, but young people are more likely to speak English to their peers (Perez y Gonzalez, 2000). Puerto Ricans encourage their youth to succeed, despite the difficulty of that goal. According to Shorris (2001), "Every Puerto Rican who survives and succeeds to any degree on the mainland is a miracle of love and will" (p. 144). Although they have not been as successful as other Latinos, especially Cubans, Puerto Ricans want to believe that such miracles are possible.

Why has the experience of Cubans been so different from that of Puerto Ricans?

The islands of Cuba and Puerto Rico have similar histories. Columbus and his men conquered the Taino Indians, inhabiting both islands and enslaving the residents. Yet by 1762, Cuba's capital city was twice the size of New York or Philadelphia; Havana was a port of such significance that the British captured the city and refused to give it back until Spain agreed to give up Florida in exchange. In addition to being a major trading center in the Caribbean, Cuba prospered because of its sugar production carried out by imported African slaves. By 1830, the combination of free and enslaved blacks was larger than the population of whites. By 1870, Cubans were trying to win independence from Spain; a few Cubans immigrated to the United States during the lengthy struggle that ended in 1898 when American troops prevailed in the Spanish-American War.

After four years of military rule, the United States agreed to make Cuba a sovereign nation, but the Platt amendment gave the United States the right to intervene in Cuba's affairs at any time to protect property and liberty in Cuba. For the next two decades, no Cuban who did not gain U.S. approval could be elected president nor stay in that office (Feagin & Feagin, 2008).

Even under American dominance, Cuba prospered; few Cubans immigrated to the United States until Fidel Castro's successful revolt against dictator Fulgencio Batista. After Castro announced that Cuba would be a communist nation, Cubans began leaving, most immigrating to Florida. The wealthiest Cubans left first. Those who followed in the 1960s were a heterogeneous group, but with a disproportionately high number of businessmen, professionals, and entrepreneurs. Many had been in the merchant navy; others were former government officials or were revolutionaries who were disillusioned with Castro (Duignan & Gann, 1998).

What happened to the Cubans who came to the United States?

A federally funded Cuban Refugee Program (CRP) was established to assist Cubans coming to Florida. CRP refugee centers provided resources rarely given to other immigrants (Portes & Bach, 1985). Cuban businessmen who had salvaged some of their wealth relied on traditional business methods called *socios* or *socioismo* where loans were approved not by an objective analysis but because the applicant was a friend. Cuban immigrants tended to be educated, and many had business experience. For the next two decades, Cubans used their resources to engage in business enterprises as well as to provide services such as grocery stores, legal assistance, and funeral homes. As Shorris (2001) stated, "The Cuban exiles, primarily middle- and upper middle-class, soon became middle- and upper middle-class again" (p. 67). Attracted by Cuban success in the United States and disenchanted with Castro's communism, more Cubans came.

The next wave of Cuban immigrants tended to be working-class people from urban areas (almost half from Havana alone). Many found work in businesses owned or managed by Cubans where they tended to earn higher wages. By the mid-1980s, Cuban Americans were the majority in Dade County and in Miami. Although 40% of Cuban immigrants settled in Florida, they also settled in New York, New Jersey, and California (Duignan & Gann, 1998). A 1953 Cuban census identified 72% of Cubans as white, but the 1970 U.S. census identified 95% of Cubans living in the United States as white (Portes & Bach, 1985).

Compared to other major Latino groups in the United States, Cuban Americans have recorded the highest median household incomes. One reason for their success is that, similar to Asian American families, they tend to have multiple wage earners in a household. According to a study of Cuban immigration from 1960 to 1980, about two thirds of Cuban American wives worked outside the home, and 27% of these households had additional family members earning income. The presence of Cubans in Florida has attracted an increasing number of tourists and entrepreneurs from both Central and South America, providing additional business opportunities.

Although Cuban immigrants have traditionally viewed themselves as a people in exile, that view is not shared by Cuban American youth. According to Shorris (2001), "Older Cubans say they will return to Cuba as soon as Castro dies or is deposed. The younger generation is interested only in going back to visit" (p. 75). Their attitudes are similar to Mexican American and Puerto Rican youth, as well as other Latinos living in the United States.

What other Latino groups live in the United States?

Other Hispanic immigrant groups coming to the United States in the twentieth century included Dominicans, Central Americans, and South Americans. Since the 1960s, there has been a small but steady stream of immigrants from the Dominican Republic, surging in the early 1980s because of the global recession that drove down sugar prices, creating a huge foreign debt and an unemployment rate of 30%. By the time the crisis was over, 10% of Dominicans had immigrated, primarily to the United States, with 90% settling in New York City (Duignan & Gann, 1998).

Immigrants from Central America have usually come to the United States to escape political turmoil and violence in countries such as Guatemala, Honduras, Nicaragua, and El Salvador. To address their needs, the Central American Refugee Committee (CRECE) was established to provide food, temporary shelter, work, and legal assistance. CRECE food distribution centers raise money to purchase food wholesale, and they ask for small

contributions from those taking food to help pay for the purchase of more food, making the centers a collaborative endeavor, not merely a charitable one (Shorris, 2001). As Central Americans have tended to settle in urban areas, CRECE has been a critical resource for them. So many Salvadorans have settled in Los Angeles that it has now become the second largest Salvadoran city after the nation's capitol of San Salvador.

Unlike Central Americans, who tend to come from impoverished areas, South American immigrants tend to have had the advantage of a good education, many having a doctoral degree. Some Chileans immigrated because of political repression, but few South Americans are refugees. Reasons for immigrating usually involve a desire for better jobs, higher salaries, and greater opportunity. Because they come with such resources, South Americans are reported to have the highest educational attainment and higher incomes than any other Spanish-speaking group in the United States (Duignan & Gann, 1998).

Why have many Americans objected to Latino immigration?

The primary motivation for all Latino immigrants is economic opportunity, but many have resorted to illegal means of gaining entry to the United States. Mexican Americans are the largest source of foreign labor in the United States, especially for manual labor jobs (Portes, 2007). Although the North American Free Trade Agreement that was implemented in the 1990s resulted in American industries building many factories just inside the Mexican border, Mexican workers have migrated to these border towns in huge numbers, creating a labor pool larger than the available jobs require. As a consequence, wages at these factories continue to be low, and many unemployed workers have crossed the border illegally to find work in the United States (Acuña, 2004).

In 1990, the U.S. Defense Department built an 11-mile fence along the Mexican border near San Diego as a strategy for keeping illegal drugs from being brought into the United States. This initiated a "militarization" of the Mexican border that has continued and has been extended to include denying entry to illegal immigrants (Acuña, 2004). Sociologist Douglas Massey argues that the border militarization has failed to stop the flow of drugs and has been equally ineffective at stopping illegal immigration. Militarizing the border has caused smuggling to become professionalized (Portes, 2007). Although professional smugglers are expensive, the odds of their being caught are reduced. By making the process of entering the United States more difficult, illegal immigrants tend to remain

> What the people want is very simple. They want an America as good as its promise.
>
> Barbara Jordan (1936–1996)

here, resulting in an outcome opposite to what people supporting border militarization wanted to achieve. Experts predict that the problem of undocumented workers will never be resolved until the U.S. government recognizes and facilitates historic patterns of cyclic immigrations for seasonal work between Mexico and the United States (Portes, 2007).

AFTERWORD

Human evolution is a story of survival, but once physical survival is assured, human beings create culture. The struggle to maintain one's culture while living in a new homeland with its own culture is no easy task, especially because physical and cultural differences have been used to create the concept of race. Race has then been used to divide human groups, creating subordinate races that are forced to struggle against a dominant race.

For the indigenous people in America, this struggle began when European colonists stepped on American shores. The roots of oppression expanded across the nation in the cultural and physical conflict that followed. The oppression eventually encompassed African slaves, Chinese and Japanese laborers, Mexican migrant workers, and other im-

migrants of color. This oppression was even directed against groups considered white today like Irish, Italian, and Slavic immigrants, but all European groups would eventually be offered the freedom and opportunity they sought in the United States while it continued to be denied to people of color.

Oppression based on race and related ethnic groups has been sustained by the descendants of the original European settlers, affecting people of color living in the United States and those who are coming with the same vision of freedom and opportunity that brought the first colonists. We are now a nation of nations with people from all over the world pursuing the happiness promised by a free society. If the United States is to be a pluralistic society embracing diverse groups, it must make sure that all people living in America are respected as part of our diverse national family.

By insisting on racial equality, Americans of color are simply demanding a chance to achieve the same American dream that has attracted so many immigrants to these shores. It is a dream not yet realized for far too many of them. In the poem "Let America be America Again," Langston Hughes (1994) speaks for all oppressed people who still pursue the American dream:

> America never was America to me,
> And yet I swear this oath—
> America will be! (p. 191)

myeducationlab

Now go to Topic #2: **Race** in the MyEducationLab (www.myeducationlab.com) for your course, where you can:

- Find learning outcomes for this topic along with the national standards that connect to these outcomes.
- Complete Assignments and Activities that can help you more deeply understand the chapter content by viewing classroom video and ABC News footage.
- Apply and practice your understanding of the core teaching skills identified in the chapter with the Building Teaching Skills and Dispositions learning units.

TERMS AND DEFINITIONS

Anglos   A term identifying white people who settled in Mexican territory, eventually becoming a generic term for white people

Black Cabinet   The Federal Council on Negro Affairs, consisting of thirty black professionals, served as an advisory group to President Franklin Roosevelt

Bracero Program   Initiated during World War II, this program continued to import Mexicans into the United States for twenty-two years as manual laborers

Brown v. Board of Education   The 1954 Supreme Court decision overturning *Plessy v. Ferguson* by declaring racial segregation as unconstitutional

Chinese Exclusion Act   An 1882 law prohibiting Chinese immigration to the United States, renewed in 1892, and making exclusion permanent in 1902

Emancipation Proclamation   Issued by President Lincoln to free slaves only in Confederate States and permitting free blacks to enlist in the Union Army

Ethnocentrism   Believing one's race, nation, or culture is superior to all other; also individual actions or institutional practices based on that belief

Gentleman's Agreement   The Japanese government assured the U.S. government it would issue no more passports (as of 1908) to Japanese workers except those already in the United States or their close relatives

Indian Sovereignty   Legal rights of Indian nations, confirmed by treaties with the U.S. government, to define themselves and to act as unique cultural and legal entities.

Indigenous people   A racial or ethnic group that is well established in an area before the arrival of a new group; a group that may be but does not need be native to the area in which it is established

League of United Latin American Citizens (LULAC)   A national organization for members of Spanish-speaking ethnic groups who are American citizens that is dedicated to promoting the value of citizenship, protesting discrimination, and advocating for civil rights for Latinos

Mexican American Legal Defense Fund (MALDEF)   An organization opposing discrimination and advocating for Mexican Americans' civil rights

Middle Passage   The ocean crossing of slave ships resulting in the deaths of an estimated 5 to 6 million Africans being transported as slaves

Model minority   The belief that Asian Americans have been successful because they have been willing to work hard, and that all other minorities could be just as successful if they emulated Asian American behavior

National Association for the Advancement of Colored People (NAACP)   An organization opposing racism and advocating for black civil rights

Nisei   The term for children of Japanese immigrants who were born in the United States and therefore possessed U.S. citizenship

Nomads   A group of persons with no single fixed abode who move from place to place in search of food and water

Operation Bootstrap   An economic plan for Puerto Rico during the 1950s and 1960s to boost its industrial base and create more manufacturing jobs

Picture bride   A modification of the Japanese system for arranged marriages involving the exchange of photographs between families negotiating a marriage for Japanese men who had immigrated to the United States

Treaty   A legal agreement between two or more nations involving terms of peace, trade, and other matters as agreed to by the negotiating parties

Underground Railroad   An organization that established "stations" where runaway slaves could get food and rest as they escaped north to freedom

Yellow Peril   The term for the belief that Chinese and Japanese immigrants could never be assimilated into American culture and therefore threatened the unity of American society

Zoot Suit Riots   Several days of mob violence in 1942 in Los Angeles that demonstrated anti-American prejudice as U.S. servicemen (later joined by civilians) attacked Mexican American youth, especially targeting those wearing zoot suits

DISCUSSION EXERCISES

Exercise #1 Understanding Recollections of Larry Kobori Activity

Directions: Read to learn the feelings that Larry recounts having had about the incident that he describes. Then, respond to the Insight Builder Questions below.

Larry Kobori's School Story

When I was young I noticed I was a little different from my friends. My father told me I was Japanese and that I should never be ashamed of being Japanese. He has emphasized this for as long as I remember.

When I started school everything was perfect until the fourth grade. Some kids called me a "Chink." I told them I'm Japanese, not Chinese. If I was going to be called a dirty name, at least use the proper dirty name. My friends always told me to forget those kids, that those kids were stupid. I was glad to hear my friends say that.

After a while the fourth grade things straightened out. But in the seventh grade we started to read about World War I and World War II. I knew that in World War II Japan attacked Pearl Harbor. So I worked real hard on World War I. I answered every question I could. But when it came to World War II, I never answered any questions. I would just slouch in my chair.

I guess I was feeling ashamed and embarrassed at the atrocities of Japan during World War II. But what I didn't understand was why the textbooks and the teacher glorified America's bombing of Hiroshima and Nagasaki. My teacher said thousands of civilians, including women and children, were killed by the atom bombs, thus making Japan surrender. She then added that the bombings had saved many American lives.

I then asked my teacher, "Wouldn't that be considered an atrocity since so many civilians died? That's the way you describe Japanese atrocities." I'll never forget the way she stared at me and said,

"There's a difference." Today that episode is still clear as a bell. It's something that I've never forgotten.

My three years in high school were the best years. I felt that now I was really being accepted. I was the varsity scorekeeper for three years in football, basketball, and baseball. I couldn't compete on the high school level so I did what I could to help. I learned the plays and found myself getting to know the other guys much better. I was then encouraged to write sport stories in the local newspaper. When these stories came out the sophomores and juniors wanted me to help them. As a result I got to know quite a few of them.

Outside of class sometimes it was a different story. Traveling with the basketball team, some blacks called me a "Jap." Remembering my promise I turned around and was about to call the blacks "Niggers." I restrained myself because I was sure it would lead to a fight. The same thing happened when some Mexicans called me a "Jap." Once again I refrained from retaliating.

I'll never understand why those people called me a "Jap."

Insight Builder Questions

1. What are your impressions of Larry Kobori?
2. Do you think Larry Kobori's responses to the racial incidents were appropriate ways to deal with the discrimination that he experienced?
3. Whether you agree it is appropriate or not, what alternatives did Larry have?
4. Which of them would you recommend as the best strategy?
5. In your opinion, how should teachers present the Japanese role in World War II? The use of atomic bombs on Hiroshima and Nagasaki?
6. What conditions were favorable in his school experiences?
7. What conditions were not favorable?
8. Suggest a generalization about Americans and race today.

Exercise #2 College Racial Incidents Activity

Directions: The following case studies illustrate a variety of incidents that occurred. Imagine that you are a college counselor or residence hall assistant when the student of color in each incident comes to you to report what happened. What sort of advice would you give to this student? Explain why your advice represents the best course of action for the student to follow.

1. A Puerto Rican American, Jorge, interviewed for a graduate assistantship position. The director discussed the role and responsibility of the assistantship position and indicated that the primary responsibility would be to supervise outreach activities for Hispanic students who were not using available student services. The director believed that Jorge would be a good role model and could convince students to use services since there were biological factors resulting in some people being able to learn more and to be more intelligent than others. Noting Jorge's negative response, the director said he just wanted to be open and honest about his opinions.

2. When in the Marine Corps, Leonard, a Lakota Sioux, had been stationed in the United States and Germany. After serving three years, he returned to his reservation and enrolled in a nearby college. Visiting a sweat lodge, Leonard's friends and older members of the tribe shared stories of their ancestors. When Leonard had been a child, he remembered listening to his father telling stories about his great-grandfather; he had always enjoyed learning about his family history. Now Leonard realized, however, that the stories had no meaning for him, and he could not understand the importance that his tribe placed on talking about individuals who no longer existed. Leonard found himself in conflict with his family and friends. He considered dropping out of college to get a job to earn enough money to leave and live elsewhere. But he knew there weren't many jobs for people with only a reservation high school diploma. Leonard became more depressed about the conflict he was experiencing and began to think that the only resolution was to drop out of college and reenlist for another full term.

3. Anthony, a Chinese American student transferring from community college to a four-year university, was invited to the new student orientation, where he met with his adviser. As he was leaving the adviser's office, the adviser said in a jovial and friendly tone of voice, "You know, the restaurant across the street sells the best wonton soup around." The more Anthony thought about it, the more upset he became.

4. Jessica, a 22-year-old Mexican American from central Illinois, left home to attend college in California. A few weeks into the semester she began to notice that the majority of the Hispanic students were able to speak both English and Spanish fluently. Although her parents spoke Spanish at home, they did not insist that their children become bilingual, so Jessica could understand Spanish if someone spoke to her, but she was not a fluent Spanish speaker. Jessica talked to the Chicano studies professor after class, who assured her that not all Mexican Americans share the same sociocultural experience, but that all people needed to understand and respect the values of others. He also suggested that if this situation continued to bother Jessica, she should consider seeing a counselor. In her English class, consisting primarily of white students, Jessica felt comfortable and relaxed; however, in a Chicano studies course, she felt out of place because she did not share the experiences of the other Hispanic students.

REFERENCES

Acuña, R. (2004). *Occupied America: A history of Chicanos* (5th ed.). New York, NY: Pearson Longman.

Presents a comprehensive overview of Chicano history beginning prior to the Spanish invasion of 1519 and subsequent occupation and ending with contemporary events.

Banks, J.A. (2009). *Teaching strategies for ethnic studies* (8th ed.). Boston, MA: Allyn & Bacon.

Describes history of racial and ethnic groups in the United States with additional information for teachers on developing a multicultural curriculum with teaching lessons and resources.

Berkhofer, R., Jr. (2004). *The white man's Indian: Images of the American Indian from Columbus to the present.* New York, NY: Vintage Books.

Examines legal manipulations by Europeans with regard to land claims in the new world. See especially "The Colonial Foundations of White Indian Policy."

Bieder, R.E. (1995). *Native American communities in Wisconsin, 1600–1960: A study of tradition and change.* Madison: University of Wisconsin Press.

Describes the history of Indian tribes in Wisconsin and examines the impact of efforts at the state and federal level to promote their assimilation.

Carson, C., & Carson, D.M. (2000). The Black Panther Party. In J. Birnbaum & C. Taylor (Eds.), *Civil rights since 1787: A reader on the black struggle* (pp. 618–620). New York, NY: New York University Press.

Provides a brief history of the Black Panther Party.

Chatters, J.C. (2001). Routes of passage. In *Ancient encounters: Kennewick Man and the first Americans* (pp. 239–264). New York, NY: Simon & Schuster.

Addresses archeological discoveries that place human beings in North and South America much earlier than can be accounted for by the Bering Strait theory of migration.

Chernow, R. (2004). *Alexander Hamilton.* New York, NY: Penguin Books.

Describes Hamilton's life, including his anti-slavery activities and his belief in racial equality.

Connolly, M.R. (2000, September/October). What's in a name?: A historical look at Native American-related nicknames and symbols at three U.S. universities. *Journal of Higher Education, 17*(5), 515–548.

Examines the Indian mascot issue by focusing specifically on efforts to change the mascots at the University of Illinois, Miami of Ohio, and Eastern Michigan University.

Cornelius, J.D. (2000). Literacy, slavery, and religion. In J. Birnbaum & C. Taylor (Eds.), *Civil rights since 1787: A reader on the black struggle* (pp. 85–89). New York, NY: New York University Press.

Describes how and why slaves tried to gain literacy skills, and how they used conversion to Christianity as a means of pursuing literacy.

Deloria, P. (2001). Sovereignty. In B. Ballantine & I. Ballantine (Eds.), *The Native Americans: An illustrated history.* North Dighton, MA: J. G. Press.

Defines and describes Indian sovereignty as a historical concept and explains why it continues to be an important concern for Native Americans.

Duignan, P.J., & Gann, L.H. (1998). *The Spanish speakers in the United States: A history.* Lanham, MD: University Press of America.

Describes the factors in their country of origin that motivated immigration and the experience in the United States of diverse Spanish-speaking ethnic groups.

Feagin, J., & Feagin, C.B. (2008). *Racial and ethnic relations* (8th ed.). Upper Saddle River, NJ: Pearson Prentice Hall.

Describes experience of major racial and ethnic groups in the United States.

Fitzgerald, F.S. (2005). Early success. In J.L. West (Ed.), *My lost city: Personal essays, 1920–1940* (pp. 184–192). Cambridge, UK: Cambridge University Press.

Describes the author's early years and initial success in writing.

Fitzpatrick, J.P. (1971). *Puerto Rican Americans: The meaning of migration to the mainland.* Englewood Cliffs, NJ: Prentice Hall.

Provides a historical overview of Puerto Rico and examines the migration of Puerto Ricans, especially to New York City, and what they have encountered.

Fong, T.P. (2000). A brief history of Asians in America. In T.P. Fong & L.H. Shinagawa (Eds.), *Asian Americans: Experiences and perspectives* (pp. 13–30). Upper Saddle River, NJ: Prentice Hall.

Provides an overview of immigration and their experience in the United States from the earliest arrivals to the most recent.

Fong, T.P., & Shinagawa, L.H. (2000). Employment and occupation. In T.P. Fong & L.H. Shinagawa (Eds.), *Asian Americans: Experiences and perspectives* (pp. 191–192). Upper Saddle River, NJ: Prentice Hall.

Describes content for the readings in the 5th chapter of their anthology after an opening comment (quoted) on the model minority myth.

Franklin, J.H., & Moss, A.A., Jr. (2000). *From slavery to freedom: A history of African Americans.* New York, NY: Alfred A. Knopf.

Begins with a description of the African cultures from which slaves came and presents a thorough description of the African American experience.

Gedicks, A. (1993). *The new resource wars: Native and environmental struggles against multinational corporations*. Boston, MA: South End Press.

Examines Indian resistance to corporate exploitation globally and efforts in Wisconsin to protect the environment by opposing mining plans of two multinational corporations.

Gell-Mann, M. (1994). *The quark and the jaguar: Adventures in the simple and the complex*. New York, NY: W.H. Freeman.

Integrates knowledge from research in the sciences, primarily physics, to explore various issues such as the need to preserve cultural and biological diversity (Chapter 21).

Glenn, E.N., & Yap, S.G.H. (2000). Chinese American families. In T.P. Fong & L.H. Shinagawa (Eds.), *Asian Americans: Experiences and perspectives* (pp. 277–292). Upper Saddle River, NJ: Prentice Hall.

Explains how Chinese American families have adapted to American society and identifies three family types that have emerged.

Hawkins, J. (2005). Smoke signals, sitting bulls, and slot machines: A new stereotype of Native Americans? *Multicultural Perspectives, 7*(3), 51–54.

Results of a review of seven popular middle and high school history textbooks as well as classrooms where the textbooks were being used.

Hendry, J. (2003). Mining the sacred mountain: The clash between the Western dualistic framework and native American religions. *Multicultural Perspectives, 5*(1), 3–10.

Contrasts patterns of Western thought with the perspective of Native Americans, especially with regard to their views of nature and the protection of the environment.

Hughes, L. (1994). Let America be America again. In A. Rampersad & D. Roellel (Eds.), *The collected poems of Langston Hughes* (pp. 189–191). New York, NY: Alfred A. Knopf.

A poem about the "dream" of America that was never fulfilled for people of color and poor whites.

Jacobs, H.A. (1987). *Incidents in the life of a slave girl*. Cambridge, MA: Harvard University Press.

Provides a personal account of the author's experience as a slave and her escape from slavery.

Jennings, F. (1976). *The invasion of America: Indians, colonialism, and the cant of conquest*. New York, NY: W.W. Norton.

Describes the conflict between the Pequot and Narragansett Indians in Chapter 13.

Josephy, A., Jr. (2005). *500 nations: An illustrated history of North American Indians*. London: Pimlico.

Provides information on conflicts between Indians and the dominant society.

Kar, S.B., Campbell, K., Jiminez, A. & Gupta, S.R. (2000). Invisible Americans: An exploration of Indo American quality of life. In T.P. Fong & E.H. Shinagawa (Eds.), *Asian Americans: Experiences and perspectives* (pp. 303–319). Upper Saddle River, NJ: Prentice Hall.

Presents the results of a survey and focus study research to identify the factors that have contributed to the quality of life for Indo-Americans.

Koppelman, K. (2001). Was Orwell wrong? In *Values in the key of life: Making harmony in the human community* (pp. 57–63). Amityville, NY: Baywood.

Discusses how language is used to label and divide people.

Le May, J.L. (Ed.). (1987). *Benjamin Franklin: Writings* (pp. 442–446). New York, NY: Library of America.

Franklin's comment is in "Securing the Friendship of the Indians: A letter to James Parker."

Lewis, D.L. (1993). *W.E.B. Du Bois: Biography of a race, 1868–1919*. New York, NY: Henry Holt.

Provides a thoroughly researched and detailed description of the first fifty years of the life of this African American scholar and social activist.

Lewis, D.L. (2000). *W.E.B. Du Bois: The fight for equality and the American century, 1919–1963*. New York, NY: Henry Holt.

Provides a thoroughly researched and detailed description of the last fifty years of the life of this African American scholar and social activist.

Loewen, J. (2008). *Lies my teacher told me: Everything your American history textbook got wrong*. New York, NY: The New Press.

Describes distortions and omissions of Americans of color in high school history textbooks.

Lomax, L.E. (1963). *The Negro revolt*. New York, NY: Signet Books.

Provides the historical context that was the foundation for the 1960s civil rights movement and explains the purpose and goals of this movement.

Louie, M.C. (2000). Immigrant Asian women in Bay Area garment sweatshops: "After sewing, laundry, cleaning and cooking, I have no breath left to sing." In T.P. Fong & L.H. Shinagawa (Eds.), *Asian Americans: Experiences and perspectives* (pp. 226–242). Upper Saddle River, NJ: Prentice Hall.

Describes the exploitation of Asian immigrant women working in the garment industry and their efforts to organize to improve work conditions.

Lowe, L. (2000). Heterogeneity, hybridity, multiplicity: Marking Asian American difference. In T.P. Fong & L.H. Shinagawa (Eds.), *Asian Americans: Experiences and perspectives* (pp. 412–421). Upper Saddle River, NJ: Prentice Hall.

Discusses the importance of recognizing differences between Asian American populations in their origins and in their American experience.

Lui, M. (2004). Doubly divided: The racial wealth gap. In C. Collins, A. Gluckman, M. Lui, B.L. Wright, & A. Scharf (Eds.), *The wealth inequality reader* (pp. 42–49). Cambridge, MA: Dollars & Sense.

Reviews the historical development of wealth in the United States to explain how people of color were not given the same opportunities as white Americans.

Malcolm X. (2000). The ballot or the bullet. In J. Birnbaum & C. Taylor (Eds.), *Civil rights since 1787: A reader on the black struggle* (pp. 589–603). New York, NY: New York University Press.

Presents a speech delivered in Cleveland on April 3, 1964 (after he had broken from the Nation of Islam) that is a call to work for human rights for all African Americans.

Matthiessen, P. (1993). *Indian country*. New York: Penguin.

Analyzes conflicts concerning land claims and land use between Indians and white people.

Mintz, S. (2004). *Huck's Raft: A history of American childhood*. Cambridge, MA: Belknap Press of Harvard University Press.

Describes historically shifting attitudes toward child raising in the United States and the diversity of approaches stemming from diverse cultural groups.

Painter, N.I. (2005). *Creating Black Americans: African-American history and its meaning, 1619 to the present*. Oxford, England: Oxford University Press.

Describes historical and aesthetic developments, using art work by blacks, to explain how certain people and events shaped black Americans.

Parfit, M., & Garrett, K. (2000). Hunt for the first Americans. *National Geographic, 198*(40), 40–64.

Explains how recent archaeological discoveries have changed the way anthropologists think about prehistoric Native Americans.

Perdue, T. (1998). *Cherokee women: Gender and culture change, 1700–1835*. Lincoln: University of Nebraska Press.

Examines the role of women in traditional Cherokee society and how that role was changed by contact with European colonists and ongoing relations with the dominant society.

Perez y Gonzalez, M.E. (2000). *Puerto Ricans in the United States*. Westport, CT: Greenwood Press.

Describes the history of Puerto Rico under Spanish and American rule, the causes of U.S. migration, and how Puerto Ricans have fared in the United States.

Pipher, M. (2002). *The middle of everywhere: The world's refugees come to our town*. New York, NY: Harcourt.

Presents stories about a variety of recent immigrants, including the conditions that forced them to immigrate and the difficulties they encounter trying to adjust to American culture.

Portes, A. (2007, October). The fence to nowhere. *The American Prospect, 18*(10), 26–29.

Discusses the attempts made to deny illegal immigrants entry into the United States and the factors that motivate that immigration; also suggests more effective ways to control it.

Portes, A., & Bach, R.L. (1985). *Latin Journey: Cuban and Mexican immigrants in the United States*. Berkeley, CA: University of California Press.

Provides historical context for Latino immigration, then describes an eight-year study of Cuban and Mexican immigrants and presents the results.

Raboteau, A. (2000). Slave religion, rebellion and docility. In J. Birnbaum & C. Taylor (Eds.), *Civil rights since 1787: A reader on the black struggle* (pp. 29–34). New York, NY: New York University Press.

Describes how Africans resisted slavery, even using Christianity as a tool to rebel against their slave owners.

Reiss, O. (1997). *Blacks in colonial America*. Jefferson, NC: McFarland.

Explains how slavery in the American colonies was different from historical antecedents and describes anti-slavery activities of both blacks and whites.

Shorris, E. (2001). *Latinos: A biography of the people*. New York, NY: W.W. Norton.

Provides a personal narrative of the diverse Latino groups in the United States using many personal stories told within a historical context.

Smedley, A. (2007). The arrival of Africans and descent into slavery. *Race in North America: Origin and evolution of a world view*. Boulder, CO: Westview.

Describes how Africans were procured for the slave trade, the arrival of Africans in America, and how they lost their equal status with other immigrants.

Smith, V. (2001). Cleanliness. In P. Sterns (Ed.), *Encyclopedia of European social history: From 1350 to 2000* (Vol. 4, pp. 343–353). New York, NY: Scribner.

Describes how attitudes and practices with regard to cleanliness have evolved since the Middle Ages (from a six-volume encyclopedia).

Spivey, D. (2003). *Fire from the soul: A history of the African-American struggle*. Durham, NC: Carolina Academic Press.

Presents African American history as an ongoing struggle against racism that takes different forms in different eras requiring different tactics.

Spring, J. (2001). *Deculturalization and the struggle for equality: A brief history of the education of dominated cultures in the United States* (3rd ed.). Boston, MA: McGraw-Hill.

Presents a concise history of racism in the United States with special attention given to the impact of school policies on members of subordinate groups.

Suzuki, D., & Knudtson, P. (1992). *Wisdom of the elders: Honoring sacred native visions of nature*. New York, NY: Bantam Books.

Provides information on Native American knowledge of herbal medicine, their perceptions of nature, and their efforts to interact harmoniously with nature.

Takaki, R. (1993). *A different mirror: A history of multicultural America*. Boston, MA: Little, Brown.

Describes the historical experience of diverse racial and ethnic groups in the United States.

Tijerina, R. (1971). Reies Tijerina's letter from the Santa Fe jail. In W. Moquin & C. Van Doren (Eds.), *A documentary history of the Mexican Americans* (pp. 484–487). New York, NY: Bantam Books.

Explains why the author is in jail for pursuing land claims based on the Treaty of Guadelupe Hidalgo (the treaty is also reprinted in this book).

Vargas, Z. (2000). Citizen, immigrant, and foreign wage workers: The Chicana/o labor refrain in U.S. labor historiography. In R.I. Rochin & D.N. Valdes (Eds.), *Voices of a new Chicana/o history* (pp. 153–165). East Lansing: Michigan State University Press.

Reviews research on the historic involvement of Chicano/a workers in the United States and their efforts to organize and confront their exploitation.

Vento, A.C. (1998). *Mestizo: The history, culture and politics of the Mexican and the Chicano*. Lanham, MD: University Press of America.

Describes the pre-Columbian cultures in Mexico, the conquest by Spain, and the evolution of Mexicans into Mestizos, Chicanos, and Mestizo-Americans.

Wallace, A. (1993). *The long, bitter trail: Andrew Jackson and the Indians*. New York, NY: Hill & Wang.

Describes the forced removal of the Cherokee to Oklahoma known as the "Trail of Tears."

Weatherford, J. (1988). *Indian givers: How the Indians of the Americas transformed the world*. New York, NY: Fawcett.

Identifies specific examples of Indian knowledge or products borrowed by Europeans and that in some instances have been associated with Europe (the Irish potato, German chocolate).

White, R. (2001). Expansion and exodus. In B. Ballantine & I. Ballantine (Eds.), *The native Americans: An illustrated history*. North Dighton, MA: J. G. Press.

Describes the failed efforts of Native Americans to reconstruct the world destroyed by contact with whites, and the institutions and values created to replace what was lost.

Whitty, J. (2005). Accounting coup. *Mother Jones, 30*(5), 57–63, 86.

Describes the efforts of a Blackfoot woman, a MacArthur Foundation Award recipient, to secure economic resources, especially by her class action suit.

Williams, J. (1987). *Eyes on the prize: America's civil rights years, 1954–1965*. New York, NY: Viking.

Describes the events that were responsible for an organized civil rights movement whose efforts resulted in the passage of the 1964 Civil Rights Act and 1965 Voting Rights Act.

Williams, W.C. (1954). The American background. *Selected essays of William Carlos Williams* (pp. 134–161). New York, NY: Random House.

Examines colonial ethnocentrism and provides several examples such as the robin.

Wilson, J. (1998). *The earth shall weep: A history of native America*. New York, NY: Atlantic Monthly Press.

Describes the history of Native American nations and relations with the dominant society.

Woo, D. (2000). The inventing and reinventing of "model minorities": The cultural veil obscuring structural sources of inequality. In T.P. Fong & L.H. Shinagawa (Eds.), *Asian Americans: Experiences and perspectives*. Upper Saddle River, NJ: Prentice Hall.

Describes the historical evolution of the model minority myth with an analysis of its popularity and persistence in the United States.

Woodward, C.V. (1966). *The strange case of Jim Crow*. Oxford, England: Oxford University Press.

Explains the origin and perpetuation of racial segregation in the South and the historic efforts of those opposed to it.

Woodward, G.S. (1988). *The Cherokees*. Norman: University of Oklahoma Press.

Presents the history of the Cherokee nation and their struggle to maintain culture and sovereignty despite the "trail of tears" and treaty violations.

Wu, C. (Ed.). (1972). *"Chink!" A documentary history of anti-Chinese prejudice in America*. New York, NY: World Publishing.

Reprints speeches, newspaper articles, and cartoons showing anti-Chinese prejudice; mob violence examples are in Chapter 3, "Chinaman's Chance."

Zia, H. (2000). *Asian American dreams: The emergence of an American people*. New York, NY: Farrar, Straus and Giroux.

Provides a personal perspective on the experiences of diverse Asian American groups and their encounters with prejudice and discrimination.

Zinn, H. (2003). *A people's history of the United States*. New York, NY: HarperCollins.

Presents historical events from the perspective of minority groups experiencing the events.

CHAPTER 6

Religion and Oppression: The Struggle for Religious Freedom

> ❝I wish you had a religion, Peter . . . Oh, I don't mean you have to be Orthodox, or believe in heaven and hell and purgatory and things. I just mean some religion. It doesn't matter what. Just to believe in something!❞
>
> **Anne Frank (1929–1945)**

The character of Anne Frank makes her comment about religion in *The Diary of Anne Frank,* a play based on the journal she kept during World War II until the Nazis found her. Her story has frequently been used to introduce students to the horrors of the Holocaust. At the play's end, Anne's father reads her diary and the audience hears Anne say, "In spite of everything, I still believe that people are really good at heart" (Goodrich & Hackett, 1956). Both comments affirm the goodness of humanity, regardless of differences between people. Neither comment seems to be controversial, yet some Christians have demanded that children not read the play because the remark about religion suggests that all religions are equally valid. Usually those who complain believe that one religion, their religion, is the only true faith.

Religious Diversity in Colonial America

Americans have confronted religious controversy since early colonial times when immigrant groups arrived with an array of diverse beliefs and minority faiths contended with the power of a dominant faith to survive. Honoring the principle of **religious freedom/religious liberty**—the right to worship according to one's individual beliefs—has been an ongoing struggle in America, and the history of our efforts to achieve it is the focus of this chapter.

Although religious freedom does not deny an individual's right to disagree with the beliefs and practice of another religion, it does require acceptance of divergent beliefs, as long as they don't infringe on the rights of others. The constitutional separation of church and state principle was established to resolve the problem of diverse faiths in America, and although the principle is appropriate, efforts to achieve religious liberty and the freedom to worship have been a source of dramatic conflict throughout American history.

How did the first colonists deal with religious diversity?

Puritans came to the New World to practice their religion freely, yet they had no intention of allowing others the same freedom. When Anne Hutchinson expressed religious sentiments contrary to Puritan teaching, she was excommunicated and then exiled in 1637. Roger Williams was exiled as well because he advocated respect for all religious faiths and for separation of church from state, a principle not inherent in either Puritan cultural heritage or that of other European immigrants. To reestablish Old World practices, dominant religious groups such as the Anglicans in Massachusetts expected their faith to be designated the **established church** of their colony and to be supported by an allotment of local tax dollars. Miller (1976) described this perspective: "The established religion with its educated ministers and stately rituals was an important element in creating or re-creating the world they left behind" (p. 26).

English colonists discovered that it was difficult to create an established church in the New World. Parishioners wishing to take care of their families could not afford to give their churches much financial support; therefore, the need for support from colonial governments was greater than had been required in England, which placed a significant fiscal burden on scarce colonial revenues. Furthermore, immigrants represented diverse faiths—Presbyterians, Quakers, Baptists—who were resentful when colonial tax revenues were expended to support a church to which they did not belong.

Religious resentment was mutual. Northern colony Puritans particularly disliked Quakers because of their ecstatic worship and their practice of allowing women to be church leaders. In Massachusetts, blasphemy laws were enacted to force Quakers out, threatening them with death if they returned. When they did return, authorities promptly arrested them; four Quakers were executed between 1659 and 1661. The executions stopped only because authorities in Britain were embarrassed, insisting that Quakers be sent to London for proper trials (Miller, 1976).

Most American colonies enacted blasphemy laws directed at those who did not belong to the colony's majority faith. Blasphemy was defined as an individual denying the truth and authority of the Bible. If anyone denied the divinity of Christ he could be executed or at least lose his property. Although violating blasphemy laws usually did not result in death, punishments could be quite severe, especially for freethinkers and atheists. According to a 1699 Maryland law, blasphemers, typically people who were using language that degraded Christ, the Apostles, or the Holy Trinity, were to be branded with a "B" for a first offense, have a hole burned through their tongue with a red-hot iron for a second offense, and have their property confiscated for a third offense. In a humanitarian gesture, some colonies allowed blasphemers to avoid punishment by publicly asking to be forgiven (Myers, 1960).

As colonies designated "established churches," blasphemy laws also required ministers from other churches to register as "dissenters" and agree to practice only after receiving colonial approval. Dissenting ministers sometimes refused to register and preached whenever they wished; however, there were consequences. In 1771, a sheriff accompanied by an Anglican minister disrupted a church service by arresting the Baptist minister, taking him to a nearby field and whipping him (Waldman, 2006). Being a minority faith, Baptist ministers were often arrested, sometimes with an effect opposite of what was intended. At one point when Baptist ministers were being aggressively pursued, arrested, and jailed for unauthorized preaching, the number of Baptist converts increased dramatically (Miller, 1976). Conversion efforts were customarily focused on those colonists who attended but were not members of a church or on those not attending a church, a majority in the colonies.

By 1775, more than 150 years since the first colonists arrived, approximately 10% of Americans were church members (Lippy, 1994). Although groups such as Puritans and Quakers came to the colonies to plant the seeds of faith in fertile ground, most immigrants came instead to escape physical destitution and moral despair. They hoped to achieve material success: to own their own land and to provide for their families. They wanted a better life on earth, not in heaven. Preachers from minority faiths focused on those who attended church with little enthusiasm or those who may have found a better material life but longed for satisfaction of spiritual needs. The competition for converts intensified the desire for religious freedom.

How did the colonies promote the concept of religious freedom?

Because of the influence of Roger Williams, William Penn, and Lord Baltimore, the colonies of Rhode Island, Pennsylvania, and Maryland declared religious freedom for those of any faith. Puritans regarded their faith as a "light to the world," so they often forced people to accept it. Williams argued that people could not develop true faith through coercion, and expressed the need for a "wall of separation between the garden of the church and the wilderness of the world" (Nord, 1995, p. 135). With a Baptist majority in Rhode Island, the arrival of Quakers tested the colony's commitment to religious freedom. Williams personally disliked Quakers and attacked them in his writings, but general tolerance prevailed as religious freedom was maintained, attracting some intolerant Puritans and a small group of Jews settling in Newport. Quakerism eventually became the dominant religion in Rhode Island (Miller, 1976).

William Penn believed that God spoke directly to individuals through the conscience and that this was the basis for a commitment to religious freedom. Penn undertook deliberate efforts to bring to Pennsylvania people from diverse faiths: Anabaptists, Presbyterians, Puritans, Roman Catholics, and others who had no religious conviction. Pennsylvania was the first colony to experiment with the idea of denominational churches instead of an established church; no church received state assistance, nor did the state interfere in church affairs. Members of a denomination were not expected to withdraw from the world but to participate in it.

As might be expected, Pennsylvania's "holy experiment" was not without problems. Because Penn was a Quaker, Quakers had more government

> (If) Papists and Protestants, Jews and Turks, may be embarked in one ship . . . none of the Papists, Protestants, Jews or Turks (should) be forced to come to the ship's prayer or worship nor compelled from their own particular prayer or worship, if they practice any.
>
> **Roger Williams (1603–1683)**

influence than other denominations, and for a time they functioned as an informal established church. Although Quaker dominance caused some friction, compared to other colonies, Pennsylvania and Rhode Island provided the clearest alternative to

the Old World tradition of state support for an established church.

Founded by Lord Baltimore, Maryland was originally intended as a refuge for English Catholics. The principle of religious freedom was self-serving because Catholics constituted a minority even among the first contingent settling Maryland, and Catholicism remained a minority faith throughout the colonial period. Still, Baltimore's commitment to religious tolerance attracted immigrants from diverse faiths. But Maryland's experiment was not successful: The Church of England became its established church in 1702. Because three other faiths—Anabaptists, Presbyterians, and Quakers—had more members, the Church of England was established on condition that religious tolerance would be maintained. Such tolerance was reserved for the currently residing religious groups; incoming Jews and Unitarians were not allowed to settle in Maryland at that time (Hudson, 1973).

How was the principle of religious freedom established in all the colonies?

As the mid-eighteenth century approached, a significant event (later termed the "Great Awakening") promoted the principle of religious freedom, beginning with ideas in the widely read writings of Jonathan Edwards and other New England ministers. Concerned about the "extraordinary dullness" of people's faith, Edwards challenged individuals to demonstrate personal commitment to their faith in their everyday lives, and he spoke of the necessity of faith being emotional as well as rational. Edwards argued that we can be told honey is sweet, but to taste honey results in a knowledge that is "direct, intuitive, certain, and rests upon experience that can be neither doubted nor denied" (Gaustad & Schmidt, 2002, p. 59). Edwards believed that such "knowledge" was the substance of genuine faith.

In 1740, English preacher George Whitefield presented his similar challenge to colonial people, with dramatic results. (See Figure 6.1.) Although Protestant ministers throughout the colonies invited him, Whitefield avoided churches, preferring to speak in open fields. His sermons stimulated people's emotions as much as their intellect, and audi-

FIGURE 6.1
Whitefield's impact on colonial America is commemorated in this statue on the University of Pennsylvania campus.

Source: Photo courtesy of the University of Pennsylvania.

ences responded enthusiastically. Whitefield insisted that being a Christian was not about belonging to a particular church, but being committed to faith and demonstrating that commitment in everyday life. Ironically, his sermons resulted in a huge increase in church attendance and church members. Nord (1995) describes a sermon in Philadelphia where Whitefield looked up to the sky and shouted:

> Father Abraham, whom have you in heaven? Any Episcopalians? No! Any Presbyterians? No! Any Independents or Methodists? No, no, no! Who have you there? . . . We don't know those names here. All who are here are Christians . . . Then God help

us to forget party names and become Christians in deed and truth. (p. 103)

The impact of the Great Awakening on religious freedom was that it denied the significance of differences between Protestant sects. Prior to the Great Awakening, Protestants belonged to one sect or another, each defining itself as the "true faith." This **sectarian** view of Christianity gave way to a consensus about what it meant to be Christian: accepting others, doing good deeds, and ignoring theological controversy. The Great Awakening replaced a sectarian approach to Christianity with a **denominational** view based on the perception of a singular Protestant church that is called—denominated—by many different names such as Anglican, Lutheran, or Baptist. Although the denominational view united Protestants, Catholics were not included.

The Emerging Concept of Religious Freedom

In the mid-eighteenth century, Europeans were making significant discoveries based on scientific inquiry. Isaac Newton alone was responsible for discovering the principles of gravitation and light; he also developed differential calculus and even had time to invent the reflecting telescope. The dissemination of ideas and inventions during this era, eventually called "the Enlightenment," created an increased respect for science and a diminished belief in miracles and the supernatural. Some argued that religious truths, like scientific truths, would be discovered by human reason, not through divine revelation. This thinking led to the birth of **Deism,** a

> I do not believe in the creed professed by the Jewish church, by the Roman church, by the Greek Church, by the Turkish church, by the Protestant church nor by any church that I know of. My own mind is my own church.
>
> **Thomas Paine (1737–1809)**

religious philosophy based on rationality that was devoid of mysticism. Deists acknowledged that God created the universe but insisted that human beings must use their intellects to understand the rational principles by which the universe functions. In response to the increased emphasis on rationality and the scientific method as the preferred means of ascertaining truth, many intellectuals rejected all religious faiths. Although some American colonists declared themselves **atheists,** denying the existence of God, the religious philosophy of Deism was more appealing than atheism to Christian intellectuals in the colonies.

What was the relationship between Deism and Christianity?

Deism dismissed much of what constituted traditional Christian beliefs. Deists believed God created the world and a system of natural laws that governed it. Although they believed that God would reward or punish the soul after death, they did not believe that God was an active force in the everyday world. Thomas Jefferson and Benjamin Franklin were among many who were attracted to Deism as a religious philosophy. Although Deists denied the divinity of Christ, they tended to admire his moral teachings; therefore, many Deists attended churches of various denominations while others never went to church. Although Deist views were not popular among the general public, the principles of Deism influenced several people who would write the documents that transformed the thirteen colonies into the United States of America. Curiously, these "enlightened" founders included little about religion in the Constitution.

Why was there so little reference to religion in the original Constitution?

Although the majority of men responsible for writing the U.S. Constitution were Protestant and of European descent, they chose to defy their European traditions and create the first secular government. For centuries, the governments of most European nations claimed to derive their authority from God; therefore, the state had both the right and the responsibility to intrude into religious issues

and attempt to resolve religious controversies, usually in favor of a majority faith and against minority faiths. The Articles of Confederation had continued that tradition by referring to "the Great Governor of the World" (Jacoby, 2005, p. 30), but

> The government of the United States of America is not in any sense founded on the Christian Religion.
>
> **John Adams (1735–1826)**

the authors of the U.S. Constitution cited "We the People" as the source of the government's power and authority, deliberately excluding any reference to God. When challenged to explain this omission, Alexander Hamilton's tongue-in-cheek response was "We forgot" (Chernow, 2004, p. 235).

They did not forget. When the delegates met in Philadelphia in 1787, they were well aware of the debate that had recently occurred in Virginia. In the early 1780s, Patrick Henry unsuccessfully lobbied to have Christianity declared Virginia's established religion. In 1784, he introduced a resolution calling for a tax on Virginians to promote Christianity but allowing them to designate their denomination or even a particular church as the recipient of their tax dollars. Those belonging to no church could contribute their taxes to a general education fund. This resolution gained wide support, even receiving George Washington's endorsement. On November 11, the Virginia legislature voted 47 to 32 in favor of the resolution, but the legislative session was dismissed shortly after this vote.

The opposition to this resolution and the legislation it called for was led by James Madison, soon to be a major contributor in drafting the U.S. Constitution. Madison saw the dangers inherent if such legislation would be enacted, and he wrote a pamphlet to describe them. Waldman (2006) cited Madison's major concern: "Who does not see that the same authority which can establish Christianity, in exclusion of all other Religions, may establish with the same ease any particular sect of Christians, in exclusion of all other Sects?" (p. 36). Madison's pamphlet was widely distributed and generated widespread support for his arguments. By the time the Virginia legislature reconvened, they were inundated with petitions and documents espousing staunch opposition to establishing Christianity as Virginia's state religion, some even coming from Christians—especially evangelical Christians.

Based on the previous passage of his resolution, Patrick Henry brought a bill to the Virginia legislature to establish Christianity as the state religion, but it was soundly defeated. Later, the legislators discussed Thomas Jefferson's "Statute for Religious Freedom," which they modified slightly before passing, making this legislation not only state law, but also a model for other states and for the first amendment that guaranteed religious freedom in the United States.

Why wasn't religious freedom guaranteed in the Constitution?

By the time of the Revolutionary War in 1776, four colonies had guaranteed the right of people to worship as they chose: Rhode Island, Pennsylvania, Delaware, and New Jersey. The Church of England remained the established church in other colonies; however, during the war one colony after another ceased providing church support. By the war's end, only Massachusetts, New Hampshire, Connecticut, and Virginia continued to have established churches. In 1786, the new nation was still struggling to function under its first constitution, entitled the Articles of Confederation, when the delegates met in Philadelphia to write the new Constitution. Especially after what had just transpired in Virginia, most of them did not question the issue of religious freedom, nor did they appear interested in debating it.

The delegates did debate other issues, however, such as what civil rights should be granted to those who were not Protestant. New Jersey's constitution stated that every officeholder had to be Protestant, a provision not revised until 1844. Some states required all those seeking public office to recite an oath that they had no allegiance to any foreign power—"ecclesiastic as well as civil" (Myers, 1960, p. 46). Of course, a devout Catholic could not take such an oath, which was the reason it was required. Some states merely demanded that an officeholder be a Christian; Maryland, which eventually permit-

ted Jews to settle, stood alone as the only state that allowed Jews to vote and hold public office. Obviously, Jefferson's wall between church and state had yet to be built.

As they wrote the Constitution, the authors affirmed the principle of religious freedom by stating, "No religious Test shall ever be required as a Qualification to any Office or public Trust under the United States" (Article VI). When completed, this was the only reference to religion, and it was not widely supported. At the debate over ratifying the Constitution in North Carolina, a minister protested that Article VI was "an invitation for Jews and pagans of every kind to come among us" (Jacoby, 2005, p. 30).

To secure consensus for the Constitution, the question of having an established church was left to each state. Because religious freedom was a well-established principle in most states, the authors may have thought there was no need to include such a statement until it became obvious that several amendments would be necessary before enough states would ratify the Constitution. Eck (2001) describes how Jefferson used the "Statute for Religious Freedom" he had written for Virginia's legislature in 1786 when he drafted the First Amendment's explicit guarantee of religious freedom.

Nord (1995) argued that much of the impetus for religious freedom stemmed from the Enlightenment belief that "natural reason, operating in a free culture, was the way to the truth" (p. 108). Yet most church leaders supported the First Amendment for similar reasons, especially evangelical Christians. They were concerned about separating church and state because they had already been persecuted and harassed. Evangelicals equated religious persecution with political persecution and insisted that Christ called for separating church and state in the statement: "render unto Caesar that which belongs to Caesar." Jefferson's letter espousing a "wall of separation between church and state" was written to Connecticut evangelicals who were pleased by his comments, saying to him in response, "Religion is at all times and places a matter between God and individuals" (Waldman, 2006, p. 38). Ministers such as Ezra Stiles believed that through competition, truth would prevail: "Here Deism will have its full chance; nor need libertines . . . complain of being overcome by any weapons but the gentle, powerful ones of argument and truth" (Hudson, 1973, p. 110).

Did the First Amendment establish religious freedom in the new nation?

Although the freedom to worship according to one's personal religious beliefs was guaranteed in the Bill of Rights, it was guaranteed in principle more than in practice. Of the two states still supporting an established church, Connecticut ended its tax subsidies to the Congregational Church in 1817, and Massachusetts did the same in 1833 (Myers, 1960). Yet having a minority faith could still affect one's political rights. As the Constitution was being ratified by the thirteen states, only three of them—Pennsylvania, Maryland, and Delaware—permitted Catholics to vote. Within five years of the Constitution's ratification, three more states—South Carolina, Georgia, and New York—granted the vote to its Catholic citizens, and eventually the remaining states did the same (Myers, 1960).

Because of their numbers, Jews exercised limited political influence, encountering intolerance early in the colonial period when Jewish immigrants were forced to depart from Boston as soon as they arrived. More than three decades after the Constitution was approved, Maryland was the only state where Jews could vote or hold public office. During the Civil War, General Ulysses S. Grant expelled Jews from areas he had reclaimed by military conquest for the United States; however, President Lincoln rescinded Grant's order (Miller, 1976). North Carolina granted civil rights to Jews in 1868; New Hampshire granted Jews the right to vote in 1876.

A Challenge to the Separation of Church and State

In 1810, Congress mandated Sunday mail service. Conservative Christian leaders lobbied aggressively against it, denouncing Sunday mail delivery as a sacrilege, but business leaders insisted on the necessity of uninterrupted mail. In 1828, the controversy came to the Senate Committee on the Post Office and Post Roads. Kentucky senator Richard M. Johnson, a war hero and devout Baptist, chaired the committee, yet in his report to Congress, he declared unequivocally that it would be unconstitutional for the federal government to engage in policy or practice that betrayed a preference for the Christian Sabbath. In the report, Johnson emphasized the history of religious persecution and intolerance that had created the need for a line separating church and state, and that "the line cannot be too strongly drawn" (Jacoby, 2005, p. 31). In the 1840s, the telegraph ended the reliance of business on daily mail service, but the principle of separation of church and state had been upheld.

Was any group actively persecuted for their religious beliefs?

Religious freedom was violently denied to the followers of Mormonism, the Church of Jesus Christ of Latter-Day Saints, which was founded on the revelations of Joseph Smith in the early 1800s. After his *Book of Mormon* was published in 1830, Smith found followers captivated by his new vision of the past and his responses to major religious controversies of the day. He aroused animosity among traditional Christian denominations by his promotion of polygamy and other ideas deemed unconventional and unacceptable in American society. Smith's first church in Ohio was not welcomed, and when the members moved to Missouri, they were attacked and forced to leave, eventually settling in Nauvoo, Illinois. They lived there for only a few years before Smith was arrested and incarcerated at nearby Carthage, where a masked mob broke into his cell, and shot and killed him. Miller (1976) declared, "The rise of Mormonism tested the American dedication to religious liberty, and the nation ultimately failed the test" (p. 111).

FIGURE 6.2 The Mormon Trail

To escape persecution, the Mormons headed west and did not stop until they had left the United States and reached the safety of Mexican territory.

Source: © by Intellectual Reserve, Inc.

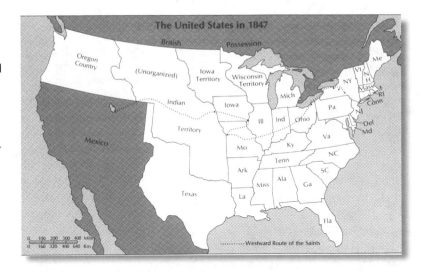

When Brigham Young was chosen to replace Smith, he was convinced that the Mormons would not be granted religious freedom anywhere in the United States, so he asked them to follow him "to a far distant region . . . where bigotry, intolerance, and insatiable oppression lose their power" (Gaustad & Schmidt, 2002, p. 178). In 1847, Young and his followers began an ambitious journey of a thousand miles, finally stopping to settle on land that belonged to Mexico. (See Figure 6.2.) One year later, as the Mexican-American War ended, the Great Salt Lake Valley where the Mormons had settled became part of the United States. Because there was no one close enough to persecute the Mormons, they successfully populated the territory of Utah and applied for statehood. Their application was denied six times until 1897, when they changed their state constitution to renounce polygamy (Kosmin & Lachman, 1993).

Religious freedom was also not extended to those who rejected religious beliefs. Atheists in Virginia could be arrested for publicly professing that God did not exist. In 1833, Abner Kneeland was arrested and incarcerated in Massachusetts for questioning the divinity of Jesus, his miracles, and his resurrection. Kneeland was convicted under the state's blasphemy law and sentenced to sixty days in jail; however, his conviction resulted in vigorous protests. Kneeland was the last person convicted of blasphemy in Massachusetts, although the law was not repealed for many years (Miller, 1976).

The Rise and Fall of Anti-Catholicism

In contrast to the slow but steady growth of members in Protestant churches, membership in the Catholic Church increased dramatically. By 1850, the number of Catholics in the United States had expanded from several hundred thousand to nearly 2 million. Between 1820 and 1865, of approximately 2 million Irish immigrants to the United States, over a million were Catholic (Kosmin & Lachman, 1993). Because of its assistance to Irish immigrants, the New York City political and labor organization known as Tammany Hall became a powerful force influencing the city and state of New York, which intensified anti-Catholic sentiments.

What was the impact of large numbers of Catholic immigrants?

Immigrants have almost always provoked hostility in some Americans, but the arrival of so many Catholics fueled Protestant fears and created an atmosphere of suspicion and distrust. Because the Catholic Church had persecuted, tortured, and even killed those who defied its authority in the past, Protestants believed that Catholics would not hesitate to employ any tactic that would convert Protestants to the Catholic faith. Several popular novels, including *The Awful Disclosures of Maria Monk,* described Protestant women being kidnapped and confined in underground cells in convents and subjected to unspeakable tortures.

Following a fistfight between laborers at a Charlestown, Massachusetts, convent and brickyard workmen, the workmen spread rumors that the convent had imprisoned a woman just as the novels suggested. Although published results of an investigation said there was no truth to the rumor, a mob gathered and set fire to the convent. No police or militia appeared. Ten fire engines responded to the call, but the fire brigades insisted they could not

> We have just enough religion to make us hate.
> But not enough to make us love one another.
>
> **Jonathan Swift (1667–1745)**

act without orders from a magistrate, so they watched as the convent was destroyed. A meeting of Protestants called by the mayor of Boston produced a formal statement denouncing the mob's actions, but the Catholic Church never received compensation for its losses (Myers, 1960).

Why was hostility directed against Catholics?

The 1830s and 1840s was the era of Native American and Know-Nothing parties promoting **anti-Catholicism** and anti-immigrant sentiments. The Know-Nothings dedicated themselves to reducing a perceived growth of Catholic power and influence. Anti-Catholic prejudices were also reflected in public school textbooks in which priests were depicted as living in luxury, oblivious to the poor and hungry, and the Catholic Church was described as the enemy of freedom and knowledge because of its history of religious persecution and its suppression of the Bible (Miller, 1976). It is not surprising that at this time the Catholic Church felt compelled to create an alternative school system, increasing Protestant animosity toward Catholics.

Protestants were not opposed to separate schools for Catholics, but in 1840, Bishop Hughes of New York created controversy when he petitioned the

New York Public Schools Society for funds to support Catholic schools. Hughes argued that separate schools for Catholic children had become necessary because of anti-Catholic materials in public schools. Protestants objected to using tax dollars to teach "Catholic dogma" and accused the bishop of trying to undermine public schools. Hughes provided excerpts from textbooks that ridiculed Catholicism, including one book in which the Catholic Church was accused of encouraging drunkenness to maintain its hold on church members who would reject the "Romish religion" if they could only think rationally (Myers, 1960). Although the New York Public Schools Society denied Hughes's petition for funds, they agreed to remove anti-Catholic content from textbooks and to exclude from school libraries books that clearly promoted anti-Catholic prejudice. Although this seemed to solve the problem in New York, growing anti-Catholic sentiment would lead to the shocking events of the Philadelphia Bible Riots.

What were the Philadelphia Bible Riots?

In 1844, the Philadelphia School Board approved the substitution of the Douay (Catholic) Bible for Catholic students when Bible reading was required. The Native American Party called for a meeting in Kensington, an Irish Catholic district in Philadelphia, to protest the use of the Catholic Bible in public schools. The meeting provoked area residents, who attacked participants and forced the meeting to end. Native American Party leaders insisted on a second meeting in Kensington, which resulted in violence that left one person dead and fifty wounded.

The following day, a large crowd gathered to approve a resolution in support of teaching the Protestant version of the Bible in public schools. The meeting soon became uncontrollable, and when the mob heard shots fired from a nearby building, they set fire to that building and went on a rampage. Troops were called in, but before they could restore order, several homes had burned, eight men were dead, and sixteen were wounded. The night was quiet, and there was no further violence the next morning. Most of the soldiers withdrew.

By midafternoon, a Protestant mob gathered once again, setting fire to a Catholic Church and a nearby row of houses whose tenants were Irish.

Troops were recalled, but before they arrived, the mob attacked another church. This time the police surrounded the church, but the mob drove them off with bricks and stones and set fire to that church and a Catholic school; then the fire spread to frame houses nearby. The troop commander summoned to Philadelphia declared martial law. Property losses from the riots included forty-five homes, two churches, and a school. Violence flared again a month later, and by the time the Philadelphia Bible Riots were finally over, 58 people had been killed and 140 wounded. The Native American Party blamed the Irish for the deaths and injuries and even for the destruction of churches and homes in Irish neighborhoods (Myers, 1960; Ravitch, 1999). Although anti-Catholic sentiment would remain strong for another decade, other issues and events would command the nation's attention.

What caused anti-Catholic sentiments in the United States to subside?

Nord (1995) concluded, "The politics of race and the Civil War put the politics of anti-Catholicism to rest" (pp. 73–74). Although the Great Awakening unified Protestant churches, they were split over the slavery issue. During the Civil War, Catholic soldiers fought and died as bravely as the Protestant soldiers beside them, and anti-Catholic sentiments declined. After the war, anti-Catholic prejudice still existed and flared up on occasion, yet it never reached the level that fostered the rise of the Native American and Know-Nothing parties. Another factor in the decline of anti-Catholic prejudice after the Civil War was that the Catholic Church was no longer the only serious opponent for Protestant churches. Religious diversity in the United States was about to increase dramatically.

How did religious diversity increase following the Civil War?

After the Civil War, immigration to the United States surpassed prewar levels. By 1900, there were 75 million Americans, 25 million of whom were foreign-born adults and their children. The number of Roman Catholics in the United States increased from 2 million in 1850 to 4 million in 1870 to 12 million by 1900. Although Protestants continued to be the dominant group, a third of Americans who claimed church membership in 1920 were members of the Catholic Church (Hudson, 1973).

Catholic immigrants came from Germany, Ireland, Poland, Italy, and Czechoslovakia, their ethnic diversity creating tension in the church. Not only did they speak different languages, but also they had different traditions and customs related to their worship. The church's inability to resolve ethnic differences led to the creation of the Polish National Catholic Church in the 1890s and the Lithuanian National Catholic Church in 1914. Protestant churches faced similar challenges. The majority of Protestant immigrants were Lutherans whose diversity resulted in Finnish, Icelandic, Swedish, Danish, German, and Norwegian Lutheran churches. According to Hudson (1973), there were at least twenty-four different kinds of Lutheran churches by 1900.

Diversity also resulted from missionaries proselytizing Native Americans and former slaves. Minimal efforts to reach either group had been made prior to the Civil War because both groups had been perceived as heathen. The Great Awakening had generated some enthusiasm for seeking Indian converts, but Native Americans who accepted Christianity usually blended new beliefs with their old ones. Following the Civil War, the federal government banned many tribal religions and provided missionaries with funding to build schools for Indian children. Protestants often established off-reservation boarding schools, whereas Catholics tended to establish boarding schools and day schools on reservations (Hendry, 2003).

Although Christian ministers were willing to evangelize and recruit slaves into the faith, many slave owners were reluctant to have their captives converted. They approved of conversion only if ministers emphasized the need for the slaves to submit to both divine and earthly authorities with the promise of eternal life as their reward for enduring slavery in this life (Lippy, 1994). After the Civil War, Protestant missionaries actively recruited the 3.5 million newly freed slaves. Former slaves who were Christians no longer wanted to attend the churches their owners had forced them to attend, especially when the church members still expected former slaves to sit in the back seats. Separate churches for freedmen were established, the majority being Baptist with Methodists a distant second. By 1916, 43% of blacks were members of a church, a higher percentage than for the white population (Hudson, 1973).

As racial and ethnic groups added to the diversity, so did the creation of new faiths. Mary Baker Eddy responded to the growing importance of scientific research by founding Church of Christ, Scientist. Eddy spoke of an Eternal Mind as the source of life, and believed that disease was a consequence of mental error. Christian Scientists sought to overcome the illusions that have been the source of all human troubles (Lippy, 1994).

William Miller was abandoned by "Millerites" in 1844 when his prediction about Jesus returning did not come true. Many of his former followers turned to Ellen Harmon White, whose spiritual revelations included hygienic practices and dietary restrictions for the faithful to ensure the return of Jesus; White's followers became Seventh-Day Adventists. Adding to the complexity of diverse faiths in the late nineteenth century, was the fact that all immigrants were not simply Christian.

What non-Christian religions were included among immigrants?

Immigrants to the United States included members of non-Christian religious groups. On the West Coast, Buddhists among Chinese and Japanese immigrants established a Young Men's Buddhist Association in 1898. On the East Coast, 1.5 million Jews came to America between 1880 and 1905 to escape anti-Semitism in Russia, Poland, Rumania, and Austro-Hungary. Hudson (1973) cites an adviser to the czar predicting the consequences of new Russian policies: "One-third of the Jews will emigrate, one-third will be baptized, and one-third will starve" (p. 332).

Diversity increased within the Jewish community as well. In 1880, most of the 250,000 Jews in the United States were descendants of German-speaking Jews from central Europe affiliated with reform Judaism; Jews emigrating later from Eastern Europe were more likely to be orthodox than reform. According to Hudson (1973), more than 3 million Jews had immigrated by 1920, with orthodox Jews outnumbering reform Jews. The largest Jewish group, larger than the total number of all religious Jews combined, comprised those not affiliated with any synagogue; many of them were Zionists whose activity was more likely to be political than religious.

America also experienced an increase in people professing no religion. Darwin's theory of evolution and other scientific advances caused many people to question the validity of religious faith. English scientist Thomas Huxley declared himself an **agnostic,** believing that one could neither prove nor disprove the existence of God. Lawyer and orator Robert Ingersoll published *Why I Am an Agnostic* in 1896 and traveled across America questioning many aspects of Christianity. Still, some scholars

> A believer is a bird in a cage: a freethinker is an eagle parting the clouds with tireless wing.
>
> **Robert Ingersoll (1833–1899)**

reconciled Darwin's ideas with religion by believing in God, just not in specific denominational doctrines. The Christian majority reacted by punishing those who strayed from conventional beliefs as well as nonbelievers. In 1878, Alexander Winchell publicly rejected the Genesis version of creation, and Vanderbilt University trustees asked him to resign. When Winchell refused, they abolished his position. In 1886, James Woodrow was removed from his faculty position at Columbia Theological Seminary for advocating the possibility of reconciling Darwin's ideas with those of the Bible (Hudson, 1973).

Did increasing numbers of non-Christians cause anti-Catholic prejudice to diminish?

Although racial prejudice became more dominant than religious prejudice after the Civil War, a large Catholic immigration fueled anti-Catholic attitudes. Protestant leaders called for tolerance, yet others said tolerance meant a lack of religious commitment and an indifference to the true faith, and urged Protestants not to give equal status to any other religion.

Forced to disband by federal troops during Reconstruction, the Ku Klux Klan was revived in 1915. In their efforts to promote and maintain white supremacy in the United States, the Klan employed tactics of intimidation including threats and violence. Although their primary targets were blacks and foreigners, as a Christian group, its

FIGURE 6.3
The Ku Klux Klan had its highest membership when the group sponsored this 1925 march in front of the nation's capitol.

Source: Library of Congress, Prints and Photographs Division

members were also hostile to Catholics and Jews. Membership in the Klan increased every year for ten years, peaking at 2 million in 1925. (See Figure 6.3.) It fell to 100,000 by 1928. At a 1941 rally in Charleston, the Grand Dragon of North Carolina was heckled and booed by many of the 3,000 who attended (Myers, 1960). The last time the Klan's anti-Catholicism would be seen on the national stage was in the presidential election of 1928.

How did the 1928 election demonstrate anti-Catholic prejudice?

The Democratic Party nominated Alfred E. Smith, the first Catholic to run for president. Some political and religious leaders hailed the nomination as evidence of growing religious tolerance; others saw it as a threat to the social order. The Klan and other anti-Catholic organizations insisted that the Vatican was directing Smith's campaign with a Jesuit committee assigned to persuade Protestants to ignore Smith's religion as an issue. Presbyterians were urged to vote for the Republican candidate. Methodists were urged to vote for the man who prayed the same way they did. Myers (1960) quoted an excerpt from an anti-Catholic magazine

claiming that Smith would get not only the Catholic vote, but also "the Jew and Negro vote . . . gamblers, the red-light and dope-ring vote . . . the Jew-Jesuit movie gang (vote) who want sex films and Sunday shows to coin millions through the corruption of youth" (p. 268).

Although anti-Catholic prejudice contributed to Smith's defeat, it is not clear how large a role it played. Democrats were the minority party, the economy was doing well, and Republican candidate Herbert Hoover was widely respected. Despite the anti-Catholic assault, Smith received 40% of the vote, more than the Protestant Democratic candidates had received in the two previous elections (34% in 1920, 28% in 1924). Smith had a higher percentage of votes than a majority of Democrats running for Congress in that election (Hudson, 1973).

After Franklin Roosevelt was elected president in 1932, Catholic participation in national politics became common, and the question of whether a Catholic could be elected president was answered in 1960 when Americans chose John F. Kennedy. It is possible that Kennedy's election was not so much a measure of increased religious tolerance as it was an indication of what has been called the "Americanization of religion." Since World War II, attitudes of

American Catholics gradually diverged from a strict recognition of Roman Catholic Church doctrine and more closely allied with attitudes of the Protestant majority. By the 1990s, polls documented Catholic

> Anti Semitism is a noxious weed that should be cut out. It has no place in America.
>
> **William Howard Taft (1857–1930)**

attitudes as similar to Protestant attitudes on such issues as abortion, birth control, ordination of women, and marriage of priests (Kosmin & Lachman, 1993).

How were Jews affected by the "Americanization of religion"?

In the late 1880s, Jews contended that they should be regarded as another denomination and accepted in the same spirit as Methodists, Baptists, or Lutherans. They were unsuccessful partly because at that time Jews were defined as a race more than a religion, a transformation that began in 1451 when the King of Castile endorsed a blood purity statute (*limpieza de sangre*), declaring that Jews who converted to Christianity could not hold office in the Catholic Church. Carroll (2001) explained that the concern for blood purity was "a shift from a religious definition of Jewishness to a racial one" (p. 347). By the nineteenth century, the transformation in Europe of societal perceptions of Jews from religious to racial was complete. Nazi Germany could justify arresting Jews who had converted to Christianity because "once born a Jew, always a Jew" (Wegner, 2002, p. 152).

Anti-Semitism in America

By 1870, American public school textbooks referred to Jews as "a race" with traditional stereotypes of Jews as greedy, selfish, and manipulating. Jews were described as unethical entrepreneurs who tried to monopolize certain professions and as the

devious power behind the throne in many European countries (Miller, 1976). In 1879, the term **anti-Semitism** was employed for the first time by a German journalist to express his opposition to the Jewish "race." In his essay, Wilhelm Marr made the paradoxical argument that although Jews were inferior to Aryans, they were a threat to Aryan world dominance (Carroll, 2001). Reacting against such pervasive stereotypes, one Jewish writer complained, "In the popular mind, the Jew is never judged as an individual, but as a specimen of a whole race whose members are identically of the same kind" (Eck, 2001, p. 303). This judgment would continue in the "popular mind" for many more decades.

From 1890 to 1914, Jews accounted for 10% of all immigrants. With increased numbers of Jews in America, anti-Semitism was at least as strong as earlier anti-Catholicism. Ironically, despite their experience of oppression, Catholics joined Protestants in vilifying Jews. In the popular press, Eck (2001) found Jews presented as undesirable aliens who could not assimilate because they were "incapable of grasping American ideals" (p. 50), although many Jews refuted the view by achieving extraordinary success, especially in higher education. As the number of Jews at Harvard escalated from 6% in 1908 to 22% in 1922, the president of Harvard proposed establishing a quota for the number of Jews Harvard would accept. Faculty rejected his plan, but Harvard still limited the number of Jews for many decades. Other colleges established quotas for Jewish enrollment at anywhere from 3% to 16% (Dinnerstein, 1994).

In what ways was anti-Semitism promoted?

Anti-Semitism had several popular advocates. In the 1920s, one was Henry Ford. In his role as publisher of a weekly newspaper, *The Dearborn Independent,* Ford printed the text of "The Protocols of the Elders of Zion," which documented the activities of a Jewish conspiracy plotting a revolution to undermine Christian civilization and establish Jewish supremacy throughout the world. Ford's popularity made it likely that his readers would take his warning seriously. In a poll taken in 1923, *Collier's* magazine reported that 260,000 people—over a third of those polled—endorsed Ford to run for president (Ribuffo, 1997).

Shortly after Ford published "Protocols," the document was exposed as a forgery concocted in the late 1890s by Russian loyalists supporting the czar. In response to this revelation and to a legal action for slander brought by a Jewish businessman, Ford wrote a letter of apology, promising not to publish anti-Semitic articles again, but the damage had been done. Ford ceased publishing his newspaper, yet he continued to maintain and express anti-Semitic attitudes. In 1938, Ford traveled to Germany to receive a medal from Adolf Hitler in honor of his anti-Semitic actions, and two years later in England during an interview with the *Manchester Guardian,* Ford insisted that "international Jewish bankers" caused World War II (Ribuffo, 1997).

In the 1930s, President Franklin Roosevelt invited many Jews into his cabinet, and over vigorous objections, he appointed a Jew to the Supreme Court, Felix Frankfurter. However, anti-Semitism found a spokesman in a priest named Charles Edward Coughlin. In his popular radio show, Father Coughlin attacked President Roosevelt, communists, and Jews. Although reprimanded for his attacks on the president, church superiors did not criticize Coughlin's anti-Semitism because he disguised it in anti-communist rhetoric (Myers, 1960).

In 1938, Coughlin revealed his anti-Semitic attitudes by reprinting "The Protocols of the Elders of Zion" despite the evidence of its forgery. Nineteen thousand people attended a gathering in Madison Square Garden where Coughlin gave a speech, surrounded by banners declaring "Smash Jewish Communism!" and "Stop Jewish Domination of Christian America!" Coughlin's use of rumor and distortions of fact to castigate Jews was challenged by Jewish groups, denounced by Protestants, and contradicted by his embarrassed superiors in the church. He was forced to abandon his radio program in 1940, but for the next three years, young men belonging to his "Christian Frontier" organization roamed the streets in several large cities, affixing obscene materials to Jewish businesses or synagogues and even assaulting Jews they chanced to encounter (Myers, 1960).

During World War II, anti-Semitism intensified. Dinnerstein (1994) quotes an Irish soldier who was

> (The Jew) always talks about the equality of all men, without regard of race or color. Those who are stupid begin to believe that.
>
> **Adolf Hitler (1889–1945)**

disturbed by the anti-Semitism of soldiers who told him,

> All the Jews stay out of the army, or if they get in, they are given commissions—the President is a Jew—you can't get a defense contract unless you are a Jew—Jews own 80% of the nation's wealth—Jews got us into the war. (p. 137)

According to a poll conducted during the war, over half of Jewish soldiers in the armed forces had changed their names to generic American surnames to avoid anti-Semitic remarks from other soldiers. Even Jews in Roosevelt's cabinet were excluded from private clubs catering to people in power. By the end of the war, 58% of Americans agreed with the statement, "Jews have too much power in the United States" (Dinnerstein, 1994, p. 146).

What influence did the Holocaust have on American attitudes?

Learning about the horrors of the Holocaust changed American attitudes toward Jews after World War II. Many returning veterans deplored anti-Semitism and other prejudices they had witnessed. Hollywood produced films exposing the prejudice and bigotry of anti-Semitism in America, and one of them, *Gentleman's Agreement,* won the Oscar for best picture in 1947. Editorials in many newspapers and magazine articles reinforced the idea that anti-Semitism was no longer acceptable in the United States. Although it was in the 1950s that "under God" was added to the Pledge of Allegiance and "In God We Trust" to U.S. currency to emphasize U.S. opposition to "godless communism," being a Catholic, Protestant, or Jew was less important than being someone who believed in the Judeo-Christian God (Fraser, 1999).

In his analysis of religion in America, *Protestant-Catholic-Jew,* sociologist Will Herberg (1955) wrote that Catholics and Jews reflected American attitudes as much as Protestants did. An "Americanization" of religion meant that each faith "regards itself as merely an alternative and variant form of being religious in the American way" (p. 278). Herberg admitted that the majority of Americans were still anti-Semitic, but they knew it was inappropriate to act on their feelings. *Look* magazine reported that Hitler had made anti-Semitism unequivocally disreputable. A series of polls in the 1950s reported Americans expressing increasingly positive attitudes toward Jews. Discrimination against Jews still occurred, especially in such prestigious professions as law and medicine, yet doors had opened, especially to colleges and universities. By 1965, *Time* magazine reported that "anti-Semitism is at an all time low," and that overt expressions of anti-Semitism were "out of fashion" (Dinnerstein, 1994, p. 171). However, a national immigration law was passed in 1965 that would challenge Americans with a new religious dilemma.

The Impact of Immigration Reform on Religious Diversity

The 1924 U.S. immigration law had prohibited Asian immigration, and strict quotas ensured that the majority of American immigrants would be white and Christian. When President Lyndon Johnson signed the Immigration and Nationality Act of 1965, not only did the racial makeup of incoming immigrants change dramatically, but their religious affiliation did as well. From 1960 to 1990, Asians constituted more than 5 million of 15 million immigrants to the United States, and from 1990 to 1999, the Asian population grew 43% to total almost 11 million people. They increased the religious diversity within and outside of Christianity; among them were 4 million Buddhists and enough Korean Christians to form 2,000 congregations. Jainists have established 60 temples and centers and Sikhs have 80 temples (Gaustad & Schmidt, 2002). Of the more than a million Hindus in the United States, 170,000 live in New York City alone. Nationwide, America can claim over 6 million Muslims, more than the number of Presbyterians and equal to the number of

Jews (Eck, 2001). There are increasing numbers of children from diverse faiths: About 20% of students attending public school in the United States identify as "religious minorities" (Clark et al., 2002).

Although proportions of those representing different religions have changed, what has not changed is the importance of religion. According to Elshtain (2001), data from the 2000 census report that 90% of Americans believed in God and 70% were members of a church, synagogue, or mosque. To appreciate this variety of faiths, Americans must confront stereotypes. We often make assumptions about an individual's religion based on his or her ethnicity, although there is religious diversity within any religion. An old stereotype is that Irish Americans are Catholic, even though the majority of Irish Americans are not. Most Asian Americans are not Buddhist or Hindu but instead are Christian, as are most Arab Americans, and most American Muslims are not Arabs (Kosmin & Lachman, 1993).

How have Americans responded to the increasing religious diversity?

Unfortunately, recent immigrants continue to encounter prejudice as Americans persist in their past religious animosities and revert to learned stereotypes. Muslim Americans have received the brunt of these negative reactions, in part because they are the largest religious minority in America. With 6 million Muslims now residing in the United States, including 4 million who were born here, Muslims have now surpassed Jews to become the second largest religious group in the nation (McCloud, 2006). But the primary reason for Barrett (2007) reporting that 75% of Muslims have personally experienced or know someone who has encountered anti-Muslim behavior is related to the terrorist activities carried out by extremist members of the Muslim faith. Americans have used the terrorist activities of some Muslims to stereotype all Muslims, including American Muslims. This has especially troubling implications for education, as illustrated by a study assessing how much pre-service teachers knew about the Islamic faith. Taggar (2006) reported the study's finding that one third of the pre-service teachers associated Islam with such negative words as "enemy," "Bin Laden," "terrorist," and "oppression of women." Only 5% of the future teachers said they would make sure their students understood that all Muslims were not terrorists.

Some American Muslims accuse television news programs of perpetuating Muslim stereotypes. Abdo (2006) has argued that: "television news programs (portray) Muslims as the new enemy of the West" (p. 5). This was illustrated following the 1995 bombing of the Murrah Federal Building in Oklahoma city when television broadcasts suggested that it was a terrorist attack and that authorities were pursuing "Middle Eastern-looking" men; the backlash was immediate. Islamic centers across the nation were sites for drive-by shootings and bomb threats. Muslim students on college campuses were assaulted. Muslim parents kept their children home for fear they would be taunted or even assaulted in school.

What the media did not report was the presence of Muslim firefighters rescuing victims of the bombing, Muslim physicians working to save victims' lives, and individual Muslims and Muslim organizations donating money to help the families of the victims. Despite their efforts, Muslims were denied an opportunity to participate in the nationally televised memorial service featuring words of consolation from President Clinton and representatives of Catholic, Jewish, and Protestant faiths.

Similar to the reaction following the Oklahoma City incident, media coverage of the 1996 crash of TWA Flight 800 prompted many Americans to suspect that Muslim terrorists were responsible despite the lack of any evidence to support their suspicions. According to Khan (2004), this was another example of American media promoting the "demonization of Islam . . . and the prejudice, hatred and intolerance it bred" (p. 100). Anti-Muslim behaviors have included arson at mosques in Minneapolis and Quincy, Massachusetts, and a shotgun attack on Muslims in Memphis.

Anti-Muslim activity increased after the destruction of New York City's World Trade Center on 9/11. More than 8,000 Muslim Americans and Arab Americans were immediately interrogated, and within a few weeks, approximately 1200 were incarcerated. This action was called a "preventive detention"; the prisoners were held without charges, they were denied the opportunity to post a bond, and they were not allowed any contact with their families (Abdo, 2006). Two months later, 600 were still held in custody, yet the FBI eventually admitted

that they had no evidence linking any of the people incarcerated to terrorist activities. Of the 82,000 Muslim immigrants who were eventually fingerprinted and interrogated under the Patriot Act, officials could only find enough evidence to declare 11 of them as "suspected" terrorists (Lee, 2004). Such actions have caused McCloud (2006) to claim that no other religion has been treated in such fashion in the history of America, noting that, "Even the Christianity of Nazi Germany (was) not demonized but considered an abomination" (p. 6). According to Nimer (2004), in the thirty days following 9/11, Muslims filed 1,700 complaints of harassment and hate crimes. One man drove his car through the plateglass doors of an Ohio mosque, a Texas mosque was firebombed, and mosques were vandalized in Tallahassee, Cleveland, and Seattle. The violence has not been restricted to Muslims; Buddhist and Hindu temples were vandalized in Boston, Houston, and Detroit. An Egyptian businessman who had resided in the United States for twenty years was shot and killed in his California store. He was a Christian.

McCloud (2004) argues that while Muslims have been accused of violence and terrorism, it was the U.S. government that imprisoned Muslims without charging them with a crime, and individual Americans who have violently attacked mosques and Muslims. It is heartening that most Americans reject the violent discriminatory acts of bigots. Neighbors and community advocates for victims of violence directed at religious groups have responded with kindness, sympathy, and offers of support. Positive responses have consistently countered negative actions against recent immigrants of diverse religious faiths. American Muslims have tried to distance themselves from terrorist activities while emphasizing Islam as a religion of peace. In 2005, the Islamic Society of North America disseminated a statement not only condemning extremism and violence, but also calling on all American Muslims to openly denounce such actions (Barrett, 2007). Some Americans have been critical of other American Muslim organizations for not making a similar statement, but the reality is that every major Islamic organization in the United States has issued a statement condemning terrorist violence (Abdo, 2006). If Americans are not aware of this, it is probably because the American media has rarely reported on these proclamations, especially the national media. In addition to denouncing terrorism, Muslims in the United States have recognized the importance of interacting with people to clarify beliefs and practices of the Islamic faith. Smith (2004) cites a Bagby survey of American Muslims reporting that 65% of them had participated in an interfaith activity.

As the United States has become home to believers from diverse faiths, some American individuals and organizations have engaged in activities to recognize this diversity and to promote interactions among members of many faiths. Since 1991, Muslim and Hindu chaplains have joined Protestant, Catholic, and Jewish chaplains to open each session of the House of Representatives and the Senate with invocations. Administrators of the Mall of America in Minneapolis, the largest enclosed shopping facility in the United States, have created an interfaith group called the Mall Area Religious Council to promote interfaith dialogue and conversations between people of different religions and cultures. Is American interfaith support a harbinger of the future as business and community leaders come to terms with the implications of religious diversity? At a Whirlpool manufacturing plant in Nashville, Tennessee, a Muslim employee quit when he was refused permission to perform his

> The First Amendment has erected a wall between church and state. That wall must be kept high and impregnable.
>
> **Justice Hugo Black (1886–1971)**

midday prayers; those Muslim employees who remained prayed secretly. After a Muslim support group intervened, Whirlpool managers agreed to schedule afternoon coffee breaks to accommodate the Islamic prayer schedule (Eck, 2001).

Universities and colleges have increasingly promoted interfaith dialogue. Wellesley College developed a Multi-Faith Council, Chapman (CA) University created an All-Faiths Chapel, and Johns Hopkins University instituted an Interfaith and Community Service Center; in each, faiths as diverse as Baha'i, Buddhist, Christian, Jewish, Muslim, and Hindu may come to worship or to talk with

members of other faiths. Interfaith discussions not only address commonalities between faiths but encourage honest dialogue concerning differences in beliefs (Eck, 2001). It is essential that students at colleges and universities engage in religious discussions because religious freedom requires understanding of different faiths. Public and private educational institutions from elementary grades through high school must also play a critical role in fostering that understanding.

How have schools taught students about the concept of religious freedom?

The history of American education reveals a gradual secularization of public schools. Public schools in the United States originally did not teach about religious freedom; they reinforced Protestant beliefs, causing Catholics and Jews to establish schools for their children in addition to or instead of public schools. History credits Horace Mann with shaping public schools in the United States, yet he was denounced as the "archenemy of the Christian church" for advocating that the Bible should be read—but not interpreted—in school because biblical interpretation should be a parental prerogative (McMillan, 1984, p. 85). When Bible reading was eliminated, *McGuffey's Reader* became the most popular public school textbook. It referred to God and used Protestant perspectives to deliver its moral lessons. Later revisions of McGuffey eliminated overt religious language but maintained a sermonizing tone. By 1870, most Protestants agreed that a sectarian religious perspective should not be presented in public schools, but that a nonsectarian Christian perspective was essential (Nord, 1995).

Starting in the 1940s, U.S. federal courts wrote several decisions related to the constitutional guarantee of religious freedom being enforced or contradicted in schools (see Table 6.1). The next sixty years of court rulings would challenge schools to eliminate their Christian bias and to become more **secular,** reflecting the civic culture and not promoting any religious perspective. U.S. courts have ruled that schools are forbidden to force students to say the Pledge of Allegiance, compel students to pray, begin the day with devotional reading from the Bible, have a minister, priest, or rabbi give a prayer at graduation, post the Ten Commandments in

TABLE 6.1 Court Rulings on Religion in Public Schools (a selection of significant cases)

1943 *West Virginia v. Barnette* (brought by a Jehovah's Witness family): No child can be forced to recite the Pledge of Allegiance.

1947 *Everson v. Board of Education:* Students attending parochial schools could be transported to their schools on buses provided for public school students.

1962 *Engel v. Vitale:* Students attending public schools could not be forced to recite state written prayers.

1963 *Abington Township v. Schempp:* Public schools could not insist that students recite the Lord's prayer or any prayer nor require "devotional Bible reading."

1968 *Epperson v. Arkansas:* An Arkansas law forbidding the teaching of Darwin's theory of evolution in school was ruled unconstitutional.

1971 *Lemon v. Kurtzman:* Established that the separation of church and state principle was not violated if the statute, policy, or practice under consideration: (1) had a secular legislative purpose; (2) did not foster excessive government entanglement with religion; (3) neither advances nor inhibits religion as its primary purpose.

1980 *Stone v. Graham:* A Kentucky law requiring a copy of the Ten Commandments posted in every public school classroom was declared unconstitutional.

1985 *Wallace v. Jaffree:* Since the intent of an Alabama law requiring a moment of silence was "to return prayer to the public schools," it was unconstitutional.

1987 *Edwards v. Aguillard:* Schools could not teach creationism as an alternative to evolutionary theory because creationism was based on religious beliefs and did not satisfy the criteria to constitute a scientific theory.

1990 *Westside Community Schools v. Mergens:* If a public school allows community groups to use its facilities, religious groups must have equal access.

1992 *Lee v. Weisman:* Schools could not include prayers offered by religious leaders (of any faith) at graduation ceremonies; if a school policy or practice has a coercive effect, it is unconstitutional.

2000 *Santa Fe School Independent School District v. Doe:* Student-led prayers at football games violated separation of church and state.

Source: The religious history of America: The heart of the American story from colonial times to today by E. Gaustad and L. Schmidt, 2002.

classrooms or hallways, or teach religion disguised as science—"creationism"—as a scientific alternative to evolutionary theory (Allen, 1996; Fraser, 1999; McMillan, 1984).

In 2002, the Ninth Circuit court created a controversy in *Newdow v. United States Congress* by ruling that the inclusion of the phrase "under God" meant the Pledge of Allegiance served a religious, not a secular purpose. The court concluded that schools could not have students recite the pledge even if they are allowed to choose to not participate because the school setting is a coercive context that puts pressure on students to conform to the majority (Pauken, 2003).

How can public schools teach about religion in a way that respects all religions?

As federal and district courts ruled on what schools could not allow, they also provided guidelines for constitutional activities. Schools were encouraged to teach objectively about all religions, and even about the Bible. As Justice Clark wrote,

It might well be said that one's education is not complete without a study of comparative religion or the history of religion and its relationship to the advancement of civilization. It certainly may be said that the Bible is worthy of study for its literary and historic qualities. (McMillan, 1984, p. 163)

Although schools cannot force students to pray, they cannot prevent a student from praying, as long as the prayer does not create a disruption. If students representing a religious group want to use school facilities, they have the same right of access as any community group.

In 1999, the U.S. Department of Education sent comprehensive guidelines on issues related to religion in public schools to every public school in the nation. A committee of diverse religious and educational leaders had developed the guidelines that include legal assurances for recommended practices (al-Hibri, 2001). Teaching *about* religions has now been incorporated into national and state standards for teachers (Douglass, 2002); following the guidelines will ensure that schools address those standards by providing accurate information about fundamental beliefs of the world's major religions.

AFTERWORD

Although historically the Protestant majority in the United States resisted accepting other faiths vigorously, at times even violently, Protestants of all denominations accepted each other on equal terms and eventually accepted Catholics and Jews. Will the faiths of new immigrants—Hinduism, Buddhism, Islam, and other non-Christian religions—become acceptable to the dominant Judeo-Christian groups in America? Although U.S. courts have consistently upheld the principle of religious freedom, schools will also have an important role to play.

In the past, public schools promoted Protestantism and reinforced anti-Catholic and anti-Semitic attitudes. As schools became more secular, they engaged less in proselytizing and contributed to the resolution of conflicts among Protestants, Catholics, and Jews. Because current immigration has increased non-Christian religious diversity in the United States, it is important that public schools continue to affirm court decisions and use the

guidelines offered by the Department of Education. Students need to learn more about other religions.

If the United States is to be successful as a religiously diverse society, it is essential that "the principal religious groups not only claim freedom for

> We establish no religion in (America), we command no worship, we mandate no belief, nor will we ever. Church and state are, and must remain, separate. All are free to believe or not to believe, all are free to practice a faith or not, and those who believe are free, and should be free, to speak of and act on their belief.
>
> **Ronald Reagan (1911–2004)**

themselves, but affirm equal freedom for others, whatever their beliefs may be" (Katz & Southerland, 1968, p. 269). As students learn about diverse religions they may also come to appreciate why religious freedom was guaranteed in the Bill of Rights, and why it has been so difficult to achieve that ideal.

myeducationlab

Now go to Topic #5: **Religion** in the MyEducationLab (www.myeducationlab.com) for your course, where you can:

- Find learning outcomes for this topic along with the national standards that connect to these outcomes.
- Complete Assignments and Activities that can help you more deeply understand the chapter content by viewing classroom video and ABC News footage.
- Apply and practice your understanding of the core teaching skills identified in the chapter with the Building Teaching Skills and Dispositions learning units.

TERMS AND DEFINITIONS

Agnostic   A belief that human beings cannot prove or disprove the existence of God

Anti-Catholicism   Expressing stereotypes about or prejudices against Catholics or discriminating against Catholics

Anti-Semitism   Having anti-Jewish prejudices or stereotypes, or engaging in discrimination against Jews

Atheism   Believing that God does not exist

Deism   A belief that God created the world and the system of natural laws that governed the world, but was not a presence (and did not play a role) in everyday life

Denominations   A perspective on diverse Protestant faiths that views all of them as a singular Protestant church with different names (denominations)

Established church   When one church is declared the official faith of a political unit (a colony or state) and tax revenues are used to fund this church

Religious freedom/religious liberty   The right to worship in any church of one's choice consistent with that church's beliefs and practices

Sectarian   A perspective on diverse Christian churches or sects in which an individual regards his or her own sect as the "true faith"

Secular   The civic culture of a society not reflective of religious perspective

DISCUSSION EXERCISES

Exercise #1 Separation of Church and State Activity

Directions: Read the situation below and decide which requests for changing school policy from the following list will be implemented (Agree) and which requests for change will be rejected (Disagree). On completion of your group's consideration of the twelve proposed rule changes, compare your recommendations with those of other groups.

The Situation: It is December 5. As a citizen and parent, you have been publicly assigned to a select committee to examine a list of new school district policies that has been proposed by a group of Jewish parents. Twenty-five percent of the students in the district are Jewish, 15% have no religious affiliation, and 60% declare some sort of Christian affiliation.

Proposed District Policies:
Breaks and Absences

1. Vacation breaks during the school year will be established without regard to religious holidays.

2. Jewish children will be excused when they are absent on Jewish holidays.
3. Jewish teachers will not be charged with personal leave when they are absent during Yom Kippur and Rosh Hashana.

Religious Holidays

4. No celebration of Christmas as part of the school curriculum.
5. No celebration of Hanukkah as part of the school curriculum.
6. No creche will be displayed in school.
7. No Christmas trees will be displayed in school.
8. No gift exchanges or Christmas parties in class.

Curricular and Extracurricular Activity

9. Impact of religious values on historic or current events and issues will be examined and discussed in the classroom.
10. The Holocaust will be studied as part of the World War II unit and as part of the history of Western civilization.

11. No extracurricular activity will be scheduled on Friday evening.
12. No songs that refer to Jesus Christ will be sung in the winter music program.

Exercise #2 Religious Freedom in the United States: What Is Your Judgment?

Directions: The following list contains incidents that have actually occurred. Determine which items you believe violate the rights of people to behave in accordance with their chosen faith.

Religious Freedom in the United States

1. Should a Sikh be allowed to wear his turban on a hard-hat job even though it appears to be a violation of safety regulations?
2. Can a soldier who is a member of Wicca practice his or her religion on an army base?
3. Should Hindus be forced to build their temple with a "Spanish" architectural style that will match the other buildings in a Southern California community instead of building it based on their traditional temple architecture?
4. Because a Jainist student attends the high school, must the cafeteria staff clearly mark the contents of the meals prepared so that the student can be assured of eating only vegetables?
5. Can a Muslim woman teaching in a public school wear her traditional head covering in her classroom?
6. Should members of the Native American Church be allowed to ingest peyote because this drug has historically been part of their religious rituals?
7. Should a Florida city council allow members of the Santeria faith to engage in animal sacrifice because it is traditionally part of their religious practice?
8. Should a Sikh student come to school with the symbolic knife (*kirpan*) he is required to wear following his initiation?
9. Should Muslim employees be given time to perform obligatory prayers during the workday?
10. Do Seventh-Day Adventist or Jewish employees have the right to be excused from work on Saturday because it is their Sabbath?

REFERENCES

Abdo, G. (2006). *Mecca and Main Street: Muslim life in America after 9/11.* Oxford, England: Oxford University Press.

Describes the efforts of a variety of Muslim Americans to live in the United States and to maintain their faith while being confronted with stereotypes, prejudice, and discrimination.

al-Hibri, A.Y. (2001). Standing at the precipice: Faith in the age of science and technology. In A. al-Hibri, J.B. Elshtain, and C.C. Haynes (Eds.), *Religion in American public life: Living with our deepest differences.* New York, NY: W.W. Norton.

Explains how the Industrial Revolution produced a mechanistic model and how it has affected the United States, including how the country approaches issues such as the separation of church and state.

Allen, R.S. (1996). *Without a prayer: Religious expression in public schools.* Amherst, NY: Prometheus.

Provides the human story behind the Supreme Court cases on religion in public schools, including the consequences for those individuals who brought those cases forward.

Barrett, P.M. (2007). *American Islam: The struggle for the soul of a religion.* New York, NY: Farrar, Straus and Giroux.

Describes the perceptions and experiences of a variety of Muslim Americans based on interviews conducted after the terrorist attacks on 9/11.

Carroll, J. (2001). *Constantine's Sword: The church and the Jews, a history.* Boston, MA: Houghton Mifflin.

Examines the history of relations between the Catholic Church and the Jews and explains the basis for the historic pattern of anti-Semitism that still exists in the church.

Chernow, R. (2004). *Alexander Hamilton.* New York, NY: Penguin Books.

Describes Hamilton's life, especially his influence on the American Federal government.

Clark, C., Vargas, M.B., Schlosser, L., & Allmo, C. (2002, Winter). It's Not Just "Secret Santa" in December: Addressing educational and workplace climate issues linked to Christian privilege. *Multicultural Education*, pp. 53–58.

Describes the ways Christianity is affirmed or promoted in subtle and blatant ways at work and in schools, and provides a religious dilemma at a worksite for group discussion.

Dinnerstein, L. (1994). *Anti-Semitism in America*. New York, NY: Oxford.

Summarizes the experience of Jews in America and the various forms of anti-Semitism they have encountered from the colonial period to the present.

Douglass, S. (2002). Teaching about religion. *Educational Leadership, 60*(2), 32–36.

Reports findings from a study of the inclusion of religion in national and state teaching standards and discusses resources and strategies for implementing these standards.

Eck, D.L. (2001). *A new religious America: How a "Christian Country" has become the world's most religiously diverse nation*. New York, NY: HarperCollins.

Examines the growth of diverse religions in the United States, especially with regard to immigration patterns since 1965, and describes both its impact and its potential.

Elshtain, J.B. (2001). Faith of our fathers and mothers: Religious belief and American democracy. In A. al-Hibri, J.B. Elshtain, & C.C. Haynes (Eds.), *Religion in American public life: Living with our deepest differences* (pp. 39–61). New York, NY: W.W. Norton.

Defines the concept of the civil society in America while examining how responsibility for religious rights has become increasingly relegated to the courts in the United States.

Fraser, J.W. (1999). *Between church and state: Religion and public education in a multicultural America*. New York, NY: St. Martin's.

Describes the history of religious diversity in the United States from the colonial beginnings to the present, and examines the critical court cases on religious freedom.

Gausted, E., & Schmidt, L. (2002). *The religious history of America: The heart of the American story from colonial times to today*. New York, NY: HarperCollins.

Describes the diversity of American religions, the historical conflicts between religious faiths, and the growing acceptance of religious diversity.

Goodrich, F., & Hackett, A. (1956). *The diary of Anne Frank*. New York, NY: Random House.

Presents ideas and events recorded in Anne Frank's diary; this Pulitzer Prize–winning play was first performed on Broadway in the fall of 1955.

Hendry, J. (2003). Mining the sacred mountain: The clash between the Western dualistic framework and Native American religions. *Multicultural Perspectives, 5*(1), 3–10.

Contrasts patterns of Western thought with the perspective of Native Americans, especially with regard to their views of nature and the protection of the environment.

Herberg, W. (1955). *Protestant-Catholic-Jew: An essay in American religious sociology*. Garden City, NY: Doubleday.

Examines the status of religion in the United States in the early 1950s and explains how the three major religions have achieved equal status in American society.

Hudson, W.S. (1973). *Religion in America: An historical account of the development of American religious life* (2nd ed.). New York, NY: Charles Scribner.

Describes the religious life of Americans from separate faiths moving toward common principles and eventually toward the pluralistic attitudes necessary for religious liberty.

Jacoby, S. (2005). Original intent. *Mother Jones, 30*(7), 29–31, 74.

Examines the historical record to argue that the founders of America did not want to create a state based on religion but separate from religion.

Katz, W., & Southerland, H. (1968). Religious pluralism and the Supreme Court. In W. McLoughlin & R. Bellah (Eds.), *Religion in America* (pp. 269–281). Boston, MA: Beacon Press.

Examines the role played by the Supreme Court in moving the United States from a nation tolerating religious diversity toward the goal of promoting religious pluralism.

Khan, M.A.M. (2004). Living on borderlines: Islam beyond the clash and dialogue of civilization. In Z.H. Buhhari, S.S. Nyang, M. Ahmad, & J.C. Esposito (Eds.), *Muslims' place in the American public square* (pp. 84–113). Walnut Creek, CA: Altamira Press.

Describes actions taken against Muslims for practicing their religion and discusses the need for acceptance of religious diversity in America.

Kosmin, B.A., & Lachman, S.P. (1993). *One nation under God: Religion in contemporary American society*. New York, NY: Crown.

Analyzes results from the 1990 National Survey of Religious Identification with data from 113,000 Americans; this was one of the most extensive religious surveys ever conducted.

Lee, E. (2004). American gate keeping: Race and immigration law in the twentieth century. In N. Foner & G.M. Frederickson (Eds.), *Not just black and white: Historical and contemporary perspectives on immigration, race and ethnicity in the United States* (pp. 119–144). New York, NY: Russell Sage Foundation.

Examines changes in racial composition of immigrants since the 1965 immigration reform.

Lippy, C.H. (1994). *Being religious, American style: A history of popular religiosity in the United States.* Westport, CT: Praeger.

Describes religious beliefs and practices of Americans from colonial times to the present that supplement or replace beliefs and practices from traditional religions.

McCloud, A.B. (2004). Conceptual discourse: Living as a Muslim in a pluralistic society. In Z.H. Buhhari, S.S. Nyang, M. Ahmad, & J.C. Esposito (Eds.), *Muslims' place in the American public square* (pp. 73–83). Walnut Creek, CA: Altamira Press.

Examines the role of the media in creating negative images of Muslims and the inconsistency of American responses to Muslims with American values.

McCloud, A.B. (2006). *Transnational Muslims in American society.* Gainesville: University of Florida Press.

Examines the experiences of Muslims who have recently become citizens of the United States and the success of their various strategies for adapting to American culture.

McMillan, R.C. (1984). *Religion in the public schools: An introduction.* Macon, GA: Mercer University Press.

Examines the historical background of the separation of church and state principle and provides the written Supreme Court decisions on major cases with minimal editing.

Miller, G.T. (1976). *Religious liberty in America: History and prospects.* Philadelphia, PA: Westminster.

Provides a history of conflicts related to religious diversity in the United States and progress made toward religious liberty with an emphasis on the period prior to the twentieth century.

Myers, G. (1960). *History of bigotry in the United States* (rev. ed.), G. Christman (Ed.). New York, NY: Capricorn.

Describes the historic targets of bigotry since colonial days, with emphasis on Catholics, Jews, and immigrants, and the actions taken against these minorities by the majority.

Nimer, M. (2004). Muslims in the American body politic. In Z.H. Buhhari, S.S. Nyang, M. Ahmad, & J.C. Esposito (Eds.), *Muslims' place in the American public square* (pp. 145–164). Walnut Creek, CA: Altamira Press.

Discusses the violence against Muslims after the Oklahoma City bombing and after 9/11, and the growing political activism of American Muslims.

Nord, W.A. (1995). *Religion and American education: Rethinking a national dilemma.* Chapel Hill: University of North Carolina Press.

Addresses current dilemmas involving religion in public schools and establishes a middle ground to accommodate religion while maintaining the principle of religious liberty.

Pauken, P. (2003, January). *I Pledge Allegiance to the Curriculum: The establishment clause and the legal balance between educational authority and individual rights.* Presented at the Hawai'i International Conference on Education, Honolulu.

Reviews court cases concerning the First Amendment's guarantee of religious liberty and the legal principles that have evolved, especially with regard to religion in the schools.

Ravitch, F.S. (1999). *School prayer and discrimination: The civil rights of religious minorities and dissenters.* Boston, MA: Northeastern University Press.

Provides an overview of the history of religious intolerance and currently legal religious practices in public schools and provides a model statute to promote religious freedom.

Ribuffo, L.P. (1997). Henry Ford and the international Jew. In J. Sarna (Ed.), *The American Jewish experience* (2nd ed., pp. 201–218). New York, NY: Holmes & Meier.

Traces Henry Ford's involvement in anti-Semitism through a series of articles in his newspaper and describes Ford's impact on anti-Semitic attitudes around the world.

Smith, J.I. (2004). Muslims as partners in interfaith encounter. In Z.H. Bukhari, S.S. Nyang, M. Ahmad, and J.L. Esposito (Eds.), *Muslims' place in the American public square* (pp. 165–197). Walnut Creek, CA: Altamira Press.

Describes seven models for interfaith dialogue and examines the problems and benefits of such dialogues in general and for Muslims specifically.

Taggar, S.V. (2006). Headscarves in the headlines! What does this mean for educators? *Multicultural Perspectives 8*(3), 3–10.

Examines teacher responses to Muslim students since 9/11, focusing on three urban high school teachers who represent distinctly different ideological perspectives.

Waldman, S. (2006). The framers and the faithful. *Washington Monthly, 38*(4), 33–38.

Discusses historical evidence that evangelical Christians were among the major supporters of the separation of church and state principle.

Wegner, G.P. (2002). *Anti-Semitism and schooling under the Third Reich*. New York, NY: Routledge Falmer.

Describes the Nazi educational philosophy and the anti-Semitic curriculum and pedagogy developed by German educators to promote Nazi ideas about race and racial purity.

CHAPTER 7

Racism: Confronting a Legacy of White Domination in America

> **❝**The problem of race remains America's greatest moral dilemma. When one considers the impact it has upon the nation, its resolution might well determine our destiny.**❞**

Martin Luther King, Jr. (1929–1968)

We have always divided people into categories based on physical differences: However, the concept of **racism,** which involves the creation of racial categories of human beings with one group superior to others, was not widely accepted until the nineteenth century. Even today, young children learn the lessons of difference.

When a city in the northwestern United States became home to a large Gypsy community, the elementary school teachers noted animosity between Gypsy children and other children. The teachers decided to implement curricula concerning Gypsy history and culture. The school district hired a consultant, Carlos Cortes, to assist them.

Cortes (2000) asked the teachers to find out what the children already knew about Gypsies, especially negative information or stereotypes. The teachers were confident that the children were too young to have learned stereotypes and believed that because the Gypsies had only recently arrived, it was highly unlikely that the children had heard much about them. Nevertheless, Cortes insisted that teachers talk to the children to find out what they knew about Gypsies. If they expressed prejudices or stereotypes, their misinformation would need to be addressed and corrected before new information could be accepted. When the teachers implemented Cortes's suggestion, they were shocked by what their children said about Gypsies: They

were dirty, they were thieves, and they kidnapped babies. It is sad to realize how easy it is for young children in America to learn to be racist; they have learned some of these lessons from their culture.

Cultural Racism

Cultural racism is the practice of recognizing activities and contributions of one racial group in preference to others within a multiracial society. From its earliest days, America had a mix of races; however, the dominant culture that emerged did not tend to include all racial groups. Andrzejewski (1996) described one aspect of oppression as an **ethnocentric** group imposing its culture on others. Because schools are regarded as institutions that instill cultural knowledge and values in the next generation, our schools are an appropriate place to begin an analysis of cultural racism.

How is racism taught to children and youth in our schools?

One misinterpretation that could be taken from the Cortes experience is that schools work to confront and reduce racial prejudice. Although this is true to some degree, too many schools do not discuss issues

> At the start of the twentieth century, over 98 percent of blacks in the United States were native-born—a much higher percentage than for whites. Blacks are as American as you can get.
>
> **Marguerite Wright (Contemporary)**

of race, and all too often, they misrepresent the role of race in the history of the United States and in contemporary American life. Students may be taught that the slave trade began because Europeans viewed Africans as a primitive and inferior people. Although some Europeans had this view, it was not shared by everyone. Evidence from English merchants engaged in trade with Africans reveals that they knew they were "dealing with people from well-organized sociopolitical systems, people who were sophisticated and intelligent" (Smedley, 1999, p. 92).

In addition, some schools celebrate African American accomplishments by identifying the first black person to achieve a particular goal or status. Providing such information may persuade students that America allows all individuals to pursue their goals, but as Smith (2004) notes, such achievements can also be viewed as a lesson in racism. Students are rarely told why a particular black person was the first to achieve a goal because that would require providing information about how the opportunity for a black person to strive for such an achievement had been denied by past racist policies and/or practices.

Cultural racism is also evidenced when teachers and textbooks largely overlook indigenous people. If students are asked who settled the country now called the United States, the answer we have been taught to give is most likely "Pilgrims" or possibly "English colonists." We don't think of—or don't know about—Africans brought to South Carolina by the Spanish and left to establish a settlement in 1526. We tend to overlook Spanish settlements (in what are now Florida and New Mexico) that existed prior to English settlements at Jamestown and Plymouth. And ironically, American elementary and secondary students are unlikely to consider American Indians as "settlers." Loewen (1995) comments,

Part of the problem is the word *settle*. "Settlers" were white, a student once pointed out to me. "Indians" didn't settle. Students are not the only people misled by *settle*. The film that introduces visitors to Plimoth Plantation tells how "they went about the work of civilizing a hostile wilderness." (p. 67)

Apparently "civilizing the wilderness" included stealing and desecrating graves. Loewen cited a colonist's journal reporting that on only their second day after arriving, two men from the Mayflower came upon an Indian dwelling where no one was at home and stole several items, noting in their journal that they intended to pay the Indians back later.

Pilgrims also took from caches where Indians stored food. During that first harsh winter when the Pilgrims were desperate for food, they dug up several Indian graves, knowing that food was buried with the bodies; then they thanked God for assisting their survival. Loewen (1995) explains the irony that Thanksgiving was never intended to be a holiday celebrating harmony between Indians and Pilgrims; it was declared a holiday by President Lincoln in the midst of the Civil War to foster patriotism. In spite of stereotypical textbook images showing Pilgrims and Indians sharing food at Thanksgiving, many Native Americans consider this holiday a form of cultural racism and do not participate in Thanksgiving celebrations.

How does society reinforce the cultural racism taught in school?

Sometimes racist messages are communicated in subtle ways. Citron (1969) identified what he called a **rightness of whiteness** concept, meaning that children learn to regard being white as normal, and to make negative judgments of those who deviate from white norms. Children grow up seeing primarily white faces on television, in movies, in advertisements. They read fairy tales and stories about Snow White and Peter Pan, request Christmas presents from a white Santa Claus, and revere white heroes in history or literature. White children and youth usually attend schools with predominantly white students, learning a curriculum that emphasizes white people's perspectives and achievements.

George (2006) argues that "Schools propagate and nurture whiteness by providing students with a steady diet of white ideology . . . [that] has resulted in a system that thinks, acts, and teaches 'white as right'" (p. 51). Consequently, white children are likely to unconsciously regard nonwhite people as less important.

In recent years, scholars have expanded Citron's insight into the concept of **white privilege,** referring to choices and behaviors white people take for granted that people of color cannot. McIntosh (2001) described white privilege as "an invisible package of unearned assets" and she identified many specific examples (p. 164). See Table 7.1 for some examples. Akbar (2010) defined white privilege as a set of options, opportunities, and opinions that are gained and maintained at the expense of people of color. To Akbar, white privilege can be as arrogant as people believing in a God who looks exactly like them or as poignant as a child reading Superman or Spiderman comic books and not needing to color the faces to identify with the heroes. Unless confronted, white privilege may create an unintended sense of white supremacy in white youth and adults, and white supremacy includes racist attitudes ranging from paternalism to antagonism.

White privilege not only fosters self-esteem and an attitude of superiority toward others, but also has provided tangible benefits. Initially excluding agricultural and domestic workers from the social security program denied hundreds of thousands of people of color a benefit that most white people enjoyed. Kivel (2002) cites a report concluding that black veterans were denied many of the benefits given to white veterans following World War II, and that veterans of color who did receive benefits were often given fewer benefits compared to white veterans. Even today, being white means a greater likelihood of being paid a higher salary, receiving promotions, and having loans approved. Hughes (2004) reports that white men are only 30% of the U.S. population, yet they have 75% of the most highly paid jobs.

White privilege is not just about economic benefits; it offers cultural benefits such as being able to shape American conceptions of reality. In our schools, white people have determined when and where philosophy begins, or mathematics or classical art. American history is said to begin when white people arrived; anything that happened prior

TABLE 7.1 White Privilege

Because of white privilege, the following activities illustrate assumptions white people can make that people of color cannot make:

1. If I should need to move, I can be pretty sure of renting or purchasing housing in an area which I can afford and in which I would want to live.
2. I can be pretty sure that my neighbors in such a location will be neutral or pleasant to me.
3. I can go shopping alone most of the time, pretty well assured that I will not be followed or harassed.
4. When I am told about our national heritage or about "civilization," I am shown that people of my color made it what it is.
5. I can be sure that my children will be given curricular materials that testify to the existence of their race.
6. Whether I use checks, credit cards, or cash, I can count on my skin color not to work against the appearance of financial reliability.
7. I can arrange to protect my children most of the time from people who might not like them.
8. I can swear, or dress in secondhand clothes, or not answer letters, without having people attribute these choices to the bad morals, the poverty, or the illiteracy of my race.
9. I can be pretty sure that if I ask to talk to "the person in charge," I will be facing a person of my own race.
10. If a traffic cop pulls me over or if the IRS audits my tax return, I can be sure I haven't been singled out because of my race.
11. I can easily buy posters, postcards, picture books, greeting cards, dolls, toys, and children's magazines featuring people of my race.
12. I can choose blemish cover or bandages in "flesh" color and have them more or less match my skin.

Source: McIntosh, P. *White Privilege: Unpacking the Invisible Knapsack.* In P. Rothenberg (Ed.), *Race, Class, and Gender in the United States: An Integrated Study.*

to that time is relegated to a largely irrelevant category termed *prehistory.* In classrooms reflecting white privilege, textbooks, bulletin boards, classroom discussions, and assignments typically focus on white people; the contributions and concerns of other racial or ethnic groups may be minimally represented or omitted. Because understanding racial and ethnic groups has not been emphasized, white students entering college may be surprised and possibly annoyed to find requirements for courses in racial and ethnic studies.

As a consequence of receiving an ethnocentric education, white Americans may regard certain people of color as foreign. Howard (2006) and others have described white people who meet Asian Americans or Latinos and ask, "Where are you from?" When a hometown such as Chicago or Miami is identified, the next question often will be, "Okay, but where are you *from?*" If the person of color responds by saying he or she has always lived in Chicago or Miami, the white person may respond: "Okay, but I mean, where did you come from?" In an attempt to ascertain the person's ethnicity, the questioner implies a perception that the other person is from outside the United States, especially because the response about their American hometown was ignored. The questioner is suggesting, "You don't look like an American." And the message that "You don't belong here" is clear to the Latino or Asian American being questioned.

Consequences of racist attitudes promoted by our culture can range from mildly annoying to tragic. A few days after the terrorists' destruction of the World Trade towers in New York City, a white man walked into a convenience store in Mesa, Arizona, and shot and killed the store clerk because he wore a turban and looked Muslim and Middle Eastern. The murder victim was not foreign, but American; he was not Muslim, but a Sikh who had emigrated from India. The killer justified his act by rationalizing that he was not racist, that his behavior was an expression of patriotism.

Individual Racism

Individual racism includes both racial prejudice and racist behavior. Racial prejudice refers to negative attitudes a person holds based on racial cate-

gories, and it is learned in many ways: from stereotypes in films to myths passed on from one generation to the next. Racist behavior occurs when someone responds to his or her racial prejudices by saying or doing something degrading or harmful toward a person or group. The murder of the Sikh man was an extreme example of individual racism; it is also illustrated by name-calling or by refusing to hire a person of color. In discussing individual racism, it is important to include an analysis of the attitudes and rationalizations used to justify racist behavior.

What denial rationalizations justify individual racism?

Although studies report a decline in racial prejudice among Americans, acts of individual racism are still prevalent. The 1954 *Brown v. Board of Education* decision said segregated schools were inherently unequal and ordered the desegregation of American schools. Communities were slow to respond to this mandate, but by the 1960s, school desegregation plans were finally being implemented. In response to legal and social pressures, school districts throughout the United States continued to develop and implement desegregation proposals. But in the 1980s, Supreme Court decisions backed away from the desegregation mandate, and the lack of aggressive political pressure brought desegregation efforts to a halt. Based on data gathered by the Harvard Civil Rights project (Orfield & Lee, 2006), schools have now become even more racially segregated than they were in the past. Yet many Americans deny that school segregation is still a problem.

Denial rationalizations often reject a reality that is well documented, and denying the resegregation of America's schools is an illustration. In 1968, almost 55% of Latino students attended segregated schools. By 1986, that percentage had risen to over 71%, and by 1998, it was at 76% and it was 77% in 2003 (Orfield & Lee, 2006; Wells, 1989). Latino students attend predominantly minority schools because the 1960s desegregation effort only succeeded in integrating students of color in urban schools. Few white students attended urban schools because their families had moved out of urban areas in a massive migration to segregated suburbs, a phenomenon called **white flight** (Thompson, 1999). Massey (2003) analyzed multiracial societies around the world and found that the only nation as segregated as the United States is today was South Africa under apartheid.

Similar to Latino students, African American students are also likely to attend segregated schools, but some states are more segregated than others. According to Orfield and Lee (2006), the states where the highest percentages of black students attend segregated schools are California (87%), New York (86%), Illinois (82%), and Texas (78%). Obviously, segregation is not just an issue for southern states. Although 29% of North Carolina's students were African American, only 37% attended segregated schools. The North Carolina percentage is still too high, but many states outside of the South are even higher. These comparisons clearly suggest the impact of white flight on public schools in America.

Some white Americans believe school desegregation ended in the 1960s, and that the passage of the 1964 Civil Rights law ended the major problems associated with racial discrimination. This denial rationalization has prompted the argument that there is no longer any need for affirmative action plans to address racial discrimination. A majority of voters in California in 1997 ended the state's affirmative action mandate; one year later the state of Washington did the same, and in the 2008 election, Nebraska voters approved a similar proposal. These voters believed that there was no longer any reason to give preference to any group because of their race or gender. Whether white or nonwhite, male or female, individuals from all groups now are supposedly competing on equal terms and with objective, unbiased criteria for scholarships, admission to college or vocational programs, and employment.

As with all denial rationalizations, this belief in a "level playing field" crumbles before even a cursory examination of the American reality. As Kozol (2005), Spriggs (2008), and Powell (2008) have documented, families of color overwhelmingly tend to live in racially segregated neighborhoods and send their children to segregated schools, which are often deteriorating facilities. A disproportionate number of people of color live in poverty, and even when people of color earn a college degree, they do not gain the same financial reward for that achievement as a white person. Further, Rehmeyer (2007) described a study that demonstrated how economic forces arising from racial segregation created economic inequities even when there was no history of discrimination between two groups. The study also concluded "even when social groups are economically equal, continued segregation may result in inequality over time" (p. 2).

In the United States, racially segregated neighborhoods and schools are not economically equal. In contrast to the deteriorating schools previously mentioned, middle- and upper-middle class white students will likely attend schools with excellent facilities and programs because of generous funding resources. Mainly white suburban school students can enjoy state-of-the-art equipment in well-financed districts, sometimes including swimming pools, tennis courts, and other luxuries that urban schools cannot afford. Meanwhile, teachers in metropolitan schools often struggle to have minimally equipped chemistry or biology laboratories and reasonably current textbooks and instructional materials. In spite of these disparities, all students take the same standardized tests to qualify for admission to colleges, technical schools, and training programs.

Another denial rationalization white people use to justify their opposition to affirmative action is to deny that racism exists. Because a disproportionate number of Americans of color live in poverty, some white people argue that poverty is the real issue, that it affects white people as well as people of color. In reality, race plays a role in *creating* poverty conditions. When white families moved to the suburbs, businesses abandoned inner cities, taking resources and jobs with them. As a result, urban schools are challenged to educate a diverse population of primarily students of color and to address problems based on disproportionate numbers of students living in poverty. Kozol (2005) cites the research finding that in 86% of schools with primarily black and Latino students, more than half of the students qualify for free or reduced-price meals.

To address the needs of students adequately, urban schools must be provided with funding equal to or greater than that for suburban schools. Instead, urban schools historically have operated with far less funding, creating a self-fulfilling prophecy for failure. When low-income students—especially students of color—are not successful in school, white people all too often insist that "those students" just aren't willing to work hard in school, a rationalization that moves beyond denial to become victim-blaming.

What victim-blaming rationalizations justify individual racism?

Surveys conducted by scholars at the University of Chicago have reported a high percentage of comments from white people that appear to blame black people and regard them as deficient. Researchers randomly selected hundreds of house-

> Most of the people I meet in America are compassionate. Why is it that individually we can be so compassionate and collectively we can be so harsh? . . . I don't have an answer to that.
>
> **Jonathan Kozol (1936–)**

holds in 300 different communities and conducted surveys concerning racial attitudes, especially white people's perceptions of African Americans (National Opinion Research Center, 1998).

A 1991 survey reported that 62% of white respondents believed that black people were more likely to be lazy than white people, 53% believed that black people were less intelligent than white people, and 56% believed that black people were more likely than white people to commit acts of violence. A 1998 survey found that 56% of white people still thought blacks were lazy. Believing blacks are lazier or less intelligent than whites can be used to justify the individual racism of an employer refusing to hire a black applicant.

Although fewer white people in 1998 thought black people were less intelligent than whites (down from 50% to 35%), white people perceiving blacks as more likely to be more violent than whites increased from 56% in 1991 to 79% in 1998. Regarding black people as violent has contributed to whites demanding more prisons and tougher sentences for violent crimes; it also affects how police officers respond to black suspects and contributes to racial profiling.

For example, Kivel (2002) cites two major reports on juvenile and adult crime in America that seem to document racial profiling. Although black youth constitute only 15% of those under eighteen,

they represent 26% of youth arrests. Although a similar number of white and black adults use drugs, there are far fewer arrests of whites than of blacks, and blacks represent two thirds of those convicted of drug use. Racial disparities continue as people move through the criminal justice system. Black youth make up 40% of those in juvenile prisons, 46% of youth tried in adult criminal courts, and 58% of juveniles incarcerated in adult prisons. The disparity continues when they become adults. In a study of thirty-seven states, black men went to prison at a rate that averaged "between 27 and 57 times the rate of white men" (p. 215).

Perhaps the most curious response to the 1991 survey was to a question eliminated from later surveys: 51% of white respondents said black people were less patriotic than white people, which is surprising because a conventional measure of patriotism in America is the willingness to risk one's life in service to the country. Buckley (2001) described African Americans who volunteered, fought, and died in every war in which the United States was involved: the Revolutionary War, Civil War, Spanish-American War, and all conflicts, large and small, in the twentieth century. (See Figure 7.1.)

What avoidance rationalizations justify individual racism?

Avoidance rationalizations propose partial or false solutions or are intended to distract attention from racism as a cause of some problem. A common avoidance rationalization stems from white people's belief that the passage of the 1964 Civil Rights Act, affirmative action plans, and a variety of other policies and programs since then have resulted in significant progress toward achieving the goal of eliminating racial prejudice and discrimination. Based on this belief, many white people have opposed a variety of programs intended to assist people of color—from recreational basketball activities to bilingual education.

Because of the highly visible role of African Americans in the civil rights movement, one would assume that they were the major beneficiaries of policies and programs developed in response to that movement, but an examination of African Americans' economic circumstances contradicts this rationalization. The good news according to Wellner

FIGURE 7.1

This photograph shows the black members of the Rough Riders who fought in the Spanish-American War; African American soldiers have rarely been acknowledged in films or in history books.

Source: North Wind Picture Archives.

ON THE BATTLE-GROUND OF LAS GUASIMAS—TROOPS GOING TO THE FRONT.

(2000) is that more than 40% of all black families today are middle class. The bad news is that almost 49% of black families earn approximately $15,000 a year or less, and they still face significant barriers stemming from race and class prejudice.

Black children are 3.5 times more likely to be part of a family living in poverty than are white children. Further, blacks are twice as likely as whites not to have health care insurance. Studies show that blacks are less likely than whites to graduate from high school or college, and about twice as likely to be employed in low-paying, low-status jobs (Morin, 2001). Despite such statistics, Morin cited a national survey conducted by the *Washington Post,* the Henry J. Kaiser Family Foundation, and Har-

> As long as you keep a person down, some part of you has to be down there to hold him down, so it means you cannot soar as you otherwise might.
>
> **Marian Anderson (1897–1993)**

vard University reporting that 40% to 60% of white Americans believe great progress has been made to reduce racial discrimination and that black people are almost economically equal to white people in the United States today.

When white Americans acknowledge problems of Americans of color, they often express no sense of responsibility. History provides numerous examples of the white majority in the United States discussing "the Negro problem" as if it had nothing to do with the white population. Novelist Richard Wright contradicted that assertion: "There isn't any Negro problem; there is only a white problem" (Lipsitz, 2008). Wright meant that the racial attitudes and behaviors of white people were the problem—that racism in America meant white racism. It is neither ethical nor practical for Americans of any color to avoid issues stemming from racism.

Institutional Racism

Jones (1997) defined **institutional racism** as "established laws, customs, and practices that systematically reflect and produce racial inequities in American society" (p. 438). We rely on institutions in America. Although individual racism is damaging, institutional racism is far more devastating because of the broader impact institutions have on people.

Institutional racism can be intentional when it is a result of a prejudiced person making a conscious decision about a person or group based on their race. Williams (2007) described a study in which pairs of black and white males, and pairs of Hispanic and white males applied for the same jobs. Identical qualifications were created on their résumés. The men were trained to present themselves in similar ways to minimize differences during interviews; still, white men received three times as many job offers as did black or Hispanic men.

We also know that institutional racism can be unintentional. Although studies have reported that people of color pay more to purchase a car than white people, especially white men, representatives of car dealerships deny that they engage in discrimination, but perhaps they are simply not conscious of it. Gladwell (2005) cites a Chicago study where 38 people dressed and identified themselves as professionals to purchase an automobile: fifteen white men, seven white women, eight black women, and five black men. They visited 242 car dealers and negotiated for a car according to strict instructions so

that their behavior would be similar. The initial offers that sales representatives made to white men tended to be about $725 above dealer's invoice compared to initial offers of about $935 above invoice given to white women. The initial offers to black women tended to be $1,200 above invoice, and for black men it was $1,690. Even after negotiating with the sales representatives, the average price of the car for black men was $1,550 above invoice, more than double what white men were offered without any bargaining.

Because most Americans seem to agree that it is wrong to discriminate based on race, ethnicity, gender, or other factors, it is important to understand

> The sad truth is that most evil is done by people who never make up their minds to be either good or evil.
>
> **Hannah Arendt (1898–1989)**

how institutional racism occurs. Whether intentional or unintentional, institutional racism results in negative consequences for people of color. Unemployment statistics document how race makes a difference when decisions are made about hiring people.

How is institutional racism reflected in statistics on employment?

Disproportionate numbers of people of color work in low-paying, low-status jobs, and people of color tend to have significantly higher unemployment rates compared to whites. The data for black youth is staggering. Tyson (1997) reported a 34% unemployment rate for black teenagers compared to 14.2% for white teenagers, and as high as 60% for black teenagers in some cities. According to Foster (2001), the employment discrepancy continues after graduation from high school. Higher percentages of African Americans are unemployed in the year after they graduate from high school than white graduates. It did not matter if the graduates were from rural or urban schools. The unemployment rate for black graduates was higher than whites regardless of socioeconomic status, the type of high school attended, or the type of academic program in which they were enrolled. Foster argued that racism is the obvious explanation of these consistently different rates.

Despite affirmative action programs, studies by the U.S. Bureau of Labor Statistics (2001) document that disparity between unemployment rates for people of color compared to whites was slightly worse in 1990 (11% versus 4%) than it was in 1960 (10% versus 5%). In 2009, the disparity in unemployment continued with an 8.4% rate for whites, 12.7% for Latinos, and 14.9% for African Americans (Bureau of Labor Statistics, 2009). Yet even with a strong economy, urban areas showed larger disparities in jobless rates for white and black workers. In a study by the Center for Economic Development at the University of Wisconsin-Milwaukee, Levine (2008) compared black and white jobless rates in Milwaukee with those in selected cities such as Chicago, Buffalo, Detroit, and St. Louis. Levine looked at jobless rates rather than unemployment rates because the latter does not include adult people in the workforce who have given up on finding a job, often because no jobs appear to be available. This is especially a problem in urban areas. Levine's data (see Table 7.2) reveals that urban black workers are almost twice as likely not to have a job as urban white workers. Milwaukee had the most significant problem with 51.1% of its black workers jobless and a disparity of 32.5% between black and white workers. Such data clearly

suggests that race, whether intentional or unintentional, was a factor in hiring employees.

How does institutional racism influence hiring decisions?

To understand why disparities in black and white unemployment exist, examine how hiring decisions are made. Studies repeatedly show that one of the most important methods used to recruit and hire employees is **word-of-mouth hiring.** If job seekers have relatives or friends already working for the company to recommend them, those job seekers have a better chance of being hired. Research suggests that 60% to 90% of blue-collar workers were hired because of recommendations from family or friends—and the same pattern has been observed in hiring decisions for white-collar jobs.

Employers feel they benefit from the word-of-mouth approach. If a trusted employee recommends someone, the employers believe that the risk in determining the quality of the person being hired is greatly reduced. Another benefit is that hiring costs are minimal; jobs are filled without paying to advertise them. Because of word-of-mouth hiring, Lipsitz (2008) found that 86% of available jobs never appeared in the classified ads of local newspapers.

Word-of-mouth hiring disadvantages people of color because of the history of segregation and discrimination in the United States. In the past, white male employees were blatantly favored over applicants who were women or people of color. At one time the preference was so obvious that state and federal governments passed anti-discrimination laws to address the problem; still, white men constituted a disproportionate share of the workforce. Schaefer (2008) reviewed social distance studies indicating that people consistently indicate a preference for people most like themselves; therefore, white people may recommend other white people simply to make sure they will be with people with whom they are comfortable.

Furthermore, because of ongoing housing segregation, white Americans have not tended to become friends with people of color. When white workers recommend a friend or relative for a job, they may insist that they are not trying to prevent a

TABLE 7.2 Black/White Jobless Rates in Selected Metropolitan Areas

Jobless Rates for Working-Age Men			
	Black	**White**	**Disparity**
1. Milwaukee	51.1	18.6	32.5
2. Buffalo	51.4	25.3	26.1
3. Detroit	50.6	25.6	25.0
4. St. Louis	46.3	21.4	24.9
5. Chicago	45.1	20.4	24.7

Source: Center for Economic Development, University of Wisconsin-Milwaukee (2008).

person of color from being hired but instead are helping someone they know. Intentional or not, word-of-mouth job recruitment offers a distinct advantage to white job applicants and contributes to discrimination documented by statistics on unemployment disparities between black and white workers.

Another way to secure employment is to join a labor union. However, admission policies of many unions still discriminate against people of color, particularly in unions for skilled trades that are historically dominated by white workers and have records of past discrimination against people of color. Unions typically accept new members based primarily on recommendations of current members. As with word-of-mouth hiring, white union members may or may not recommend people of color, but they are more likely to know and recommend someone who is white (Feagin & Feagin, 1986; Lipsitz, 2008).

Discrimination also occurs in decisions regarding company location. Because neighborhoods in the United States still reveal a pattern of racial segregation, a company's decision to locate in a white suburb means that the employees hired will be primarily or exclusively white. Studies show that when a new company selects a location or an established company expands to a new location, employees who live within a 30- to 40-mile radius of the worksite tend to be hired.

In the 1990s, Wilson (1996) reported a trend toward the *suburbanization of industry,* especially among retail trade companies. The trend has continued. White suburbs are advantaged because they tend to be more affluent than urban areas and usually offer more incentives to influence a company's decision to relocate. Wilson reported that when a number of low-income blacks were placed in suburban apartments, they were significantly more likely to find work than the low-income blacks placed in apartments in the city; the reason was the higher availability of jobs in the suburbs. Leondar-Wright (2009) cites a study of forty-five urban areas reporting that 25% to 50% of black unemployment was a result of jobs being shifted to the suburbs. A company's reasons for selecting a location may have more to do with economic incentives than with race, but the consequences of that decision have a racial impact.

How has institutional racism influenced the development of segregated neighborhoods?

Studies report that neighborhoods in the United States continue to reveal a pattern of racial segregation (Bonilla-Silva, 2001; Farley, 2010; Massey, 2001; Orser, 1990). Although there has been some improvement since the 1980s, Massey (2003) describes the level of black and white segregation in urban areas:

> The most common measure of residential segregation is an index that ranges from 0 to 100, where 0 indicates that blacks and whites are evenly distributed among neighborhoods and 100 means that blacks and whites share no neighborhood in common. Scores greater than 50 are considered to be "high"; those above 70 are "extreme." . . . The most segregated U.S. metropolitan area is Detroit, with an index of 85, followed by Milwaukee (82), New York (81), Newark, N.J. (80), and Chicago (80). Other areas with "extreme" segregation scores include Buffalo, Cincinnati, Cleveland, Kansas City, Philadelphia, and St. Louis. (p. 22)

Past practices of discrimination were overt, including the use of covenants by which homeowners guaranteed other homeowners in their neighborhood that if they sold their home it would not be sold to a family of color. Today such tactics are illegal, but other discriminatory practices still occur.

Some people believe American attitudes are changing. Foster (2001) cites a 1958 study in which white people were asked if they would leave their neighborhood if a black family moved in next to

An illustration of the craving people have to attach favorable symbols to themselves is seen in the community where white people banded together to force out a Negro family that had moved in. They called themselves 'Neighborly Endeavor' and chose as their motto the Golden Rule.

Gordon Allport (1897–1967)

them: 44% of them said they would, but in a 1997 study only 1% of white respondents said they would move. In the 1958 study, 80% of white respondents said they would leave their neighborhood if a large number of black families moved in, but in the 1997 study, only 18% said they would leave. Yet Foster and others have cited studies documenting that white families will stay in a neighborhood as long as black families do not exceed 7% or 8% of its residents. Once that percentage is exceeded, white families leave (Bonilla-Silva, 2001).

Neighborhood segregation is assured when realtors engage in a practice known as **steering.** The term refers to keeping files of homes for sale in white neighborhoods separate from those for sale in areas consisting predominantly or exclusively of families of color. Realtors show their clients homes in neighborhoods based on their race (Jenkins, 2007). Clients may be shown homes in integrated neighborhoods, if there are any, in response to a specific request. If accused of racism, realtors may claim that white homeowners who don't want people of color moving into their neighborhoods will not list their home with a realtor whom they believe will show their home to people of color. Realtors could insist that they are not being racist but are simply respecting the wishes of their clients.

Zoning ordinances might also contribute to racial segregation of neighborhoods. City councils often approve ordinances excluding multifamily dwellings in certain residential areas. The cost of homes in such areas is usually well beyond the means of many families of color. The rental price of units in a multifamily dwelling might be affordable to many clients of color. So the passage of a zoning ordinance expressly prohibiting multifamily housing virtually eliminates the possibility of families of color moving into the neighborhood.

Segregation aside, it is often more difficult for people of color to finance the purchase of homes. A study of the Federal Reserve Bank of Boston reported almost three times as many mortgage loans in low-income neighborhoods consisting of white homeowners than in those consisting of African American homeowners. Home loan officers seem more willing to dismiss the credit record problems of white applicants. Lipsitz (2008) also cites a Los Angeles study that found different standards of eligibility for white and black loan applicants. A study of a Houston bank reported that 13% of middle-

income white applicants were denied loans compared to 36% of middle-income black applicants; a study of home loan institutions in Atlanta found that they approved five times as many loans to whites as to blacks.

Between 1998 and 2008, banks and other lending institutions began to approve more home loans to people of color as part of the infamous subprime mortgage fiasco. During the financial collapse that took place in 2008, many critics blamed the lenders for making too many bad loans to people, especially people of color, whose finances were inadequate to pay off the home loans they received. Yet data was collected over the same ten-year period from the Community Advantage Program that facilitated loans to families with low incomes or single-headed households, and the data reveals that even though these clients presented a greater risk, they were no more likely to default on conventional home mortgage loans than the rest of the population (Oliver & Shapiro, 2008). The problem with sub-prime mortgage loans was that they involved hidden costs, wildly adjustable rates, and severe pre-payment penalties. Adding insult to injury, African American families who qualified for conventional mortgages often were steered to the more profitable sub-prime home loans. As a consequence, three times more families of color were given sub-prime mortgages than white families, and twice as many African American and Latino homeowners ended up losing their homes because they defaulted on the sub-prime loans. One estimate of the loss of wealth to African American homeowners was somewhere between $72–$93 billion (Oliver & Shapiro, 2008). These foreclosures not only harmed families who lost their homes, but also diminished the value of surrounding homes in the neighborhood. Since U.S. neighborhoods tend to be racially segregated, homeowners who were people of color were more likely to suffer a loss in the value of their homes because of foreclosures in their neighborhood. And reductions in home values result in fewer tax dollars to support the schools in these areas.

How does institutional racism occur in schools?

As the statistics given earlier in the chapter illustrate, American schools are racially segregated, in fact, more segregated than ever. The last significant effort by the U.S. Congress to support racial integration in schools was a 1972 law providing funds for schools attempting to desegregate. According to Gary Orfield of the Harvard Civil Rights Project, schools in the United States were desegregating in compliance with court-ordered desegregation for slightly more than two decades, and data from that period show that the numbers of students of color graduating from high school increased significantly and the racial divide in test scores decreased substantially (Kozol, 2005). As schools began resegregating in the 1990s, racial test scores widened once again. Orfield's research shows that this ongoing process of resegregation has resulted in 75% of African American and Latino students attending schools with predominantly minority populations, with more than 2 million of them attending "schools which we call apartheid schools" (Kozol, 2005, p. 19).

Some school districts, especially in urban areas, have attempted to overcome the impact of racial segregation by implementing multicultural curricula to make subject matter more inclusive, yet most elementary and secondary schools do not address adequately issues concerning people of color. In part, this problem stems from textbooks that continue to demonstrate a Eurocentric bias in history, literature, art, and music (Kirp, 1991; Loewen, 1995; Sleeter & Grant, 1991). Indeed, textbook bias can be a problem at all levels of education. In a review of college economics textbooks, Clawson (2002) found African Americans were disproportionately described as low-income families and were not usually featured in contexts such as the 1930s depression where readers might be more sympathetic to the poor. Textbook bias requires that conscientious teachers develop supplementary materials to provide students with information about multicultural perspectives. This is a difficult task because the major function of teaching is delivering curriculum, and teachers have limited time and resources to develop new material.

Another example of racism in schools is **tracking**—grouping students into categories by ability and assigning them to specific, ability-related classes. Most public elementary, middle, and high schools in America engage in some form of tracking. Based on supposedly objective tests of intellectual ability, children whose first language is not

English have been inappropriately placed in remedial classes or even classes for cognitively disabled students (Fattah, 2001). Students of color tend to be overrepresented in classes for slow learners, underrepresented in accelerated classes, and placed in vocational or remedial classes in disproportionate numbers (Kershaw, 1992; Oakes, 2005; Oakes &

> If we were to select the most intelligent, imaginative, energetic, and stable third of mankind, all races would be represented.
>
> **Franz Boas (1858–1942)**

Wells, 1996; Oakes et al., 2004). Nieto (2008) explained how tracking children who are still going through puberty influences economic and occupational outcomes when they become adults.

Research has found that tracking provides minimal value for accelerated learners, and it harms students tracked at lower levels, especially those at the lowest level. Because a large percentage of low-income students are racial minorities, tracking usually results in both race and class segregation because low-income students are typically placed in different tracks than middle- or upper-class students. Tracking has been justified by the argument that it improves education for all students, allowing teachers to teach to the students' level so they learn more efficiently. Research does not support this assumption. Academic outcomes for high-achieving students do not appear to be compromised in heterogeneous classes. Middle- and low-achieving students appear to benefit by interacting with high-achieving students; scholastic development is curtailed significantly when they are stratified with other equally low-achieving students (Oakes, 2005; Oakes & Wells, 1996; Oakes et al., 2000).

It is difficult for people of color to confront institutional racism in jobs, housing, and schools because that requires political power at local, state, and federal levels. Institutional racism curtails opportunities to be elected to local governing bodies—school boards, city councils, county commissions—and makes it even more difficult to win party primaries or elections at the state and national levels.

How does institutional racism affect politics?

Although the situation is improving in some state legislatures, people of color still tend to be underrepresented in the House of Representatives and Senate at both state and federal levels (Bonilla-Silva, 1999). Although people of color constitute more than 35% of the U.S. population, only 17% of

> In a democracy the majority of citizens is capable of exercising the most cruel oppressions upon the minority.
>
> **Edmund Burke (1729–1797)**

the members of the House of Representatives and 5% of the Senate are people of color (Amer & Manning, 2009). There are many problems for candidates of color to overcome.

In New Mexico, some Hispanic candidates have been successful emphasizing their Spanish (i.e., white) ancestry. Shorris (2001) noted that such candidates were elected to local and state offices "long before other Latinos could get past gerrymandering, ward politics, and at-large elections" (p. 167). The use of **at-large candidates** involves members of city councils or school boards being elected by the entire city, instead of by their respective districts or wards. If the majority of voters in a city are white, electing at-large candidates will assure all-white representation on councils or boards, despite having areas within the city consisting primarily or exclusively of people of color. Imagine a city that is composed of twelve wards, where three wards are predominantly Mexican American. If each ward elects its own council member, it is likely that three of the twelve city council members would be Mexican American. To reduce or even eliminate that possible outcome, a city can require at-large elections to fill any available position. Each year, when city council elections are conducted, voters in all twelve districts vote to fill all vacancies, with candidates receiving the most votes being elected. Because nine of the twelve wards consist

predominantly of white voters, they can cast enough votes to elect white candidates at each election, making it very difficult for a Mexican American candidate to be elected to the city council.

In the 2008 presidential campaign, the Democratic Party exemplified the changing face of America by fielding three highly regarded candidates who were not white males. The Latino candidate, Governor Bill Richardson (New Mexico), dropped out of the race after the early primaries, but Hillary Rodham Clinton and Barack Obama competed for the nomination through the entire primary season. Perhaps the most significant achievement of Obama's campaign organization was its ability to overcome fundraising problems that have tended to disadvantage candidates of color at all levels in the past. For example, when Jesse Jackson ran for president in the Democratic primaries in 1984 and 1988, he used his celebrity status to compensate for his lack of funds because the national media gave extensive coverage to his campaign. Obama's phenomenal fundraising during the primaries was surpassed after he received the party's nomination for President, setting a record by raising $65 million in August and then shattering that record by raising $150 million in September. Much of the fundraising was done on the Internet as 3.1 million contributors gave an average of $86.

Despite Senator Obama's fundraising success and his impressive oratory, pundits still wondered if white voters would vote for an African American candidate or if they would merely tell pollsters they were voting for him but then vote for the Republican candidate, Senator John McCain, or one of the other white male candidates on the ballot. This phenomenon was called the *Bradley effect* because of the 1982 California Governor's race in which Tom Bradley, the popular African American Mayor of Los Angeles, was defeated despite being ahead in the polls. Despite the doubts and fears, Barack Obama emerged triumphant on election night, becoming the first African American and the first openly biracial individual to become President of the United States. His election was viewed by many as a stunning blow against institutional racism in the United States, and as a sign of hope that institutional racism may be challenged and diminished even more in the future.

FIGURE 7.2

President Barack Obama's nomination of Judge Sonia Sotomayor meant that she would become the first Latina to serve on the Supreme Court. Although widely regarded as one of the best qualified nominees in recent years, Republican opponents demonstrated the persistence of historic prejudices as they questioned her abilities and even accused her of being "a racist" for arguing that her ethnicity provided a valuable perspective for her judicial decisions.

Source: Whitehouse.gov, Stacey Ilyse Photography

How can institutional racism be reduced in the United States?

Institutional racism involves complex problems that are not easily solved. In the 1970s, scholars began to emphasize that *intent* was not necessarily relevant to the issue of whether institutional policies and practices created advantages for white people and disadvantages for people of color. In the 1980s, however, the U.S. Supreme Court ruled that to prove a claim of discrimination, plaintiffs had to demonstrate that the intended purpose of institutional policies or practices was to discriminate against a particular group. Producing statistics documenting racial inequities was not enough; plaintiffs had to prove that those who developed policies or engaged in practices alleged as discriminatory

were guilty of an *evil intent*. As Bonilla-Silva (1999) noted,

> The standards that the Supreme Court enacted . . . on discrimination (plaintiffs carrying the burden of proof in discrimination cases and the denial of statistical evidence as valid proof of discrimination) help to preserve intact contemporary forms for reproducing racial inequality in America. (p. 85)

The Supreme Court's ruling illustrates the difficulties involved in making much progress on institutional racism unless the people of the United States and the legal system acknowledge that evil intent is not always the cause of discrimination. When courts are willing to examine the issue of who is advantaged or disadvantaged by institutional policies or practices—regardless of the original goals that these policies or practices were intended to address—then we may see progress in the United States against subtle but widespread institutional practices of racism. In the meantime, people of color must rely on affirmative action programs and legal recourse to respond to blatant discrimination within American institutions. Affirmative action has been effective to a degree, but it also has produced vigorous criticisms.

How do advocates and critics assess the effectiveness of affirmative action programs?

Advocates of affirmative action cite studies beginning in the 1960s showing that the number of workers of color decreased in their traditional occupations and increased significantly in other occupations. For example, the percentage of African Americans employed as domestic servants or other service occupations decreased while their numbers have increased in the ranks of bank tellers, firefighters, electricians, and police officers. Professionals of color have moved into high-status positions in larger numbers than ever before. Critics of affirmative action argue that gains have primarily benefited people of color who were already middle class. They propose changing affirmative action policies to focus on socioeconomic status rather than race, but Waller (2001) described extensive racism encountered by middle-class people of color despite their economic success.

Critics of affirmative action charge that these programs engender **reverse discrimination** by giving applicants of color preferential treatment over whites, especially white men. Studies do not support this allegation. Kivel (2002) summarizes a report reviewing opinions rendered by U.S. District Courts and Courts of Appeal for over four years. There were 3,000 discrimination cases of which 100 alleged reverse discrimination. The courts found merit in only 6 of the 100 claims and ordered restitution. Kivel concluded that charges of reverse racism were part of a strategy "to counterattack attempts to promote racial justice" (p. 61). Affirmative action advocates agree, and they also argue that white men have benefited from preferential treatment, beginning with the U.S. Constitution and sustained in most policies and practices implemented since then. Because racial discrimination still exists, they believe that affirmative action programs are essential to combat it.

Countering the historical argument, critics of affirmative action insist that it be eliminated because reverse discrimination is the more serious problem today. To support this allegation, studies have been cited showing that African Americans represented approximately 40% of new hires for police officers in U.S. cities from 1970 to 2000 (Reaves & Hickman, 2002). Because African Americans constitute only 12% of the population in the United States, this appears to justify the accusation that urban police departments are hiring an excessive number of African Americans.

African Americans actually constitute much more than 12% of the population in most urban areas, yet Jones (1997) reported that 95% of urban police officers in 1970 were white. To determine if hiring decisions by police departments have been fair, a useful measure would be to compare the percentage of officers of color with the percentage of people of color in an urban community. In police departments of many cities in the United States, the percentage of police officers of color still does not equal the percentage of the city's residents of color.

According to a Justice Department report, 63% of the police force in Detroit was African American, but African Americans comprise 82% of Detroit's population. Almost 39% of Baltimore's police officers were African American, but 65% of Baltimore's citizens are black. New York City's finest included 13.3% African American police officers, half of what it should be to equal the percentage of black people in New York City (Reaves & Hickman, 2002).

Such discrepancies do not just affect African Americans. Latinos represented 26% of New York City's population, but only 18% of NYPD. San Diego's police force was 16% Hispanic, but Latinos constituted 26% of the population; 18% of Houston's police officers were Hispanic, less than half of the percentage of Latinos living in Houston; and 12% of Phoenix police officers are Hispanic, but a third of its citizens are Latino (Reaves & Hickman, 2002). Although people of color have constituted a significant percentage of the police officers hired over the past thirty years, claims of reverse discrimination can be countered by the argument that the hiring decisions were a justifiable effort to correct a history of discrimination.

What are some consequences of racial discrimination?

One consequence that has been addressed by numerous critics is the incarceration of disproportionate numbers of African Americans, especially males. The Sentencing Project has calculated the racial disparity rates for each state in the United States (see Table 7.3). Many Americans still associate overt racism with southern states, but there is not a single southern state among the top states with the most disproportionate numbers of African Americans in prison. Researchers suggest two major reasons to explain this disparity: (1) different levels of involvement in criminal activity and racially biased penalties imposed during the judicial process, and (2) institutional biases resulting in different outcomes for minority defendants (Rome, 2008). For example, even the FBI's Universal Crime Reports Index (UCRI) reflects biases in our society. UCRI provides data on street crime, but excludes white-collar crimes, and white people are the majority of offenders with regard to white-collar crime. Rome (2008) also explains that police are given wide latitude in how they enforce the law and how they make arrests, and that police are likely to spend far more time monitoring minority neighborhoods than middle- or upper-class neighborhoods. Referring to findings from sociological research, Rome argues that class and race biases are revealed in police judgments about whom they are more likely to perceive as "troublemakers," and there is evidence that police are more likely to make an arrest if the complainant is white and less likely to arrest someone who appears to be white and middle class.

Another consequence of racial discrimination can be seen in the asset inequalities based on race. According to Oliver and Shapiro (2007), for each dollar of net worth owned by white Americans, Hispanic Americans own only 9 cents and African Americans own just 7 cents. In addition, Packer (2005) provides the calculations of a Fannie Mae consultant about how life would be different for African Americans if the United States had achieved racial equality. In education, 2 million more African Americans would have graduated from high school, and another 2 million would have graduated from college. With regard to employment, almost 2 million more African Americans would have professional and managerial jobs, and they would have

TABLE 7.3 Racial Disparities between Blacks and Whites in Prison

State	Disparity Index Rating*
1. New Jersey	13.15
2. Connecticut	12.77
3. Minnesota	12.63
4. Iowa	11.63
5. Wisconsin	11.59
6. Pennsylvania	10.53
7. New York	09.47
8. New Hampshire	09.26

Source: Cited in Rome (2008), data came from the Sentencing Project in Washington D.C.

*Index indicates the disparity between minorities and whites in prison as a percentage of their respective populations in that state.

almost $200 billion more in income. In terms of housing, about 3 million more African Americans would own their own homes, with $760 billion more in home equity value. Finally, if racial equality existed in the United States, African Americans would have $120 billion more in their retirement accounts, $80 billion more in their bank accounts, and the wealth they controlled would be $1 trillion

> Washing one's hands of the conflict between the powerful and the powerless means to side with the powerful, not to be neutral.
>
> **Paulo Freire (1921–1997)**

higher than it is today. This is an indication of only economic consequences of racism, but it is important that the cost to African Americans and other people of color in this country be understood and acknowledged. As Kivel (2002) says, all Americans "are responsible for the daily choices we make about how to live in a racist society. We are only responsible for our own part, (but) we each have a part" (p. 41).

What remedies have been proposed to address institutional racism?

To speak of remedies for problems as complex and widespread as those stemming from institutional racism is to speak of partial solutions and of good faith efforts. Ongoing research must be conducted on institutional racism because racist outcomes of policies and practices often are not easily identified and vary from one region and one institution to the next. Solutions will require cooperation and commitment, but whatever progress can be made represents a step forward. With each step, America comes closer to resolving race problems.

Remedies proposed to address problems stemming from racism have come from scholars such as Massey (2001); Wilson (1996); and Feagin and Feagin (1986). Among their proposed solutions for institutional racism are the following:

1. A national agency should be created that has regional offices to coordinate anti-discrimination activities across the nation. Such an agency would improve enforcement of anti-discrimination legislation and provide better documentation and dissemination of information. Most experts agree there are adequate laws against discrimination, but enforcement of those laws is not adequate because the responsibility for enforcement is currently assigned to the Justice Department, which has so many other areas of responsibility.

2. There must be a national and statewide commitment to stop the deterioration of inner cities in America. By providing resources, we could better address conditions that create misery and despair. Examples of resources include tax incentives to attract businesses to inner cities, federally funded jobs similar to the 1930s Works Progress Administration, training programs to give people skills related to available jobs, and day care subsidies to provide quality and affordable child care so that more people could work.

3. There must be active monitoring of real estate practices pertaining to advertising and marketing. Such oversight would ensure that practices are consistent with guidelines established in federal fair-housing legislation.

4. A commitment must be made to improve public elementary, middle, and high schools serving low-income students. Schools in low-income areas include many students of color who could be provided opportunities to develop the abilities and skills needed to function effectively in our highly technical, global economy. Resources will be required to remodel or build new schools, replacing the deteriorating buildings that low-income students often have to attend. Resources will also be required to develop and implement multicultural curriculum and to redesign teacher preparation programs.

5. Teachers must be taught how to work effectively with diverse student populations. They need to learn about the diversity of their students, not just students of color, but students with disabilities, low-income students, and students marginalized by the society or by other students. Teachers must learn how to support positive intergroup relationships between students in their classrooms. They also must be able to identify bias in instructional materials and to teach students how to recognize bias. Until textbooks reflect multicultural content, schools must have resources to purchase multicultural instructional materials to supplement textbooks.

AFTERWORD

In *The Souls of Black Folk* published originally in 1903, W. E. B. Du Bois (1994) wrote that the problem of America was the problem of the "color line," that skin color divided America as if it were a line drawn in the sand, never to be crossed. The color line continues to prevent Americans from being united by a common vision, strengthened by an appreciation of diversity. Du Bois challenged Americans to solve the problem of the color line in the twentieth century. That challenge still has not been met at the beginning of the twenty-first century.

What must Americans do to confront the problem of the color line? For people of color, the challenge continues to be the same as it was for Du Bois, to overcome barriers created by racism. The challenge for white Americans is first to acknowledge

> [America is] a vast and quarrelsome family, a family rent by racial, social, political and class division, but a family nonetheless.
>
> **Leonard Pitts (1957–)**

the existence of racism, then to understand blatant and subtle ways it operates in society, and, finally, to join with Americans of goodwill to reduce racism in America's schools, neighborhoods, and institutions. If those of us who will commit to this goal are successful, we will bring this society closer to the ideals for which it stands: freedom, equality, and the opportunity for all people to pursue their vision of happiness. When we come closer to that goal, it will not just be a victory for Americans of color, it will be a victory for America.

myeducationlab

Now go to Topic #2: **Race** in the MyEducationLab (www.myeducationlab.com) for your course, where you can:

- Find learning outcomes for this topic along with the national standards that connect to these outcomes.
- Complete Assignments and Activities that can help you more deeply understand the chapter content by viewing classroom video and ABC News footage.
- Apply and practice your understanding of the core teaching skills identified in the chapter with the Building Teaching Skills and Dispositions learning units.

TERMS AND DEFINITIONS

At-large candidates Refers to candidates for local offices being elected by an entire community rather than by districts or wards within that community

Cultural racism The societal recognition and promotion of activities and contributions of one racial group in preference to others within a multiracial society; the superimposition of history and traditions of one racial group over other racial groups

Ethnocentrism The belief that one's race, nation, or culture is superior to all others; also individual actions or institutional practices based on that belief

Individual racism Prejudiced attitudes and behavior against others based on skin color demonstrated whenever someone responds by saying or doing something degrading or harmful about people of another race

Institutional racism Established laws, customs, and practices in a society that allow systematic discrimination between people or groups based on skin color

Racism The creation of categories of human beings according to color, with one group establishing an artificial superiority to others; an attitude, action, or institutional structure that subordinates or limits a person on the basis of his or her race

Reverse discrimination The allegation that people of color are receiving preferential treatment with regard to decisions about hiring, promotion, participation, and admission to schools

Rightness of whiteness The belief that white people are the human norm against which all persons of color must be judged

Steering The practice of realtors of showing homes to prospective buyers in neighborhoods where residents are predominantly or exclusively of the same race

Tracking The process in which students are divided into categories so that they can be assigned in groups to various kinds of classes

White flight The migration of white families from an urban to a suburban location because of court rulings to desegregate urban schools

White privilege A set of options, opportunities, and opinions that are gained and maintained at the expense of people of color

Word-of-mouth hiring Employment of a job applicant based on the recommendation of current employees

DISCUSSION EXERCISES

Exercise #1 My Feelings About Race—A Personal Questionnaire

Directions: The twelve statements below could be a reaction that you might hear concerning another person's feelings about race. Create a response you think would be appropriate.

1. People should not be forced to integrate if they don't want to.
2. I don't believe I'm racist, but when it comes right down to it, I wouldn't marry a person of another race.
3. On the whole, the educated, the upper classes, the more sophisticated, or the more deeply religious people are much less racist.
4. I don't want to hear any more about the past and broken treaties; I should not be held responsible for what white people did to Indians a hundred years ago.
5. When I am around angry blacks, it makes me feel defensive because it's as if they want me to feel guilty or something.
6. Other ethnic groups had to struggle, so why should it be any different for Mexican Americans? Why should they get bilingual education and other special accommodations?
7. These days, whenever a black man sneezes, thirty-seven white people rush up to wipe his nose.
8. How can I be pro-Indian without being anti-white?
9. Don't tell me that blacks aren't more violent than whites. If you look at the statistics, you have to admit that there is a higher crime rate in the ghetto.
10. In many situations, minorities—especially Jews and blacks—are paranoid and oversensitive; they read more into a situation than is really there.
11. Because of the civil rights legislation passed in the mid-1960s, great opportunities are now available to racial minorities, and it is up to them to take more responsibility for exploiting those increased opportunities.
12. No, I'm not going to take the *Understanding Diversity* course because I'm not interested in learning about minorities; further, I've been told that it's a white-bashing course; male-bashing, too.

Exercise #2 My Experiences with Culture, Race, and Ethnicity

Directions: Reflect on what age(s) over your life span you have had personal, direct contact with someone of a different culture, race, and ethnicity. Begin with the earliest recollection and move forward to the present.

1. Identify your first personal experiences with people different from you. What was the setting: home, school, family? What was the basis for the contact: dinner guest, classmate, and playmate? What was your age at the time? Who and how was the person different?
2. Identify your earliest exposures to people who were different from you through movies or television shows, including newscasts. What was the story about? What was your age at the time? Who and how was the person different? What impressions did you gain from each of these visual media experiences?
3. Identify your earliest exposure to different others through newspapers, storybooks, novels, or magazines. What was the story about? What was your age at the time? Who and how was the person different? What did you learn about people different from you because of these reading experiences?

Follow-up: Explain to others the impressions these experiences made on you at the time and your reactions to them then and now. Have your reactions changed over time?

REFERENCES

Akbar, N. (2010). Privilege in black and white. In K. Koppelman (Ed.), *Perspectives on diversity*. Boston, MA: Allyn & Bacon.

Discusses white privilege and ways that blacks collaborate with white privilege.

Amer, M.L., & Manning, J. E. (2009). Membership of the 11th Congress: A profile. Retrieved on September 21, 2009 from www.senate.gov.

Provides demographic details on members of the House of Representatives and the Senate.

Andrzejewski, J. (1996). Definitions for understanding oppression and social justice. In J. Andrzejewski (Ed.)., *Oppression and social justice: Critical frameworks* (5th ed., pp. 52–58). Needham, MA: Simon & Schuster.

Provides definitions for a variety of terms essential for discussing intergroup relations.

Bonilla-Silva, E. (2001). *White supremacy and racism in the post-civil rights era*. Boulder, CO: Lynne Rienner.

Examines why blacks and other racial minorities remain behind whites financially, in educational attainment and other social indicators (see residential segregation on pp. 95–96).

Bonilla-Silva, E. (1999). The new racism: Racial structure in the United States, 1960s–1990s. In P. Wong (Ed.), *Race, ethnicity, and nationality in the United States: Toward the twenty-first century* (pp. 55–101). Boulder, CO: Westview.

Examines research on housing, education, politics, and social interactions to describe how the new racism perpetuates social and economic control of African Americans.

Buckley, G. (2001). *American patriots: The story of blacks in the military from the Revolution to Desert Storm*. New York, NY: Random House.

Includes statistics and stories about African Americans who fought in America's wars.

Citron, A. (1969). *The rightness of whiteness*. Detroit: Michigan-Ohio Regional Educational Laboratory.

Describes how cultural images create racial ethnocentrism in the United States.

Clawson, R. (2002, January). Poor people, black faces: The portrayal of poverty in economics textbooks. *Journal of Black Studies, 32*(3), 352–361.

Examines images of African Americans in college economics textbooks and relates findings to previous studies of how women and minorities are portrayed in college textbooks.

Cortes, C. (2000). *The children are watching: How the media teach about diversity*. New York, NY: Teachers College Press.

Analyzes media images, including news and entertainment, to identify themes and values related to diversity and describes media influence on public perceptions of diversity issues.

Du Bois, W. E. B. (1994). *The souls of black folk*. New York, NY: Dover.

Includes the famous "color line" phrase in "The Forethought" that precedes essays affirming African Americans and rejecting accommodations to white supremacy. For those interested in learning more about Du Bois, read David Lewis Levering, *W.E.B. Du Bois: Biography of a race (1868–1919)* (1993), and *W.E.B. Du Bois: The fight for equality and the American century, 1919–1963* (2000), both published by Henry Holt.

Farley, J. (2010). *Majority-minority relations* (6th ed.). Upper Saddle River, NJ: Prentice-Hall.

Provides an overview of racial segregation in the United States in Chapter 10, and examines the basis and consequences of busing in Chapter 12,

Fattah, C. (2001, October). *Racial bias in special education*. FDCH Congressional Testimony, Washington DC: eMediaMillWorks.

Testimony on special education issues, including a description of the boy placed in a low-functioning category who graduated from school and obtained a PhD.

Feagin, J., & Feagin, C. (1986). *Discrimination American style* (2nd ed.). Malabar, FL: Krieger.

Describes theories of discrimination and examples of discrimination in employment, housing, politics, education, and more.

Feagin, J., & Sikes, M.P. (1994). *Living with racism: The black middle class experience*. Boston, MA: Beacon.

Examines overt and subtle discrimination experienced by middle-class African Americans.

Foster, M. (2001). Education and socialization: A review of the literature. In W.H. Watkins, J.L. Lewis, & V. Chou (Eds.), *Race and education: The roles of history and society in educating African American students* (pp. 200–244). Boston, MA: Allyn & Bacon.

Reviews research on racial attitudes and interracial behaviors in school and society.

George, R.G. (2006). The race card: An interactive tool for teaching multiculturalism. *Multicultural Perspectives, 8*(3), 51–55.

Discusses how white is presented as the norm in schools and how whiteness functions as a system of institutional oppression, and describes a pedagogical tool to teach about race.

Gladwell, M. (2005). *Blink: The power of thinking without thinking.* New York, NY: Little, Brown.

Discusses evidence for cognitive activity below the level of consciousness.

Howard, G.R. (2006). *We can't teach what we don't know: White teachers, multiracial schools.* New York, NY: Teachers College Press.

Integrates theory, research, and personal experiences to describe problems created by racism and white privilege and discusses actions to bring about positive changes.

Hughes, R. (2004). The dwindling pool of qualified professors of color: Suburban legends. In D. Cleveland (Ed.), *A long way to go: Conversations about race by African American faculty and graduate students* (pp. 81–93). New York, NY: Peter Lang.

Discusses strategies for the recruitment and retention of students of color in higher education.

Jenkins, A. (2007, May). Inequality, race and remedy. *The American Prospect, 18*(5), A8–A11.

Examines the legacy of past racial discrimination in the present, evaluates the role of racial discrimination in promoting poverty, and suggests ways of addressing racial barriers.

Jones, J. (1997). *Prejudice and racism* (2nd ed.). New York, NY: McGraw Hill.

Integrates data from psychology, sociology, and history to explain the relationship between prejudice and racism in their appropriate sociocultural historical context.

Kershaw T. (1992). The effects of educational tracking on the social mobility of African Americans. *Journal of Black Studies 23*(1), 152–170.

Analyzes criteria used to determine student placement in tracking systems; explains how black students are discriminated against and the negative consequences of such decisions.

Kirp, D.L. (1991, Summer). Textbooks and tribalism in California. *Public Interest, 104,* 20–37.

Discusses the dissatisfaction expressed by various minority groups with textbooks being considered for adoption by California's curriculum commission.

Kivel, P. (2002). *Uprooting racism: How white people can work for racial justice.* (Rev. ed.). Gabriola Island, British Columbia: New Society Publishers.

Examines the dynamics of racism and white privilege in society and offers strategies to work for social justice.

Kozol, J. (2005). *The shame of the nation: The restoration of apartheid schooling in America.* New York, NY: Crown.

Examines evidence of segregation in American schools based on race and social class and discusses the moral and societal implications of maintaining this segregation.

Leondar-Wright, B. (2004). Black job loss deja vu. In C. Collins, A. Gluckman, M. Lui, B.L. Wright, & A. Scharf (Eds.), *The wealth inequality reader* (pp. 95–105). Cambridge, MA: Dollars & Sense.

Discusses low unemployment for blacks in the 1990s, the high percentage of blacks laid off during recessions, and other economic factors affecting income and wealth for black families.

Levine, M. (2008). *Research update: The crisis of male joblessness in Milwaukee, 2007.* Retrieved June 10, 2009 from www.uwm.edu/ced/publications.cfm

Explores unemployment and joblessness in Milwaukee and surrounding areas and compares the economic conditions for blacks in Milwaukee with other urban areas.

Lipsitz, G. (2008). The possessive investment in whiteness. In P. Rothenberg (Ed.), *White privilege: Essential readings on the other side of racism* (pp. 61–84). New York, NY: Worth.

Discusses the economic benefits of racism for white people in the United States.

Loewen, J. (1995). *Lies my teacher told me: Everything your American history textbook got wrong.* New York, NY: The New Press.

Describes distortions and omissions concerning the role of people of color in U.S. history.

Massey, D.S. (2001). Residential segregation and neighborhood conditions in U.S. metropolitan areas. In N. Smelser, W. Wilson, & F. Mitchell (Eds.), *America becoming: Racial trends and their consequences.* East Lansing, MI: National Center for Research on Teacher Learning. (ERIC Document Reproduction Service No. ED449286)

Describes how segregation has increased in recent years, especially for blacks, as well as the nature of segregation for Hispanics and Asian Americans.

Massey, D.S. (2003). The race case. *The American Prospect, 14*(3), 22.

Describes the current status of housing segregation in the United States, especially in urban areas.

McIntosh, P. (2001). White privilege: Unpacking the invisible knapsack. In P. Rothenberg (Ed.), *Race, class, and gender in the United States: An integrated study* (5th ed., pp. 163–168). New York, NY: Worth.

Describes how her understanding of white privilege emerged from a feminist analysis of male privilege and provides a list of twenty-six examples of white privilege.

Morin, R. (2001, July 11). Misperceptions cloud whites' view of blacks. *Washington Post.* Retrieved June 11, 2009, from http://www.washingtonpost.com

Presents the results of a poll of 779 randomly selected white Americans in terms of their perceptions of the economic status of and opportunities available to black Americans.

National Opinion Research Center. (1998). *Race surveys.* University of Chicago. Retrieved August 10, 2003, from www.norc.uchicago.edu/projects/gensoc4.asp

Access survey information dealing with racial attitudes on this Web site by going to "General Survey Data and Information Retrieval System."

Nieto, S. (2008). *Affirming diversity: The sociopolitical context of multicultural education* (5th ed.). Boston, MA: Pearson.

Provides a comprehensive analysis of how schools are failing to meet the needs of students of color and suggests strategies to improve schools.

Oakes, J. (2005). *Keeping track: How schools structure inequality.* New Haven, CT: Yale University Press.

Documents how tracking practices have perpetuated racial and social class inequalities.

Oakes, J., Quartz, K.H., Ryan, S., & Lipton, M. (2000). *Becoming good American schools: The struggle for civic virtue in school reform.* San Francisco, CA: Jossey-Bass.

Describes the effort of sixteen schools in five states to move away from tracked classes and implement other reforms to improve the education of all students.

Oakes, J., & Wells, A.S. (1996). *Beyond the technicalities of school reform: Policy lessons from detracking schools.* Los Angeles, CA: UCLA Graduate School of Education and Information Studies.

Describes problems affecting students in tracked classes and strategies for detracking schools.

Oliver, M.L., & Shapiro, T.M. (2008, October). Subprime as a black catastrophe. *The American Prospect, 19*(10), A9–A11.

Describes how families of color, especially African Americans, were adversely affected by the sub-prime mortgage crisis.

Oliver, M.L. & Shapiro, T.M. (2007, May). Creating an opportunity society. *The American Prospect, 18*(5), A27–28.

Discusses the need to implement asset-building strategies so that more Americans can acquire property and increase their wealth.

Orfield, G., & Lee, C. (2006). *Racial transformation and the changing nature of segregation.* Cambridge, MA: The Civil Rights Project at Harvard University.

Examines the transformation of the racial composition in American schools from 1954 to 2003, with special attention to the period from 1991 to 2003.

Orser, W.E. (1990). Secondhand suburbs. *Journal of Urban History, 16*(3), 227–263.

Describes blockbusting tactics and white flight occurring in Baltimore in the 1950s and 1960s and the economic consequences for black homeowners.

Packer, Z. (2005). Sorry, not buying. *The American Prospect, 16*(12), 46–48.

Analyzes efforts by political conservatives to attract black voters on moral issues and the difficulties they face because of their reluctance to address current racial inequities.

Powell, J.A. (2008, October). Race, place, and opportunity. *The American Prospect, 19*(10), A21–A23.

Describes current consequences of ongoing segregation for people of color in the United States and some of the historic efforts that have been made to address it.

Reaves, B.A., & Hickman, M.J. (2002). *Police departments in large cities, 1990–2000.* United States Department of Justice. Retrieved June 9, 2009, from http://www.ojp.usdoj.gov/bjs.

A special report from the Bureau of Justice Statistics agency that includes statistics in the text and in tables concerning police departments in major U.S. cities.

Rehmeyer, J.J. (2007). Separate is never equal. *Science News.* Retrieved Nov. 7, 2008, from http://blog.sciencenews.org (select Math Trek, search for separate_is_never_equal).

Highlights a study that applied a mathematical model to a segregated community to explore the interaction between segregation and inequality.

Rome, D. (2008, Spring). How stereotypes become acts of discrimination: A look at racial disparities in Wisconsin prisons. *Kaleidoscope II,* The University of Wisconsin Institute on Race and Ethnicity, pp. 2–5.

Examines issues related to the disparity between blacks and whites incarcerated in prisons nationally and specifically in the state of Wisconsin.

Schaefer, R.T. (2008). Prejudice. In *Racial and ethnic groups* (11th ed., pp. 37–65). Upper Saddle River, NJ: Pearson Education.

Discusses causes and consequences of prejudice including the findings from research using the Social Distance Scale.

Shorris, E. (2001). *Latinos: A biography of the people.* New York, NY: W.W. Norton.

Provides a personal narrative of the diverse Latino groups in the United States using many personal stories told within a historical context.

Sleeter, C.E., & Grant, C.A. (1991). Race, class, gender and disability in current textbooks. In M. Apple & L.K. Christian-Smith (Eds.), *The politics of the textbook* (pp. 78–110). New York, NY: Routledge.

A textbook analysis instrument was employed to examine forty-seven elementary and middle-school textbooks in social studies, reading, language arts, science, and mathematics.

Smedley, A. The arrival of Africans and descent into slavery. *Race in North America: Origin and evolution of a world view.* Boulder, CO: Westview.

Describes the arrival of Africans to America and how they lost their equal status with other immigrants.

Smith, W.A. (2004). Black faculty coping with racial battle fatigue: The campus racial climate in a post–civil rights era. In D. Cleveland (Ed.), *A long way to go: Conversations about race by African American faculty and graduate students* (pp. 171–190). New York, NY: Peter Lang.

Explores race relations in the United States and consequences for African Americans in higher education.

Spriggs, W.E. (2008, October). The economic crisis in black and white. *The American Prospect, 19*(10), A2–A5.

Analyzes trends in economic data concerning income and wealth of African Americans compared to white Americans.

Thompson, H.A. (1999). Rethinking the politics of white flight in the postwar city. *Journal of Urban History, 25*(2), 163–199.

Discusses the pattern of white flight in Detroit up to 1980 and explains how white flight has contributed to the economic devastation of Detroit's inner city.

Tyson, J.L. (1997). Jobless rate for blacks falls to 23-year low. *Christian Science Monitor, 89*(214), 8.

Describes the decline in unemployment for black Americans in the 1990s while noting problems that remain, such as high unemployment for black youth.

U.S. Bureau of Labor Statistics. (2009, June 5). Employment Situation. Retrieved on June 10, 2009, from www.bls.gov/cps/#news.

Provides unemployment data as recorded for May of 2009.

U.S. Bureau of Labor Statistics. (2001). Counting minorities: A brief history and a look at the future. In *Report on the American Workforce.* Washington, DC: U.S. Department of Labor (www.bls.gov/opub).

Analyzes statistics pertaining to the American workforce and the role and nature of the participation of women and minorities in that workforce.

Waller, J. (2001). *Face to face: The changing state of racism across America.* Cambridge, MA: Perseus Books Group.

Refutes myths about the decline of racism in America and describes various forms of contemporary racism in the United States.

Wellner, A.S. (2000). The money in the middle. *American Demographics, 22*(4), 56–64.

Examines the impact of the economic prosperity of the 1990s on incomes of racial and ethnic minorities and immigrant populations in the United States.

Wells, A.S. (1989). *Hispanic education in America: Separate and unequal.* ERIC Document Reproduction Service.

Presents data on the growth of the Hispanic population of the United States, the percentage of Hispanic students in segregated schools, and the need for desegregation.

Wilson, W.J. (1996). *When work disappears: The world of the new urban poor.* New York, NY: Knopf.

Discusses the causes of unemployment in inner cities and provides recommendations to address the problem. The study of blacks placed in suburbs is on pp. 38–39.

Williams, C. (2003) Managing individuals in a diverse workforce. In *Management* (2nd ed., pp. 434–471). Versailles, KY: Thompson Southwestern.

Explains the benefits of diversity in the corporate world and principles for managing diverse employees effectively.

PART THREE

Issues in Multicultural Education

CHAPTER 8

Multicultural Education and School Reform

Rachel Ilana Shuman, *Providence/Hope*. Mixed media collage, 2005.

66We don't need multicultural education here; most of our students are White.99

66I don't see color. All my students are the same to me.99

66We shouldn't talk about racism in school because it has nothing to do with learning. Besides, it'll just make the kids feel bad.99

66Let's not focus on negative things. Can't we all just get along?99

66I want to include multicultural education in my curriculum, but there's just no time for it.99

66Oh, yes, we have multicultural education here: We celebrate Black History Month, and there's an annual Diversity Dinner.99

❝Multicultural education is just therapy for Black students.❞

❝Multicultural education became irrelevant after 9/11. It's divisive because it focuses on differences. Now, more than ever, we need to stress our similarities.❞

In discussing multicultural education with teachers and other educators over many years, we have heard all these comments and other similar remarks. Statements such as these reflect a profound misconception of multicultural education.

When multicultural education is mentioned, many people first think of lessons in human relations and sensitivity training, units about ethnic holidays, education in inner-city schools, or food festivals. If multicultural education is limited to these issues, the potential for substantive change in schools is severely diminished. Moreover, those who called for an end to multicultural education after September 11, 2001, missed the boat. Rather than eliminating it, we believe that 9/11 underscored the need to emphasize multicultural education more than ever. In fact, we believe that nothing is more divisive than a monocultural education, because such an education excludes so many people and perspectives from schools' curricula and pedagogy.

When broadly conceptualized, multicultural education can lead to more understanding and empathy. It can also help to address the four areas of potential conflict and inequity to be addressed in Part 2—namely, racism and discrimination, structural conditions in schools that may limit learning, the impact of culture on learning, and language diversity. However, it is necessary to stress that multicultural education is not a panacea for all educational ills. Because schools are part of our communities, they reflect the stratification and social inequities of the larger society. As long as this is the case, no school program alone, no matter how broadly conceptualized, can change things completely without addressing inequalities in the larger society. It will not cure underachievement, eliminate boring and irrelevant curriculum, or stop vandalism. It will not automatically motivate families to participate in schools, reinvigorate tired and dissatisfied teachers, or guarantee a lower dropout rate.

Despite these caveats, when multicultural education is conceptualized as broad-based school reform, it can offer hope for real change. Multicultural education in a sociopolitical context is both richer and more complex than simple lessons on getting along or units on ethnic festivals. By focusing on major conditions contributing to underachievement, a broadly conceptualized multicultural education permits educators to explore alternatives to a system that promotes failure for too many of its students. Such an exploration can lead to the creation of a richer and more productive school climate and a deeper awareness of the role of culture and language in learning. Seen in this comprehensive way, educational success for all students is a realistic goal rather than an impossible ideal.

This chapter proposes a definition of multicultural education based on the context and terminology demonstrated in the preceding chapters and analyzes the seven primary characteristics included in the definition. These characteristics underscore the role that multicultural education can play in reforming schools and providing an equal and excellent education for all students. This definition of multicultural education emerges from the reality of persistent problems in our nation's schools, especially the lack of achievement among students of diverse backgrounds. A comprehensive definition emphasizes the context and process of education rather than viewing multicultural education as an add-on or luxury disconnected from the everyday lives of students.

In spite of some differences among major theorists, during the past 30 years there has been remarkable consistency in the educational field about the goals, purposes, and reasons for multicultural education.[1] But no definition of multicultural education can truly capture all its complexities. The definition we present here reflects one way of conceptualizing the issues; it is based on our many years of experience as students, teachers, researchers, and teacher educators. We hope that it will serve to encourage further dialogue and reflection among readers. So, although we propose seven characteristics that we believe are essential in multicultural education, you might come up with just three, or with 15. The point is not to develop a definitive way to understand multicultural education but instead to start you thinking about the interplay of societal and school structures and contexts and how they influence learning.

What we believe is essential is an emphasis on the sociopolitical context of education and a rejection of the notion that multicultural education is either a superficial addition of content to the curriculum, or, alternatively, the magic pill that will do away with all educational problems. In the process of considering our definition of multicultural education, it is our hope that you will develop your own ideas, priorities, and perspective.

A Definition of Multicultural Education

We define multicultural education in a sociopolitical context as follows: Multicultural education is a process of comprehensive school reform and basic education for all students. It challenges and rejects racism and other forms of discrimination in schools and society and accepts and affirms the pluralism (ethnic, racial, linguistic, religious, economic, and gender, among others) that students, their communities, and teachers reflect. Multicultural education permeates schools' curriculum and instructional strategies as well as the interactions among teachers, students, and families and the very way that schools conceptualize the nature of teaching and learning. Because it uses critical pedagogy as its underlying philosophy and focuses on knowledge, reflection, and action (praxis) as the basis for social change, multicultural education promotes democratic principles of social justice.

The seven basic characteristics of multicultural education in this definition are as follows:

1. Multicultural education is antiracist education.
2. Multicultural education is basic education.
3. Multicultural education is important for all students.
4. Multicultural education is pervasive.
5. Multicultural education is education for social justice.
6. Multicultural education is a process.
7. Multicultural education is critical pedagogy.

Multicultural education is antiracist education

Antiracism, indeed antidiscrimination in general, is at the very core of a multicultural perspective. It is essential to keep the antiracist nature of multicultural education in mind because, in many schools, even some that espouse a multicultural philosophy, only superficial aspects of multicultural education are apparent. Celebrations of ethnic festivals are the extent of multicultural education programs in some schools. In others, sincere attempts to decorate bulletin boards with what is thought to be a multicultural perspective end up perpetuating the worst kind of stereotypes. Even where there are serious attempts to develop a truly pluralistic environment, it is not unusual to find incongruencies. In some schools, for instance, the highest academic tracks are overwhelmingly White, the lowest are populated primarily by students of color, and girls are nonexistent or invisible in calculus and physics classes. These are examples of multicultural education without an explicitly antiracist and antidiscrimination perspective.

Because many people erroneously assume that a school's multicultural program automatically takes care of racism, we stress that multicultural education must be *consciously antiracist*. Writing about multicultural education over 25 years ago, when the field was fairly new, Meyer Weinberg asserted:

> Most multicultural materials deal wholly with the cultural distinctiveness of various groups and little more. Almost never is there any sustained attention to the ugly realities of systematic discrimination against the same group that also happens to utilize quaint clothing, fascinating toys, delightful fairy tales, and delicious food. Responding to racist attacks and defamation is also part of the culture of the group under study.[2]

Being antiracist and antidiscriminatory means being mindful of how some students are favored over others in school policies and practices such as the curriculum, choice of materials, sorting policies, and teachers' interactions and relationships with students and their families. Consequently, to be inclusive and balanced, multicultural curriculum must, by definition, be antiracist. Teaching does not become more honest and critical simply by becoming more inclusive, but this is an important first step in ensuring that students have access to a wide variety of viewpoints. Although the beautiful and heroic aspects of our history should be taught, so must the ugly and exclusionary. Rather than viewing the world through rose-colored glasses, antiracist multicultural education forces teachers and students to take a long, hard look at everything as it was and is, instead of just how we wish it were.

Too many schools avoid confronting in an honest and direct way the negative aspects of history, the arts, and science. Michelle Fine has called this the "fear of naming," and it is part of the system of silencing in public schools.[3] To name might become too messy, or so the thinking goes. Teachers often refuse to engage their students in discussions about racism because it might "demoralize" them. Too dangerous a topic, it is often left untouched.

Related to the fear of naming is the insistence of schools on "sanitizing" the curriculum, or what Jonathan Kozol many years ago called "tailoring" important men and women for school use. Kozol described how schools manage to take the most exciting and memorable heroes and bleed the life and spirit completely out of them because it can be dangerous, he wrote, to teach a history "studded with so many bold, and revolutionary, and subversive, and exhilarating men and women." He described how, instead, schools drain these heroes of their passions, glaze them over with an implausible veneer, place them on lofty pedestals, and then tell "incredibly dull stories" about them.[4] Although he wrote these words many years ago, Kozol could just as well be writing about education in today's U.S. schools.

The process of sanitizing is nowhere more evident than in depictions of Martin Luther King, Jr. In attempting to make him palatable to the U.S. mainstream, schools have made King a milquetoast. The only thing most children know about him is that he kept "having a dream." School bulletin boards are full of ethereal pictures of Dr. King surrounded by clouds. If children get to read or hear any of his speeches at all, it is his "I Have a Dream" speech. As inspirational as this speech is, it is only one of his notable accomplishments. Rare indeed are allusions to his early and consistent opposition to the Vietnam War; his strong criticism of unbridled capitalism; and the connections he made near the end of his life among racism, capitalism, and war. This sanitization of Martin Luther King, a man full of passion and life, renders him an oversimplified, lifeless figure, thus making him a "safe hero."

Most of the heroes we present to our children are either those in the mainstream or those who have become safe through the process of what Kozol referred to as "tailoring." Others who have fought for social justice are often downplayed, maligned, or ignored. For example, although John Brown's actions in defense of the liberation of enslaved people are considered noble by many, in our history books he is presented, at best, as somewhat of a crazed idealist. Nat Turner is another example. The slave revolt that he led deserves a larger place in our history, if only to acknowledge that enslaved people fought against their own oppression and were not simply passive victims. However, Turner's name and role in U.S. history are usually overlooked, and Abraham Lincoln is presented as the Great Emancipator as if he single-handedly was responsible for the abolition of slavery (and with little acknowledgment of his own inconsistent ideas about race and equality). Nat Turner is not considered a safe hero; Abraham Lincoln is.

To be antiracist also means to work affirmatively to combat racism. It means making antiracism and antidiscrimination explicit parts of the curriculum and teaching young people skills in confronting racism. A school that is truly committed to a multicultural philosophy will closely examine both its policies and the attitudes and behaviors of its staff to determine how these might discriminate against some students. The focus on school policies and practices makes it evident that multicultural education is about more than the perceptions and beliefs of individual teachers and other educators. Multicultural education is antiracist because it exposes racist and discriminatory practices in schools.

Racism is seldom mentioned in school (it is bad, a dirty word) and, therefore, is not dealt with. Unfortunately, many teachers think that simply having lessons in getting along or celebrating Human Relations Week will make students nonracist or nondiscriminatory in general. But it is impossible to be untouched by racism, sexism, linguicism, heterosexism, ageism, anti-Semitism, classism, and ethno-centrism in a society characterized by all of them. To expect schools to be an oasis of sensitivity and understanding in the midst of this stratification is unrealistic. Therefore, part of the mission of the school becomes creating the environment and encouragement that legitimates talk about inequality and makes it a source of dialogue. Teaching the missing or fragmented parts of our history is crucial to achieving this mission.

Although White students may be uncomfortable by discussions about race, Henry Giroux has suggested that bringing race and racism into full view can become a useful and positive pedagogical tool to help students locate themselves and their responsibilities concerning racism.[5] In addition, Beverly Daniel Tatum's groundbreaking work on bringing discussions of race out of the closet proposes discussing race and racism within the framework of racial and cultural identity theory. Doing so, she contends, can help students and teachers focus on how racism negatively affects all people and can provide a sense of hope for positive changes.[6]

What about teachers? Because many teachers have had little experience with diversity, discussions of racism often threaten to disrupt their deeply held ideals of fair play and equality. Most teachers are uneasy with these topics, and therefore fruitful classroom discussions about discrimination rarely happen. If this continues to be the case, neither unfair individual behaviors nor institutional policies and practices in schools will change. Students of disempowered groups will continue to bear the brunt of these kinds of inequities. The dilemma is how to challenge the silence about race and racism so that teachers can enter into meaningful and constructive dialogue with their students. In speaking specifically about confronting this issue in teacher education, Marilyn Cochran-Smith writes, "To teach lessons about race and racism in teacher education is to struggle to unlearn racism itself—to interrogate the assumptions that are deeply embedded in the curriculum, to our own complicity in maintaining existing systems of privilege and oppression, and to grapple with our own failure."[7]

For example, in research with teachers from around the country, Karen McLean Donaldson found that many teachers were in denial about racism and its effects in schools. On the other hand, those who became active in antiracist projects broadened their understanding and were able to use their new skills in creating affirming learning environments for all their students.[8]

One of the reasons schools are reluctant to tackle racism and discrimination is that these are disturbing topics for those who have traditionally benefited by their race, gender, and social class, among other advantageous differences. Because instruction in, and discussion of, such topics place people in the role of either the victimizer or the victimized, an initial and logical reaction, for example, of European American teachers and students in discussing race, is to feel guilty. But being antiracist does not mean flailing about in guilt and remorse. Although this reaction may be understandable, remaining at this level is immobilizing. Teachers and students need to move beyond guilt to a state of invigorated awareness and informed confidence in which they take personal and group action for positive change rather than hide behind feelings of remorse.

The primary victims of racism and discrimination are those who suffer its immediate consequences, but racism and discrimination are destructive and demeaning to everyone. Keeping this in mind, it is easier for all teachers and students to face these issues. Although not everyone is directly guilty of racism and discrimination, we are all responsible for it. What does this mean? Primarily, it means that working actively for social justice is everyone's business. Yet it is often the victims of racism and other kinds of discrimination who are left to act on their own. Fern Sherman's case study, which follows Chapter 9, is a good example. Being the only Native American student in her entire school was difficult. For one, it meant that Fern felt a tremendous responsibility to confront, on her own, the racism she saw in texts and in the curriculum. Having allies to support her would have shifted the responsibility from her shoulders to others so that it could become a shared responsibility. Everybody loses out when a particular group of students is scapegoated. Rebecca Florentina's case study is another example. As a lesbian, Rebecca felt the need to personally confront the heterosexual biases in her school, but this should have been viewed as everyone's responsibility. Indeed, we will have come a long way when everybody feels this same obligation.

Multicultural education is basic education

Given the recurring concern for teaching the "basics," multicultural education must be understood as basic education. Multicultural literacy is just as indispensable for living in today's world as reading, writing, arithmetic, and computer literacy. When multicultural education is peripheral to the core curriculum, it is perceived as irrelevant to basic education. One of the major stumbling blocks to implementing a broadly conceptualized multicultural education is the ossification of the "canon" in our schools.

The canon, as understood in contemporary U.S. education, assumes that the knowledge that is most worthwhile is already in place. This notion explains the popularity of E. D. Hirsch's series *What Every [First, Second, Third . . .] Grader Needs to Know.*[9] Geared primarily to parents, this series builds on the fear that their children simply will not measure up if they do not possess the core knowledge (usually in the form of facts) that they need to succeed in school. According to this rather narrow view, the basics have, in effect, already been defined, and the knowledge taught is inevitably European, male, and upper class in origin and conception. In a recent response to Hirsch's view of cultural literacy, Eugene Provenzo faults Hirsch for a limited and rigid understanding of cultural literacy that is ultimately impoverished, elitist, antidemocratic, and even un-American in that it excludes so much that is uniquely American.[10]

The idea that there is a static and sacred knowledge that must be mastered is especially evident in the arts and social sciences. For instance, art history classes rarely consider other countries besides France's, Italy's, and sometimes England's Great Masters, yet surely other nations besides Europe have had great masters. "Classical music" is another example. What is called "classical music" is actually European classical music. Africa, Asia, and Latin America define their classical music in different ways. This same ethnocentrism is found in our history books, which portray Europeans and European Americans as the "actors" and all others as the recipients, bystanders, or bit players of history. The canon, as it currently stands, however, is unrealistic and incomplete because history is never as one-sided as it appears in most of our schools' curricula. We need to expand the definition of *basic* education by opening up curricula to a variety of perspectives and experiences.

This is not to say that the concern that the canon tries to address is not a genuine one. Modern-day knowledge is so dispersed and compartmentalized that our young people learn very little about commonalities in our history and culture. There is little core knowledge to which they are exposed and this can be problematic, but proposing static curricula, almost exclusively with European and European American referents, does little to expand our actual common culture.

At the same time, it is unrealistic, for a number of reasons, to expect perfectly "equal treatment" about all groups of people in school curricula and instruction. A "force-fit," which tries to equalize the number of African Americans, women, Jewish Americans, gays, and so on in the curriculum, is not what multicultural education is about. A great many groups have been denied access to participation in history. Thus, their role has not been equal, at least if we consider history in the traditional sense of great movers and shakers, monarchs and despots, and makers of war and peace. But, even within this somewhat narrow view of history, the participation of people of diverse backgrounds and social identities has nevertheless been appreciable. These heretofore ignored participants deserve to be included. The point is that those who have been important and/or prominent in the evolution of our history, arts, literature, and science, yet invisible, should be made visible. Recent literature anthologies are a good example of the inclusion of more voices and perspectives than ever before. Did these people become "great writers" overnight, or was it simply that they were "buried" for too long?

We are not recommending simply the "contributions" approach to history, literature, and the arts.[11] Such an approach can easily become patronizing by simply adding bits and pieces to a preconceived canon. Rather, missing from most curricula is a consideration of how generally excluded groups have made history and affected the arts, literature, geography, science, and philosophy on their own terms.

The alternative to multicultural education is monocultural education, which reflects only one reality and is biased toward the dominant group. Monocultural education is the order of the day in most of our schools. What students learn represents only a fraction of what is available knowledge, and those who decide what is most important make choices that are influenced by their own limited background, education, and experiences. Because the viewpoints of so many are left out, monocultural education is, at best, an incomplete education. It deprives all students of the diversity that is part of our world.

No school can consider that it is doing a proper or complete job unless its students develop multicultural literacy. What such a conception means in practice will no doubt differ from school to school, but at the very least, we should expect all students to be fluent in a language other than their own, aware of the literature and arts of many different peoples, and conversant with the history and geography not only of the United States but also of African, Asian, Latin American, and European countries. Through such an education, we should expect students to develop social and intellectual skills that help them understand and empathize with a wide diversity of people. Nothing can be more basic than this.

Multicultural education is important for all students

There is a widespread perception—or rather, misperception—that multicultural education is only for students of color, for urban students, or for so-called "disadvantaged" or "at-risk" students. This belief probably grew from the roots of multicultural education: the Civil Rights and Equal Education Movements of the 1960s. During that era, the primary objective of multicultural education was to address the needs of students who historically had been most neglected or miseducated by the schools, especially students of color. Those who first promoted multicultural education firmly believed that attention needed to be given to developing curriculum and materials that reflected these students' histories, cultures, and experiences. This thinking was historically necessary and is understandable even today, given the great curricular imbalance that continues to exist in most schools.

More recently, a broader conceptualization of multicultural education has gained acceptance. It is that all students are miseducated to the extent that they receive only a partial and biased education. Although it is true that the primary victims of biased education are those who are invisible in the curriculum, everyone misses out when education is biased. Important female figures, for example, are still largely absent in curricula, except in special courses on women's history that are few and far between. Working-class history is also absent in virtually all U.S. curricula. The children of the working class are deprived not only of a more forthright education but, more important, of a place in history, and students of all social class backgrounds are deprived of a more honest and complete view of our past. Likewise, there is a pervasive and impenetrable silence concerning gays and lesbians in most schools, not just in the curriculum but also in extracurricular activities. The result is that gay and lesbian students are placed at risk in terms of social well-being and academic achievement.[12]

Teachers in primarily White schools might think that multicultural education is not meant for their students. They could not be more wrong. White students receive only a partial education, which helps to legitimate their cultural blindness. Seeing only themselves, they may believe that they are the norm and thus most important and everyone else is secondary and less important. A recent book that challenges this perception (*What If All the Kids Are White?*) provides excellent strategies and resources for teachers working in mostly White communities.[13]

Males also receive an incomplete education because they (not to mention their female peers) learn little about women in their schooling. The children of the wealthy learn that the wealthy and the powerful are the real makers of history, the ones who have left their mark on civilization. Heterosexual students receive the message that gay and lesbian students should be ostracized because they are deviant and immoral. Only the able-bodied are reflected in most curricula, save for exceptions such as Helen Keller, who are presented as either bigger than life or as sources of pity. The humanity of all students is jeopardized as a result.

Multicultural education is, by definition, *inclusive*. Because it is *about* all people, it is also *for* all people, regardless of their ethnicity, ability, social class, language, sexual orientation, religion, gender, race, or other difference. It can even be convincingly argued that students from the dominant culture need multicultural education more than others because they are generally the most miseducated or uneducated about diversity. For example, European American youths often think that they do not even have a culture, at least not in the same sense that easily culturally identifiable youths do. At the same time, they feel that their ways of living, doing things, believing, and acting are "normal." Anything else is "ethnic" and exotic.

Feeling as they do, young people from dominant groups are prone to develop an unrealistic view of the world and of their place in it. These are the children who learn not to question, for example, the name of "flesh-colored" bandages, even though they are not the flesh color of 75 percent of the world's population. They do not even have to think about the fact that everyone, Christian or not, gets holidays at Christmas and Easter and that the holidays of other religions are given little attention in our calendars and school schedules. They may automatically assume that all children are raised by heterosexual biological parents and may be surprised to learn that many children are instead raised by just one parent, adoptive parents, grandparents, or lesbian or gay parents. Whereas children from dominated groups may develop feelings of inferiority based on their schooling, dominant group children may develop feelings of superiority. Both responses are based on incomplete and inaccurate information about the complexity and diversity of the world, and both are harmful.

In spite of this, multicultural education continues to be thought of by many educators as education for the "culturally different" or the "disadvantaged." Teachers in predominantly European American schools, for example, may feel it is not important or necessary to teach their students anything about the Civil Rights Movement. Likewise, only in scattered bilingual programs in Mexican American communities are students exposed to literature by Mexican and Mexican American authors, and ethnic studies classes are often only offered at high schools with a high percentage of students of color. These are ethnocentric interpretations of multicultural education.

The thinking behind these actions is paternalistic as well as misinformed. Because anything remotely digressing from the "regular" (European American) curriculum is automatically considered soft by some educators, a traditional response to making a curriculum multicultural is to water it down. Poor pedagogical decisions are then based on the premise that so-called disadvantaged students need a watered-down version of the "real" curriculum, whereas more privileged children can handle the "regular" or more academically challenging curriculum. But, rather than dilute it, making a curriculum multicultural inevitably enriches it. All students would be enriched by reading the poetry of Langston Hughes or the stories of Gary Soto, by being fluent in a second language, or by understanding the history of Islam.

Multicultural education is pervasive

Multicultural education is neither an activity that happens at a set period of the day nor another subject area to be covered. Having a "multicultural teacher" who goes from class to class in the same way as the music or art teacher is not what multicultural education should be about either. If this is a school's concept of multicultural education, it is little wonder that teachers sometimes decide that it is a frill they cannot afford.

A true multicultural approach is pervasive. It permeates everything: the school climate, physical environment, curriculum, and relationships among teachers and students and community.[14] It is apparent in every lesson, curriculum guide, unit, bulletin board, and letter that is sent home; it can be seen in the process by which books and audiovisual aids are acquired for the library, in the games played during recess, and in the lunch that is served. *Multicultural education is a philosophy, a way of looking at the world,* not simply a program or a class or a teacher. In this comprehensive way, multicultural education helps us rethink school reform.

What might a multicultural philosophy mean in the way that schools are organized? For one, it would probably mean the end of rigid forms of ability tracking, which inevitably favors some students over others. It would also mean that the complexion of the school, both literally and figuratively, would change. That is, schools would be desegregated rather than segregated along lines of race and social class as they are now. In addition, there would be an effort to have the entire school staff be more representative of our nation's diversity. Pervasiveness would be apparent in the great variety and creativity of instructional strategies, so that students from all cultural groups, and females as well as males, would benefit from methods other than the traditional. The curriculum would be completely overhauled and would include the histories, viewpoints, and insights of many different peoples and both males and females. Topics usually considered "dangerous" could be talked about in classes, and students would be encouraged to become critical thinkers. Textbooks and other instructional materials would also reflect a pluralistic perspective. Families and other community people would be visible in the schools because they offer a unique and helpful viewpoint. Teachers, families, and students would have the opportunity to work together to design motivating and multiculturally appropriate curricula.

In other less global but no less important ways, the multicultural school would probably look vastly different. For example, the lunchroom might offer a variety of international meals, not because they are exotic delights but because they are the foods people in the community eat daily. Sports and games from all over the world might be played, and not all would be competitive. Letters would be sent home in the languages that the particular child's family understands. Children would not be punished for speaking their native language. On the contrary, they would be encouraged to do so, and it would be used in their instruction as well. In summary, the school would be a learning environment in which curriculum, pedagogy, and outreach are all consistent with a broadly conceptualized multicultural philosophy.

Multicultural education is education for social justice

All good education connects theory with reflection and action, which is what Brazilian educator Paulo Freire defined as *praxis*.[15] Developing a multicultural perspective means learning how to think in more inclusive and expansive ways, reflecting on what is learned, and applying that learning to real situations. Nearly a century ago, educational philosopher John Dewey described what happens when education is not connected to reflection and action when he wrote "information severed from thoughtful action is dead, a mind-crushing load."[16]

Multicultural education invites students and teachers to put their learning into action for social justice. Whether debating a difficult issue, developing a community newspaper, starting a collaborative program at a local senior center, or organizing a petition for the removal of a potentially dangerous waste treatment plant in the neighborhood, students learn that they have power, collectively and individually, to make change.

This aspect of multicultural education fits in particularly well with the developmental level of young people who, starting in the middle elementary grades, are very conscious of what is fair and unfair. If their pronounced sense of justice is not channeled appropriately, the result can be anger, resentment, alienation, or dropping out of school physically or psychologically.

Preparing students for active membership in a democracy is also the basis of Deweyian philosophy and it has frequently been cited by schools as a major educational goal. But few schools serve as sites of apprenticeship for democracy. Policies and practices such as inflexible ability grouping, inequitable testing, monocultural curricula, and unimaginative pedagogy contradict this lofty aim. The result is that students in many schools perceive the claim of democracy to be a hollow and irrelevant issue. Henry Giroux, for example, has suggested that what he calls "the discourse of democracy" has been trivialized to mean such things as uncritical patriotism and mandatory pledges to the flag that the 9/11 disaster has exacerbated.[17] In some schools, democratic practices are found only in textbooks and confined to discussions of the American Revolution, and the chance for students to practice day-to-day democracy is minimal.

The fact that controversial topics such as power and inequality are rarely discussed in schools should come as no surprise. As institutions, schools are charged with maintaining the status quo, and discussing such issues might seem to threaten the status quo. But schools are also expected to promote equality. Exposing the contradictions between democratic ideals and actual manifestations of inequality makes many people uncomfortable, including some educators. Still, such matters are at the heart of a broadly conceptualized multicultural perspective because the subject matter of schooling is society, with all its wrinkles and warts and contradictions. Ethics and the distribution of power, status, and rewards are basic societal concerns; education *must* address them.

Although the connection between multicultural education and students' rights and responsibilities in a democracy is unmistakable, many young people do not learn about these responsibilities, about the challenges of democracy, or about the central role of citizens in ensuring and maintaining the privileges of democracy. Results from a recent study about the First Amendment, in which over 112,000 high school students were surveyed, is a chilling example of how little students understand about democracy. The project, which was funded by the John S. and James L. Knight Foundation, found that when the First Amendment was quoted to students, more than one-third of them felt that it went too far in the rights it guarantees. The report concluded that "It appears, in fact, that our nation's high schools are failing their students when it comes to instilling in them appreciation for the First Amendment."[18] In this situation, social justice becomes an empty concept.

Multicultural education can have a great impact in helping to turn this situation around. A multicultural perspective presumes that classrooms should not simply allow discussions that focus on social justice, but also welcome them and even plan actively for such discussions to take place. These discussions might center on issues that adversely and disproportionately affect disenfranchised communities—poverty, discrimination, war, the national budget—and what students can do to address these problems. Because all of these problems are pluralistic, education must be multicultural.

Multicultural education is a process

Curriculum and materials represent the content of multicultural education, but multicultural education is, above all, a process, that is, it is ongoing and dynamic. No one ever stops becoming a multicultural person, and knowledge is never complete. This means that there is no established canon that is set in stone. Second, multicultural education is a process because it primarily involves relationships among people. The sensitivity and understanding teachers show their students are more crucial in promoting student learning than the facts and fig-

ures they may know about different ethnic and cultural groups. Also, multicultural education is a process because it concerns such intangibles as expectations of student achievement, learning environments, students' learning preferences, and other cultural variables that are absolutely essential for schools to understand if they are to become successful with all students.

The dimension of multicultural education as a process is too often relegated to a secondary position, because content is easier to handle and has speedier results. For instance, staging an assembly program on Black History Month is easier than eliminating tracking: The former involves adding extracurricular content, and, although this is important and necessary, it is not as decisive at challenging fundamental perceptions about ability, social class, and race through the elimination of tracking. Another example: Changing a basal reader is easier than developing higher expectations for all students. The former involves substituting one book for another; the latter involves changing perceptions, behaviors, and knowledge, not an easy task. As a result, the processes of multicultural education are generally more complex, more politically volatile, and even more threatening to vested interests than introducing "controversial" content.

Because multicultural education is a process, it must debunk simplistic and erroneous conventional wisdom as well as dismantle policies and practices that are disadvantageous for some students at the expense of others. Through their teacher education programs, future teachers need to develop an awareness of the influence of culture and language on learning, the persistence of racism and discrimination in schools and society, and instructional and curricular strategies that encourage learning among a wide variety of students. Teachers' roles in the school also need to be redefined, because empowered teachers help to create learning environments in which students are empowered. Also, the role of families needs to be expanded so that the insights and values of the community can be accurately reflected in the school. Nothing short of a complete restructuring of curricula and the organization of schools is required. The process is complex, problematic, controversial, and time consuming, but it is one in which teachers and schools must engage to make their schools truly multicultural.

Multicultural education is critical pedagogy

Knowledge is neither neutral nor apolitical, yet it is generally treated by teachers and schools as if it were. Consequently, knowledge taught in our schools tends to reflect the lowest common denominator—that which is sure to offend the fewest (and the most powerful) and is least controversial. Students may leave school with the impression that all major conflicts have already been resolved, but history, including educational history, is still full of great debates, controversies, and ideological struggles. These controversies and conflicts are often left at the schoolhouse door.

Every educational decision made at any level, whether by a teacher or by an entire school system, reflects the political ideology and worldview of the decision maker. Decisions to dismantle tracking, discontinue standardized tests, lengthen the school day, use one reading program rather than another, study literature from the Harlem Renaissance or Elizabethan period (or both), or use learning centers rather than rows of chairs, all reflect a particular view of learners and of education.

All the decisions we, as educators, make, no matter how neutral they seem, may have an impact on the lives and experiences of our students. This is true of the curriculum, books, and other materials we provide for them. State and local guidelines and mandates may limit what particular schools and teachers choose to teach, and this too is a political decision. What is excluded is often as revealing as what is included. Much of the literature taught at the high school level, for instance, is still heavily male-oriented, European, and European American. The significance of women, people of color, and those who write in other languages (even if their work has been translated into English) is diminished, unintentionally or not.

A major problem with a monocultural curriculum is that it gives students only one way of seeing the world. When reality is presented as static, finished and flat, the underlying tensions, controversies, passions, and problems faced by people throughout history and today disappear. To be informed and active participants in a democratic society, students need to understand the complexity of the world and the many perspectives involved. Using a critical perspective, students learn that there

is not just one way (or even two or three) of viewing issues.

To explain what we mean by "using a critical perspective," we will be facetious and use the number 17 to explain it: Let's say there are at least 17 ways of understanding reality, and, until we have learned all of them, we have only part of the truth. The point is that there are multiple perspectives on every issue, but most of us have learned only the "safe" or standard way of interpreting events and issues.

Textbooks in all subject areas exclude information about unpopular perspectives or the perspectives of disempowered groups in our society. These are the "lies my teacher told me" to which James Loewen refers in his powerful critique of U.S. history textbooks.[19] For instance, Thanksgiving is generally presented as an uncomplicated celebration in which Pilgrims and Indians shared the bounty of the harvest, but it is unlikely that the Wampanoags experienced Thanksgiving in this manner. One way to counter simplistic or one-sided views is to provide alternative or multiple views of the same topic. A good example is a book published by the Boston Children's Museum that presents a multiplicity of perspectives on Thanksgiving, including the Wampanoag perspective.[20] Likewise, few U.S. history texts include the perspective of working-class people, although they were and continue to be the backbone of our country. To cite another example, the immigrant experience is generally treated as a romantic and successful odyssey rather than the traumatic, wrenching, and often less-than-idyllic situation it was (and still is) for so many. The experiences of non-European immigrants or those forcibly incorporated into the United States are usually presented as if they were identical to the experiences of Europeans, which they have not at all been. We can also be sure that, if the perspectives of women were taken seriously, the school curriculum would be altered dramatically. The historian Howard Zinn provides one of the few examples of such a multifaceted, multicultural, and complex history. In his classic, *A People's History of the United States* (most recently updated in 2005), we clearly see a history full of passion and conflict with voices rarely included in traditional history texts.[21] All students need to understand these multiple perspectives and not only the viewpoints of dominant groups. Unless they do, students will continue to think of history as linear and fixed and to think of themselves as passive and unable to make changes in their communities and the larger society or even in their personal interactions.

According to James Banks, the main goal of a multicultural curriculum is to help students develop decision-making and social action skills.[22] By doing so, students learn to view events and situations from a variety of perspectives. A multicultural approach values diversity and encourages critical thinking, reflection, and action. Through this process, students are empowered. This is the basis of critical pedagogy. Its opposite is what Paulo Freire called "domesticating education,"—education that emphasizes passivity, acceptance, and submissiveness. According to Freire, education for domestication is a process of "transferring knowledge," whereas education for liberation is one of "transforming action."[23] Education that is liberating encourages students to take risks, to be curious, and to question. Rather than expecting students to repeat teachers' words, it expects them to seek their own answers.

How are critical pedagogy and multicultural education connected? They are what Geneva Gay has called "mirror images."[24] That is, they work together, according to Christine Sleeter, as "a form of resistance to dominant modes of schooling."[25] Critical pedagogy acknowledges rather than suppresses cultural and linguistic diversity. It is not simply the transfer of knowledge from teacher to students, even though that knowledge may challenge what students previously learned. Critical literacy, which developed from critical pedagogy and focuses specifically on language, has a similar goal. According to educational researcher Barbara Comber, "When teachers and students are engaged in critical literacy, they will be asking complicated questions about language and power, about people and lifestyle, about morality and ethics, about who is advantaged by the way things are and who is disadvantaged."[26]

A multicultural perspective does not simply operate on the principle of substituting one "truth" or perspective for another. Rather, it reflects on multiple and contradictory perspectives to understand reality more fully. The historian Ronald Takaki expressed it best when he said, "The multiculturalism I have been seeking is a serious scholarship that includes all American peoples and challenges the traditional master narrative of American history."

He concludes that "[t]he intellectual purpose of multiculturalism is a more accurate understanding of who we are as Americans."[27] This means that, in our pluralistic society, teachers and students need to learn to understand even those viewpoints with which they may disagree—not to practice "political correctness," but to develop a critical perspective about what they hear, read, or see. Individuals with this kind of critical perspective can use the understanding gained from mindful reflection to act as catalysts for change.

Ira Shor has proposed that critical pedagogy is more difficult precisely because it moves beyond academic discourse: "Testing the limits by practicing theory and theorizing practice in a real context is harder and more risky than theorizing theory without a context."[28] Yet the typical curriculum discourages students from thinking critically. In this sense, critical pedagogy takes courage. What does it mean to teach with courage? A few examples are in order. For teachers Darcy Ballentine and Lisa Hill, the purpose of teaching reading to their second, third, and fourth graders meant challenging the children to take up "brave books" that included what the teachers called "dangerous truths." These books broached topics such as racism and inequality, issues generally avoided in children's books (although certainly present in the lives of many children). Ballentine and Hill reflected on their experience in this way: "In the year that we taught these two texts, as well as many other brave books, our children's voices—in discussion, in explanations of their art, and in their dramatic enactments—continually reminded us that the risks we were taking in our teaching made sense."[29]

More recently, teacher Vivian Vasquez, in her book *Negotiating Critical Literacies with Young Children*, documented her experiences in using a critical literacy approach with three- to five-year-olds. Among the many examples she cites, one concerns what happened when the children in her class realized that a classmate had not eaten at the annual school barbecue because he was a vegetarian and only hot dogs and hamburgers had been served. On their own initiative—but having learned to think critically about social action—the students drew up a petition about providing vegetarian alternatives and gave it to the event committee. The next year, vegetarian alternatives were provided. In her beautiful and hopeful book, Vasquez demonstrates that critical literacy is not about despair and anger but rather about joy and inclusion. She also affirms that even the youngest children can learn to think critically and positively about their ability to effect change through their actions.[30]

History is generally written by the conquerors, not by the vanquished or by those who benefit least in society. The result is that history books are skewed in the direction of dominant groups in a society. When American Indian people write history books, they generally say that Columbus *invaded* rather than *discovered* this land, and that there was no heroic *westward expansion,* but rather an *eastern encroachment.* Mexican Americans often include references to Aztlán, the legendary land that was overrun by Europeans during this encroachment. Many Puerto Ricans remove the gratuitous word *granted* that appears in so many textbooks and explain that U.S. citizenship was instead *imposed,* and they emphasize that U.S. citizenship was opposed by even the two houses of the legislature that existed in Puerto Rico in 1917. African American historians tend to describe the active participation of enslaved Africans in their own liberation, and they often include such accounts as slave narratives to describe the rebellion and resistance of their people. Working class people who know their history usually credit laborers rather than Andrew Carnegie with the tremendous building boom that occurred in the United States, and the rapid growth of the U.S. economy, during the late 19th century and the 20th century. And Japanese Americans frequently cite racist hysteria, economic exploitation, and propaganda as major reasons for their internment in U.S. concentration camps during World War II.

Critical pedagogy is also an exploder of myths. It helps to expose and demystify as well as demythologize some of the truths that we take for granted and to analyze them critically and carefully. Justice for all, equal treatment under the law, and equal educational opportunity, although certainly ideals worth believing in and striving for, are not always the reality. The problem is that we teach them as if they are, and were always, real and true, with no exceptions. Critical pedagogy allows us to have faith in these ideals while critically examining the discrepancies between the ideal and the reality.

Because critical pedagogy begins with the experiences and viewpoints of students, it is by its very nature multicultural. The most successful education is that which begins with the learner and, when a multicultural perspective underpins education, students themselves become the foundation for the curriculum. However, a liberating education also takes students beyond their own particular and therefore limited experiences, no matter what their background.

Critical pedagogy is not new, although it has been referred to by other terms in other times. In our country, precursors to critical pedagogy can be found in the work of African American educators such as Carter Woodson and W. E. B. DuBois.[31] In Brazil, the historic work of Paulo Freire influenced literacy and liberation movements throughout the world. Even before Freire, critical pedagogy was being practiced in other parts of the world. Almost half a century ago, Sylvia Ashton-Warner, teaching Maori children in New Zealand, found that the curriculum, materials, viewpoints, and pedagogy that had been used in educating them were all borrowed from the dominant culture. Because Maori children had been failed dismally by New Zealand schools, Ashton-Warner developed a strategy for literacy based on the children's experiences and interests. Calling it an "organic" approach, she taught children how to read by using the words they wanted to learn. Each child would bring in a number of new words each day, learn to read them, and then use them in writing. Because Ashton-Warner's approach was based on what children knew and wanted to know, it was extraordinarily successful. In contrast, basal readers, having little to do with Maori children's experiences, were mechanistic instruments that imposed severe limitations on the students' creativity and expressiveness.[32]

Other approaches that have successfully used the experiences of students are worth mentioning. The superb preschool curriculum developed nearly two decades ago by Louise Derman-Sparks and the Anti-Bias Curriculum Task Force is especially noteworthy. Another recent example is Mary Cowhey's approach. A first- and second-grade teacher, Cowhey has written about how she uses critical pedagogy to help create a strong community as well as to teach her students to question everything they learn. Catherine Compton-Lilly, in her role as a first-grade teacher and later a reading teacher, uses a critical perspective to develop classroom strategies to "change the world" by confronting assumptions about race, poverty, and culture. Instructional strategies based on students' languages, cultures, families, and communities are also included in wonderful books by the educational organizations Rethinking Schools and Teaching for Change. Ira Shor's descriptions of the work he does in his own college classroom are further proof of the power of critical pedagogy at all levels. In the same category, Enid Lee, Deborah Menkart, and Margo Okazawa-Rey have developed an exceptional professional development guide for teachers and preservice teachers.[33]

SUMMARY

Multicultural education represents a way of rethinking school reform because it responds to many of the problematic factors leading to school underachievement and failure. When implemented comprehensively, multicultural education can transform and enrich the schooling of all young people. Because multicultural education takes into account the cultures, languages, and experiences of all students, it can go beyond the simple transfer of skills to include those attitudes and critical, analytical abilities that have the potential to empower students for productive and meaningful lives.

This discussion leads us to an intriguing insight: In the final analysis, multicultural education as defined here is simply good pedagogy. That is, all good education takes students seriously, uses their experiences as a basis for further learning, and helps them to develop into informed, critically aware, and empowered citizens. What is multicultural about this? To put it simply, in our multicultural society, all good education needs to take into account the diversity of our student population. Multicultural education is good education for a larger number of our students. Is multicultural education just as necessary in a monocultural society? In response, we might legitimately ask whether even the most ethnically homogeneous society is truly monocultural, considering the diversity of social class, language, sexual orientation, physical and mental ability, and other human and social differences that exist in all societies. Our world is increasingly interdependent, and all students need to understand their role in a global society, not simply in their small town, city, or nation. Multicultural education is a process that goes beyond the changing demographics in a particular country. It is more effective education for a changing world.

To Think About

1. What do you see as the difference between a broadly conceptualized multicultural education and multicultural education defined in terms of "holidays and heroes"?
2. Do you believe it is important for antiracism and antidiscrimination, in general, to be at the core of multicultural education? Why or why not?
3. Would you say that European American students are miseducated if they are not exposed to a multicultural curriculum? What about males if they do not learn about women in history? Why?
4. Think of a number of curriculum ideas that conform to the definition of multicultural education as social justice. How might students be engaged through the curriculum to consider and act on issues of social justice? Give some specific examples.
5. How do you define multicultural education? Explain your definition.

Activities for Personal, School, and Community Change

1. Prepare a public presentation on the benefits of multicultural education for your colleagues, a group of new teachers, or a group of parents. What might you include in your presentation to convince skeptics that multicultural education, broadly defined and implemented, is necessary for your school?

2. Ask to be on your school's hiring committee when the next teaching position becomes available. How can you use your influence to define the job qualifications and job description in a way that includes multicultural education? What should these be?

3. With a group of colleagues, develop an art, science, or math project that builds on multicultural education as critical pedagogy. How would you do this? In what activities would students be involved? How would these activities motivate them to think critically? Discuss the results with your colleagues.

Companion Website

For access to additional case studies, weblinks, concept cards, and other material related to this chapter, visit the text's companion website at **www.ablongman.com/nieto5e.**

Notes to Chapter 8

1. A comprehensive resource on the history, goals, and concerns of multicultural education is *Handbook of Research on Multicultural Education*, 2nd ed., edited by James A. Banks and Cherry A. McGee Banks (San Francisco: Jossey-Bass, 2004).

2. Meyer Weinberg, "Notes from the Editor." *A Chronicle of Equal Education* 4, no. 3 (November 1982): 7.

3. Michelle Fine, *Framing Dropouts: Notes on the Politics of an Urban Public High School* (Albany: State University of New York Press, 1991).

4. Jonathan Kozol, "Great Men and Women (Tailored for School Use)." *Learning Magazine* (December 1975): 16–20.

5. Henry Giroux, "Rewriting the Discourse of Racial Identity: Towards a Pedagogy and Politics of Whiteness." *Harvard Educational Review* 67, no. 2 (Summer 1997): 285–320.

6. Beverly Daniel Tatum, *Why Are All the Black Kids Sitting Together in the Cafeteria? and Other Conversations About Race* (New York: Basic Books, 1997).

7. Marilyn Cochran-Smith, "Blind Vision: Unlearning Racism in Teacher Education." *Harvard Educational Review* 70, no. 2 (Summer 2000): 57–190.

8. Karen B. McLean Donaldson, *Shattering the Denial: Protocols for the Classrooms and Beyond* (Westport, CT: Bergin and Garvey, 2001).

9. Published by Delta beginning in 1994, these texts include the "core" knowledge that children are supposed to know at different grade levels in order to do well in school. As an example, see *What Your Fourth Grader Needs to Know: Fundamentals of a Good Fourth-Grade Education* (*The Core Knowledge*), edited by E. D. Hirsch (New York: Delta, 1994).

10. Eugene F. Provenzo, Jr., *Critical Literacy: What Every American Ought to Know* (Boulder, CO: Paradigm, 2005).

11. For a discussion of different levels of curriculum integration in multicultural education, see James A. Banks, *Teaching Strategies for Ethnic Studies*, 7th ed. (Boston: Allyn and Bacon, 2003).

12. See, for example, Joan Roughgarden, *Evolution's Rainbow: Diversity, Gender, and Sexuality in Nature and People* (Berkeley: University of California Press, 2005); and Ian Ayres and Jennifer Gararda Brown, *Straightforward* (Princeton, NJ: Princeton University Press, 2005).

13. Louise Derman-Sparks, Patricia G. Ramsey, Julie Olsen Edwards, and Carol Brunson Day, *What If All The Kids Are White? Anti-Bias Multicultural Education With Young Children and Families* (New York: Teachers College Press, 2006).

14. A good example of how a multicultural approach includes educators, students, and families can be found in Patricia G. Ramsey, ed., *Teaching and Learning in a Diverse World: Multicultural Education for Young Children*, 3rd ed. (New York: Teachers College Press, 2004).

15. Paulo Freire, *Pedagogy of the Oppressed* (New York: Seabury Press, 1970).

16. John Dewey, *Democracy and Education* (New York: Free Press, 1966; first published 1916): 153.

17. Henry A. Giroux, "Democracy, Freedom, and Justice After September 11th: Rethinking the Role of Educators and the Politics of Schooling." *Teachers College Record* 104, no. 6 (September 2002): 1138–1162.

18. "Future of the First Amendment." John S. and James L. Knight Foundation, 2005. Available at: http://firstamendmentfuture.org

19. James W. Loewen, *Lies My Teacher Told Me: Everything Your American History Textbook Got Wrong* (New York: New Press, reissue edition, 2005).

20. Children's Museum, Boston, *Many Thanksgivings: Teaching Thanksgiving—Including the Wampanoag Perspective* (Boston: The Children's Museum, 2002).

21. Howard Zinn, *A People's History of the United States, 1492–Present* (New York: Harper Perennial, 2001; 1st ed., 1980).

22. James A. Banks, *Teaching Strategies for Ethnic Studies*, 7th ed. (Boston: Allyn and Bacon, 2003).

23. Paulo Freire, *The Politics of Education: Culture, Power, and Liberation* (South Hadley, MA: Bergen and Garvey, 1985).

24. Geneva Gay, "Mirror Images on Common Issues: Parallels Between Multicultural Education and Critical Pedagogy." In *Multicultural Education, Critical Pedagogy, and the Politics of Difference*, edited by Christine E. Sleeter and Peter L. McLaren (Albany: State University of New York Press, 1996): 155–189.

25. Christine E. Sleeter, *Multicultural Education and Social Activism* (Albany, NY: State University of New York Press, 1996): 2.

26. Barbara Comber, "Critical Literacies and Local Action: Teacher Knowledge and a 'New' Research Agenda." In *Negotiating Critical Literacies in Classrooms*, edited by Barbara Comber and Anne Simpson. (Mahwah, NJ: Lawrence Erlbaum, 2001): 271.

27. Joan Montgomery, "A Different Mirror: A Conversation with Ronald Takaki," *Educational Leadership* 56, no. 7 (April 1999): 9–13.

28. Ira Shor, *When Students Have Power: Negotiating Authority in a Critical Pedagogy* (Chicago: University of Chicago Press, 1996): 3.

29. Darcy Ballentine and Lisa Hill, "Teaching Beyond Once Upon a Time." *Language Arts* 78, no. 1 (September 2000): 11–20.

30. Vivian Vasquez, *Negotiating Critical Literacies with Young Children* (Mahwah, NJ: Lawrence Erlbaum, 2004).

31. See, for instance, Carter G. Woodson, *The Miseducation of the Negro* (Washington, DC: Associated Publishers, 1933); W. E. B. DuBois, "Does the Negro Need Separate Schools?" *Journal of Negro Education* 4, no. 3 (July 1935): 328–335. For a historical analysis of multicultural education and critical pedagogy, see James A. Banks, "Multicultural Education: Historical Development, Dimensions, and Practice." In *Handbook of Research on Multicultural Education*, 2nd ed., edited by James A. Banks and Cherry A. McGee Banks (San Francisco: Jossey-Bass, 2004).

32. Sylvia Ashton-Warner, *Teacher* (New York: Simon & Schuster, 1963).

33. See, for example, Louise Derman-Sparks and the A.B.C. Task Force, *Anti-Bias Curriculum: Tools for Empowering Young Children* (Washington, DC: National Association for the Education of Young Children, 1989); Mary Cowhey, *Black Ants and Buddhists: Thinking Critically and Teaching Differently in the Primary Grades* (Portland, ME: Stenhouse, 2006); Catherine Compton-Lilly, *Confronting Racism, Poverty, and Power: Classroom Strategies to Change the World* (Portsmouth, NH: Heinemann, 2004); Bill Bigelow, Linda Christensen, Stanley Karp, Barbara Miner, and Bob Peterson, eds., *Rethinking Our Classrooms: Teaching for Equity and Justice*, vol. 1 (Milwaukee, WI: Rethinking Schools, 1994); Bill Bigelow, Brenda Harvey, Stan Karp, and Larry Miller, eds., *Rethinking Our Classrooms: Teaching for Equity and Justice*, vol. 2 (Milwaukee: Rethinking Schools, 2001); Ira Shor, *When Students Have Power: Negotiating Authority in a Critical Pedagogy* (Chicago: University of Chicago Press, 1997); and Enid Lee, Deborah Menkart, Margo Okazawa-Rey, *Beyond Heroes and Holidays: A Practical Guide to K–12 Anti-Racist, Multicultural Education and Staff Development* (Washington, DC: Network of Educators on the Americas [NECA], 1998). Also, two educational organizations, Teaching for Change and Rethinking Schools, have many excellent resources available. See the Appendix for contact information.

Structural and Organizational Issues in Schools

❝I've noticed if you're getting D's and F's, they don't look up to you; they look down. And you're always the last on the list for special activities, you know?❞

—Fern Sherman, interviewee

Andrea D. Cardoso and Brianna Millor-Hammond in Liz Brennan's and Layla Cady's art class. *Self-portraits.* Relief prints, 2006.

Nearly a century ago, John Dewey warned, "Democracy cannot flourish where the chief influences in selecting subject matter of instruction are utilitarian ends narrowly conceived for the masses, and, for the higher education of the few, the traditions of a specialized cultivated class."[1] As Dewey feared, our public schools, as currently organized, are not fulfilling the promise of democracy. Certain school policies and practices exacerbate the inequality that exists in society. Although some of these policies and practices may have evolved in an attempt to deal more equitably with student diversity, just the opposite may be the result. This is the case with *tracking*, which often is meant to help those students most in academic need. Some practices are so integral to the schooling experience that they are hardly disputed even though there may be little evidence for their effectiveness. This is the case with *retention*, or holding students back a grade. Some may not be official policies, but rather unquestioned practices that can lead to disempowerment. This is the case with the limited roles that teachers, students, and parents have in school.

Policies and practices can end up becoming rigid structures that are difficult to change. Many of these structures, unfortunately, run counter to the grand and noble purposes that Dewey described, yet they have come to define schooling itself. These include the general similarity of curriculum and schedules, particular patterns of resource allocation, and an unswerving faith in test scores as measures of ability or success. The case studies that follow this chapter provide other examples of organizational practices and policies that can harm students. Avi Abramson, for example, was adamant that teachers' pedagogy can either motivate or turn off students. For Fern Sherman, the content of the curriculum sometimes made her feel alienated and angry. As these cases demonstrate, all school policies and practices need to be critically evaluated if we are serious about developing the kind of public education that Dewey deemed necessary.

It is legitimate to ask how structural and organizational issues such as school policies and practices are related to multicultural education. When multicultural education is thought of as simple additions of ethnic content to the traditional curriculum, a discussion of school policies and practices may seem irrelevant. However, when defined comprehensively, multicultural education questions the total context of education, including curriculum, student placement, physical structure of schools, school climate, pedagogical strategies, assumptions about student ability, hiring of staff, and parent involvement, among other issues. In this sense, organizational structures are central to the development of a comprehensive multicultural education.

The following discussion provides examples of classroom and school-based policies and practices that may reinforce social inequities by inhibiting the educational success of some students. Because the focus is on the classroom and school rather than society, the impression may be that issues such as school financing, residential housing patterns, unemployment opportunities, racism and other institutional biases, and the ideological underpinnings of education are not as important. On the contrary, as we made clear in Chapter 1, all of these larger structural issues are profoundly implicated in school failure. We urge you to keep these societal issues in mind to understand how they directly influence inequities at the classroom and school levels.

Because larger structural issues have been discussed in previous chapters, this chapter focuses on school and classroom-based policies and practices. Each of the following is briefly described and examined:

- Tracking
- Retention
- Standardized testing
- Curriculum
- Pedagogy
- Physical structure
- Disciplinary policies
- Limited role of students
- Limited role of teachers
- Limited family and community involvement

Tracking

One of the most inequitable and, until two decades ago, relatively undisputed practices in schools is tracking. The term *tracking* generally refers to the placement of students into groups that are perceived to be of similar ability (homogeneous groups) within classes (e.g., reading groups in self-contained classes), into classroom groups according to perceived abilities and subject areas (e.g., a low-level math group in seventh grade), or into groups according to specific programs of study at the high school level (e.g., academic or vocational).[2] In most schools, some kind of tracking is as much a part of school as are bells and recess.

Tracking may begin at the very earliest grades and decisions about student placement may be made on tenuous grounds. These can include social indicators such as information provided on registration forms, initial interviews with parents, and teachers' prior knowledge about specific students. Furthermore, research over many years has confirmed that tracking is frequently linked with racial, ethnic, and social-class differences. For example, research by Jeannie Oakes and Gretchen Guiton found that economically advantaged Whites and Asians in three high schools that they studied had much greater access to high-status, academically rigorous courses than Latinos whose achievement was similar.[3]

Tracking decisions are rarely innocent and their effects are not benign; on the contrary, they can have devastating consequences. Students in elementary school may be targeted for years to come, sometimes for their entire academic careers and beyond. As they get older, students may need to make decisions about future programs of study. For example, they may need to decide on a vocational school, an academic track, a secretarial or "business" track, or what is sometimes called a "general" track. Through their choices, they may pursue a college education, a low-paying job, or almost certain joblessness. Thus, at young ages, students are expected to make choices that can virtually chart the course of their entire lives. Young people 13 or 14 years of age are hardly prepared to make such monumental decisions on their own, and many parents are unable to help them. In addition, most schools lack adequate staffs to help students and their families make these decisions. Because of the labeling that low-track students often experience, they may not feel capable of handling more demanding programs of study.

Another consequence of tracking is that students may develop enduring classroom personalities and attitudes. They may begin to believe that their placement in these groups is natural and a true reflection of whether they are "smart," "average," or "dumb." Although students may feel that they themselves are deciding which courses to take, these decisions may actually have been made for them years before by the first teacher who placed them, for example, in the "Crows" rather than the "Blue Jays" reading group. The messages children internalize because of grouping practices are probably more destructive than we realize, and their effects more long lasting than we care to admit.

A further result of tracking is that students who most need excellent and experienced teachers have the least access to them. Considering the way in which scheduling decisions are made, teachers with the most experience are frequently given the "plum" assignments, and this usually means teaching high-ability classes. For example, in their research in high schools around the country, Milbrey McLaughlin and Joan Talbert found that teachers assigned to low-track classes were often poorly prepared in their subject matter and new to teaching.[4]

Tracking leaves its mark on pedagogy as well. Students in the lowest levels are the most likely to be subjected to rote memorization and static teaching methods, as their teachers often feel that these are the children who most need to master the "basics." Until the basics are learned, the thinking goes, creative methods are a frill that these students can ill afford. Children living in poverty and those most alienated by the schools are once again the losers, and the cycle of school failure is repeated. The students most in need are placed in the lowest level classes and exposed to the drudgery of drill and repetition, school becomes more boring and senseless every day, and the students become discouraged and drop out.

This is not to imply that students at the top ability levels always receive instruction that is uplifting, interesting, and meaningful. They too are exposed to methods and materials similar to those used for students at the bottom levels. If innovative methods and appealing materials exist at all, however, they tend to be found at the top levels. Knowledge becomes yet another privilege of those who are already privileged.

The effectiveness of tracking is questionable. In her 1985 pioneering research study of 25 junior and senior high schools around the country, Jeannie Oakes found that the results of tracking were almost exclusively negative for most students. Many other studies since then have been consistent with this finding. In a recent edition of her groundbreaking study, Oakes reviewed the field over the past 20 years and concluded that tracking as a practice is still largely grounded in ideologies that maintain race and social class privilege.[5] If the purpose of tracking is to provide access to opportunity for those who have most been denied this access, it has failed badly. In many instances, it has had the opposite effect.

Despite the extensive evidence that it does not work for most students, tracking is in place in most schools throughout the United States. Although its effects may be contrary to statements about its intended outcomes, tracking has been an immutable part of the culture of middle and secondary schools for many years, partly because the culture of the school is resistant to change. Once an idea has taken hold in schools, it seems to develop a life of its own, regardless of its usefulness or effectiveness. Moreover, schools respond poorly to pressure for change, particularly if it comes from those most jeopardized but least powerful.

If tracking were unanimously acknowledged as placing all students at risk, it would have been eliminated long ago. The truth is that powerful vested interests are at play in preserving it. Although tracking affects most students negatively, it may help a few. The evidence is mixed, but there is some indication that high-achieving students benefit from being tracked in honors and high-level classes. It is not surprising, then, that it is frequently the parents of high-achieving students who are most reluctant to challenge tracking because they perceive it as beneficial to their children. In addition, as mentioned previously, tracking decisions and race are often linked. This was found to be the case in a three-year longitudinal case study by Oakes and her colleagues. In their review of ten racially and socioeconomically mixed secondary schools participating in detracking reform, the researchers concluded that one of the greatest barriers to detracking was the resistance of powerful parents, most of whom were White. Through strategies such as threatening to remove their children from the school, the parents of students who traditionally benefited from tracking made detracking difficult, if not impossible.[6]

As we have seen, tracking is largely propped up and sustained by social class interests. Because it

sorts and classifies students, tracking helps prepare them for their place in the larger society. Students in the top tracks generally end up attending college and having a better shot at becoming professionals; those in the bottom tracks frequently drop out or, if they do finish high school, become unskilled workers. Without lapsing into a mechanistic explanation for a complex process, it is nevertheless true that some students benefit and others lose because of tracking. Teachers and schools may compound the problem by seeing tracking as the only alternative to handling student differences and as a "natural" and even "neutral" practice.

We want to make it clear, however, that grouping per se is not always a negative practice. Good and experienced teachers have always understood that short-term and flexible grouping can be very effective in reviewing a particular skill or teaching intensively a missing piece of social studies or math or science. Grouping in such instances can be effective in meeting temporary and specific ends. But because rigid ability-group tracking is linked with, and supported by, particular classist and racist ideologies, grouping of any kind needs to be done with great care.

What are the alternatives to tracking? One approach is to "detrack," that is, to do away with tracking based on so-called ability differences. However, detracking alone will do little unless accompanied by a change in the school's culture and norms. In one study of six racially mixed high schools undergoing detracking, Susan Yonezawa, Amy Stuart Wells, and Irene Serna found that the schools' low- and middle-track students, mostly Latino and African American, resisted entering high-track classes even when they were academically capable of taking them because they "hungered for 'places of respect'—classrooms where they were not racially isolated and their cultural backgrounds were valued."[7] Because tracking is supported by a complex set of structures that reinforce cultural assumptions and influence students' identities, the authors concluded that "freedom of choice" for students to select their own classes is by itself an empty concept *without* altering the other structures and ideologies that help perpetuate existing track hierarchies. They suggest that, to work, tracking needs to be accompanied by "safe spaces" such as ethnic studies classes that can make students feel valued. Anne Wheelock, who also has written extensively on the subject of tracking, has suggested that de-tracking combined with strategies such as coopera-tive learning, peer tutoring, multilevel teaching, shared decision making with students, and de-emphasizing the use of textbooks, while challeng-ing racist and classist notions of ability, can also result in inspired stories of improved learning and intergroup relations.[8]

Although students differ from one another in many ways, and such differences need to be taken into account in order to provide students with a high-quality education, tracking alone has not proved to be the answer. At the same time, tracking alone cannot be blamed for inequality in learning. Singling out any particular policy or practice as the culprit is an insufficient explanation for schools' lack of success with particular students. In his ex-tensive review of educational research, Joseph D'Amico found that other aspects of schools play a crucial role: the quality of teaching and the attitudes of teachers, the nature of the curriculum and in-struction, the level of material resources available to students and teachers, and class size (among oth-ers).[9] Thus, it is a constellation of factors that create school failure, and the discussion that follows con-siders some of these factors.

Retention

Retention, or the practice of holding students back a grade, is another common practice in schools. Like tracking, retention is intertwined with other poli-cies and practices that exacerbate inequality. For in-stance, it is related to testing because retention decisions are often made as a result of test scores. This is especially evident in the high-stakes testing context of the past several years.

One review of the literature on the effect of re-tention begins with the pointed question, "Making students repeat a grade hasn't worked for 100 years, so why it is still happening?" Susan Black, the au-thor, goes on to say that according to some esti-mates, almost 2.5 million children are retained in U.S. classrooms and low-income students, boys, and students of color are overrepresented in this number. Aside from a short-term benefit for some students—a benefit that has been found to have no lasting effects—there is no evidence that retention

brings children up to grade level. On the contrary, Black reviewed several decades of research that showed retention fails to improve achievement. Also, retention is linked in a very obvious way with dropping out of school: Students who are retained once are 40–50 percent more likely to drop out of school than those who have never been retained; for those retained twice, the risk is 90 percent.[10]

Students are typically retained in a particular grade when a determination is made, usually by the teacher (sometimes in consultation with coun-selors, the principal, and parents) that a student is incapable of performing the work that is required in the coming grade. As in the case of tracking, these decisions are generally made with good intentions: Often, teachers want to protect students from fur-ther failure or believe that, during the following year (in the same class), students will learn the ma-terial that they have not yet learned. As in the case of tracking, this reasoning is often erroneous. The largest number of students is retained in first grade, although researchers have found that first graders usually benefit the least from the practice.[11] In addi-tion, as more pressure is placed on kindergarten to become more like first grade, there is a related pres-sure for kindergarten teachers to have their stu-dents "ready to learn" in first grade. As a consequence, more retentions are occurring in kindergarten. Yet, as one large study found, there is no evidence whatsoever that a policy of grade re-tention in kindergarten improves average achieve-ment in math or reading. In fact, the evidence points in the opposite direction: Children who are retained actually learn less than they would have, had they been promoted.[12]

What, then, is the alternative? Considering the widespread public opposition to "social promo-tion"—promoting students to the next grade even if they have not learned the subject matter of their current grade—it is unrealistic to expect that reten-tion as a policy will be abandoned. It is also unfair to simply move students on to the next grade even if they are unprepared for it and to expect them to catch up on their own. Because of this dilemma, more schools are implementing alternative inter-vention programs such as mandatory summer school and after-school tutoring programs. How-ever, these measures are likely to produce few re-sults unless accompanied by comprehensive school-wide reform involving other practices and policies. For example, extracurricular activities have been found to have a positive influence on student retention.[13] The connection between academic success and cocurricular and extracurricular activities is also clear in the case studies in this book, yet poor urban schools, where the need is greatest, have fewer of these activities.

Standardized Testing

Another practice that impedes equity in schools is the uncritical use of standardized testing, particularly when employed to sort students rather than to improve instruction. Originally designed almost a century ago to help identify children who were la-beled "mentally retarded", the use of standardized tests expanded greatly afterward, influenced by the tremendous influx of new immigrants into the country. As a result, the original aims of standardized tests were subverted to include rationalization of racist theories of genetic inferiority.[14] An extensive review of how test use changed during this period is not called for here. Nonetheless, it should be pointed out that standardized tests have frequently been used as a basis for segregating and sorting students, principally those whose cultures and languages differ from the mainstream. Moreover, the relationship between IQ tests and repressive and racist social theories and policies is not a historical relic. Unfortunately, there are contemporary examples of this relationship.[15]

What You Can Do

Become Informed

In collaboration with colleagues, use professional days to visit schools that have successfully implemented detracking. Recommend that staff development sessions address directly tracking, detracking, and alternative kinds of grouping. It would be critical for schools considering detracking to view the video *Off-Track* (developed by Michelle Fine and her colleagues and available from Teachers College Press). In it, students and staff address the benefits and challenges of detracking. In addition, as part of a team of colleagues, you might ask for the opportunity to prepare seminars in which staff members share ideas for detracking or for creative grouping in classrooms.

Detrack Extracurricular Activities

Tracking also occurs in extracurricular activities. As the case studies and snapshots demonstrate, extracurricular activities were significant in the academic success of most of the students interviewed or described. Nevertheless, extracurricular clubs or organizations are often seen by students as exclusive clubs with limited membership. The school newspaper, for instance, is generally an activity in which highly intellectual and academically successful students engage, whereas sports is usually often the major domain of less academically oriented students. School activities and clubs frequently perpetuate the social class groupings that students develop instead of helping to counter the stereotypes on which they are based.

Although the message "You need not apply" is not purposely given, many students infer it from the recruitment policies and activities of some clubs and organizations. You can help make clubs and other organizations appealing to a wider range of students by, for instance, becoming a faculty sponsor for a group and actively recruiting and encouraging students of diverse backgrounds to join. Also, you could print recruitment materials in a number of languages, post them in neighborhood centers, and do outreach with families of students underrepresented in extracurricular activities to encourage their children to join.

Testing and tracking have often been symbiotically linked. Joel Spring has used a variety of primary sources ranging from real estate publications to newspaper accounts to demonstrate these links.[16] Lewis Terman, a psychologist who experimented with intelligence tests at the beginning of the 20th century, stated, with absolute conviction, after testing only two American Indian and Mexican American children, "Their dullness seems to be racial, or at least inherent in the family stock from which they came. . . . Children of this group should be segregated in special classes . . . they cannot master abstractions, but they can often be made efficient workers."[17] The same reasoning was used on other occasions to explain the "inferior" intelligence of Blacks, Jews, and Italians; practically every new ethnic group that has come to the United States has fared badly on standardized tests.[18]

Although today comments about specific groups tend not to be as blatantly racist as Lewis Terman's, the kind and number of standardized tests to which we continue to subject our students are staggering. This situation is especially related to the No Child Left Behind (NCLB) law that mandates annual mandatory testing in reading and math and—starting in the 2007–2008 school year, in science—at least once in elementary, middle, and high school. The testing requirement is based on the dubious reasoning that more tests will somehow lead to more learning and higher standards. Students now spend entire days, sometimes weeks, taking standardized tests. On top of the actual testing days, a great deal of time is spent on teaching children how to take tests, time that could be better spent in teaching, and the students' learning, actual content. In fact, Barbara Miner, writing for *Rethinking Schools,* has estimated that 17 tests—not including city and classroom-based test—are now required by NCLB each year.[19] One teacher we know told us that in her school, every year the fourth graders need to take a whopping 35 standardized tests!

In addition, the fact that textbook companies and other companies that develop tests earn huge profits from test construction and dissemination is often unmentioned, yet it, too, is a reality. The Government Accounting Office (GAO) reported that states would spend somewhere between $1.9 billion to $5.3 billion between 2002 and 2008 to implement NCLB-mandated tests. These, according to Barbara Miner, are just the *indirect* costs; if teacher time was added, the figure would be many times higher. Moreover, Miner found that the private testing companies that control the market operate with little or no public accountability, which is ironic considering the calls for "accountability" in schools.[20]

Despite its purported intent, NCLB has focused little attention on changes in curriculum or instructional practices, on improvements in teacher education, or on equalizing funding for school districts. Richard Elmore, a respected educational researcher whose work has centered on school improvement, has called this legislation "the single largest—and the single most damaging—expansion of federal policy over the nation's education system."[21] In reviewing the history of this legislation, Elmore argues that a school's ability to make improvements has much more to do with the beliefs and practices of the people in the school than with a demand that students in those schools reach a particular performance level on tests. According to him, the work of improving schools consists of improving "capacity," that is, the knowledge and skills of teachers, by increasing their command of content and how to teach it.

A concern for equity is a common reason cited for "high stakes" testing, that is, for linking test scores to the success of schools, teachers, and students. Certainly, equity is a significant concern because, as we have seen, schools for poor children of diverse backgrounds are often inferior to others; however, there is little evidence to support the contention that standardized tests lead to greater achievement. A number of reviews of testing legislation and practice have concluded that, rather than improving learning outcomes, such legislation is actually having a detrimental impact because gross inequities in instructional quality, resources, and other support services are being ignored. Researchers and educators concerned with social justice in education have become alarmed at these results. For instance, in a comprehensive volume devoted to the topic of standardized tests and equity, its editors, Gary Orfield and Mindy Kornhaber, conclude that "high-stakes tests, even those intended to raise standards for all students, can and have created barriers, especially for the nation's most vulnerable students."[22] Moreover, the efficacy of using such tests to improve student learning has been called into serious question. In a large multi-state study on the impact of high-stakes testing funded by the Rockefeller Foundation, researchers Audrey Amrein and David Berliner came to the conclusion that if the intended goal of using high-stakes tests is to increase student learning, then it is not working. Evidence from the study of 18 states is that in almost every case, student learning was unchanged or actually *went down* when high-stakes testing policies were instituted.[23] Also, as pointed out in the discussion of retention, because more states are now requiring that students pass a standardized test before they can graduate from high school, tests are resulting in increased urban dropout rates.

Standardized test scores are also inequitable because they correlate highly with family income. This reality exposes the myth that in the United States there is equality of opportunity regardless of social class and race. In a review of abundant national and international studies, David Berliner found overwhelming evidence of a positive and high relationship between social class and test scores.[24] This correlation has consistently been shown to be the case with the Scholastic Achievement Test (SAT), a test that is required for admission to most colleges and universities. Even the College Board, which administers the SAT, has demonstrated the correlation between income and scores: In their own analysis, the College Board found that a student whose family makes less than $10,000 a year scores nearly 250 points less on the SAT than a student whose family earns more than $100,000 a year.[25]

In addition, standardized testing affects other practices that impede equity. For example, testing may have a harmful effect on curricula by limiting teachers' creativity. This is because teachers in schools in which children have poor test scores may be forced to "teach to the test" rather than create curricula that respond to the real needs of learners. The result may be "dumbing down" or restricting the curriculum to better reflect the content and approach of tests. This is precisely the conclusion reached by Linda McNeil, who investigated the so-called Texas miracle (that is, the claim that student achievement in Texas increased as a result of more rigorous testing). What she found was that, instead, the testing mandates narrowed the curriculum and

created conditions hostile to learning. In addition to reducing teacher motivation, more standardized testing led to higher dropout rates among students.[26] Other research corroborates this conclusion. One study found that the most pervasive finding on the effects of high-stakes testing on instruction has been the narrowing of the curriculum.[27] In addition, a national survey of 12,000 teachers reported that the extent of curriculum narrowing due to testing was directly associated with the nature of the stakes involved—that is, the higher the stakes, the greater the teachers' focus on tested content.[28]

Pedagogy may also be negatively affected by standardized testing. Many critics of high-stakes testing have found that when standardized tests were required, there was a decline in the use of such innovative approaches as student-centered discussions, essay writing, research projects, and laboratory work.[29] Because of the growing pressure to raise test scores, teachers may reason that they have little time for innovative approaches. This, in turn, affects teacher autonomy because it removes curriculum decision making from the teacher to the school, district, city, or even state level. The result is that the further the curriculum is from the teacher and the school, the less it reflects the lives of the students in the school.

Regrettably, the concern for engagement in meaningful activities is missing in many state-mandated testing programs, and students who are most vulnerable are once again the major victims. In a vicious cycle of failure, students perceived as needing more help are placed in classes in which the curriculum is diluted and higher levels of thinking are not demanded and in which instruction is bland and formulaic. As a result, the academic achievement of students may fall even further behind. Michael Sadowski, who has done a careful review of the issues, asks the timely question, "Are high-stakes tests worth the wager?"[30]

Although standardized tests ostensibly are used to provide teachers and schools with information about the learning needs of students, in fact they are often used to sort students further. John Dewey minced no words in expressing his views of rigid assessments: "How one person's abilities compare in quantity with those of another is none of the teacher's business. It is irrelevant to his work,"

Dewey wrote. He went on to state, "What is required is that every individual shall have opportunities to employ his own powers in activities that have meaning."[31]

In spite of the shortcomings of high-stakes standardized testing, we need to understand why there is so much popular support for them. For one, many people view standardized tests as highly objective and reliable measures of what students know, even if this is not the case. In addition, parents whose children attend poor schools have become weary of the poor achievement of their children. It is true that many teachers who work in poor urban and rural schools are highly competent and devoted to their students; they demonstrate their care through high expectations and rigorous demands. On the other hand, as we saw in Chapter 4, in schools where few teachers know much about the students they are teaching, expectations of student achievement are likely to be quite low. As a result, some schools have been chronically underserved for many years, with very little actual teaching taking place. It is little wonder that some children in these circumstances have failed to learn and that their parents have become staunch advocates of stringent accountability measures, including standardized testing. As we have seen, however, standardized tests alone rarely guarantee equality; in fact, they may exacerbate inequality.

There is, nevertheless, a need to have reliable and effective assessment of student learning. Teachers and schools must be held accountable for what students learn or fail to learn, especially in the case of those who have received low-quality schooling. This means that schools, districts, states, and the federal government need to rethink testing policies and practices so that they are more equitable. One response has been to promote alternative assessments, for example to replace or at least complement norm-referenced tests with *performance-based assessments*, also called authentic assessments. Some examples of more authentic assessment are portfolios, performance tasks, and student exhibitions. The alternative assessment movement represents an important shift in thinking about the purpose and uses of tests, from sorting and separating students toward ensuring more equitable opportunities for all children to learn at high levels of achievement.

However, even if performance-based assessments are positive alternatives to norm-referenced assessments, they are not necessarily more equitable, especially if they are used in the same way as externally developed and mandated tests.[32] Once again, *how* assessment is used is just as important as *what kind* of assessment is used.

The Curriculum

Broadly defined, *curriculum* is the organized environment for learning. This means that it concerns *what* should be learned and *under what conditions* it is to be learned. Although it may seem that this is a fairly clear-cut process, it is not. Because curriculum defines what is deemed important for students to know, it also involves the knowledge, attitudes, and traditions valued in society. Thus, curriculum is an inherently *political* matter. To illustrate this point, we turn to curriculum theorist Michael Apple, who has suggested a number of essential questions to keep in mind when thinking about the curriculum—questions that are particularly significant within a multicultural framework. Some of them are: "Whose knowledge is it? Who selected it? Why is it organized and taught in this way?"[33] If we consider these issues when developing or implementing the curriculum, it becomes clear that any curriculum is deeply ideological. Because only a tiny fraction of the vast array of available knowledge finds its way into state curriculum standards and frameworks, district guides, textbooks, and teachers' instructional manuals, it is obvious that the curriculum is never neutral. Instead, it represents what is perceived to be consequential and necessary knowledge, generally by those who are dominant in a society. Furthermore, curriculum decisions in public schools are usually made by those furthest from the lives of students—namely, central and state boards of education, with little input from teachers, parents, and students.

The curriculum lets students know whether the knowledge they and their communities value has prestige within the educational establishment and beyond. The problem is that the curriculum is often presented as if it were the whole, unvarnished, and uncontested truth. It is more appropriate to think of curriculum as a decision-making process. If we think of it in this way, we realize that *somebody* made decisions about what to include. For example, it is rare for Black English to be incorporated into the established curriculum. It only becomes part of the curriculum when students who speak Black English are corrected by their teachers. Hence, even when present in the curriculum, Black English tends to be viewed in a negative light. As a result, students may pick up the powerful message that the language variety they speak has little value in our society. On the other hand, if teachers were to use students' language—including Black English, or *Ebonics*—as a bridge to Standard English or to discuss critical perspectives about the role that language and culture play in their lives, the value of students' identity is affirmed. This is the case with Bob Fecho, who used his students' vernacular to discuss broader issues about language and power in his urban high school English classroom.[34] Unfortunately, however, talk about such issues is frequently silenced, and in this way, the curriculum serves as a primary means of social control. Often, students learn that what is meaningful at home is negated in school.

The life of the school is often separate and distinct from the life of the community in ways that are abundantly clear as soon as one steps inside the school; and this is especially evident in schools in urban and poor rural areas. As an example, it is not unusual to see urban classrooms in which young children learn about "community helpers" without ever studying about people in their own communities. They learn about police officers, fire fighters, and mail carriers, all of whom may live outside their

What You Can Do

Be Proactive About Tests

Tests exert a powerful influence on most educational decisions. Yet, as we have seen, they correlate more with family income than with intelligence or ability. The specific strategies that each teacher, school, and school district chooses to engage in may vary, depending on how they use tests, whether the tests are grossly biased or not, and the testing skills that students already have. There are two basic strategies: Either challenge the use of tests, or focus attention on test taking and how to use it to the advantage of the students. In fact, these need not be either-or strategies. We know of one teacher, for instance, who campaigns against standardized tests because he knows they unfairly jeopardize his students. At the same time, he developed after-school tutorial sessions in which he teaches his students specific test-taking skills so that they might be more successful in taking these required tests.

In affluent schools and neighborhoods, students often learn specific test-taking skills that help them do very well on tests. A recent study found that test coaching, contrary to previous claims, boosted math SAT scores by 18 points.* More affluent families also have the means to pay for tutoring and other classes to help their children do well on tests. Less affluent students, especially students living in poverty, do not generally have the same kind of access to learning these skills.

With a group of interested colleagues and parents, you can approach the local school committee and ask that standardized tests be kept to a minimum, that the results be used in more appropriate ways, and that students not be placed at risk because of the results of such tests. Like the previously mentioned teacher, you might decide that given the pervasiveness of testing and the power it exerts on the options of young people, your energy might be better spent in teaching students how to take tests more critically and effectively. To help even the playing field, you can start an after-school test-tutoring program for students in your school. Try to get funding from your school system or PTA, or even from a local business.

*Jack Kaplan, "The Effectiveness of SAT Coaching on Math SAT Scores, Chance 18, no. 2 (2005).

immediate neighborhood. Students learn about doctors and lawyers and people who own large businesses, but they may never have met one of these people in their own neighborhood. The people the children do see every day—the owner of the corner "bodega," the local factory worker, or community service providers—are rarely mentioned as "community helpers." In like manner, the curriculum hardly ever includes the study of non-Christian holidays or history, and this fact helps explain why Avi Abramson, whose case study follows this chapter, had a hard time adjusting to public school.

Another example: When studying the "food pyramid," it is not unusual for children to make up fictitious breakfasts in order to satisfy their teachers. This is because to admit having eaten bread and butter and coffee or cold noodles for breakfast is to admit that they are doing something wrong, at least in the eyes of the school. Similarly, a teacher with a mandate to teach her second graders about Holland may struggle to find relevant ways to describe the lives of Dutch children, while at the same time neglecting to include the heritage and backgrounds of some of the children who are sitting in her own classroom. And there is the incongruous but typical situation of Mexican American, Puerto Rican, and other Latin American children who are fluent in Spanish yet being forced to learn "Castilian Spanish" because their teachers have accepted the premise that it is more "correct." Paradoxically, these same students are often prohibited from speaking Spanish outside of Spanish class.

This is not meant to suggest that children should study *only* about themselves and their communities. Doing so would fly in the face of one of the major objectives of education, that is, to broaden students' experiences and perspectives beyond their own particular life circumstances. One of my (Sonia Nieto's) favorite books when I was a child was *Heidi*, a story that was as distinct from my own experience as night is from day. What could I, a relatively poor Puerto Rican child growing up in New York City, possibly get out of the story of an orphan sent to live in the Alps with her cantankerous grandfather? I knew nothing about mountains, had spent little time outside of urban Brooklyn, and didn't even have a grandfather. But I understood Heidi because hers was a story of close family relationships and resilience in the face of considerable obstacles, and I could relate to these things. I could also relate to a

girl who loved reading and exploring life. It was precisely because I could identify with these things on a personal level that I was able to benefit from *Heidi*. The point is that a curriculum needs to *build on* rather than neglect students' life experiences in order to broaden their worlds.

Children who are not in the dominant group have a hard time finding themselves or their communities in the curriculum. If they do "see" themselves, it is often through the distorted lens of others. American Indian children may read about themselves as "savages" who were bereft of culture until the Europeans arrived; African Americans often read sanitized versions of slavery; Mexican Americans read of the "westward expansion," with no information about the fact that their ancestors were already living on the lands to which Europeans were "expanding"; working-class children learn virtually nothing of their history, except perhaps that the struggle for the eight-hour workday was a long one; and females may be left wondering how it is that half of humanity has consistently been left out of the curriculum. Little wonder, then, that school curricula and real life are often at polar extremes.

In contrast to a traditional approach to curriculum design, James Banks has proposed a *transformative approach* that "changes the canon, paradigms, and basic assumptions of the curriculum, thus letting students learn about issues, concepts, and problems from a variety of perspectives and points of view."[35] For example, learning how people from different communities feel about a topic such as immigration or terrorism—matters that are paramount in current news stories and in the lives of many students as well—would help them develop a more nuanced way of understanding the world.

Another way to transform the curriculum is to use students' own experiences and identities to help frame it. A good example of such an approach is a long-term collaborative-action research project in which two university researchers, Judith Solsken and Jerri Willett, worked with a teacher researcher, Jo-Anne Wilson Keenan. The project was based on the premise that parents and other family members of children from widely diverse backgrounds can enhance their children's learning. Proj-ects in which parents are invited to speak about their culture and to share food or teach youngsters particular crafts are not new, but the research by Solsken,

Keenan, and Willett instead focused on how parents' talents and skills could be used to promote student learning. The researchers explained how the visits of students' families to their second-grade classroom "changed the nature of the conversation in Room 8." They added that the families "opened the conversation to many aspects of the children's language and lives that had not previously had a place in the classroom, and they created many different opportunities for everyone to connect to one another and to the academic discourse of school."[36]

Another way to develop a transformative approach to the curriculum is to bring up difficult or conflicting issues in the curriculum and class discussions, something that many teachers are reluctant to do. Yet these issues are frequently central to students' lives. Chapter 4 discussed how teachers and prospective teachers are socialized in this attitude. Michelle Fine has called this *silencing*, that is, determining "who can speak, what can and cannot be spoken, and whose discourse must be controlled."[37] One topic that seems to hold particular saliency for many young people, regardless of their background, is that of biases and discrimination, but teaching about these things is staunchly avoided in most classrooms. This may be due to several factors: Most teachers are unaccustomed to, afraid of, or uncomfortable discussing discrimination and inequality; they feel pressure to "cover the material," and these topics are not included in the traditional curriculum; they are used to presenting information as if it were free of conflict and controversy; and they may feel that bringing up issues concerning conflict will create or exacerbate animosity among students. In the words of one of the teachers in Michelle Fine's study, discussing such issues would be a mistake because "it would demoralize the students, they need to feel positive and optimistic—like they have a chance,"[38] a comment based on the spurious assumption that students are not already demoralized, or that they would have a hard time handling the truth. Racism and discrimination and other "dangerous" topics, students quickly find out, are not supposed to be discussed in school.

Unfortunately, however, these issues do not simply vanish because they are excluded from the curriculum. On the contrary, quashing them reinforces students' feelings that school life is unrelated to real life. In spite of teachers' reluctance to broach issues such as racism, slavery, inequality, genocide, and so

on, a number of studies suggest that discussing them can be tremendously beneficial to students if they are approached with sensitivity and care. An example comes from a recent study in which the researchers found that providing information about racism had a positive impact on the racial attitudes of both White students and students of color.[39]

That contentious and difficult issues need to be confronted honestly and directly is the underlying premise behind the Facing History and Ourselves (FHAO) School. The school, located in New York City, promotes in-depth examination of some of history's most troubling incidents (the Nazi Holocaust, the Armenian genocide, and U.S. slavery, to name a few) as a key to encouraging young people to work for a socially just and democratic society. FHAO, a nonprofit organization with headquarters in Brookline, Massachusetts, and regional offices around the country and connections around the world, advances the idea that young people are capable of reflecting critically on such issues as scapegoating, racism, and personal and collective responsibility in order to become productive and concerned adults. One article described the curriculum as deeply connected with the pedagogy and underlying assumptions about young people:

> Facing History's approach is more than curriculum, however; it's a method of inquiry. The emphasis is not on lectures or memorizing names and dates. Students read memoirs, write essays, create artwork, debate in class, take field trips, and meet activists and Holocaust survivors. They work on small group projects to learn teamwork and keep journals to discover their own hearts, minds, and voices.[40]

This stance makes learning more complex and knotty, to be sure, but it also makes learning more meaningful for students. Maxine Greene, addressing the matter of complexity in the aftermath of 9/11 said, "The curriculum has to leave so many questions open so that children will explore and wonder and not believe there is a final answer, because they can only be devastated when they find out there isn't."[41] Murray Levin, an educator who taught at Harvard University and Boston University and later at the Greater Egleston Community School in Boston, provides a vivid example. Levin believed that even the most marginalized students learn when education is meaningful to their lives. The title of his book documenting the experiences he had at the school is *'Teach Me!' Kids Will Learn When Oppression Is the Lesson*.[42] We would do well to heed these words.

The relationship between curriculum and democracy is significant, especially in this post-9/11 era. In light of our nation's expressed support for equality and fair play, students need to learn that patriotism means standing up for individual and collective freedom, and this is sometimes unpopular. Actions that we now recognize as patriotic may have been very unpopular at the time they took place. For example, the general public largely reviled the actions of those who took part in the Civil Rights Movement, yet today the view that all Americans deserve equal rights is largely accepted, at least in principle. The same is true of women's rights, considered a radical idea just a few decades ago. The issue of gay rights, still controversial in many quarters, hopefully will follow the same course.

Students need to learn that putting democracy into action may mean taking unpopular stands. There is frequently a tremendous chasm between expounding on democracy and actual democratic actions in schools. Providing students with both the *rhetoric* and the *reality* of democracy may help them to become agents of positive social change. However, curriculum transformation is needed if we believe that one of the basic purposes of schooling is to prepare young people to become productive and critical citizens of a democratic society.

Democratic principles are thwarted by the lack of access to knowledge in other ways as well. For example, sometimes the curriculum is "watered down" by teachers who believe that such accommodations will better meet the needs of learners from socioeconomically disadvantaged backgrounds. On the face of it, this practice may seem equitable, but the truth is that it may reflect teachers' lower expectations of some students. All children can benefit from high expectations and a challenging curriculum, but some students are regularly subjected to diluted, undemanding, and boring educational programs because teachers and schools do not tap into their strengths and talents. Typically, though, what students want are *more* demands rather than fewer, as you can see in the case studies in this book. In fact, according to researcher Linda Darling-Hammond, "unequal access to high-level courses and challenging curriculum explains much of the so-called 'achievement gap.' "[43]

For instance, sociologists have found patterns of disproportionately low achievement and participation in science, math, and other high-status courses among female students, students of color, and students of low-income families.[44] Low-income students and students from inner city and poor rural schools, therefore, generally have fewer opportunities to learn, and as we have already seen, they also have fewer material resources, less engaging learning activities in their classrooms, and less qualified teachers.

Textbooks, a considerable component of the curriculum in most schools, may also be at odds with democratic and pluralistic values. Textbooks tend to reinforce the dominance of the European American perspective and to sustain stereotypes of groups outside the cultural and political mainstream. This situation is not new. A 1949 comprehensive analysis of 300 textbooks revealed that many of them perpetuated negative stereotypes of "minority" groups.[45] This finding has been reiterated time and again in more recent years.[46] A similar situation has been documented in children's literature, which, until just a few decades ago, largely omitted or stereotyped the lives and experiences of African American, Latino, Asian American, American Indian, and other groups.[47]

Even in recent textbooks, the lack of adequate representation of women and people of color is striking; critical and nondominant perspectives are also largely missing. According to James Loewen, most history textbooks are filled with half-truths or myths. Loewen points out how both textbooks and public monuments have perpetuated the myths that are the basis for much of the U.S. history taught in school.[48]

Pedagogy

Pedagogy refers to the strategies, techniques, and approaches used by teachers in their classrooms, that is, *teachers' practices*. It means more than these things, however. Pedagogy also includes how teachers perceive the nature of learning and what they do to create conditions that motivate students to become critical thinkers. For example, most classrooms, through their practices, reflect the belief that learning can best take place in a competitive atmosphere—that is, the most prevalent approaches used in the classroom stress individual achievement and extrinsic motivation. These include ability grouping, testing of all kinds, and rote learning. Although learning in such classrooms can be fun or interesting, students may learn other unintended lessons as well: that learning equals memorization, that reciting what teachers want to hear is what education is about, and that independent thinking has no place in the classroom.

The observation that schools are tedious places where little learning takes place and where most students are not challenged to learn is hardly new. It is particularly true of secondary schools, where subject matter dominates pedagogy and classes are too often driven by standardized tests as "gatekeepers" to promotion and/or accreditation. The case studies of both Avi Abramson and Fern Sherman provide enlightening examples of pedagogy that is engaging or boring. Avi contrasted teachers that "teach from the point of view of the kid" with those who "just come out and say, 'All right, do this, *blah, blah, blah.*'" Fern mentioned that she would have liked more "involved activities" in which more students take part, "not making only the two smartest people up here do the whole work for the whole class."

Avi and Fern's impressions are confirmed by research. In his comprehensive and classic study on secondary schools, John Goodlad found that textbooks were used frequently and mechanistically, whereas other materials were used infrequently, if at all; that teaching methods varied little from the traditional "chalk and talk" methodology commonly used over 100 years ago; and that routine and rote learning were favored over creativity and critical thinking.[49] Most students today would likely agree. In a three-year study of students in Philadelphia middle schools, Bruce Wilson and H. Dickson Corbett discovered that, more than anything, students wanted teachers who taught content meaningful to their lives and who had high expectations of them.[50] Specifically, students most frequently mentioned projects and experiments as the kind of work they liked doing best and that most helped them learn. Rather than focusing only on just

teachers' personalities or their sense of humor, students cared about *how* their teachers taught.

Martin Haberman uses the term *pedagogy of poverty* to refer to a basic urban pedagogy that encompasses a body of specific strategies that are limited to asking questions, giving directions, making assignments, and monitoring seatwork. Unsupported by research, theory, or even the practice of the best urban teachers, this pedagogy of poverty is based on the dubious assumption that children of culturally, racially, and linguistically diverse backgrounds and poor students cannot learn in creative, active, and challenging environments. Suggesting instead that exemplary pedagogy in urban schools actively involves students in real-life situations and allows them to reflect on their own lives, Haberman finds that good teaching is taking place when, among other things, the following occur:

- Students are involved with issues they perceive as vital concerns (e.g., rather than avoid controversies as censorship of school newspapers or dress codes, students use these opportunities for learning).
- Students are involved with explanations of differences in race, culture, religion, ethnicity, and gender.
- Students are helped to see major concepts, big ideas, and general principles rather than isolated facts.
- Students are involved in planning their education.
- Students are involved in applying ideals such as fairness, equity, and justice to their world.
- Students are actively involved in heterogeneous groups.
- Students are asked to question common sense or widely accepted assumptions.[51]

Expanding pedagogical strategies alone, however, will not change how and what students learn in school. Let us take the example of cooperative learning, generally praised as a useful instructional strategy. In reviewing virtually hundreds of studies of cooperative learning over the past three decades, Laurel Shaper Walters concluded that there is a positive correlation between cooperative learning and student achievement.[52] In spite of its commendable qualities, however, cooperative learning should be

What You Can Do

Use the Curriculum Critically

Use the current curriculum as the basis for helping students develop a more critical per-spective and better research skills. For example, when studying the Revolutionary War, have students investigate the experiences of African Americans, American Indians, women, working people, loyalists, and others whose perspectives have traditionally been excluded from the curriculum. When studying the Industrial Revolution, ask students to explore the role of the nascent workers' movement and of children and young women factory workers, as well as the impact of European immigration on the rise of cities. Students can also concentrate on the emergence of scientific discoveries through inventions by African Americans, women, and immigrants during the late 19th century.

When teaching different mathematical operations, ask students to investigate how they are done in other countries. A variety of materials, such as an abacus and other counting instruments, can be demonstrated. If traditional U.S. holidays are commemorated in the curriculum, try to include other perspectives as well. For example, for Columbus Day, discuss the concept of "discovery" with students so that they understand that this was the perspective of the Europeans, not the Indians. Alternative activities can focus on October 12th as the encounter of two worldviews and histories rather than on the "discovery" of one world by another. (Rethinking Columbus,* from Rethinking Schools, is an excellent publication that includes many lesson plans and other resources for classrooms.) Thanksgiving, considered by many American Indians to be a day of mourning, is another holiday that can be presented through multiple perspectives.

Create an emerging multicultural curriculum by using the experiences, cultures, and languages of every student in your class. Encourage them to "bring their identities" into the classroom, for example, by inviting their parents to teach the class about their particular talent, job, or interest. These talents do not have to be culture specific: For instance, a parent who is a seamstress might teach the children how to sew a hem. Although a talent may not be particular to a specific ethnic heritage, it helps students to see that people from all backgrounds have skills and worthwhile experiences.

Activities such as these are particularly effective at the early elementary level, but they can be equally relevant for secondary students studying specific subjects. For example, if older students are learning calligraphy, invite a local Chinese artist to give them some pointers, or, if they are learning about operating a small business, invite a local store owner to speak to them.

Oral history projects that focus on students and their family experiences are another good way to make the curriculum multicultural. Ask students to collect stories, poems, and legends from their families, either tape recorded or written down, to create a multicultural library. More elaborate activities might include dramatizations for the school assembly, videotaping parents and other community members reciting the poems and stories, and readings by older students to children in the younger grades.

*Bill Bigelow and Bob Peterson, Rethinking Columbus: The Next 500 Years, 2nd ed. (Milwaukee, WI: Rethinking Schools, 1998).

viewed as no more than a means to an end. Cooperative learning is based on the premise that using the talents and skills of all students is key to designing successful learning environments. But, if it is viewed unproblematically, cooperative learning has little chance of changing the fundamental climate of learning in the classroom. In this regard, research by Mary McCaslin and Thomas Good found that small-group work too often allowed some students to become even more passive and dependent learners than if they were in whole-class settings.[53] This is a good reminder that particular methods can become, in the words of María de la Luz Reyes, "venerable assumptions" that take on a life of their own, disconnected from their educational purposes or sociopolitical context.[54]

Another pedagogical approach growing in popularity is constructivism.[55] This approach is based on the notion that students' background knowledge can be enormously significant in their learning and that their interpretations of new information is influenced by their prior knowledge and experiences. Through this approach, teachers encourage students to use what they know to develop deeper understandings rather than simply to learn random and unrelated facts. Constructivist teaching is characterized by such practices as inquiry activities, problem-posing strategies, and dialogue among peers. In this approach, learning is viewed as an interactive rather than a passive process, and students' creativity and intelligence are respected. Although this sounds promising, constructivism—or any other approach, for that matter—is not necessarily effective with all students and cannot be simply "applied" as if it is the answer to all learning problems. In a critique of constructivism, Virginia Richardson, who is herself a proponent of the approach, claims that using it indiscriminately may be counterproductive. One problem in doing so is that it ignores the fact that the approach reflects a dominant view of pedagogy: Constructivism does not take into account the experiences and wishes of those who would rather learn differently. Richardson writes, "The most serious problem with the use of the constructive pedagogy construct occurs when it becomes valued as best practice for everyone."[56]

Who has access to constructivist teaching? Although conventional wisdom might lead us to believe that only students in high-ability groups receive this kind of instruction, the opposite has actually been found. In their investigation of the use of constructivist versus didactic teaching, Becky Smerden and her colleagues found that *less able* students in science classes received *more* constructivist instruction than did more able students. The researchers did not greet this finding with optimism. Instead, they were troubled by this finding because they discovered that a great many of the teachers who used this type of instruction in lower level courses were not trained in science and did not have certification as science teachers. Because

they had a weak base of scientific knowledge, they used constructivism to cover this fact. If this is the case, the researchers concluded, methods alone do not guarantee high-quality educational experiences for students.[57]

We need to view all approaches and methods with a critical eye, even with skepticism, because no method will solve learning problems for all students. This is the problem with any pedagogical approach that is uncritically elevated to the level of "best practice" as if a particular practice is appropriate for all students in all contexts. Lilia Bartolomé suggests that, instead of devotion to a particular instructional strategy, teachers need to develop a "humanizing pedagogy" that values students' cultural, linguistic, and experiential backgrounds.[58] To underscore the secondary place of particular strategies, Jim Cummins cautions that "good teaching does not require us to internalize an endless list of instructional techniques. Much more fundamental is the recognition that human relationships are central to effective instruction."[59]

Climate and Physical Structure

Climate refers to the nature of the environment. In schools, the climate can either encourage or stifle learning. In urban areas, and increasingly in some suburban areas as well, for instance, it is not unusual to find schools with police officers standing guard. In some schools, students are frisked before entering. Teachers sometimes feel afraid unless they lock their classrooms. Climate is often, although not always, associated with the *physical structure* of schools, that is, the architecture, classroom resources, cleanliness, order, and even such things as the color of the paint in the hallways and the condition of the plumbing in the bathrooms. The physical structure of schools can also either promote or inhibit educational equity. In some schools, desks are nailed to the floor; halls and classrooms are airless and poorly lit; and shattered glass can be found in courtyards where young children play. To understand the connection that exists between climate and physical structures, we turn to Ron Berger, a long-time teacher, who describes how the various elements of a school's culture affect students:

The aspects of a school that most clearly engrave the school experience on children are often in the "other stuff" category: the physical appearance of the school building, outside and in; the manner in which school property and personal property are respected and cared for in the school; the levels of physical safety and emotional safety that children and adults in the building feel; the way routines of arrival, class transitions, lunch times, and dismissal are handled; the ways authority is exercised; the tone of courtesy, kindness, and acceptance in peer culture; the ways in which students' achievements are shared with the school community and outside of it; the aspects of the school that define it in the larger community. These things are every bit as important as curriculum.[60]

One dramatic example of how school climate can influence student behavior was reported by Valerie Lee and David Burkam. Using a sample of 3,840 students in 190 urban and suburban high schools, they found that the structures and organization of high schools may influence students' decisions to stay in school or drop out. Some of the conditions that fostered staying in school were school size of fewer than 1,500 students, a curriculum offering mainly academic courses and few nonaca-demic courses, and positive relationships between students and their teachers. Lee and Burkam concluded that explanations for dropping out that rely solely on students' social background and school behaviors are inadequate.[61]

In addition, a survey of the literature associated with school facilities reported that there is indeed a relationship between poor student achievement and the condition of school buildings. These conditions include poor lighting, inadequate ventilation, inadequate or too much heating, school safety, class size, and air quality.[62] Also, disturbing statistics about the physical condition of schools have been reported: One in four U.S. schools is overcrowded and 3.5 million children attend public schools that are in very poor or even nonoperative condition— this in the wealthiest country in the world.[63] Add the lack of relevant and culturally appropriate pictures, posters, and other instructional materials, and we are left with environments that are scarcely inviting centers of learning.

In many instances, of course, schools are un-inviting, fortresslike places precisely because school

What You Can Do

Punch Up Your Pedagogy!

The case studies and snapshots in this book highlight the fact that the standard pedagogy used in many schools is unappealing to most students. Although textbooks may be important teaching and learning tools, they often become the entire curriculum and are used as the only basis for pedagogy, to the exclusion of materials that may be more appealing. Go beyond textbooks and use additional resources to make the curriculum more inviting for students, for example, audiovisual materials such as camcorders and cameras, guest speakers, and alternative reading material. To create a real sense of history among students, use primary documents and involve students more directly as "history sleuths" to uncover history.

Develop a variety of approaches that will engage students. Although a straight lecture, what has been called "chalk and talk," may be appropriate sometimes, it treats students as passive learners and receptacles of knowledge. It is also culturally inappropriate for many students. To help students become more active learners as well as to provide a multiculturally sensitive learning environment, encourage group work, individualized tasks, collaborative research, peer tutoring, cross-age tutoring, group reflection, dialogue, and action projects in the school and community. The last of these might include volunteer activities at a local senior center or day-care center or a letter-writing campaign about a community issue (e.g., the need for a traffic light at a nearby intersection).

officials are trying to protect students and teachers against vandalism, theft, and other acts of violence. Although violence in schools has diminished in the past several years, it is still a major problem. The violent crime victimization rate at school declined from 48 per 1,000 in 1992 to 28 per 1,000 in 2003. In spite of this decline, students 12 years of age or older were victims of about 740,000 violent crimes such as bullying, and another 1.2 million were victims of theft.[64] Moreover, a recent survey of 32,000 students in 108 urban schools found that 25 percent of the students surveyed said they felt uncertain about their safety in school, and fully half indicated that they had seen other students being bullied at least once a month.[65]

Schools alone are not to blame for violence, however. Violence in schools is a reflection of the violence that takes place in society, and teachers and administrators often struggle heroically to contain it and to make schools places of learning and joy. Yet, frequently it is students from these very schools who do the damage. Boredom and rage are implicated in these actions, particularly when schools show little regard for students by silencing their voices and negating their identities in the curriculum. Destructiveness and violence by students sometimes represent a clear message that school structures are incompatible with students' emotional and physical needs. For instance, the U.S. Department of Education reported that large and impersonal schools, and those with hostile and authoritarian teachers and administrators, were more likely to be vandalized than schools characterized by cooperation among teachers and administrators and clear expectations for students.[66]

The resemblance of some schools to factories or prisons has been mentioned many times over the years.[67] The size of schools alone is enough to give them this institutional look. High schools hold sometimes 2,000, 3,000, or even 4,000 students, and it is easy to understand the students' and teachers' feelings of alienation and insecurity that can result. Also, schools that are in good repair may help to retain both teachers and students. One study found that facility quality was an important predictor of the decision of teachers to stay or leave, probably even more important than a pay increase.[68] Another project has experimented with the color of walls: Publicolor, a program in which students are

encouraged to paint over the industrial shades of their schools' walls, has been found to lower dropout rates, decrease discipline problem, and increase attendance.[69]

Because school size makes a difference in student learning, many schools are developing schools within schools, teams, or other approaches to encourage more familylike environments and closer relationships among students and teachers. School size may also influence students' feelings of belonging, and thus their engagement with learning. One recent study concluded that elementary schools of fewer than 400 students tend to display stronger collective teacher responsibility for student learning and greater student achievement in math.[70] Small classes also have been proven to have an effect on student learning. A widely cited study by Jeremy Finn and his associates found that when students started early and continued in small classes or classes with teachers' aides for at least three years, they performed significantly better in all grades than students in full-size classes or without teachers' aides. In addition, those benefits lasted: Students who attended small classes in grades K–3 continued to perform better in all subjects up to the eighth grade.[71] Class size alone, however, may not be the most important factor in influencing student engagement in learning. Simply making schools smaller will not have a major impact if the climate within schools remains unchanged.[72]

Not all schools are large and impersonal, however. In general, the farther away from urban or poor rural communities, the less institutional the appearance of the school. Suburban schools or schools in wealthy towns tend to look strikingly different from schools that serve the poor. Not only do the former usually have more space, bigger classrooms, and more light, but they also have more material supplies and generally are in better physical condition, partly because the level of financing for the education of poor students is lower than for children in more affluent districts. Wealthier schools tend to have smaller classes as well, another condition that is related to higher quality education for students.

The physical environment of schools can also reflect the expectations that educators have of the capabilities of students. If students are perceived to be deficient, the educational environment may reflect a no-nonsense, back-to-basics drill orientation. However, if students are perceived as intelligent and motivated and as having an interest in the world around them, the educational environment tends to reflect an intellectually stimulating and academically challenging orientation, a place where learning is considered joyful rather than tedious. Given this reality, we might well ask what would happen if the schools attended by youngsters in poor urban and rural areas were to miraculously become like the schools that middle-class and wealthy youngsters attend. Might there be a change in educational outcomes if all students had access to generously endowed, smaller, and more democratically run schools? We cannot know the answer to this question until we try such an approach, but one thing is for certain: The physical environment in many schools provides a stark contrast to the stated purposes of teaching and learning. When schools are not cared for, when they become fortresses rather than an integral part of the community they serve, and when they are holding places instead of learning environments, the contradiction between goals and realities is a vivid one. This chasm between ideal and real is not lost on the students.

Disciplinary Policies

Disciplinary policies, especially in middle and secondary schools, may be at odds with the developmental level of students and, as a result, can aggravate the sense of alienation felt by some students. Research that supports this hypothesis is compelling. Two decades ago, using longitudinal data from the national High School and Beyond study, researchers Gary Wehlage and Robert Rutter found that certain conditions in the schools themselves can *predict* the dropping-out behavior of students.[73] These conditions include disciplinary policies perceived by students to be unfair and ineffective, especially those that are imposed rather than negotiated. Consequently, there is a serious problem with what Wehlage and Rutter refer to as the *holding power* of school. They concluded that certain student characteristics in *combination with* certain school conditions are responsible for students' decisions to drop out.

Interpretations of student behavior may be culturally or class biased, and this poses an additional barrier to enforcing disciplinary policies fairly. For example, students in poor schools who insist on wearing highly prized leather jackets in class may be doing so because of a well-founded fear that they will be stolen if left in the closet. Latino children who cast their eyes downward when being scolded probably are not being defiant but simply behaving out of respect for their teachers, as they were taught at home. African American students are especially vulnerable to unfair policies if they follow particular styles. For example, in her study of an urban school undergoing restructuring, Pauline Lipman described the case of an African American male student who was given a 10-day in-school suspension for wearing his overall straps unsnapped, a common style among African American males, whereas White students who wore their pants with large holes cut in the thighs, a widespread style among White students, were not even reprimanded.[74]

Students living in poverty and students of color are also more likely to be suspended and to be victims of corporal punishment. This inequity is frequently related to poor communication among administrators, teachers, and students. For example, in a two-month investigation, the *Seattle Post-Intelligencer* found that Black students were two and a half times more likely to be suspended or expelled than other students. Although common explanations for this situation include poverty and broken homes, the investigation found that Black students were far more likely than others to be suspended or expelled *regardless of their home lives and poverty*. In this case, too, school climate and size can make a difference. The report of this investigation cited one school that had become a "small school" by creating a more intimate and sensitive environment. The result was that suspensions and expulsions had been reduced across the board, although a racial gap still existed. "A school culture that prides itself on being color-blind," the report concluded, "might be better off taking a hard look at race."[75]

Discipline can be an issue even among more economically privileged students who are culturally different from the mainstream. For instance, Avi Abramson, one of the case studies that follows this chapter, pointed out how he was the subject of several anti-Semitic incidents. Because teachers were

What You Can Do

Enliven Your Environment
There are some things in your physical environment that you can do little about but there are others that you can change, both inside classrooms and out.

Make your classroom inviting and comfortable. Ask parents, students, and colleagues to help with ideas and resources. In the younger grades, create engaging activity corners, a cozy place to read, comfortable chairs or a couch, and a place for group work. In the older grades, have a quiet place for individual work and a space for collaborative research. From time to time, place seats in a horseshoe arrangement in order to create a more amenable space for dialogue. From preschool through high school, posters, maps, pictures, books, and music help create a sense of belonging in a classroom.

Outside the classroom, graffiti and garbage around a school, or broken toilets and nonfunctioning science labs, give the message that the children who attend that school are not valued. Help organize families, colleagues, and children for clean-up brigades. If there are more serious problems, inform parents and other community members about some of the policies and practices that make school uninviting so that they can organize to help solve these problems. These issues can be brought up at parent–teacher association (PTA), school board, and even city council meetings. Unless demands are made to change the negative messages these school-environment problems send, children will continue to be the victims.

uncertain how they should respond, Avi felt that he had to take matters into his own hands. One time, he said, "I went up to the teacher and I said to her, 'I'm either gonna leave the class or they leave.'"

A lack of awareness of cultural and social factors on the part of teachers and schools can lead to misinterpretations and faulty conclusions. Although it is usually students who experience the least success in school who bear the brunt of rigid school policies, all students who differ from the cultural mainstream are jeopardized.

The Limited Role of Students

That many students are alienated, uninvolved, and discouraged by school is abundantly clear. This fact is most striking, of course, in dropout rates, the most extreme manifestation of disengagement from schooling. Students who drop out are commonly uninvolved and passive participants in the school experience.

Usually, schools are not organized to encourage active student involvement. Although school is a place where a lot of talk goes on, it is seldom student talk, and teachers and other staff lose out on an opportunity to learn firsthand from students about their educational experiences and what could improve them. Students and teachers who spend the most time in schools and classrooms often have the least opportunity to talk about their experiences.

Although it is true that students are nominally represented in the governance structure of many schools, often this representation is merely window dressing that has little to do with the actual management of the school. Rather than being designed to prepare students for democratic life, most schools are more like benign dictatorships in which all decisions are made for them, albeit in what schools may perceive to be students' best interests. They are more often organized around issues of control than of collaboration or consultation. That is, students are expected to learn what is decided, designed, and executed by others. Often, it is not the teacher or even the school that determines the content but some mythical "downtown," school board, or state education department.

In the classroom itself, the pedagogy frequently reflects what Paulo Freire called *banking education*, that is, a process by which teachers "deposit" knowledge into students, who are thought to be empty receptacles. It is education that promotes powerlessness. In a characterization of what happens in most schools, Freire contrasted the expected roles of the teacher and the students:

- The teacher teaches, and the students are taught.
- The teacher knows everything, and the students know nothing.
- The teacher thinks, and the students are thought about.
- The teacher talks, and the students listen—meekly.
- The teacher disciplines, and the students are disciplined.
- The teacher chooses and enforces his or her choice, and the students comply.
- The teacher acts, and the students have the illusion of acting through the action of the teacher.
- The teacher chooses the program content, and the students (who were not consulted) adapt to it.
- The teacher confuses the authority of knowledge with his or her own professional author-ity, which he or she sets in opposition to the freedom of the students.
- The teacher is the subject of the learning process, while the pupils are mere objects.[76]

What impact does involvement of students have on their school experiences and achievement? Little research has been done on this issue, but researcher Ernest Morrell, in a multiyear critical ethnographic study of—and with—urban students, sought to understand the relationship between apprenticing urban youth as critical researchers of their realities and the development of their academic literacy. Working on a college access project with students of color from Pacific High School (a pseudonym) during two summers, they took on the issue of the tremendous disparity that existed in the high school, based on ethnicity and social class background, effectively making it seem like two separate high schools. Morrell saw students develop from novices to productive writers, researchers, and speakers at national education conferences who published their research as a form of social action. He concluded,

> Through their writings, presentations, personal conversations, and subtle interrogations, the project participants forced nearly all of the major power brokers at the school and in the district to respond to the two-school situation at Pacific Beach High

What You Can Do

Create Inclusive Disciplinary Practices

Investigate how disciplinary policies and practices affect students of different groups unfairly by looking at rates of detention, suspension, and assignments to "special" classes or alternative programs in your school. If students in these programs are overwhelmingly from one social or racial group or gender, ask the principal to set up study or inquiry groups to look into this problem. Suggest appropriate steps to address the problem directly.

At the classroom level, ask your students to help design disciplinary policies. Think about how to involve all your students as class citizens. At the school level, rather than rely on those who happen to be on the student council—generally a rather limited group of students—suggest a forum in which a broad range of student voices are heard. This forum can include academic classes, assemblies, and other student activities such as sports and clubs.

School and to design and implement strategies to overcome the problem.[77]

In addition, students became more passionate learners. Some who had never dreamed about going to college were so changed by this experience that they were determined to do so. Unfortunately, however, as Morrell found, such changes cannot be sustained in the absence of a broader political movement in which students, families, and educators mobilize to radically alter the status quo in schools and districts. Nevertheless, the message should not be lost on teachers and schools: When students are involved in directing their own education in some way, they are more enthusiastic learners.

The Limited Role of Teachers

As a group, teachers are shown little respect by our society and are usually poorly paid and infrequently rewarded. In school, they are sometimes the victims of physical and verbal threats and attacks, and they feel a lack of parental support and involvement. Moreover, teachers are traditionally discouraged from becoming involved in decision-making processes in the schools. Moreover, they have become more alienated in the current climate of reform because more decisions about curriculum and instruction are being made by others, while accountability is being more and more determined by high-stakes tests and imposed standards. Alienated and discouraged teachers can hardly be expected to help students become empowered, critical thinkers. Michelle Fine, for instance, reported research findings that teacher disempowerment correlates highly with disparaging attitudes toward students—that is, the more powerless teachers feel, the more negative they are toward their students. In contrast, teachers who feel that they have autonomy in their classrooms and in decisions about curriculum generally also have high expectations of their students.[78]

New structures such as teacher-led schools, job sharing, and time, on a weekly basis, for professional development and other activities may help make teachers more active players in their schools. In addition, a number of recent studies have found that, in order to create a sense of teaching as intel-

lectual work, it is vital to develop schools as professional communities of practice.[79] Changing the nature of professional development in schools so that teachers take more responsibility for their own learning is imperative, but the professional climate in schools is only one aspect of a larger problem. Teachers are disempowered for many reasons, and these do not correspond simply to school structures. Their disempowerment also has a lot to do with their status within the professional hierarchy. For example, many teachers become angry at the lack of respect with which they are treated by administrators and the general public. They also resent the fact that they are frequently overlooked when it comes to making decisions about curriculum and instruction. More recently, with the growing standardization of curriculum in public schools and the greater use of high-stakes tests, teachers have even less say on these issues than before. Restructuring schools to be more respectful of teachers' professionalism is, therefore, crucial if they are to become places where teachers feel engaged and empowered.

Nevertheless, restructuring and greater teacher efficacy, by themselves, are no guarantee that schools will become more effective learning environments for students. For example, in research on a restructuring school, Pauline Lipman found that even in an environment where teachers were included in developing policies, some policies remained largely untouched. Tracking was never challenged, disciplinary practices primarily continued to jeopardize students of color, and a general silence concerning issues of racism and inequality pervaded the school.[80] It is clear, then, that making the school environment better for teachers will not necessarily make it better for students. Structural changes to broaden the roles, responsibilities, and status of teachers need to be accompanied by changes in (1) the general public's attitudes about teachers' professionalism, (2) teachers' beliefs about their own capabilities, and (3) the dynamic possibilities for learning that students' diversity creates. Thus, in spite of the restrictions imposed by high-stakes standardized testing and the bureaucratization of schools, when teachers deliberately choose to work together to promote change, and when they focus on learning about their students' realities, tremendous positive changes can begin to take shape.

Limited Family and Community Involvement

The findings of research on the effectiveness of family and community involvement are clear. In programs with strong family involvement, students are consistently better achievers than in otherwise identical programs with less family involvement. In addition, students in schools that maintain frequent contact with their communities outperform students in other schools. These positive effects persist well beyond the short term.[81]

There are many definitions of parent involvement, and each is more or less effective, depending on the context. Becoming involved in activities such as attendance at parent–teacher conferences, participation in parent–teacher associations (PTAs), and influence over children's selection of courses can help improve student achievement. But involvement of this kind is becoming more and more scarce in a society increasingly characterized by one-parent families or two-parent families in which both work outside the home. Thus, defining involvement only in these traditional ways is problematic. PTA meetings held during the day, parent–teacher conferences held during school hours, and the ubiquitous parent-sponsored cake sale are becoming relics of the past. Currently, most families, regardless of cultural or economic background, find it difficult to attend meetings or to otherwise become involved in the governance of the school or in fund-raising.

Cultural and economic differences also influence family involvement. Families of linguistically and culturally diverse communities and from working-class neighborhoods frequently have difficulty fulfilling the level and kind of parent involvement expected by the school, such as homework assistance and family excursions. Not taking part in these activities should not be interpreted as noninvolvement or apathy, however. Families of all backgrounds generally have high expectations and aspirations for their children, although school personnel may not realize this. In addition, there is a general lack of awareness among school staff concerning the cultural and linguistic resources of families of diverse backgrounds. One study found that when Mexican American families were encouraged to participate in a home-school partnership, their involvement with school increased and their children's engagement with learning also increased. Similar conclusions have been reached in studies of families of other backgrounds.[82]

Family involvement is a complex issue, and teachers and other educators are often intimidated by family involvement or are reluctant to reach out to families. For one, most educators have had little

What You Can Do

Vigorously Promote Family Outreach

First, recognize and acknowledge that most families are involved in the education of their children through the values they foster at home and in the implicit and explicit expectations they have of their children. At the same time, encourage families to become more involved in the day-to-day life of the school if they can.

Most important, communicate with families regularly through a weekly or monthly newsletter, phone calls, meetings at school or home, or a combination of these methods. Mary Cowhey, a teacher we know, visits every family of her students in the two weeks prior to the beginning of school. She says she learns more about her students, about who loves them, and about what's important to them through these visits than any other way.

When school meetings are to take place, ask administrators to provide child care, translation of the proceedings into languages spoken by the families, and transportation. Encourage family members to bring activities and materials that are significant to them and their children into the classroom.

preparation for working with families.[83] Also, families and school personnel may have little knowledge of one another's realities. One interesting poll found that there was a wide gap in the way parents and principals perceived their relationship: Although 93 percent of the principals said that their relationships with parents was "satisfactory," only 64 percent of the parents polled expressed the same feeling.[84] Furthermore, teachers and other school staff often do not understand the cultural values of different families and the goals that parents have for their children; typical involvement strategies may further estrange families who already feel disconnected from the school. This was one of the conclusions reached by Guadalupe Valdés in a study of ten Mexican immigrant families in the Southwest. She found that although the beliefs and practices of the families were perfectly reasonable in their former cultural contexts, they did not always work in their new setting. Schools do not always know how

to negotiate these different worlds, and common strategies such as "parenting classes" tend to worsen the situation. In the words of Valdés,[85]

> Relationships between parents and schools do, in fact, reflect the structural locations of these individuals in the wider society. Simply bringing parents to schools will not change the racist or classist responses that teachers may have toward them and their behaviors. Parenting classes alone will not equalize outcomes.

In spite of the challenges of parent involvement—especially when it comes to poor and immigrant families—it still represents a potential avenue for bringing community values, lifestyles, and realities into the school. When families become involved, it also means that their language and culture and the expectations they have for their children can become a part of the dialogue, and it is through dialogue that true change can begin to happen.

SUMMARY

The organization and structures of schools often are contrary to the needs of students, the values of their communities, and even to one of the major articulated purposes of schooling—to provide equal educational opportunity for all students. The result is that policies and practices in schools more often than not reflect and maintain the status quo and the stratification of the larger society. But schools by themselves cannot change this situation. Witness the sobering words of Jeannie Oakes and her colleagues. In a longitudinal study of 16 schools around the country undergoing reform, these researchers reached the reluctant conclusion that the educational reforms they studied "did little to interrupt or disrupt the course of the nation's history, flaws, and inequity, its hegemony and racism." They added, "Asking to disrupt a nation is a tall order—one that, we have become convinced, schools will eagerly follow but should not be expected to lead."[86]

In spite of our fondest wishes, therefore, schools cannot, by themselves, become an oasis of equity in a land of inequity. This does not mean, however, that the situation is hopeless. On the contrary, there is much for teachers and other educators to do, both in classrooms and out. This is the subject of subsequent chapters.

To Think About

1. Ability-group tracking decisions are often based on ideologies concerning intelligence. The "nature versus nurture" argument in explaining intelligence has been raging for many years. That is, while some people believe that intelligence is primarily dependent on genetic makeup ("nature"), others believe that the environment ("nurture") plays a more important

role. What are your thoughts on this debate? Why? What is the basis for your conclusions?

2. Think about the curriculum in classrooms where you have been a student. How have your experiences and culture and those of your classmates been included? If they have not, what do you think the effect has been on you and others? In a journal, write to a former teacher and tell her or him what kinds of changes in the curriculum would have made you a more enthusiastic and engaged student.

3. Design a school for either the elementary or secondary level that would provide a suitable environment for learning. Explain why you've designed it in the way that you have.

4. The criticism has been made that because schools do not provide opportunities for either teachers or students to exercise critical thinking or leadership, they subvert the very purpose of education as preparation for civic life and democratic participation. Do you believe this to be the case? How? Discuss some ways in which schools might provide more opportunities for teachers and students to be more fully engaged.

5. Research the disciplinary policies in your district. How do suspensions compare across racial, ethnic, and gender groups? How would you interpret these data? If there are inequities, what can you do—alone, with colleagues, or with parents and other community members—to address them?

Activities for Personal, School, and Community Change

1. Observe a number of similar classrooms, some that are tracked and others that are not. What are the differences in these classrooms? Be specific, citing student engagement with work, expectations of student achievement, level of academic difficulty, and teacher-student and student-student relationships. What are your conclusions about tracking? What can you do about it?

2. Get some evaluation checklists for textbooks at your library or, working with colleagues, design your own. Review and evaluate the textbooks used in your local school. Are they biased against students of any group? How? Give specific examples based on the checklists you have used.

3. Observe a classroom and indicate the kind of pedagogical strategies used by the teacher. Are all students engaged in learning? Who are not, and what might engage them?

4. With a group of colleagues, prepare a workshop for other teachers on retention and alternatives to it. Present some actual data from your school or district about the effects of retention.

Companion Website

For access to additional case studies, weblinks, concept cards, and other material related to this chapter, visit the text's companion website at **www.ablongman.com/nieto5e.**

Notes to Chapter 9

1. John Dewey, *Democracy and Education* (New York: Free Press, 1916): 175.

2. For the purpose of consistency, the term *tracking* rather than *ability grouping* will be generally used in the discussion that follows.

3. Jeannie Oakes and Gretchen Guiton, "Matchmaking: The Dynamics of High School Tracking Decisions." *American Educational Research Journal* 32, no. 1 (Spring 1995): 3–33. For a comprehensive review of this history, see Jeannie Oakes, *Keeping Track: How Schools Structure Inequality,* 2nd ed. (New Haven, CT: Yale University Press, 2005).

4. Milbrey W. McLaughlin and Joan E. Talbert, *Professional Communities and the Work of High School Teaching* (Chicago: University of Chicago Press, 2001).

5. Jeannie Oakes, *Keeping Track: How Schools Structure Inequality* (New Haven, CT: Yale University Press, 1985). See also *Keeping Track: How Schools Structure Inequality,* 2nd ed., 2005.

6. This research is reviewed in the new edition of *Keeping Track.* See Note 5.

7. Susan Yonezawa, Amy Stuart Wells, and Irene Serna, "Choosing Tracks: 'Freedom of Choice' in Detracking Schools." *American Educational Research Journal,* 39, no. 1 (Spring 2002): 37–67.

8. Anne Wheelock, *Crossing the Tracks: How "Untracking" Can Save America's Schools* (New York: New Press, 1992).

9. Joseph J. D'Amico, "A Closer Look at the Minority Achievement Gap." *ERS Spectrum* (Spring 2001): 4–10.

10. Susan Black, "Second Time Around." *American School,* 191, no. 11 (November 2004). Available at: www.asbj.com/researcharchive/index.html

11. Karen Kelly, "Retention vs. Social Promotion: Schools Search for Alternatives." *Harvard Education Letter* 15, no. 1 (Jan/Feb 1999): 1–3.

12. Guanglei Hong and Stephen W. Raudenbush, "Effects of Kindergarten Retention Policy on Children's Cognitive Growth in Reading and Mathematics." *Educational Evaluation and Policy Analysis* 27, no. 3 (Fall 2005): 205–224.

13. See, for instance, Nilda Flores-González, "The Structuring of Extracurricular Opportunities and Latino Student Retention." *Journal of Poverty* 4, nos. 1, 2 (2000): 85–108.

14. See Steve Selden, *Inheriting Shame: The Story of Eugenics and Racism in America* (New York: Teachers College Press, 1999).

15. For a more recent example of how IQ tests are used to "prove" the social and intellectual inferiority of some groups, see Richard J. Herrnstein and Charles Murray, *The Bell Curve: Intelligence and Class Structure in American Life* (New York: Free Press, 1994).

16. Joel Spring, *American Education,* 12th ed. (New York: McGraw-Hill, 2006).

17. Lewis Terman, *The Measurement of Intelligence* (Boston: Houghton Mifflin, 1916).

18. See examples of the connection between IQ testing and eugenics in Selden, *Inheriting Shame: The Story of Eugenics and Racism in America* and in Stephen Jay Gould, *The Mismeasure of Man,* revised and expanded ed. (New York: W. W. Norton, 1996).

19. Barbara Miner, "Testing Companies Mine for Gold." *Rethinking Schools* 19, no. 2 (Winter 2004): 5–7.

20. *Ibid.*

21. Richard F. Elmore, "Testing Trap," *Harvard Magazine* (September–October 2002). Available at: www.harvardmagazine.com/online/o902140.html

22. Gary Orfield and Mindy L. Kornhaber, eds., *Raising Standards or Raising Barriers? Inequality and High-Stakes Testing in Public Education* (New York: The Century Foundation Press, 2001).

23. Audrey I. Amrein and David C. Berliner, "High-Stakes Testing, Uncertainty, and Student Learning," *Education Policy Analysis Archives* 10, no. 18 (2002). Available at: http://epaa.asu.edu/epaa/v10n18/

24. David C. Berliner, "Our Impoverished View of Educational Reform." *Teachers College Record.* Available at: www.tcrecord.org/content.asp?contentID=12106

25. College Board, "2004 College Bound Seniors' Test Scores: SAT." In *College-Bound Seniors 2004: A Profile of SAT Program Test Takers* (New York: Author, 2005).

26. Linda McNeil, *Contradictions of School Reform: Educational Costs of Standardized Testing* (New York: Routledge, 2000).

27. James W. Pellegrino, Naomi Chudowsky, and Robert Glaser, *Knowing What Students Know: The Science and Design of Educational Assessment* (Washington, DC: National Academy Press, 2001).

28. Joseph J. Pedula, Lisa M. Abrams, George F. Madaus, Michael K. Russell, Miguel A. Ramos, and Jing Miao, *Perceived Effects of State-Mandated Testing Programs on Teaching and Learning: Findings from a National Survey of Teachers* (Boston: National Board on Educational Testing and Public Policy, Boston College, 2003).

29. Many recent books and monographs have weighed in on the debate about standardized tests. Most have come out squarely against the overuse and misuse of high-stakes standardized tests. Besides Linda McNeil's *Contradictions of School Reform,* some of the most important titles are Kathy Swope and Barbara Miner, *Failing Our Kids: Why the Testing Craze Won't Fix Our Schools* (Milwaukee: Rethinking Schools, 2000); Deborah Meier, *In Schools We Trust: Creating Communities of Learning in an Era of Testing and Standardization* (Boston: Beacon Press, 2003); M. Gail Jones, Brett D. Jones, and Tracy Hargrove, *The Unintended Consequences of High-Stakes Testing* (Lanham, MD: Rowman & Littlefield, 2003); and Sharon Nichols and David C. Berliner, *The Inevitable Corruption of Indicators and Educators Through High-Stakes Testing.* (Tempe, AZ: Educational Policy Studies Laboratory, Educational Policy Research Unit, Arizona State University, March 2005). Available at: http://edpolicylab.org

30. Michael Sadowski, "Are High-Stakes Tests Worth the Wager?" In Minority *Achievement,* edited by David T. Gordon (Cambridge, MA: *Harvard Education Letter* Focus Series no. 7, 2002).

31. Dewey, *Democracy and Education,* 172.

32. Several of the chapter authors in Gary Orfield and Mindy Kornhaber's *Raising Standards or Raising Barriers?* discuss alternatives to high-stakes standardized tests and also offer some caveats about them.

33. Michael W. Apple, *Identity and Curriculum,* 3rd ed. (New York: RoutledgeFalmer, 2004).

34. Bob Fecho, *Is This English? Race, Language, and Culture in the Classroom* (New York: Teachers College Press, 2003). See also Lisa Delpit and Joanne Kilgour Doudy, eds., *The Skin That We Speak: Thoughts on Language and Culture in the Classroom* (New York: New Press, 2002).

35. James A. Banks, *An Introduction to Multicultural Education,* 4th ed. (Boston: Allyn and Bacon, 2007).

36. Judith Solsken, Jo-Anne Wilson Keenan, and Jerri Willett, "Interweaving Stories: Creating a Multicultural Classroom Through School/Home/University Collaboration." *Democracy and Education* (Fall 1993): 16–21.

37. Michelle Fine, *Framing Dropouts: Notes on the Politics of an Urban Public High School* (Albany: State University of New York Press, 1991): 33.

38. *Ibid.,* 37.

39. J. M. Hughes and Rebecca S. Bigler, "Addressing Race and Racism in the Classroom." In *Lessons in Integration: Realizing the Promise of Racial Diversity in American Schools* by Gary Orfield and Erica Frankonburg, eds. (Charlottesville: University of Virginia Press, 2007).

40. Fran Smith, "Candor in the Class." Available at: http://edutopia.or/magazine/ed1article.php?id=Art_1499&issue_apr_06

41. Maxine Greene, "Reflections: Implications of September 11th for Curriculum." In *Division B: Curriculum Studies Newsletter* (Washington, DC: American Educational Research Association, Fall 2001).

42. Murray Levin, *'Teach Me!' Kids Will Learn When Oppression Is the Lesson* (Lanham, MD: Rowman & Littlefield, 2001).

43. Linda Darling-Hammond, "New Standards and Inequalities: School Reform and the Education of African American Students." In *Black Education: A Transformative Research and Action Agenda for the New Century,* edited by Joyce E. King (Mahwah, NJ: Lawrence Erlbaum; and Washington, DC: American Educational Research Association, 2005).

44. For an excellent analysis of this phenomenon, see Kathleen Demarrais and Margaret LeCompte, *The Way Schools Work: A Sociological Analysis of Education,* 4th ed. (Boston: Allyn and Bacon, 2007).

45. Study by the American Council on Education in 1949; cited by Gordon Allport, *The Nature of Prejudice* (Reading, MA: Addison-Wesley, 1954): 202.

46. See Christine E. Sleeter, *Un-Standardizing the Curriculum: Multicultural Teaching in the Standards-Based Classroom* (New York: Teachers College Press, 2005) for a recent review.

47. Violet J. Harris, ed., *Using Multiethnic Literature in the K–8 Classroom* (Norwood, MA: Christopher-Gordon, 1997); Arlette Willis, ed., *Teaching and Using Multicultural Literature in Grades 9–12: Moving Beyond the Canon* (Norwood, MA: Christopher-Gordon, 1998).

48. James W. Loewen, *Lies My Teacher Told Me: Everything Your American History Textbook Got Wrong* (New York: New Press, reissue edition, 2005); and James W. Loewen, *Lies Across America: What Our Historic Sites Got Wrong* (New York: New Press, 2000).

49. John Goodlad, *A Place Called School,* 20th Anniversary ed. (New York: McGraw-Hill, 2004).

50. Bruce L. Wilson and H. Dickson Corbett, *Listening to Urban Kids: School Reform and the Teachers They Want* (Albany: State University of New York Press, 2001).

51. Martin Haberman, "The Pedagogy of Poverty versus Good Teaching." *Phi Delta Kappan* 73, no. 4 (December 1991): 290–294.

52. Laurel Shaper Walters, "Putting Cooperative Learning to the Test." *Harvard Education Letter* 16, no. 3 (May/June 2000): 1–7.

53. Mary McCaslin and Thomas L. Good, "Compliant Cognition: The Misalliance of Management and Instructional Goals in Current School Reform." *Educational Researcher* 21, no. 3 (April 1992): 4–17.

54. For a discussion of these issues, see María de la Luz Reyes, "Challenging Venerable Assump-

tions: Literacy Instruction for Linguistically Different Students." *Harvard Educational Review* 62, no. 4 (Winter 1992): 427–446.

55. D. C. Phillips, ed. *Constructivism in Education*. National Society for the Study of Education Yearbook, 99, issue 1. (Chicago: University of Illinois at Chicago, 2000).

56. Virginia Richardson, "Constructivist Pedagogy," *Teachers College Record* 105, no. 9 (December 2003): 1623–1640, p. 1635.

57. Becky A. Smerden, David T. Burkham, and Valerie E. Lee, "Access to Constructivist and Didactic Teaching: Who Gets it? Where is it Practiced?" *Teachers College Record* 101, no. 1 (Fall 1999): 5–34.

58. Lilia I. Bartolomé, "Beyond the Methods Fetish: Toward a Humanizing Pedagogy." *Harvard Educational Review* 64, no. 2 (Summer 1994): 173–194.

59. Jim Cummins, *Negotiating Identities: Education for Empowerment in a Diverse Society* (Ontario: California Association for Bilingual Education, 1996): 73.

60. Ron Berger, "What Is a Culture of Quality?" In *Going Public With Our Teaching: An Anthology of Practice*, edited by Thomas Hatch, Dilruba Ahmed, Ann Lieberman, Deborah Faigenbaum, Melissa Eiler White, and Desiree H. Pointer Mace (New York: Teachers College Press, 2005): 35.

61. Valerie E. Lee and David T. Burkam, "Dropping Out of High School: The Role of School Organization and Structure." *American Educational Research Journal* 40, no. 2 (Summer 2003): 353–393.

62. "Public School Facilities: Providing Environments That Sustain Learning." *ACCESS* (Quarterly Newsletter of the Advocacy Center for Children's Educational Success With Standards), 4, no. 1 (Winter 2004): 1.

63. Sara Mead, "Schoolings' Crumbling Infrastructure: Addressing a Serious and Unappreciated Problem," 2005. Available at: www.edweek.org/ew/articles/2005/06/15/a40mead.h24.html

64. Jill DeVoe, Peter Katharin, Margaret Noonan, Thomas Snyder, and Katrina Baum, *Indicators of School Climate and Safety: 2005* (Washington, DC: Bureau of Justice Statistics, and the National Center for Education Statistics, 2005).

65. Brian K. Perkins, *Where We Learn: The CUBE Survey of Urban School Climate* (Washington, DC: Urban Achievement Task Force, Council of Urban Boards of Education and the National School Boards Association, 2006).

66. Many of these ideas are addressed in an informative article by Susan Black, "The Roots of Vandalism," *American School Board Journal* (July 2002). Available at: www.asbj.com/current/research.html

67. David B. Tyack, *The One Best System: A History of American Urban Education* (Cambridge, MA: Harvard University Press, 1974); Michael B. Katz, Class, *Bureaucracy, and the Schools: The Illusion of Educational Change in America* (New York: Praeger, 1975).

68. Jack Buckley, Mark Schneider, and Yi Shang. "Fix It and They Might Stay: School Facility Quality and Teacher Retention in Washington, DC." *Teachers College Record* 107, no. 4 (May 2005): 1107–1123.

69. "Do Brighter Walls Make Brighter Students?" Available at: www.cnn.com/2005/EDUCATION/12/19/paint.in.schools.ap/index.html

70. Valerie E. Lee and S. Loeb, "School Size in Chicago Elementary Schools: Effects on Teachers' Attitudes and Students' Achievement," *American Educational Research Journal* 37 (2000): 3–31.

71. Jeremy D. Finn, Susan B. Gerber, Charles M. Achilles, and Jayne Byrd-Zaharias, "The Enduring Effects of Small Classes." *Teachers College Record* 103, no. 2 (April 2001): 145–183.

72. For the benefits and potential pitfalls of small schools, see Deborah Meier, " 'As Though They Owned The Place': Small Schools as Membership Communities." *Phi Delta Kappan* 87, no. 9 (May 2006): 657–662.

73. Gary G. Wehlage and Robert A. Rutter, "Dropping Out: How Much Do Schools Contribute to the Problem?" In *School Dropouts: Patterns and Policies*, edited by Gary Natriello (New York: Teachers College Press, Columbia University, 1986).

74. Pauline Lipman, "Restructuring in Context: A Case Study of Teacher Participation and the Dynamics of Ideology, Race, and Power." *American Educational Research Journal* 34, no. 1 (1997): 3–37.

75. "School Discipline: An Uneven Hand," *Seattle Post-Intelligencer*, July 1, 2002. Available at: www.seattlepi.nwsource.com/disciplinegap/

76. Paulo Freire, *Pedagogy of the Oppressed* (New York: Seabury Press, 1970): 59.

77. Ernest Morrell, *Becoming Critical Researchers: Literacy and Empowerment for Urban Youth* (New York: Peter Lang, 2004).

78. See Fine, *Framing Dropouts: Notes on the Politics of an Urban Public High School.*

79. See, for example, Sonia Nieto, *What Keeps Teachers Going?* (New York: Teachers College Press, 2003) and McLaughlin and Talbert, *Professional Communities and the Work of High School Teaching.*

80. Pauline Lipman, *Restructuring in Context.*

81. For the literature on the importance of family–school partnerships, see Anne T. Henderson and Karen L. Mapp, *A New Wave of Evidence: The Impact of School, Family, and Community Connections on Student Achievement* (Austin, TX: Southwest Educational Development Laboratory, 2002).

82. Concha Delgado-Gaitan, *Involving Latino Families in Schools: Raising Student Achievement Through Home-School Partnerships* (Thousand Oaks, CA: Corwin Press, 2004). See also Carmen I. Mercado and Luis Moll, "Student Agency Through Collaborative Research in *Puerto Rican Communities.*" In *Puerto Rican Students in U.S. Schools,* edited by Sonia Nieto (Mahwah, NJ: Lawrence Erlbaum, 2000).

83. Joyce L. Epstein's *School, Family, and Community Partnerships: Preparing Educators and Improving Schools* (Boulder, CO: Westview, 2001), a textbook for courses that focus on family involvement, fills this void.

84. Harris Interactive, Inc., *Survey of the American Teacher: An Examination of School Leadership* (Rochester, NY: Author, 2003). Available at: www.metlife.com/Applications/Corporate/WPS/DCA/Pagegenerator/0,1674,P2315,00.htm/

85. Guadalupe Valdés, *Con Respeto: Bridging the Distance Between Culturally Diverse Families and Schools* (New York: Teachers College Press, 1996): 39.

86. Jeannie Oakes, Karen Hunter Quartz, Steve Ryan, and Martin Lipton, *Becoming Good American Schools: The Struggle for Civil Virtue in Education Reform* (San Francisco: Jossey-Bass, 2000): xxi.

CHAPTER 9 CASE STUDIES

Avi Abramson

Some teachers teach from the point of
view of the kid. They don't
just come out and say, "All right, do this,
blah, blah, blah."
They're not so one-tone voice.

Talbot is a small, quiet, and aging working-class town in eastern Massachusetts a few miles from the busy metropolis of Boston. Its total area is a mere 1.6 square miles, and it has a population of approximately 20,000. With the exception of salt marshes and surplus federal installations, there is little vacant land in Talbot.

One gets a sense of the community's aging by its housing. More than half of the dwellings are at least 75 years old, and this is partly due to the nature of the population. In the past two decades, the number of youths has been declining, with younger adults and families moving to more prosperous areas. The older residents remain, continuing to live in homes that long ago lost their newness and modern veneer. Both public and parochial school enrollment have been dwindling over the past two decades. One of the three elementary schools was turned into condominiums. The one high school in town, Talbot High School, has approximately 700 students.

Avi Abramson,[1] the subject of this case study, lived in Talbot at the time of his interview over a decade ago. Talbot was home to many Italians and

Irish and to smaller concentrations of other European American immigrants. The percentage of people of color was quite low—only a handful of families. Although there had been a thriving community in Talbot just a generation before, the number of Jewish families was very small at the time of Avi's interview. There were two synagogues in town, one known as the "big synagogue" and the other as the "small synagogue." Many Jewish families moved to other communities, and the remaining Jews were mostly senior citizens; many of them were religiously observant and went to temple regularly. According to Avi, many people in his community were close to 85 years of age. The high school had no more than ten Jewish students.

Avi had lived in Talbot almost all his life, except for a year when his family moved to North Carolina. He went to first and second grade in public school, then went to a Jewish day school until eighth grade. When interviewed, he was 16 years old and a senior at Talbot High School. As he explained during his interviews, Avi had not always been a successful student, and he had had a hard time adjusting to public school because the curriculum was so different from what he had experienced in the Jewish day school. His plans were to go to college the following year, and he had given some thought to becoming either a history teacher or a graphic designer. Because both his parents had been teachers and because drawing was one of his hobbies, these choices were not unexpected.

Avi lived on the water-tower hillside of this quaint old town in a quiet neighborhood of single and multifamily homes. During the Christmas season, his house was easily spotted: It was the only one on the street without Christmas lights. He described his town as peaceful, and he said he enjoyed living there. Avi and his family developed good relationships with their neighbors, whom he described with fondness ("Everybody looks out for each other," he said). Nevertheless, he clearly longed to live in a community where he was not perceived as being so "different."

Avi lived with his mother and a brother who was 10 years his elder. His older sister lived in New York City with her husband and two children. Avi's father had originally come from Israel and had met his Jewish American wife in the United States,

where he had remained. He had died after a long illness six years before Avi's interview. He had been a much-loved teacher in various Hebrew schools. Avi's mother was also a Hebrew teacher, and, although she loved teaching, there was not much call for Hebrew teachers in the area, so she began studying computers to prepare for a new career.

Exuding a warm glow of familiarity and old, comfortable furniture, Avi's home was filled with the aroma of latkes (potato pancakes) during the Hanukkah season and of many other Jewish foods at other times of the year. Books and artifacts were everywhere, reflecting the family's respect for tradition and history.

In many ways, Avi was a typical American teenager. He had a girlfriend and enjoyed frequent telephone conversations with friends. His bedroom was crammed with posters, comic books, encyclopedias, track team gear, woodworking projects, Star Trek memorabilia, drawing pads full of his own comics, and, underneath it all, bunk beds. However, in other ways, Avi was different from many other American youths. His serious, wise demeanor was evident in the profound respect and love that he had for his culture and religion. Few young people of any religion would dedicate every Saturday, as he did, to leading the last elderly remnants of his community in their Sabbath prayers at the small synagogue (what one might call a "role model in reverse"). He enjoyed speaking Hebrew, loved the Jewish holidays, and devoted a great deal of time to religious and cultural activities. An energetic and thoughtful young man, he enjoyed school as well as sports and other hobbies. But Avi was not what one would call a "nerd." Although he was serious about his studies, he had not always excelled in school and did not spend an inordinate amount of time studying.

Three basic themes were revealed in Avi's interviews. One was his *sense of responsibility*—to himself, his family, and his community—as well as his persistence in fulfilling this responsibility. This trait was especially evident in the respect and care with which he treated his culture and religion. *The joy and pain of maintaining them* was another theme frequently discussed by Avi. *The role of positive pressure*, from peers and family, and through activities such as track, was the third.

Independent responsibility and persistence

I'm fairly religious. I mean, I work in a temple on Saturdays, so I keep myself Orthodox. I try to keep the law, you know, for Shabbos [Yiddish for Sabbath], 'cause I'm reading the Torah [holiest book for Jews], so it would be nice if the person who's reading at least [should follow it]; if you're reading the law, then you might as well follow it. Set an example, in a way. Again, I don't know how much of a role model I can be to 85-year-olds [laughs sadly].

I'm currently working, or helping out, in Temple Solomon, with their services. A lot of people here too, they come to temple but some of them don't understand exactly what they're doing. They come, and if there weren't certain people here, they wouldn't know what to do and they wouldn't come at all, probably. So, I guess one of the reasons why I probably do what I'm doing is . . . well, I enjoy it 'cause I enjoy doing the services. I enjoy being that kind of leader. To help them.

I was going to temple every Saturday when I was little. I didn't follow along, but I just listened to them every time, and I got the tune and everything. It wasn't hard for me at all to learn the service for my Bar Mitzvah 'cause I already knew half of it in my head. Yeah, it's fun . . . it is.

The price of maintaining language and culture

There were more [Jews] years ago. Yeah, and now everybody has aged, and all the young ones are gone and left. So, there's not too many young ones coming up, 'cause there's not too many families— young families. The average age is probably 50s.

[In school] I'm the only, really, person that I guess follows the [Jewish Orthodox] laws. So I wouldn't go out on a Friday night or something like that. Right now, most people know that I don't usually come out on a Friday night. But when I started high school, people used to say sometimes, "Ya coming out tonight?" I'm like, "No, I can't. . . . " In a way, it brought me away from those people. I mean, I have different responsibilities than most people.

If I miss track and say, "'cause it's not exactly the holiday, it's the day before and I have to go home and prepare," most people won't understand. "What do you mean, you have to prepare?" or, "I

thought the holiday was tomorrow?" Most other religions don't have so many holidays during the year, so there's not that much preparation that they have to do, I guess.

[How would you feel if you lived in a place where everybody was Jewish?] [I'd] have a good feeling every day, 'cause everybody knows there's a holiday. It would be fun, 'cause I mean, it wouldn't be boring on Shabbos 'cause when you can't . . . really do anything, there's always somebody around. That's why I go to [Jewish] camp, too.

There's not too many other Jewish children around [here]. I'm sure there's some families. I know there are a few families that live in Talbot, but they aren't religious or they . . . just don't have time to send their children to temple.

We just had Simchas Torah here the other day. . . . It was really pathetic. I mean, on Thursday night, there were four little kids there, and there were less than 20 people all together. And then, Friday morning, there were 11 men at the big shul [temple], and there were 10 at the little shul.

When I have kids, I want to bring them up in a Jewish community. And from the looks of it here, there might be a Jewish community. I mean, there is one now, but it's dwindling away, or starting to rebuild itself. But it will probably take a while before it actually becomes a large Jewish community again, when people start coming and bringing their children to the temple and actually doing something.

And I'd like to be in a place myself, even if I'm not married, I'd like to be in a place where I could walk to the temple on Saturday, or I could just go down the street and I won't have to travel so far to where I could get some good kosher meat. Or things like that. Some place where there's always something to do, [so] you don't have to travel too far.

If the other people that are out there, if the reason that they don't come is also probably 'cause their parents [don't] . . . 'cause I remember, I was just speaking to a friend of mine last week who's Jewish, and I said to him, "When was the last time you were in temple? I'm just curious." I was just joking around with him, of course. And, he was like, "Yeah, I haven't been there in a while, you know. It's pretty sad. My parents don't follow anything, so I don't," he basically said.

A couple of years ago, I had some anti-Semitic things happen. But that was cleared up. I mean, it wasn't cleared up, but they, I don't know.

. . . There's a few kids in school that I still know are anti-Semites. Basically Jew haters.

I was in a woods class, and there was another boy in there, my age, and he was in my grade. He's also Jewish, and he used to come to the temple sometimes and went to Hebrew school. But then, of course, he started hanging around with the wrong people, and some of these people were in my class, and I guess they were making fun of him. And a few of them started making swastikas out of wood. So I saw one and I said to some kid, "What are you doing?" and the kid said to me, "Don't worry. It's not for you. It's for him." And I said to him, *"What?!?"* And he walked away. And after a while, they started bugging me about it, and they started saying remarks and things and. . . . Finally, it got to a point where I had them thrown out of class . . . 'cause I just decided to speak up.

And there was one kid that I didn't have thrown out because I didn't think he was as harmful as they were. But it turned out, as the year went on, I had a little incident with him too.

It was one of the last days of school, and I was wearing shorts, and it was hot out, you know. And I came into the class and I said to myself, "This is it. If he says something to me today, I'm gonna go hit him." So I walked in there and I was just walking around, and he started bugging me again, so I did the same thing. I just went up to him and I pushed him, and he must've been 300 pounds. And I just started pushing him and I said, "Come on, let's go already. I'm sick of you. . . ." I don't remember exactly what happened, but I know I got pulled away. And he walked by me again and he goes, "You ready for the second Holocaust?"

And then I think I had him thrown out. Yeah, you see, I went up to the teacher and I said to her, "I'm either gonna leave the class or they leave."

It was funny 'cause one of the kids I got thrown out actually wasn't that harmful. I don't know, he was just like a little follower on the side. And it turns out last year, I was on the track team and he decided to do track, and I became friends with him. And I got to know him, and . . . apparently his grandfather had converted to Judaism before he died. This year, I'm pretty good friends with him, and every time I'm talking to him, he's always mentioning Judaism. And he's very interested in Judaism and he told me that he would like to convert himself. He just asked me last week if he could come to the temple.

He understands a lot now. So, I mean, he was hanging around with the wrong [crowd]. They didn't care. I mean, they weren't doing anything in the class, anyways. They were just sitting around. Yeah, druggies basically.

[*Do your teachers understand your culture?*] Yeah, when I tell them I'm gonna be out of school for the holidays and they say, "Okay, don't worry. Make up, don't worry." They know about Rosh Hashanah and Yom Kippur [major Jewish holidays], but they don't know about Succos. There's the first day and the last day. After Yom Kippur, I say I'm gonna be out these other days and they go, "Oh, I thought the holidays were over with," and I go, "No, there's a few more." But they're nice about it anyway. I mean, sometimes, once in a while, someone gets a little frustrated. You know, if I come in the next day after a holiday and I'm not ready for the test 'cause I couldn't write or do anything to study for it, but I make up my work in pretty good time. And I don't usually have any trouble.

[*How do you celebrate holidays with your family?*] With pride and tradition! [*laughs*] I usually have to stay around here 'cause I work in the temple. But if we can, we invite somebody over for the Seder [Passover dinner]. It's nice to have people over for the holidays. It makes the holiday more enjoyable.

I like the taste of chicken on a Friday night—that I've waited for all week long. It's just not the same on Wednesday night. You can't even smell it the same. It's different. I like deli stuff: corned beef, a nice sandwich, a little pickle, you know. I like kugel too. All the Jewish food's good. On like Shavuos or Pesach or Succos, we usually get special fruits, like the new spring fruits, the first fruits of the harvest.

[Pesach, or Passover] is my favorite holiday. I love the preparation for it. I don't like it after the third day because there's no more seders, and there's nothing left to do except for waiting it out. I mean, it wouldn't be so bad. . . . You see, if I have to go to school, I have to go to school in the middle. But if I didn't have to go to school, then I could sit home and kind of enjoy it. But I have to go to school, and I just say it's not the same when you see other food that you can't eat. I mean, it would be a whole different feeling if you saw so many other people eating matzoth or whatever.

When I went to [Jewish] day school, it was nice to have people who were Jewish around you. I mean, it made you understand. When I came [to public school] in the ninth grade, it was hard 'cause I didn't hardly know anybody, and I didn't know what to expect 'cause it was such a different curriculum. I didn't know anybody, like I said, and you just walked around, you know, tried to speak to people, see who you could make friends with, who was right to make friends with.

The role of positive pressure

[Good grades] give you confidence, show you what you're doing. . . . and [help you] keep on going.

I haven't done really bad in a while. . . . I mean occasionally, I'll do bad on a test or something, but I'll just bring it back up after. 'cause I'll feel bad after. "Ugh, I really did bad. I should have done really well." And I just try and do it better the next time. . . . Let myself slip a little bit and then I'll go back. I'll take a break and go on.

Growing up at an early age, [my parents taught me] like what was right and wrong and the basics of Judaism. . . . One summer, my mother was teaching me Hebrew. My mother actually taught . . . sat me down and actually taught me.

She's fair. . . . She doesn't keep me bound, keep me in. You know, "Stay here; don't go anywhere. You can't go out if you have to." She trusts me. . . . Most of the time, I can see why she wouldn't want me to do some things.

Most [teachers] are understanding. I mean, if you don't know how to do something, you can always just go ask them. And ask them again and again and again [*he singles out one particular teacher, a math teacher he had in ninth grade*] 'cause I never really did good in math 'til ninth grade and I had him. And he showed me that it wasn't so bad, and after that I've been doing pretty good in math and I enjoy it.

There's some teachers that understand the kids better than other teachers. . . . They teach from the point of view of the kid. They don't just come out and say, "All right, do this, *blah, blah, blah.*" I mean, in a way, they like, sometimes joke around with the kid. They try to act like the student. . . . They're not so *one-tone voice.*

[A bad teacher is] one who just . . . for example, some student was doing really bad on his tests, test after test after test. The teacher would just correct them and that's it. Wouldn't say anything to the student. . . .

I try to run [track] as often as I can. I mean, during the season you kinda have to run every day just to keep in shape. But I like to run anyways, 'cause when you run you think about everything and just . . . it gives you time, in a way, [to] relax, and just get your mind in a different place.

I do a lot of drawing. I've been drawing for years. Just sometimes—it's nothing special. Sometimes it's just doodling or drawing strange designs or things like that. But I enjoy it. It relaxes me to sit down, flip on my radio, anything I want to listen to and just draw away. It just puts you away from the rest of the world.

Some of my friends have an influence on me, too, to do well in school. My friends from camp, I mean, they all do pretty good in school and we're all close friends. Whenever one of us gets in, if we ever got into some sort of trouble, we'd bail each other out of it. Because, well, I mean, we all trust each other, basically. We keep in touch a lot. We'll always be friends.

I run up my phone bill talking to them 'cause they're all out of state. [My mother] tells me to write letters [*laughs*]. But sometimes it's hard 'cause sometimes, in a way, I live off my friends. They're like a type of energy, like a power source.

Commentary

When asked to describe himself, Avi said he was "fun loving and religious," adjectives that might not ordinarily be juxtaposed in this way, yet, curiously, his description was an apt one. Deeply involved in his religion, as was apparent from his earnest and responsible attitude about his work at the synagogue, he was also a gregarious and playful teenager who enjoyed camp, sports, and practical jokes. A little digging may reveal how Avi was able to develop these seemingly divergent qualities.

Because both of his parents were teachers, and given the immensely important role of scholarship within religious education in the Jewish culture, it was no surprise that Avi had done well in school. However, the perception that all Jewish children are good students, what has often been called a "positive stereotype," has placed an undue burden on many youths. Like the "model minority" myth surrounding the academic achievement of Asian students, the consequences of this "positive stereotype" are negative in that they treat a whole class of students in the same way, without allowing for individual differences.

The enormous commitment he had to his religious community in the "small synagogue" was evident. Avi spoke Hebrew and worked hard at it. He studied the Torah and was open about the love he had for his culture and religion. But the price Avi was paying for upholding his religion and culture was often steep. The mismatch of his culture with that of the school was evident in many ways, especially when it came to organizational policies and practices. For example, during his interviews, Avi said that he had accepted that most of his teachers and classmates did not pronounce his name correctly. He appreciated that most of them tried to be understanding about the Jewish holidays, although they usually did not understand what holiday observance meant within the religious context of Judaism. His days off were always at odds with those of the other students, and the curriculum was at odds with his experience. Because remaining somewhat unassimilated is a hard choice, Avi's desire to move from Talbot when he had his own family was not surprising.

Other problems Avi talked about concerned his social life and the lack of friends in his community. For a teenager, making the decision between staying home on Friday evening with family or going out with friends can be difficult. Incidents of anti-Semitism in school were also painful reminders that being different from the majority can still be dangerous in our society. The decisiveness with which he handled these particular incidents revealed his self-confidence and desire to take control of his life (by "having them taken out of the class"), although in his hesitant explanation, it was also evident that he felt powerless ("But that was cleared up. I mean, it wasn't cleared up, but they, I don't know . . ."). The incidents also revealed his own stereotypes and social class biases about those he called "druggies."

Straddling two worlds, Avi was constantly confronted with the need to accommodate the outside world. This is a challenge historically faced by most immigrants. As expressed by Stephan Brumberg in describing the experience of Jewish immigrants in New York City at the turn of the century, "In the immigrant world, learning to live simultaneously in two worlds may have been required for successful adaptation."[2] What is unique in Avi's case is that this balancing act was increasingly taking place with those who had been here for more than one or two generations, not simply with new arrivals.

Jewish culture is intertwined with religion and tradition, rather than with nationality as in other groups, and this may make maintaining cultural ties more difficult. Although our society claims to be secular, clearly it is not. Rather, it is openly a Christian nation, as can be seen in the abundance of Christian symbols and artifacts, from the daily prayer in Congress to the crèches that adorn small towns in New England, where Avi comes from, at Christmas. Added to this is the weight of centuries of oppression, minority status, and marginality to which Jews have been subjected. Even in societies where they have been assimilated, Jews have often been victimized and treated as scapegoats.[3] Given this long history of oppression, Jews throughout the world have had to think long and hard about the balance between the degree of accommodating to host societies and maintaining their cultural traditions. The results have ranged widely—from becoming completely assimilated and losing all traces of their roots to remaining within religious and cultural enclaves removed from any but the most basic and necessary exchanges with non-Jews.[4]

Pressure toward assimilation and the accommodations made to it are only one reflection of the diversity in the Jewish community in the United States, which has often been portrayed in a unidimensional manner. However, Jews differ in religiosity, tradition, political viewpoints, language, and social class, among other characteristics. The religious tenets in Judaism itself—that is, Orthodox, Reform, and Conservative elements—reflect this diversity. In addition, some Jews who are not religious at all—secular Jews—are still profoundly Jewish in terms of cultural values. Some Jews speak Hebrew and others speak Yiddish, although others speak neither. Jews differ in their viewpoints on relations with the Arab world and on Zionism.

Besides his religion and track, another source of positive pressure for Avi were his Jewish friends, who are, in his eloquent phrase, "a type of energy . . .

like a power source." That peers can have this kind of influence on young people is often overlooked by schools and parents, yet it is the very reason for the existence of such institutions as Portuguese American schools, Hebrew camps, and Saturday culture schools in the Chinese community.

Avi Abramson was straddling two worlds, trying to be both an American and a Jew. He was maintaining a difficult balancing act between complete assimilation into the mainstream of U.S. life and holding onto his religion and culture. This is not easy, even for seasoned adults. For Avi, it meant not giving in to assimilationist forces while also accommodating those parts of his life to U.S. society that would not compromise his values. With the help of his family, friends, and religious community, and with the support of his non-Jewish community, he would no doubt be able to do it.[5]

Reflect on this case study

1. What, in your view, keeps Avi Abramson so involved in his synagogue?

2. Do you think Avi's school life would be different if he were not on the track team? How? What implications can you draw from this for schools?

3. The United States officially supports "separation of church and state," but is it possible for teachers to affirm Avi's culture and background without bringing religion into the school? Think about some ways this might be done. If you do not believe it is possible, list some of the ways that the separation of church and state is violated in schools and other institutions. What is the alternative to this practice?

4. Friends are, in Avi's words, "like a power source." How can teachers use this power source to good advantage? Think of strategies that teachers and schools might develop to build on positive peer pressure.

5. It is obvious that Avi has little respect for those he calls "the druggies." Do schools help perpetuate stereotypes about students in different social groups? How? If you were a teacher in his school, what might you do about this problem? What if you were the principal?

Fern Sherman

If there's something in the
history book that's wrong,
I should tell them that it is wrong.

Springdale, a small city in Iowa, is surrounded by farm country. With a population of close to 50,000, the city is a haven from the problems of more populated midwestern cities, yet it affords the advantages of a large university and other cultural activities. The city is not very ethnically diverse: Most of the residents of Springdale identify as "American," with no ethnic classification. Many have been here for several generations. The African American community numbers just over 1,000 and there are fewer than 800 Latinos. There are slightly more than 3,000 Asians, the largest non–European American group. The number of Native Americans in the entire city is minuscule, totaling only about 60.

When she was first interviewed, Fern Sherman[1] was 14 years old and an eighth grader in the middle school in town. Of Chippewa, Ponca, Norwegian, German, and English heritage, Fern identified as Native American. She and her sisters were registered as both Turtle Mountain Chippewa and Northern Ponca, an Indian Nation that was reinstated after being "terminated" (no longer recognized by the federal government) in 1966. Tribal affiliation designations are so complex and bureaucratic that Fern and her sisters were classified as $^{237}/_{512}$, or slightly over half Indian. This kind of identification is arbitrary and clearly a social construct, having little to do with self-identification. American Indians are unique in having this kind of definition in the United States.[2]

The American Indian community is extremely heterogeneous. In 2002, the U.S. Census Bureau reported that it numbered almost 2.5 million, nearly triple the 1970 U.S. census.[3] About 500 Nations are recognized by the federal government, of which more than 200 have a land base or reservation. There are others that are not officially recognized. About two-thirds of all American Indians now live away from reservations in other communities, primarily in urban areas. Although a growing number speak only English, one-third regularly speak another language as well. Currently, more than 200 languages are spoken, and some are still vigorously maintained. For example, more than 70 percent of Navajo children enter school speaking Navajo as their native language. Several Indian Nations have declared their languages to be official, designating English as a "foreign language."[4] American Indians are also very diverse in cultural traditions, physical appearance, religion, and lifestyle. In spite of these vast differences, a pan-Indian identity has emerged in the past several decades, probably the result of several factors: the many values shared by most Native peoples; the need to develop greater political strength; and intermarriage among Native groups, as was the case in Fern's family.

There are currently more than half a million American Indian/Alaska Native students (the designation used by the Census Bureau) in U.S. public schools.[5] Fern was the only Native American in her entire school, although she said she wished there were more. Before moving to Springdale, she had attended a tribal reservation school for kindergarten and first grade, and later a public school where there were a large number of Indian students. In that school, there had been some Indian teachers, an Indian Club, an Indian education program with special tutors, and other support services. In both of those schools, Fern and her sisters had felt comfortable and accepted, which had not always been the case after they moved to Springdale.

Fern lived with her father, two sisters, and young nephew. Her father was a professor of political science at the local university, and her mother, who lived in another city, was a truck driver. Her parents had been separated for years, and Fern and her sisters rarely saw their mother, who had taken little responsibility for their upbringing and education. Two of Fern's other sisters lived with their mother. Instrumental in raising her nephew, Daryl, who was two years old when she was interviewed, Fern had seen firsthand what raising a child was like and wanted to delay having children of her own for a long time. She said, "I want to get my life started and on the go before I have a family."

Fern's sisters, Juanita and Rose, were 16 and 17 years old at the time of the interview. Despite not being their biological father, Mr. Sherman had taken responsibility for raising Juanita and Rose as well as his own daughter. Both of the older girls had a history of alcohol and drug abuse. Rose was in an out-of-state treatment center but was expected to move back home in a few months; Juanita was living at an alcohol and drug abuse residential center. She had begun drinking a number of years earlier because, according to her father, "She just never fit in." Isolated and alone at school, she sought relief through alcohol.

Mr. Sherman had worked valiantly to help Juanita and Rose overcome their addiction. Having seen firsthand the results of drug and alcohol abuse, he was convinced that they are linked to poor self-esteem and lack of success in school. As a result, he had pushed his daughters to excel in school. Having lived through the nightmare of addiction with his family, he thought a lot about the role that schools should play. He ruefully asked, "Do we have to intervene in every Indian kid's life that goes into these school systems in such drastic manners?" Although he did not place the blame entirely on teachers for his children's problems, he thought there were too many misunderstandings in school that could lead to failure. Getting a good education was an essential that he felt his children could not afford to neglect. As a result, he was tireless in his pressure on them to study, get good grades, and prepare for college. At the time of the interview, Fern was in eighth grade and doing very well academically. Her father was keeping his fingers crossed that she would continue to do so, although his agonizing experiences with his other daughters had tempered his optimism.

Becoming aware and proud of their heritage was another message that Mr. Sherman had given his daughters. They did not speak a language other than English at home, but he sometimes taught them words in Ponca. They perceived his pressure on them to succeed and to identify as Native American as sometimes overbearing, but they also appreciated him for giving them strength in their culture and the determination to get ahead.

Fern and her family lived in a middle-class neighborhood close to the university. Although it was a friendly and close-knit community, like many suburbs it provided little recreation for youths. Although they were the only Native American family in the area, Fern described her community as a "really nice neighborhood" and "one big happy family." She said that her neighbors were always there to help one another out and that they were understanding and kind.

Saying that the middle school she attended was "kinda stuck on itself," Fern nevertheless acknowledged that it was a good school. She was taking classes in science, math, English, home economics, art, physical education, and family and consumer science, her favorite subject because it included experiences in childcare. Her grades were very good, although not necessarily reflective of her interests. Her highest grade was in English, her least favorite subject; and her worst grade, C, was in her favorite subject, science. Her grades were, however, a reflection of the particular teachers who taught these subjects that year. Fern was very active in school activities such as chorus, cooking club, and sports and in out-of-school activities such as dance.

Aware of the role of teachers' expectations on her achievement, Fern spoke about her reaction to different teachers and schools. Family pressures and responsibilities, the isolation she felt as the only Native American student in her school, and identifying as a successful student were the other dominant themes that emerged during Fern's interviews.

The role of teachers' expectations

I'd rather go through school and get A's and B's than D's and F's. . . . In Springdale, I've noticed if you're getting D's and F's, they don't look up to you; they look down. And you're always the last on the list for special activities, you know?

Most of my friends were from the same culture or background [in my former school in South Dakota] 'cause there are a lot of Native Americans there. And you weren't really treated different there. You were all the same and you all got pushed the same and you were all helped the same. And one thing I've noticed in Springdale is they kind of teach 25 percent and they kinda leave 75 percent out. . . . [Teachers] really push us hard, but, if we're getting bad grades, they don't help us as much.

Being at the top of my class, always being noticed as a top person, grade-wise [made me feel good]. I mostly got straight A's and B's until I moved to Springdale. And I got like a C and D the first semester, in science and math here because they just push you to your limits. I mean, it's just incredible

the way they think you're like "Incredible Woman" or something.

I don't like being pushed to my limit. I mean, I think you should have a little bit of leeway. Like, this past week, I had three different reports due in three different classes. I think [teachers] should have at least a little bit of communication, not to give you three reports due in the same week.

I like going to math or, like, science to do different experiments. I've always liked science, but it's not really my best subject. I like American history because sometimes I'll know more than the teacher just because my dad has taught me stuff. I don't really like English . . . because I hate when they make you cut off at 400 words. If you can't write what you're gonna write, why write it?

In science, if you don't understand something, and the science teacher doesn't get in until 8:00 and the bell rings at 8:10 . . . In 10 minutes, you can't learn something. . . . Like, if you don't have your assignment done, and you need help on it, you have 10 minutes to go in, get help, get it done. Because if it's not done by class time, you'll have detention.

[*What would you do to make school more interesting?*] More like involved activities in class, you know? . . . 'cause, like, when you're sitting in class, and the teacher is lecturing, I usually feel like falling asleep, 'cause it's just blah. And in chorus, there's, like, this rap about history, you know? It's really fun. . . . More like making the whole class be involved, not making only the two smartest people up here do the whole work for the whole class.

Family pressure, expectations, and responsibilities

I try [to do well in school] for my dad, but I mostly do it for myself. [My sisters] are always like, "Yeah, you're daddy's girl, just 'cause you get A's and B's." It's how they put me down for what I'm doing, for how I'm succeeding.

He's always involved in what's happening in school, unlike most parents. . . . My dad is just always [at school]. He's always been there, every school activity, I mean, unless our car breaks down. . . . I sure remember, we were having a musical and it was set up with, like, 300 kids. And our car had a flat tire. And so my dad put this air stuff in so he could get me to the musical [*laughing*]. And he went and got the tire fixed and he made the guy give him a ride back to school so he could see it! . . . He's always been involved, so I really don't know what it's like to not be involved.

He thinks [school] is heaven! When he was young, he only got A's and B's. C was an F to him. And I sometimes have to stop him and say, "Hey, I'm not you!" But I'm glad he's pushing me.

Just from my family breaking up so many times, I've learned to always stick with it. I've learned really to stick with my family. I've always been told to love everybody the same in your family, but sometimes that's really hard for me because I've always been so close to Juanita. So, I really feel that Juanita's my mom. . . . My dad's probably the first person I go to, and Juanita's probably someone I can go to, you know, for "woman help."

[Dad] always tries to comfort me, telling me that he's always there for me. He can always arrange for me to talk to somebody if I'm hurting. But I try to explain to him that he's the only person I really need. He's always been understanding. . . . [When things go bad], I talk to my dad.

My dad is more or less a brick wall that you can't get through [*laughing*]. He's really set, like you always get those stupid lectures: "Well, my dad did it this way. . . ." But, Dad, *you're* not your dad. I know I might grow up and treat my children a little bit the same way as my dad, but knowing how much it hurts me inside when he says, "Well, you know, I was a straight A student when I was little. . . ." I'm not gonna do that to my kids because it just makes them want to fail more. When you're mad at your parents, you try to find something to get them back with. And I think grades are a very good way to get them back with.

He's a kid at heart. He doesn't try to be "Macho Parent" or "Mercedes Man." He doesn't try to fit in with people. He's himself, and he's always been himself. And if people don't like the way he is, tough Sherlock!

He's a one-of-a-kind dad. I'll always love him for what he is. I've really not known [my mother] that much. From just what my dad's told me and what I've seen, she is really hard to get along with. She's, like, very emotional. She makes all these excuses . . . "Yeah, my phone bill's really high. I'm sorry I can't call you." Well, if the stupid boyfriend's more important than calling her own daughter, you

know, that's not my fault. She's always been mean, in my eyes, but nice when she's face to face with me.

I think I'm gifted to have a family like this, but I'm glad we're not a Leave-it-to-Beaver-Cleaver family. I've got friends that their families are perfect, no problems. But I'm sure there are problems inside the locked doors, but not really showing it. But in my family, if I'm angry, I'm going to go out and tell them. I hate people who try to hide it.

You know how counselors say "dysfunctional" and "functional" families? I think every family's dysfunctional, in their own way. I mean, every family is gonna have a fight about what they're gonna eat for supper, or who gets the family car tonight, or whatever.

The isolation of being Native American

Sometimes I get sick of hearing about [being Native American]. I mean, like my dad just goes on and on, and finally, I just space out and pretend like I'm listening to him. Because I've already heard all of it. And he always tries to make me what I'm not . . . make me more Native American. And since I'm the only Native American in the Springdale school district almost, he tries to make me go to the principal and say, "We need this." There's no use, because there's no other Native Americans to help me!

I'm really not noticed as a Native American until something . . . like the ITBS test. The woman was giving us our codes. She called "Native Americans," and she goes, "Well, I don't think there is any." And the whole auditorium goes, "Fern!" I think it's really neat. I don't hide it. I express it.

[South Dakota] was more like everybody was a family. You would go to your backyard and have a banquet with the whole neighborhood, you know? It was like the whole town was one big family.

[My teachers don't understand my culture.] Like if I say, "This isn't done in my culture. This isn't the way it's done. . . ." Like, talking about abortion in history or something. For Native Americans, abortion is just . . . like, you should really put the mother in jail for it. Because the baby is alive, just like we are. And that's the way I feel. And when they sit there and say, "It's the mother's right to do it," well, I don't think it's the mother's right because it's not the baby's fault the mother doesn't want it. And so, when I try to tell them, they just, "Oh, well, we're out of time." They cut me off, and we've still got half an hour! And so that kinda makes me mad.

If there's something in the history book that's wrong, my dad always taught me that, if it's wrong, I should tell them that it is wrong. And the only time I ever do is if I know it's exactly wrong. Like we were reading about Native Americans and scalping. Well, the French are really the ones that made them do it so they could get money. And my teacher would not believe me. I finally just shut up because he just would not believe me. . . . Just my arguments with them, they just cut it off.

[Other people] are not going to understand me as much, if I start talking about spirituality. But I don't feel like people put me down or put me up for being Indian. I always get good praises from people, you know. "I'm glad you're sticking in there, not being ashamed of being Native American."

We do have different values. We do have different needs, and we do have different wants. I mean, I'm sure every family needs love. Love is a very, very top thing in our list of needs. For White people, it's usually shelter over their heads. For Native Americans, usually number one . . . family love.

It can be different. Like my family sits down and eats corn soup and fried dough. It would be different from, "Well, my family goes out for pizza."

I don't know why other Native Americans have dropped out of Springdale schools. Maybe it's because I just haven't been in high school yet. But I remember one time, my sister came home and she was just mad. They said that "Geronimo was a stupid chief riding that stupid horse," and my sister got mad!

I've always been taught to be kind to elders, to always look up to them. And my dad's always taught me that everybody's really the same. I mean, there's no difference between Black and White. . . . Really everybody's the same to me, because we're all the same blood, you know?

Identifying as successful

I found school fun. I liked to do homework. I got moved: I didn't go to kindergarten. I went straight from Head Start to first grade because I was too bored in the classes, and I wouldn't do the work because I fought with the teachers and told them I already did it because I had done it the year before. And so my dad made them move me out because

there was no use for me to stay back if I wasn't gonna learn anything new.

I like sports a lot . . . volleyball and basketball. I like sports and I'm just glad they offer them 'cause some schools don't have enough funding. Basketball is mostly my sport. I compare it to stuff, like, when I can't get science, or like in sewing, I'll look at that machine and I'll say, "This is a basketball; I can overcome it. . . ."

One [of my friends], she's really understanding. If I have family problems, she's always there to talk to. We're really close. We're, like, involved in the same sports, and we love basketball. Natalie, I can always talk to. . . . I mean, she's like free counseling!

I've, like, always wanted to be president of the United States, but I figured that was too hard [laughs]. . . . I don't know, I kinda wanna be a fashion lawyer. I've always wanted to be president and I think it's just because, like, I'll see so many mess-ups and . . . I don't know, just George Bush [the elder] right now. . . . I was infatuated with Ronald Reagan the whole time he was in office. And, like, I'd make posters for Dad and tell him, "Yeah, this is me." And I just like the idea of being head honcho!

[What is the reason for going to school?] To learn and make something out of yourself when you're older, so you're not just, I don't know, a person on welfare or something.

I sure remember the day I got my first B; I started crying. Most of my friends, you know, get A's and B's, and everything. And it's not to impress them; it's to show them that I'm just as good, you know? It's mostly just for me, to make me know that I'm just as good as anybody else and that I can really do it.

I'm ambitious. I always want to get things done. Like, say, I'm running for copresident for the school, I want to get my campaign done [way] ahead, not the day before.

I succeed in everything I do. If I don't get it right the first time, I always go back and try to do it again.

Commentary

Teachers' expectations play an important role in the academic achievement of many students, including Native American students. They certainly had an impact on Fern's school achievement. Although she said she did not like being pushed, it was obvious that when teachers held high expectations, she was able to live up to them. Although Fern was a successful student, the dropout rate for Native American students as a whole is estimated to be among the highest of any other group—more than 30 percent.[6] This percentage is misleading, however, because many students drop out before even reaching high school, as early as elementary school.

Fern's father, who promoted both academic achievement and ethnic pride and awareness for his daughters, was obviously the major influence in her life. Having been a successful student himself, he knew the value of education. And, as an American Indian, he was convinced that the only way to progress, both individually and for the community, was by getting a good education. These are the messages Fern had been listening to since early childhood and they had a profound impact on her. She said that she tried to be successful for herself, her father, and her friends ("to show them that I'm just as good"). The need to excel on an individual basis contradicts a deeply held cultural value of collective progress in American Indian communities. Striving to excel for one's family, Nation, or community is a much better way of motivating children, which is why Fern's father stressed "making Grandmother proud." Providing a learning environment that emphasizes cooperative learning rather than individual competition is one important, culturally appropriate strategy for schools to consider. Others include using traditional ways of knowing in constructing the curriculum and providing meaningful activities that affirm and build on students' culture.[7]

Being the only American Indian student in school is a theme that came up repeatedly during Fern's interviews. At times, she felt that the pressure of being the only one was unbearable, especially when her father expected her to confront every issue dealing with Native people head on. At other times, being the only one meant being unique and special (she identified being singled out for this kind of interview as one of the benefits). Although some teachers, such as her English teacher, made accommodations in the content and structure of their curricula, most others did not. For instance, her feeling that a Native American perspective was missing from school curricula was likely correct. Also, when giving students writing assignments about their families, her English teacher allowed each student ample flexibility to discuss differences, and, although Fern loved science, she felt that her

teacher was not very helpful and probably the "last person for me to go talk to." Being the only Native American in her school also meant always being different. Fern was an extremely strong young woman, but this kind of pressure is exceedingly difficult for adolescents experiencing the traumas of identification and peer acceptance.

Education was sometimes used to separate American Indian children physically, emotionally, and culturally from their families. A particularly graphic example of this practice is the 1895 *Annual Report* of the Indian commissioner to the Secretary of the Interior, in which the government's intent in educating Indian children was described as "to free the children from the language and habits of their untutored and oftentimes savage parents."[8] Such blatant expressions of racism probably would not be used today, but many of the patronizing attitudes stemming from this belief are still apparent in the curriculum and texts used in schools.

According to Sharon Nelson-Barber and Elise Trumbull Estrin, a majority of teachers do not recognize the knowledge or learning strategies that American Indian students bring to science and math; because of this, teachers miss out on ways to involve students more meaningfully in their learning.[9] Ironically, however, traditional American Indian ways of knowing, such as modeling and providing time for observation and practice, are consistent with current constructivist notions of learning.[10] When schools are culturally aware and make sense to students, the students tend to succeed. Teresa McCarty's in-depth study of Rough Rock Community School in Arizona is moving testimony to this truth.[11] This school, in existence for over 40 years, has been a model and inspiration for many other schools for Indigenous groups that are attempting to create affirming and high-quality learning environments.

American Indian children are faced with other difficult situations as well. Suicide is much more prevalent among reservation Indians than in the general population; the rate of adult unemployment among American Indians is extraordinary, reaching as high as 50 percent; health care, particularly on reservations, is either completely absent or inadequate; infant mortality is higher among American Indians than the national average; there are widespread nutritional deficiencies in this group; and alcoholism may affect the lives and functioning of more than 60 percent of all American Indian children.[12] Struggling against these odds is an awesome responsibility; school sometimes takes a back seat. Fern developed a number of successful strategies to deal with these overwhelmingly negative barriers to success: She was unabashedly ambitious and she wanted to succeed in school and beyond and was quite certain that she would ("I succeed in everything I do," she said confidently). In fact, when asked what she likes most about herself, she was quick to single out her ambition.

In helping to raise her nephew, supporting her sister Juanita during a difficult time, adjusting to a school where she was culturally different from all her peers, and confronting the dual challenges of academic success and parental pressures, no matter how positive they may be, Fern Sherman was contending with tremendous responsibilities at an early age.

Reflect on this case study

1. Fern's feeling of isolation in a city with so few American Indians affected her life in a great many ways. When have you been the only ___ (fill in the blank) in a particular setting? What impact did this have on you? Describe how you felt in school, at home, and in your community. What might have made you feel less isolated? What are the implications of this situation for you as a teacher?

2. What is meant by the statement that tribal affiliation is a "social construction"? Who determines what a person is? Why do you think that identity has been determined *for* some people in our society, while other people have been able to determine their own identity?

3. Based on Fern's case study, what do you think are some of the pressures that can lead to alcohol and drug abuse for young people? What specific situations in the American Indian community can exacerbate this problem? What can schools do to help alleviate it?

4. If you could talk with Fern about remaining a successful and confident student, what would you say?

5. What approaches might work to lower the dropout rate of American Indian students? What can schools, communities, and families do together to help?

6. Work together with a small group of your colleagues and plan a science lesson in which you incorporate some American Indian ways of knowing (you may want to read the article by Nelson-Barber and Estrin cited in the case study). How might it differ from another science lesson? Would Indian students be the only ones to benefit from such lessons? Why or why not?

Notes to Chapter 9 Case Studies

Avi Abramson

1. We appreciate Diane Sweet's work in finding and interviewing Avi and in providing extensive background information for this case study. Diane teaches courses in language and writing at the Wentworth Institute of Technology in Massachusetts.

2. Stephan F. Brumberg, *Going to America, Going to School: The Jewish Immigrant Public School Encounter in Turn-of-the-Century New York City* (New York: Praeger, 1986): 2.

3. See Meyer Weinberg's extensive history of anti-Semitism in 12 countries, *Because They Were Jews: A History of Anti-Semitism* (Westport, CT: Greenwood Press, 1986); Chapter 12 deals with the United States. See also Leonard Dinnerstein, *Anti-Semitism in America* (New York: Oxford University Press, 1994).

4. For an examination of the pressure Jews feel to become assimilated in U.S. society, see Seymour Martin Lipset and Earl Raab, *Jews and the New American Scene* (Cambridge, MA: Harvard University Press, 1995) and Alan M. Dershowitz, *The Vanishing American Jew* (New York: Simon & Schuster, 1998).

5. For an update on Avi's life, see the *Epilogue* on the *Affirming Diversity* Web page.

Fern Sherman

1. We wish to thank Carlie Collins Tartakov for the extensive interviews with Fern Sherman, her sister Juanita, and their father. After 23 years of teaching in elementary schools in California and Massachusetts, Carlie became a faculty member

in the Department of Curriculum and Instruction at Iowa State University, from which she recently retired.

2. Cornel Pewewardy, "Will the 'Real' Indians Please Stand Up?" *Multicultural Review* (June 1998): 36–42.

3. U.S. Census Bureau, *Census 2000 Summary File 1* (Washington, DC: U.S. Department of Commerce, 2002).

4. The Northern Ute Nation, for example, declared English a foreign language in 1984; see Jon Reyhner, "Native American Languages Act Becomes Law." *NABE News* 14, no. 3 (December 1, 1990).

5. National Center for Education Statistics, *State Nonfiscal Survey of Public Elemetary/Secondary Education* (Washington, DC: U.S. Department of Education, 2001).

6. See K. Tsianina Lomawaima, "Educating Native Americans." In *Handbook of Research on Multicultural Education,* 2nd ed. edited by James A. Banks and Cherry A. McGee Banks (San Francisco: Jossey-Bass, 2004). See also Donna Deyhle and Karen Swisher, "Research in American Indian and Alaska Native Education: From Assimilation to Self-Determination." In *Review of Research in Education,* 22, edited by Michael W. Apple (Washington, DC: American Educational Research Association, 1997).

7. See, for example, Deyhle and Swisher, "Research in American Indian and Alaska Native Education: From Assimilation to Self-Determination"; Sharon Nelson-Barber and Elise Trumbull Estrin, "Bringing Native American Perspectives to Mathematics and Science Teaching." *Theory into Practice* 34, no. 3 (Summer 1995): 174–185; and K. Tsianina Lomawaima and Teresa L. McCarty, "When Tribal Sovereignty Challenges Democracy: American Indian Education and the Democratic Ideal," *American Educational Research Journal* 39, no. 2 (Summer 2002): 279–305.

8. As cited in Jon Reyhner, "Bilingual Education: Teaching the Native Language." *In Teaching the Indian Child: A Bilingual/Multicultural Approach,* edited by Jon Reyhner (Billings: Eastern Montana College, 1992): 39.

9. Nelson-Barber and Estrin, 1995.

10. *Ibid.*

11. Teresa L. McCarty, *A Place to Be Navajo: Rough Rock and the Struggle for Self-Determination in Indigenous Schooling* (Mahwah, NJ: Lawrence Erlbaum, 2002). See also Reyhner, "Bilingual Education: Teaching the Native Language."

12. See, for example, Mei L. Castor, Michael S. Smyser, Maile M. Taualii, Alice N. Park, Shelley A. Lawson, and Ralph A. Forquera, "A Nationwide Population-Based Study Identifying Health Disparities Between American Indians/Alaska Natives and the General Populations Living in Select Urban Counties," *American Journal of Public Health* 96, no. 8 (2006): 1478–1484; for the latest data, including on reservations, see the National Council of Urban Indian Health Services website (www.ncuih.org).

Linguistic Diversity in U.S. Classrooms

❝Being Latino, it's good 'cause a lot of people tell me it's a good advantage for me to know two languages. I like that.**❞**

—Alicia Montejo, interviewee

Sezin Ugor Aksoy. *They took it and only left this.* Collage mixed media, 2006.

anguage is intimately linked to culture. It is a primary means by which people express their cultural values and the lens through which they view the world. This link was described by Henry Trueba in the following way:

> Whatever knowledge we acquire, it is always acquired through language and culture, two interlocked symbolic systems considered essential for human interaction and survival. Culture and language are so intricately intertwined that even trained scholars find it impossible to decide where language ends and culture begins, or which one of the two impacts the other the most.[1]

The language practices that children bring to school invariably affect how and what they learn, yet native language issues are frequently overlooked in multicultural education; race and ethnicity have been emphasized almost exclusively.[2] That language issues often go unaddressed in multicultural education is apparent in the lack of relevant terms concerning linguistic diversity. Terms that describe discrimination based on race, gender, and class are part of our general vocabulary (*racism, sexism, ethnocentrism, anti-Semitism, classism*), but until recently, no such term existed for language discrimination, although this does not mean that language discrimination did not exist. Tove Skutnabb-Kangas, by coining the term *linguicism* to refer to discrimination based specifically on language, has helped to make the issue more visible.[3]

This chapter explores the influence that language differences may have on student learning. How teachers and schools view language differences, whether and how they use these differences as a resource in the classroom, and different approaches to teaching language minority students, that is, those whose first language is not English, are all reviewed.

Definitions and Demographics

There are numerous terms to identify students who speak a language other than English as their native language. The term currently in vogue is *English Language Learners*, or *ELLs*. This term has become popular as a substitute for the more contentious

bilingual (more information on the controversies surrounding bilingual education is given in a subsequent section of this chapter), although bilingual itself was a misnomer because most students to whom this label was applied were not really bilingual but rather *monolingual* in their native language, or *becoming bilingual* in their native language and English. (Nonetheless, the term usually was accurate for describing the *program* in which many of these students were placed.) The terms ELL or ESL (English as a Second Language), on the other hand, focus only on students' need to acquire English. Although *ELL* has become the preferred term in the current anti-bilingual education climate, a decade or two ago, the most common term was *limited English proficient*, or *LEP*, an unfortunate acronym to which many people objected. Another popular term used for these students is *language-minority students*, which reflects the fact that they speak a minority language in the United States. No term is completely accurate or appropriate. In this text, we have chosen to use either *ELL* or *language minority* to refer to students who are learning English as a second or additional language.

Who are the ELLs to whom we refer in this chapter? In the United States, the population of those who speak a language other than English as their native language has increased tremendously in the past several decades. By the 2000 census, nearly 46 million people, or about 18 percent of the total population, spoke a native language other than English. The number and variety of languages is over 450—from Urdu to Punjabi to Yup'ik—although by far the largest number (28 million) and percentage (about 60 percent) speak Spanish.[4] Table 10.1 enumerates the most widely spoken languages in the nation's schools. The growth of the population that speaks native languages other than English is also reflected in public school enrollments. While the national growth of the school-age population—that is, those from 5 to 17 years of age—increased by 17 percent from 1990 to 2000, during the same time period, the percentage of English-language learners increased by a staggering 46 percent.[5] Even more dramatic, the growth of this population, compared to that during the previous decade, was over 100 percent (see Figure 10.1).

The demographic changes indicated by these statistics are part of a larger trend of immigration to the United States, which, since the late 1970s, has been responsible for a remarkable shift in our population. The reasons for this trend are varied, from a worsening economic situation in many countries, to a rise in the number of refugees from countries where the United States was involved in aggression (as was the case in Central America and Southeast Asia), to the loosening of immigration restrictions for some parts of the world. Unlike the earlier massive wave of immigration at the turn of the 20th century, the greatest number of immigrants are now from Asia and Latin America. All the states have felt the impact of this immigration, but the states with the largest enrollment of language-mi-

Table 10.1
United States—Ability to Speak English by Language Spoken at Home for the Population 5 Years and Over: 2000

Language Spoken at Home	Total	Speak English "very well"		Speak English "well"		Speak English "not well"		Speak English "not at all"	
	Number	Number	Percent	Number	Percent	Number	Percent	Number	Percent
Population 5 years and over	262,375,150	(X)	(X)	(X)	(X)	(X)	(X)	(X)	(X)
Speak only English	215,423,555	(X)	(X)	(X)	(X)	(X)	(X)	(X)	(X)
Speak language other than English	46,951,595	25,631,190	54.6	10,333,555	22.0	7,620,720	16.2	3,366,130	7.2
Spanish or Spanish Creole	28,101,055	14,349,795	51.1	5,819,410	20.7	5,130,400	18.3	2,801,450	10.0
Other Indo-European languages	10,017,975	6,627,685	66.2	2,091,450	20.9	1,078,915	10.8	219,925	2.2
French (incl. Patois, Cajun)	1,643,840	1,228,800	74.8	269,460	16.4	138,000	8.4	7,580	0.5
French Creole	453,365	245,855	54.2	121,915	26.9	70,960	15.7	14,635	3.2
Italian	1,008,370	701,220	69.5	195,900	19.4	99,270	9.8	11,980	1.2
Portuguese or Portuguese Creole	564,630	320,445	56.8	125,465	22.2	90,410	16.0	28,310	5.0
German	1,383,440	1,079,695	78.0	219,465	15.9	79,560	5.8	4,720	0.3
Yiddish	178,940	123,160	68.8	35,455	19.8	17,295	9.7	3,030	1.7
Other West Germanic languages	251,135	182,050	72.5	58,290	23.2	9,420	3.8	1,375	0.6
Scandinavian languages	162,255	137,615	84.8	19,110	11.8	5,165	3.2	365	0.2
Greek	365,435	262,850	71.9	65,025	17.8	33,345	9.1	4,215	1.2
Russian	706,240	304,890	43.2	209,055	29.6	148,670	21.1	43,625	6.2
Polish	667,415	387,695	58.1	167,235	25.1	95,030	14.2	17,455	2.6
Serbo-Croatian	233,865	119,270	51.0	61,255	26.2	42,970	18.4	10,370	4.4
Other Slavic languages	301,080	176,715	58.7	72,945	24.2	41,860	13.9	9,560	3.2
Armenian	202,710	108,555	53.6	48,470	23.9	31,870	15.7	13,815	6.8
Persian	312,085	198,040	63.5	70,910	22.7	32,960	10.6	10,175	3.3
Gujarathi	235,985	155,010	65.7	50,635	21.5	22,520	9.5	7,820	3.3
Hindi	317,055	245,190	77.3	51,930	16.4	16,680	5.3	3,255	1.0
Urdu	262,900	180,020	68.5	56,735	21.6	20,815	7.9	5,330	2.0
Other Indic languages	439,285	274,140	62.4	108,510	24.7	43,395	9.9	13,240	3.0
Other Indo-European languages	327,945	196,470	59.9	83,685	25.5	38,720	11.8	9,070	2.8
Asian and Pacific Island languages	6,960,070	3,370,045	48.4	2,023,310	29.1	1,260,260	18.1	306,455	4.4
Chinese	2,022,140	855,690	42.3	595,330	29.4	408,595	20.2	162,525	8.0
Japanese	478,000	241,705	50.6	146,615	30.7	84,020	17.6	5,660	1.2

(continued)

Table 10.1 (Continued)

Language Spoken at Home	Total Number	Speak English "very well"		Speak English "well"		Speak English "not well"		Speak English "not at all"	
		Number	Percent	Number	Percent	Number	Percent	Number	Percent
Korean	894,060	361,165	40.4	268,475	30.0	228,390	25.6	36,030	4.0
Mon-Khmer, Cambodian	181,890	77,620	42.7	51,650	28.4	41,460	22.8	11,160	6.1
Miao, Hmong	168,065	65,865	39.2	55,910	33.3	34,405	20.5	11,885	7.1
Thai	120,465	57,630	47.8	43,250	35.9	17,635	14.6	1,950	1.6
Laotian	149,305	67,565	45.3	43,175	28.9	32,100	21.5	6,465	4.3
Vietnamese	1,009,625	342,595	33.9	340,060	33.7	270,950	26.8	56,020	5.6
Other Asian languages	398,440	282,565	70.9	81,740	20.5	28,000	7.0	6,135	1.5
Tagalog	1,224,240	827,560	67.6	311,465	25.4	79,720	6.5	5,495	0.5
Other Pacific Island languages	313,840	190,085	60.6	85,640	27.3	34,985	11.2	3,130	1.0
Other languages	1,872,485	1,283,660	68.6	399,395	21.3	151,125	8.1	38,305	2.0
Navajo	178,015	115,025	64.6	42,975	24.1	14,390	8.1	5,625	3.2
Other Native North American languages	203,465	149,020	73.2	41,010	20.2	12,430	6.1	1,005	0.5
Hungarian	117,975	79,600	67.5	28,310	24.0	9,005	7.6	1,060	0.9
Arabic	614,580	403,395	65.6	140,055	22.8	58,595	9.5	12,535	2.0
Hebrew	195,375	158,450	81.1	28,575	14.6	7,770	4.0	580	0.3
African languages	418,500	294,455	70.4	87,135	20.8	30,875	7.4	6,035	1.4
Other and unspecified languages	144,575	83,715	57.9	31,335	21.7	18,060	12.5	11,465	7.9

[Data based on a sample. For information on confidentiality protection, sampling error, nonsampling error, and definitions, see http://www.census.gov/prod/cen2000/doc/sf3.pdf]
(X) Not applicable.
Source: Anneka L. Kindler, *Survey of the States' Limited English Proficient Students and Available Educational Programs and Services, 2000–2001 Summary Report.* (Washington, DC: National Clearinghouse for English Language Acquisition and Language Instruction Educational Programs, October 2002).

nority students are California (with over one-third of all students for whom English is a second language), Texas, Florida, New York, Illinois, and Arizona. At the same time, the greatest growth in the percentage of students with limited English proficiency were in states that had previously had very low numbers of such students. Georgia topped the list with a 113 percent increase, followed by Mississippi with a 79 percent increase.[6]

These changes in the population of the United States have profound implications for education. For one, approaches and programs to teach language-minority students need to be expanded. Most states have legislative provisions for students with limited English proficiency. However, although these services may include English as a second language (ESL) instruction, bilingual or dual language instruction, or both, the number of students in bilingual classrooms has decreased in the past several years. In 2000, for instance, only 22 percent of language minority students were receiving any instruction in their native language, although this does not mean that they were in bilingual programs.[7] The reasons for the decline of bilingual education programs also vary, from an ideological resistance to approaches based on native language instruction to legislative changes (bilingual education, for instance, has been eliminated in

FIGURE 10.1 Relative Growth of Limited English Proficient Student Enrollment, 1989–2002

Source: U.S. Department of Education's Survey of the States' Limited English Proficient Students and Available Educational Programs and Services, 1989–90 through 2001–02 summary reports. Supplemented by state publications (1998–99 data), and enrollment totals from NCES.

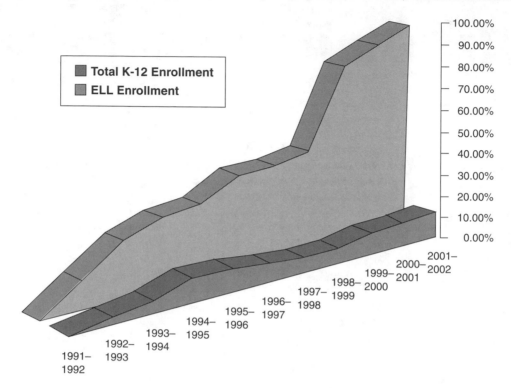

a number of states since the late 1990s). Finding qualified personnel has been another major problem. For instance, a survey of teachers concerning their preparedness to teach language-minority students found that only 20 percent of teachers felt "very well prepared" to teach them.[8]

A Brief Overview of the History of Language Diversity in U.S. Schools

The notion that children who do not yet speak English lack language altogether is a prevalent one in the United States, and it is linked with the mainstream perception that cultures other than the dominant one lack significance. In our nation, linguistic diversity has commonly been viewed as a temporary, if troublesome, barrier to learning. After students learn English, the thinking goes, learning can then proceed unhampered. Forgetting their native language is seen as a regrettable but necessary price to pay for the benefits of citizenship. As a result of this thinking, the traditional strategy in most schools has been to help students rid themselves as quickly as possible of what is perceived as the "burden" of speaking another language. Yet we lose a valuable resource, on both a personal and a national level, when we pressure students who speak a language other than English as their native language to drop that language and replace it with English. A far more productive strategy would be to encourage the maintenance of heritage languages while also promoting the learning of English.

Entire communities have been denied the use of their native language, not only for instruction in schools but also for social communication of all kinds. Throughout our history, the language rights of substantial numbers of people have been violated, from prohibiting enslaved Africans from speaking their languages to the recent imposition of "English Only" laws in a growing number of states.[9] Joel Spring provides many compelling historical examples of the strategy of linguistic "deculturalization" used in the schooling of Native Americans, Puerto Ricans, Mexican Americans, and Asian Americans.[10]

U.S. language policies and practices have by no means been uniform. Rather, they have ranged widely from "sink or swim" policies (i.e., immersing language-minority students in English-only classrooms to fend on their own) to the imposition of English as the sole medium of instruction, to allowing and even encouraging bilingualism. By 1900, for example, at least 600,000 children, or about 4 percent of students enrolled in public and parochial elementary schools, were being taught in bilingual German/English bilingual schools. Smaller numbers were taught in Polish, Italian, Norwegian, Spanish, French, Czech, Dutch, and other languages.[11]

The zigzag of support and rejection of languages other than English demonstrates the ambivalence with which language diversity has been viewed in the United States. Today, misgivings concerning native-language maintenance, particularly bilingual education, still exist. The public has always been deeply divided over bilingual education, and this is more true today than ever before. There is a general reluctance to support bilingual education because it involves the use of not only English but also a language other than English for instruction. The fact that bilingual education has as one of its fundamental goals the *learning of English* often goes unmentioned by opponents. They focus their opposition on the practice of using students' native language in instruction because they perceive it to be a threat to national unity. But it is a myth that English has been a unifying force. In the words of James Crawford, who has exhaustively researched language policies in the United States, "Such notions obscure a multilingual tradition that is unsurpassed in its variety and richness, while inventing for English a unifying role that it rarely enjoyed."[12]

In the United States, language use and patriotic loyalty have often been linked, and patriotism has been measured by how quickly one abandons his or her native language and replaces it with English. Such views hold sway today for any number of rea-sons, from the massive number of new immigrants crossing our borders, to the incidents of September 11, 2001. Being fluent in another language, even if one is also fluent in English, is often viewed with suspicion, at least in the case of immigrants. Consequently, where language issues are concerned, everyone has gotten into the fray. As President Theodore Roosevelt, a spokesperson for the restrictive language policies at the beginning of the 20th century that were a response to the huge influx of primarily East European immigrants to the United States, said: "We have room for but one language here, and that is the English language; for we intend to see that the crucible turns our people out as Americans, of American nationality, and not as dwellers in a polyglot boardinghouse."[13] Roosevelt's views were widely shared by many people who felt threatened by the new wave of immigrants.

At times, restrictive views of language have resulted in counterproductive policies that inhibit or even prohibit the learning of foreign languages, as was the case with the teaching of German in the period between World War I and World War II. More recently, in 1998, the controversy surrounding native-language use resulted in the passage of California's Proposition 227, in which bilingual education was weakened considerably. Arizona followed suit in 2000, and Massachusetts in 2002. (A similar proposition failed in Colorado in 2002.) The implications of these measures for the rest of the country need to be considered within the context of U.S. Society, which is becoming more, not less, linguistically diverse. That our society continues to be ignorant of other languages and cultures is self-evident. That it is now jeopardized by this monolingualism and monoculturalism in a world becoming increasingly interdependent is also becoming more and more apparent.

Linguistic Diversity and Learning

All good teachers know that learning builds on prior knowledge and experiences. In the case of language-minority students, we seem to forget this truth as we effectively rob students of access to their prior learning, thus contradicting how learning takes place and the crucial role of language in the process. One's native language is a foundation for future learning. If we think of language development as the concrete foundation of a building, it makes sense that it needs to be strong to sustain the stress of many tons of building materials that will be erected on top of it. This is analogous to what takes place when students enter school in the United States: They use the language they know as a foundation for learning the content of the curriculum. For English speakers, this is a seamless process. For English-language learners, however, not knowing English is a tremendous disadvantage, not because their native language is ineffectual for learning, but because it is not usually viewed by their teachers and schools as a resource for learning. Extending the metaphor further, it would be as if the strong foundation that had been created were abandoned and the building materials were placed on top of a sand lot across the street. Needless to say, the building would crumble in short order.

According to Jim Cummins, "There is general agreement among cognitive psychologists that we learn by integrating new input into our existing cognitive structures or schemata. Our prior experience provides the foundation for interpreting new information. No learner is a blank slate."[14] As a rule, however, teachers and schools disregard language-minority students' native languages and cultures for what they believe to be good reasons: Because they link students' English-language proficiency with their prospective economic and social mobility, they may view English language learners as "handicapped" and thus urge students, through both subtle and direct means, to abandon their native language. For example, teachers and administrators ask parents to speak English to their children at home, they punish children for using their native language, or they simply withhold education until the children have mastered English, usually in the name of protecting students' futures.

Even if they have gifted and caring teachers, language-minority students may experience trauma when learning their new language. No doubt, the stress of immigration and the reasons for leaving their home countries play a part in this trauma for some of them, but just the process of learning a new language can be a devastating experience for many. In recounting her extensive experience teaching immigrant children, Cristina Igoa suggests that sheer weariness is one consequence: "A recurring theme regarding the inner world of the immigrant child is a feeling of exhaustion, not only from the sounds of a new language but also from the continual parade of strange sights and events in a new culture."[15]

Although some teachers may treat the fact that students speak a language other than English as a problem, lack of English skills alone cannot explain the poor academic achievement of language minority students. It is tempting to point to English "sink or swim" programs as the solution to the problem of academic failure, but confounding English-language acquisition with academic achievement is simplistic at best. For example, a study of a rural high school in northern California by Rebecca Callahan found that issues other than English proficiency were much more salient influences on the academic achievement of language-minority students. Specifically, track placement proved to be more significant because many English learners were enrolled in low-track curricula that do little to prepare them for college and other post-secondary school opportunities. More than anything, then, teachers' and schools' perception of the abilities of English-language learners get in the way of student achievement. In Callahan's words, "Constructions of English learners as deficient, bilingual programs as compensatory, and ESL classrooms as linguistic rather than academic speak to the marginalization of English learners in U.S. schools."[16]

In contrast to negative perceptions of bilingualism, a good deal of research confirms the positive influence of knowing more than one language. Native-language maintenance may act as a buffer against academic failure by simply supporting literacy in children's most developed language. For example, Lourdes Díaz Soto's research among 30 Hispanic families of young children with low and high academic achievement found that the parents of the higher achieving children favored a native-language environment to a greater extent than those of the lower achieving youngsters.[17] Patricia Gándara, in analyzing the impressive academic achievements of 50 Mexican American adults who grew up in poverty, found that the largest percentage of these successful adults grew up in households where *only* Spanish was spoken, and a re-markable two-thirds of them began school speaking *only* Spanish.[18]

That students' native language is an asset that can enhance their academic achievement was also found to be true by Ana Celia Zentella in a study of 19 families in El Barrio, a low-income, predominantly Puerto Rican community in New York City. In her research, the most successful students were enrolled in bilingual programs and were the most fluent bilinguals.[19] Also, in their review of research studies concerning the adaptation and school achievement of immigrants of various backgrounds, Alejandro Portes and Rubén Rumbaut came to a striking conclusion: Students with limited bilingualism are far more likely to leave school than those fluent in both languages. Rather than being an impediment to academic achievement, bilingualism can act to promote learning.[20]

Conclusions such as these contradict the common advice given to language minority parents to "speak English with your children at home." In contrast, Catherine Snow, a respected researcher in literacy and language acquisition, suggests that "the greatest contribution immigrant parents can make to their children's success is to ensure they maintain fluency and continue to develop the home language."[21] This makes sense, of course, and it leads us to reflect on the innate wisdom of many immigrant mothers, including my (Sonia's) mother, who ignored teachers' pleas to speak to us in English. Had it not been for my mother's quiet but obstinate resistance, my sister and I would probably now be monolingual English speakers rather than fluent bilinguals.

The problem of language-minority children has often been articulated as a problem of not knowing English. But the real problem may be what Luis Moll has labeled the "obsession with speaking English,"[22] as if learning English is the solution to all the other difficulties faced by language-minority students, including poverty, racism, poorly financed schools, and lack of access to excellent education. Learning English is, of course, important and necessary for all students; this is a given. But, rather than supporting the suppression or elimination of native language use at home and school, the research reviewed here supports promoting native-language literacy as a way to promote learning English more effectively. If this is the case, the language dominance of students is not the real issue; rather, *the way in which teachers and schools view students' language may have an even greater influence on their achievement.*

The way in which languages other than English are perceived by the schools and teachers, and whether modifications in the curriculum are made as a result, are therefore crucial issues to keep in mind. For this reason, language diversity needs to be placed within a sociopolitical context to understand why speaking a language other than English is not itself a handicap. On the contrary, it can be a great asset to learning. The myths regarding language use are part of the sociopolitical context. For example, in the United States, the prevailing view about knowing languages other than English is that, among culturally dominated groups, bilingualism is a burden, yet among middle-class and wealthy students, it is usually seen as an asset. It is not unusual to find in the same high school the seemingly incongruous, ironic situation of one group of students having their native language wiped out while another group of students struggles to learn a foreign language, a language they will never be able to use with any real fluency. There are more affirming approaches to teaching language-minority students, and they need to be used more widely than is currently the case. Recent research on how to build on students' languages and literacies provide a more hopeful direction in the education of language-minority students.[23]

Approaches to Teaching Language-Minority Students

Given the dramatic increase in the number of English-language learners in our country in the past several decades, every classroom in every city and town has already been, or will soon be, affected. This reality is in stark contrast to the conventional wisdom that only specialists teach these children. For instance, a 2002 survey reported that *more than 40 percent* of all teachers in the nation reported that they taught students who were limited in their English proficiency, yet only 12 percent of these teachers had eight or more hours of training in how to teach these students.[24] More recently, in 2005, a survey of over 5,000 California teachers found that

Snapshot

Liane Chang

Liane is a ninth-grade student at a comprehensive high school in a midsize town in the Northeast. Her father is European American, and her mother is Chinese. Liane is fortunate because her efforts to learn Chinese, her mother's native language, are supported in the school system. Her pride and excitement in developing fluency in Chinese speaks to the affirmation she experiences in both her school and home settings. Liane's experience points to the power of a school experience that can support students in maintaining or reclaiming their family language.

If I look at how my different ethnicities have influenced my education, I would have to say that it has impacted my confidence in expressing my cultures to others. When people ask me to tell them how I identify, I reply, "Eurasian" [and] their reaction is always a very positive comment, the sort of thing that could start a whole conversation. I think that being Eurasian is about the coolest identity a person could have. Many might think that it would be embarrassing to be anything other than what is said to be "American" but through my teachers' and peers' influence, I see it as an opportunity to be an individual.

Now I am learning Chinese in school (with the help of my mom). I felt that, since I am Chinese, I should learn the language so that, when my mom and I go to China, I can understand and speak the language also. My love of the Chinese language has always been great throughout my childhood. I used to dream and wonder what it would be like for me to speak a different language, and my inspiration came from my mother's conversations with her Chinese friends, either on the phone or in person. Late at night, right before I was tucked into bed, my mother would always say goodnight to me in Chinese.

My lesson on how to say "Thank you" in Chinese was useful when I went to Chinese restaurants or people's homes. Many trips yearly to New York City's Chinatown were also a great inspiration in my early childhood. This language and culture inspired me to choose to learn the language through my middle and high school world-language programs. Now that I'm learning Chinese, it's like I'm more related to my mom. It gave me more of a personal connection with my mom . . . something that I'll always share with her. She can help me because she understands it, and [it is] just something between her and me . . . very special. It can be very, very difficult at times because, when she corrects me, it doesn't seem like I know the language very much. But she helps me in a way that I can't be helped at school, and she gives me a new outlook on the language. It's a neat experience.

My grandparents on the European side of me are the only grandparents I have ever known. They have taught me hard work ethics and frugality that they learned through their daily lives. From these cultures, I have received what my grandparents learned through generations and have passed down to my parents and myself. And because these were the only grandparents I have ever known during my life, their stories and memories were also passed to me to treasure and to pass on to other generations. Through their hardships growing up in Europe during World War II and their few choices, I feel that I can appreciate my opportunities here to receive a good education. During World War II, my grandpa in

Poland was captured by the Germans and forced to do manual labor, but he did not have to go to a concentration camp. When he got out, he went to France, because he couldn't return to Poland. Then he married my Grandma, so my dad is French-Polish.

Somewhere else, people might think I'm not American because I don't look like the typical American, but here, in this school system, it's sort of the opposite. Being different makes you cool, and you can have your own individuality and you can differentiate yourself from different people. It's sort of a good thing, here, to be different—and I've never had someone be racist about my different cultures—except when you are really little, you know, the rhyme when they pull back their eyes? But that's little-kid stuff.

In seventh grade, I went to China with my Chinese teacher. It was a really good chance to see it . . . to be in an environment where I was actually a minority—being American—instead of being in an environment where everybody's similar, you feel not part of their culture, because it is so different from what you are used to. My language skills were new then. I knew basic questions of survival. The experience was really overwhelming at times, but really exciting too. We went to visit a Chinese high school, and we were each set up with a Chinese student, and we tried to communicate with, and ask them about their life. Actually it was the school that my mom's dad went to when he was in China. Isn't that neat?

In seventh grade art, I completed a project about myself, expressing various symbols that had meaning [for me]. Though I did not have many symbols, each of them represents a lot about my life and heritage. For example, the flags that I put on my collage symbolize more than my heritage. They symbolize the people who come from there and are a big part of my life.

In my picture, I have the flags of my heritage flowing out of my fingernails like smoke. There are a total of three: the Chinese, French, and Polish flags. The Chinese flag represents my heritage on my mom's side. Both of her parents were born in China and immigrated to Taiwan during the Chinese Revolution. On the other hand, in my painting, my dad is both French and Polish. Polish and French are a big part of my family. Last of all, I have an American flag for the background of my project. This, of course, represents the place my sister Jillian and I were born. Since it is the biggest part of my life, it is the largest in the collage. I am proud to be American and that is the most important thing of all that I symbolized in the project.

Commentary

Liane's snapshot can help us think about what it might mean to have more school systems support students' identities by offering language courses from various language groups and even trips to the countries where those languages are spoken. Although not every language can be offered and trips are out of the question for many schools, it is intriguing to see how Liane's experience was made so much more positive by studying Chinese. Not only was Chinese one of the languages of her heritage, but it also promoted a closer relationship with her mother. We can adapt this approach for language-minority students in our schools: those who enter school without English but are our future citizens.

they were largely ill prepared to meet the needs of the state's nearly 1.6 million ELLs because they had received little professional development geared specifically to the task of teaching these students.[25] It is clear that the responsibility for educating language-minority students can no longer fall only on those teachers who have been trained specifically to provide bilingual education and ESL services. This responsibility needs to be shared by *all* teachers and *all* schools, yet most teachers have had little training in language acquisition and other language-related issues.

What do all classroom teachers need to know to help them be better teachers of language minority students? How can they best prepare to teach students of different language backgrounds and varying language abilities? Fortunately, more attention is being paid to these questions than has been the case in the recent past.[26] In the following sections, we suggest a number of steps that teachers and schools can take to effectively educate English-language learners. Before doing so, however, we want to emphasize that we are not suggesting that teachers will automatically produce results by simply following a set of prescribed strategies. Although learning new approaches and techniques may be very helpful, teaching students successfully means, above all, changing one's attitudes toward the students, their languages and cultures, and their communities. Anything short of this will result in repeating the pattern of failure that currently exists.[27] As Jim Cummins has eloquently stated, "Fortunately, good teaching does not require us to internalize an endless list of instructional techniques. Much more fundamental is the recognition that human relationships are central to effective instruction."[28]

Understanding language development, second-language acquisition, and the sociopolitical context of education

All teachers need to understand how language is learned—both native and subsequent languages. This knowledge is often reserved for specialists in bilingual and ESL education, but it should become standard knowledge for all teachers. For example, Stephen Krashen's significant theories of second-language acquisition and his recommendations that teachers provide students for whom English is a second language with *comprehensible input*—that is,

cues that are contextualized in their instruction—is useful for all teachers who have language-minority students in their classrooms.[29] Likewise, related knowledge in curriculum and instruction, linguistics, sociology, and history are all helpful for teachers of language-minority students. Consequently, all teachers should have:

- Familiarity with first- and second-language acquisition
- Awareness of the sociocultural and sociopolitical context of education for language-minority students
- Awareness of the history of immigration in the United States, with particular attention to language policies and practices throughout that history
- Knowledge of the history and experiences of specific groups of people, especially those who are residents of the city, town, and state where they are teaching
- The ability to adapt curriculum for students whose first language is other than English
- Competence in pedagogical approaches suitable for culturally and linguistically heterogeneous classrooms
- Experience with teachers of diverse backgrounds and the ability to develop collaborative relationships with colleagues that promote the learning of language-minority students
- The ability to communicate effectively with parents of diverse language, cultural, and social class backgrounds[30]

According to Lily Wong Fillmore and Catherine Snow, besides appropriate preservice experiences and positive attitudes about ELL students, basic coursework in edu-cational linguistics is "the bare minimum" for preparing teachers for today's schools.[31] Unfortunately, however, many teachers have not had access to this kind of knowledge during their teacher preparation or even in their professional development after becoming teachers. Consequently, they may need to acquire this knowledge on their own. They can do this by attending conferences in literacy, bilingual education, multicultural education, and ESL; participating in professional development opportunities in their district and beyond; subscribing to journals and newsletters in these fields; setting up study groups with colleagues to discuss and practice different strategies; and returning to graduate school to take relevant courses or to seek advanced degrees.

Developing an additive bilingual perspective

Additive bilingualism refers to a framework for understanding language acquisition and development that *adds* a new language rather than *subtracts* an existing one.[32] This perspective is radically different from the traditional expectation in our society that immigrants need to exchange their native language for their new language, English. Many educators and others are now questioning whether it needs to be this way. Abandoning one's native language leads not only to individual psychological costs but also to a tremendous loss of linguistic resources to the nation. Additive bilingualism supports the notion that two is better than one—that English *plus* other languages can make us stronger individually and as a society.

The challenge is that many teachers do not speak the native languages of their students. Nevertheless, all teachers, even those who are monolingual English speakers, can create a learning environment that supports and affirms the native languages of their students. A good example comes from researchers David Schwarzer, Alexia Haywood, and Charla Lorenzen, who described their collaborative work within a multiliterate preschool classroom in Central Texas.[33] They suggest, for example, that teachers can tap into some of the resources available in students' native languages by creating a multiliterate learning community with the help of students, their families, elders, and other community members. Some of the ideas they suggest for doing this are creating a multiliterate print environment in the classroom; using literature in students' native languages; learning some key words in students' first languages; creating audiotapes of greetings, simple conversations, songs, and stories in students' first languages; and so on. It is clear that teachers—even those who do not speak the native languages of their students—can demonstrate an appreciation and support for these languages in numerous ways. There are many reasons for doing so, including the affirmation it gives students who do not yet speak English. Even more important, nurturing native-language literacy is supported by research demonstrating that the skills students develop in their native language are usually easily transferred to a second or third language.[34] This being the case, how can we continue to view bilingualism as a deficit?

Consciously fostering native-language literacy

As we saw in the previous examples, developing an additive approach to language acquisition counters the false assumption that students must forget their native language. Even small gestures in the classroom can convey this message of inclusion of native languages. In her work with immigrant students, for instance, Cristina Igoa reserved the last period of the day, three times a week, for students to listen to stories or to read in their native languages. Because she did not speak all the languages of her many stu-

What You Can Do

Accept Students' Identities

Learn to say each child's name correctly. Don't change *Marisol* to *Marcy* or *Vinh* to *Vinny*. As simplistic as it may sound, this basic rule of respect is violated daily in classrooms around the nation. Given the pressure to conform that all students face, some of them readily accede to having their names changed so that they can fit in. Although learning many names in different languages may be time consuming for teachers, it is a first step in affirming who students *are* rather than who we may want them to become.

dents, she recruited college students who were fluent in various languages to help out.[35]

Teachers can also make a commitment to learn at least one of the languages of their students. When they become second-language learners, teachers develop a new appreciation for both the joys and the struggles experienced by language-minority students—including exhaustion, frustration, and withdrawal—when they are learning English. This was what happened to Bill Dunn, a veteran teacher who decided to, in his words, "come out of the closet as a Spanish speaker." He realized that, after teaching for 20 years in a largely Puerto Rican community, he understood a great deal of Spanish, so he decided to study it formally and to keep a journal of his experiences. Although he had always been a wonderful and caring teacher, putting himself in the place of his students helped him understand a great many things more clearly—from students' grammatical errors in English to their boredom and misbehavior when they could not understand the language of instruction.[36] As a result, he developed more targeted pedagogical strategies for teaching them as well as a renewed respect for the situation of students who are learning English.

The responsibility to create powerful learning environments for English-language learners should not rest on individual teachers alone, however. Entire schools can also develop such environments: They can, for instance, make a conscious effort to recruit and hire bilingual staff members who can communicate with parents in their native languages. A major challenge, however, is that few teacher-preparation programs are currently preparing teachers and administrators to create positive conditions for English-language learners. Programs that do so are based on the premise that diversity is a resource to be cherished. Consequently, they provide a number of elements for preservice teachers and administrators: courses in language acquisition and development, field placements in schools that are successful with English-language learners, experiences in a second language, and others.[37]

These recommendations are based (1) on the assumption that all students come to their learning with skills and talents that can be used as resources and (2) on the notion that biliteracy is a value in itself, a case that has been made by numerous researchers including María de la Luz Reyes, John Halcón, María Fránquiz, María Torres-Guzmán, and many others.[38] Native-language literacy is a resource that should be cherished, and it is the basis for bilingual education, which we consider next.

Language Diversity and the Case for Bilingual Education

The freedom to maintain and use one's native language is thought by some linguists and human rights advocates to be a basic human right. The proposal for a Declaration of Children's Linguistic Human Rights, for instance, places linguistic rights on the same level as other human rights.[39] This proposal includes the right to identify positively with one's mother tongue, to learn it, and to choose when to use it. Although these rights may be self-evident for language-majority children (in the United States this means native English speakers), they may not be so apparent for those who speak a language that carries a stigma, as is the case with most language-minority students in the United States.

Just as racial integration was considered a key civil right for those who were forcibly segregated, bilingual education is viewed by many language-minority communities as equally vital. There is a significant link between bilingual education and equity. Although frequently addressed as simply an issue of language, it can be argued that using students' native language in instruction is a civil rights issue. Doing this provides some measure of assurance that children who do not speak English will be educated in a language they understand. Without it, millions of children may be doomed to a future of educational underachievement and limited occupational choices.

In 1974, the U.S. Supreme Court recognized the connection between native-language rights and equal educational opportunity. In 1969, plaintiffs representing 1,800 Chinese-speaking students had sued the San Francisco Unified School District for failing to provide students who did not speak English with an equal chance to learn. They lost their case in San Francisco, but by 1974 they had taken it all the way to the Supreme Court. In the landmark

Lau v. Nichols case, the Court ruled unanimously that the civil rights of students who did not understand the language of instruction were indeed being violated. Citing Title VI of the Civil Rights Act, the Court stated, in part:

> There is no equality of treatment merely by providing students with the same facilities, textbooks, teachers, and curriculum; for students who do not understand English are effectively foreclosed from any meaningful education. Basic skills are at the very core of what these public schools teach. Imposition of a requirement that, before a child can effectively participate in the educational program he must already have acquired those basic skills is to make a mockery of public education.[40]

Although the decision did not impose any particular remedy, its results were immediate and extensive. By 1975, the Office for Civil Rights and the Department of Health, Education, and Welfare issued a document called *The Lau Remedies,* which served as the basis for determining whether or not school systems throughout the United States were in compliance with the *Lau* decision. This document provided guidance in identifying students with limited proficiency in English, assessing their language abilities, and providing appropriate programs. Bilingual programs became the common remedy in most school systems.

The Equal Educational Opportunities Act (EEOA) of 1974 has also been instrumental in protecting the language rights of students for whom English is not their native language. This law interprets the failure of any educational agency to "take appropriate action to overcome language barriers that impede equal participation by its students in its instructional programs" as a denial of equal educational opportunity.[41] In both the *Lau* decision and the EEOA, bilingual education emerged as a key strategy to counteract the language discrimination faced by many students in our schools.

There is a dizzying array of program models and definitions of bilingual education,[42] but in general terms, *bilingual education* can be defined as an educational program that involves the *use of two languages of instruction* at some point in a student's school career. This definition is broad enough to include many program variations. For example, a child who speaks a language other than English,

let's say, Vietnamese, may receive instruction in content areas in Vietnamese while at the same time learning ESL. The cultures associated with both the native language and English are generally part of the curriculum as well. This approach, sometimes called *bilingual/bicultural education,* is based on the premise that the language and culture children bring to school are assets that must be used in their education.

In the United States, a primary objective of bilingual education is to develop proficiency and literacy in the English language. As such, ESL is an integral and necessary component of all bilingual programs because it goes hand in hand with native-language instruction in content areas. When provided in isolation, however, ESL cannot be called *bilingual* education because the child's native language is not used in instruction. Although they are learning English, students in ESL programs may be languishing in their other subject areas because they do not understand the language of instruction. Their education usually consists only of learning English until they can function in the regular English-language environment.

In spite of opposition to bilingual education in many places, various models of bilingual education can still be found in schools throughout our nation. *Transitional bilingual education* is probably the most common model of bilingual education in the United States. In this approach, students receive their content-area instruction in their native language while learning English as a second language. As soon as they are deemed ready to benefit from the monolingual English-language curriculum, they are "exited" or "mainstreamed" out of the program. The rationale behind this model is that native-language services should serve only as a transition to English. Therefore, there is a limit on the time a student may be in a bilingual program—usually three years. This limit was established in 1971 by Massachusetts, the first state to mandate bilingual education, and although bilingual education, as such, no longer exists in Massachusetts (it was replaced by a one-year English immersion program in 2002 through a ballot initiative), it has served as a model for other states.

Developmental or maintenance bilingual education can be characterized as a robust version of bilingual education because it provides a more comprehensive and long-term approach. As in the transitional approach, students receive content-area instruction in their native language while learning English as a second language. The difference is that generally no limit is set on the time students can be in the program. The objective is to develop students' fluency in both languages, or *biliteracy*, by using both for instruction. The longer the students remain in the program the more functionally bilingual they become and therefore the more balanced the curriculum to which they are exposed. That is, the students can potentially receive equal amounts of instruction in English and their native language.

Two-way bilingual education, also called *two-way immersion*, is another model. This approach integrates students whose native language is English with students for whom English is a second language. The goal of this approach is to develop bilingual proficiency, academic achievement, and positive cross-cultural attitudes and behaviors among all students. The approach lends itself to cooperative learning and peer tutoring because all students have considerable skills to share with one another. There is generally no time limit, although some two-way programs are part of existing transitional programs and therefore have the same entrance and exit criteria, at least for the students who are learning English. Two-way programs hold the promise of expanding our nation's linguistic resources and improving relationships between majority and minority language groups.

A variety of approaches and strategies are used in two-way programs, depending on the students enrolled, the program design, and the particular community. Most two-way programs use students' native or second language at different stages, and most are Spanish-English programs. Results of the two-way model have been very positive. In a longitudinal study of students who had been in two-way immersion (TWI) Spanish/English programs, researchers Elizabeth Howard, Donna Christian, and Fred Genesee found impressive levels of performance in reading, writing, and oral language in both English and Spanish. Students, both native English speakers and native Spanish speakers, had very high levels of English fluency, and while native English speakers scored lower on reading Spanish than native Spanish speakers, their oral Spanish proficiency was quite high.[43] Another study of a two-way program found that a high number of high school students who had been enrolled in a two-way program throughout elementary school had positive attitudes toward school

and expectations of attending college. Many of the Hispanic students in the study credited the two-way program with keeping them from dropping out of high school. The researchers, Kathryn Lindholm-Leary and Graciela Borsato, pointed to the development of a sense of "resiliency" among the Hispanic students in the study, especially those who were from low-income families.[44]

The fact is that bilingual education is generally more effective than other programs such as ESL alone, not only for learning content through the native language but also for learning English. This finding has been validated by many studies and meta-analyses throughout the years, most recently by a comprehensive summary of research conducted by the National Literacy Panel on Language-Minority Children and Youth.[45] This apparently counterintuitive finding can be understood if one considers that students in bilingual programs are educated in content areas *along with* structured instruction in English. Students in bilingual education programs are building on their previous literacy, but this may not be the case in ESL programs that concentrate on English grammar, phonics, and other language features out of context with the way in which real, day-to-day language is used.

Bilingual programs may have secondary salutary effects. These include motivating students to remain in school rather than dropping out, making school more meaningful and, in general, making the school experience more enjoyable. This was certainly true for Manuel Gomes, whose case study follows this chapter. Because of the close-knit relationships between his Crioulo-speaking teachers and their students, Manuel's transition to English was far easier than it might otherwise have been. A related phenomenon may be that bilingual education reinforces close relationships among children and their family members, promoting more communication than would be the case if they were instructed solely in English.

Why the Controversy Over Bilingual Education?

Why is there such controversy over bilingual education despite research findings of its effectiveness?

The truth is that bilingual education has always been controversial. Both its proponents and its opponents have long recognized its potential for empowering traditionally powerless groups. Thus, the issue is not so much whether bilingual education works, but rather the real possibility that it *might*. Bilingual education challenges conventional U.S. educational wisdom that native language and culture need to be forgotten in order to be successful students and "real Americans." Bilingual education continues to be controversial because it generally represents the class and ethnic group interests of traditionally subordinated groups and it comes out on the side of education as an emancipatory proposition. In the end, children who could benefit from bilingual education are, as Jim Cummins asserts, caught "in the crossfire."[46]

In spite of its sound pedagogical basis, bilingual education is, above all, a political issue because it is concerned with power relations in society. Understanding the political nature of bilingual education, and of multicultural education in general, is therefore essential if we are to develop effective programs for all students. For example, through an extensive review of programs for ELLs, the 2006 National Literacy Panel report concerning literacy for English language learners—a panel hand-picked and appointed by President George W. Bush—found that good bilingual programs produce faster results in developing English fluency than good English-only programs. Because this finding contradicted the administration's English-only agenda, it was not made public through official government channels. In an unusual move, both the *New York Times* and the *Los Angeles Times* urged the government to release the findings. Ultimately, the report was published privately.[47]

Nevertheless, although bilingual education is a political issue, we need to emphasize that it is *also* a pedagogical issue. Successful bilingual programs have demonstrated that students can learn through their native language while learning English *and also* achieving academically. This achievement contradicts the conservative agenda, which calls for a return to traditional curriculum and pedagogy. Successful bilingual education threatens to explode the myth of the "basics" if the basics means only valuing a Eurocentric curriculum and the English language. In fact, fluency in English, although

necessary, is no guarantee that students of language-minority backgrounds will succeed in school or later in life. If this were the case, all language-minority students who have never been in bilingual programs or who were mainstreamed into regular classes years ago, would be doing quite well academically, but as we know, this is far from the case. Additionally, research by Alejandro Portes and Rubén Rumbaut found that the students they studied from nationalities that speak English best (including West Indians and Filipinos) are not necessarily those who earn the highest incomes or have the highest number of managers and professionals among their ranks. On the other hand, Chinese and other Asians and Colombians and other Latin Americans, with relatively low fluency in English, earn considerably more. English-language fluency, then, is not the only explanation. In some cases, according to Portes and Rumbaut, the way in which immigrants have been received and incorporated into the society also matters a great deal.[48]

Promising Practices for Language-Minority Students

Although bilingual education represents a notable advance over monolingual education, it is unrealistic to expect it to work for all English-language learners. It is often perceived as a panacea for all the educational problems of language-minority students, but even with bilingual education, many children are likely to face educational failure. No approach or program is a panacea for all the problems, educational and otherwise, facing young people. Essential issues such as poverty, racism, reception and incorporation into the society, and structural inequality also need to be faced. Simply substituting one language for another, or using books in Spanish with Dick and Jane in brownface, will not guarantee success for language-minority students. Expecting too much of even good programs is counterproductive because, in the absence of quick results, the children are again blamed.

As we have seen, effective pedagogy is not simply teaching subject areas in another language, but instead finding ways to use the language, culture, and experiences of students meaningfully in their education. Even when bilingual programs are more effective than ESL or immersion programs, the pedagogy in such classrooms all too frequently replicates the traditional "chalk and talk" or "transmission" methods found in most classrooms. If bilingual education is to challenge this kind of pedagogy, a far different and more empowering environment needs to be designed.

Another problem with bilingual programs has to do with the manner in which they usually define success. Bilingual programs, particularly weak models with a transitional focus, are meant to self-destruct within a specified time, generally three years. Success in these programs is measured by the rapidity with which they mainstream students. Therefore, their very existence is based on a compensatory-education philosophy, whereby students who enter school knowing little or no English are regarded as needing compensation. Their knowledge of another language is considered a crutch to use until they master what is considered the real language of schooling. Little wonder, then, that such programs are often viewed by parents and educators alike as ineffectual. In addition, because most bilingual programs are for poor children who attend high-poverty schools, they suffer from the same lack of adequate resources as other programs for poor children, including poorly trained teachers and few curricular materials.

Given this reality, it is not surprising that some parents do not want their children in bilingual programs or that these programs are often isolated and ghettoized in the schools. The message underlying this reality is not lost on students either. As a result, some language-minority children unconsciously jeopardize their language development by refusing to speak their native language in school: They stop using a language that could benefit their academic achievement by allowing them to access higher level cognitive skills than they employ when they use English, which they do not speak as well.

Contrary to the "quick exit" philosophy that undergirds most bilingual programs, research has documented that students generally need a minimum of five to seven years to develop the level of English proficiency needed to succeed academically in school.[49] Because most programs permit students to remain a maximum of just three to four years, only partially positive results can be expected. In spite of this, many programs are successful because they are

better than programs that provide no native-language support at all.

Equally troublesome for some school districts is that in their student population, they have numerous language groups called *low incidence populations* (i.e., students who speak a particular language for which there may not be sufficient speakers to entitle them legally to a bilingual program). This is often the case with Asian languages and some European languages. Providing a bilingual program for each of these small groups would be not only impractical but impossible. In this situation, the most common programmatic practice is some kind of ESL approach.

The fact that most bilingual programs are based on the need to separate students is also problematic. Bilingual education has been characterized by some as tracking because students are separated from their peers for instruction. Although the reasons for this separation are legitimate and based on sound research and pedagogy, tracking as a practice flies in the face of equal educational opportunity. This makes it a particularly thorny issue in a democratic society. Add the research evidence suggesting that students should remain in bilingual classrooms until they develop sufficient academic competency in English, and we are left with some students in segregated language settings for a major part of their schooling. Nevertheless, it must be remembered that a great deal of segregation of language-minority students took place *before* there were bilingual programs (and it continues even more strongly today in sheltered English and ESL pullout-type programs). Yet very little criticism has been lodged against segregation in these cases.

In fact, Latino students, who represent by far the highest number in bilingual programs, are now the most segregated population in U.S. schools, and bilingual education has nothing to do with this.[50] Instead, "White flight," a retrenchment in busing policies, and segregated residential housing patterns are largely to blame. We must conclude that sometimes criticisms that students in bilingual programs are unnecessarily segregated are based more on an ideological opposition to bilingual education than concern about protecting students' civil rights.

It is also true, however, that every bilingual program has numerous opportunities for integrating students more meaningfully than is currently the case. Students in bilingual programs can take art,

What You Can Do
Accept Students' Language

Accept students' language, including language used by both new speakers of English and those who speak another variety of it, without overcorrection. Overcorrecting can jeopardize learning. Although all students need to learn Standard English, especially those who have been traditionally denied access to higher status learning, it is equally crucial that teachers accept and value students' native languages or dialects. Rather than always directly correcting students' language, model Standard English in your responses or statements. Students soon pick up the message that there are different ways of saying the same thing and that some are more appropriate in certain settings.

physical education, and other nonacademic classes with their English-speaking peers. Bilingual programs can also be more structurally integrated into the school, instead of separated in a wing of the building, so that teachers from both bilingual and nonbilingual classrooms can collaborate. This seldom happens because bilingual teachers bear the burden of the "bilingual" label in the same way as their students. These teachers are suspected of being less intelligent, less academically prepared, and less able than nonbilingual teachers—this in spite of the fact that those who have been adequately prepared are fluent in two languages and have developed a wide range of pedagogical approaches for teaching a diverse student body. Because many bilingual teachers are from the same cultural and linguistic backgrounds as the students they teach, they bring a necessary element of diversity into the school, but most schools have not found a way to benefit from their presence.

Two-way bilingual programs provide another opportunity for integration and heightened academic achievement. As we have seen, children at all grade levels and from all ethnic, linguistic, and social class backgrounds can benefit from two-way programs, thus fulfilling both social and educational goals.

Finally, a word about the need to differentiate between *language-minority* students and the larger category of *immigrant* students. As Lin Goodwin rightfully has pointed out, it is often the case that these are conflated, as if all immigrant students are limited in their English proficiency or all students who are English-language learners are immigrants.[51] Neither of these is the case. In fact, there are many English language learners who are citizens (Puerto Ricans, for example, or others who are second or even third generation); there are also immigrants for whom English is a native language (Jamaicans, for instance). It is necessary, therefore, for teachers to understand that native language and national origin are different.

SUMMARY

There are numerous ways in which language differences may affect students' learning. These differences are not necessarily barriers to learning, but the history of linguicism in our society has resulted in making them so. Language policies and practices in the United States have ranged from a grudging acceptance of language diversity to outright hostility. We have seen the positive impact that recognizing and affirming students' native languages can have on their learning. Even teachers who do not speak the languages of their students can successfully teach them. In fact, they must be successful with them, because English language learners are found in all classrooms throughout the nation. As such, these students are the responsibility of all teachers, not just specialists in ESL and bilingual education. This requires that all teachers become familiar with theories and pedagogical approaches to second-language acquisition and development and have, or develop, positive attitudes about their language-minority students.

Bilingual education cannot completely reverse the history of failure for linguistic minority students; it is both unreasonable and naive to expect it to do so. Nevertheless, bilingual education has proved to be an effective program for students for whom English is a second language, because it is based on a fundamental critique of the "assimilation equals success" formula on which much of our educational policy and practice is based. The fact that it, alone, cannot change the achievement of students is an indication of the complexity of factors that affect learning.

We have also pointed out some of the problems that arise when programs for English language learners have low status and when these students are separated from other students for instruction. Even in bilingual programs, for example, when there is an emphasis on low-level rote and drill and there are low expectations for students, little learning takes place. In contrast, researcher Luis Moll has suggested that when schools exemplify "educational sovereignty"—that is, when they challenge the arbitrary authority of the dominant power structure, in this case manifested through English-only and high-stakes testing policies—English language learners will be successful. In a longitudinal study of a dual-language school in the Southwest, he found that all students in the school, regardless of their sociocultural characteristics, became literate in both languages. This success was due to several factors, including a highly qualified and diverse teaching staff, close and caring relationships between teachers and students, and the teachers' ideological clarity in understanding that teaching is above all a political activity. Moll concludes,

> The school, consequently, is not only successful in producing biliterate students, a rare achievement in U.S. schools, but also successful despite the heavy ideological and programmatic pressures of the state to dismantle bilingual education, a consequence of the state's English-only policy, and the current emphasis on high-stakes testing, also conducted only in English.[52]

Moll's study makes it clear that, while there is no magic solution for all the educational problems of English language learners, a good place to begin would be to honor and affirm students' native languages, their families, their communities, and the resources they bring to their education.

To Think About

1. Research the English-only movement. Do you consider it an example of linguicism? Why or why not?
2. Why do you think bilingual education has been less controversial at some times than at others? Review the cases of referenda in California, Arizona, Colorado, and Massachusetts as examples.
3. The argument "My folks made it without bilingual education; why give other folks special treatment?" has often been made, particularly

by descendants of European American immigrants. Is this a compelling argument? Why or why not?

4. If you were the principal of a school with a large population of language-minority students, how would you address this situation? What if you were a parent of one of those children? A teacher?

5. Some people are offended when the term *English as a Second Language (ESL)* is used. They believe that English should be the first language of everyone who lives in the United States. Why do people react in this way? What would you say to someone who said this?

Activities for Personal, School, and Community Change

1. If you do not currently speak a language other than English, enroll in a course to learn one (preferably a language spoken by a number of your students). Keep a journal of your reflections, noting what you're learning; what it feels like to be a learner of another language; whether or not your relationship with your students changes; and if and how your teaching strategies change as a result.

2. Ask your students to do a "language inventory"—that is, ask them to find out how many members of their families speak or used to speak another language; what language or languages they speak or spoke; and, if they no longer speak it, why they do not. Encourage them to interview family members and even to audiotape them, if possible. Have them bring the results to class and use them as the basis for a lesson or unit on language diversity in the United States.

3. Find out what policies your school has concerning the use of languages other than English in the classroom, on the playground, and in other areas of the school. If there is an "English Only" policy in any of these, find out how it came about. Ask other staff members and families what they think about it. If you disagree with the policy, develop an action plan to address it.

Companion Website

For access to additional case studies, weblinks, concept cards, and other material related to this chapter, visit the text's companion website at **www.ablongman.com/nieto5e.**

Notes to Chapter 10

1. Henry T. Trueba, "Culture and Language: The Ethnographic Approach to the Study of Learning Environments." In *Language and Culture in Learning: Teaching Spanish to Native Speakers of Spanish,* edited by Barbara J. Merino, Henry T. Trueba, and Fabián A. Samaniego (Bristol, PA: Falmer Press, 1993): 26–27.

2. This is changing as more authors are beginning to include language as an important component of multicultural education. See, for example, James A. Banks and Cherry McGee Banks (eds.), *Handbook of Research on Multicultural Education,* 2nd ed. (San Francisco: Jossey-Bass, 2004). Language issues are included in several chapters of the handbook. Donna Gollnick and Philip Chinn also include linguistic diversity as a separate issue in their conceptualization of multicultural education: Donna M. Gollnick and Philip C. Chinn, *Multicultural Education in a Pluralistic Society,* 7th ed. (New York: Prentice-Hall, 2006).

3. By *linguicism,* Skutnabb-Kangas means "ideologies and structures which are used to legitimate, effectuate and reproduce an unequal division of power and resources (both material and nonmaterial) between groups which are defined on the basis of language." See Tove Skutnabb-Kangas, "Multilingualism and the Education of Minority Children." In *Minority Education: From Shame to Struggle,* edited by Tove Skutnabb-Kangas and Jim Cummins (Clevedon, England: Multilingual Matters, 1988): 13.

4. U.S. Census Bureau, *Ability to Speak English by Language Spoken at Home for the Population 5 years and Over: 2000.* Census 2000, released October 29, 2004 (Washington, DC: Author, 2004).

5. *English Language Learners and the U.S. Census, 1990–2000.* These and many other data are avail-

able from the National Clearinghouse for English Language Acquisition and Language Instruction Educational Programs (NCELA) at www.ncela.gwu.edu

6. Anneka L. Kindler, *Survey of the States' Limited English Proficient Students and Available Educational Programs and Services: 1999–2000 Summary Report* (Washington, DC: U.S. Department of Education, Office of English Language Acquisition, Language Enhancement, and Academic Achievement for Limited English Proficient Students [NCELA], 2002).

7. *Ibid.*

8. National Center for Education Statistics, *Indicator of the Month: Teachers' Feelings of Preparedness.* Available at: nces.ed.gov/pubs2000/qrtlyspring/4elem/q4-6.html

9. James Crawford, *Hold Your Tongue: Bilingualism and the Politics of "English Only"* (Reading, MA: Addison-Wesley, 1992); see also James Crawford, *At War with Diversity: U.S. Language Policy in an Age of Anxiety* (Clevedon, England: Multilingual Matters, 2000).

10. Joel Spring, *Deculturalization and the Struggle for Equality: A Brief History of the Education of Dominated Cultures in the United States,* 5th ed (New York: McGraw-Hill, 2006).

11. Crawford, *Hold Your Tongue: Bilingualism and the Politics of "English Only."*

12. Crawford, *Hold Your Tongue,* 11.

13. As quoted in Crawford, *Hold Your Tongue,* 59.

14. Jim Cummins, *Negotiating Identities: Education for Empowerment in a Diverse Society* (Ontario, CA: California Association for Bilingual Education, 1996): 75.

15. Cristina Igoa, *The Inner World of the Immigrant Child* (New York: St. Martins Press, 1995): 50.

16. Rebecca M. Callahan, "Tracking and High School English Learners: Limiting Opportunity to Learn." *American Educational Research Journal* 42, no. 2 (Summer 2005): 305–328, p. 322.

17. Lourdes Díaz Soto, *Language, Culture, and Power: Bilingual Families and the Struggle for Quality Education* (Albany: State University of New York Press, 1997).

18. Patricia Gándara, *Over the Ivy Walls: The Educational Mobility of Low-Income Chicanos* (Albany: State University of New York Press, 1995).

19. Ana Celia Zentella, *Growing Up Bilingual: Puerto Rican Children in New York* (Malden, MA: Blackwell, 1997).

20. Alejandro Portes and Rubén G. Rumbaut, *Legacies: The Story of the Immigrant Second Generation* (Berkeley: University of California Press, and New York: Russell Sage Foundation, 2001).

21. Catherine Snow, "The Myths Around Bilingual Education." *NABE News* 21, no. 2 (1997): 29.

22. Luis C. Moll, "Bilingual Classroom Studies and Community Analysis: Some Recent Trends." *Educational Researcher* 21, no. 2 (1992): 20–24, p. 20.

23. Ana Celia Zentella, ed., *Building on Strengths: Language and Literacy in Latino Families and Communities* (New York: Teachers College Press, 2005).

24. National Center for Education Statistics, *Schools and Staffing Survey, 1999–2000: Overview of the Data for Public, Private, Charter, and Bureau of Indian Affairs Elementary and Secondary Schools* (Washington, DC: U.S. Department of Education, 2002): Table 1.19, pp. 43–44. Available at: nces.ed.gov/pubsearch/pubsinfor.asp?pubid+2002313

25. Patricia Gándara, Julie Maxwell-Jolly, and Anne Driscoll, *Listening to Teachers of English Learners* (Santa Cruz, CA: Center for the Study of Teaching and Learning, 2005).

26. Following are two excellent resources that focus on strategies and approaches for nonspecialist teachers who have ELLs in their classrooms: Carolyn Temple Adger, Catherine E. Snow, and Donna Christian, eds., *What Teachers Need to Know About Language.* Washington, DC: Center for Applied Linguistics, 2002; and Zeynep Beykont, ed., *The Power of Culture: Teaching Across Language Difference* (Cambridge, MA: Harvard Education Publishing Group, 2002).

27. Sonia Nieto, *The Light in Their Eyes: Creating Multicultural Learning Communities* (New York: Teachers College Press, 1999).

28. Jim Cummins, *Negotiating Identities: Education for Empowerment in a Diverse Society* (Ontario, CA: Calfornia Association for Bilingual Education, 1996): 73.

29. Stephen Krashen, *Second Language Acquisition and Second Language Learning* (New York: Pergamon Press, 1981).

30. For a more in-depth discussion of this issue, see Sonia Nieto, "Bringing Bilingual Education Out of the Basement, and Other Imperatives for Teacher Education." In *Lifting Every Voice: Pedagogy and Politics of Bilingual Education*, edited by Zeynep Beykont (Cambridge, MA: Harvard Educational Review, 2000).

31. Lily Wong Fillmore and Catherine E. Snow, "What Teachers Need to Know About Language." In *What Teachers Need to Know About Language*, edited by Carolyn Temple Adger, Catherine E. Snow, and Donna Christian (Washington, DC: Center for Applied Linguistics, 2002): 7–43, p. 43.

32. For early research on additive and subtractive bilingualism, see Wallace E. Lambert, "Culture and Language as Factors in Learning and Education." In *Education of Immigrant Students*, edited by A. Wolfgang (Toronto, Canada: Ontario Institute for Studies in Education, 1975).

33. David Schwarzer, Alexia Haywood, and Charla Lorenzen, "Fostering Multiliteracy in a Linguistically Diverse Classroom." *Language Arts* 80, no. 6 (July 2003): 453–460.

34. Terrence G. Wiley, *Literacy and Language Diversity in the United States*, 2nd ed. (Washington, DC: Center for Applied Linguistics, 2005).

35. Igoa, *The Inner World of the Immigrant Child*.

36. For a more extensive discussion of Bill Dunn's experience, see Nieto, *The Light in Their Eyes: Creating Multicultural Learning Communities*.

37. See, for example, Meg Gebhard, Theresa Austin, Sonia Nieto, and Jerri Willett, " 'You Can't Step on Someone Else's Words': Preparing All Teachers to Teach Language Minority Students." In *The Power of Culture: Teaching Across Language Difference*, edited by Zeynep Beykont (Cambridge, MA: Harvard Education Publishing Group, 2002).

38. See, for instance, María de la Luz Reyes and John Halcón, eds., *The Best for Our Children: Critical Perspectives on Literacy for Latino Students* (New York: Teachers College Press, 2001); Berta Pérez and María E. Torres-Guzmán, *Learning in Two Worlds: An Integrated Spanish/English Biliteracy Approach*, 3rd ed. (Boston: Allyn and Bacon, 2002); and María E. Fránquiz and María de la Luz Reyes, "Multicultural Language Practices: Opportunity, Inclusion and Choice." *Primary Voices* 8, no. 4 (2000): 3–10.

39. Skutnabb-Kangas, "Multilingualism and the Education of Minority Children." In *Minority Education: From Shame to Struggle*, edited by Tove Skutnabb-Kangas and Jim Cummins (Clevedon, England: Multilingual Matters, 1988).

40. *Lau v. Nichols*, 414 U.S. 563 (1974).

41. *Equal Educational Opportunities Act of 1974*, 20 U.S.C. ¶ 1703(f).

42. For in-depth descriptions of the many program models and their implications, see Terrence G. Wiley, *Literacy and Language Diversity in the United States*, 2nd ed. (McHenry, IL: Center for Applied Linguistics and Delta Systems, 2005).

43. See Elizabeth R. Howard, Donna Christian, and Fred Genesee, *The Development of Bilingualism and Biliteracy From Grade 3 to 5: A Summary of Findings From the CAL/CREDE Study of Two-Way Immersion Education* (University of California, Santa Cruz: Center for Research on Education, Diversity, and Excellence, 2004).

44. Kathryn J. Lindholm-Leary and Graciela Borsato, *Impact of Two-Way Bilingual Education Programs on Students' Attitudes Toward School and College* (Santa Barbara, CA: Center for Research on Education, Diversity, and Excellence, 2001).

45. Diane August and Timothy Shanahan, eds., *Developing Literacy in Second-Language Learners* (Mahwah, NJ: Lawrence Erlbaum; and Washington, DC: Center for Applied Linguistics, 2006). See also Wayne Thomas and Virginia Collier, *National Study of School Effectiveness for Language Minority Students' Long-Term Academic Achievement* (Santa Cruz, CA: Center for Research on Education, Diversity, and Excellence, 2003); Kellie Rolstad, Kate Mahoney, and Gene V. Glass, "The Big Picture: A Meta-Analy-sis of Program Effectiveness Research on English Language Learners." *Educational Policy* 19, no. 4 (September 2005): 572–594; and Stephen Krashen, "Bilingual Education Accelerates English Language Development." Available at: www.nabe.org/documents/krashen_intro.pdf. James Crawford also does an excellent job of summarizing the research on the effectiveness of bilingual education. See James Crawford, *Educating English Learners: Language Diversity in the Classroom*, 5th ed. (Los Angeles: Bilingual Education Services, 2004).

46. Jim Cummins, *Language, Power, and Pedagogy: Bilingual Children in the Crossfire* (Clevedon, England: Multilingual Matters, 2000).

47. See Editorial, "Tongue-Tied on Bilingual Education." *The New York Times,* September 2, 2005; and Bruce Fuller, "Good Bilingual Education Programs Produce Faster Results Than Good English-Only Programs." *Los Angeles Times,* August 24, 2005.

48. Portes and Rumbaut, *Legacies: The Story of the Immigrant Second Generation.*

49. Wayne Thomas and Virginia Collier, *National Study of School Effectiveness for Language Minority Students' Long-Term Academic Achievement* Santa Cruz, CA: Center for Research on Education, Diversity, and Excellence, 2003).

50. Gary Orfield and John T. Yun, *Resegregation in American Schools* (Cambridge, MA: Civil Rights Project at Harvard University, 1999).

51. A. Lin Goodwin, "Teacher Preparation and the Education of Immigrant Children." *Education and Urban Society* 34, no. 2 (February 2002): 156–172.

52. Luis C. Moll, "Sociocultural Competence in Teacher Education," Journal of *Teacher Education* 56, no. 3 (May/June 2005): 242–247.

CHAPTER 10 CASE STUDIES

Manuel Gomes

It's kind of scary at first, especially if you don't know the language.

The first thing you would notice about Manuel was that he was constantly on the move, as if the engine had started and he was ready to shift to fourth without moving through the other gears. Of slight stature and with a somewhat rumpled look, Manuel had an infectious and lively sense of humor and a generally positive attitude about life.

Manuel Gomes[1] had emigrated to Boston with his family from Cape Verde when he was 11 years old. When he was first interviewed, Manuel was 19 years old and was to graduate from high school that year. In many urban high schools, 19 is no longer a late age to graduate. In fact, many immigrant students graduate quite late. Immigrant and refugee students are more likely to be retained in-grade, to be inappropriately placed in special education, and to be at risk for being placed in low academic tracks on the basis of language differences or slow academic progress. That Manuel was soon to graduate from high school is noteworthy because the dropout rate for foreign-born students is close to 70 percent.[2]

Even before gaining its independence from Portugal in 1975, Cape Verde, an archipelago of ten large and several smaller islands off the West Coast of Africa, had a huge out-migration of its population. Official documents estimate that close to 180,000 Cape Verdeans emigrated voluntarily between 1970 and 1973, some 20,000 to the United States alone. The process of emigration had begun with the arrival of North American whaling boats from New England in the late 17th century. By the end of the 19th century, there was already a sizable Cape Verdean community in Massachusetts. Currently, well over twice as many Cape Verdeans reside abroad than live at home. The 325,000 who live in the United States (about equal to the number who reside on the islands) represent the largest Cape Verdean community outside of Cape Verde.[3]

Having suffered from more than 400 years of colonial neglect under Portugal, Cape Verde was left in poor economic and social condition. For example, the literacy rate in 1981 was 14 percent, a dramatic indication of the lack of educational opportunities available to the majority of the people. Since independence, the situation improved remarkably, and the literacy rate in 1987 was more than 57 percent.[4] Although the official language of the islands is Portuguese, the lingua franca is Crioulo, an Afro-Portuguese Creole.

Most Cape Verdeans in the United States live in New England, primarily in Rhode Island and Massachusetts. Manuel's family, like most, came to the United States for economic reasons. Although formerly farmers in Cape Verde, they quickly settled into the urban environment. Manuel's father found a job cleaning offices downtown at night, while his mother stayed home to take care of their many children. They came to Boston, which has a large Cape Verdean community, and they lived in a three-decker home with apartments occupied by other members of the large family. The neighborhood, once a working-class Irish community, had become multiracial, with a big Catholic church close by and Vietnamese and Cape Verdean restaurants up the street. The older homes, the din on the street, and the crowding all created to the sense of an aging but still vibrant urban community.

Manuel was the youngest of 11 children, and he would be the first in his family to graduate from high school. He had been in a bilingual program for several years after arriving in Boston. The language of instruction in the program was Crioulo. The State Assembly of Massachusetts passed legislation in 1977 distinguishing Crioulo as a language separate from Portuguese and required that Crioulo-speaking students be placed in separate programs from those for Portuguese-speaking students. The result was a scramble to find Crioulo-speaking teachers and aides and to develop appropriate materials, because few or none existed. The rationale for placing Cape Verdean students in a separate program, notwithstanding the administrative problems it could create, was pedagogically sound because students should be taught in the language they speak and understand, not in their second or third language.

A benefit of separating the program was that a strong sense of community among teachers, students, and parents developed. Some of the teachers and other staff in the program were intimately involved in the life of the community, and the separation that often exists between school and home, especially for immigrant children, was alleviated. Manuel's participation in the bilingual program proved to be decisive in his education because it allowed a less traumatic transition to the English language and U.S. culture. Nevertheless, he constantly referred to how hard it had been to "fit in," both in school and in society in general.

Boston, like most big cities in the United States, is a highly diverse metropolitan area. It is not unusual to walk from street to street and hear languages from all over the world, smell the foods of different continents, and hear the music of a wide variety of cultures. In spite of this diversity, and perhaps in part because of it, the city is not without its tensions, including diverse economic vested interests and interethnic hostility. These tensions are evident in many arenas, including the schools. The attendant problems of segregation, with a long and tumultuous history in the city, are still apparent. The city's schools, for example, have experienced a vast decrease in the percentage of White and middle-class students since court-ordered desegregation and, although once highly regarded, have lost both resources and prestige.

Manuel's plans for the future were sketchy, but when interviewed, he was working in a downtown hotel and wanted to use the accounting skills he learned in high school to find a job at a bank. His positive experience in a theater class as a sophomore, along with his great enthusiasm and expressiveness, also sparked a desire to continue in the acting field. He had also talked of continuing his education by attending a community college.

Manuel was excited and proud of graduating from high school but reflected on the pain and fear of immigration. This is the major theme that characterized Manuel's experiences, both as a student and as an immigrant to this society. The role reversals within his family is another central theme that emerged. Finally, the *mediating role of bilingual education* in his success as a student was evident. Each of these themes is further explored in the following sections.

The pain and fear of immigration

We have a different way of living in Cape Verde than in America. Our culture is totally different, so we have to start a different way of living in America. It's kind of confusing when you come to America, you know.

I liked going to school in Cape Verde, you know, 'cause you know everybody and you have all your friends there. In our country, we treat people different. There's no crime. You don't have to worry about people jumping you, taking your money, or walking at night by yourself. There's no fear for that, you know. In Cape Verde, you don't have to worry about something happening to your child, or you don't have to worry about using drugs.

My father and mother used to work on plantations. We used to grow potatoes; we used to grow corn; we used to grow beans and stuff like that. We had a lot of land. Every season, we farmed. We had cows. Me and my brother used to feed the cows and take them to walk and give them water to drink and stuff like that. We used to sell our milk to rich folks, and I used to deliver [it]. It was kinda fun. These rich people, every time I'd go there, they'd feed me, which I liked very much [*laughs*]. They used to give me cake and stuff like that, cookies. I liked that. We'd have a lot of crops and we'd give some away to poor people, those that don't have any. We had a lot of friends and stuff like that.

When we came to America, it was totally different.

In Cape Verde, they have this rumor that it's easier to make a living up here. So everybody wants to come up here. They have this rumor that once you get here, you find money all around you, you know. So, when you're, like, coming up here, they make a big commotion out of it: "Oh, you're going to America, rich country", and stuff like that. So they think once you come here, you got it made . . . you're rich. People in our country actually think that we're rich here, that we are filthy rich, that money surrounds us—we eat money!

I was disappointed in a lot of ways [when we came here], especially with the crime, especially with the kids. They don't respect each other; they don't respect their parents. It's very different here. It's very tough.

I was afraid. I had people jumping me a few times, trying to take my wallet and stuff like that. It's a scary situation. It didn't really bother me, but like what got to me, is, if they try to start a fight with you, you go to tell, like, a teacher, they couldn't do nothing about it. That's what got to me, you know?

It was a few students. I know this kid, this big Black kid. He tried to fight me, like, three times. Then I had a brother that was going to the same middle school, so he had a fight with my brother, my big brother. After that, it calmed down a little bit, you know?

Kids might try to stab you if you probably step on them. That happened to me once. I stepped on this kid's sneaker once, and he tried to fight me. He

said, "What you doing?" I said that I'm sorry and he said, "That's not enough," and he tried to punch me. He didn't, but he was very furious.

You gotta get used to it. That's why a lot of Cape Verdean kids, when they get here, they change. They become violent, like some of the kids in America. So, it's sad. It's very hard for the parents. The parents are not used to that, and it's happening [to] a lot with parents in our neighborhood. It's happening to our family. I have a cousin, and his mother tried to commit suicide because her son was dealing drugs and hanging with the wrong crowd, with all these hoods. The son almost died because someone beat him up so bad. And it's sad, you know?

They try to be strict about it, you know. But with kids, they try to copy kids that were born here. They try to be like them. They try to go out and do the stuff that *they're* doing. It's like teen pressure, you know? So, it's very hard, you know? You want to fit in. You like to fit in with the crowd. If you hang with the wrong crowd, you're going to be in big trouble. You just change . . . and you're going to be a person that you don't want to be. You'll probably end up in jail.

I been here eight years, and I never hang with the wrong crowd. I've never used drugs in my life. I've never *smelled* cigarettes. So, I really hate when I see other kids doing it. It's sad when you see especially your friends doing it. So I had to say, "Go away. I don't want that life." So I had to separate from them. I had a hard time finding friends that wasn't doing that stuff like they were doing. It's very hard if you hate what your friends are doing.

Start learning the language was hard for me. And then start making friends, because you gotta start making new friends. When American students see you, it's kinda hard [to] get along with them when you have a different culture, a different way of dressing and stuff like that. So kids really look at you and laugh, you know, at the beginning.

It was difficult like when you see a girl at school that you like. It's kind of difficult to express yourself and tell her the way you feel about her, you know? When you don't even know the language, it's kind of hard. I had a hard time. It's kind of scary at first, especially if you don't know the language and, like, if you don't have friends there. Some people are slow to learn the language and some just catch it up easy. It wasn't easy for me . . . like, the pronunciation of the words and stuff like that. Like, in Portuguese and in English, they're different. It's kinda hard, you know?

I don't think I want to be an American citizen. To tell you the truth, I don't like America at all. [Well], I *like* it, but I don't like the lifestyles. It's different from my point of view. What I'm thinking of doing is work in America for 10 years and go back to my country, because America's a violent country. It's dangerous with crime, with drugs.

Role reversals within the family

I took [my father] to the hospital. Then I found out that he had cancer. I didn't wanna tell him. The doctor told me that he had cancer. I didn't wanna tell him because he hates to get sick and he hates to die! He hates to die. If you tell him he's gonna die, he'll kill you before he dies!

This happened when I was in school, so I was missing school a lot. I was the only one that was able to understand the language and stuff like that. It actually got to the point that I had to tell him. It was, like, sad when I had to tell him because it's very hard to tell him that he had cancer.

Because they don't speak English, I have to go places with them to translate and stuff like that. So I'm usually busy. We have a big family, you know. I have to help them out.

If I felt like I had support from my family, if they only knew the language. . . . If they were educated, I could make it big, you see what I'm saying? I would've had a better opportunity, a better chance.

I'm very happy about [graduating]. It means a lot to me. It means that I did something that I'm very proud [of]. It feels good, you know? And I'd really like to continue in my education because, you know, I'm the first one. And I want to be successful with my life. I just wanted to help them, you know? I wanted to be the one to help them. They didn't support me, but I wanted to support them.

My mother's proud of me. My father is too. It was tough for me when I found out that my father had cancer because, you know, I really wanted to graduate. I just want to show him that I can be somebody, you know? I actually did this, try to graduate from high school, for him, you know?

Bilingual education as linguistic and cultural mediator

A Cape Verdean person is usually, he looks like he's a nice person, educated, you know? Not all of them, but like 70 percent of Cape Verdeans, they look educated. They're not violent. You can tell someone is Cape Verdean . . . if he starts pointing at you. That's a sign that he's Cape Verdean automatic. If he starts staring at you, he's Cape Verdean. We have problems when we look at American people. They might think we are talking about them and stuff like that, so we have to change that behavior. We have to get used to not pointing at people and not looking at them very much, because American people are not used to people staring at them.

What we do in our country, we *observe* people. It don't mean nothing to us Cape Verdeans. It's just normal. But if we do it to an American person, it makes that American person nervous, I guess, and he would ask you, "What are you looking at?" or "Why are you looking at me?" and start questioning and probably start trouble with you.

It's normal to us. That's why other people got to understand that not everybody has the same culture; not everybody is the same. So some people don't understand.

Like a Spanish [Hispanic] person, what he usually do, they use their body in a different way. With [Hispanic people], what they do, they point with their lips. They go [*demonstrates puckering of the lips*]. So, that's different. Other cultures, they might use their head; they might use their eyebrows.

It's good to understand other people's culture from different countries. America is made up of different countries, and we all should know a little bit about each one's cultures.

I think [teachers] could help students, try to influence them . . . that they can do whatever they want to do, that they can be whatever they want to be, that they got opportunities out there. Most schools don't encourage kids to be all they can be.

What they need to do is try to know the student before they influence him. If you don't know a student, there's no way to influence him. If you don't know his background, there's no way you are going to get in touch with him. There's no way you're going to influence him if you don't know where he's been.

You cannot forget about [your culture], you know? It's part of you. You can't forget something like that. . . . You gotta know who you are. You cannot deny your country and say "I'm an American; I'm not Cape Verdean." That's something that a lot of kids do when they come to America. They change their names. Say you're Carlos—they say, "I'm Carl." They wanna be American; they're not Cape Verdean. That's wrong. They're fooling themselves.

I identify myself as Cape Verdean. I'm Cape Verdean. I cannot be an American because I'm not an American. That's it.

[*Describe yourself as a student*] I'm not a genius [*laughing*]! [But] I know that I can do whatever I want to do in life. Whatever I want to do, I know I could make it. I believe that strongly.

Commentary

Manuel was eloquent in expressing his concerns as an immigrant and student, concerns related to his academic success and his motivation for graduating and possibly continuing his education. But, behind the sometimes forced enthusiasm he displayed, Manuel's voice was also tinged with sadness at what might have been. His expression changed when talking about his early experiences in Cape Verde. In spite of the obviously difficult circumstances of going to school—where he was in a crowded, one-room schoolhouse with many other students of all ages and where corporal punishment was a common practice—over the years, Manuel had idealized his experiences there. He seemed to have forgotten the harsh life he had in Cape Verde, although he did admit that he did not like farming. In spite of the difficulties, life there was, at least when he reflected on it years later, easier and more familiar. Manuel often contrasted the crime and violence in the United States with his romanticized memories of a bucolic childhood in Cape Verde.

With obvious pain, Manuel described what it was like being perceived as different by his peers when he first arrived in the United States. For example, other kids would call him names (" 'foreigner' and stuff like that") and ridicule him ("It really gets to a student when other students make fun"). The situation

had changed after he reached high school, but those first years were indelibly etched in his memory.

The distress caused by immigration is multifaceted. Not only do immigrants leave behind a country that is loved and an existence that is at least familiar, if not comfortable, but they also leave a language and culture that can never find full expression in their adopted country. In addition, they are coming into a situation that, although it may offer many exciting possibilities, nonetheless is often frightening and new. Manuel was ambivalent about his experience in the United States.

Several of the painful incidents described by Manuel focus on interethnic rivalries and violence. This situation is a guarded secret, especially at many urban schools. School officials, perhaps fearful of being labeled racists, are reluctant to confront the prejudicial behaviors and actions of one group of students toward another, whether they involve conflicts between Black and White students or between different students of color, yet the issue is real and is becoming more apparent all the time. Racial stereotypes and epithets are commonplace, voiced by even the most seemingly sensitive students. For example, Manuel's comment about a "big Black kid" reinforces the negative stereotype of African American as frightening and violent.

Many immigrant children experience role reversals with their parents as a result of their parents' lack of English fluency as well as their lack of knowledge of U.S. customs. Based on their extensive studies of immigrant children, Alejandro Portes and Rubén Rumbaut explain: "This role reversal occurs when children's acculturation has moved so far ahead of their parents' that key family decisions become dependent on the children's knowledge."[5] Manuel had the role of "language broker" in his family because his was the public face that interacted with the greater community. Manuel's role as translator was especially prominent when his father developed cancer a few years before. Because his parents spoke little English, Manuel was placed in the extraordinary position of being the one to tell him that he had cancer. This experience had a great impact on Manuel, especially because the cancer was considered terminal. He also had to tell his father that he needed an operation, not an easy task given his father's memories of Cape Verde, where surgery was used only as a last resort and where, according to Manuel, the chances of recovery were slim. Although his father recovered from the cancer against all the odds, the experience left Manuel shaken. His grades also suffered during that period.

Many immigrant students play the role of family interpreter and arbiter, resulting in the transfer of authority and status from parents to children, which in turn can lead to further conflicts at home. In addition, teachers not accustomed to this kind of adult responsibility often interpret students' absences and lateness as a sign that their parents do not care about education or that the students are irresponsible. Frequently, just the opposite is true. Immigrant parents are not oblivious to the benefits of education, but they often need support in attending to their basic needs. Here is where the school, as an advocate of children and their families, can come in. The school can help by finding needed services or by helping parents devise ways to attend to family needs without keeping their children out of school.

There may also be different perceptions of family involvement among immigrant parents. Manuel's parents, for example, rarely visited his school. This is not surprising: Parent involvement in schools in most countries is minimal because, in these countries, the feeling is that, after children begin school, it is the school's responsibility to educate them. The parents, in essence, hand over their children to the school, trusting that the school will educate them. To jump to the conclusion that these parents do not care about education is to miss the mark. On the contrary, most economically oppressed parents see the role of education as extremely important and stress this to their children constantly.

By the time he got to high school, Manuel had learned enough English to be able to speak up. He said that the bilingual program at the high school provided a safe environment for him and other Cape Verdean students. It was a rather large program, much larger than the one at the middle school, and most of the teachers and some of the other staff were Cape Verdean as well. Cape Verdean students in the city had a strong identification with this high school and looked forward to attending it. In fact, it was always one of the more constructive and distinguishing characteristics of this particular urban school. That the bilingual program acted as a linguistic and cultural mediator was evident in many of Manuel's comments. For example, he was extremely perceptive about culture and its manifestations. This perceptiveness is a common by-product of bilingual programs, in which culture and language become a natural aspect of the curriculum. The description of how his Latino classmates use their lips to point rather than their fingers demonstrates Manuel's sensitivity and sophistication in understanding nonverbal cues. Many teachers, even those who work with students from different cultures, fail to pick up these sometimes subtle cues.

Manuel spoke fondly of his experiences with the teachers and students in the program. He said that it was "more comfortable" for him there. The program also helped mediate his experiences in the rest of the school and in his community in general. For example, he remembered the theater workshop that he took as a sophomore (a project that was unfortunately eliminated shortly thereafter). Although it was not part of the bilingual program and all the skits were in English, it focused on issues that were relevant to immigrant and language-minority students. Manuel recalled with great enthusiasm a monologue he did about a student going to a new school, a situation he could identify with because it was so reminiscent of his own experiences.

The significance of the bilingual program in Manuel's life cannot be over-emphasized, and this has been true for many Cape Verdean and other language-minority students in Massachusetts. It is especially ironic, then, that Massachusetts became one of the latest casualties in the national attacks against bilingual education. Massachusetts, the first state to pass legislation mandating bilingual education in 1971, became one of the states to eliminate it in 2002. The bilingual program helped Manuel retain his language and culture and, with it, his ties to his family and community. It gave him something to "hold onto." Even this kind of program, however, is not enough if it is not part of a larger whole that affirms the diversity of all within it. It and other bilingual programs like it become tiny islands in a sea of homogeneity and pressure to conform.

One of the ways Manuel dealt with finding a place to fit in was by joining and becoming very active in a fundamentalist Christian church. As Manuel so eloquently expressed it, "That's the place I belong to. I fit there. I felt that God had moved there. Jesus got hold of me. He said, 'Calm down.' " A number of issues were apparently influential in leading Manuel to this particular church. It was about this time that his father developed cancer and Manuel was immersed in his role as "the man of the family." It was also around the time that he decided to drop some of his friends (as he said, "It's very hard if you hate what your friends are doing"). In looking for something to keep him on track, as the bilingual program and other cultural supports had done previously, he looked toward the community. Although Manuel had been raised a Catholic, the local Catholic church was completely unappealing to him. This, too, became an issue of "fitting in." Manuel said that the Catholic church had made few accommodations to its newest members, many of whom were immigrants who spoke little or no English. His new church, however, seems to have gone to great lengths to welcome Cape Verdeans, and Manuel felt he had finally found a place to fit in.

The tension of fitting in was well articulated by Manuel when he pitted being Cape Verdean against being American. He did not perceive the possibility that he could be *both* Cape Verdean *and* American as an option. That is, if he identified with being American, he felt he was abandoning his culture and country; on the other hand, if he chose to remain Cape Verdean, his possibilities in this society might be limited. These are hard choices for young people to make and are part of the pain of living in a culture that has a rigid definition of "American."

Reflect on This Case Study

1. Considering some of the ways in which Manuel's experiences as an immigrant were frightening and painful, what can teachers and schools do to help?

2. Why do you think Manuel idealized his former life on the Cape Verde Islands?

3. What can account for Manuel's highly developed sensitivity to cultural differences? What can teachers and schools learn from this?

4. Given Manuel's many absences from school during his father's illness, it is probable that school authorities and teachers assumed that his family was wrong in keeping him home to attend to family business. What do you think? What could the school have done to accommodate his family's needs?

5. Why was it important for Manuel to graduate "for" his father?

6. How do you think the bilingual program acted as a linguistic and cultural mediator for Manuel? What can teachers in nonbilingual programs learn from this?

7. Do you understand why Manuel felt reluctant to identify himself as "American"? How would you approach this issue if he was one of your students?

Alicia Montejo

My sister uses the word Hispanic or Latino; I'm Mexican: I am really Mexican.

When she was first interviewed, Alicia Montejo[1] was finishing ninth grade at Red Rock High School in greater Denver, Colorado. Alicia's mother had died three years earlier and she had moved a few times since then. She was born and raised in a mid-size Texas border city and had been living there with her stepdad. His family served as her legal guardians for about 18 months. Then she moved to Colorado with her older sister, who became her legal guardian just six months before this interview.

Alicia attended preschool through sixth grade in a South Texas school district where school records cite the student population as 98 percent Hispanic and 93 percent economically disadvantaged. The district also lists the K–12 population as 51 percent Limited English Proficient. Being Mexican, speaking Spanish, and experiencing economic struggles were inseparable realities central to Alicia's life, both at home and school.

The school that Alicia attended for her freshman year is a public high school that had been created during massive district-wide reform as part of the Colorado Small Schools Initiative (CSSI),[2] which was funded by a grant from the Bill & Melinda Gates Foundation.[3] The school district, serving 5,700 students, transformed one large high school into seven distinct, small high schools, offering students a choice of enrollment. In Alicia's case, Red Rock High School met some of the district's objectives to create "personalized secondary learning environments that challenged and engaged students, supporting high standards for all."[4] However, it fell short in challenging Alicia to her fullest potential. The built-in option to transfer to one of the seven new high schools within the district appealed to Alicia, who said that she hoped to transfer to another school where she "could be pushed harder."

A 2006 report from the National Research Council on the perils of underinvestment in U.S. Hispanic youth paints a distressing portrait of Mexican American students' academic achievement and the difficulties they face.[5] According to the report, in 2003, the poverty rate for Mexican origin children was estimated at 28 percent, well above the national average of 17 percent for those under age 18.[6] Complex socioeconomic circumstances, combined with severely unequal schooling conditions from preschool through high school, create devastating and enduring consequences for Mexican American youth.[7] Among many factors that conspire to perpetuate this situation are low expectations of teachers and brutally under-resourced schools.[8] In a 20-year comparison of test scores reported in the National Assessment of Educational Progress, Hispanic students continue to lag behind Whites throughout middle and high school. These gaps are widest for Mexican Americans, the fastest-growing segment of the elementary school population.[9]

Even though the number of Hispanic college graduates has reached an all-time high, too many students of Mexican origin are still not completing high school.[10] When examining data on those who make it through high school, the dropout rate—or what some activists and researchers have called the *pushout rate*—is holding steady.[11] Tara J. Yosso's analysis of the data on the "K–12 educational pipeline" revealed that for every 100 Chicana/o students entering elementary school, only 44 graduate from high school. Her study also showed that for every 100 Chicana/o students, only 7 graduate with a bachelors degree, 2 earn a masters, and 1 earns a doctorate degree.[12]

Within this sociopolitical context, three themes emerge from Alicia's case study; she tells us a great deal about her perspective on her Mexican heritage and education. The role of Spanish language in shaping her identity is pervasive throughout these themes: *desire for academic challenge; family, respect, and expectations;* and *interconnectedness of language, identity, and learning,* with which we begin.

Interconnectedness of language, identity, and learning

My dad and my mom, they came from Mexico. They moved here before I was born, but I was born here; Mexican American. All I say is that I am Mexican; my sister uses the word *Hispanic* or *Latino;* I'm Mexican: I am really Mexican.

Being Latino, it's good 'cause a lot of people tell me it's a good advantage for me to know two languages. I like that. Sometimes it's frustrating. I know English, but not perfect English. Sometimes it gets frustrating that you don't know what something's called in English.

By the time I was in first grade, I already had all my English. The school did have a program [for English language learners], but I didn't have to go to it. It worked out for me pretty good. Nobody at home taught me. I just learned from my friends in preschool and my teachers. My parents, they didn't speak English, so I guess I pushed myself really hard to learn English. My parents were pushing me really hard to learn English, they were, like, "You gotta learn it!"

I remember my pre-K teacher 'cause she helped me a lot. She taught me English. She spent time with me after school and everything. I had no friends then, and my teachers made me feel good. They were there for me and they helped me out. There was this one time where I didn't really know much English, but my friend next to me, she had to do her homework and she spoke pure Spanish, and I helped her out. That made me feel really good that I helped other people out with what they didn't know and what they did know. But still, I get frustrated sometimes when my friends need help or whatever and I don't know to help them out.

Now, in Colorado my friends are a little different. There are a lot of Mexican people here, but not as much as there were in Texas. There's mountains. You could see some of the mountains from here. There's different kinds of people, like African Americans, Latinos, White people, Asians. In Texas, I had friends from other kinds of groups, but mostly Mexican. In Texas, almost everybody spoke Spanish. Here in Colorado, some people speak Spanish, but lots don't. Here the Mexicans come from lots of different [regions in Mexico]. In Texas, everybody was from the same place. Here, even some of the Mexicans don't speak Spanish.

A lot of White people do not know Spanish. White people don't know how to pronounce stuff in Spanish, or they don't know Spanish at all. And they have a hard time communicating. Then there's some kids at our school that know pure Spanish, and they want to communicate with them but they can't. It's probably frustrating for them to not be able to talk to each other—communicate to other people that know a different language or something. But I can talk to everybody.

[If I could give advice to the school] I would tell teachers to help the Mexican kids who don't speak English. Help them a little but don't leave them behind, and don't do the work for them. Have a special class for them at one point in the day at least, but mostly regular classes. Then have a time when they can learn and use Spanish, and flash cards with the different languages—and learning how to speak better English—and learn in English and Spanish, both languages in school.

If a new Latino student came to our school, I would tell them not to give up. I mean, if they only know Spanish, not to give up. Just to try and understand as much as you can, or try to ask somebody that speaks both languages. It might be frustrating for them not to understand what their teachers are saying, but don't give up.

What I would advise teachers is to learn Spanish so they can teach [ELL Latino students]. Latinos that know pure Spanish, they get frustrating just to sit there and not be able to know what the teacher's talking about. They just sit there and they get a worksheet. They don't know what to do with it and they have to ask somebody. It would be frustrating. And then the [bilingual] students might not be able to explain to them right, and they get frustrating. Tell teachers just not to get frustrated with students that speak Spanish or other languages. Just try your best to communicate with them. The school does have teachers come in and translate the lessons for the Mexican kids, but all I saw was one for that one class.

When teachers understand our culture they speak to us in Spanish. Mr. Thomas, my humanities teacher, he knows Spanish 'cause he's married to a Mexican woman. He talks to everybody in Spanish! The people that know Spanish come to him and he tells me to translate to them something that I need to help them with, like a worksheet. You can tell if a teacher understands our culture by other stuff, too. Like in the art room, there's, like, Mexican stuff put up and all that: Mexican flag, Mexican paintings.

To get to know my culture, I would tell teachers to understand my language. Take a course or something; take courses. The other way they can learn about our culture is by asking us about it. Ask us.

Family, respect, and expectations

The person that I most admire is my sister. She went through a lot when she was small. She married a good husband. He doesn't do drugs, he don't cuss, he don't smoke or nothing. He's got a nice job. He's respectful to her. She made a lot of good choices. Like when she was a teenager, she didn't get pregnant or anything 'til now that she's married and she got a nice job. She really made a lot of good choices. Her and her husband. They act like my parents.

My mom talked to me about me growing up and having a good life. Not to let myself go with any guy or whatever, not to have sex: to protect myself. Nothing is holding me back from getting a good education, unless I get pregnant, which I probably won't. I'm scared for that. But, nothing's keeping me back. I'm more into school than that. Right now, I wouldn't be ready for a kid. I want to go on in school. I want to go straight to college and get a career and after I have a career and then maybe have children. One of my friends just had a baby and she's really struggling. I wouldn't want to be like that. I'm gonna do the same thing my sister did. I'm gonna wait till I grow up, have a nice job, and then think about babies.

My family taught me just to value school. Value what I have. All my family is positive about school. Since my dad was Mexican, he didn't really have many chances—he's like a construction [worker] or something like that. He told me that Mexicans don't have a lot of choice in work 'cause they're not legal from the United States. Doing good in school is to get a chance to do stuff that most of my family hasn't been able to do; to get a good job and have money, be able to raise a family.

From my family, I learned respect and manners. Well, my mom passed away in 2002; she's not here with us anymore. But she was really positive about school. My dad, he works—he's still alive but he's working off in a place [far from here]. They just tell me to get an education, to grow up and have a good job and a good family.

I was a good student when I was younger and I still am. My family, they taught me well. How to be respectful and everything, and how much school is important. Sometimes I think about ditching, but I don't, 'cause I'm a really good student. I have to do my work 'cause school is important to me. I know I complain a lot, but it is important to me. I'm friendly. I am respectful, most of the time. I help other people when they need help and if I know how, I'll help them. Pretty much, I'm responsible. Not all the time, but I'm responsible. But, when I'm having a bad day, or when teachers really get on my nerves, that's when I'm not that respectful. I talk back or I ignore them. I just tell them "Leave me alone," "Don't talk to me," or I'll just don't talk to them. I'll listen to them, but I won't talk to them. And you can tell right away whenever I have that look or whenever I roll my eyes.

My sister, she's very positive about me going to school. She wouldn't want me to drop out or anything like that. Her husband, he's the same way. They're really positive about school. He tells me stories, like, to get a good job. 'Cause not a lot of people have that chance to get an education and have a good job. People [who drop out] are usually [working] at Burger King or McDonalds or something, or a grocery store.

My sister is involved in the school. She works at a school. She's a teacher's aide with four-year-olds in the . . . pre-school. She likes it. She's thinking of getting a degree and her own job, I mean her own classroom for herself where she's teaching. She wants me to go to college. She's told me before and she talks to me about it a lot. [She asks about] what colleges do I want to go into, or whatever. My sister and her husband, they're there whenever I need help. They're fun to be around. But, my sister's a little bit uptight because she's never had to take care of a teenager.

Grades are important to me. I don't like a C or below. I love to make my family happy. Making them feel good, letting them know that I do good in school and that I try to keep my grades up high. Grades are

important at home. My sister and her husband, they would want a B or above. They would prefer an A. They'll talk to me and they'll help me out with whatever I need, but they would rather an A. But they're not too happy with the C's. I mean they're OK with it, but they would rather an A.

Desire for academic challenge

School ended up pretty good freshman year [at Red Rock High School]. It was pretty good; it could have been a lot better. I liked how we actually could go out in fieldwork and actually learn stuff, not in school but the actual place where history happened. I wouldn't mind getting pushed a little bit harder. When there was a little bit more of a challenge, I did good. I got As, Bs, and Cs. I only got one D in my whole life. When I got that D, me and the teacher, we kinda knocked heads. We didn't work together. I could do better. I could be pushed more.

I want to go to Mountain Academy—they push you a little harder there. They don't really get to go out on field trips as much, but I want a new environment. I want something that's going to help me a little bit more—push me a little harder. Mountain Academy is more challenging. I want to be pushed harder. I want to meet new people. I want to see what's better for me.

I think [the teachers at Red Rock High School should] maybe get it to the next level. Mainly, when we wrote stuff, they don't push you hard. For your last final grade for the trimester, they would just pick your highest grade and give you that. Other kids passed when they were just not really doing the work in class. I feel like I slacked off a bit. I am a talkative person and sometimes I talked too much.

[In school] we have talked about what we want to do or be, but we don't talk much about college. In the future, I see me being a person that actually has nice work that's got money. I could support my kids that I have and the family. Help my family out and everything. Just a nice future. I am thinking of going into the medical field when I graduate, or the law enforcement field. Nobody is talking with me about helping me choose classes. [I am hoping to become] a doctor for children, a pediatrician or else law enforcement, border patrol . . . I am not interested in law enforcement as much as I was when I lived in Texas, but I am still thinking about it. When I lived in Texas, I lived near the border, and I saw the border patrol trucks all over the place. Now I am thinking a doctor—helping children.

Commentary

The fusion of language and cultural identity became obvious during Alicia's interview. Her family and home community deeply influenced the intertwined relationship of her mother tongue and distinctive ways of life. She seemed shocked to discover that in Colorado, there are Mexicans who don't speak Spanish. As she changed communities and geographic region, the role of her bilingualism changed. Her perspective grew from taking her bilingualism for granted as intrinsic to everyday life, to perceiving her language skills as a precious asset, realizing that "some kids lose their Spanish, their own language." Although she had been academically bilingual since first grade, Alicia referred to Spanish as her language and equated knowing it with knowing her culture.

Notably, Alicia referred to the monolingual Spanish-speaking Mexican students as "knowing pure Spanish." At no time in the interview did she use deficit labels commonly heard in school policies and practices such as "non-English speaking"; "students without English"; or "limited English proficient." She consistently referred to those peers as "pure Spanish speakers" and supported bilingual education even though she herself did not participate in such a program.

In terms of advice for teachers, Alicia urged them to get to know her culture by learning to understand her language. She emphasized the importance of being patient with pure Spanish speakers and recommended offering support while still providing challenge. In addition, she encouraged teachers to "ask the kids." Her statements echo my (Patty's) research findings that urban students continually urge teachers to "just ask kids about their culture."[13] Alicia's insistence on being challenged academically also resonates with a great deal of other research that has found that many students view school curriculum as not challenging enough, contributing to decisions to drop out.[14] In a broad survey of more than 500 students who did not com-

plete high school, 47 percent cited boredom and irrelevant curriculum as reasons for dropping out, challenging the myth that these students may be incapable of the work.[15]

Carlos Cortés points out that negative societal views and racial stereotypes are pervasive in mass media and popular culture.[16] Alicia's refusal to settle for limited opportunities and to accept stereotypical messages contributed to the construction of a "counterstory." Moreover, Alicia's words resonate with the work of researcher Tara J. Yosso who writes about the "very serious leaks" in the Chicana/Chicano educational pipeline. The harmful stereotypes stem from a "majoritarian story" that assumes all people enjoy access to equal education, faulting Chicana/o students for not taking advantage of that equal opportunity. In Yosso's work, counterstories point out the bias in the majoritarian story and reveal the structural, practical, and discursive influences that facilitate the high dropout (pushout) rates along the Chicana/o educational pipeline.[17]

Supporting and working for family and strong identification with, and solidarity among, family members are qualities that are held in high esteem in most Mexican communities.[18] Because of the centrality of the role of family in Mexican culture, and Alicia's perspective as a contemporary Latina and an academic high-achiever, she may have been zig-zagging through multiple cultural intersections in trying to negotiate statements about what is expected of Mexicans. Straddling the realms of race, class, and gender are especially challenging for a youth in her position.

Despite the various social and institutional structures that can impede academic success, Alicia was committed to continuing her academic achievement by trying to enroll in a different high school that would offer "more of a push." Her statements about the importance of school and grades express her family's values and teachings of *respeto*. Linking the completion of high school with a "nice future," she said she had aspirations to go to college and become a professional: either a medical doctor or a border patrol officer. While the latter may seem an ironic choice for a first-generation Mexican American, the social context reveals a great deal. In her economically strapped community on the Texas border, one of the only professional opportunities to which she was exposed was driving a border patrol truck. Her imagined engagement in border patrol also indexes what Ricardo D. Stanton-Salazar refers to as "playing host to the system." He argues, following the work of Bowles and Gintis, as well as Freire, that for many Mexican-origin urban youth, the diminished pool of resources, lack of institutional support, structured segregation, and cultural alienation lead community members to reproduce the unequal, hierarchical relations of the racialized, patriarchal capitalist society.[19]

Alicia's goals are visibly tied to making her family proud and her hope to adequately provide for a future family. These perspectives point to the urgency of wide-ranging curriculum choices and the role of expansive career and college counseling, especially for youth who are first-generation college-bound students, as their parents/guardians may be unfamiliar with the complexities of the U.S. educational system.[20] The cultural capital and social fluency required to be admitted to, and eventually succeed in, a quality college cannot be underestimated.

Alicia certainly demonstrated agency (i.e., her role as an agent in her own success). She was actively seeking supportive institutional structures. It remains to be seen if the structures and cultural processes at her new school provide the robust academic challenge and collaborative relationships that would help her succeed. With the median age of the Chicana/o population at 24 years and the Mexican and Mexican American community as the largest growing students of people of color in U.S. schools, the educational opportunities available to Alicia and her peers is a matter of moral urgency.

Notes to Chapter 10 Case Studies

Manuel Gomes

1. We are grateful to Carol Shea for the interviews and transcriptions and for many valuable insights in the development of this case study. After over 30 years in urban education, mostly at Madison Park High School in Boston as an English and theatre arts teacher and then as a school counselor, Carol is now involved in counselor training and in developing resources and support programs that assist young women in meeting their personal and educational needs.

2. Gary Orfield, ed., *Dropouts in America: Confronting the Graduate Rate Crisis* (Cambridge, MA: Harvard Education Press, 2004): 1–11.
3. Colm Foy, *Cape Verde: Politics, Economics, and Society* (London: Pinter, 1988).
4. Foy, *Cape Verde*.
5. See Alejandro Portes and Rubén Rumbaut, *Legacies: The Story of the Immigrant Second Generation* (Berkeley, CA: University of California Press; and New York: Russell Sage Foundation 2001).

Alicia Montejo

1. We appreciate the work of Stephanie Schmidt, an art teacher at Bear Creek High School in Colorado, who interviewed Alicia and helped us with many details for the case study.
2. For more information about the Colorado Small Schools Initiative (CSSI), see www.coloradosmallschools.org.
3. The Bill & Melinda Gates Foundation states on its website, www.gatesfoundation.org/Education, that "the Bill & Melinda Gates Foundation is committed to raising the high school graduation rate and helping all students—regardless of race or family income—graduate as strong citizens ready for college and work." The Gates Foundation has made a positive impact in many urban communities, yet questions remain about the use of private money for funding public schools. For a critique of the current movement to privately fund school reform, using the "small schools" banner, and a cautionary statement about abandoning the social justice concerns of the early small schools movement, see Michelle Fine, "Not in Our Name: Reclaiming the Democratic Vision on Small School Reform." *Rethinking Schools* 19, no. 4 (Summer 2005).
4. To protect the participant's anonymity, the school documents are not disclosed here.
5. See Marta Tienda and Faith Mitchell, eds., *Multiple Origins, Uncertain Destinies: Hispanics and the American Future: Panel on Hispanics in the United States*. Committee on Population, Division of Behavioral and Social Sciences and Education (Washington, DC: The National Academies Press, 2006). Electronic PDF version, accessed July 2006. http:fermat.nap.edu/catalog/11314.html

6. Tienda and Mitchell, eds., *Multiple Origins, Uncertain Destinies: Hispanics and the American Future,* 97. Also see U.S. Census Bureau, Hispanic Population Passes 40 Million, 2005. Available at: www.census.gov/PressRelease/www/releases/archives/population/005164.html; accessed July, 2006.

7. On the topic of unequal schooling, numerous studies provide data on the structural and institutional inequalities of the schooling of children of Mexican origin, noting the detrimental outcomes as well as the resilience of many students. See, for example, Robert Crosnoe, "Double Disadvantage or Signs of Resilience? The Elementary School Contexts of Children from Mexican Immigrant Families." *American Educational Research Journal* 42 no. 2 (2005): 269–303; and Robert Crosnoe, Monica Kirkpatrick, and Glen H. Elder, Jr., "School Size and the Interpersonal Side of Education: An Examination of Race/Ethnicity and Organizational Context." *Social Sciences Quarterly* 85 no. 5 (2004): 1259–1274. For more context, also see Richard R. Valencia, *Chicano School Failure and Success: Past, Present, and Future* (New York: Routledge/Falmer Press, 2002).

8. See, for example, B. Schneider, S. Martinez, and A. Owens, "Barriers to Educational Opportunities for Hispanics in the United States." In *National Research Council, Hispanics and the Future of America"* by Panel on Hispanics in the United States, Committee on Population, Division of Behavioral and Social Sciences and Education (Washington, DC: The National Academies Press, 2006): Chap 6.

9. National Center for Education Statistics, *Status and Trends in the Education of Hispanics.* NCES 2003-008. (Washington, DC: U.S. Department of Education, 2003).

10. Tienda and Mitchell, eds., *Multiple Origins, Uncertain Destinies: Hispanics and the American Future,* 87.

11. For more about "pushouts," see Tara J. Yosso, *Critical Race Counterstories Along the Chicana/Chicano Educational Pipeline* (New York: Routledge, 2006): 4; and Daniel G. Solórzano, Maria C. Ledesma, Jeanette Pérez, Maria R. Burciaga, and Armida Ornelas, "Latina Equity in Education: Gaining Access to Academic Enrichment Programs." In *Latino Policy & Issues Brief, 4* (Los Angeles: UCLA Chicano Studies Research Center 2003).

12. Yosso, *Critical Race Counterstories, Along the Chicana/Chicano Educational Pipeline,* 2–3.

13. Patricia Bode, "Multicultural Art Education: Voices of Art Teachers and Students in the Postmodern Era," diss., University of Massachusetts Amherst, 2005.

14. John M. Bridgeland, John J. Dilulio, Jr., and Karen Burke Morison, *The Silent Epidemic: Perspectives of High School Dropouts.* A Report by Civic Enterprises with Peter D. Hart Research Associates for the Bill & Melinda Gates Foundation (Washington, DC: Civic Enterprises: March 2006). Available at: www.gatesfoundation.org/nr/downloads/ed/TheSilentEpidemic3-06FINAL.pdf; accessed June 2006.

15. Bridgeland, Dilulio, Jr., and Burke Morison, *The Silent Epidemic: Perspectives of High School Dropouts.*

16. Carlos E. Cortés, *The Children are Watching: How the Media Teach about Diversity* (New York: Teachers College Press, 2000).

17. Yosso, *Critical Race Counterstories Along the Chicana/Chicano Educational Pipeline.*

18. Nitza M. Hildago, "Latino/a Families' Epistemology." In *Latino Education: An Agenda for Community Action Research,* edited by Pedro Pedraza and Melissa Rivera (Mahwah, NJ: Lawrence Erlbaum, 2005): 375–402; and Tienda and Mitchell, *Multiple Origins, Uncertain Destinies: Hispanics and the American Future,* 19.

19. Ricardo D. Stanton-Salazar, *Manufacturing Hope and Despair: The School and Kin Support Networks of U.S.–Mexican Youth* (New York: Teachers College Press, 2001): 252. Also see Paulo Freire, *Pedagogy of the Oppressed,* translated by Myra Bergman Ramos (New York: Continuum, 1970) and Samuel Bowles and Herbert Gintis, *Schooling in Capitalist America: Education Reform and Contradictions of Economic Life* (New York: Basic Books, 1976).

20. Tienda and Mitchell, *Multiple Origins, Uncertain Destinies: Hispanics and the American Future,* 85.

Toward an Understanding of School Achievement

❝ There's so much to learn and that's all I want to do is just learn, try to educate my mind to see what I could get out of it. **❞**

—Paul Chavez, interviewee

Paul Quackenbush, Khalea Glasgow, and Alexander Sasi Wallace in Tara Farley's art class. *Collaborative poetry painting.* Tempera, 2005.

s improbable as it might sound, the words quoted on the previous page are those of a young man who was suspended and expelled from school on many occasions. A gang member with a difficult family life, Paul Chavez had managed to be accepted into an alternative school, where he was experiencing academic success for only the second time in his life. As you will see in his case study, which follows this chapter, Paul was resolute about continuing his education and becoming a teacher or counselor in order to help young people like himself. However, given his background and experiences, few people would have believed that he was capable of learning. Conventional theories of academic success or failure do not explain cases such as Paul's.

The simplistic dichotomy traditionally used to explain the school failure of students, particularly those from culturally diverse and poor backgrounds, can be summarized as follows: School failure is the fault either of the students themselves, who are genetically inferior, or of the social characteristics of their communities, which suffer from economic and cultural disadvantages and thus are unable to provide their children with the necessary preparation for academic success.[1] Alternative explanations are that school failure is caused by the structure of schools, which are static, classist, and racist and represent the interests of the dominant classes, or it is caused by cultural incompatibilities between the home and the school.[2]

This chapter reviews these and other theories about the complex conditions that may affect school achievement and then considers how these conditions may collectively influence the academic success or failure of students. After the discussion of these theories, the case studies of two students who have not been successful in school, Paul Chavez and Latrell Elton, are presented. Both of these young men were written off by their respective schools and teachers as incapable of becoming successful students. Their cases demonstrate that learning can take place even in the most difficult personal and societal circumstances.

Deficit Theories Revisited

The theory that genetic or cultural inferiority is the cause of academic failure has been a recurrent theme in U.S. educational history. Throughout the past half century, much of the research on school failure has focused on the inadequacy of students' home environment and culture. In an early review of research concerning the poor achievement of Black children, for instance, Stephen and Joan Baratz found that most of the research was based on the assumption that Black children were deficient in language, social development, and intelligence. This assumption resulted in blaming students' failure to achieve on their so-called deficits. Singled out for blame were children's *poorly developed language* (more concretely, the fact that they did not speak Standard English); an *inadequate mother* (the assumption being that low-income Black mothers were invariably poor parents); *too little stimulation* in the home (that their homes lacked the kinds of environments that encouraged learning); *too much stimulation* in the home (their homes were too chaotic and disorganized or simply not organized along middle-class norms); and a host of other, often contradictory hypotheses. Baratz and Baratz found that the homes and backgrounds of Black children and poor children, in general, were classified in the research as "sick, pathological, deviant, or underdeveloped."[3] Such caricatures, which continue to exist, are of little value to teachers and schools who want to provide their students with a high-quality education.

The case studies of Paul and Latrell that follow this chapter are compelling examples of life in difficult circumstances: Both lived in poverty with families headed by single mothers; both had been involved in antisocial and criminal behavior; and both had had negative school experiences. One might be tempted to write them off because of these circumstances, but, as their case studies demonstrate, both Paul and Latrell had begun achieving academic success in alternative schools. Deficit explanations of school achievement cannot explain their success.

Although more comprehensive explanations of academic achievement have been proposed in recent decades, the theories of genetic inferiority and cultural deprivation popularized during the 1960s have left their mark on the schooling of children living in poverty and children of color. These theories are not only classist and racist but are also simply inadequate in explaining the failure of so many students. Although the social and economic conditions of their communities and families *can* be significant contributing factors in the academic failure of students, they alone are not the cause of student failure or success. As an early critic of deficit theories, the late William Ryan turned the argument of cultural deprivation on its head by claiming that it was a strategy to "blame the victim." In a book that had a great impact in challenging the theory of cultural inferiority during its heydey in the 1960s, Ryan was eloquent in his critique:

> We are dealing, it would seem, not so much with culturally deprived children as with culturally depriving schools. And the task to be accomplished is not to revise, amend, and repair deficient children, but to alter and transform the atmosphere and operations of the schools to which we commit these children.[4]

Students' identities—that is, their sense of self based in part on their race, ethnicity, social class, and language, among other characteristics—can also have an impact on their academic success or failure, but it is not these characteristics per se that cause success or failure. Rather, it is the school's *perception* of students' language, culture, and class as *inadequate* and *negative*, and thus the devalued status of these characteristics in the academic environment, that help explain school failure. In Paul Chavez's case, his early gang affiliation had had a decided negative effect on teachers' academic expectations of him. Teacher and author Linda Christensen provides another powerful example. Christensen, a talented high school teacher of students of diverse background, describes how she helps her students understand the power of their own language patterns *while at the same time* they learn Standard English without humiliation. Christensen recalls her own painful experiences as a working class child in the classroom of Mrs. Delaney, her ninth-grade English teacher, who taught her to be ashamed of her language, something that Christensen refuses to do with her own students:

> For too long, I felt inferior when I spoke. I knew the voice of my childhood crept out, and I confused that with ignorance. It wasn't. I just didn't belong to the group who made the rules. I was an outsider, a foreigner in their world. My students won't be.[5]

That the behaviors of middle-class parents of any race or ethnic group tend to be different from those of poor parents is amply documented. Parents living in poverty may be either unaware of the benefits of what middle-class parents know by experience or may be unable to provide certain activities for their children. Middle-class parents, for example, usually speak Standard English. They also tend to engage in school-like prereading activities much more regularly than working class parents. Schools deem other activities in which middle-class parents and their children participate as essential to educational success: going to the library on a consistent basis, attending museums and other cultural centers, and providing a host of other experiences that schools and society have labeled "enriching."

Whether these activities are, in fact, enriching is not in question; the problem is that the activities of poor families, some of which may also be enriching, are not viewed in the same way. For example, many poor families travel either to their original home countries or to other parts of the United States from where they originally came. Children may spend summers "down South" or in Jamaica or Mexico, but what they learn on these trips is usually ignored by the school in spite of its potentially enriching character. I (Sonia) recall, for example, that it never occurred to me that my own experience of visiting family in Puerto Rico between fifth grade and sixth grade might be of interest to my teacher or classmates. My teachers never told me this directly, but I had already gotten the message that issues of consequence to my family carried no great weight in school. When I think of the giant tarantula I caught, froze, and brought home, or of the many things I learned about living on a farm, or of how my Spanish substantially improved that summer, I can only conclude that these things might have been as interesting to my teacher and classmates as they were enlightening for me.

Students' ability to develop literacy and other academic skills, as traditionally defined by schools, is necessary for academic success, but if defined only in this way, academic success is limited because it encourages students to abandon part of their identity in the process. Students' abilities to use the skills, talents, and experiences learned at home and in the community to further their learning must *also* be included in a definition of academic success.

Shirley Brice Heath's classic research with a Black community that she called "Trackton" is a persuasive example. She found that the kinds of questioning rituals in which parents and other adults engaged with children were not preparing the children adequately for school activities.[6] In observing the White middle-class teachers of these children, she found that the questions they asked the students were qualitatively different from the kinds of questions the children were accustomed to being asked at home. Teachers' questions, for example, concerned pulling attributes of things out of context and naming them (e.g., to identify size, shape, or color). In contrast, in their homes the children were asked questions about whole events or objects as well as about their uses, causes, and effects. The questions their parents asked them often required the children to make analogical comparisons and understand complex metaphors. These questions frequently were linguistically complex, and they required a sophisticated use of language on the part of the children. Usually, there was no one "right" answer because answers involved telling a story or describing a situation.

Heath discovered that the result of the different kinds of questions asked in the different contexts was a perplexing lack of communication in the school: Normally communicative students were silent and unresponsive to teachers' questions, and teachers assumed that their students were deficient in language or were unintelligent. There was nothing wrong with the questions asked by the families in Trackton. They were simply different from those asked in school and therefore placed the children at a disadvantage for school success.

Through a research project with Heath, the teachers became aware of the differences in questioning rituals, and they began to study the kinds of questions that adults in Trackton asked. Some of these could be called *"probing questions,"* and teachers began using them in their school lessons as a basis for asking more traditional "school" questions, to which children also needed to become accustomed if they were to be successful in school. The results were powerful. Children became active and enthusiastic participants in these lessons, a dramatic change from their previous passive behavior.

This fortuitous example of learning to use the culture of students in their education contradicts the scenario of failure in many schools, where parents are expected to provide help in ways they may be unable to do. Some parents are unaware of how to give their children concrete support in areas such

as homework, but this lack of support, in itself, does not necessarily produce school failure. Blaming parents or children for academic failure begs the question, for the role of schools is to educate *all* students from all families, not only the most academically gifted students from economically advantaged, mainstream, English-speaking, European American families. Moreover, students' home and family situations are seldom subject to change by the school. Because schools cannot change the living conditions of students, the challenge is to find ways to teach children effectively in spite of the poverty or other disabling conditions in which they may live. Instead of focusing on students' life circumstances, it makes sense for schools to focus on what they can change: themselves. As we discussed in Chapter 10, schools sometimes view children living in poverty and children of color as if they were blank slates, in effect tearing down the building blocks the children already have in order to start from a middle-class foundation. School-related skills are, of course, necessary for academic success, but there is no reason why they cannot be built on the linguistic, cultural, or experiential foundation that children already have. The fact that some children come to school with a rich oral tradition is a case in point. Perhaps their parents never read stories to them but instead *tell* them stories. This experience can either be dismissed by schools as trivial, or it can be used as the basis for learning.

Genetic and cultural inferiority theories are not a thing of the past. As recently as 1994, Richard Herrnstein and Charles Murray resurrected the argument that genetic inferiority was the root cause of the academic failure among African American students.[7] Although widely discredited by serious scholars as both ethnocentric and scientifically unfounded, genetic and cultural inferiority theories have survived because they provide a simplistic explanation for complex problems.[8] That is, by accepting theories of genetic and cultural inferiority, the detrimental effects of structural inequality, racism, and poverty on student learning do not have to be considered.

We also need to understand the power of what has been called the *cultural capital* of dominant groups. According to Pierre Bourdieu, cultural capital can exist in three forms: dispositions of the mind and body; cultural goods, such as pictures, books, and other material objects; and educational qualifications. In all three forms, transmission of cultural capital is, according to Bourdieu, "no doubt the best hidden form of hereditary transmission of capital."[9] That is, the values, tastes, languages, dialects, and cultures that have most status are invariably associated with the dominant group. As a consequence, the weight of cultural capital cannot be ignored. To do so would be both naive and romantic because it would deny the reality that power, knowledge, and resources are located in the norms of dominant cultures and languages. To imply that working class students and students from dominated groups need not learn the cultural norms of the dominant group is effectively to disempower the students who are most academically vulnerable. However, the curriculum should also be relevant to the cultural experiences and values of students from subordinated groups. A complete education needs to include both the norms and canon of the dominant culture and those of the dominated cultures. Including diverse culturally relevant curriculum is a valuable way to challenge a monocultural canon.

Economic and Social Reproduction Revisited

The argument that schools reproduce the economic and social relations of society and therefore tend to serve the interests of the dominant classes, articulated first during the 1970s by scholars such as Samuel Bowles, Herbert Gintis, and Joel Spring, placed schools squarely in a political context.[10] According to this theory, the role of the schools was to keep the poor in their place by teaching them the proper attitudes and behaviors for becoming good workers, and to keep the dominant classes in power by teaching their children the skills of management and control that would presumably prepare them to manage and control the working class. Schools, therefore, reproduced the status quo and not only reflected structural inequalities based on class, race, and gender but also helped to maintain these inequalities.

Economic and social reproduction theorists maintain that the *sorting function of schools,* to use a term coined by Spring, is apparent in everything from physical structure to curriculum and instruction. For example, the schools of the poor are generally factory-like fortresses that operate with an abundance of bells and other controlling mechanisms, whereas the schools of the wealthy tend to be much more "open" physically and psychologically, allowing for more autonomy and creative thinking on the part of students. Likewise, relations between students and teachers in poor communities reflect a dominant–dominated relationship much more so than in middle-class or wealthy communities. The curriculum also differs. More sophisticated and challenging knowledge is generally taught in wealthy schools, whereas the basics and rote memorization are the order of the day in poor schools. The sorting function of the schools results in an almost perfect replication of the stratification of society. Although the theories of the economic and social reproduction theorists generally concerned the United States, they are true of all societies.

This thinking revolutionized the debate on the purposes and outcomes of schools and placed the success or failure of students in a new light. The benign, stated purpose of U.S. schooling to serve as an "equalizer" is seriously questioned by these theories. For example, following the logic of this thinking, it is no accident that so many students in urban schools drop out; rather, it is an *intended outcome* of the educational system. That is, some students are intentionally channeled by schools to be either fodder for war or a reserve uneducated labor force. Schools do just exactly what is expected of them: They succeed at school failure.

The arguments of the social reproduction theorists are compelling, and they have had an enormous impact on educational thinking since the 1970s. However, by concentrating on the labor-market purpose of schooling, these theories tend to offer static, oversimplified explanations of school success or failure. According to these theories, school life is almost completely subordinated to the needs of the economy, leaving little room for the role that students and their communities have in influencing school policies and practices. These analyses assume that schooling is simply imposed from above and accepted from below. In reality, schools are complex and perplexing institutions, and things are not always this neat or apparent.

While economic and social reproduction theories provide a more persuasive analysis of academic failure than either genetic and cultural inferiority or cultural incompatibility theories by placing schools in a sociopolitical context, these analyses are incomplete. They can fall into mechanistic explanations of dynamic processes, assuming a simple cause–effect relationship. Such theories fail to explain why students from some culturally dominated communities have managed to succeed in school or why some schools in poor communities are extraordinarily successful in spite of tremendous odds. By emphasizing only the role of social class, these social and economic reproduction theories fail to explain why schools are also inequitable for females and for students of racially and culturally subordinated communities. In addition, these theories overlook the lengthy struggles over schooling in which many communities have been historically involved: the desegregation of schools, bilingual education, multicultural education, and access to education for students with special needs as well as for females. If education were simply imposed from above, these reforms would never have found their way, even imperfectly, into schools. Some theorists, such as Michael Apple, have suggested that schools are a product of conflicts among competing group interests and that the purposes of the dominant class are never perfectly reflected in the schools but, rather, are resisted and modified by the recipients of schooling.[11]

Economic and social reproduction theories help explain how academic failure and success are not unintended outcomes but rather are logical results of differentiated schooling. They also help remove the complete burden of failure from students, their families, and communities to the society at large, and they provide a macroanalytic, or societal, understanding of schooling. Social reproduction theories, however, are incomplete because they generally fail to take cultural and psychological issues into account.

Cultural Incompatibilities Revisited

Another explanation for school failure is that it is caused by cultural incompatibilities—that is, because school culture and home culture are often at odds, the result is a "cultural clash" that produces school failure. According to this explanation, it is necessary to consider the differing experiences, values, skills, expectations, and lifestyles children have when they enter school and how these differences, in being more or less consistent with the school environment, affect their achievement. The more consistent that home and school cultures are, the more successful students will be. The opposite is also true. The more that students' experiences, skills, and values differ from the school setting, the more failure that they will experience.

This explanation makes a great deal of sense, and it explains school failure more convincingly than simple deficit theories. That some students learn more effectively in cooperative settings than in competitive settings is not a problem per se. What makes it a problem is that many schools persist in providing competitive environments *only*. Given this reality, cultural differences begin to function as a risk factor. This reasoning turns around the popular concept of "children at risk" so that the risk comes not from within the child, but develops as a result of particular school policies, practices, and structures.

Likewise, the fact that some students enter school without speaking English is not, itself, a satisfactory explanation for why some of them fail in school. Rather, the interpretation of their non-English speaking status and the value, or lack of value, given to the child's native language also matter. Whereas in some schools a student might be identified as *non–English speaking,* in another school that same child might be called *Khmer speaking.* The difference is not simply a semantic one. In the first case, the child is assumed to be missing language, but in the second case, the child is assumed to possess language already, even if it is not the majority language. And because language ability is the major ingredient for school success, how schools and teachers perceive children's language is significant.

The cultural mismatch theory is more hopeful than deterministic explanations such as genetic inferiority or economic reproduction theories because it assumes that teachers can learn to create environments in which all students can be successful learners. It also respects teachers as creative intellectuals rather than as simple technicians. Teachers are expected to be able to develop a critical analysis of

What You Can Do

Expand Perspectives of Success

In conversation with fellow teachers—both casual chats and formal faculty meeting discussions—the topic of childrens' family life frequently arises. Too often these comments link family culture to underachievement. These statements are often made with an air of authority or by people in positions of authority, making them difficult to challenge and confusing to understand. There are ways to challenge prejudicial assumptions without alienating yourself from your peers or losing your job.

While other chapters, especially Chapter 12, focus on what you can do to get to know more about families' and students' cultural identities, this chapter focuses more on what you can do through your own reading and research. Teachers are smart and intellectually curious by nature. Their intellectual prowess deserves to be cultivated and supported. Teachers may also be overworked and have too much to read, so finding ways to integrate the most current research into school discussions can be helpful. Some strategies are described below.

Build Relationships for Solidarity

The PERSONAL level: A colleague says something that rings of stereotyping and misinformation, for example, "Well, you know, Puerto Ricans, as a culture, do not value education." As upset as you may be, it is guaranteed that a full-blown confrontation will not have positive results. Let your colleague know that you are uncomfortable, but that you want to talk more. Their perspective has been developed over time and thus will take some time to change. It is also unlikely that any single retort or conversation will change their view, so start out with little things, such as "Oh, I am surprised to hear that point of view. It doesn't match up with the families that I know. Did you read about that somewhere? Because I would like to know more."

Try to keep your conversations rooted in research. For example, at an opportune moment, share some anecdotes about your positive experiences with Puerto Rican families in the school. At another time, share your excitement about, for example, the children's literature and cultural resources created by Edwin Fontánez of Exit Studio as great curriculum supplements.* Many teachers learn a great deal of cultural information from the children's resources they use in their classrooms. At another time, bring up some educational research that helps teachers support the academic achievement of Puerto Rican students, for example, such as the book *Puerto Rican Students in U.S. Schools I* (Sonia) edited.† Also refer to work that examines the education of Latinos more broadly, for example, *Latino Education: An Agenda for Community Action Research* edited by Pedro Pedraza and Melissa Rivera.‡

Honor and Support Teachers as Scholars and Intellectuals

The SCHOOL-WIDE level: Follow up your personal relationship building with school-wide action. Suggest to your principal, department chair, or curriculum director that a forthcoming faculty or department meeting be dedicated to reading some educational research about student achievement. A meeting that allows time for reading and discussion is the most effective, since many teachers may not have time to read in preparation for the meeting. This chapter is filled with citations of books, chapters, and articles about particular topics. You may choose a single article or a book chapter. Or, for a more comprehensive view, such as that which this chapter provides, break the faculty into small groups and assign each group a short article or portion of a chapter to read. Re-group the whole faculty and ask each group to have a member report on the findings of the article or chapter section and what the implications may be for your particular school community, thereby co-constructing a wider range of group knowledge.

Even if this seems like an untenable request of your administration, ask anyway. How do you know unless you try? If the first level of administration, let's say the principal, rejects the idea, try another level (department head, grade-level chair, team leader, district-wide curriculum director, or superintendent). If all else fails in your attempts to organize "sanctioned" in-school study-group discussions, try an after-school voluntary group. Whether the study groups are voluntary or assigned, be sure you document the time and get professional development points or credits for all participants. These strategies may be applied to a range of educational research topics.

*See www.exitstudio.com for books, CDs, and videos about Puerto Rican culture.

†Sonia Nieto, ed., Puerto Rican Students in U.S. Schools, (Mahwah, NJ: Lawrence Erlbaum, 2000).

‡Pedro Pedraza and Melissa Rivera, eds., Latino Education: An Agenda for Community Action Research (Mahwah, NJ: Lawrence Erlbaum, 2005).

their students' cultures and to use this analysis to teach all their students effectively. In terms of the kind of knowledge teachers need to know about their students' realities, the late Paulo Freire eloquently described their responsibility:

> Educators need to know what happens in the world of the children with whom they work. They need to know the universe of their dreams, the language with which they skillfully defend themselves from the aggressiveness of their world, what they know independently of the school, and how they know it.[12]

Gloria Ladson-Billings, in coining the term *culturally relevant teaching,* has suggested that this kind of pedagogy is in sharp contrast to "assimilationist" teaching, whose main purpose is to transmit dominant culture beliefs and values in an uncritical way to all students. In the same vein, Geneva Gay's work in defining and explicating what she calls *culturally responsive teaching* has also been tremendously significant.[13]

Although the cultural mismatch theory is more comprehensive than the cultural or genetic deficit theories and is without their implicit racist and classist overtones, the cultural mismatch theory, too, is insufficient to explain why some students succeed and others fail. The extraordinarily high dropout rates among American Indian and Alaska Native students (higher than all other racial or ethnic groups in the United States) is a case in point. According to Richard St. Germaine, addressing cultural discontinuities through the curriculum can help, but this strategy alone is only a partial solution because the structural inequality that produces enormous poverty is left untouched.[14]

Newer research points to a major weakness in the theory of cultural discontinuity: Insufficient attention is given to cultural accommodation or biculturation, just to mention two responses to cultural diversity experienced by immigrants. No culture exists in isolation, and a rigid interpretation of the theory of cultural discontinuity presupposes that all children from the same cultural background experience school in the same way, yet we know this is far from true. The result of a cultural discontinuity perspective is that individual and family differences, school conditions, or the broader sociopolitical context that can also influence learning may be disregarded. In fact, a rigid interpretation of this theory hovers dangerously close to stereotyping students from particular cultural groups, resulting in *limiting* views of them and thus limited educational opportunities for them.

For instance, Gloria Ladson-Billings notes that the way the concept of culture is used by some teachers and students in preservice teacher education can exacerbate the problem and perpetuate stereotypes. These constructed meanings have evolved from notions such as "the culture of poverty" asserted by Oscar Lewis and Michael Harrington in the 1960s.[15] Ladson-Billings points out that a growing number of teachers use the term *culture* as a catchall for a wide variety of behaviors and characteristics when discussing students and parents who are not White, not English speaking, or not native-born U.S. citizens. For example, some teachers muse that "maybe it is part of their culture" for groups of students to be noisy or for parents to be absent from Open House night. Not only are these assessments inaccurate, they turn attention away from socioeconomic reasons or school practices that precipitate these behaviors. Parents may be absent from Open House night for any one of a number of reasons: For example, they may be working night shift or caring for younger children; they may have no transportation; they may feel isolated or unwelcome in the school; or they may not have had a translation of the Open House information into their language. Groups of children may be loud simply because they are groups of children, not because of their skin color or another reason related to "their culture."[16]

Another problem with the cultural discontinuity theory is that it cannot explain why students from some cultural groups are academically successful, even though, by all indications, they should not be. For example, Margaret Gibson's ethnographic research has documented that although Punjabi students are culturally very different from most of their peers, they have been quite successful in U.S. schools.[17] Their grades and high school graduation rates equal or surpass those of their classmates in spite of severe handicaps: Their families are primar-

ily farm laborers and factory workers, and many are illiterate and speak little or no English. They generally have to become fluent in English in nonbilingual settings, very few of them have received any special assistance, and they have been subjected to tremendous discrimination by both peers and teachers. Also, their home values and the values practiced by the school are in sharp contrast. Given this situation, their cultural background should predispose them to school failure. That this is not the case leads us to other explanations, some of which may be the combination of social, economic, and cultural compatibility theories and others that are subsequently described in this chapter.

Combining Perspectives of Social, Economic, and Cultural Compatibility Theories

Examining cultural incompatibilities as well as social and economic inequities, and their resulting negative educational consequences, can assist in ascertaining how schools are effective or ineffective within the broader social picture. Richard Rothstein's research asserts that, outside of school, myriad factors related to social class and how families in some groups are stratified in society, profoundly influence learning in school.[18] Robert Evans extrapolates further on social and economic conditions, pointing to a "crisis in childrearing" that negatively affects school achievement.[19] These researchers' conclusions are double edged. They emphasize the powerlessness of schools to achieve educational equity without massive social reforms, while they also argue that educational reform efforts that do not take into account the social and economic conditions outside of schools can be only partially successful. At the same time, these researchers' frameworks are beneficial in their investigations of ways in which lack of health care, inadequate nutrition, inadequate housing, and unstable family life impinge on school experiences. Their writings assertively address social supports that are required for schools to be successful in educating all children. However, some argue that isolating social and economic reforms from school reform unnecessarily shifts the attention for resources and action away from schools. Pedro Noguera challenges this implication and argues that since poor children typically attend schools that are overcrowded, underfunded, and staffed by inexperienced teachers, schools need to be viewed as an integral part of social solutions. Noguera points out that "reducing poverty and improving schools should not be treated as competing goals."[20]

Moreover, both Rothstein and Evans stress the sociological backgrounds of families in poverty as risk factors for failure, exposing what some may unfortunately interpret as a shadow of the notion of cultural inferiority. Evans' theory is at particular risk for being reduced to the simplistic conclusion that families are to blame, which will certainly not advance social or educational reforms. Nevertheless, because both Rothstein and Evans shine light on the ways in which dominant cultural practices, specifically racial discrimination, perpetuate structural inequities, their work contributes to the overall efforts of multicultural school reform. They elaborate on how systemic biases, particularly institutionalized racism, influence family life, shape parents' preparation of children for school, and eventually affect students' attachment to school.

In the current environment of No Child Left Behind and high-stakes testing, these theories make a compelling case for examining and reforming social structures outside of the institution of the school in order to promote academic achievement for all children, especially those from low-income families. Specifically, these perspectives support teachers, particularly those who work in the most economically strapped neighborhoods, by widening the lens through which their communities of teaching and learning are viewed. Mark Simon reports on members of a teachers' study group who were inspired to take further action in response to Rothstein's book. They took walking tours of their students' neighborhoods and got to know families, fought for expansion of Head Start and other preschool programs, and initiated district conversations to reconsider the overemphasis on testing, which they viewed as devaluing many noncognitive aspects of their students' performance.[21]

Bearing in mind the insights and cautions about theories that focus on the interactive characteristics of social class, racial identity, culture, and academic achievement, we now move to another theory that has had a great impact on educational thinking in the past three decades.

Cultural-Ecological Theory: The Immigrant Experience versus the "Minority" Experience

A traditional argument used to explain differences in academic achievement is that it takes students from certain cultural groups who are not doing well in school a generation or two to climb the ladder of success, just as it took all other immigrants to do so. While this argument may largely be true for European immigrants (but by no means for all), it is a specious argument for others because it fails to explain the educational and historical experiences of African Americans, American Indians, Asian Americans, and Latinos, which are markedly different from those of European ethnic groups. For one, American Indians, African Americans, and many Mexican Americans can hardly be called new immigrants. Many have been here, on U.S. soil, for generations, and some for millenia. Furthermore, some Asians have been here for four or five generations, and although many do well in school, others are not as successful.

It is clear that certain groups represent unique cases of subjugation in U.S. history. This is true of American Indians, who were conquered and segregated on reservations; African Americans, who were enslaved and whose families were torn apart; Mexican Americans, whose land was annexed and who were then colonized within their own country; and Puerto Ricans, who were colonized and whose country is still under the domination of the United States. In addition, and probably not incidentally, they are all people of color, and the issue of race remains paramount in explaining their experiences.

In an alternative explanation of school failure and success, John Ogbu developed what he called the *cultural-ecological* theory that goes beyond cultural discontinuities. Ogbu with Herbert Simons suggested that it is necessary to look not only at a group's cultural background but also at its situation in the host society and its perceptions of opportunities available in that society.[22] Ogbu classifies most immigrants in the United States as *voluntary immigrants,* and racial minority group immigrants as either *voluntary* or *involuntary minorities,* that is, those who come of their own free will as compared with those who were conquered or colonized.[23] The latter groups were incorporated into U.S. society against their will. These included American Indians, Africans, Mexicans, and Puerto Ricans, among others. According to Ogbu, voluntary immigrants include all European and some Asian, African, and Central American immigrants, among others. The distinction is not always true, of course, because those who appear on the surface to be voluntary immigrants may not be so at all, and vice versa. Witness, for example, the current situation of millions of Mexicans who not only come voluntarily but risk their lives to do so. Nevertheless, the categories, imperfect as they are, help explain the present condition and educational experiences of some groups.

Ogbu concluded that students from particular backgrounds experience a great variability in academic performance and this variability often can be explained by the sociopolitical setting in which they find themselves. These students are not always racially d fferent from the dominant group in a society, but they have lower social and political status. Other differences may also help explain their marginal status, especially their social class, gender, and native language. It is not their differences that make them marginal but rather the value placed on those differences by the dominant society. Several extensive reviews have documented that socially and politically dominated groups have experienced the most severe academic disadvantage.[24] In Japan, for instance, students of Korean descent and students from the Buraku caste tend to do quite poorly in Japanese schools because both are perceived in Japan as less valued than the majority population. When they emigrate to the United States, however, they are equally successful in school as immigrants from the Japanese majority. In addition, their IQ scores, a supposedly immutable indication of intelligence, also rise when these children emigrate to another society. Their dominated and devalued status in their home country seems to be the deciding factor because those who are in minority positions in their own countries are not subject to the same

castelike status in another society and may therefore be more successful in school.

The same phenomenon has been found among Finns, who do poorly in Swedish schools but quite well in schools when they emigrate to Australia. Their history of colonization and subsequent low status in Swedish society seems to be the key ingredient. In New Zealand, the native Maori perform less well in school than immigrant Polynesians (who share a similar language and culture), and the Samis in Norway and Irish Catholics in Belfast also do less well than their dominant-group peers.

Similar results have been found closer to home. For example, in the United States, newly arrived immigrants tend to do better in school and have higher self-esteem than those born here.[25] Their self-esteem and school success depend not just on their ethnicity but also on their interaction with U.S. society and on the strength of the self-concepts they have developed in their home countries, where they are not seen as "minorities." Similarly, some research has concluded that American Indian students, especially those in urban settings who are almost completely cut off from their tribal roots, suffer negative consequences both for their self-esteem and their staying power.[26] Again, the differences in these situations seem to be the sociopolitical context of schooling.

The visions, hopes, dreams, and experiences of voluntary and involuntary minorities also need to be kept in mind. According to Ogbu, most voluntary minorities have a "folk theory" of school success: They see the United States as a land of opportunity where one gets ahead through education and hard work. According to this view, even a relative newcomer with few skills and little education can succeed economically, and their children can experience even more success if they work hard in school, largely because these immigrants have great faith in the "American Dream." As a result, they apply themselves to achieve it. They understand that, in order to achieve success, they may have to endure, for example, racism, economic hardships, and working at several menial jobs at the same time. These are accepted as the price they have to pay for success. Immigrants coming from war-torn countries or refugee camps and those who have experienced the death of loved ones may not consider living in an urban ghetto and engaging in

Snapshot

Nini Rostland

Nini Rostland[1] is a fifteen-year-old freshman at Avery High School in a mid-size college town in the Midwest. She describes herself as racially and ethnically mixed. Her mother is Black South African and her father is Polish American. Her family moved from South Africa to the United States when she was in kindergarten, so most of her education has been in U.S. public schools. This snapshot of Nini emphasizes that many students of mixed heritage negotiate labels, assumptions, and expectations with friends and teachers in school settings.

It kind of makes me mad that they always try to put people into a certain box. You have to check a box every time you fill out a form. I don't fit in a box. Especially these days, more people are getting more and more racially mixed. I don't identify myself as Black or as White. I usually put "both" or "other", because I'm not either; I'm both.

My cultural identity is really important to me. It makes me mad when people say, "Oh, you are not White." Well, I know I'm not White. I'm not Black either. People automatically assume that I'm not Caucasian, and they are automatically, "You're Black". And I'm, like, "Not necessarily". It makes me mad sometimes.

Being of mixed heritage is kind of difficult sometimes because it's hard finding where you fit in. For me, for a while I didn't really know what kind of people would accept me. Now I find people who accept me just as I am, not for trying to be like them. Now I try to hang out with people who are of all different races. I hang out with the Black people, the mixed people, the White people, Asian, everything. I don't like to be classified as a certain thing. The Black people treat me like I'm one of them. I find that Black people are more accepting of people in their group. More of the White people are, like, "You're not rich and you're not White, so you can't be in our group". Most likely, if you are mixed with some Black, the group of Black people will accept you.

Some of my friends would say that you can be attracted to both, that White people can like you, mixed people can like you, and Black people can like you. My closest group of friends, there's a foursome of us, and we all became really close over the summer at this camp for people of mixed heritage or of other ethnic backgrounds. And over that camp we have become really, best friends. That was in seventh grade. So for two years now, we've all been really close. And three of my friends are both like me: mixed with Black and White, and my other friend is African.

It's difficult because you don't really fit anybody's expectation. I think expectations may be holding me back a little bit. I think when people see me, they assume, "Oh, she's Black". They automatically assume, "Oh, she's not going to achieve well". That is kind of holding me back because it's sort of like a psychological thing where you think, "Well, if that's what people expect you to achieve", then you kind of think, "Oh, I might achieve that". I'm trying to turn that around, and be, like, "Well I can achieve anything I want to."

I think school in some ways is kind of like mainstreaming. It's what we are all forced into doing when we're young. You have to go to school, you have to get an education, you have to go to college so you can get a good job. But really, I think if you look back at history, the people who went out of the way of the expectations of society, they were the ones who went on to be really great. I understand that there is a good reason why I should go to school, because I don't want to be working at McDonald's my entire life. But I also think that it's important that I be able to explore other things.

School's really not that challenging to me. One of the classes that I actually learn something in and enjoy is art class because I am learning a lot of new techniques. But most of my other classes are just memorization, and I'm really not learning anything from it. I have found very few teachers who actually teach classes in an interesting way that makes me really want to work. But, when I see all the stuff that my mom did, it makes me feel like my mom went through a lot harder stuff than I have ever went through, so I should try my hardest at what I'm doing right now. One way that I think school is really important is through my mom. Because I have seen that to get to where she came from, she had to put in a lot of effort and go through a lot of high-level schooling just so that she could come to the U.S.

Both of my parents taught me about each of their heritages. I can just identify with that because that's me. I learned about my dad's Polish background because his parents are Polish and they make a lot of Polish dishes. We even went to a traditional Polish dinner where they made Polish meals and stuff like that. My dad has told me about some of the traditions they had when he was younger. Also, from my dad I've learned about social issues and what's going on in the world. I learn so much about government and that kind of stuff from my dad. From my mom I've learned ethnic pride. I'm really proud of my heritage. My mom is South African and she came through a lot just so that she could be here. I know a lot of history about what happened in South Africa and what my mom and my brother both lived through. They've told stories about what happened to them and stuff like that. But my parents don't really know what it's like to be of mixed heritage.

Commentary

Racial, ethnic, and cultural identities are constantly under construction, and adolescence is an especially vulnerable time for this formation. Messages from peers, family, popular culture, and school strongly influence a young person's perspectives on their cultural heritages, identities, and school engagement. Nini appears to possess a strong sense of identity and she articulates an appreciation for her mixed heritage. Her parents provide her with familial, historical, and cultural appreciation, and she has formed powerful bonds, through a summer camp experience, with a small group of peers with similar roots. Simultaneously, she struggles with feelings of acceptance within certain groups and the threat of negative anticipations. The tensions she experiences around racial identity extend beyond peer groups and are felt in teacher expectations as well. Can schools offer the level of affirmation that the summer camp provided while simultaneously creating a robust academic atmosphere? Can we develop learning communities that help students and teachers cross racial boundaries to cultivate more full individual selves within deeply connected communities? If, as Nini says, "These days, more people are

(continued)

getting more and more racially mixed," what are the implications for developing learning communities that affirm multiple histories and multiple forms of cultural knowledge?

1. We appreciate the work of Dr. Carlie Tartakov, who interviewed Nini and provided background information for the snapshot, and that of John Raible, who helped transcribe the interview.

backbreaking work to be a severe hardship. Marcelo Suarez-Orozco, for example, documents the extraordinary success of many Central Americans, who go to the same schools and live in the same impoverished and crime-filled neighborhoods as Mexican Americans who have been much more unsuccessful in school.[27]

For Ogbu, the major problem in the academic performance of children from what he calls *castelike minorities* is not that they possess a different language, culture, or cognitive or communication style. The problem lies instead in the nature of the history, subjugation, and exploitation they have experienced, together with their own responses to their treatment. Castelike minorities in the United States tend to perceive schooling as providing unequal returns: In their communities, the children do not see their elders getting jobs, wages, or other benefits commensurate with their level of education.

Also, according to Ogbu, because of the long history of discrimination and racism in U.S. schools, involuntary minority children and their families are often distrustful of the educational system. Children in these communities have routinely been subjected to what Jim Cummins calls *identity eradication*,[28] whereby their culture and language have been stripped away as one of the conditions for school success. These negative experiences result in their perception that equal educational opportunity and the folk theories of getting ahead in the United States are myths. The folk theories, however, are readily accepted by immigrants who have not had a long history of discrimination in this country. Given this situation, Ogbu claims that it is not unusual for students from castelike minorities to engage in what he calls *cultural inversion*, that is, to resist acquiring and

demonstrating the culture and cognitive styles identified with the dominant group. He asserts that these behaviors are considered "White"; include being studious and hardworking, speaking standard English, listening to European classical music, going to museums, getting good grades, and so on. Instead, involuntary minority students may choose to emphasize cultural behaviors that differentiate them from the majority and are in opposition to it—that is, demonstrate what Ogbu calls *oppositional behavior*. Such behaviors include language, speech forms, and other manifestations that help to characterize their group but are contrary to the behaviors promoted by the schools.

Even extremely bright students from involuntary minority groups may try just to "get by" because they fear being ostracized by their peers if they engage in behaviors that conform to the mainstream culture. They must cope, according to Signithia Fordham and John Ogbu, "with the burden of acting White."[29] These students, assert Fordham and Ogbu, see little benefit from academic success, at least in terms of peer relationships. Those who excel in school may feel both internal ambivalence and external pressures not to manifest such behaviors and attitudes. In research conducted in a predominantly African American school, Fordham and Ogbu found that successful students who were accepted by their peers also were either very successful in sports or had found another way to hide their academic achievement. According to Ogbu, involuntary minority parents, who themselves have a long history of discrimination and negative experiences at school, may subconsciously mirror these same attitudes, adding to their children's ambivalent attitudes about education and success.

Newer Perspectives About Cultural-Ecological Theories and Immigrant and "Minority" Experiences

Cultural-ecological theories have been helpful in explaining differences in the school experiences of students of various backgrounds. But the theories have also come under great scrutiny and criticism for being incomplete, ahistorical, and inflexible in allowing for individual differences. For example, Ogbu's theory may result in placing an inordinate responsibility on students and families without taking into account conditions outside their control that also affect learning. In addition, Ogbu's theories do not explain the long struggle of African American and other involuntary minorities for educational equality, nor do they explain the tremendous faith so many of these communities have had in the promise of public education. His explanation of oppositional culture has been criticized as being dangerously close to the old concept of the "culture of poverty," a deficit theory developed by Oscar Lewis in the 1960s that persists even today, and has been roundly criticized for its racist and ethnocentric overtones.[30]

More recent research has posed a direct challenge to Ogbu's framework, especially because of its inability to account for intragroup variability (see the section "Complicating Theories of Identities and Cultures Within School Structures" on page 296). That is, why do some involuntary minorities do well in school while others do not? Some scholars and educators have found Ogbu's theories too dichotomous and deterministic. For example, the typology does not neatly fit all groups, such as Mexican Americans, who share elements of both voluntary and involuntary minorities. Also, recent studies—most notably, one by Margaret Gibson—have found that the second generation of voluntary minorities is experiencing as much school failure as more established involuntary minorities because they do not wholeheartedly accept the folk theory of success as did their parents. They are also less likely to perceive the long-term benefits of hard work and study.[31]

Another criticism has to do with the role and influence of oppositional culture. As viewed by Ogbu, oppositional culture is detrimental to academic success because, in rejecting behaviors and attitudes that can lead to success, students are, in effect, jeopardizing their own futures. The possibility that African American students could be *both* oppositional *and* academically successful is not presented as a possibility in Ogbu's theory. David Gillborn, who has studied youths of various backgrounds in Great Britain, suggests that the dichotomy between resistance and conformity is too simplistic because it overlooks the great complexity of students' responses to schooling. That is, accommodation does not guarantee that success will follow, nor is it the only way to be academically successful; similarly, opposition does not necessarily lead to failure.[32] To understand this process more clearly, we now turn to a consideration of the concept of resistance.

Resistance Theory

Resistance theory, as articulated by scholars such as Henry Giroux, Jim Cummins, and Herbert Kohl, adds another layer to the explanation of school failure.[33] According to this theory, not learning what schools teach can be interpreted as a form of political resistance. Frederick Erickson maintains that, whereas cultural differences may cause some initial school failures and misunderstandings, it is only when they become entrenched over time that *not-learning*, a consistent pattern of refusing to learn, becomes the outcome of schooling.[34]

Resistance theory is helpful because it attempts to explain the complex relationship between disempowered communities and their schools. Students and their families are not only victims of the educational system but also actors. They learn to react to schools in ways that make perfect sense, given the reality of the schools, although some of these coping strategies may in the long run be self-defeating and counterproductive. On the other hand, Herb Kohl, describing *not-learning* as the response of students who refuse to learn, has concluded, "Over the years I've come to side with them in their refusal to be molded by a hostile society and have come to look upon not-learning as positive and healthy in many situations."[35]

There are numerous examples of students' resistance and they range from innocuous to dangerous: Inattention in class, failure to do homework, negative attitudes toward schoolwork, poor relationships with teachers, misbehavior, vandalism, and violence are all illustrations of students' resistance. We see many of these manifestations of resistance in the case studies of Paul Chavez and Latrell Elton that follow this chapter.

Students who develop a critical consciousness may also end up resisting education. Such students are often branded and punished as loudmouths and troublemakers. Although some drop out, others choose to no longer actively participate in the "game" of school. They might still show up, but they may adopt a passive or passive-aggressive stance. Others end up cutting many of their classes. Students who do continue coming to class may "dumb down" their own critical responses to the curriculum or to their teachers' pedagogy because they know instinctively that being seen as too critical or too much of a leader is potentially dangerous. Teachers, on the other hand, are often frustrated by apparently disinterested youth, even in honors classes, who look bored and disengaged or who allow themselves to engage only minimally and only with the more interesting and inventive strategies used by creative teachers. As a result, many capable and critically aware students are intellectually "on strike" even though they may be physically present in school.[36]

Dropping out is an extreme form of refusing education. Michelle Fine's 1991 study of a large urban school found two major reasons for students' decisions to leave: a political stance of resistance and disappointment with the "promise of education." Many of the students she spoke with were articulate in their resistance to school; even some of those who stayed in school were unsure about what benefits they would derive from their education.[37]

What causes students to resist education and otherwise engage in behaviors that might ultimately jeopardize their chances of learning? There is no simple answer to this question, but one probable element is a school climate that rejects students' identities. This is nowhere more evident than in the case studies that follow this chapter. Both Paul and Latrell were eloquent in describing how their backgrounds were not reflected in the school structures and curriculum. Latrell, especially, had perceived few positive messages in his school experience.

The nature of teachers' identities is also important. For example, in his research among Yup'ik

students and teachers, Jerry Lipka found that resistance was virtually nonexistent, and he concluded that resistance theory "makes much less sense in a classroom where the teacher is your uncle or your aunt and where most of the school employees come from your community."[38] This being the case, what are the implications for students from culturally dominated groups? Does it mean that they always need to be taught by teachers from their own cultural communities? This might be appropriate in some situations, but it is untenable and unrealistic in others. Moreover, believing this to be the case would imply that teachers can never be successful with students of backgrounds different from their own. This is not true, as we have seen in much of the literature cited, and as you will also see in the case studies of Paul and Latrell, both of whom had some caring and respectful teachers who did not share their ethnicity. Furthermore, in a society that claims to be democratic and pluralistic, believing that only teachers of particular backgrounds can teach students of the same background is unacceptable. A more comprehensive view of students' academic success or failure is needed.

Complicating Theories of Identities and Cultures Within School Structures

Dissatisfied with the cultural-ecological explanations of school failure like those derived from Ogbu and Fordham's theories on "acting White," and likewise unconvinced by resistance theories such as those previously described, some alternative theories are emerging from scholars such as Prudence Carter, Gilberto Conchas and D. Bruce Jackson.[39] These researchers present research in which students' perspectives, voices, and experiences are centered. Both Conchas and Carter take a sociological view of the ways in which culture and identity are discussed and enacted by urban students. Jackson, speaking from his experience as a high school teacher, focuses on the academic identities and agency—that is, self-advocacy and proactive engagement—of students. Conchas warns, for example, that minority group categories used in cultural-ecological theoretical frameworks do not allow for variations in the school experiences of racial minorities.[40]

Likewise, Carter cautions against creating master narratives that try to speak of all members of "involuntary minority groups" as if each student in these groups had identical experiences and perspectives.[41] For instance, she points out that recent research has shown that African Americans subscribe to the basic values of education as much as Whites do, or in some case, even more so. Nearly all of the participants in Carter's study agree that education is the key to success. They believe in the so-called American Dream that education may bring good jobs, home and car ownership, and intact families.

To more fully discuss what results in academic achievement, Carter points to *attachment to* and *engagement in* school, as explained by Monica Johnson, Robert Crosnoe, and Glen Elder.[42] *Attachment* is the affective component, or the degree to which students feel a sense of belonging and feel welcome and a part of school. *Engagement* is the behavioral component: whether students put in effort, are attentive, complete their homework, and so on. While attachment and engagement are conceptually distinct, they are often confused with valuing education. Carter maintains this distinction while allowing that both attachment and engagement influence achievement.

By interviewing 68 youths from low-income communities who identified as African American or Latino/Latina, Carter challenges the framework of "oppositional culture." She pays close attention to the ways in which culture is discussed influence student engagement and achievement:

> Students use culture as a vehicle to signal many things, ranging from the stylistic to the political. The oppositional culture framework, however, ignores the full spectrum of why and how culture becomes a social and political response to schooling by discounting the positive values and functions of these students' culture.[43]

Carter highlights youths' positive cultural assertions that contribute to their success, and she argues that their ethno-racial cultures are not adaptations to the limits created by a dominant culture. She maintains that focusing on a student's culture as a maladaptive response to social marginalization ignores the roles and values of nondominent cultural practices in the lives of minority youth.

Carter also found that gender is enacted in specific ways that affect school achievement within the lives of female and male students in marginalized communities. That girls and boys take up academic achievement by developing attachment, and committing to engagement, in differing ways, is often ignored in research about low income students of color. So much of the focus has been on disparities among racial and ethnic groups that the gender story *within* the groups has gone untold. Furthermore, the students, both girls and boys, in Carter's study did not equate academic achievement with "acting White." Instead, students recognized the unfairness in, and were critical of, the representation of what counts as knowledge, and the linking of intelligence (or what it means to be smart) with certain styles that acculturate toward "White" middle class ways.

Within the ethno-racial groups in her study, Carter noted three categories of characteristics that describe how students manage their identities: *noncompliant believers, cultural mainstreamers,* and *cultural straddlers.* Of these three, the noncompliant believers were found to have the widest disparity in their belief in the benefits of school, their engagement, and their achievement. The cultural mainstreamers embrace the dominant cultural repertoire, although they also express their own racial or ethnic background as a central part of their identity. Cultural straddlers obey school rules just as the cultural mainstreamers do, but they navigate between multiple cultures, including ethnic groups, peer groups, communities and schools, to simultaneously create meanings with their co-ethnic peers. According to Carter, cultural straddlers critique the school's cultural exclusivity and "negotiate schooling in a way that enables them to hold onto their native cultural styles and also embrace dominant cultural codes and discourses," making them more successful with their African American and Latino peers than cultural mainstreamers.[44]

Carter asserts that culture *does* matter in the achievement of African American and Latino students. She notes that students draw upon both dominant cultural capital and nondominant cultural capital to construct academic success. Three forces—race/ethnicity, class, and gender—dictate much about how "acting Black," "acting Spanish," or "acting White" get integrated into the identities of students. She is clear that African American and

Latino students need tools to make them literate, self-sufficient, politically active, and economically productive. Educators cannot disregard the values of different groups' cultural repertoires; they need to build upon the powerful cultural dynamics permeating the school.

Conchas's study also holds implications for how educators address the cultural identities within schools. He focused on a group of students, most of whom identified as African American, Latino, and Vietnamese. Conchas is emphatic about the different ways that these students embraced and asserted their cultural and academic identities within and between groups. By examining and comparing specific programs that follow the structural model of "school-within-a-school," Conchas addressed the institutional mechanisms of programs that create alienation among some successful students of color. Examining students' ideology in such programs revealed that they "embraced the importance of individualism and meritocracy, while simultaneously downplaying the significance of race, class, and gender equity."[45] Conchas found mechanisms in some programs that acted as a "mediating force against racial disparity."[46] Some programs supplied youth with both cultural and social capital, and encouraged cooperative experiences of academic achievement.

Conchas found that nurturing, mentoring relationships within schools are significant for students' development of multiple forms of social capital that may contribute to educational success. As such, he suggests that concentrated efforts are needed to reduce ethnic segregation and equalize all students' access within schools to mentoring and encouragement. Conchas also points to structural models supporting sociocultural processes that can develop a high-achieving academic culture of success. He cites the benefits of smaller, intimate school-within-a-school structures or small learning communities. His findings note that school structures directly contribute to differing patterns of school adaptation within and between racial groups. Moreover, some institutional arrangements are much better at creating a supportive cross-ethnic community of learners, while the sense of exclusion and competition in some programs contributes to racial tensions in schools.

Conchas's description of a culture of academic achievement, the social capital created by school relationships, and the call for small learning communities reverberate with some assertions made by D. Bruce Jackson. Jackson points out that students who are successful in school take on and sustain what he calls *academic identity*. Academic identity is an understanding of self within the context of school, in which intellectual activities within and outside of school are valued. Jackson acknowledges the many forces that influence student identity but argues that, despite the range of theories about student success or failure, success depends on what students decide to do or not do. Although teachers can influence those decisions, ultimately it is students who really direct how they spend their time. They are critical agents in their own education.

Although the theories developed by Carter, Conchas, and Jackson stem from a range of research projects conducted from diverse perspectives, they share a concern for the ways in which students' identities intersect with school cultures. They all maintain that while sociocultural factors and discriminatory histories may influence students' perception of their academic identities and their academic achievement, these factors do not *predetermine* academic success. These scholars are optimistic about the opportunity to tap into youths' dynamic, multiple ways of shaping self and their diverse means of expressing cultural identities. Within this lively interplay lies the potential for taking up academic identity and all the strategies for success that comprise it. It would be simple-minded to assert that simply wanting to succeed magically grants one an academic identity. That is why the focus of these theories holds particular promise: Rather than designing a particular roadmap to success, their focus is more like a global positioning system for teachers and students to view the multifaceted aspects of identity and the web of structures that support academic achievement.

The Impact of Educators' Caring

Another essential component in promoting student learning that has received great attention in the past two decades is what Nel Noddings has called the "ethic of care."[47] Noddings's impressive contribution to the conversation concerning student engagement with schooling cannot be overemphasized. For her, educators' caring is just as important—and in some cases, even more so—than larger structural conditions that influence student learning. Noddings postulates that whether and how teachers and schools care for students can make an immense difference in how students experience schooling. Her research is corroborated by a nation-wide survey of several hundred 13- to 17-year-old students who were asked whether they work harder for some teachers than for others. Three out of four said "yes" and that the reason was that these were the teachers who cared most for them. The survey authors concluded that effective schooling relies almost entirely on creative and passionate teachers.[48] Angela Valenzuela, in a three-year investigation of academic achievement among Mexican and Mexican American students in a Texas high school, provides compelling examples of care among a small number of teachers.[49] Teachers showed they cared through close and affirming relationships with their students, high expectations for students' capabilities, and respect for their students' families. This was the case in spite of the general context of the school that provided what Valenzuela called *subtractive schooling*, that is, a process that divested students of the social and cultural resources they brought to their education, making them vulnerable for academic failure. Her research led Valenzuela to locate the problem of "underachievement" not to students' identities or parents' economic situation but to school-based relationships and organizational structures. Nilda Flores-Gónzales, in a study among Latino students in Chicago, came to similar conclusions.[50] For both of these researchers, care was of immense significance.

The problem is that educators sometimes think of caring only as outward shows of affection—something that teachers might find difficult or even inappropriate. Hugging students, however, is not the only way to demonstrate care. One parent described a teacher to us who loved her students but did not hug them. She explained, "She loves them with her eyes!" She went on to say that this teacher also loved her students with her encouragement, her demands, and her expectations. Hence, *care* does not just mean giving students hugs or pats on the back. Care means loving students in the most profound ways: through high expectations, great support, and rigorous demands.

Another example comes from Susan Roberta Katz in research done among Central American and Mexican immigrant students in a California high school. Exploring the tensions between these students and their teachers, she found striking differences in the perceptions of each. Although teachers felt they were doing their best under difficult circumstances, students described these same teachers as racist and uncaring. Katz's analysis was that students' perceptions may have been linked to structural conditions in the school such as rigid ability tracking and high teacher turnover, conditions that contributed to rendering the possibility of consistent caring relationships remote. She found that both teachers' caring and high expectations were essential in fostering positive learning outcomes for students. Specifically, Katz concluded,

> High expectations can result in setting goals that are impossible for the student to reach without adult support and assistance. On the other hand, caring without high expectations can turn dangerously into paternalism in which teachers feel sorry for "underprivileged" youth but never challenge them academically.[51]

A further example comes from a study that also focused on students of Mexican descent in California. Here, too, the climate of the educational program was found to influence students' engagement with learning. In this migrant-education program, researchers Margaret Gibson and Livier Bejínez discovered that staff members facilitated students' learning in various ways: caring relationships, access to institutional support, and activities based on students' cultural backgrounds. The researchers concluded that caring relationships were at the very heart of the program's success. Specifically, in spite of students' vulnerable status (including their migrant status, poverty, and the fact that only 7 percent had parents who had completed high school), there was a remarkably high degree of school persistence. Nearly halfway through their senior year, amazingly, 75 percent were still attending high school. As in other research highlighted here, the researchers explain *caring* not just as affection but as close and trusting relationships that, most importantly, create a sense of *belonging* in the school community. This sense of belonging is especially meaningful, they conclude, for Mexican American and other students of color because of the power differential that exists between them and people of the dominant society. Specifically, Gibson and Bejínez state that "students who feel they can bring their whole selves to school and have their multiple identities affirmed, or at the very least allowed, are more likely to feel they belong in school and are more likely to engage with the schooling process than those who do not."[52]

These ideas resounded in two distinct recent research projects we (Sonia and Patty) each conducted. In my (Sonia's) research with teachers, when I asked them to explain why they teach, I found five qualities that describe caring and committed teachers: *a sense of mission; solidarity with and empathy for students; the courage to challenge mainstream knowledge; improvisation;* and *a passion for social justice.*[53] All of these are rooted in caring and committed practices, but here we focus on the second quality: *solidarity with and empathy for* students. Solidarity and empathy can also be described as love, although love is not a word that one hears very often when discussing teaching. Within the context of schools, love means that teachers have genuine respect, high expectations, and great admiration for their students. *Solidarity* means remembering what it was like to be a child, and forming a community of learners. The combination of empathy and solidarity is demonstrated in numerous ways, including valuing students' families, understanding what life is like for different children, and anticipating the diverse worlds they encounter.

Patty's study echoed Sonia's. When I (Patty) interviewed students in urban schools, I asked them what teachers needed to know to be effective in diverse classrooms. Their answers consistently pointed to solidarity with, and empathy for, students. One of the implications that my study asserts is that reconceptualized multicultural teacher education may need to consider ways to teach what were previously called *unteachable qualities* such as solidarity, empathy, and compassion to influence high academic achievement.[54]

Another theory closely connected with the ethic of caring is described by Ricardo Stanton-Salazar as a "social capital networks framework." This theory focuses on the centrality of social relations and networks between adults and youth, particularly vulnerable youth who rarely have access to the social capital that more privileged students take for granted. According to Stanton-Salazar, these networks function to reproduce or deny privilege and power. In the end, Stanton-Salazar argues, it is the power of institutional agents, such as teachers, counselors, and other adults who can manipulate the social and institutional conditions in and out of school, that determines who "makes it" and who doesn't. What exactly are the kinds of networks and institutional supports to which he refers? As examples, he cites various kinds of knowledge, including particular discourses and social capital: *bridging* (i.e., providing access to gatekeepers and to other opportunities usually closed to disenfranchised students), advocacy, role modeling, emotional and moral support, and advice and guidance.[55] These supports are linked with caring because it is only through trusting and close relationships with teachers that some students gain access to such networks. Through these networks, students can learn to "decode the system" and to participate in power while that they continue to honor their identities. In turn, these networks provide students with the skills and resources they will need to successfully navigate the broader society.

Developing a Comprehensive Understanding of Student Learning

No simple explanation accounts for student achievement or failure. As we have seen in this chapter, most explanations have been inadequate or incomplete. Some have failed to consider the significance of culture in learning; others have not taken into account the social, cultural, and political context of schooling; and still others have placed all the responsibility for academic failure or success on students and their families. Even the persistence of racism and discrimination, the presence of unjust policies and practices in schools, and the role that schools play in reproducing existing societal inequities do not fully explain school failure.

Broad societal structures, for instance, make a difference in student learning. Newer perspectives concerning the education of new and old immigrant groups of color in the United States have emerged in the past several years, and they add significantly to our understanding of the achievement of these groups. For example, Alejandro Portes and Rubén Rumbaut, in a series of long-term, comprehensive studies of immigrant families of various backgrounds, conclude that the process of "growing up American," in their words, "ranges from smooth acceptance to traumatic confrontation depending on the characteristics that immigrants and their children bring along and the social context that receives them."[56] Portes and Rumbaut found that race is a paramount factor in whether and how groups are accepted into the mainstream, and it can overpower the influence of other factors such as social class, religion, or language.

In addition, the context of immigrants' arrival is also consequential. Portes and Rumbaut suggest that immigrants fleeing from communism are received more favorably than those fleeing economic exploitation. As examples, they cite the case of Haitian, Nicaraguan, and Mexican immigrants, who have significantly lower earnings than Cubans and Vietnamese, even after controlling for level of education, knowledge of English, and occupation. Also, no matter how long they have been here, the earnings of Mexicans, Nicaraguans, and Haitians remain flat, while those of Vietnamese and Cubans increase each additional year of residence in the United States. Portes and Rumbaut come to this astonishing conclusion: "Hence, no matter how educated a Mexican or Haitian parent is, his or her chances of moving ahead economically are significantly constrained by the social environment in which his or her group has become incorporated."[57] Thus, for these groups, a college degree yields no improvement in earnings. This conclusion flies in the face of conventional wisdom that education equals economic advancement. Clearly, additional factors—race, context of incorporation, and others—are at work here.

Even in the face of these larger structural conditions, however, the school context *can* make a difference. Underachievement, as Jim Cummins has suggested, is also the result of the interactions between teachers, students, and their families.[58] When teachers respect and affirm the identities and experiences of students and their families, they also change the nature of the interactions they have with them, and this can help promote student achievement. In Paul Chavez's case, for instance,

the staff's closeness with him and his family paid off in his growing association with school and learning.

Also, how students and communities *perceive* and *react* to schools is another consideration in explaining school achievement. However, in spite of the perceptions and reactions of particular groups to schools, there are always individual exceptions. The students in Prudence Carter's and Gilberto Conchas's studies make clear that not all African American students, even those from economically oppressed communities, fail; many do not see school success as "acting White"; and not all voluntary immigrants are successful in school. Unless we look at individual cases as well as at entire groups, we fall into rather facile, inaccurate explanations of failure. These can lead to stereotypes and inappropriate educational expectations.

School climate makes a difference in other ways as well. When teachers and schools believe their students are capable learners and they create appropriate learning environments for them, young people are given a clear and positive message about their worth and abilities. The policies and practices of schools, and the hopes and expectations they have for students, are also key variables in explaining student academic achievement. In Paul's case study, you will see the positive effect that participating in developing the school rules had on him. In the case of Latrell, he characterized the atmosphere in his school as negative: "Like I'm just a prisoner, like I'm a bad person." On the other hand, he described the school's teachers as supportive: "They've been helping me out a lot, a way, way lot. 'Cause I've got after-school tutorial, and we got more help after school. I'm a good student right now". Latrell's case illustrates that school policies are not always consistent with teachers' practices, presenting the student with a challenging landscape to navigate.

Looking beyond just cultural and social class characteristics as determinants of school achievement can be empowering because it shines light on what teachers and schools can do to improve student learning. As we saw in Chapter 9, characteristics of the school environment and culture that make a positive difference include an enriched and more demanding curriculum, respect for students' languages and cultures, high expectations for all students, and encouragement of parental involvement. However, reforming school structures alone will not lead to substantive improvement in student achievement if such changes are not accompanied by profound changes in what we believe students deserve and are capable of learning. In short, changing school policies and practices is a necessary but insufficient condition for improving academic achievement. As we have seen in the discussion about care, the nature of the relationships among students, teachers, and schools also matter a great deal. This is where the issue of caring and mentoring matter most.

Learning environments that may seem at first glance to be totally culturally inappropriate for some students can in fact be effective. The so-called "Catholic school effect" is a case in point. In some ways, nothing seems more culturally incompatible for African American and Latino students than a Catholic school: Bilingual programs are usually unavailable, classes tend to be overcrowded, and formal environments that stress individual excellence over cooperation are common. In spite of these conditions, Catholic schools have been successful environments for many Latino and African American children, especially those from poor communities. The literature points to the fact that Catholic schools, because of restricted resources, tend to offer all students a less differentiated curriculum, less tracking, and more academic classes. They also

have clear, uncomplicated missions and strong social contracts.[59] What may at first glance appear to be incongruous in terms of cultural compatibility is explained by school structures that imply high expectations for all students.

This discussion leads us to the conclusion that school achievement can be explained only by taking into account multiple, competing, and dynamic conditions: the school's tendency to replicate society and its inequities; cultural and language incompatibilities; the unfair and bureaucratic structures of schools; the nature of the relationships among students; students' multiple and dynamic ways of asserting ethno-racial, gender and cultural identities; teachers' relationships with the communities they serve; and the political relationship of particular groups to society and the schools. It is tricky business, however, to seek causal explanations for school success and failure. Understanding how numerous complex conditions are mediated within the school and home settings can also help explain students' academic success or failure. Understanding all these conditions contributes to a more comprehensive explanation of the massive school failure of many students. This is the sociopolitical context of multicultural education, and it forms the basis for the conceptual framework that has been developed in this book.

SUMMARY

In this chapter, we have explored a number of theories regarding conditions that influence school failure and success. The deficit theories popularized in the 1960s were responsible for much of our educational policy during that era; their influence has continued into the present. These theories assumed that children from families whose cultural backgrounds differed from the majority, or from poor neighborhoods, were either genetically or culturally inferior to culturally dominant children from the middle class.

An alternative explanation developed during the 1970s was that schools were responsible for school

failure because they reproduced the existing economic and social inequities, and therefore, replicated structural inequality. During this time, the cultural mismatch theory was also developed. According to this theory, schools are unsuccessful in educating a substantial number of students because there is a mismatch between their home cultures and the culture of the school. Social class and family background have re-emerged in recent research as forces outside of schools that influence underachievement. These theories argue for the necessity of changing social policy in order to support achievement among students marginalized by race and class. The theories of John Ogbu and others, developed during the late 1970s, argue that there is a crucial distinction between castelike minorities and immigrant minorities. These theorists argue that cultural differences alone cannot explain the differential school achievement of distinct "minority" groups.

Resistance theory also has helped us understand that students and their families are frequently engaged in some form of resistance to the education to which they are exposed. Resistance may be either passive or active, and it may have consequences that are counterproductive to the interests of the students who engage in it. Alternatively, resistance can lead to a critical awareness of structural inequality and a desire to succeed academically in order to make change, as we shall see in both case studies that follow this chapter illustrate.

Challenges to Ogbu's cultural-ecological theories and to resistance theories come from Prudence Carter and Gilberto Conchas. The majority of low-income students of color in urban schools who participated in their studies did not equate "acting White" with high academic achievement. The students were critical of social and education stratification that devalued expressions of knowledge differing from middle-class White norms. Carter and Conchas cited ways in which the students constructed academic identities that intersected with their ethno-racial cultures, gendered selves and socioecomnic experiences. These theories refute labeling nondominant school behaviors and academic performance as maladaptive responses to the dominant framework.

Finally, the significance of caring relationships among students and their teachers has taken on great significance in the recent past. There is a growing awareness of the tremendous difference that teachers—and the school climate in general—can make in the lives and futures of young people. Teachers and schools that affirm students' identities, believe in their intelligence, and accept nothing less than the best have proved to be inspirational for young people, even if they live in otherwise difficult circumstances. In fact, the case can be made that such relationships are one of the most important elements of student learning.

We have attempted to develop a comprehensive view of school achievement by providing an analysis and critique of a number of theories. It is clear that no single explanation of academic achievement is sufficient to explain why some students succeed in school and others fail. Rather, we need to understand school achievement as a combination of *personal, cultural, familial, interactive, political, relational,* and *societal* issues, and this requires an understanding of the sociopolitical context in which education takes place.

To Think About

1. What did William Ryan mean by "culturally depriving schools"? Can you give some examples?
2. Think of your own students. How accurate do you think John Ogbu's classification of "voluntary" and "involuntary" minorities is? Consider both the advantages and disadvantages of this theory.
3. Think about schools and classrooms with which you are familiar. Have you noticed examples of student resistance? If so, what are they, and what is their effect?
4. Consider Prudence Carter's categories: cultural mainstreamers, cultural straddlers, and noncompliant believers. How can these categories help you understand your students and their achievement? Does your teaching style and philosophy support one of these categories more than another? Is there a category you would like to support more?
5. You and a group of your colleagues need to determine why a particular student has been doing poorly in your classes. What will you look at? Why?

Activities for Personal, School, and Community Change

1. If you teach in an elementary school, plan a visit to the homes of your students to get to know their families. Use the occasion to find out about the children: what they like and what motivates them to learn. Ask the families about some of the culturally enriching activities they are engaged in within their communities. If you teach in a middle or high school class in which you have many students, making home visits unlikely, ask students to describe some of the activities they do with their families. How can you

use what you've learned to create a more culturally affirming classroom?

2. Think about a teacher who has made a difference in your life. Try to get in touch with her or him. Tell that person how he or she influenced you, and ask for advice on how you can have the same impact on your students. How can you apply what you have learned from this to your own teaching?

3. Get together with a group of colleagues to discuss how students in your school display "resistance" behaviors. What exact behaviors are they? Are these behaviors getting in the way of their engagement with school? If so, what can you do about them? You may also want to visit one another's classrooms to lend a pair of "fresh eyes" to the situation. Decide on a plan of action for your classrooms, and come together again to talk about the results.

Companion Website

For access to additional case studies, weblinks, concept cards, and other material related to this chapter, visit the text's companion website at **www.ablongman.com/nieto5e.**

Notes to Chapter 11

1. For full expositions of these arguments, see, for example, Carl Bereiter and Siegfried Englemann, *Teaching Disadvantaged Children in the Preschool* (Englewood Cliffs, NJ: Prentice-Hall, 1966); Arthur R. Jensen, "How Much Can We Boost IQ and Scholastic Achievement?" *Harvard Educational Review* 39 no. 1 (1969): 1–123; Frank Reissman, *The Culturally Deprived Child* (New York: Harper & Row, 1962).

2. See Samuel Bowles and Herbert Gintis, *Schooling in Capitalist America: Educational Reform and the Contradictions of Economic Life* (New York: Basic Books, 1976); Joel Spring, *The Rise and Fall of the Corporate State* (Boston: Beacon Press, 1972).

3. Stephen S. Baratz and Joan C. Baratz, "Early Childhood Intervention: The Social Science Base of Institutional Racism." In *Challenging the Myths: The Schools, the Blacks, and the Poor,* Reprint Series no. 5 (Cambridge, MA: Harvard Educational Review, 1971).

4. William Ryan, *Blaming the Victim* (New York: Vintage Books, 1972): 61.

5. Linda Christensen, "Whose Standard? Teaching Standard English." In *Language Development: A Reader for Teachers,* edited by Brenda Miller Power and Ruth Shagoury Hubbard (Englewood Cliffs, NJ: Merrill, 1996).

6. Shirley Brice Heath, *Ways with Words* (New York: Cambridge University Press, 1983).

7. Richard J. Herrnstein and Charles Murray, *The Bell Curve: Intelligence and Class Structure in American Life* (New York: Free Press, 1994).

8. Steve Fraser, ed., *The Bell Curve Wars: Race, Intelligence, and the Future of America* (New York: Basic Books, 1995) provides a collection of essays by leading scholars that refute the assertions of Herrnstein and Murray. Also see "The Bell Curve: Laying Bare the Resurgence of Scientific Racism." *American Behavioral Scientist* 39, no. 1 (September/October 1995).

9. Pierre Bourdieu, "The Forms of Capital." In *Handbook of Theory and Research for the Sociology of Education,* edited by John G. Richardson (New York: Greenwood Press, 1986): 246.

10. See Bowles and Gintis, *Schooling in Capitalist America: Educational Reform and the Contradictions of Economic Life,* and Spring, *The Rise and Fall of the Corporate State.*

11. Michael W. Apple, *Teachers and Texts: A Political Economy of Class and Gender Relations in Education* (Boston: Routledge and Kegan Paul, 1986).

12. Paulo Freire, *Teachers as Cultural Workers: Letters to Those Who Dare Teach* (Boulder, CO: Westview Press, 1998): 72–73.

13. Gloria Ladson-Billings, *The Dreamkeepers: Successful Teachers of African American Children* (San Francisco: Jossey-Bass, 1994). See also Geneva Gay, *Culturally Responsive Teaching: Theory, Research, and Practice* (New York: Teachers College Press, 2000).

14. Richard St. Germaine, "Drop-out Rates Among American Indian and Alaska Native Students: Beyond Cultural Discontinuity." In *ERIC Digest, Clearinghouse on Rural Education and Small Schools* (Charleston, WV: Appalachia Educational Laboratory, November 1995).

15. Oscar Lewis, *La Vida: A Puerto Rican Family in the Culture of Poverty—San Juan and New York* (New York: Random House, 1965); and Michael Harrington, *The Other America: Poverty in the United States* (New York: Scribner, 1997/1971).

16. Gloria Ladson-Billings, "It's Not the Culture of Poverty, It's the Poverty of Culture: The Problem with Teacher Education." *Anthropology and Education Quarterly* 37, no. 2 (June 2006): 104–109.

17. Margaret A. Gibson, "The School Performance of Immigrant Minorities: A Comparative View." *Anthropology and Education Quarterly* 18, no. 4 (December 1987): 262–275.

18. Richard Rothstein, *Class and Schools: Using Social, Economic and Education Reform to Close the Black–White Achievement Gap* (New York: Economic Policy Institute, Teachers College, 2004).

19. Robert Evans, *Family Matters: How School Can Cope With the Crisis in Childrearing* (San Francisco: Jossey-Bass, 2004); also see Robert Evans, "Reframing the Achievement Gap." *Phi Delta Kappan* 86, no. 8 (April 2005): 582–589.

20. Pedro Noguera, "Social Class, But What About Schools?" *Poverty & Race* 13, no. 5. Washington, DC: Poverty & Race Research Action Council, (September/October 2004): 11–12.

21. Mark Simon, "What Teachers Know." *Poverty & Race* 13, no. 5. Washington, DC. Poverty & Race Research Action Council (September/October 2004): 16.

22. John U. Ogbu and Herbert D. Simons, "Voluntary and Involuntary Minorities: A Cultural-Ecological Theory of School Performance with Some Implications for Education." *Anthropology & Education Quarterly* 29, no. 2 (1998): 155–188.

23. John U. Ogbu, "Variability in Minority School Performance: A Problem in Search of an Explanation." *Anthropology & Education Quarterly* 18, no. 4 (December 1987): 312–334.

24. For a more extensive discussion, see Evelyn Jacob and Cathie Jordan, eds., *Minority Education: Anthropological Perspectives* (Norwood, NJ: Ablex, 1993).

25. María E. Matute-Bianchi, "Situational Ethnicity and Patterns of School Performance Among Immigrant and Nonimmigrant Mexican-Descent Students." In *Minority Status and Schooling*, edited by Margaret A. Gibson and John U. Ogbu. Also, research by Susan Katz with Central American and Mexican immigrants found that those who were born in the United States or who had arrived here before the age of 5 had the most difficulties at school in terms of both academics and behavior. See Susan Roberta Katz, "Where the Streets Cross the Classroom: A Study of Latino Students' Perspectives on Cultural Identity in City Schools and Neighborhood Gangs." *Bilingual Research Journal* 20, nos. 3, 4 (Summer/Fall 1995): 603–631.

26. Donna Deyhle and Karen Swisher, "Research in American Indian and Alaska Native Education: From Assimilation to Self-Determination." In *Review of Research in Education* 22, edited by Michael W. Apple (Washington, DC: American Educational Research Association, 1997): 113–194.

27. Marcelo M. Suarez-Orozco, " 'Becoming Somebody': Central American Immigrants in the U.S." *Anthropology & Education Quarterly* 18, no. 4 (December 1987): 287–299.

28. Jim Cummins, *Negotiating Identities: Education for Empowerment in a Diverse Society* (Ontario, CA: California Association for Bilingual Education, 1996).

29. Signithia Fordham and John U. Ogbu, "Black Students' School Success: Coping with the 'Burden of Acting White.' " *Urban Review* 18, no. 3 (1986): 176–206.

30. For Oscar Lewis's theory of the culture of poverty, see *La Vida: A Puerto Rican Family in the Culture of Poverty—San Juan and New York* (New York: Random House, 1965).

31. Margaret A. Gibson, "Conclusion: Complicating the Immigrant/Involuntary Minority Typology." *Anthropology and Education Quarterly* 28, no. 3 (September 1997): 431–454.

32. David Gillborn, "Ethnicity and Educational Performance in the United Kingdom: Racism, Ethnicity, and Variability in Achievement." *Anthropology & Education Quarterly* 28, no. 3 (September 1997): 375–393.

33. Henry A. Giroux, *Theory and Resistance in Education: A Pedagogy for the Opposition* (South Hadley, MA: Bergen & Garvey, 1983); see also Cummins, *Negotiating Identities: Education for Empowerment in a Diverse Society;* and Herbert Kohl, *'I Won't Learn From You' and Other Thoughts on Creative Maladjustment* (New York: New Press, 1994).

34. Frederick Erickson, "Transformation and School Success: The Politics and Culture of Educational Achievement." In *Minority Education*, edited by Evelyn Jacob and Cathie Jordan.

35. Kohl, *'I Won't Learn From You' and Other Thoughts on Creative Maladjustment*, 2.

36. We are grateful to John Raible for these insights.

37. Michelle Fine, *Framing Dropouts: Notes on the Politics of an Urban Public High School* (Albany: State University of New York Press, 1991).

38. Jerry Lipka, "Toward a Culturally-Based Pedagogy: A Case Study of One Yup'ik Eskimo Teacher." In *Transforming Curriculum for a Culturally Diverse Society,* edited by Etta R. Hollins (Mahwah, NJ: Lawrence Erlbaum, 1996).

39. Prudence L. Carter, *Keepin' It Real: School Success Beyond Black and White* (New York: Oxford University Press, 2005); Gilberto Q. Conchas, *The Color of Success: Race and High-Achieving Urban Youth* (New York: Teachers College Press, 2006); D. Bruce Jackson, "Education Reform as if Student Agency Mattered: Academic Microcultures and Student Identity." *Phi Delta Kappan* 84, no. 8 (April 2003): 579–585.

40. Conchas, *The Color of Success: Race and High-Achieving Urban Youth,* 12–13.

41. Carter, *Keepin' It Real: School Success Beyond Black and White,* 8.

42. Monica K. Johnson, Robert Crosnoe, and Glen H. Elder, Jr. "Students' Attachment and Academic Engagement: The Role of Race and Ethnicity." *Sociology of Education* 74, no. 4 (2001): 318–334.

43. Carter, *Keepin' It Real: School Success Beyond Black and White,* 8.

44. Carter, *Keepin' It Real,* 30–31.

45. Jackson, "Education Reform as if Student Agency Mattered: Academic Microcultures and Student Identity."

46. Conchas, *The Color of Success: Race and High-Achieving Urban Youth,* 115.

47. Nel Noddings, *The Challenge to Care in Schools: An Alternative Approach to Education* (New York: Teachers College Press, 1992).

48. S. Crabtree, "Teachers Who Care Get the Most from Kids." *Detroit News,* June 4, 2004, 9.

49. Angela Valenzuela, *Subtractive Schooling: U.S.-Mexican Youth and the Politics of Caring* (Albany: State University of New York Press, 1999).

50. Nilda Flores-González, *School Kids, Street Kids: Identity and High School Completion Among Latinos* (New York: Teachers College Press, 2002).

51. Susan Roberta Katz, "Teaching in Tensions: Latino Immigrant Youth, Their Teachers, and the Structures of Schooling." *Teachers College Record* 100, no. 4 (Summer 1999): 809–840.

52. Margaret A. Gibson and Livier F. Bejínez, "Dropout Prevention: How Migrant Education Supports Mexican Youth." *Journal of Latinos and Education* 1, no. 3 (2002): 155–175.

53. Sonia Nieto, *Why We Teach* (New York: Teachers College Press, 2005): 204.

54. Patricia Bode, "Multicultural Art Education: Voices of Art Teachers and Students in the Postmodern Era," diss., University of Massachusetts Amherst, 2005.

55. Ricardo Stanton-Salazar, "A Social Capital Framework for Understanding the Socialization of Racial Minority Children and Youth." *Harvard Educational Review* 67, no. 1 (Spring 1997): 1–40.

56. Alejandro Portes and Rubén Rumbaut, *Legacies: The Story of the Immigrant Second Generation* (Berkeley: University of California Press, and New York: Russell Sage Foundation, 2001). Valerie E. Lee, Linda F. Winfield, and Thomas C. Wilson, "Academic Behaviors Among High-Achieving African-American Students." *Education and Urban* Society 24, no. 1 (November 1991): 65–86.

57. *Ibid.,* 80.

58. Cummins, *Negotiating Identities: Education for Empowerment in a Diverse Society.*

59. See, for example, Anthony S. Bryk, Valerie E. Lee, and Peter B. Holland, *Catholic Schools and the Common Good* (Cambridge, MA: Harvard Educational Review Press, 1993) and Jacqueline Jordan Irvine and Michele Foster, *Growing Up African American in Catholic Schools* (New York: Teachers College Press, 1996).

CHAPTER 11 CASE STUDIES

Paul Chavez

I don't want to speak too soon, but I'm pretty much on a good road here.

Speaking in an earnest and intense tone, Paul Chavez[1] thought carefully before sharing his thoughts about the importance of school, the "hood," and his family. Paul was 16 years old at the time of his interview, and he had already lived a lifetime full of gang activity, drugs, and disappointment. The signs were evident, from his style of dress to the "tag" (tattoo) on his arm, to his reminiscence of "homeboys" who had been killed. Describing himself as Chicano and Mexican American, Paul's was the third generation in his family to be born in Los Angeles. He did not speak Spanish but said that both his mother and grandmother did, even though they too were born and raised here.

Paul lived with his mother, two brothers ages 19 and 9, and two younger sisters. Another brother, 21, was not living at home. His mother was trying to obtain her high school equivalency diploma; she had failed the test once, but was studying hard to try to pass it the next time. She and Paul's father had been separated for about four years, and Paul described the entire family as "Christian." His mother was a church leader, and his brother was a Bible study leader. Even his father, a recovering alcoholic, who had lived on the streets for years and spent time in prison, was living in what Paul called a "Christian home," probably a halfway house.

The one-family homes in Paul's East L.A. neighborhood mask the poverty and despair that are easier to see in other urban ghettos, with their high-rise tenements and projects. Here, the mostly Latino families struggle to maintain a sense of community in the well-kept homes on small lots. However, signs of gang activity are apparent in the tags on buildings and walls. Paul said that an outsider suspected of belonging to another gang was likely to get jumped merely for walking down the street.

School problems began for Paul when he was in third or fourth grade, and he had been suspended on numerous occasions for poor behavior. The problem was not lack of ability (his teachers always felt he was smart) but rather lack of interest. He was more interested in belonging to a "school gang," a group of young boys looking for boys in other classes to fight. In spite of the lure of gangs, he remembered fifth grade as the best year he had had in school, and he attributed this to Ms. Nelson, the most caring teacher he had until he went to his current school. Paul already wore gang-affiliated attire, and he had a reputation as a troublemaker, but she did not let this get in the way of her high expectations of him. It was in her class that he became interested in history, and he recalled being fascinated by the American Revolution.

By the time Paul began junior high school, peer pressure, family problems, and street violence brought the situation to a head. Seventh and eighth grades were his worst years. He was expelled in eighth grade, and although he was told by school authorities to attend an alternative school in another district, he refused to go and instead stayed home for six months. By ninth grade he was heavily involved in gang activity, joining the 18th Street Gang, a gang with thousands of members not only in L.A. but also in other cities and even in other states. Thirteen of his cousins were or had been in the same gang, as was an older brother, so the role of gang as "family" was even more revelant in his case. An uncle and a cousin had both been killed as a result of their gang activity.

Encouraged by his mother, Paul tried to enroll in another program but was again expelled after a few months. Then he heard about and applied to the Escuela de Dignidad y Orgullo (School of Dignity and Pride), a high school for students who had dropped out of other schools. With a large Chicano population, the school was characterized by a multicultural curriculum with a focus on Chicano history, and it relied on student and staff involvement in its day-to-day operations. All talk of gangs was discouraged, and the staff tried hard to create a different kind of community here, one not affiliated with gang culture. The staff included counselors, a psychologist, a probation officer, and several teachers. Although Paul had not formally been arrested, because of his previous problems, he agreed to a voluntary placement with the probation officer, just to "keep me on the right road," he said.

The new road Paul had taken was far from easy for him, however. He had also been expelled from Escuela de Dignidad y Orgullo, and it was only after trying another program and then spending several months on the street that he had realized he wanted to return. All of his friends had quit school, and he feared ending up like them. He had been accepted at Escuela once again and had done well since returning two years before. At the time he was interviewed, Paul was spending most of his time at school, doing homework every day when he got home, and working after school at the local city hall, a job the school found for him. Paul described Escuela as different from any other he had attended because the entire staff cared about and encouraged the students and because Chicano culture and history were central to the curriculum, making it a more exciting place to learn.

Paul's philosophy at this point was to take life one day at a time because the lure of gang life was still ever-present. He had not yet quit the gang, and it was obvious that he was at a crossroads in his life. The next several months might determine which direction his life would take: either an escalating life of crime on the streets or a promising future of education and work.

Paul's case study highlights two goals he had had for a long time: *to be respected* and to make something of himself, two goals that are frequently at odds. Another theme is his determination to *"make it better,"* and the third is the *importance of family support.*

"Everybody's Gotta Get Respect"

I grew up ditching school, just getting in trouble, trying to make a dollar, that's it, you know? Just go to school, steal from the store, and go sell candies at school. And that's what I was doing in the third or fourth grade. I was always getting in the principal's office, suspended, kicked out, everything, starting from the third grade.

My fifth grade teacher, Ms. Nelson, she put me in a play and that, like, tripped me out. Like, why do you want me in a play? Me, I'm just a mess-up. Still, you know, she put me in a play. And in fifth grade, I think that was the best year out of the whole six years [of elementary school]. I learned a lot about the Revolutionary War, you know? The fifth grade was a grade I'll always remember. Had good friends. We had a project we were involved in. Ms. Nelson was a good teacher. She just involved everyone. We made books, this and that. And I used to like to write, and I wrote two . . . three books. Was in a book fair and this and that. She did pretty nice things. She got real deep into you, just, you know, "Come on, you can do it." That was a good year for me, the fifth grade.

My most troubled years was my junior high years. Seventh grade, first day of school, I met this guy and then, from there, we started to form. And every junior high, you're gonna have a group, okay? You're gonna have a group that you hang around with. And it got to we just started always starting trouble in classes. Whatever period we had, we just started trouble in. And me, I have a great sense of humor, right? I can make people laugh a lot. So then I was always getting kicked out of the classroom. And so what that got me was kind of, I guess popular, right? Where girls were always around me. I had a big group. But, like, I was always the one clowning, getting in trouble. So it kind of like set a path for me where I was, like, all right, so I clown and get popularity. All right, I understand now the program.

I [wasn't] in a gang, but I was dressing pretty . . . still gang affiliated. And so people looked like, "Well, where you from?" "I ain't from nowhere." And that kind of like got me to want to be from somewhere so I could tell 'em, "Well, I'm from here. . . ." Those were the years in seventh grade, and I was fighting with eighth graders. I'd be in a dance, a little Oriental kid would come up to me and she goes, "I know you, you're Paul," this and that. They would know me. It made me feel good.

Being in a gang, you think about who you're retaliating, you know, just another Chicano brother. And that's kind of deep. Well, why you're gonna be from a neighborhood [gang], have pride, this and that, and take out your own *Raza*, you know?[2] So that kind of always caught me in my mind. You see a lot of your own people just going down because of your neighborhood. And it's a trip. And you got a lot of homeboys that come out from the system, the jails, and it's real segregated in there, you know, the Blacks and Chicanos. And they even got the border brothers, the ones from Mexico who don't speak no English. They're even separated from the Chicanos, the Sureños, that's right from South L.A. Okay, they're paranoid in there, and everybody is, like, "What's up with the Blacks? It's on, it's on. We're gonna have a war." And everybody, then they turn little things into big things. So it's really just a race war going on in the inside, and they bring it out to us.

It has a great hold on you, and it's, like, I talk to my cousin. He's still into it real deep. I'm not really. Don't get me wrong: I'm from the neighborhood, but I'm not really deep into it. You know what I mean? But it's, like, I talk to 'em. "Yeah, we were with the homeboys on the Eastside, blah, blah, blah, this and that," and I'll be like, "Damn," and I think, "I wish I was there getting off on drinking and shit."

I had a cousin, he was 16 in '89 when he passed away. He was my cousin . . . family . . . from 18th Street, too. And what happened, see, he passed away and that's another tragedy. It's just, you see so much. I'm 16, and I see so much. First his dad passed away and then my cousin . . . my uncle and my cousin. And you think, "Man, all this because of a gang!" And there's times when you just sit and you think, you sit and you think, and you say, "Why? Why? Why? What is this?" But you don't know why, but you have it so much inside of you. It's hard, it's not easy to get rid of. I don't want to get rid of, but you just got to try to focus on other things right now. I'm from a gang and that's it, and just 'cause I'm from a gang doesn't mean I can't make myself better.

But me, I do care. I have a life, and I want to keep it. I don't want to lose it. I have two little sisters, and I want to see them grow up too, and I want to have my own family. So, I got the tag. I got a big 18 on my arm where everybody could see it, and that's the way I was about a year ago. You know, man, if you would be talking a year ago I'd be, like, "I'm from the neighborhood." I'd be talking to you in slang street all crazy, you know? Now I'm more intelligent.

I try not to get influenced too much . . . pulled into what I don't want to be into. But mostly, it's

hard. You don't want people to be saying you're stupid. "Why do you want to go to school and get a job?" I was talking to my homeboy the other day, so [he said] ". . . school? Drop out, like. . . ." "Like, all right, that's pretty good. Thanks for your encouragement" [*laughs*]. See, they trip like that, but they just mess around. That's just a joke, but it's, like, you just think about things like that. I guess your peers, they try to pull you down and then you just got to be strong enough to try to pull away.

I got to think about myself and get what I got to get going on. Get something going on, or else nobody else is going to do it. It's where you're starting to think a little different. You sort of know what's happening. All they're thinking about is partying, this and that. Nothing wrong with it, but I got to try to better myself.

Making It Better

I guess in a lot of ways, I am [successful] . . . a lot of things I'm trying to achieve. Starting something, already you're successful, you know? But finishing it, it's gonna make you more complete . . . successful and complete. Got to have your priorities straight. Get what you got to get done, and get it done, and just be happy when you're doing something.

I came to this school, and it was deep here. They got down into a lot of studies that I liked, and there was a lot going on here. But see, I was me, I was just a clown. I always liked to mess around, so they gave me chance after chance. I took it for granted, and they kicked me out. They booted me out, right? So I went back to that other school and it was like, "This thing is boring. Nothing going on." And so I called over here and I go, "I need another chance," this and that, to get back into school. So they gave me another chance and that's why I'm here right now, 'cause they gave me a chance.

They get more into deeper Latino history here, and that's what I like. A lot of other, how you say, background, ethnic background. We had even Martin Luther King. We had Cesar Chavez. We had a lot of things.

I never used to think about [being Chicano] before. Now I do . . . being Brown and just how our race is just going out. You know, you don't want to see your race go out like that.

[Mexican American], it's what you make it, you know? Let's say I'm Chicano and I dress like a gang member. They're gonna look at you like one of those crazy kids, you know, Mexican kid, Chicano kid. But if you present yourself nice or whatever, it really depends how your outer appears. Like, people say it's just *from the inside,* but it's really what's *on the outside* . . . how you look on the outside, like tattoos and that. So it's, like, I get discriminated because of a lot of things, and I can't really pinpoint it. So it's, like, I don't really know if it's 'cause I'm Brown or if it's 'cause of my gang tattoo, so I can't really pinpoint. But for me, as far as me being Chicano, it's prideful, it's pride of your race, of what you are.

[Chicano young people] have some pretty trippy insights of life. It's like they know how to talk to people, and they know how to give presentations, you know what I mean? Like what we're doing right now [*referring to the interview*]. A lot of the things they say is pretty deep.

[In this school], they just leave the killings out and talk about how you can make it better, you know what I'm saying? Try to be more of the positive side of being a Brown person, that's what I'm talking about. A lot of the other alternative schools you can't go because of your gang. It's all gang affiliated. Every single alternative school is gang affiliated. This is the only one where it's all neutral.

[To make school better I would] talk about more interesting things, more things like what I would like, students would like. And I would just get more involved . . . get more people involved. Get things going, not just let them vegetate on a desk and "Here's a paper," . . . teach 'em a lesson and expect them to do it. You know, get all involved.

Put some music in the school. I mean, put some music and get some like drawings. Get a better surrounding so you feel more like the 'hood, you could learn more, you'll feel more comfortable. This [school] is pretty good, but if you had somebody kicking it, put like a character on the wall of something . . . yeah, like a mural or something, it would be more like a more comfortable setting to work.

Try to find out what we think is important. Try to do the best you can to try to get it. The kids want it. They're gonna use it. If they don't want it, they're not, so. . . . I remember the *Diary of Anne Frank.* I was pretty deep into the Nazis and Jews, and so that was pretty cool.

I think [multicultural education] is important because that goes back to segregating. You got to get to

know everybody more better. If you understand them better, you're gonna get along better. So, yeah, I think that would be good.

I'm getting out all I can get out [from this school]. There's so much to learn and that's all I want to do is just learn, try to educate my mind to see what I could get out of it. Anything I can, I'm gonna get out of it.

I was here when they barely opened this school. I brought my mom and my dad, and we had a couple of kids here and the staff here. What we did was wrote all the rules, just made an outline of how the school was gonna be: People are gonna get treated right, what you could wear. Everything was done with each other, you know? It wasn't just talked about with the staff and brought to the students. It was the students *and* the staff.

[*What would have made school easier for you?*] If you had asked me that question a year ago, I would have said, "No school!" School would have been made easier if it wasn't so early in the morning [*laughs*]. But school, it will be better if more activities [are] going on. People wouldn't just think of it as a routine. People got into it really where it really meant something. But it's both on the students' part and the teachers' part. It takes both.

The classes [should have] more better learning techniques. It's an advanced age. We got a lot of computer things going on. Get a lot of things going with computers and a lot of things that are going to draw the eye. Catch my eye and I'm gonna be, "Oh, all right," and gonna go over there and see what's up.

I think they should get more of these aides, assistants, to be parents, okay? 'Cause the parents, I notice this: A parent in a school is more, like, they got love. That's it, they got love and they give it to you. They give it back to more students. I think they should get more, like, parents involved in the school, like, to teach this and that. Get more parents involved in the classroom, too. Parents have a lot of things to say, I would think, about the schools.

[Teachers should] not think of a lesson as a lesson. Think of it as not a lesson just being taught to students, but a lesson being taught to one of your own family members, you know? 'Cause if it's, like, that they get more deep into it, and that's all it takes. Teach a lesson with heart behind it and try to get your kids to understand more of what's going on. And don't lie to your kids . . . like, to your students, saying "Everything is okay and 'just say no to drugs'; it's easy." Let them know what's really going on. Don't beat around the bush. Let them know there's gangs, drugs. "You guys got to get on with that. That's for kids. Do what you got to do and stay in education." They're starting to do that more now. Try to get a dress code going on. I never used to like that, but that's a pretty good idea, you know? But not really a strict dress code, but just where you can't wear gang attire.

It just catches up to you later on. It does because when you're in the 10th grade and you sit down to do fractions and you can't do a problem 'cause you didn't really learn the basics, it all catches up. When I was in junior high, I didn't do math the whole seventh and eighth grade. I never did a math paper. Maybe turned one or two in, but it was, like, I don't like math, and it all catches up to you.

Now I take every chance I get to try to involve myself in something. Now it's like I figure if I'm more involved in school, I won't be so much involved in the gang, you know? . . . It's what you put into it, what you're gonna get out of it. And you know, sometimes I tell myself, like, accountants are always working with numbers, and I say, "I want to be an accountant because I want to do something where I got to work hard to try to get it, and show that I could learn math and do it real good." That's just the kind of person I am, where if I can't do something, like, just to trip myself up, I want to do this. You know, just so I can learn it more real good and show 'em that I can . . . try to make an example out of myself, of everything I do.

[Good grades] make you feel good, getting A's. See this gang-member-type man getting A's. I get pretty good grades. I get A's, B's, and C's. That's better than all F's on report cards that I used to get, all failures in all six subjects.

After when I get my diploma, it's not the end of school, it's the beginning. I still want to learn a lot more after that. I basically want to go to college. That's what I want to do. Get more schooling so I could learn more.

Probably I would want to be either a teacher, a counselor, something like working with youngsters to share my experience with them, you know? 'Cause I know there's a lot of people out there who talk down to youngsters, you know what I'm saying? Instead of talking *with* them. And just try to understand what they're going through.

I mean, you can't get a teacher, put 'em in a classroom with a bunch of kids from the neighborhood, and the teacher lives in [another neighborhood] and expect to understand. I have problems at home, a lot of problems. And to come into school and for a teacher to come with a snotty attitude, I'm gonna give it back. That's the way it is.

I don't want to speak too soon, but I'm pretty much on a good road here. I'm pretty much making it. Trying to make something out of myself. I'm on that way, you know . . . I'm going that way.

You can't talk about next month, at least at this time. I'm just today, get it done. That's it. The best I can.

And I just, I'm tripping out on myself. I don't believe I'm doing this. But I don't really like to build myself too high . . . because the higher you are the harder you're gonna fall. I don't want to fall.

Family Support: "I Had a Love That Kept Me Home"

I like kids. I like kids a lot. They see me and, "Gee, that guy is scary. He's a gang member. . . ." This experience the other day when I was at work: I was working in [a daycare center], and I walked in and the kids were looking at me like and whispering. And this one kid, this Oriental kid, came up and we started playing. The next thing I know, she was sitting on my lap and all these kids just started coming towards me. And they know: They could feel I love kids.

You need to educate your mind. Somebody gets born and throw 'em into the world, you know, they're not gonna make it. You get somebody, you born 'em, you raise 'em, you feed 'em and encourage 'em, and they're gonna make it. That's what the reason for going to school is. A lot of it, of my going to school, is 'cause of my mom. I want her to be proud and her to say that I made it and this and that.

My mom used to run with gangs when she was young. My mom and my father both belonged to gangs. They're out of it. They don't mess around no more.

I learned a lot of morals from my mother. Respect, how to respect people. If my mom wasn't in church, she wouldn't be there for us, I don't think. She would be trying to find a way to seek to comfort herself, you know what I mean?

My mom, she's real strong and real understanding. Not strict, but more understanding, you know? She don't really compromise with me. Usually what she says is what she says, that's it. My mom, I wouldn't change nothing, nothing [about her]. My dad, I would . . . just have him be there for me when I was younger. I could have turned out different if he was there, you never know.

It's hard for me to talk to my mom or my dad, but I talk to my mom about a lot of things like girlfriends, things that happen. Like when homeboys die, I don't go talking to nobody else but my mom. My homeboy just passed away about a month ago or two months ago, and I just remember I was in my mom's room. My mom was ironing and I just started crying, and I don't cry a lot. I started crying and I started telling her, "I hurt, Mom. I don't know why, but I hurt so much." 'Cause I had been trying to, how do you say, run from it, I'd been trying to put it off, like my homeboy's gone, 'cause we were pretty close. So I was like, "It hurts, Mommy." She said, "I know, in your gut," like this and that. So we talked. We get pretty much into it.

She dropped out in the tenth grade, and she was pregnant. And she says, "I want you to do good. Don't be like me, going back to school when it's already kind of late, you know." It's never too late, but you know what I'm saying. She was like, "Just learn now, Paul. Do it the first time right and you won't have to do it again."

My mom wants me to go to school basically so I could have a good house and home when I build up my family, and so we won't have to be five people living in a three-bedroom home, with not that much money to live on, you know?

My mom makes a good living, not in money but in moral standards. We're happy with what we've got and that's just the bottom line. So I go to school for my mom, try to help her and try to help me.

My mom, she's not really [involved in school]. She's too busy doing her own thing. She gets out of school, makes dinner, cleans the house, goes to church, comes home, irons for my two sisters. She doesn't really have time for all this. She'll come in and she'll talk to my probation officer, talk to Isabel [*a staff member*], different people, yeah, pretty much involved when she can be.

You're gonna realize that you got to learn from day one and education will never end. It's only when you stop it. I realize that now. But see, me, I never really had somebody to push me. My mother pushed me, and my mom, she just got tired. "Paul, you're too much for me." My father, he never really pushed me. He talked to me. That was, like, "Education, Paul, education," you know? And getting letters from my dad in jail, "Stay in school," and that's all. He said some pretty deep things, understanding things to me. And my dad always knew the right words to say to me that kind of encouraged me. And my mom. They both encouraged me.

If it wasn't for the family, the love I get from my family, I would look for it in my homeboys. I never had to do that. I just wanted my homeboys to party. A lot of my friends, they go to homeboys to look for just to kick it with somebody. See, me, I had a love that kept me home, that kept me in my place.

I remember I used to just take off from Friday night to Monday morning, come home. My mom be worrying all night, "Where is this guy?" and I was in the street. And that was like every weekend. 'Til now, I stay home every day and I'm just going to school. . . . I come from work, do my homework, whatever. Go to work, come home, go to church, 'cause I go to church with my mother.

My mom, she's really proud of me. My friend was telling me that she was at church, at Bible study, a gathering at home of church people. And [my mom] was crying. She was proud. [My friend] said, "Your mom was talking about you, and she was crying. She's real proud." And that's my mom, she's real sensitive. I love my mom so much it's even hard to explain. And she thinks . . . she tells me, "You don't care about me, Paul," this and that, 'cause like it's hard for me. . . . It's hard for me to show my feelings.

Commentary

Luis Rodríguez, author of *Always Running, La Vida Loca: Gang Days in L.A.*, whose experiences parallel Paul's in many ways, describes gangs as young people's search for a sense of belonging.[3]

Looking back on his own youth and fearing for the future of his son, who was following the same path, Rodríguez wrote his book to encourage people to understand that gangs, in spite of providing belonging, respect, and protection to their members, represent an unhealthy and self-destructive response to oppression. Gangs emerge when communities are deprived of basic human rights. According to Rodríguez, few young people would choose gangs if they were given decent education, productive jobs, and positive channels for social recreation.

Schools may unwittingly contribute to young people's gang involvement by failing to provide the strong cultural identity and support that students need. In fact, James Diego Vigil has suggested that neighborhoods (streets) and schools interact in ways that can interfere with the learning of many Chicano students. According to him, understanding this connection can help educators create a more positive school experience for Chicano students. Vigil suggests that schools can develop a balanced strategy of *prevention, intervention,* and *suppression.*[4] For example, *prevention* would focus on strengthening families and addressing some of the conditions that lead children to street life and gangs. *Intervention* would address students' behavioral problems, and *suppression* would confront the most destructive behavioral aspects of gang culture. However, suppression can also unintentionally lead to creating school dropouts, for instance, when dress codes that may appear to be neutral rather than targeted at only gang members, drive gang members out of school. Even in the early grades, when Paul began to dress like a gang member, teachers' negative reactions—if not specific dress codes—made him feel that school was not a place for him. That is why he so vividly remembered Ms. Nelson, the one teacher who treated him kindly despite his attire.

The yearning for respect, which is, after all, just another word for a sense of competence, is what Paul described when he talked about joining first what he called a "school gang" and later the full-fledged street gang. Young men and women in desperate economic straits are turning in ever larger numbers to "*la vida loca,*" or the crazy life of gangs. In 1991, when Paul was interviewed, Los Angeles alone was estimated to have 100,000 gang members in 800 gangs. In that peak year for gang activity, nearly 600 youths were killed, mostly by other youths.[5]

The rage felt by young people when their dreams are denied or suppressed is turned inward, resulting in such things as drug abuse or suicide, or turned outward. The unspeakably violent actions of Chicanos against their own *Raza,* so poignantly expressed by Paul, is an example of the latter. Rodríguez describes this violence as emanating too often from the self-loathing that is the result of oppression: "And if they murder, the victims are usually the ones who look like them, the ones closest to who they are—the mirror reflections. They murder and they're killing themselves, over and over."[6]

Nevertheless, blame for gangs and for other manifestations of oppression in our society cannot be placed on schools. The issues are too complicated for simplistic scapegoating; they include massive unemployment, a historical legacy of racism and discrimination, and a lack of appropriate housing and health care, among others. In addition, families struggling to survive on a daily basis can seldom do much to counteract the lure of gangs and drugs, with their easy money and instant popularity, that influences so many of their children. As Paul said, his mother, try as she might, just got tired: "Paul, you're too much for me," she said.

Although schools can neither do away with gangs nor put a stop to the violence taking place in communities across the United States every day, they can make a difference. Paul was quick to place the responsibility for his past on his own shoulders rather than blaming teachers. However, when he thought more deeply about it, he also recognized that particular teachers and schools *did* make a difference. This is nowhere more evident than in the case of Ms. Nelson or, years later, the teachers in his alternative school.

Chicano parents and their children often have high aspirations, but, unless these are somehow incorporated into the culture of schools, they will make little difference. For instance, Alejandro Portes and Rubén Rumbaut, in their extensive research on various immigrant communities, found that the strengths of these communities are frequently disregarded by schools. In the specific case of Mexican Americans, they concluded that "In many Mexican families, the *only* thing going for the children is the support and ambition of their parents. These aspirations should be strengthened rather than undermined."[7] This finding compels us to shift the focus to the context and structure of schools rather than to focus only on the shortcomings of students and their families. In other words, policies and practices need to be reviewed to make education more engaging and positive for all students. In this regard, schools need to develop strategies that use a more culturally congruent approach rather than an approach based on culture as a deficit.

Paul's suggestion that his school hire more parents as school aides because they "got love and they give it to you" reminds us of the powerful influence of family on Hispanic/Latino culture. Even families in difficult circumstances want the best for their children but often are unaware of how to provide it for them. His father's insistence on "Education, Paul, education," if unaccompanied by structural support to help him stay in school, is of little help. Paul clearly understood this when he said that, although his parents supported him, they never really pushed him.

Paul Chavez was fortunate to be in the alternative school he was attending, and it seemed to be serving as a safeguard to keep him at some distance from his gang. The policies and practices of his school were geared toward creating a positive learning environment. There was no tracking; staff interactions with students were positive and healthy; students were involved in the school's governance; there were high expectations and demanding standards of all students; and their languages and cultures were an integral part of the school's curriculum. Nevertheless, an insightful observation by Vigil is worth noting here. Alternative schools, he says, may replicate street gang culture by concentrating a critical mass of gang members in one place. Thus, these schools can act as "temporary warehouses," or in the words of some of the gang members quoted by James Vigil, as "preparation for prison."[8]

One cannot help but remember, however, that at the time of his interview, Paul was only 16 years old, a tender age, and he had so many difficult situations and easy temptations still facing him. In spite of Paul's strong motivation and eloquent insights, his school's caring, his mother's love and strict discipline, and his growing realization that gang life is no solution to the problems facing Chicano youth, he still had a long and hard road ahead of him.

Reflect on This Case Study

1. What can teachers and schools learn from Paul's fifth-grade teacher, Ms. Nelson? Give specific suggestions.
2. What support services do you think are needed in schools such as those in Paul's neighborhood? Why?
3. Take a look at the recommendations that Paul made to improve schools. Which do you think make sense? Why?
4. Why do you think Paul never thought about being Chicano before? What kinds of ethnic studies would be important for students at different levels?
5. How can schools use the tremendously positive feelings about family that Paul and other Latinos have?

Latrell Elton

I wanna do positive stuff now. I wanna do something positive with my life.

At the time he was interviewed, Latrell Elton,[1] a 16-year-old African American young man, was finishing his sophomore year of high school in Atlanta, Georgia. After starting at his local high school, the district transferred him to Bowden County Alternative High School, a school for students who had been expelled from their home schools. While the alternative school claimed to develop self-esteem, self-discipline, trust, lifelong learning, and respect for others, Latrell's description of his experience there raises many concerns about the gaping divide between a school's missions and the messages, both explicit and implicit, that students receive from the school's policies and practices.

Latrell reported that the alternative school is 100 percent segregated: "The school is—all it is—is Black. The students are all Black and the teachers are all Black," aligning it with Jonathan Kozol's description of apartheid schools.[2] Within this environment, Latrell's narrative pointed to three distressing themes: *his school experience as resembling prison; the detrimental messages about his racial identity;* and his *low expectations for the future.*

Prison Analogy

We're in school; but it ain't like the regular school. When you go in the school, they check you tucked in your shirt. And then you gotta go through the metal detectors. When you go through the metal detectors, they search you. After they search you, you go on to the cafeteria—you sit down. Goin' through metal detectors at school, I don't feel uncomfortable with it. Well, truly it shouldn't be happenin' but I don't be feelin' uncomfortable with it, you know what I'm saying? Every day we go in school, they searchin' us like we prisoners and stuff. I put my own self in a predicament to go to that school. I didn't really wanna go. But they were, like, "Well Mr. Elton, we can't let you in school until you go and do a year in there." And I was, like, "All right. I'll do what I gotta do." The main thing I'm focused on is trying to get up out that school. As soon as I get up out that school I'll be a happy person.

We ride on a bus that have two Bowden County motorcycle mans right here. They have marked police in the front, one in the middle and one in the back, and they have each marked police on each bus. Man, make me feel like I'm in jail. Like I'm just a prisoner, like I'm a bad person. My bus have burglary bar windows. They got cameras on there. You can't get up out your seat.

Detrimental Messages and Racial Identity

I'm African American. Y'all don't want to hear what I got in my blood. I got the N-word in my blood. 'Cause I'm just, I just don't like sitting down, I can't stay seated. I just wanna run around, get my energy out. It's negative. Right now I'm trying to control it at school. When I was in [my previous] school, I used to run around, can't sit down in class, sit on top of the desk, cut. But now I don't. I sit down.

I feel like Black folk these days, we doin' stupid stuff, we wanna kill each other over little stupid stuff like a car. We wanna go out here and break into houses. To tell you the truth, the whole jail system is made for us only. That's why they build jails and welfare: for Black people. 'Cause they know what we're gonna do. [Black people] put themselves in a predicament. I ain't gonna lie.

Say, for instance, a Black person would have got shot right here and we call the ambulance. You know how long it's gonna take them? About an hour to 35 minutes just to come. Just to come. Oh, this Black person, they got shot. That's one less Black person we got to worry about on the street. One person we ain't got to do nothing for. But if it's like a mixed person being shot, they be on the scene in less than five min-

utes. You hear the sirens and everything. You got helicopter, news, and everything.

About my neighborhood, I would tell you: Be safe. Be careful. Don't trust nobody around here. People around here, they steal, they'll lie to you. Everything. They'll do everything around here. People around here, they just don't care. Like, you trying to cross the street, they won't slow down. They'll just keep flying by you. Just go on.

The community people are all Black folk. That's what all it is. That's what I said, nothing but black folks all on the street. They like this because they ain't been in no real life, you know what I'm saying? With people who got quieter streets, who like respect, like neighborhood watch. We ain't got no neighborhood watch. It's just people out there doing stupid stuff. Where I'm from, when we had neighborhood watch, they wouldn't be doing what they doing now.

Future Expectations

I hope when I get out of Bowden Alternative School, I can go ahead and go back to regular school. And when I get on to regular school, first thing I'm gonna be looking for is basketball tryout. When I find out when they having basketball tryout, I'm gonna stay after school. I'm just gonna play basketball. And when I play basketball, I'm gonna try and go pro. I'm trying to go to the top. Trying to be the best I can be in basketball. My teacher told me I could be a comedian. I got jokes. I got some jokes. I could joke. I'm gonna try and be a comedian too if basketball don't happen.

I see all these folks out here, they be like, "Yeah cous', do this, selling drug gonna get money." Selling drugs ain't gonna get you nowhere. Drug money don't last long. And then drugs get you locked up and stuff. I wanna do positive stuff now. I wanna do something positive with my life. I don't wanna keep on doing no negative stuff. Can't keep on doing that. It just ain't right. 'Cause I see all this money, there's money out here. I tell people, there's money out here. You got cars you can wash—you even got— even yards to cut . . . cut grass all day, you know what I'm saying? I don't like cutting yards, but I cut 'em. Only why I cut 'em is because, sometimes when I'm feeling broke and I got more to cut.

It make me feel good about myself [to have a job cutting grass] 'cause I know I ain't gotta go out here and ask nobody for no money, you know what I'm saying? 'Cause I don't want my momma see me in a couple more years on the street asking folks for 50 cents. I want her to see me coming in a car. So clean. With a big old house, with a bag full of money. Just say, "Momma, for all the years of hard work you put me through, there you go, right there. There you go, a brand new set of car keys, there go you some house keys, there you go." See my momma there, up in the house. I got big plans for when I get out of school.

'Cause if I keep on putting my mind on right things, positive things, I ain't got to worry about no niggaz' still trying to get through my brain and trying to make me mess up. 'Cause right now, since I been in these sports and stuff, it's helped me out a lot. Because I know I'm with safe people. People who I really can trust. People who I ain't gotta worry about got illegal drugs. I know I ain't gotta worry about all that. I'm on the right track. I can do this and that to make my life positive.

Now, since I'm in the alternative school, they've been helping me out a lot, a way, way lot. 'Cause I've got after-school tutorial, and we got more help after school. I'm a good student right now. I consider myself a good student. [What makes me a good student right now is] my behavior, the way I done calmed down. Going to school on time. Getting A's. Passing all my classes. I ain't got to worry about none of this. Last year, [at my previous school] I didn't have nothing but stress. I didn't know what to do with my work. Until I met this lady named Miss Kathy. So when I met her, I showed her my report card and I talked to her about getting me a mentor. And then when she had found me this mentor, and ever since, I been coming home with good grades, passing. Look, yo, I show her every Tuesday, look at my progress report. You see, I done did good. I done finally learned something. I don't worry about falling asleep in class, not doing no work. I used to fall asleep every-day in class.

In literature class now my average is a D. It's between a C and a D. By the end of the semester, I'm hoping to have A's, A's, A's, A's, A's by paying attention, doing what I'm doing every day all day. Working. Trying not to go to sleep.

The school I went to before, I went there and I just kept causing trouble. I had so many friends that I knew from middle school, you know what I'm saying? They trying to tell me, "Do that. Go do that, mess with that right there". But like I told my mom when I get out that school system and stuff I ain't got to worry about it. Gotta be a grown man. I can make my own decisions, do what I wanna do. I ain't gotta worry about people telling me what to do, and I just be free.

Commentary

Latrell is a bright, perceptive young man who was painfully aware of the ravages of institutionalized racism in his community. His poignant comments point to both the responsibilities of school structures and the limits of the school's reach within under-resourced and over-exploited communities. Latrell said he was "not uncomfortable" about entering the school house through metal detectors, implying that he viewed it as a necessary reality.

He equated having the "N-word in my blood" with struggling to conform to classroom expectations, apparently having absorbed the message that staying seated and overcoming restlessness are racial traits. It is evident that Latrell's perspective of his racial identity and cultural group had become skewed by experiences of racism, marginalization, and violence.

While Latrell's hopeful outlook on the future was courageous, it also pointed to a lack of adequate guidance and academic preparation for professional goals. In the overwhelming shadow of American popular culture, it has become the norm for many young people, especially young men, to dream of becoming professional athletes or entertainers. While these are noteworthy possibilities that should not be dismissed, both are exceptionally competitive careers, considering the percentage of individuals who actually secure personal and financial success in such pursuits. Strong guidance and career counseling services in some schools help students with such aspirations follow their hearts *and* prepare for a collegiate trajectory that supports their vision. For example, thoughts of pursuing a career in sports medicine, sports management, physical education, theater studies, entertainment management, or entrepreneurial endeavors did not even appear in Latrell's vocabulary. Regrettably, he is not alone.

In Gilberto Conchas's research of successful programs for urban youth of color, he found a common thread among the low-income African American males in the school that he studied. Even in a highly successful program that boasted strong graduation rates and consistent levels of matriculation into two- and four-year colleges, low-income African American males placed higher value on athletic fame than on their collegiate path. Conchas writes, "They knew college was important but they really wanted to play football or basketball or perhaps become entertainers."[3] Conchas's research illustrates that although these particular low-income African American males were provided with the social and academic support systems essential for college, "their perceptions of social mobility were seemingly no different than the general stereotype."[4] Despite the tenacious power of negative stereotypes, Conchas concludes that schools can take steps to counteract the negative consequences of linking racial identity and academic performance. He insists, "We must remain critical of larger historical and structural forces that impact African American youth's perceptions of the opportunity structure."[5]

By indicting systemic social injustices, Latrell was perceptive about the opportunity structures that limit students' life options. He linked standard-of-living disparities to institutionalized oppression. In his daily life, he witnessed the slow response of emergency services as a reflection and reinforcement of the pervasive messages about the disposability of Black people. He perceived the lack of cooperation among members of his community as a response to the constraints of living immensely unequal lives.

Many urban schools recognize the toll that inhumane socioeconomic conditions have taken on minority students' perceptions of themselves and their racial identities. Some school administrations have implemented self-esteem programs and attempted to include culturally affirming curriculum. While such efforts may be commendable, they are insufficient shields against the forces of historically rooted racist beliefs and structures of racism. Reflecting on the myriad methods of self-esteem-building tactics that have become commonplace in many urban schools, Jonathan Kozol asserts,

We are in a world where hope must be constructed therapeutically because so much of it has been destroyed by the conditions of internment in which we have placed these children. It is harder to convince young people that they "can learn" when they are cordoned off by a society that isn't sure they really can.[6]

Kozol's assessment concurs with Latrell's: "They like this because they ain't been in no real life." Yet, this is Latrell's real life, as it is the real life of his family, his peers, and his neighbors.

The poetic nuance of Latrell's phrase exposes his feeling that having a different kind of life was unrealistic or even other-worldly. However, despite his indictment of institutional inequities and community challenges, Latrell's perspective is explicitly hopeful. He recognized that mowing lawns pays less than selling drugs, but he deliberately chose cutting grass as a means of resisting the prevalent opportunities for drug dealing. He saw the analogies to prison in his school structures but yearned for academic success. He revealed his awareness of his responsibility in achieving higher grades, but it is unclear whether the adults in his world were hearing his hopeful voice. What will it take for Latrell and his peers to attend a U.S. urban school where the notion of metal detectors seems foreign and out of place? Why does it seem only imaginary for Latrell to engage in a rigorous curriculum that promotes fluency in multiple academic disciplines, with participation in co-curricular activities that promote healthy athleticism and artistic accomplishments and with teachers and guidance counselors supporting achievable, fulfilling goals?

Reflect on This Case Study

1. Latrell's racial identity was continually developing, especially as a young adult. Given the negative perceptions of school that Latrell articulated, what can you, as an individual teacher, do, and what can the school, as an institution, do to positively influence Latrell's racial identity development?

2. Conchas's research suggests ways that schools can create structures to counteract the negative consequences of the linkage between racial identity and academic performance. How might a small group of dedicated teachers embark on

changing structures in schools? Identify the stakeholders the group would have to bring on board to effect change.

3. What perceptions do you think most teachers would have of Latrell? What information would you share with those teachers to advocate for Latrell's participation in rigorous academics, arts, and athletics? What support structures would you build to help Latrell be successful?

4. What do you think about Latrell's assessment of having metal detectors in his school entrance and bars on the bus windows? Do you think such measures are necessary? Might there be alternative safety strategies?

5. Imagine you are Latrell's teacher. How does your memory of your high school experience compare to Latrell's? How do the communities and neighborhoods in which you grew up compare to Latrell's? What can you do as a teacher to come to know the realities of your students' daily lives? Does it matter?

Notes to Chapter 11 Case Studies

Paul Chavez

1. We are grateful to Dr. Mac Lee Morante for the interview and background information for Paul's case study. Dr. Morante is a bilingual school psychologist for the Anaheim City Schools and also works as a counselor at Santa Ana College in California.

2. *Raza* refers to the people of Mexican and Mexican American origin.

3. Luis J. Rodríguez, *Always Running, La Vida Loca: Gang Days in L.A.* (New York: Simon & Schuster, 1993): 250.

4. James Diego Vigil, "Streets and Schools: How Educators Can Help Chicano Marginalized Gang Youth." *Harvard Educational Review* 69, no. 3 (Fall 1999): 270–288.

5. Rodríguez, *Always Running, La Vida Loca: Gang Days in L.A.*

6. Rodríguez, *Always Running, La Vida Loca*, 9.

7. Alejandro Portes and Rubén Rumbaut, *Legacies: The Story of the Immigrant Second Generation* (Berkeley, CA: University of California Press and New York: Russell Sage Foundation, 2001), 280.

8. James Diego Vigil, "Streets and Schools: How Educators Can Help Chicano Marginalized Gang Youth." *Harvard Educational Review* 69, no. 3 (Fall 1999): 270–288.

Latrell Elton

1. We want to thank Vera Stenhouse for conducting the interview with Latrell. Vera is currently a doctoral candidate at Emory University where her research explores how new teacher preparation programs educate teachers to work with diverse students. Vera also provided follow-up information about Latrell's school to add depth to the case study.

2. Jonathon Kozol, *Shame of the Nation: The Restoration of Apartheid Schooling in America* (New York: Crown, 2005).

3. Gilberto Q. Conchas, *The Color of Success: Race and High-Achieving Urban Youth* (New York: Teachers College Press, 2006): 113–115.

4. Conchas, *The Color of Success*, 56.

5. Conchas, *The Color of Success*, 59.

6. Kozol, *Shame of the Nation*, 37.

PART FOUR

Teaching for Intercultural Competence

Learning from Students

> **❝**To keep us from forgetting our culture's language, schools could still have reading sessions in our culture's language. I think that would help the Asian students.**❞**
>
> **—Savoun Nouch, interviewee**

Timothy Burbank, Nyima Smith, Ben Hastings in Ben Sear's art class. *Self-portrait.* Relief print. 2005.

The voices of the students in the case studies and snapshots in this book are testimony to the vitality and spirit of youth. Despite a variety of conditions that might severely test the mettle and aspirations of others in similar circumstances, these youths have demonstrated a staunch determination to succeed in school and in life. Most define themselves as successful students, and they are proud of this fact, so understanding the insights of these particular students can be enlightening for educators interested in providing effective learning environments for all young people. Students who have not been as fortunate also have important messages for us, for they challenge our prevailing assumptions about learning and teaching.

In this chapter, four major issues that emerged from the case studies and snapshots are reviewed:

- A redefinition of success and achievement
- The conflicted nature of culture and language
- The key role of activities outside of academics in sustaining students' enthusiasm and motivation for school
- The central role of family, community, and school in providing environments for success

The Meaning of Success

Many young people have a conception of education that is distinct from that commonly held by schools. For instance, the role of hard work in becoming educated was mentioned by most of the students. During his interview, for instance, Kaval Sethi said that intelligence rather than hard work was rewarded in his school. He said, "I don't think school is fair for people who are not as intelligent as other people. . . . It is very rigid." Others also made it clear that intelligence is not an innate ability or immutable quality—something that one is born with—as it often is defined in U.S. society. Intelligence is, in fact, something that one cultivates, studies hard to attain, and eventually achieves. Being smart is a goal, not a characteristic. Being smart is also the result of family and community support and the quality of care shown by teachers and schools. In this sense, intelligence is within everyone's reach.

Grades are a major indicator of academic success in our schools, and their importance is increasing in the current climate of accountability and high-stakes standardized tests. Grades were significant for most of the students we interviewed, but contrary to what many teachers and schools might believe, academically successful students may not consider grades to be as meaningful as other manifestations of their success. Many of the students we interviewed mentioned being satisfied with a grade for which they worked hard even if it was not the best grade. On the other hand, Fern Sherman's A's in English were not particularly satisfying to her because the class was neither engaging nor challenging. Fern's and Yahaira León's science classes, which were far more demanding classes in which they did not get as high a grade, were nevertheless their favorites.

The purposes of education are much broader and more noble for many students than the limited goals schools often set. Thus, although teachers often talk in terms of future employment and career goals, many of the students interviewed saw education as far more. While some did mention hope for a good job in the future (certainly a positive aspiration), a more nuanced interpretation of their words reveals deeper goals. More than a concern about the quality of their future job, many students exhibited a desire to fulfill their potential as human beings and as family members. For Hoang Vinh, going to school had one purpose: to become educated. He considered a good job to be secondary. Yahaira said, "The reason for going to school is to educate your mind."

A word needs to be said, however, about the vague or romantic ideals some female students tend to have regarding their future. Alicia Montejo, Fern Sherman, and Linda Howard all talked about dual and seemingly contradictory career goals. Alicia wanted to be either a medical doctor or a border patrol officer; Fern, a fashion lawyer or U.S. president; and Linda, a teacher or a world famous singer. Particularly for females, the reality of limited choices in the past, and the continuing sexualization of their identities, have an impact. Most of these young women selected what seems to be a glamorous choice or one that appears to wield social power. Besides culture, language, and social class, gender also mediates what students may consider realistic goals for their future.

But females' ethnic cultures not only *limit* their choices; they may also *expand* them. Girls are often subject to limited role expectations and gender stereotyping, but they may also receive affirming and powerful cultural messages about being female. A study done by Pilar Muñoz and Josette Henschel illustrates this seeming contradiction. They interviewed ten Puerto Rican women to determine what messages these women had received during their childhood regarding their future role in society. All the women reported that they had been taught to be submissive, quiet, long-suffering, and patient by their mothers and grandmothers. These were the *verbal* messages they heard throughout their youth. However, they also learned *nonverbal* attitudes and behaviors from their mothers and grandmothers—that women need to be resourceful, intelligent, and stronger than men. These dual and apparently conflicting messages were not lost on the women interviewed, all of whom were extraordinarily strong and resilient and had learned to "take care of themselves."[1]

Pride and Conflict in Culture

One of the most consistent, and least expected, outcomes to emerge from our interviews was the resoluteness with which young people maintained pride and satisfaction in their culture and the strength they derived from it. This does not mean that their pride was sustained without great conflict, hesitation, or contradiction. Because young people's positive sense of cultural identification challenges the messages and models of an essentially assimilationist society, it creates its own internal conflicts, but the fact that almost all of the students mentioned a deep pride in their culture cannot be overlooked. Students volunteered that their culture helped them in many ways and that they felt proud of who they were. Vanessa Mattison was an exception; she was uncomfortable even describing herself in ethnic terms. She reflected pride and shame in her cultural background, but for a different reason: because of the unfair privilege she derived from it as a white person.

Moreover, many of them understood that their culture was not what they *do,* but who they *are.* These young people seemed to understand intuitively that their heritage informed and enriched them, but they were also clear that it did not define them. For many, strong self-identification was understood as a value. "You gotta know who you are," is how Manuel Gomes expressed it. At the same time, they resisted essentialist notions of identity. Instead, they understood, to a much greater extent than most adults, that they were *cultural hybrids.* "I mix a lot of American values into my culture" is how Kaval described this hybridity.

We have written elsewhere, with colleagues Eugenie Kang and John Raible, about young people's growing awareness of the multiple influences on their identities and cultures. These influences draw from categories of race and identity but do not adhere to stable, fixed notions or labels.[2] Likewise, Nadine Dolby questions formulations of identity that rely on absolute categories and argues that multicultural education must embrace a more dynamic and nuanced notion of self. In her one-year ethnographic study of a multiracial high school in Durban, South Africa, she found that students "actively produce self" as a "changing, not reified, formation".[3] The young people described in this book's case studies and snapshots defined culture as an active, dynamic interplay of their home, school, youth, traditional and contemporary cultures, and more, as they created and recreated identities.

Conflict and ambivalence

Pride in culture was neither uniform nor easy for these young people. Eugene Crocket, whose snapshot appears at the end of Chapter 13, spoke about the difficulty of being "out" concerning his gay dads when he was in middle school: "I wasn't ashamed, but more embarrassed. I don't know . . . I didn't want people to think of me as different." He went on to explain the conflict: "At home everything is normal, like everyone else's family. Going out in public is a little more different." The experiences of other students in the case studies and snapshots are similar in their negotiation between love for family and comfort in family culture, and confrontation with mainstream expectations.

Pierre Bourdieu's theory of *cultural capital* and of the role of schools in determining what knowledge has greatest status is helpful here.[4] This theory postulates that because schools primarily reflect the knowledge and values of economically and culturally dominant groups in society, they validate and reinforce the cultural capital that students from such groups already bring from home. This validation takes place through the overt and covert curriculum and the school climate. According to Bourdieu, the confirmation of the dominant culture's supremacy results in a *symbolic violence* against groups that are devalued. The cultural model held up for all is not within easy reach of all, and only token numbers of students from less-valued groups can achieve it. If they learn and take on this cultural capital—abandoning their own culture, language, and values—they may succeed. In this way, although few students from dominated groups are permitted to succeed, the myth of a meritocracy is maintained.

Some examples of the symbolic violence suffered by the students we interviewed help illustrate this point. James Karam's Lebanese culture was missing from all school activities, although other, more "visible" cultures were represented. Rashaud Kates longed for the presence of African American historical figures in his school curriculum. Nadia Bara, a Muslim American, and Kaval, a Sikh, both mentioned that their cultures were virtually nonexistent in their schools before September 11, 2001. After that date, they became visible, but mostly in negative ways. The invisibility of Native American content in Fern's schools and in the school's books and curriculum is another example of the devaluation of knowledge. Students may perceive that what is not taught is not worthy of learning.

In contrast, the language and culture of Manuel was highly evident in his schools, and teachers often referred to them explicitly both in curricular and extracurricular activities, giving them even more status. Liane Chang, whose middle school offers classes in Chinese, felt affirmed in her desire to become fluent in the native language of her mother. The schools of these two students demonstrate, in a concrete way, respect for students' identities. In the case of Manuel, the bilingual program was at least partly responsible for his success. In Liane's case, teaching a language visible in the community makes a statement about the importance of that language to the *entire* community. Savoun Nouch, whose case study is at the end of this chapter, and Paul Chavez, although not previously successful in school, became empowered by the multicultural curriculum at their alternative schools.

It is hardly surprising that symbolic violence causes conflict in students from devalued groups. This problem is not unique to the United States; it is evident wherever one group is dominant and held up as the appropriate model. The Finns, who were formerly colonized by the Swedes, and who live in Sweden are a case in point. Finns who emigrate to Sweden are often perceived in negative and sometimes hostile ways. In the words of a young Finn who was educated in Sweden and experienced this firsthand, "When the idea had eaten itself deeply into my soul that it was despicable to be a Finn, I began to feel ashamed of my origins." The result can be a conflict that is difficult to resolve. This particular young man concluded that such conflict was the price he had to pay: "In short, in order to live in harmony with my surroundings, I had to live in perpetual conflict with myself."[5]

The painful alienation from family and culture is not inevitable, although it is a particularly difficult dilemma for first-generation immigrants. Even though the task of trying to fit together what are, at times, contradictory values takes its toll, it need not always result in the complete loss of language and culture. The case studies and snapshots in this book demonstrate that students struggle to maintain both, in spite of the difficulty of doing so.

Although they learned to feel proud of themselves for many things, including their culture, their dexterity in functioning in two worlds, and their bilingualism, several of the students interviewed also learned to feel ashamed of their culture and of the people who reflect it. They faced what they saw as irreconcilable choices: denying or abandoning their identity to succeed, or holding onto it and failing in school and society. Sometimes, students blame their families and communities for perceived failures while absolving the school of almost all responsibility.

Latrell Elton sometimes used words to describe his community that either victimized or blamed people for their failure: "They [Black people] put themselves in a predicament," and "doin' stupid stuff," some of the very words used by those outside the African American community to criticize it. Although demanding accountability from one's own community is necessary, the critical analysis that must accompany it is missing. Latrell's case, however, is complex. For instance, he did not place all of the responsibility on his own community. He also considered the role that social structures, schools, and teachers play by having low expectations of Black students. Nini Rostland's comments concurred with Latrell's perspective: "I think expectations may be holding me back a little bit. I think when people see me, they assume, "Oh, she's Black." They automatically assume, "Oh, she's not going to achieve well."

Nini's snapshot provides a window into negotiating identity as a multiracial youth. In school, she often felt that neither her Polish American identity nor her African heritage were recognized. Assumptions based on her appearance were exacerbated by institutional racism. The strong influence of her family, friends, and summer camp environment supported her assertions of multiple perspectives, but her interview also revealed the weight of always being a boundary crosser and cultural bridge between groups. Some students who are not supported as strongly as Nini may try to ignore or disregard cultural identity, an unfortunate and ultimately counterproductive strategy.

Vanessa's case is especially notable and poignant. Because she was actively opposed to racism and other forms of discrimination (note her actions beginning in elementary school and her stand against heterosexism), she attempted to distance herself from the privileges she earned simply as a result of her ethnic background. Vanessa knew that she had benefited because of being White, but she thought this was unfair. Consequently, she took the position that one's culture and race are unimportant, accepting colorblindness as the ultimate expression of fairness.

Others for whom the conflict is simply too great are expelled or drop out, either physically or psychologically. This was the case with Paul and Savoun. For many students who drop out of school, the reason is not that they are incapable of doing the work, but that the school is an unaffirming place. For example, in an extensive review of literature on the education of American Indian students, Donna Deyhle and Karen Swisher concluded that the major reason for leaving school was students' perceptions that the school curriculum was not connected to their lives.[6] More recent research by Sandy Grande on the education of American Indians proposes *red pedagogy,* that is, paying particular attention to contemporary students' multifaceted identities in order to assertively address their realities.[7]

As we have seen, most of the young people in the case studies have struggled to remain true to themselves, but the process of fitting into a culture different from their family culture is a complex one. Moreover, the students are also challenging the dichotomy between being culturally different from the majority and succeeding academically. This dilemma has been aptly described by Laurie Olsen in her comprehensive study of a highly diverse urban high school in California. One young woman interviewed by Olsen talked about the pressure from peers and teachers to stay within strictly defined cultural borders. She observed, "They want to make you just their culture and if you try to be who you are, and try to be both American and yourself, forget it. It won't work. It's not allowed."[8]

Self-identification and conflict

Like the student in Olsen's study, another conflict that some of the students in the case studies and snapshots felt was expressed as an inability to identify both as "American" and as belonging to their cultural group. Their sense of pride in culture precluded identification with the United States because, for these students, claiming both meant denying their background or being a traitor to it. Why some young people make this choice is no mystery. Ethnicity in the United States, according to

Stanley Aronowitz, has been "generally viewed as a temporary condition on the way to assimilation."[9] This being the case, it is no surprise that Manuel, for example, was emphatic about saying "I'm Cape Verdean. I cannot be an American because I'm not an American. That's it."

Later in this chapter, Christina Kamau marked out her identity when she said, "I'm not Black American, I'm African and I came from Kenya." Yahaira, who was born in the United States, as were her parents, stated, "I'd say I'm Puerto Rican and Dominican" with no reference to the American context. Our society has forced many young people to make a choice, and the students in the case studies and snapshots sometimes made it in favor of their heritage and family culture. Considering their youth and the negative messages about ethnicity around them, this is a courageous stand, but it can also be a limiting one. The consequences of such a choice probably affect what they think they deserve and are entitled to in our society. Having no attachment to the dominant society, they may also feel they have no rights. That is, they may feel they have no right to claim their fair share of society's power and resources or even to demand equality within it. Exclusive identification as a member of their cultural group may also exacerbate the conflict of feeling separate, different, and, consequently, powerless.

But are these the only choices? Fortunately, recent research is pointing in a healthier direction. In their longitudinal research among young people of various immigrant backgrounds, Alejandro Portes and Rubén Rumbaut came to the conclusion that the most positive path to identity was what they called *selective acculturation,* that is, a process by which children of immigrant backgrounds acculturate to the host society in a measured and careful way while at the same time maintaining ties with their ethnic communities. Portes and Rumbaut state,

> This path is closely intertwined with preservation of fluent bilingualism and linked, in turn, with higher self-esteem, higher educational and occupational expectations, and higher academic achievement . . . Children who learn the language and culture of their new country without losing those of the old have a much better understanding of their place in the world. They need not clash with their parents as

often or feel embarrassed by them because they are able to bridge the gap across generations and value their elders' traditions and goals.[10]

The preservation and intersection of languages, cultures, and identities were also salient themes advanced by the 26 immigrant youth interviewed by Judith Blohm and Terri Lapinsky. Their book emphasizes the diverse ways in which students claim their identities inside and outside the home, and it offers curriculum and activities to affirm them.[11] Another example of the tension felt in making choices can be seen in the following snapshot of Gamini Padmaperuma, who sometimes felt pressure to identify in one way or the other. Gamini wrote about his identity for a project done in my (Patty Bode's) art class, in which students developed *identity portraits*, both in writing and graphically. Gamini's portrait accompanies his words.

The way the young people in our case studies and snapshots sustained culture is fascinating. In more than one case, they maintained their "deep culture," particularly values and worldviews, although they may have abandoned more superficial aspects such as food and music preferences. These modifications are a function not only of clashing messages from school and home but also of young peoples' involvement with a peer culture with its own rituals and norms. Although peer culture acts as a primary assimilating structure of our society, we should not assume that individuals have completely abandoned their family's culture simply because they act like other young people their age.

Creating new cultures

Identity is constantly being negotiated and renegotiated by young people. Gamini Padmaperuma presents a good example of this negotiation. His snapshot demonstrates in a graphic way how complicated identity can be, but even adolescents of similar backgrounds have starkly different senses of their personhood. For instance, a recent volume co-edited by Clara Park, A. Lin Goodwin, and Stacey Lee advances a comprehensive perspective of how "American identities" are shaped by Asian and Pacific Americans.[12] Similarly, an exploration of how adolescents negotiate their multiple identities, and what teachers and schools can learn from them, is described in a book edited by Michael Sadowski.[13] Throughout the chapters in the book, various au-

thors demonstrate why identity matters so much to adolescents.

That young people are involved in creating new cultures is evident in the remarks of the students in the snapshots and case studies. Their native cultures do not simply disappear, as schools and society might expect or want them to. Rather, aspects of the native culture are retained, modified, reinserted into different environments, and recast so that they are workable in a new society. Yahaira, for instance, loved rap and hip hop music, not salsa. Nevertheless, the influence of the Latino culture (as well as other cultures) on these musical forms cannot be denied.

Fashioning a new culture is no easy task. It involves first the difficult and painful experience of learning to survive in an environment that may have values and behaviors at polar extremes from those in the home, for instance, the often-cited example of Latino children looking down when being reprimanded. Whereas these children have been taught in their homes to look down as a sign of respect, in U.S. mainstream society, such behavior is generally interpreted as disrespectful. Children who misbehave are expected to "take their medicine"; they are told "Look me straight in the eye." This is an example of how the behaviors expected at home and at school may be diametrically opposed. Even five-year-old children are expected to understand the subtle nuances of these behaviors. They usually do, although their teachers may be completely unaware of the conflicts involved or of the great strain students may experience because of such competing expectations. This example only scratches the surface of cultural clashes.

On the other hand, even knowing about such "cultural behaviors" may lead teachers to have stereotypical expectations of all students of a particular background. For instance, expecting that all Latino students will look down as a sign of respect is unrealistic because Latinos are a heterogeneous group. Some Latinos have been in this country for a few days, while others have been here for many generations; some have been raised in more traditional ways and some in less traditional ways; they come from various social and economic backgrounds; and they may speak Spanish only or English only, or a combination of the two. In addition, their individual differences also make each person a unique individual. Because of all these differences

Snapshot

Gamini Padmaperuma

At the time of his interview, Gamini was an eighth-grade student in a midsize town in the Northeast. His parents speak Singhalese, their native Sri Lankan language. In spite of his youth, Gamini powerfully articulated the struggle to learn Singhalese in the United States, a society with a strong and growing monolingual stance. In his snapshot, he pondered the problems and promises of crossing cultures in U.S. schools.

In art class, we have been working on A Portrait of Our Hands as a painting, in unison with curriculum of other classes. Our hand paintings are supposed to give a visual image of how we identify ourselves.

As one first looks at my painting, they will see the following: an American flag on the left side of a road, on the other side of the road is the Sri Lankan flag, and handle bars of a bike with my hands on it. The handlebars of the bike with my gloved hands on it represent my passion for biking. I like biking because it's a place where I can get away from everything and just concentrate on one thought, whatever that may be, while still paying attention to the road ahead.

My cultural background has played an influence on my educational experience since the beginning of my schooling: Sri Lankan by nationality, I have seen how it has made me more conscious about my culture. I realize who I am, what makes me different from many of my peers, and how that relates me to my surroundings.

Being Sri Lankan hasn't really affected how my teachers treat me but rather what is expected of me from myself and my family. In Sri Lanka, when I was traveling there, I realized how valued academics and an education are. There, it is the highest priority of any child, not sports, not being popular, but totally focused on learning. My parents didn't leave those values behind; they still would expect me to succeed in school, which is an expectation of myself as well. But in Sri Lanka, a given student's social status, in school (that is, how "cool" or popular), isn't important. But in the American culture, kids tend to take school for granted, and they're more concerned about what they wear and how popular they are.

When I look at my parents, I see how far they have come. Coming from Sri Lanka to America is a big thing, so I should not shame my parents—they've worked so hard. If I blow off school, it would really upset them. This poses a problem between myself and my parents, for they have trouble understanding how important it is to spend time with friends, and doing school work. Well, I can do both. The schools my parents had gone through—the school that my dad went to was an all boys' school since he was in kindergarten through high school, and the school that my mom went to was an all girls' school. So my parents aren't so comfortable with how in America we have boys and girls going to the same school. Like, sometimes when I have a girl over, just like as a friend, they aren't as comfortable as the other American parents. But my parents are working really hard for us. My mom has a long ride to work because the job is better paying so she and my dad can earn enough to send me and my other two brothers to go to college. They work so hard for us.

I've lived in the U.S. all of my life, and I consider myself an American, but the Sri Lankan culture has been weaved into my life since I was young. Every so often my family will have religious ceremonies so my brothers and I can experience the traditions from the "Old Country." I can't speak Singhalese, which is the official language of Sri Lanka, so when I travel there I generally can't speak to some of the kids who haven't learned English yet. When I traveled there two summers ago, it was the first time I was surrounded by people who are like me, but I could not really communicate with them. I got to stay with my relatives, and I actually spent a day in the Sri Lankan school where my mom had gone [co-ed now]. It is a very big difference. I really noticed how teaching is a lot stricter there and the kids take it a lot more seriously. But I also now see how we take for granted the things we have in our school here, like lots of textbooks, and even the classroom and the building. It also taught me so much about cultures and societies. Educationally, I feel like I should start working harder and live up to my parents' expectations. It made me think a lot.

I have been trying to learn the language. I can understand what my parents are saying because they talk to one another, and I have picked up words, but I feel ashamed that I can't speak Singhalese. Especially when I see some of my other friends who speak their language with their parents. It makes me feel that I should really work on that. There are kids who are born here, and they can speak their parents' language.

See, when I was younger, I knew English, and I didn't care about my parents' language. I wouldn't want to go to the grocery store and start talking to my mom in Singhalese, like if she asked me to go get milk. I knew what she was talking about, but I felt embarrassed, I felt weird because people start looking at you and wonder about your language and stuff. But now I see my cousin, who lives in England, but he lived in Sri Lanka for a year, and he is learning the language. I am pretty amazed because he can come back and speak Singhalese. It makes me wish I could do something like that. A lot of Sri Lankan kids tend to lose the language when they go to American, English-speaking schools. You speak it at home, but then you go to school in kindergarten and it just goes out the window.

But if you look at my painting, you see that the road I'm headed on splits, one towards America, one to Sri Lanka, and one in the middle. It represents a choice I have to make. Should I turn onto the road and take a bite of Americana? Should I turn towards Sri Lanka, continue Buddhism, learn about the language, have the culture take a larger portion of me? Or should I take the middle path? I don't know where it leads. Is it rough? Is it tough? I don't know.

Commentary

Most students, particularly adolescents, make choices about how much of their culture and language to embrace and how much to be influenced by those around them while shaping a self-image. They may do so consciously or subconsciously, but they do choose. Do Gamini's choices have to be "rough" or "tough"? Can we create a school environment and a society where Gamini and other students like him feel proud to speak their family's language—where they can create a new road rather than face difficult choices of "American" or home culture?

and others, teachers should be cautious about expecting students of the same background to behave in the same way.

In creating new cultures, young people also need to choose from an array of values and behaviors, selecting those that fit in the new society and discarding or transforming others. The process is neither conscious nor planned. Those whose values and behaviors differ from the mainstream's are inevitably involved in this transformation every day. Whether children or adults, students or workers, they are directly engaged in changing the complexion, attitudes, and values of our society. In the process, they may experience the pain and conflict that the young people in our case studies and snapshots articulated so well.

The point to remember is that U.S. society does not simply impose its culture on all newcomers. The process is neither as linear nor as straightforward as those who claim complete success for the process of *anglo-conformity* might have us believe,[14] but neither has the result been a truly pluralistic society. Although the United States is, in fact, multicultural, it is sometimes so in spite of itself, that is, it is not always the result of a conscious goal. For the most part, our society still reflects and perpetuates European American values and worldviews, but it has always also reflected, albeit at times poorly or stereotypically and against its will, the values of less respected and dominated groups as well. Latino heritage, for instance, can be seen in innumerable ways, from architecture in the Southwest to the myth of the cowboy. Jazz, widely acknowledged to be the greatest authentic U.S. music, is primarily African American in origin rather than European American.

What is "American" is neither simply an alien culture imposed on dominated groups nor an immigrant culture transposed indiscriminately to new soil. Neither is it an amalgam of old and new. What is "American" is the result of interactions of old, new, and created cultures. These interactions are neither benign nor smooth. Often characterized by unavoidable tension and great conflict, the creation of new cultures takes place in the contexts of the family, the community, and the schools.

Creating new cultures is made even more complicated by schools which, consciously or not, perceive their role as needing to shape all students to fit the middle-class, European American model. "They want to *monoculture* us," says a student in a video of successful Hispanic students in a Boston high school speaking about their identities and their schooling.[15] As we can see in the case studies and snapshots, students of diverse backgrounds respond in numerous ways to the pressures of an assimilationist society that is attempting to do away with differences. By refusing to accept either assimilation or cultural rejection, they force us to look at new ways of defining success.

Identity and learning

Students pick up competing messages about language and culture from teachers, schools, and society. This was evident in the remarks of the students in our case studies and snapshots. One of the messages to emerge can be stated as follows: *Culture is important,* something that most of the students are proud of and maintain, However, students also learn that *culture is unimportant* in the school environment.

Research corroborates the perspectives of many of the case study students, that is, that culture is significant and that it can support learning. One intriguing lesson that can be gleaned from the case studies and other related research is this: The more that students are involved in resisting complete assimilation while maintaining ties to their ethnic and linguistic communities, the more successful they will be in school. There are, of course, many examples to the contrary, that is, of people who have assimilated in order to succeed in school. Nevertheless, based on the case studies and snapshots in this book, as well as recent research highlighted here, we can legitimately ask whether it is necessary to abandon one's identity to be successful. That is the question that young people are asking themselves and us, as educators.

In our case studies and snapshots, most students suggest an alternative route to academic success. For them, maintaining cultural connections seems to have had at least a partially positive influence on academic achievement. Although it is important not to overstate this assertion, it is indeed a real possibility and one that severely challenges the "melting pot" ideology that has dominated U.S. schools and society into the 21st century. As discussed in Chapter 10, similar findings in terms of language maintenance have been consistently reported by researchers. That

What You Can Do

Encourage the Expression of Multiple Identities in the Classroom

Design some classroom activities to help students express themselves as cultural beings and to provide opportunities for you to learn from, and affirm, those expressions. An example follows.

With your students, make a classroom list of the many different group affiliations that students move in and out of throughout their school week: family, neighborhood, sports teams, faith communities, hobby groups/clubs, performing arts groups, lunch groups, locker buddies, after-school classes, chat rooms, various classrooms/course activities, circles of friends, and so on. Make another list of the behaviors that "go with" each of these group affiliations. Make another list of how some behaviors may clash or cause tension if they are demonstrated in a different setting. Make a list of behaviors that are transferable and useful across multiple settings. Discuss what this means for cultural identities. Help students understand that most of us are influenced by multiple cultures and have more than one way of identifying ourselves. Brainstorm how you may learn from one another, as a classroom community, about affiliation groups that are less visible in your school.

From time to time, revisit this activity to help you and your students delve deeper into identity. Play the card game "Go Fish" and pretend that each card represents an aspect of identity. Keep written journals about what it is like to have somebody "fish away" an aspect of your identity and what it feels like to "fish away" somebody else's identities. Don't be surprised if your students decide to change the rules of the game.

is, when students' language is used as the basis for their education—when it is respected and valued—students tend to succeed in school.

The notion that assimilation is a prerequisite for success in school or society is contested both by the research reviewed here and by the case studies and snapshots. The experiences of these young people call into question the often-cited claim that students who are not from European American backgrounds have poor self-images and low self-esteem. It is not that simple. In fact, schools and society may be complicit in *creating* low self-esteem. That is, students do not simply develop poor self-concepts out of the blue; self-concepts are also the result of policies and practices of schools and society that respect and affirm some groups while devaluing and rejecting others. Although young people might partially internalize some of the many daily negative messages about their culture, race, ethnic group, class,

and language, they are not simply passive recipients of such messages. They also actively resist negative messages through more positive interactions with peers, family, and even school. The mediating role of families, communities, teachers, and schools helps to contradict detrimental messages and to reinforce more affirming ones.

The conclusion that sustaining native language and culture nurtures academic achievement turns on its head not only conventional educational philosophy, but also the policies and practices of schools that have done everything possible to eradicate students' identities in order, they maintain, for all students to succeed in school. We suggest that the opposite is true: School policies and practices that stress cultural knowledge, build on students' native-language ability, and emphasize the history and experiences of the students' communities would be much more productive.

Beyond Academics

In nearly all the case studies and snapshots of students who were successful in school, significant involvement in activities beyond academics emerged as a key component. Whether through school-related organizations, hobbies, religious groups, or other activities, students found ways to support their learning. Often, although the activities promoted learning, they had little to do with academics. These activities had several important roles, both academic and nonacademic: keeping students on track, removing them from negative peer pressure, developing leadership and critical thinking skills, and giving them a feeling of belonging.

While such activities take place in a range of settings, from organized or structured formal programs to extended family or neighborhood settings, the role of organized after-school programs for youth development cannot be overstated. A burgeoning field of research is documenting the influence of these community activities on young people's lives. Robert Halpern's research describes the historical development of after-school programs and empha-sizes their critical role, especially in the lives of children from economically strapped communities.[16] In another study, Barton J. Hirsch studied six Boys and Girls Clubs across the country and, through the voices of students, documented how recreation and relationship building create a "second home" for these urban youth.[17] Similarly, in a study of a math and science enrichment program, Annie Bouie outlined the successes that can spring from focusing on the inherent strengths and resilience of young people's cultures and communities.[18] The research and practice of these community workers and others points to the growing importance of after-school programs and their relationships to schooling.

Keeping on track

One way in which activities other than school help is by keeping students "on track." That is, non-school activities focus students' attention on the importance of school while simultaneously providing some relief from it. This finding is consistent with other research. For instance, Jabari Mahiri's research on the literacy activities of 10- to 12-year-old

---

What You Can Do

Widen Horizons by Acknowledging What You Do Not Know

Study your list of students who you are currently teaching. Do any of them have cultural experiences or backgrounds with which you are unfamiliar? Pick two students who may represent groups of which you have little knowledge. For the purpose of example, we'll use two groups that Eugene mentions in his snapshot in Chapter 10: Tibetans and lesbian, gay, bisexual, and transgender (LGBT) people.

Assignment for the Teacher: Make a KWL chart for each of the two students you have selected: what I KNOW, what I WANT to know, What I LEARNED). Make a plan to fill in the charts within one month. Use at least one print source as resources: Read a book or an article. Also, take at least one field trip that immerses you in each family's culture: Visit a community event, a performance, or the students' family. Perhaps you can also visit an arts event, go to a Tibetan cultural gathering, attend a political rally or meeting to support gay marriage rights, or take each student's family out for ice cream.

After you fill in "what I learned," choose two other students' families and start with two new KWL charts. Continue throughout the year.

African American males during participation in a neighborhood basketball association found that this sport had immense motivational value in inspiring them to engage in literacy activities.[19]

In the case studies and snapshots, extracurricular activities also had a definitive influence, and these extended beyond simply sports. Rashaud, for example, spoke about his membership in Future Business Leaders of America. This after-school group engaged in community service in children's hospitals and nursing homes. In addition to a sense of fulfillment, these activities provided a framework for understanding the role of the business leader beyond that as somebody who focuses on making money. Involvement in the Gay-Straight Alliance was significant in carving out a place where Rebecca Florentina and other LGBT students could feel at home. Melinda Miceli's research documents the social and political impact of the Gay-Straight Alliance. She emphasizes the role of the first student leaders who create these organizations within their communities as vehicles of change within schools.[20] Such after-school activities taught Rashaud, Rebecca, and their peers essential life skills, and it also gave them the impetus and energy to educate others.

Many researchers have documented the important role of the arts in cocurricular, extracurricular, and out-of-school activities in developing rich multicultural student expression. A collection of essays by Maxine Greene provides a critical account of the role of the arts in social change. She argues that releasing students' imagination and artistic expression asserts multicultural student voices while developing skills in academic disciplines.[21] To illustrate the power of arts in after-school communities, Shirley Brice Heath and Laura Smyth, in collaboration with researcher Milbrey Mclaughlin, created a documentary film and guidebook. The film and book present four case studies of high-quality after-school arts programs that defy stereotypical public perceptions of urban youth.[22]

Shields against peer pressure

The negative peer pressure to which students are subjected can be very difficult to resist, but most of the students in the case studies were successful in doing so. One reason was the activities in which they were involved, which for some, shield them against negative influences. This was described vividly by Paul, who had not yet totally succeeded in resisting the pressure to be in a gang but nevertheless said, "Now it's like I figure if I'm more involved in school, I won't be so much involved in the gang, you know?" As you will see, Savoun also explained the role of peers in his former choices: "I was unwilling to focus on my education life. I chose friends over education, and one thing led to another and I dropped out there."

For other students as well, involvement in these school-related and community activities took up nonschool time, acting as a preventive strategy for discouraging less productive, although at times more alluring, activities. This was the reason, for example, that Manuel dropped some of his friends; at just about the same time, he joined a church in which he became deeply involved. Linda's devotion to music and Avi's insistence on honoring the Sabbath can probably be understood in this way as well.

Developing critical thinking and leadership skills

Extracurricular and after-school activities also contribute to the development of important skills such as critical thinking and leadership qualities. Through a theater workshop based on students' experiences and ideas, Manuel was able to analyze critically his own experience as an immigrant to this country. This workshop gave him a place to reflect on his experiences more deeply and to articulate consciously and clearly the pain and fear that he felt in his first years here.

James's involvement with bicycle racing, his self-acclaimed first love, consumed both his time and attention. Before his bike accident, he was riding 40 miles per day. James's involvement in bicycling extended beyond racing itself, however. He subscribed to all of the related magazines, got his racing license, and was actively recruiting others interested in the sport to start a biking club. He was also planning to approach local bicycle merchants with the idea of obtaining financial support to sponsor the team. Gamini expressed a similar attachment to biking, an activity that helped him sort out his thoughts.

Avi's work in the synagogue is another powerful example of how extracurricular activities can develop leadership skills. Not only did his involvement in the temple require a great deal of study and sacrifice, but it also made him a role model for others in his community. The same was true of Nadia's involvement in her mosque and of Kaval's work in the Gurudwara, the Sikh house of worship. Vanessa's work with a peer education group helped her develop important leadership qualities and a growing critical awareness and sensitivity to issues of exclusion and stratification.

Belonging

The feeling of belonging, so important for adolescents, is also a benefit of participating in extracurricular activities. Young people seek to fit in and belong in any way they can. Some meet this need by joining gangs or taking part in other harmful activities in which they feel part of a "family." For many young people, the satis-faction of belonging is particularly evident in activities related to their ethnic group. Paul and Savoun were notable exceptions to participation in out-of-classroom activities. Transportation, finances, and obligations to care for his sisters prevented Savoun from joining the football team at his former school. Paul and Savoun succumbed to the lure of some of the only "extracurricular" activities in their neighborhoods— gangs and criminal activity—yet, when provided with more positive outlets, they blossomed.

Manuel, James, Kaval, Nadia, and Avi found their niche through, among other things, their houses of worship. In these cases, their religious commitment affirmed their ethnicity as well. For Manuel, a Protestant sect was much more in tune with his culture than the Catholic church typically associated with Cape Verdeans. As he so dramatically stated during one of his interviews, "I felt that God had moved there," implying that a cultural resonance was missing in the local Catholic church. Combining his cultural and religious activities, Rashaud was active in a local Black church. Kaval not only attended the Sikh Gurudwara, but he also helped out in the soup kitchen. Nadia not only attended her mosque to pray, but she also was considering teaching Arabic to some of the younger children whose families attended.

The role of faith communities in young people's lives also needs to be understood in a cultural context. For many people with deep connections to re-ligion, their spiritual lives are not an add-on or an extracurricular activity. The youth groups or committees that emerge from religious communities may be extracurricular, but in many cases, they have inextricable connections with cultural identities. Khyati Y. Joshi's research on the experiences of second-generation Indians offers a framework for understanding the relationships of ethnicity and race to religion in America. Joshi argues for educational curricular reforms and, more broadly, for recognition of religion as a form of social identity.[23] In this context, young people's activities in their re-ligious communities may be significant factors in their identity development.

These are valuable illustrations of how extracurricular activities in school, as well as activities outside school, including hobbies and religious and cultural organizations, support student learning. Rather than detracting from students' academic success by taking time away from homework or other school-related activities, such involvement helps young people by channeling their creative and physical energy. In some cases, the activities may also have academic benefits.

Family, Community, and School Environments for Success

Successful students are surrounded by messages that encourage success, including direct and indirect support from family and friends, activities that enhance, rather than detract from, success, and teachers and other school staff who demonstrate their care.

The crucial role of family

The ways families support children in their learning are complex and sometimes not what one might expect. Non–middle-class families, in particular, may not have much experience with academic involvement or achievement, but they do what they can to help their children in other ways. One way that families demonstrate their support for academic success is through high expectations. Education was highly valued by the families of all these students, regardless of their economic background. In fact, in some instances, working class parents and parents living in poverty had even *more* hope in education than middle-class parents, for obvious reasons.[24] They could not always help their children with homework or in learning English, and because they often lacked the "cultural capital" valued in society at large, they could not pass it down to their children. As a result, the ways they manifested high expectations were sometimes indirect, but the messages they verbalized to their children were clear. Vinh said his uncle supported him by saying, "Next time, you should do better." Alicia explained, "Doing good in school is to get a chance to do stuff that most of my family hasn't been able to do." Rashaud told us about his parents' concern: "It matters to me, because if they didn't care, I wouldn't care. Since they do, I really do. I really want to make them proud."

Family messages that communicate high expectations, although powerful, are not always enough. Many of the young people described in the case studies and snapshots had great respect and appreciation for their families and understood the sacrifices that had been made on their behalf. Nevertheless, this appreciation did not always make their school experiences any easier or more tolerable. Because their parents were not always able to give them concrete help and tangible guidance, students sometimes lacked a sense of direction. Manuel put it most poignantly when he said, "If I felt like I had support from my family, if they only knew the language . . . If they were educated, I could make it big, you see what I'm saying?" Although parents' inability to speak English is not a liability in itself, it can become one if the school does not provide alternative means for student learning through such structures as bilingual programs and homework centers.

Given the kind of help middle-class parents are able to provide for their children, Manuel was absolutely right when he concluded, "I would've had a better opportunity, a better chance." A good example comes from Barbara Comber's research that focused on early literacy experiences of children in Australia. Comber explains that children's families do not just "disappear" when the children start school. On the contrary, children bring with them their privileges and disadvantages and everything they have learned prior to beginning school. Discussing three specific children, she argued that children's lives aren't simply "background" information for teachers, and, in describing Mark, one of the children, she explained:

> At home, Mark did not have a collection of books and nobody read him bedtime stories. But he did have knowledge and dispositions which counted for quite a lot in making the transition to school. He knew how to be a "good boy." He knew what counted as important practices in the classroom (e.g., looking after books, answering questions).[25]

Even families who lack formal education and have limited experience with the means for achieving academic success frequently do a great deal to prepare their children for school. They often compensate by providing other critical support to their children. In the case of students from different linguistic backgrounds, parents and other family members frequently maintain native language use in the home, despite contrary messages from school and society. Such language use helps students develop literacy and prepares them for school. The more students are able to use language in a variety of ways and in diverse contexts, the more they replicate the literacy skills necessary for successful schoolwork.

This is a crucial message for teachers to understand. Although the children in their classrooms might not have the specific skills called for in school, they *do* have attitudes, skills, and capabilities that can be tapped to advance their learning.

Maintaining native-language communication at home also implies nurturing cultural connections through such activities as family rituals and traditions, not to mention the even more meaningful underlying cultural values that help form young people's attitudes and behaviors. Savoun put it plainly: "I would never want to leave my culture or my language; I always want to learn more." "Apprenticeship" in their families, and the consequent learning of culture, language, and values, is a primary way in which children receive and internalize the message that they are important.

Encouraging communication within the family is another way parents support the academic success of their children. The importance of talking with their parents about issues central to their lives was mentioned by a number of young people. Alicia recalled significant conversations with her mother, when she was still alive, about "protecting herself," sexual responsibility, and the importance of school. Yahaira stated that she talked to her mother about "almost everything," including school achievement. As you will see in Nadia's case study, she described each member of the family as forming a piece of the "puzzle" and communication as central to maintaining this close connection. For Vinh, even long-distance communication was meaningful. He wrote to his parents weekly and was in turn revitalized by their messages. Linda's description of shared dinnertime in her family is a moving expression of the value of communication.

In numerous ways, academically successful students in the case studies and snapshots made it clear that they dedicated their school success to their parents, almost as a way of showing their gratitude for the sacrifices their parents made for them. These young people frequently mentioned that their parents were the motivating force behind their success, even if the parents did not always completely understand or appreciate what it meant. For example, Paul was inspired to return to school by his mother's own return to school. Gamini said that he wanted to do well for his family because of all they had sacrificed for him and his brothers. More than one student mentioned making her or his parents *happy*. This focus on parents' happiness, not what one might expect from modern, sophisticated adolescents, is a theme that emerged time and again.

Students in the case studies and snapshots often described their parents in remarkably tender and loving ways. From Yahaira's "my mom is the person I admire the most in the world," to Vanessa's "they're caring and they're willing to go against the norm," students made it clear that they had warm, close-knit relationships with their parents, which had a significant influence on their lives and the formation of values. Savoun described his affection for his family thus: "It's been great to be a member of my family. Sometime they don't understand me, but I still love them." Linda said that her parents were "always there for me, all the time" and even that she understood the "twisted reasons" for their rules and limits.

This is not to say that parents whose children are not successful in school have *not* provided affirming environments. There are a multitude of complex reasons why students are successful in school, and a close and warm relationship with parents is only one of them. Notwithstanding the caring and loving environments that parents may provide their children, their children may still be rebellious, alienated, or unsuccessful in school. A good example is Paul, who maintained that, "If it wasn't for the family, the love I get from my family, I would look for it in my homeboys. . . . I had a love that kept me home." While earnestly stating this, Paul was still engaged in the gang. Latrell expressed his earnest desire to avoid drug dealing and "negative stuff" so he could make his mother proud. His interview demonstrated the many forces that he had to negotiate to accomplish his goal of a positive future.

Other issues also influence academic success. What Carlos Cortés called *the societal curriculum*, that is, influences of the general society—including the mass media, gender-role expectations, anti-immigrant hysteria, and rampant violence—are another layer of the sociopolitical context of education that needs to be considered.[26] Other influences may also affect school achievement: rank within family; other family dynamics, including relationships among siblings; and simple personality and idiosyncratic differences. It appears, however, that a close and open relationship between children and their parents or guardians is a necessary but incomplete element of school success.

Although their relationships with their parents and other family members were obviously prominent in the academic success of these students, with some exceptions, the family was uninvolved in the school, according to the traditional definition of parent involvement: Most of the students' families did not go to school unless called, did not attend meetings or volunteer in school activities, and were not members of parent organizations. This was somewhat surprising, considering the research on the relationship between parental involvement and their children's academic achievement, which is reviewed in Chapter 9. The fact that some of these parents did not speak English, that they themselves had not always had positive experiences in schools, and that they were inhibited by the impersonal and unreceptive nature of many schools may be partial explanations. Conflicting work schedules, child care needs, and other situations also help explain their noninvolvement.

Teachers, Schools, and Caring

Many of the students in the case studies and snap-shots mentioned particular teachers, programs, or activities in school that helped them succeed. The key role teachers play in the achievement of their students is not surprising. The most important characteristic students looked for in their teachers was "caring." Students evaluated their teachers' level of caring by the amount of time they dedicated to their students, their patience, how well they prepared their classes, and how they made classes interesting.

For Manuel, caring came in the form of an entire program. The bilingual program, in his case, was critical to his eventual school success. For Liane, the fact that her school offered Chinese as a language of study was a powerful message that the language was valued in the school community. In many ways, students remembered the teachers who had affirmed them, whether through their language, their culture, or their concerns.

Students are empowered not only by studying about their *own* culture but also by being exposed, through a variety of pedagogical strategies, to different perspectives. Numerous students mentioned this, including Paul, who was empowered when he read *The Diary of Anne Frank* in elementary school. It was not only the subject matter but also how it was taught that made history come alive for him. Several students mentioned the desire to learn more about world regions and the cultural groups involved in current events. Several mentioned wishing they were taught more about the war in Iraq and expressed a desire to learn about Iraqi experiences and Islamic traditions.

Teachers of the same background as students also make a difference. Several recent studies have pointed to the positive influence that same-group identity among a teacher and students can have. A study by Sabrina Zirkel, for instance, found that students with race- and gender-matched role models had better academic performance, had more achievement-oriented goals, and thought more about their future, compared to students who did not have such matched role models.[27] However, the fact that the teachers and other staff members who understand and call on the students' cultures are often from the same background does not mean that only educators from the students' ethnic group can teach them or be meaningful in their lives. Having teachers from students' ethnic backgrounds cannot be underestimated, but students in the case studies also named teachers not from the same background who had made a difference in their lives. These teachers had either learned the students' language or were knowledgeable about, and comfortable with, the students' cultures, or they were simply sensitive to the concerns of young people.

What can teachers and other educators learn from these examples? For one, it is apparent that how educators view their role in relation to their students can make a powerful difference in the lives of students. This role definition is not about strategies as much as it is about attitudes. In the words of Jim Cummins, "The interactions that take place between students and teachers and among students are more central to student success than any method for teaching literacy, or science or math."[28]

In a related area, the lesson that *relationships* are at the core of teaching and learning is reinforced through these case studies. Students mentioned teachers who cared about them and how these teachers helped to make them feel that they belonged. When students feel connected to school, they identify as *learners,* and they have a far greater chance of becoming successful students. When they feel that they do not belong, identifying as a learner is more difficult.

Finally, educators can learn that there are many ways to show caring. Accepting students' differences is one way; another is to have rigorous and high expectations of them. Also, becoming what Ricardo Stanton-Salazar has called *institutional agents,* providing social networks for students, is equally meaningful. These networks, from information on college admissions, to securing needed tutoring services, are generally unavailable to culturally marginalized students or those living in poverty, but they can make the difference in achieving academic success.[29] Prudence Carter builds on that notion by calling for "multicultural navigators" who are fluent in the social and cultural capital of college admissions, scholarship acquisition, and the like, yet do not totally acculturate, or give in, to the establishment. According to Carter, navigators are needed who can demonstrate:

What You Can Do

Expand the "Comfort Zone" for You and Your Students

The students in the snapshots and case studies told us about crossing cultural boundaries and negotiating multiple worlds. How often do you consider the many realms that students are required to juggle to meet school success? Here is a little experiment to help you consider life through the eyes of students whose lives may not be easily integrated into mainstream cultures.

Your Comfort Zone: Two Weeks in the Life of a Teacher

Week One: Consider your daily routines, environments, and communications as a teacher and also as a member of your community. For one week, keep brief journal entries that describe these experiences: What is your usual journey to and from work? Where do you purchase your food? How do you take care of your laundry? Who are the people you see in these events? Do you have a regular "pit-stop" in your weekly routine: visiting a neighbor or family member, stopping at a coffee shop, an exercise class, a library, escorting young ones to activities or elders to appointments? In what language do you speak when you engage in these activities? Write down the mundane and the ordinary.

Week Two: Change your daily routine. Try a different route to get to work. Purchase your food from a merchant you have never or rarely visited. Cook a recipe or purchase prepared food you have never tasted. Fold your laundry in a different way. Travel to an unfamiliar neighborhood. Change the day of some routines that do not have prescribed schedules. Learn at least two sentences in a language you have never spoken. Keep brief journal entries. What did you notice? How did you feel? How well did you function? Did these changes have positive aspects? Were there negative aspects?

Everyday experiences such as getting to work, purchasing food, and folding laundry are not necessarily cultural events, but cultural life is enacted and comprised of everyday experiences. To cultivate empathy for, and solidarity with, students who are perceived as different—or perceive themselves as different—it is useful to reflect on how familiarity and routine create comfort. You don't have to plan a heritage festival to develop awareness of how identities are asserted and affirmed in our daily lives.

This exercise will help you imagine how students may feel when their perspectives and identities are negated or ignored. In turn, the significance of the little things that make a difference in students' school day, such as a warm smile, an extra moment of patience in an explanation, or acknowledgement for "little" accomplishments, take on fresh meaning. Imagine a classroom where all the students and teachers work from such a perspective.

Your Students' Comfort Zones: Adapt this activity for your classroom but do not assign it until you have done it yourself!

how to overcome poverty with critical, self-loving, and other respecting perspectives, who do not make them ashamed of who they are but rather proud of how far they will go.[30]

Whether they are in traditional or alternative schools, whether they are from mainstream or non-mainstream backgrounds, whether they speak students' native languages or not, *all* teachers can make a significant difference in their students' lives. The young people in our case studies and snapshots have provided much food for thought in how this can happen.

SUMMARY

In this chapter, we reviewed the major themes that emerged in the case studies, with particular attention to four themes related to academic achievement:

- A redefinition of education and success
- Pride and conflict in culture and language
- The role of activities not related to academics in sustaining school success
- The important support of family, community, and teachers

Cultural, linguistic connections can play a key role in students' academic success. In most of these cases, language and culture have been reinforced in the home and sometimes in the school as well. When reinforced in both settings, the message that language and culture are valued is clear and powerful. If they are valued only in the home, students may develop conflicted feelings about them.

The larger society also plays a key role in student learning. If young people see their culture devalued in such things as political initiatives (e.g., propositions to abolish bilingual education or to ban gay marriage), they are certain to develop conflicted attitudes concerning their ethnic group and family culture. However, in spite of sometimes harsh attacks on their culture, successful students have been able to maintain considerable pride in their ethnic group, family culture, and community. In the process, they reject both the pressure to assimilate and the pressure to give up. They are transforming culture and language in order to fit in, but on their own terms.

Involvement in activities outside the classroom also plays a part in promoting students' academic achievement. Most successful students we interviewed were involved successfully in extracurricular activities and other activities outside of school. Whether such activities are sports, social clubs, religious groups, or other community activities does not seem to matter. Students' involvement in such activities may help them develop a sense of fulfillment, leadership, and other skills that reinforce academic achievement and remove them from possible negative peer pressures.

Finally, families, communities, and schools work in different, complementary ways to motivate students to succeed. Although families from culturally nondominant and economically poor communities are sometimes unable to give their children the tangible help and support that dominant and economically secure families are able to, they serve an indispensable role in their children's school accomplishments. The families of all the successful students we have studied—from middle class to low-income families—have provided support in the following ways:

- Maintaining native language and ethnic connections in the home
- Having high expectations of their children at all times
- Providing loving and supportive home environments
- Communicating with their children on a consistent basis

Teachers and schools also play an essential role in students' success. We have seen that teachers who care, who take time with students, and who affirm their students' identities are the most successful. School policies and practices that support students in their learning are also critical. Students were explicit in pointing out the classroom activities and school practices that helped them learn from help after school to small-group work. As the students pointed out, when schools and families work together, school success can become a reality.

To Think About

1. What characteristics do you think define academic success? Do they differ from how you think most teachers define it? Do you think your cultural values influence your definition? How?

2. If it is true that pride in culture and language is important for academic success, what does this mean for school policies and practices? Discuss policies and practices related to culture and language that you think schools should consider to promote educational equity for all students.

3. Caring on the part of teachers, schools, and parents was highlighted by a number of students. What might schools do to give students the message that they care? How would these practices compare with current practices?

Activities for Personal, School, and Community Change

1. The crucial role of families in providing environments for success was highlighted by many of the students in the case studies, but their families' role was often different from that which schools traditionally define as *involvement*. Come up with an action plan for working with parents to develop environments for success while also respecting their specific contexts. For example, not all families have computers, so requiring that they provide them for their children is unrealistic. Likewise, not all families speak English fluently, and asking them to do so might be counterproductive. What can you do in such cases to encourage families to motivate their children to become academically engaged?

2. Involvement in school and community activities emerged as a major support for the academic success of students in the case studies. Brainstorm some ways that your school can promote such activities. Be specific, citing concrete examples.

3. If you don't already do so, begin a weekly "Letter to Parents" in which you highlight some of the classroom activities their children have been doing. You can ask for their advice on curriculum issues, encourage them to volunteer in the classroom, and so on. You might also include children's work in the letters from time to time.

Companion Website

For access to additional case studies, weblinks, concept cards, and other material related to this chapter, visit the text's companion website at **www.ablongman.com/nieto5e.**

Notes to Chapter 12

1. Pilar Muñoz and Josette Henschel interviewed ten Puerto Rican women who differed in age, social class, marital status, and length of stay in the United States. I am grateful to Josette and Pilar and to the women they interviewed for this example.

2. Sonia Nieto, Patty Bode, Eugenie Kang, and John Raible, "Pushing the Boundaries of Multicultural Education: Retheorizing Identity, Community and Curriculum." In *Handbook of Curriculum and Instruction*, edited by F. Michael Connelly, Ming Fang He, and Joanne Phillion (Thousand Oaks, CA: Sage, 2007).

3. Nadine Dolby, "Changing Selves: Multicultural Education and the Challenge of New Identities." *Teachers College Record* 102, no. 5 (2000): 898–912.

4. Pierre Bourdieu, "The Forms of Capital." In *Handbook of Theory and Research for the Sociology of Education*, edited by John G. Richardson (New York: Greenwood Press, 1986). Also see David Halpern, *Social Capital* (Cambridge, England: Polity Press, 2005) for a re-view of the burgeoning literature and definitions of social capital.

5. Antti Jalava, "Mother Tongue and Identity: Nobody Could See That I Was a Finn." In *Minority Education: From Shame to Struggle,* edited by Tove Skutnabb-Kangas and Jim Cummins (Clevedon, England: Multilingual Matters, 1988): 164–165.

6. Donna Deyhle and Karen Swisher, "Research in American Indian and Alaska Native Education: From Assimilation to Self-Determination." In *Review of Research in Education,* vol. 22, edited by Michael W. Apple (Washington, DC: American Educational Research Association, 1997): 113–194.

7. Sandy Grande, *Red Pedagogy: Native American Social and Political Thought* (Lanham, MD: Rowman & Littlefield, 2004).

8. Laurie Olsen, *Made in America: Immigrant Students in Our Public Schools* (New York: New Press, 1998): 55.

9. Stanley Aronowitz, "Between Nationality and Class." *Harvard Educational Review* 67, no. 2 (Summer 1997): 188–207.

10. Alejandro Portes and Rubén Rumbaut, *Legacies: The Story of the Immigrant Second Generation* (Berkeley, CA: University of California Press; and New York: Russell Sage Foundation, 2001): 274. Also see Alejandro Portes and Rubén Rumbaut, *Immigrant America: A Portrait,* 3rd ed. (Berkeley: University of California Press, 2006).

11. Judith M. Blohm and Terri Lapinsky, *Kids Like Me: Voices of the Immigrant Experience* (Boston: Intercultural Press, 2006).

12. Clara C. Park, A. Lin Goodwin, and Stacey J. Lee, *Asian American Identities, Families, and Schooling: Research on the Education of Asian and Pacific Americans.* (Charlotte, NC: Information Age, 2003).

13. Michael Sadowski, ed., *Adolescents at School: Perspectives on Youth, Identity, and Education* (Cambridge, MA: Harvard Education Press, 2003).

14. *Anglo-conformity* refers to the pressures, both expressed and hidden, to conform to the values, attitudes, and behaviors representative of the dominant group in U.S. society.

15. The excellent video *How We Feel: Hispanic Students Speak Out* was developed by Virginia Vogel Zanger and is available from Landmark Media, Falls Church, VA. The contact information is www.landmarkmedia.com and (800)342-4336.

16. Robert Halpern, *Making Play Work: The Promise of After-School Programs for Low-Income Children* (New York: Teachers College Press, 2003).

17. Barton J. Hirsch, *A Place to Call Home: After-school Programs for Urban Youth* (New York: Teachers College Press, 2005).

18. Annie Bouie, *After-School Success: Academic Enrichment with Urban Youth* (New York: Teachers College Press, 2006).

19. Jabari Mahiri, *Shooting for Excellence: African American and Youth Culture in New Century Schools* (Urbana, IL: National Council of Teachers of English; and New York: Teachers College Press, 1998).

20. Melinda Miceli, *Standing Out, Standing Together: The Social and Political Impact of Gay-Straight Alliances* (New York: Routledge, 2005).

21. Maxine Greene, *Releasing the Imagination: Essays on Education, the Arts, and Social Change* (San Francisco: Jossey-Bass, 2000).

22. Art*Show,* to be understood as "arts show how," comprises a dual package of resource guide and documentary video. The resource guide summarizes the project from which a focus on the linguistic and cognitive aspects of learning in the arts emerged. The project and the guide–video package are the culmination of ten years of research on youth organizations by Shirley Brice Heath, Laura Smyth, and Milbrey W. McLaughlin. See the book: Laura Smyth and Shirley Brice Heath, *ArtShow: Youth and Community Development* (Washington, DC: Partners for Livable Communities, 1999). Also see the documentary film *ArtShow* directed by Shirley Brice Heath. The documentary video was produced for Partners for Livable Communities and for distribution to PBS, 1999. (Winner of Gold Award, Worldfest Video and Film Festival, Houston, 2000; Winner of Chris Award, 2000.) For more information see www.shirleybriceheath.com

23. Khyati Y. Joshi, *New Roots in America's Sacred Ground: Religion, Race, and Ethnicity in Indian America* (New Brunswick, NJ: Rutgers University Press, 2006).

24. See Alejandro Portes and Rubén Rumbaut, *Legacies.* Also see Prudence Carter, *Keepin' It Real: School Success Beyond Black and White* (New York: Oxford University Press, 2005).

25. Barbara Comber, "What *Really* Counts in Early Literacy Lessons." *Language Arts* 78, no. 1 (September 2000): 39–49.

26. Jim Carnes, "Searching for Patterns: A Conversation with Carlos Cortés." *Teaching Tolerance* no. 16 (Fall 1999): 10–15.

27. Sabrina Zirkel, " 'Is There a Place for Me?' Role Models and Academic Identity Among White Students and Students of Color." *Teachers College Record* 104, no. 2 (March 2002): 357–376.

28. Jim Cummins, *Negotiating Identities: Education for Empowerment in a Diverse Society, 2nd ed* (Ontario, CA: California Association for Bilingual Education, 2001).

29. Ricardo D. Stanton-Salazar, *Manufacturing Hope and Despair: The School and Kin Support Networks of U.S.–Mexican Youth* (New York: Teachers College Press, 2001).

30. Carter, *Keepin' It Real: School Success Beyond Black and White*, 155–156.

CHAPTER 12 CASE STUDIES

Nadia Bara

I could never really stand in other
people's shoes but now . . .
I kind of feel for the people that had
racists against them because
now I kind of know how they feel.

In some ways, it's hard to believe that Nadia Bara[1] was just 14 years old when she was first interviewed. Talking about school, her family, her religion, or the joys and difficulties of being different, she was at once a wise older spirit and a teenager.

A ninth grader in a high school known throughout the state as an excellent school, Nadia lived with her mother and father in Linden Oaks, a comfortable, upper middle-class suburb in the Midwest that boasts the highest yearly median income in the state. Her sister Layla, 18, was a first-year student at the state university, also a well-regarded institution in the Midwest. Layla lived on campus a couple of hours from home but frequently returned home on weekends. Nadia's mother, Sarah, and her husband, Omar, both physicians, had lived in the United States for nearly two decades. Sarah was born in the United States, but while still a child, she had returned with her family to Syria, where she was raised and completed her education, including her medical training. Omar was born in Kuwait and attended medical school in Egypt. They met and married in Kuwait and came to live in the United States shortly before the birth of their first daughter, Layla.

The entire family visits Syria for at least two weeks every year to see family and friends and reconnect with their roots. During these trips, they usually visit at least one new place, too. They had recently been to Holland, Germany, Austria, and Maui. These trips had increased Nadia's motivation to travel, which she loved because, as she said, "I love seeing all the different types of people anywhere." During her interview, Nadia spoke fondly about her experiences in Syria, while also describing her status as an insider/outsider both in Syria and the United States.

The Bara family is a close-knit and fairly religious one. They belong to a relatively sizable Muslim community in Linden Oaks, and they try, in the midst of the fast-paced and postindustrial society of the United States, to live as Syrians and Muslims. This is not always possible, and Nadia and her sister both spoke of the tribulations they've faced because of their identities.

Nadia and her family are part of a growing Arab and Muslim presence in the United States. In 2000, the U.S. Census Bureau counted 1.2 million Arabs in the United States, or about 0.4 percent of the U.S. population, although Muslims continue to arrive in the United States, and a growing number of non-Arabs in the United States are converting to Islam.[2] Arabs are a remarkably diverse group, hailing from some 20 countries in the Middle East and Northern Africa. Most Arabs in the world are Muslims, but Arabs are only 20 percent of all Muslims in the world (estimated to be more than 1 billion in number). In fact, Islam is the fastest growing religion in the world.[3] Nevertheless, only a quarter of Arabs in the United States are Muslim. Arabs live in many parts of the United States, settling in places that would surprise many people. According to Diana Eck, for example, about a century ago, three small communities in North Dakota were home to an early group of Muslim immigrants, and one of the first mosques in the country was built in 1920 in the town of Ross, North Dakota. In addition, the Muslim community in Cedar Rapids, Iowa, goes back more than 100 years. Thus, from the start, the Midwest has been a destination for Muslims from various countries.[4]

Reasons for making the United States their destination vary greatly, but economic and political reasons account for why many come. Although Arabs are not new to the United States, the challenges they face have become more apparent in the recent past. These include negative stereotyping, racism, discrimination, and misinformation about their history and culture, a theme echoed by Nadia. Schools are some of the places where these problems are most visible.

The Bara family chose public schools for their daughters. This decision was not an easy one to make, particularly because of differences in religion and religious practices. Both Nadia and Layla have done very well in school. Layla, for instance, graduated with a 4.0 grade-point average from the same high school that Nadia was attending. Nadia loved school and was also doing well academically, having received a special award for earning straight A's in eighth grade. She was involved in many nonschool activities, especially sports (soccer, tennis, track, and volleyball), as well as school activities, including student council, theater productions, and the school newspaper.

As pointed out in the case of James, the Christian Maronite student whose case study appears after Chapter 9, until recently, Arabs and Arab Americans were often "invisible" in schools. This invisibility disappeared after the events of September 11, 2001, when they became all too visible. Nevertheless, Arabs are still frequently invisible in curricula and in other school policies and practices. Consequently, Islam is the religion about which most Americans have the least information and the most biases.[5]

In the case study that follows, we see a young woman who reflects on these issues in a thought-ful and mature way. The major themes that surfaced in Nadia's interviews were *belonging and the challenge of difference, the call to activism,* and *the centrality of family.*

"I'm torn right in the middle": belonging and the challenge of difference

I'm Nadia. I'm fourteen years old, and I am a freshman at Linden Oaks High School. I speak Arabic, English, and I've been in Spanish since first grade. One of my best friends is Jewish, and a lot of my friends are Protestant and Catholic, and I have many Black, White, everything [background of friends] . . . it's good.

I think the thing I like the most about myself is, I guess, how I can be funny and make people feel better. All my friends, they say I can cheer people up. I would much rather be laughing than thinking about bad stuff. I think that's a good thing, being optimistic.

I'm Arabic, and my parents are both Syrian. When I come here, you know I feel like I belong and . . . I mean I feel American, but I also go back to my race, you know? But when I go to Syria, for some strange reason, I feel like I belong even more. I'm, you could say, the only Syrian at my school right now, but there's lots of other people from the Middle East. But it's never been a problem, and I don't know, at first, after September 11th it was a little shaky, and I didn't want to tell people that I was Arabic because you got the weird looks, or when I went to camp someone asked me, they said, "Are you . . . you kind of look Afghani?" That's when it's a bit of a burden, just when you get singled out. People look at you different when they find out you're Arabic, especially now. Before [before] it wasn't [that way] at all. But now, especially when we're in restaurants or something as a family, my parents are talking Arabic, the waitresses will come and [ask] "Where are you from?" My parents will tell them, and they all give us weird looks like it's scary.

But I love going back to Syria. It's one of the greatest places in the world, and I love to be there, and I love my religion. I love it. I mean it's just there's times when it's a little hard, but it's no big deal. Before, I never thought about it very much. Going to Syria makes it all much better. It's so fun because you don't have to hide anything about your religion there, and you can be completely religious. It's great because everyone's the same.

Being Muslim and being American is hard because, here, I guess you know how the traditional Muslims, they wear the hajab over their head? There's a lot of stuff that I guess we're not too religious about, and it's really hard to be that religious here when you have friends. I mean, I don't have a boyfriend. Lots of my friends are dating, and they all go and that's what's a little hard about it. You feel kind of different and singled out. Sometimes if I wanna go out with friends and stay 'til eleven [my parents] won't let me. All my friends stay out 'til twelve, and I come home at ten. My parents are a lot stricter than all my other friends' [parents] and I don't date and I don't talk to boys on the phone. I'm not allowed to do that. Like, it's a lot stricter, but sometimes I think it's for the better but other times . . . I mean, I get frustrated a lot with it because these are the times when everyone is dating and everyone is going out, and I'm not allowed to go out, like, every day of the weekend. But I pray and I fast during Ramadan, and we give to charity and everything like that. It's just lots of stuff is hard to keep up with when you're a teenager growing up in America, trying to be Muslim, and trying to be Arabic, and trying to be American. Sometimes it's a lot but . . . I love everything.

A lot of my friends or just people at my school, they're not that religious, and they don't really have much to fall back on. And I guess it's very humbling maybe, just to go back and be at home and know that, even if you don't belong at school or even if that didn't work out, you have your religion and you have your culture and you know that that's never gonna change. And that makes you who you are.

Going back to Syria, I feel very much at home. But there's also times in Syria when I feel like I don't know as much as everyone there knows and I guess especially now, this year, when I went back there's a little more hostility towards . . . I mean, not my family, but people that we would see on the street if they heard us talking English. Just because of everything that's going on in Palestine, there's a little more hostility towards Americans I guess. And that's when it becomes a little hard, because I'm torn right in the middle, you know? But going to Syria, being Muslim, in a Muslim group, I'm not the strongest, most religious Muslim, but I have the

beliefs. When you're in Syria, sometimes it makes you feel bad because I look around I'm like "Wow, I'm not religious enough and when I go home I'm going to be very good," but then, when you get home, you don't know what to do because it's a back and forth thing really.

[In school], the weird thing was they never really asked us our nationality or anything until [after 2001]. They would ask you in every class, and you had to raise your hand [saying] what you were and they went through every culture except they didn't have Middle Eastern. And so I never raised my hand, and they're, like, "What *are* you?" And I [would say] "Arabic" and then they would um . . . I mean the teachers, they never gave me, like, weird looks or anything like that. It's just sometimes kids are . . . especially after September 11th, everyone's shaky.

The thing that was really cool is my friends have stuck with me through and through. They know who I am and they know my family and they've known I'm Arabic and they haven't changed at all. My friends have stayed the same. My teachers don't care at all. It's just every now and then you'll get a weird look or you'll get a weird feeling . . . kind of feel singled out sometimes, but it's nothing too big at all.

We were on a field trip one time. We were coming back on the bus, and there's another boy who goes to my mosque, and he's made fun of a lot. I don't really know why. And a boy that's normally my friend, he made fun of the other boy that's Muslim and he told him (this is after September 11th), he told him something like "Well at least, I don't believe in blowing planes into buildings" and I felt bad because Khallid, the boy that goes to my mosque, he didn't really say anything, and I was infuriated, so I yelled at my friend. Which was really an uncomfortable feeling because I hated to yell at my friend, but I was so sad and hurt that he would say something like that. And I just told him "How could you say something when you don't know?" Now he kind of held a grudge about it, and we're kind of friends, but it was just really an uncomfortable feeling to be in that situation because Khallid didn't say anything, and I think he was really just too scared to get into it.

Most of the time I just tell myself, especially with that boy, he doesn't know any better. I feel bad because he's uneducated . . . it's kind of like looking at a German and saying "Oh, they're a Nazi." It's just stereotypes, and I think that's horrible and I just try to tell myself "Don't get mad, don't let it get to you. Just tell him that that's not right and try to educate him that that's completely wrong."

I think now, after the events of September 11th, it's become more of an issue. And the weird thing was when we would learn about racism and just stuff like that, I never really knew what it felt like, and I could never really stand in the people's shoes, but now I kind of feel for the people that had racists against them. People that I know have been discriminated against, but I haven't myself as much. I think now I just have a bigger . . . I'm trying to think of the word, like I feel for them, I guess, a little more. I kind of know how they feel, and I'm more understanding because I've been through it, I guess.

I know adults are a lot more smart about the whole thing, and they know that not all Arab people are terrorists, and I just wouldn't want [teachers] to associate everything that I say or do with my ethnicity or with my religion, and I'm not a representative of it. I know I'm a representative of it *to an extent*, but what I do does not portray what every other Arabic Muslim would do. We're all different, and no one is the same.

My friend Chelsea, she's Jewish, Russian. All our lives we never even *thought* about me being Muslim and her being Jewish and how anywhere else that would have been such a big deal, and we never thought about it, and we've been best friends since, like, second grade, and she's such a great person. Now, after September 11th, when we hear about all this stuff and when we hear about the fights going on in Israel and Palestine, it's really hard. But her mom is so open-minded. I love our friendship because it's against what everyone would say in the Middle East. It proves that it doesn't matter where you're from or what religion you are, you can still be getting along well.

The call to activism

Just a couple of weeks ago I was confronted by one of the leaders of the mosque to see if I could teach the little kids, the ones that don't know . . . like the ones from Bosnia and the ones that don't know Arabic hardly at all, if I could teach them Arabic. I haven't heard from the lady again, but that sounds like fun. My sister did that before she went off to college, and she said it was really fun. I like kids.

My dad came to me, and one of his friends had asked him [to speak to me]. They were having a rally for peace in the Middle East. It was just a lot of people from our mosque trying to put something together, and they wanted a youth speaker, and I jumped at the chance 'cause I like speaking and I like writing. So I wrote a speech up in, like, the end of May, and the rally was in the beginning of June, and so I went and I gave a speech, and it was really great. I got interviewed for the newspaper, and a different lady came from this world newspaper. She interviewed me, and so we got a copy of those. It was really fun. I like to get really involved.

Most of the time I hate hearing about what's going on in Palestine, [and] Israel you know, 'cause it's heart wrenching. We can't do much over here to help, and I feel like the littlest thing [can help]. Just do whatever you can to help, so I jumped at the chance to do that.

I love being in front of people. Like I love doing speeches, and just being in front of a crowd is fun for me. When they asked me if I would do that speech, I wanted to do it so bad, but then I was also, like, "This could be kind of weird, if I'm in the newspaper and someone sees it." And I was really hesitant sometimes, but just to give people a good feeling of what it is to be Arabic and what it is to be Muslim. And just to show them that we're not all terrorists and we're not all radicals.

The centrality of family

My parents are very family oriented, and they always want us to have a family dinner hour. Like, especially on Sundays, we all come together, and we just do something together just like how they grew up. Everything's family oriented. We celebrate [holidays], especially since there's not very much of our family here. Everyone's in Syria. We get as much as we can, especially during our holiday. My parents try to make it a very big deal, since me and my sister aren't that religious. They try and make it a very big deal, so we can get close to our religion, at least for that part of time. A while ago we had to drive to Florida, and it was a 17-hour drive, very long drive. I learned so much in that 17 hours in the car with my parents, them talking about their backgrounds with their families and everything. I guess they taught [my culture] to me in a way that I think I won't ever forget it. Instead of a teacher teaching it to you. They love their culture, and they love going back to Syria, as do I. And so, pretty much everything I know came from them, and all my religious beliefs came from them.

My sister, I followed in her footsteps a lot. Pretty much, we're almost the exact same, but there's so many things about her that I love. . . . I'm pretty good at looking at the bright side of things, especially with my sister. So if I'm having a horrible day, she can just cheer me up right away and the same with [me]. I can cheer her up in a second. [My parents] want to hear about friends. It's good to tell them, but once again you can't tell your parents everything . . . I tell lots of stuff to my parents, and I tell lots of stuff to my sister. It's good to have that, I guess.

I have learned lots of things [from my parents], most of them when I was younger, but one of the main ones was be proud of who you are and be confident. Because when I was younger . . . I mean now I'm starting to not have as much insecurities, but I've always had lots of insecurities, and they were always there just to make me feel a lot better about myself and bring the self-esteem up and just make you feel very good. You know, they always say, "Don't be afraid of who you are—be confident. No one's better than you, but you're not better than anyone else."

I can sit with my dad on the couch for like ten hours just watching TV and just joking around. He's the biggest joker, and we have so much fun, and I guess when I want something, I go to my dad and, you know, it's kind of like "daddy's girl." We have a lot of fun; we both have the same interest in sports, and so we connect like that, and he's very good at boosting self-esteem and all that, and he's the best compliment giver. And also with my mom, I guess, mom and daughter always have a little harder time, but my mom is great. She's always so busy; I don't think any of my friend's moms work as much. . . . But she always has time to come home and drive me to places I need to go, and she's always there for advice. And I feel for her because I know it's hard because sometimes she doesn't understand. That's what I tell her when I'm upset with her, I say, "You don't understand." But she really does, I guess.

I'm the youngest and I've always had my spot. I guess we're all like a puzzle. Without one of us, it's not the same. Like especially now with my sister gone, it's a little harder, so we're all trying to make

up for it, and so I'm trying to mature a little more because I know that my mom, especially my mom, she's having the hardest time with it. They're not used to that 'cause, where they grew up, you go to college [and] you come home at the end of the day and you stay at your house. So they're not used to this at all, and so it's hard on them. I guess, like I said, without every piece of the puzzle, it doesn't go together. So we're all trying to work together a bit more, and I'm sympathizing with my parents more, and I'm not fighting with them as often. I know that I'm needed in the family just as everyone else is. It really feels good to have that spot, and you know it's never gonna go away . . . We all make a difference.

When we're all together, we talk about pretty much anything, especially now we mostly talk about, like, my sister's college and how everything's changing. A lot of the times we talk about what's going on in the Middle East, although it hurts. I don't like to talk about that stuff very much because I feel so helpless, and I can't do anything, and my parents get so frustrated, and they watch like the Arabic news 'cause we have Arabic channels. Arabic news show a lot more. They show like a dead person, and they show like what happened when someone got shot. It's so, so heart wrenching, and you feel so helpless, and it's horrible. So sometimes I get very frustrated, and I don't want to talk about it, but it's always gonna be there, I guess, and so you have to face it. And we talk about school and we talk about doctor stuff a lot. My parents always have funny stories about patients, and so it's fun.

I think that lots of happiness doesn't just come from grades, but [from being] with friends and with family.

Commentary

In Nadia's voice, we hear some of the complexities involved in finding a way to manage family, school, religion, and other activities. Nadia wore a necklace with "God is good" written on it; at the same time, she played soccer and spoke publicly against racism and bigotry. This is a complex balancing act for a young person of Nadia's age, but she was nevertheless managing admirably.

It was clear throughout the interview with Nadia and her family that she was deeply attached to her religion and culture. She was simultaneously living with the challenges of fitting in and belonging in two very distinct cultural worlds. As a result, she felt, at times, both comfortable and uncomfortable in one or the other. Generally, Nadia was comfortable in her school and in her city. At other times, she felt the sting of discrimination, something that, prior to September 11, 2001, she said she had not really experienced. When she and her family traveled to Syria, Nadia sometimes was more at home there than here, while at other times, she felt like an outsider. Her musings about fitting in were poignant, and they reflect the experiences of a growing number of young people of diverse backgrounds in our society.

School could be a place where these differences are negotiated, but this has not been the case for Nadia. She mentioned that, before September 11th, no one had even mentioned Syria or Muslims. Afterward, being Muslim became a negative thing. When she said "teachers don't care" that she's Muslim, she said it in a positive way, meaning that they didn't discriminate on the basis of her background. But neither did they make it part of the curriculum, something that might have helped Nadia feel more included while also educating other students about her community.

There are several ways in which Nadia was negotiating these dilemmas of diversity. For one, as we saw, diversity was not an empty concept to Nadia. Her best friend was Jewish, and she also had an African American friend who was teaching her to cook soul food. In addition, even at this young age, Nadia was becoming outspoken about justice and fair play. This was evident in her participation in Heart Connection at school. She had also agreed to teach Arabic to young Muslim children. Her willingness, even eagerness, to speak publicly at a rally condemning bigotry against Muslims was another indication of her commitment to social justice.

But it was in her strong family connection that Nadia and her sister were able to negotiate their identities most powerfully. The Bara family was a close-knit and loving family, a family that insisted on maintaining certain cultural and religious values as a foundation for their daughters' futures. Nadia didn't like all their rules, but it was obvious that she appreciated them nevertheless. Although she would rather have stayed out later with her friends, or she might have liked the opportunity to talk to boys on the phone, she was grateful for her parents'

values. The metaphor of a puzzle, and of each piece having a particular and crucial place in the puzzle, is a fitting one. She wanted to "fit in" but not in a cookie-cutter way. Nadia is a unique piece of our American puzzle, and it is young people like her who can make it work.

Reflect on this case study

1. What do you think Nadia meant when she said that she was "torn right in the middle"? As a teacher, what could you do about this?
2. Since 9/11, have you noticed any changes in your students' perceptions or actions concerning Muslim students? What are some ways to address these issues in the curriculum?
3. Nadia said that her parents weren't very involved in her school (in such activities as PTA, for instance) because they were very busy. Can you think of some ways they might be "brought into" the school by becoming involved at some level? How? What might you ask them to do?
4. If you were one of Nadia's teachers and had seen the newspaper article in which she was featured, would you have said or done anything about it? Why or why not? If so, what would you do?

Savoun Nouch

When people look at me as an Asian I say, "No I'm not Asian, I'm Cambodian." There are other Asian kids, but I am the only Khmer kid.

Savoun Nouch[1] said that he had "traveled quite a distance" to start to his senior year at Watershed High School in Providence, Rhode Island. His mother arrived in New England as a refugee from Cambodia. Savoun was born in New England, but he and his mother migrated to California when he was a small child. He said, "I think of California as my actual home." His mom chose Stockton, California, because of its sizable Cambodian community (over 10,000 in a city of 285,000 in 1990). A friend welcomed them into her home there.

In Stockton, Savoun attended a large city high school with 2,500 students. The student population was diverse, and according to Savoun, almost 25 percent of the student body was Asian, primarily Cambodian. The school also included a small percentage of Native American and Filipino students and more sizable percentages of White, African American, and Latino students. About 8 percent of the students were English Language Learners. Furthermore, just over half the students participated in meal-assistance programs.

The school community struggled with racial tensions that played out in harmful ways. Savoun described how school gangs dominated his early high school experiences: "My school was very segregated, basically Asians. We Cambodians, we were the Asians. We got together and we were feuding with other nationalities. Almost every single day we would get into arguments and it would escalate into a fight with Blacks and Latinos. Every day. Mostly fist fights, but a few times there were some weapons. Some people outside of school got wounded or lost their lives."

The Cambodian population in U.S. schools today is a diverse group in terms of religious practices, language, education, and more. Some are first-generation immigrants, recently arrived from Cambodia or Thailand, where many refugee camps were located. Others are second- and third-generation Americans, with the perspectives and languages common to mainstream American teens. Some Cambodian families hold Buddhist beliefs close to their daily lives, others are secular, and still others practice Christianity or other religions.[2] In spite of their varied experiences, the Khmer community shares a common tormented history and a determined resiliency.

Thirty years have passed since the genocide carried out by Pol Pot's regime of the Khmer Rouge. The four years from 1975 through 1979 saw the death of 1.7 million people by execution, starvation, disease, and overwork in labor camps. The Khmer Rouge's "Democratic Kampuchea," a horrific campaign of social, ethnic, and racial cleansing wiped out a large percentage of Cambodia's population (estimates range from 20 percent to 48 percent). Pol Pot tried to exterminate the Cham, Vietnamese, Thai, and Lao minorities in Cambodia.[3] For many Cambodians in America, the tragedies of that holocaust and the efforts to sustain cultural memory persistently influence daily life.[4]

The political struggles that created the Cambodian diaspora and the resulting widespread post-traumatic stress among Cambodians are notable. Political analysts from the 1970s through today assert that President Richard M. Nixon's bombing campaign of Cambodia, which was implemented without Congressional approval, set the stage for civil-war-torn Cambodia to be relinquished to Pol Pot's regime.[5] Estimates are that between 100,000 and 600,000 civilians lost their lives and two million were rendered homeless by the United States bombings, ostensibly done to push the communist North Vietnamese away from the Cambodian border. Instead, the Vietnamese moved deeper inside Cambodia, and the U.S "carpet bombings" followed, inflicting greater devastation on the peasant civilians. To escape the violent chaos of internal civil war and the bombings, hundreds of thousands of Cambodian people fled their country to seek refuge in neighboring countries. These horrendous experiences led to more than 235,000 Cambodian refugees' resettling overseas between 1975 to 1992, including 180,000 in the United States.[6]

Escaping violence was a theme that shaped Savoun's life in many ways. His parents' escape from the Khmer Rouge in Cambodia was echoed by his deliberate break away from racially motivated gang violence in California. He dropped out of the large high school and twice made efforts to re-enter school through different alternative programs. But the gang activity persisted, and as he explained,

> [I]t was a very rocky road, and I decided that this was not the way life should be for me. I realized if I stayed, there was nothing there for me. I finally decided to drop everything and leave.

With the company and moral support of a good friend, Savoun got on a bus headed for the East Coast and got off by mistake in Providence, Rhode Island. Since he had a cousin in Providence who welcomed him "with open arms," he stayed with her and enrolled in a new high school, with a fresh start.

Because of the history of violence that had affected Savoun and his family, the major theme that reappeared many times in his interview was a *determination to escape violence*. Yet, just as powerful were the themes of *family pride and academic achievement* as well as *cherishing culture and language.*

Cherishing culture and language

It's great to be Cambodian; I'm proud of it. I love this culture, love everything about it. You have your culture to 'represent'—to cherish. I am different from somebody in Cambodia; I have the opportunity to learn English and to have more hope and to have a better life, but I have not been to Cambodia. Identity and culture is important to me. I am proud of my culture because of where I was born from. Being Khmer has been a big part of my upbringing. I have learned from my parents my culture, how I was brought up, everything. They have been through a whole lot of devastating moments back in Cambodia. So what we have now, we should cherish it. The people in Cambodia don't have what we have now. [My parents] really don't talk about it, because it brings bad memories for them. So I ask them myself, so they answer my questions, but I have to ask.

My mother carried the Cambodian culture a lot with her when she came to the United States. They worked in the past, grew crops back in Cambodia, near Phenom Penn. But there's not a lot of Khmer farmers around here. She wanted to stay in the Cambodian environment; my neighborhood in California was all Cambodian people. Every single day she could be there and talk with her friends, just chat with Cambodian people. They are very isolated from the world. They don't really go out that much unless they go to their friends. Mostly all their friends are Cambodian. They do not interact with other cultures very much.

We are different from other American families. We don't celebrate holidays as much as other cultures. That's a big difference. We do celebrate some, like Thanksgiving and Christmas, now—and birthdays. Cambodian New Year is the only Khmer holiday. For me, for my birthday, I would just get a present—no cake; no friends come over; I did not invite people over. My parents were not into inviting people over. It was like, "We keep it really simple. Here's your gift and don't ask for more." We have our family—we have how our family acts—how we are brought up different . . . So, we act different, we cook different, things like that. For Thanksgiving, my parents do cook American food.

So on a Thanksgiving dinner table, it is a mixture of Cambodian food and American food: Turkey, with stuffing, and we have mashed potatoes, Cambodian soup . . . all those things together.

When I was in California, my parents take me to temple [to] get some blessings, and we participate in Cambodian activities. My parents would take me there, see the monks to get my blessings. I would ask them why. They would tell me to "vanish all the bad things." I went to temple once a year. My parents would go much more often to the temple. I did not like to go for the prayers that much when I was younger, but when it was Cambodian New Year, I was always there! In the future, definitely, I would like to go to the temple more on my own, to be more involved in my parents, to get a good feel for why they go to the temple . . .

The first person I learned from was my parents . . . to speak Cambodian. I don't know that much, but I know enough to speak it. Mom speaks Khmer at home. When I got to school, [learning English] was a process between elementary school and toward junior high. I just had to figure out. There were teachers' assistants who translated English for kids who did not know English. At times, we had reading sessions where she would actually read in Cambodian, teach the lessons so we could learn in Cambodian and English. There was a balance of Cambodian and English when I was growing up. I would never want to leave my culture or my language; I always want to learn more.

I got the hang of English ever since I hit junior high. I was speaking, like, intermediate English. I was actually speaking a balance of Cambodian and English, but at junior high there was no more reading sessions, no more culture lessons. None of it. Basically, I was speaking all English throughout the junior high and the high school. There was no more of my culture's language in the school. The only time I would speak my language was to my family members and with some friends.

As I learn more and more English, I am forgetting my culture's language right now. To keep us from forgetting our culture's language, schools could still have reading sessions in our culture's language. I think that would help the Asian students. Reading sessions would help . . . because a lot of the students right now, they are forgetting their culture's language and they really do not know how to speak as much as they used to. We would love to learn more. We wish we would. I just try to speak as much Cambodian at home as possible. When I am at home and speak to the other people and older people, I only speak Cambodian.

When I lived with my parents, I did a lot of translation. It was hard for me because I don't speak Cambodian that well, and when you translate back and forth, there are words in English that do not translate into Cambodian. I talked to my parents pretty well. They can understand me. It's been great to be a member of my family.

Sometime they don't understand me, but I still love them. Growing up, it was a problem. It was hard for them to know what I've been through. They think it is very easy for me because I was born in America, I had the opportunity to go to school. [But] I had to deal with all these peer pressures. Gang stuff. Stuff they don't know anything about. They think it's a perfect world out there. They seen hard stuff back in Cambodia.

Determination to escape violence

I would describe my neighborhood I live in now [in Rhode Island] as a pretty good community . . . no violence, a lot of nice people, a lot of Hispanic. But at my old school [in California] what I remember most was—there was a lot of violence. A lot of racial issues between we Asians and other cultures such as African American and Hispanics. You can say that it was gang related. It's more about who is the boss of the school, who won the school. I was part of a gang. It's all about what you are going to say and who is going to kick whose ass. I had my peers with me. I had my friends, so I felt very comfortable. I would say 90 percent of my friends in California dropped out of school because of gangs and violence. A few got shot, a few ended up in the hospital, a few got locked up. Only a few are still thinking about life.

Everything got rough for me because I was in a gang. I did not really have the support that I needed. I was the type of kid . . . I always wanted to play sports, but, money wise, the football uniform, and transportation from practice . . . it was very hard, it would be too hard, and my sisters, I had to look after them after school. I didn't have the support from my family, so everything was a big whole downfall for me because, during my junior year my average was

like less than a 2.0 GPA. I stopped going to school. One thing led to another and I dropped out of my junior year at Avery High School.

I wouldn't say [the school administrators and teachers] didn't try to help me. It wasn't really that. They didn't really have any interventions to help students with the whole bureaucracy to get kids through. All you had to do was go to the guidance counselor and they would transfer you. I went to two different high schools. The first one was a model alternative school. The same thing happened. My friends were there, and there wasn't a lot of support. I was unwilling to focus on my education life. I chose friends over education, and one thing led to another and I dropped out there.

They are my friends, but they have different goals in life. I feel bad for them. I moved out here to change. I would hope the same thing for them. I would hope they could move out here with me. I can't control another person's life. When you are in the gang, [you don't realize there are] more things than being in a gang. I think about the future. Like what does life bring to you. There are things like life and education. You got to get your education, think more about life . . . than gang bangin' 'cause that's not gonna get you nowhere in life.

To get to Watershed High School now, in Providence, my cousin talked to the co-founder of the school and asked for me to get an interview. I went there and they interviewed me and ever since then, I fell in love with it. I fell in love with it because [of] the diversity, how personal the teachers get with you. It is no typical school. At the interview there are not teachers who interview you; it was students. That breaks that barrier, like kids-to-kids. I talked to a few kids. There was no Asians at all, only one girl. Everyone else was different nationalities and I was so surprised and the way they welcomed me, I was like "this school must be very great and there is no one feuding or fighting or nothing." I was so surprised there was no one feuding or anything. I was the only Asian kid, and the diversity was really great because even though I was the only Asian (and lots of—majority was Spanish and African American), [there were] no racial problems at all. Nobody feuding. I just loved it!

It has changed my whole perspective about school. Going to school here, because the teachers are so involved with you either at school or at home—always there for you, ready to talk to you and everything—about your education. They call me up at home to talk to me.

Family pride and academic achievement

You got to have an education. It is important. In order to pursue your dream, what you want in life, get your education first. For my family, my parents, it is important for other people to see their reputation, how they raised their child to be, to go to school, and it is the opportunity America gives to you, so get that opportunity and make it useful. They make a great deal about their reputation, their reputation for the son they're raising. They don't want to have a son who is a bad kid, with other people talking about them. They want you to be good. If you do bad things, the community will hear about you. They will often spread rumors, the gossip in the Khmer community.

My parents support me being here in Providence 100 percent, and my cousin supports me being here with her 100 percent. My cousin welcomed me with open arms. I believe in education 100 percent. My parents want to hear good things, like if I'm getting my work done, how I'm getting my work done, all the details. My advisor contacts them and tells them the things they need to know and what I need to know. I never had my parents back in California participate in what the teachers had to offer, so this is a very new experience.

It is important to me to be Cambodian in my school. Definitely I stand out from the crowd because I am the only Cambodian person at my school. One of the teachers, she tried to learn more about my culture, so then I did a book report and everything. I wanted to do it on Cambodian and Khmer, on my culture. She tells me she is very fascinated by my culture. She knows something about the Khmer Rouge genocide, a little something about it.

The way the school works, they wouldn't just pass out work and have it just turned in. It has to be completed and 100 percent revised. So every time she handed out an assignment, we would continually revise it until it reached its perfection. We went through that whole process for the whole entire junior year and senior year. The way she was, the way she treated us, the way she made that connection—it made me work. She would contact me, out

of school, to see what I was doing. We would have conversations, like friend to friend. That made us bonded very well and then I opened up.

To improve schools, if they could change the system the way they teach, that would be great idea, but even if they can't change the system, have a good relationship with the students and be in contact with them, always be in contact with them. Call them up. And, of course, I would love to learn more about my culture. If the teachers would make, like, an elective about my culture, that would be it. Learn more about the history, the war, the whole South East Asian history. The politics, who and what—a lot of information that is hard to get if you don't learn it in school. My mother told me about her escape from Cambodia. It was hard living in Cambodia. She lived in a refugee camp for awhile. That's about it. But she did not tell me much about the war.

My advisor helped me plan my future—give me prep for college, looking for scholarships, looking for college, everything—the whole 9 yards. What would help me be successful into the future is: Be more involved with me—I tend to procrastinate a lot. I need someone there telling me I need to get stuff done. My advisors are very hard on me. They call me up at home. But that makes me successful.

[In the future,] I definitely want to go back to California to be closer to my mom. The person I most admire is my mother because of what she's been through in the past and how she's got me here. I want to go to college first for four years. So I can at least support my mom when I go back. I don't want to leave with nothing and go back with nothing.

Commentary

Maintaining and reshaping cultural traditions is a work in progress for Savoun. In Chapter 6 we cautioned about the pitfall of essentializing culture and the importance of understanding culture as an evolving process rather than as a static product. A cultural-historical approach, as defined by Kris Gutierrez and Barbara Rogoff, illustrates the flexibility of cultural identity in Savoun's life.[7] Savoun's identity evolves through a process of amalgamation of his parents' perspective as Cambodian farmers and refugees from civil and international warfare, transplanted to Stockton, California, living in a primarily Khmer-speaking neighborhood; of his multiple perspectives in urban youth cultures, with the expressiveness of hip-hop; and then of his experiences in and out of gang affiliations. For Savoun, his culture is something to be "cherished," yet its history, traditions, religious practices, and language appear to be elusive. While certain Cambodian practices and beliefs may be lost to Savoun, other new understandings are gained.

Nancy Smith-Hefner's research reveals the efforts of Khmer Americans to maintain and reinvent culture in the aftermath of the violence of the holocaust. In her ethnographic study of Cambodians residing in metropolitan Boston, Smith-Hefner portrays the attempts to preserve Khmer Buddhism by the elders in the community. Her study provides a context for understanding how cultural heritage may influence the performance of Khmer children in U.S. schools.[8] In a more recent study of Cambodian children, Roberta Wallitt suggests that, in addition to gaining insights from studies such as Smith-Hefner's, more contemporary studies are needed. As the Cambodian population in the United States ages, cultural values and influences will fluctuate.[9]

Issues of cultural identity dominated Savoun's school experiences. He moved from a school where about 25 percent of the student body was Cambodian, to being the only "Khmer kid" at Watershed High School. As much as Savoun appreciated his new school, with its personalized approach and supportive infrastructure, he was conscious of his isolation as the only Cambodian student. The isolation was underscored by his own—and his teachers'—lack of knowledge about his cultural history. His comments point out how the refugee experience is often invisible or misrepresented in school curriculum. Similarly, in Roberta Wallitt's study, she found that "one of the greatest sources of alienation was the absence of their history and culture in the curriculum."[10]

Despite the lack of Cambodians and the absence of a culturally specific curriculum in his current high school, Savoun was deeply affirmed and felt a strong sense of solidarity with his peers and teachers at Watershed. There, he was pleasantly surprised to learn that racial diversity does not necessarily lead to violence. The importance of cultivating a safe learning environment that develops racial inclusion is articulated in Savoun's affection-

ate description of his new school life: "No racial problems at all. Nobody feuding. I just loved it!"

In terms of academic achievement, Savoun compared his new school to his old school and explained, "They wouldn't just pass out work and have it just turned in." He proudly noted that his teachers expected nothing less than perfection in his final drafts of schoolwork. Teacher communication was another hallmark of his experience at Watershed. On multiple occasions, he mentioned that his teachers "call me up at home." Likewise, another recommendation from Wallitt's study concerned the essential role teachers, advisors, and mentors can play when they develop cultural competency and reach out to support students through home visits, phone calls, navigation of college applications, and attending cultural events.[11] The effort to reach out to Savoun outside of school hours left an enduring imprint of caring support and high expectations on him.

When we last checked in with Savoun, he had just graduated from Watershed High School. He was ecstatic about making his family proud through his accomplishments and was looking forward to starting community college in the fall "and then transferring credits to a bigger college." With the support of his advisor, he transformed his interest in car repair and auto mechanics to a goal of achieving a degree in business, with the hope of eventually opening his own car dealership. The outcome of this vision is still a few years away, but his willfulness to make sound educational choices, combined with his sincerity to "represent his culture" by providing for his mother and a future family of his own, appears to have pointed him toward success.

Reflect on this case study

1. Savoun mentioned that his teacher "wouldn't just pass out work and have it just turned in. It has to be completed and 100 percent revised." How might teachers present the revision process as motivation of pride and accomplishment, as Savoun expressed?

2. Savoun said "To keep us from forgetting our culture's language, schools could still have reading sessions in our culture's language." That may not have been possible because Savoun was the only Cambodian student in his school, but what are

some strategies that could have been implemented in the school to affirm and cultivate his language?

3. Receiving phone calls from teachers left a lasting impression on Savoun. What are the implications for your classroom practice? How can you integrate such personal communication with students outside of the school day?

4. In almost every school, there are students who may feel that they are "the only one" of a cultural, religious, ethnic, language, sexual orientation, class, or ability group. How can you and your colleagues affirm the students' identities in meaningful ways that make them feel more "visible" and understood while also challenging them academically?

5. Gang activity affects the school lives of countless students and families in U.S. schools. What can we learn from Savoun's case study about the teacher's role in helping students resist gang activity?

Christina Kamau

If you could just go, to have a chance to go
to some countries that are
suffering and see the difference . . .
you will be so shocked.

As a 16-year-old junior in high school, Christina Kamau[1] expressed viewpoints common to many immigrant teens in the United States. At the same time, her individual perspectives, based on personal life experiences, are evident. Christina's family is from Kenya where she attended school until fifth grade. They moved to Botswana, where she attended middle school in her early teens. At the beginning of her freshman year of high school, her family immigrated to the United States—to Shephardstown, a mid-size college town surrounding a large state university in the heart of the Midwest.

Christina's family is much like many of the over 1 million African immigrants currently living in the United States. The U.S. Census Bureau reports over 50 percent of this population arrived between 1990 and 2000, making African immigrants significantly more visible in U.S. schools in recent years.[2] In the 1990s, the highest numbers came from Nigeria, Ethiopia, and Ghana.

The influence of African immigrants in the United States is evident in the cultural, linguistic, political, business, and religious life of big cities and small towns throughout the country. Larger urban areas such as New York, Washington, DC, Houston, Atlanta, and Chicago are home to the largest numbers of recent African immigrants, but increasingly, small towns and suburbs, especially in the Midwest, are the destination for families such as Christina's.

Since culture, language, religion, and political frameworks are so diverse within the continent of Africa, the sociopolitical contexts of African immigrants vary greatly. Media coverage of African immigrants often focuses on refugees. The difficulties faced by immigrant refugees cannot be underestimated, but within the broad scope of African immigrant demographics, refugees account for only 10 percent of the immigrant population admitted to the United States in the 1990s. Of these, more than 40,000 were Somalis, and approximately 21,000 came from Ethiopia, while 18,500 arrived from the Sudan.[3] The children of refugee families bring values such as a vibrant connection to family and religious communities, steadfast determination to maintain multiple languages, and strong traditions. In addition, they often have vivid memories of human suffering in their homeland, which has continuing strife due to civil wars, human rights abuses, political unrest, corrupt governments, natural disasters, and the ravages of economic policies gone awry under globalization. The most recent difficulties in Sierra Leone, the Democratic Republic of Congo and Darfur, Sudan, attest to the widespread difficulties and challenges faced by many African states.

The detrimental effects of these struggles should not be diminished, but there is a propensity in the West, especially in the United States, to view Africa condescendingly and as if it were a monolith. The widespread misperceptions of Africa affect mainstream America's perspective on immigrants from the African continent. For instance, most people in the United States do not know that the majority of immigrants from Africa are highly skilled professionals who intend to establish permanent homes in the United States.[4] Christina's father, for example, is a university professor, and her mother is a medical student. While the influx of highly educated immigrants continues, their employment in the United States does not always match their talents. Their opportunities are limited for a variety of reasons, including immigration documentation and the fact that university degrees from oversees are often not recognized here. Many with prestigious credentials work as cab drivers, restaurant servers, or parking lot attendants, striving for the American Dream through any opportunity that may be available. Frequently, it is more than economics that motivates this community. In his comprehensive assessment of contemporary African immigrants, Joseph Takougang points out, "The new African immigrant is no longer just interested in making money; they are also interested in building stronger communities and organizing themselves in order to become a more powerful political and economic force in their respective communities."[5]

Racism also influences wages and job opportunities. Despite their hard work and determined outlook, Takougang reveals that, not surprisingly, many African immigrants encounter racism. Many do not have a history of experience with race relations in the United States and are naive about the confrontations with institutional racism and negative stereotypes.[6] A tragic illustration of racist violence, the 1999 killing of Amadou Diallo, an African immigrant from Guinea, by New York police officers, has become a metaphor for the way African immigrants are perceived and treated by some law enforcement authorities.[7]

Christina entered U.S. schools in ninth grade within this challenging yet hopeful and complex social, political, economic and cultural matrix. Relocating several times into vastly diverse cultures and language communities, she cultivated her perspectives on friendship, learning, and the meaning of academic achievement. The viewpoints she expressed during her interview highlight three themes: *adapting to new cultures and school structures, preconceptions and stereotypes,* and *educational achievement for social action.*

Adapting to new cultures and school structures

Just push yourself into being the best you can be, and try to strive the best you can be. Just remember where you came from. You know, remember your origin in Africa. You're not American; you're African first. Always keep that in mind.

After being in Kenya my whole life, Botswana was difficult. I started to go to a Christian, American type of school. And the school was way different for me, honor roll and all this stuff I didn't understand. There was no corporal punishment, you understand. [I did not know] what detention was. In Kenya, you get beaten by the teacher and you go home, even though you didn't do anything wrong. [Teachers] call your parents most of the times.

But I got used to Botswana. Our teacher was never like one-to-one, and she would teach a whole class and just gives you books to help yourself. Never checked to see who was correct, just give you points for completion. I didn't understand that, because in Kenya [there is] step by step and explaining. You know what to know. When I went to the American-type-school in Botswana, I found it very different to be trying all these different things. The funny thing was, in my math class, they let us use calculators, which I never did in Kenya. You had to know your time's tables and your subtraction and addition and all your facts. You have to do that on your paper. You can't use a calculator to solve those problems. So, in sixth grade I was introduced to a calculator. I was, like, "I don't know how to do this"! I found it strange and exciting too. It made my life easier in school terms because I can do homework much faster and go play and go do something else. So it was different for me for awhile.

Then, in seventh grade I moved to another school. It was, like, a private school and it had from elementary all the way to high school. That was different because I couldn't speak the same language as everybody else because each country in Africa has their own languages and their own native language. I spoke Swahili, and then in Botswana, you speak Botswanan. I couldn't speak Botswanan. I had to get used to learning how to interact with other students without them making fun of me trying say things. I had to speak in English all the time. That made me practice my English a lot because I couldn't communicate with them in any other way except in my English.

To make friends and do all those other things were hard for me because all the other students were, you know, cliquish. Because they had their own languages and they knew how to talk to each other without having to speak English, which I had to do all the time. But school became easier for me because my teacher could talk to me all the time in English and try to teach me a little bit of Botswana and interpret the other students. So that was pretty nice.

When I came here [to the United States] I was really shocked by the high school. We entered the parking lot, I kept asking Mom, "Are all these cars for the teachers or all for the students?" She was, like, "Yeah, all for the students." I couldn't believe how many students have such nice cars, so many cars, it was so crazy. Also the building was, like, wow, I always thought high school [was like] in TV and stuff in movies. I always wonder what it would be like to go to school in America.

School was crazy in the U.S. at first. First, projectors. I have never seen a projector before in my whole life. I got used to that, I guess, even the markers. Writing on the board in Africa, we used chalk, chalkboards in Africa. I miss that. I wish we had that here. Because markers smell strange, I don't know, it's hard for me to see up there with the projector. So I couldn't understand how you could look there at your answers, to check your answers to see if your answers are correct.

And at the beginning of the first semester, it was my world studies class, the teacher says we have to go to the media center, and I don't know where the media center is, and I didn't know what that was. So all of us go, open the door, and it's a bunch of kids and computers everywhere! I was, like, "cool", 'cause I never seen so many computers before! It was really hard for me to get used to going to Microsoft and going, oh, check tool, and check spell, check all these stuff. First day at school, my teacher said, "You have to research on different regions"; it's like research on Hinduism because we're studying India. He said, "OK, log on, get your password and get your stuff and get to the Internet and go to Google and start searching". I didn't know I *had* a log name. I could see other kids looking at me, wondering, "Why she is not knowing all these things?" We didn't have all these stuff. So I started looking for the Internet, so many programs—Microsoft Excel, PowerPoint, school printing, and all these stuff. All by myself, was trying to get to the Internet. So the other teacher kind of sees me sitting. "OK, I can help you." By the way, he is Laotian, he is from Laos, so he told me that he had a hard time. He knows how I feel.

I noticed that on the next day for my English class, all we did was type up papers, like every week. Every Friday, double-spaced page of essay. So I was used to writing with my hand, all my rough drafts, I could write them. Handwriting, you have really good handwriting, good grammar in Africa. But, the first paper, I didn't know how to type, so I asked. She, at least took half of the points off because it wasn't typed. I tried to explain to her, I was still learning. But she was, like, "You need to get a move on because you have to catch up with these people." Now I'm pretty good at typing and stuff and I'm trying to encourage my sister to get that stuff done because it's a big deal when it comes to high school. If you don't know how to use computers you are in a big trouble, because that's all we use all the time to research for classes. It is really big deal for us.

Preconceptions and stereotypes

When I couldn't get that computer stuff, some girls were calling me an "African girl" because "an African girl doesn't know anything." That's not really nice of you to say that. Even the teacher went to her and said, "That's not really nice for you to say. It's not like you who have the privilege to go Internet everyday and get all these things. She's still getting accustomed to all these stuff."

I guess some other people really help me. Like the way my best friend was to the lunch lady. So I go to the line to get my food first day. I couldn't understand how this huge cafeteria, all of us could sit and talk, so noisy! Everybody's trying to get food and huge line. She told me, "You gotta move on, you know, you have to get your food." I go to line and have my ID card and going to my line and get my food. She tells me to swipe my card so that we can get my food and get out. And I swiped my card and it didn't go through. She was like, "Wait, your card is not yet activated." I have no idea how to do that; it was my first day! She was really mean, I could tell. Maybe she didn't have a good day. So some girls behind me, some African girls behind me, heard my accent, "Oh are you from Africa?" I was, like, "Yes!" They say, "OK, we will pay for you." I am like, "Really? That's so sweet of you." They paid for me, and got out. We sat down and they were, like, "Is this your first day? We could tell, because the same thing happened to us!" I was like, "OK." [*giggle*]. So we have something common, that's only my best friends, they are from Ghana. We are good friends now.

I really have a big deal with people calling me *Black American*. I don't like being called that because I noticed that people in our school use that to get a sympathy from other people. "Oh yeah, my ancestors struggle for this and that" and you know what? That's gone. It's gone, so you can't use it now to defend yourself. Because you are creating another stereotype for you. In our school, there is very few Black people. And I'm sad for the fact that I'm not being able to interact with them that well 'cause they are not open to me. They always say, "Oh that's African culture." I think that I have more White friends than Black friends. I can still talk to them and I always say hi. I always say, "I'm not Black American, I'm African and I came from Kenya."

All the teachers are really nice to me. They all are interested about Africa. Africa is really cool. [They] always ask me, "Is it how we see on TV?" I tell them, "No, it's no way. [On TV] it's like a jungle place. We have CDs, we have cars and computers; it depends on what level class you come from." They all are interested, and for my English class that's all I did, my life comparing to American and African. Yeah, even in my speech class, that's all I did. My teacher was like, "Let's learn about Africa," all the time.

I joined track as an after-school activity. That's because my coach was, like, "Are you from Africa, from Kenya?" I was, like, "Yes." "Well, you have to join the track for me." The funny thing is that I have never run before. [*laughter*] He found out that I couldn't run that well, but he taught me, and pushed me, and it was fun. I met a lot of people; it was a good experience for me.

Educational achievement for social action

Freshmen year, it was not good for me, even my GPA reflected that, and my parents were disappointed. I was really disappointed myself because less than 3.0 GPA was a really big shock for me. All my teachers told me, "You have a lot of potentials, just try to get used to the school." And so, in my sophomore year, I tried really hard; I did all my homework and always ask questions. Even after school—I went to school earlier and stayed later than everyone and my GPA was able to go higher to 3.8. That was really good thing for me. I'm hop-

ing to do the same thing this year—try to even get 4.0 GPA.

I just want to get my degree and go help people somewhere. I want to be somewhere in Africa or somewhere in China. Somewhere where I know I am useful to help people. For me right now, going to school is a really big deal because I want to help people. That's the only way for me to get that education through school. For me, that is the reason for going to school. For me, it's getting a better education. I have seen in Africa that people give up. You know, here you can drop out of school and go to try your GED after a while. In Africa you don't get to do that. When you drop out of school, it's a failure; it's like an embarrassment to your family.

Also this year, Mr. Gervisay is recommending me to join the model UN, like a club. I'm really opinionated. Especially like in Mr. Gervisay's class, he encourages you to talk about politics, what's going in the world. Most people would be not interested, [they say] "Oh, the war, it's not in the U.S." How could you be so ignorant about something that happened to you? It's gonna affect you for the rest of your life, you know. If you could just go, to have a chance to go to some countries that are suffering and see the difference. You are so sheltered here that you can't step away; you will be so shocked.

I have the privilege of being here. For me, being here, my parents always say, "The land of opportunities, take them." You know, it's really hard, for many people dream to be here. And some of the best schools are here, like the state university. [My parents] want me to go to school because I can be a better person. I can help them raise [my] little sisters, you know, when they are older, look after myself, and I wouldn't get that chance if I didn't have that education to be able to get a job. Be better myself and be independent.

[For my future] I'm really battling between being a doctor or UN advocate, like maybe a lawyer. To see the wrongs of all the countries' policies and those stuff. I wish I could be, not a secretary general of the United Nations, but just trying to see a way of being able to tell other countries, you know, if you did something wrong you have to face the consequences. Right now, in the world, any country, as long as you have the power, you don't face up to what you did wrong. Because my parents punish me, you know, when I get something wrong—always have the consequences, you always have to face it. I notice that other countries don't do that, and I always believe in the UN. Bunch of countries always together, you know, try to make the world a better place. But, being a doctor for me would be fine, to do like doctor's organizations, Doctors Without Borders. Maybe in Africa, help a bunch of orphan kids and that would be a good thing. I don't know—it's a hard one, maybe a pediatrician. Because I like kids, but I don't know.

I guess being the fact that I am an international student, I have to push myself harder. I have to work harder and to prove that I do have the intelligence as everybody else and I should get the same opportunity as everybody else, especially with college. You can be anything. It doesn't matter what color you are and what shape, what country, what language you speak.

Commentary

Christina demonstrated remarkable resilience in adapting to school structures in various countries and cultures. When she described each school experience, she eloquently noted a range of approaches to curriculum, instructional methods, and homework practices. She compared administrative policies regarding student behavior, parent involvement, dress code, and more. She analyzed her school achievement the first year in Shepardstown High School, considering all those factors, and made explicit adjustments in her approach to her studies, such as staying after school for help and practicing technology skills.

The importance of having peers in school who share some perspectives was evident throughout Christina's interview. From her description of the language differences in Botswana to the lunch line rescue by the Ghanaian students in the U.S. high school, it was clear that immigrant students are often isolated in facing the academic and social realms of school. However, unlike many immigrant students, Christina already spoke English, which established a common ground in academics and social endeavors. Yet, Christina's language of origin, nationality, African identity, and more, influenced her integration into the school. She emphasized that there were very few Black students in her school, highlighting racial identity concerns. Some students feel desperately alone despite spending their day in

a school building with hundreds, or even thousands, of other students and adults.

The issue of cultural isolation affects students' views of school life, and it has curricular and structural implications. The more teachers get to know students through the curriculum, the more insight they may gain into students' perspectives, thereby cultivating authentic connections in relationships and in curricular adaptations. Judith Blohm and Terri Lapinsky provide several examples of "linking classroom to community" in a book that includes interviews with more than 2 dozen teen immigrants.[8] As structural remedies, some schools create buddy systems, ambassador programs, and other "safety nets" to assist new students, especially immigrants, to navigate the mystifying structures of the school year. Too often, the quick-fix approach is used. For example, Christina told us, "I had an ambassador at the first day at school to show me all the classes, and she did help me, but, like, the second day of the school, she left."

In addition to the challenge of establishing peer groups, adapting to new technologies and teaching methods, and navigating surprising new institutional structures, fighting bias was a major theme in Christina's school life. The perceptions of some teachers and peers about the capabilities of an "African girl" did not sway Christina's determination to achieve academically, but it did make her feel that she had to prove herself. Simultaneously, she spoke affectionately of most teachers' efforts to learn about her heritage and to weave her experiences in Africa into her schoolwork. When confronted with a so-called positive stereotype—that all Kenyans are talented runners—she laughed out loud. She demonstrated a graceful capacity to recognize the damaging implications of stereotypes while overcoming the limits of prejudicial encounters. Such wisdom and stalwart determination is to be commended, but it most certainly added tremendous weight to the challenge of adapting to a new culture and new school.

By emphasizing markers of her identity as a Kenyan, and more broadly as an African, Christina distinguished her language and her continent of origin as powerful affinities, but she also differentiated herself from her African American counterparts. She stressed that she had a "big deal with people calling me Black American," pointing to the differences in historical heritage between recent African immigrants and African Americans. The dynamic between African American communities and African immigrant communities is a complex and multilayered phenomenon.[9] A report from the New York Public Library Schomberg Center for Research in Black Culture observes that for many immigrants from Africa,

> [I]dentity as "black" is often perceived as a negation of culture and origin, which Africans regard as the most important elements of identity. They are keenly aware that they encounter racism and discrimination as black people; but they generally reject the imposition of an identity they feel does not completely reflect who they are.[10]

Despite confronting racism and the implications of being Black in America, Christina holds a classic view of the American dream. "You can be anything. It doesn't matter what color you are and what shape, what country, what language you speak," she asserts. For Christina, this may well be true because of the combination of many dynamics. Her family's social class advantage and their expectations that education will make her a better person are undergirded by Christina's and her parents' models of academic achievement. Her peer support helps navigate the confusing cultural conflicts, and the dedication of many teachers advances her academic achievement. From these sources, and clearly from within her own strength, Christina had resolved to get her degree and "go help people somewhere." Christina's accomplishments and determination raise the question about how schools may support rigorous academic engagement of students who are culturally, linguistically, and racially different: Specifically, how might schools influence all students to view successful education as a means to serve others and to help fight injustice?

Reflect on this case study

1. Christina described some examples of teachers' and students' demonstrating solidarity with, and empathy for, her. How do these scenarios change her school experience? Imagine her school experience without these demonstrations of solidarity and empathy. How might a school encourage a mindset that manifests these gestures by staff members and students, especially toward students who are culturally, racially, and linguistically different?

2. In her new school, several assumptions were made about Christina's prior knowledge and skills, ranging from technology to athletics. When do preconceived notions become damaging stereotypes? Give examples of how teachers can explore the prior knowledge of students and build on it in an affirming way to engage students in academic rigor.

3. What do you think about Christina's differentiation between African Americans and Africans? What tensions are revealed in her statements? What is the role of the school in recognizing and taking action regarding these tensions?

4. The practical aspects of daily school life can be a struggle for any new student. What makes some of these challenges particularly difficult for international students? How could Christina's first experiences with the media center, cafeteria, locker combinations, and the like, be made more welcoming? If such welcoming strategies are not in place in your school, what might you and your colleagues do to call attention to the need for them and what suggestions for effective change might you make?

5. Christina brings a critical and international perspective to current events and political struggles that appears to differ from the viewpoint of many of her fellow students who were born and raised in the midwestern college town. How can a teacher integrate diverse voices in classroom discussions to co-construct knowledge? What is the teacher's responsibility in framing multiple perspectives while cultivating socially responsible student understanding?

Notes to Chapter 12 Case Studies

Nadia Bara

1. We appreciate Dr. Carlie Tartakov, who located the Bara family and spent a day interviewing the daughters Nadia and Layla, and Sarah, their mother. Dr. Tartakov also sent information about the city in which they live and the Muslim community there. In addition, she transcribed all the

interviews, going above and beyond our expectations. All of these things made the job of developing this case study a great deal easier than it might have been.

2. U.S. Census Bureau, *Census 2000*. Table DP-2. "Profile of Selected Social Characteristics: 2000." (Washington, DC: U.S. Department of Commerce, 2000).

3. P. Hajar, "Arab Americans: Concepts, Strategies, and Materials." In *Teaching Strategies for Ethnic Studies*, 7th ed., edited by James A. Banks (Boston: Allyn and Bacon, 2003).

4. Diana L. Eck, *A New Religious America: How a "Christian Country" Has Become the World's Most Religiously Diverse Nation* (New York: HarperCollins, 2001).

5. Eck, *A New Religious America*.

Savoun Nouch

1. We appreciate the work of Keonilrath Bun, who interviewed Savoun for this case study. Keo is a graduate of Rhode Island School of Design, currently preparing to apply to architecture school.

2. See, for example, Stephanie St. Pierre, *Teenage Refugees from Cambodia Speak Out: In Their Own Voices* (New York: Rosen, 1995); see also Ji-Yeon O. Jo, "Neglected Voices in the Multicultural America: Asian American Racial Politics and Its Implication for Multicultural Education." *Multicultural Perspectives* 6, no. 1 (2004): 19–25.

3. Ben Kiernan, *The Pol Pot Regime: Race, Power, and Genocide in Cambodia Under the Khmer Rouge, 1975–79*, 2nd ed. (New Haven, CT: Yale University Press, 2002).

4. For a study that focuses on resilience and Cambodian life in the United States, see Nancy Smith-Hefner, *Khmer American: Identity and Moral Education in a Diasporic Community* (Berkeley: University of California Press, 1999); also, for a first person account of survival of the Khmer Rouge and resilience, see Chanrithy Him, When Broken Glass Floats: Growing Up Under the Khmer Rouge (New York: W. W. Norton, 2001).

5. Ben Kiernan, *How Pol Pot Came to Power: Colonialism, Nationalism, and Communism in Cambodia*, 2nd ed. (New Haven, CT: Yale University Press, 2004).

6. United Nations, High Commission for Refugees Report, *The State of The World's Refugees 2000: Fifty Years of Humanitarian Action*, "Chapter 4: Flight from Indochina," 79–103. (Accessed June 2006 at www.unhcr.org/cgibin/texis/vtx/publ/ opendoc.pdf?tbl=PUBL&id=3ebf9bad0); also see W. Courtland Robinson, *Terms of Refuge: The Indochinese Exodus and the International Response* (London, England: Zed Books, 1998).

7. Kris Gutierrez and Barbara Rogoff, "Cultural Ways of Learning: Individual Traits or Repertoires of Practice." *Educational Researcher* 32, no. 5 (July 2003): 19–25.

8. For considerations of how Khmer culture may influence children's school engagement, see Smith-Hefner, *Khmer American: Identity and Moral Education in a Diasporic Community*. For more context on Cambodian youth and school engagement, see Margaret E. Goldberg, "Truancy and Dropout among Cambodian Students: Results from a Comprehensive High School." *Social Work in Education* 21, no. 1 (January 1999): 49–63.

9. Roberta Wallitt, "Breaking the Silence: Cambodian Students Speak Out About School, Success, and Shifting Identities," diss. University of Massachusetts Amherst, 2005.

10. Wallitt, "Breaking the Silence," 296.

11. Wallitt, "Breaking the Silence."

Christina Kamau

1. We appreciate the work of Dr. Carlie Tartakov, who interviewed Christina and provided support for this case study. Dr. Tartakov is Professor Emerita at Iowa State University.

2. U.S. Census Bureau. Available at: www. census.gov/; see also Baffour Takyi, "The Making of the Second Diaspora: On the Recent African Immigrant Community in the United States of America." *Western Journal of Black Studies* 26, no. 1 (2002): 32–43.

3. U.S. Census Bureau. Available at: www. census.gov/. For a more in-depth analysis of the Sub-Sahara African Diaspora, see John Arthur, *Invisible Sojourners: African Immigrant Diaspora in the United States* (Westport, CT: Greenwood Press, 2000).

4. Gumisai Mutume, "Reversing Africa's 'brain drain': New initiatives tap skills of African expatriates." *Africa Recovery* 17, no. 2 (July 2003): 1. See also the United Nations Web page

www.un.org/ecosocdev/geninfo/afrec/vol17no2/172brain.htm

5. Joseph Takougang, "Contemporary African Immigrants to the United States." *Irinkerindo: A Journal of African Migration,* issue 2 (December 2003). Available at: www.africamigration.com/?CFID=662515&CFTOKEN=14479383

6. Xue Lan Do Rong and Frank Brown, "Socialization, Culture, and Identities of Black Immigrant Children: What Educators Need to Know and Do." *Education and Urban Society* 34, no. 2 (February 2002): 247–273.

7. Delario Lindsey, "To Build a More 'Perfect Discipline': Ideologies of the Normative and the Social Control of the Criminal Innocent in the Policing of New York City." *Critical Sociology* 30, no. 2 (2004): 321–353. See also Maxwell S. Hines, "Remembering Amadou Diallo: The Response of the New Teachers Network." *Phi Delta Kappan* 84, no. 4 (December 2002): 303–306.

8. Judith M. Blohm and Terri Lapinsky, *Kids Like Me: Voices of the Immigrant Experience* (Boston: Intercultural Press, 2006).

9. Mojubaolu Olufunke Okome, "Emergent African Immigrant Philanthropy in New York City." *Research in Urban Sociology* 7 (2004): 179–191. See also Takougang, "Contemporary African Immigrants to the United States." (December 2003).

10. Howard Dodson and Sylviane A. Diouf, eds., *In Motion: The African-American Migration Experience* (New York: The New York Public Library Schomberg Center for Research in Black Culture, August 2006). Available at: www.inmotionaame.org/migrations/landing.cfm?migration=13

CHAPTER 13

Adapting Curriculum for Multicultural Classrooms

> 66 The curriculum is never simply a neutral assemblage of knowledge, somehow appearing in the texts and classrooms of a nation. It is always part of a selective tradition, someone's selection, some group's vision of legitimate knowledge. 99
>
> —Michael Apple
> "The Politics of Official Knowledge," Teachers College Record, 1993.

Diana Corley, in Gina Simm's class. *Family portrait.* Mixed media, 2005.

A question that we hear time and time again is "What does a truly multicultural curriculum look like?" Teachers are swamped with data about achievement and models of so-called "best practices." It can be difficult to sort out trendy jargon from effective teaching.

When considering the implications of the previous chapters, it is clear that multicultural education is a multifaceted, complex process. Nowhere is this process more visible than in the curriculum teachers implement in their class-rooms. Many teachers in PK–12 classrooms acknowledge the need to adapt the curriculum and their practices to meet the needs of their increasingly diverse student populations. However, there are many challenges they face in developing a multicultural curriculum.

In keeping with our commitment to making curriculum culturally relevant to specific learning communities, we do not provide specific lesson plans or "canned" curriculum in this book. Instead, we present three cases of curriculum with which teachers and students have demonstrated success. There are myriad ways in which curriculum may be conceived and designed. We do not advocate any one, single model. The three approaches described in this chapter include concrete, hands-on examples to provide educators with both inspiration and ideas for developing a parallel unit on a similar or different theme or to spin off an activity and add their own creative questions. The three cases include:

1. Studying specific cultures and geographic regions: a study of Cambodia and the Cambodian American experience
2. Transforming pedagogy: detracking math
3. A thematic approach: expanding definitions of Family

In addition to the three cases described here, a fourth example can be found on the Companion Website atwww.ablongman.com/nieto5e. The curriculum case focuses on teaching about current events in a unit called "Hurricane Katrina and the Opportunity for Change."

One approach to transforming curriculum through a more multicultural perspective is the strategy of teaching about a specific geographical region and the cultural experiences of its people. This approach can develop rich, robust questions and understandings about specific groups, their histo-

ries, and their traditions. However, if the topic of a certain cultural group is approached as merely "adding color" to the curriculum, teachers run the risk of stumbling into any one of a number of pitfalls that run counter to the critical multicultural approach we have advanced in the previous chapters. Such pitfalls include perpetuating stereotypes by painting a group of people with a broad brush, "exoticizing" the "other" through a shallow "tourist" approach or, even more damaging, developing new pigeonholes by reinforcing a limited understanding of the experiences of a group of people. Out of concern for these pitfalls and fear of the unfamiliar, teachers may shy away from presenting a unit about specific cultural groups.

On the other hand, using a problem-posing approach and constructing curriculum with students on topics that both teachers and students want to explore creates an authentic learning experience. This is not to suggest that teachers enter blindly into creating curriculum on a random topic or subject area. Some preparation is always necessary. When teachers announce their own curiosity and model their own struggle with ignorance, students are empowered to ask previously hushed questions and uncover misconceptions. For instance, in a study of Cambodia and the Cambodian American experience, students who are unfamiliar with the topic may feel sanctioned to voice confusions that they might otherwise feel inhibited to ask—for example: "I thought Cambodians and Vietnamese kids were the same. How are they different?" "Why did Cambodian families move here to our community?" Or some students may point to social discrepancies that they feel uncomfortable about voicing: "I'm Cambodian and all my relatives are Cambodian, and we all live together with our relatives in the apartments at the edge of town. Why don't most White kids live with their relatives?"

Students' questions can reveal how social structures create stereotypes and lack of information that may lead to tension, alienation, and conflict. Attentive teachers can invite those questions and affirm a classroom culture that creates trustful, respectful dialogue. Such dialogue reveals that many of us are wondering about these things and why it is so crucial to use our academic skills to demystify the questions. By modeling an inquisitive mindset that takes a social justice stance, educators can encourage students to express their wonderment. Teachers can do this by making statements such as, "There is a growing Cambodian community here in our town. The first Cambodian families immigrated here in the 1970s, yet 30 years later, we study very little about the Cambodian culture or the experience of Cambodian American families in our school. Do you think it is worth exploring this community?" Dialogue can help promote academic rigor directed by a classroom community's curiosity.

Curricular Adaptation 1: A Study of Cambodia and the Cambodian American Experience

In what follows, we offer an example of a curriculum that was developed by a team of teachers of middle school students in an effort to stimulate intellectual growth, deepen understandings, support curiosity, and affirm the identities of students from all backgrounds. Besides describing the curriculum that the team of teachers developed, this example provides suggestions for expanding it.[1] We hope this sample curriculum will be viewed within the framework of critical pedagogy and multicultural education. It is one of many models that can be transferred and expanded to other curriculum units of regional studies and cultural groups, and it lends itself to continual adaptation by teachers for their specific learning communities.

What we don't know

A team of seventh grade teachers was concerned about the academic achievement of their Cambodian students, so they developed and implemented a curriculum about Cambodia. They called themselves *Team C* and included teachers of science, math, social studies, English, and art. These teachers noticed that while there was a small population of Cambodian students—an average of 8–10 in a school of about 630 students—the Cambodian students expressed their culture in several distinct ways. Team C teachers also noticed, with distress, that many of the Cambodian students in the school were experiencing low academic achievement. The

individual teachers on the team brought a range of philosophies and perspectives to their classrooms, but something on which they all agreed was that they lacked knowledge about Cambodia and the Cambodian American experience.

Preparation

Supported by the school system's staff development funds, the team of teachers met during the summer to study the topic of Cambodia. They enrolled in a course called *Cambodian Culture, American Soil: Conflict, Convergence and Compromise* co-taught by a Cambodian teacher in their district, and his colleague, an activist in the community.[2] In addition to taking the course, the principal also provided each teacher with copies of the book *First They Killed My Father: A Daughter of Cambodia Remembers* by Loung Ung.[3]

While many school districts may not support such in-depth staff development, an alternative approach to a study group could be for teachers to read primary sources and have book discussions. Such an approach requires commitment of considerable time and energy, but the results can be transformative. Many appropriate books and resources are listed at the end of this case.[4]

Whether preparation for curriculum development comes through coursework, reviewing literature, or field research, there is rarely a moment when teachers think they know everything they should to embark on creating a curriculum. On the contrary, thoughtful teachers are intensely aware of the endless boundaries of knowledge on any given subject. Rather than avoid the unknown, a problem-posing teacher launches into the topic by asking the students stimulating questions. Herein lies the tension between over-preparing structured curriculum, which may exclude student voices, and including student questions in the actual development of the curriculum. Teacher preparation as a foundation is essential, and setting some goals for framing students' questions is helpful.

Goal setting

When setting goals from a multicultural perspective for a curriculum unit about a geographical region or specific cultural group, teachers need to think beyond content, facts, and figures to consider the unit of study as intellectual and cultural work. Teachers who plan curriculum with a social justice mindset bring far-reaching goals to the curriculum design by considering what ideas will endure long after the books are closed and years after the students leave their classrooms. Grant Wiggins and Jay McTighe refer to these concepts as *big ideas* or *enduring understandings* and assert that depth of understanding is developed if these concepts are clearly articulated in the classroom when embarking on a unit of study, as opposed to content only to be tested at the end.[5]

A multicultural curriculum with enduring understandings based on a social justice perspective can help motivate teachers and students to work together toward social change. A unit about Cambodia and the Cambodian American experience could be designed with the following enduring understandings:

- Knowledge about historical events can help us understand current social conditions.
- War, genocide, and forced migration deeply influence people's lives for many generations.
- Recovering, preserving, and renewing cultural identity is an ongoing process of education, artistic expression, and cultural exchange.
- Awareness of the oppression and resistance experienced by a group of people can motivate them, and others, to work toward social change.

These enduring understandings could be taught through many content areas within a range of thematic topics, and they are transferable to other cases of war and displacement. Overarching goals such as the ones listed above can serve as guidelines when teachers get into the nitty-gritty work of planning objectives for their daily lessons and activities to uncover specific content. Team C teachers formulated the following specific objectives for the unit:

- All students will understand the history of Cambodia and its relationship with the United States.
- All students will develop inquiry about the Cambodian presence in western Massachusetts: What do we know? What do we wonder? (What is our knowledge? What are our questions?)

- All students will engage in direct involvement with the Cambodian community: at the Cambodian community garden, at the Buddhist temple with the monks, with high school "buddies" from the Cambodian club, and other community events.
- The curriculum will affirm identity of Cambodian students and families.
- The curriculum will build understanding among all students of all backgrounds.

The first two objectives are traditionally academic in nature, pointing to understanding history and current events. The academic achievement *embedded* in the overarching enduring understandings and in the specific objectives for the content underscores that multicultural education is *basic education*, as emphasized in Chapter 8. Likewise, the editors of *Rethinking Schools* have consistently asserted that multicultural curriculum and classroom practice must be academically rigorous.[6] The deliberate intellectual work of this unit disputes the misperception that multicultural curriculum is just about making people feel good, as detractors may claim. Each of the objectives addresses academic engagement in a variety of ways. Throughout this curriculum, you will see many opportunities for students to develop and increase skills.

The work of learning

One of the first questions teachers often ask is, "How long should I spend on this unit?" The unit about Cambodia and the Cambodian American experience was developed and operated as three different schedule plans: (1) events throughout the school year, (2) intensive study for one to three weeks and (3) the focus group week. We will give examples of the activities for the three different schedule plans.

The School Year   While the major framework and implementation of the unit work happened within a one- to three-week schedule, many other experiences reinforced the overarching enduring understandings throughout the year. Team C teachers had a great deal of other curriculum on many other topics to teach, yet they viewed the entire school year as having opportunities for teaching and learning about the Cambodian experience unit.

Some of the activities throughout the year included visitors and field trips.

Visitors

A Community Member   The social studies teacher invited a man who was a teacher in their school and a member of the Cambodian community (Mr. Mao) to visit her classes for four different sessions. The students were captivated by Mr. Mao's memories of his childhood, his family, his village, and his strategies for survival when captured by the Khmer Rouge. He showed the students how he had to trick the Khmer Rouge soldiers into believing he was a peasant farmer by demonstrating that he knew how to make rope from raw fibers. Mr. Mao's visits emphasized the grim tragedies of surviving genocide as well as the resilience of human nature. His warm nature and sparkling wit overcame the seventh graders' discomfort with the difficult topic of genocide, creating a community of honest questioners. The personal accounts Mr. Mao related to the class were reinforced by a series of videos about the history of Cambodia and the devastation caused by Pol Pot's regime, which the students had previously viewed.

High School Khmer Culture Club   Other guests included high school students from the district's Khmer Culture Club. The high school students shared their experiences as Cambodian American teenagers. They discussed the challenges of negotiating multiple cultural perspectives and the tension between traditional Cambodian family structure and mainstream U.S. teen culture. Many of the high school students had never been to Cambodia; they were born in the United States or had emigrated as very young children from refugee camps. Their experiences of Cambodia were vicarious, derived from collective memories of the elders in their families. Some teens were second-generation Cambodian Americans. Some were fluent in Khmer and English and some spoke no Khmer. They articulated the responsibilities of being bilingual youth in a culture in which most of the adults with literacy skills had been murdered in the genocide. The challenge of becoming assimilated into the U.S. mainstream while simultaneously maintaining cultural solidarity with their families had often been compounded by their struggles against institutionalized racism and poverty.

The teens also shared and taught traditional art forms, such as Cambodian folk dance and poetry, to the middle school youth. In addition, they talked about their favorite music and forms of entertainment in U.S. popular culture. The high school students' visits provided a dialogue and demonstration of the perspectives of many postmodern youth who are fluent in family language, Hip-Hop culture, Standard English, and multiple ways of expressing their academic and artistic knowledge. By making multiple perspectives visible and embodied, these encounters expanded the notion of what it means to be Cambodian American.

Master Musician   Another visitor, provided through the Cambodian Masters in the Classroom Program, played traditional Cambodian music and demonstrated traditional musical instruments to the whole team.[7]

Field Trips

Cambodian Community Garden   In the early fall, the entire team took a trip to the local Cambodian Community Garden. The vegetables grown in the garden were sold to restaurants and farmers' markets to raise funds for rebuilding temples and schools in Cambodia. The whole team picked vegetables to contribute to the community effort.

Khmer Dance Performance   A combination of serendipity and resourcefulness brought Team C to a performing arts event at a nearby university. The Asian Dance Program was hosting a performance of the award-winning Cambodian Angkor Dance Troupe from Lowell, Massachusetts.[8] Since the teachers were alert to gleaning from the community all available knowledge related to the Cambodian experiences, and energetic enough to write grants to fund the trip, all seventh graders, including Team C students, attended the dynamic dance performance. The Angkor Dance Troupe features teen Cambodian dancers who are mastering the classical Cambodian traditional dance forms as well as developing hybrid performances that integrate break dance and other Hip-Hop forms into their movements. One of the seventh graders, Eric, made this observation about the performance: ". . . I wish I was a Cambodian dancer. Those guys can break dance mad-cool and then they know their culture, too. I wish I had something like that."

In lieu of a lucky coincidence of a live performance within walking distance of one's school, teachers can use videos, DVDs, and websites projected onto a large screen to bring the performing arts to their students. For example, *Monkey Dance* is a recent documentary film about three teens from the Angkor Dance Troupe coming of age in Lowell, Massachusetts. The website about the film explains, "Children of Cambodian refugees inhabit a tough, working class world overshadowed by their parents' nightmares of the Khmer Rouge. Traditional Cambodian dance links them to their parents' culture, but fast cars, hip consumerism, and good times often pull harder."[9]

The Peace Pagoda and the Nipponzan Myohoji Sangha Buddhist Temple   Teachers made connections with the monks at the nearby Buddhist temple[10] in Leverett, Massachusetts, where many of the Cambodian families gather for prayer and meditation as well as for education and celebration. A field trip was planned in early April so that Team C students could help clean the grounds and plant flowers in anticipation of the annual Cambodian New Year celebration. As is not unusual during spring in New England, it had snowed several inches on the day of the field trip and the gardening plans turned into a snow-shoveling project, which also included a snowball battle with the monks! The monks taught Team C students about many of the symbols in the physical space of the temple as well as the role of Buddhism in many Cambodian families.

Team C scheduled these visitors and field trips between September and June. The teachers witnessed a sustained interest in the topic of Cambodia and the Cambodian experience long after the one- to three-week immersion study. Giving the students some breathing room to consider the topic, and the questions throughout the school year, reinforced the intellectual depth of the study.

One to Three Weeks   The teachers developed an intensive classroom unit of study that can last from one to three weeks. (These time frames are flexible, depending on how often teachers meet with their classes and the depth of study on the topic. Since this curriculum was enacted in a middle school, each Team C teacher taught in a specific discipline.) *English Class*   The English teacher led an in-depth investigation of Cambodian and Southeast Asian folk tales. Students read from children's picture books (traditional prose translated into English

from the Khmer source) and saw videos of storytellers. Specific attention was focused on how folktales use humor and metaphor to teach lessons. These activities met the state's framework standards and were integrated with a wider body of literature about cross-cultural folktales in the English department curriculum. Students could draw similarities and differences about the literature while viewing the Cambodian folktales as a means for reclaiming and reinvigorating cultural symbols that had been threatened by extinction in the aftermath of the genocide.[11]

Science Class   During the two years that this curriculum was implemented, there were two science teachers. One year, a science teacher led an investigation of endangered species in Southeast Asia. Students developed research projects on specific animals and species. They expressed their findings in text and artistic forms to create over-size classroom books. The books of illustrated scientific research were donated to the local elementary school, which served a large population of Cambodian students. In addition, the seventh graders created bookmarks depicting a synopsis of their research. They sold the bookmarks in a fund-raising effort to purchase protected areas of rainforest acreage in Southeast Asia.

Another year, a science teacher integrated his science curriculum with a study of the local Cambodian Community Garden. While at the garden, the science teacher led groups in measuring the space with global positioning satellite (GPS) devices; students worked in partner groups to map the surface area while learning about technology and computation. At school, they went to the computer lab and learned how to download and analyze the data. These science activities met the state's framework and standards for studying ecosystems and using technology for collection and analysis of data.

Social Studies Class   The social studies teacher engaged the students in an exploration of the refugee experience. They scrutinized the legal and social implications of refugee status, giving specific attention to the ravages of war and the conditions that cause a population to be forcibly displaced and become "refugees." They developed questions about the plight of people in many regions, from Afghanistan and Cambodia to the United States. In addition to studying groups from abroad who have been named political refugees under U.S. policy, they also critically examined the history of American Indian groups and compared their status in their native land as similar to the refugee experience.

Math Class The math teacher worked with concepts of ratio, proportion, and scaling to compare and contrast the amount of space used in a typical house in Cambodia with the amount of space in a typical house in the United States. The math teacher worked with the Cambodian community teacher, who provided lots of photographs and illustrations of houses in Cambodian villages and cities. The students designed a scale model of a house that reflected the typical size and shape of a Cambodian house. Meeting the seventh grade math standards, they worked from their individual design of a flat net that could be folded into a three-dimensional structure.

The math teacher also worked closely with the science teacher on a map activity. Students divided the maps into sections and analyzed Cambodia's ecosystems in science class. In the math activity, they developed an analysis of the total Cambodian population compared to the population densities in specific areas of the country. Using computational skills, they created a visual graph to illustrate their understanding of how people are dispersed regionally. This activity was integrated with the social studies investigation of the refugee experience to learn what the population looked like before and after the war.

Art Class In art class, the seventh graders studied the history, architectural design, and sculptural relief work of the temple of Angkor Wat. Studying the 12th century temple as an example of architectural accomplishment and cultural endurance helped bring alive the intersection of spiritual beliefs, political struggles, and environmental changes in Cambodia's history. Students explored Cambodia's cultural junctions of India and China through the presence of Hindu and Buddhist traditions, multiple language influences, and the stories illustrated by the seemingly endless sculptural murals of the temple.

By studying the symbolism, stories, and mind-boggling technical prowess demonstrated in the construction of the temple, the seventh graders gained insight into the depth of history and the significance of the temple in present-day Cambodia. One student exclaimed, "No wonder they put it in the middle of their flag!"

Continuing with the art exploration, the students, using clay and plaster, created their own relief sculptures depicting the animals they studied in science class and the folktales they explored in English. When some students asked about copying illustrations of the goddesses that are carved on Angkor Wat, they had a group discussion about religious iconography and who had the right to appropriate religious imagery. They imagined what it might be like for a classroom to produce 25 crucifixes or 25 images of the Star of David. They also looked at the work of some contemporary artists who use religious imagery in their work—whether reverently or irreverently—and noticed that most of these artists have a personal connection with the religious images they use. Such open discussions helped students make informed, deliberate decisions about whether or not they chose to imitate the statues of the goddesses of Angkor Wat.

Focus Groups After their intensive one- to three-week studies in the separate disciplines—visiting each teacher throughout their school day as middle school students usually do—Team C students chose a focus group in which to work. Each focus group worked in a single discipline for a full school week. Students spent the entire day with one teacher, working in depth on a single project. As the seventh graders said, it was "just like elementary school!" Each focus group visited the art room daily to work on a visual art component of the focus group project. Students chose from the following focus group activities:

- The English teacher led a focus group of students to dramatize the folktales the team had studied. Students collaboratively made decisions while directing plays, memorizing lines, creating costumes, and managing props and scenery. In art class, they worked on scenery and props for the plays inspired by illustrations from the picture books and by their study of Angkor Wat.
- The science teacher led a focus group in the construction of a scale model of the Cambodian Community Garden. Students used the data

Resources for Teaching about the Cambodian Experience

These resources are listed in two categories: professional and classroom.

PROFESSIONAL RESOURCES from which to draw information or excerpts for classroom curriculum (for adult readers)

Altman, Linda: J., *Genocide: The Systematic Killing of a People* (Berkley Heights, NJ: Enslow, 1995).

"Pol Pot: Secret Killer" *A&E Biography* (New York: A. E. T. Networks, 1997). DVD.

Brown, Karen, *Trauma and Recovery* (Amherst, MA: WFCR, NPR, 2002). Radio broadcast.

Nath, Vann, *A Cambodian Prison Portrait: One Year in the Khmer Rouge's S-21* (Bangkok, Thailand: White Lotus, 1998).

Ung, Loung, *First They Killed My Father* (New York: HarperCollins, 2000).

Ung, Loung, *Lucky Child: A Daughter of Cambodia Reunites with the Sister She Left Behind* (New York: HarperCollins, 2005).

CLASSROOM RESOURCES suitable for student use, including folktale picture books

Bartok-Baratta, Mira, and Roberta Dempsey, *Stencils Indonesia, Cambodia, and Thailand* (Glenview, IL: Scott Foresman, 1996).

Canesso, Claudia, *Cambodia* (New York: Chelsea House, 1989).

Carrison, Muriel P., *Cambodian Folk Stories from the Gaitloke* (Rutland, VT: Charles E. Tuttle, 1987).

Chamrouen, Yin, *In My Heart. I Am a Dancer* (Philadelphia: Philadelphia Folklore Project, 1996).

Chiemruom, Sothea, *Dara's Cambodian New Year* (Cleveland, OH: Modern Curriculum Press, 1992).

Coburn, Jewell, *Khmers, Tigers and Talismans from the History and Legends of Mysterious Cambodia* (Thousand Oaks, CA: Burn, Hart, 1994).

Coburn, Jewell, *Angkat, The Cambodian Cinderella* (Auburn, CA: Shen's Books, 1998).

Criddle, Joan D., *Bamboo and Butterflies: From Refugee to Citizen* (Davis, CA: East/West BRIDGE, 1992).

Criddle, Joan D., and Thida Mam, *To Destroy You Is No Loss* (New York: Doubleday, 1987).

Dagens, Bruno, *Angkor: Heart of an Asian Empire* (New York: Harry Abrams, 1995).

De Silva, Dayaneetha, *Cambodia* (Milwaukee: Gareth Stevens, 2000).

Ho, Minfong, *The Clay Marble* (New York: Farrar, Straus and Giroux, 1991).

Ho, Minfong, and Saphan Ros, *Brother Rabbit* (New York: Morrow, 1997).

Knight, Margy Burns, *Who Belongs Here? An American Story* (Gardiner, ME: Tilbury House, 1993).

Kodish, Deborah, and Deborah Wei, *Teacher's Guide to In My Heart, I Am a Dancer* (Philadelphia: Philadelphia Folklore Project, 2001).

Lipp, Fred, *The Caged Birds of Phnom Penh* (New York: Holiday House, 2001).

Maryknoll World Productions, *Beyond the Killing Fields* (Maryknoll, NY: Author, 1993). Video Magazine.

Norton, Ann W., *The Spirit of Cambodia . . . a Tribute* (Providence, RI: Providence College, 2002).

Pastore, Clare, *Journey to America: Chantrea Conway's Story: A Voyage from Cambodia in 1975* (New York: Berkley Jam Books, 2001).

Ray, Nick, *Cambodia* (Melbourne, Australia: Lonely Planet, 2000).

Sam, Sam-Ang, and Patricia S. Campbell, *Silent Temples, Songful Hearts: Traditional Music of Cambodia* (Danbury, CT: World Music Press, 1991).

St. Pierre, Stephanie, *Teenage Refugees from Cambodia Speak Out* (New York: Rosen, 1995).

Ung, Loung, *First They Killed My Father* (New York: HarperCollins, 2000).

Ung, Loung, *Lucky Child: A Daughter of Cambodia Reunites with the Sister She Left Behind* (New York: HarperCollins, 2005).

Wall, Lina Mao, and Cathy Spagnoli, *Judge Rabbit and the Tree Spirit* (San Francisco: Children's Book Press, 1991).

from their GPS activity to re-create the plot of land they had visited on the field trip. To investigate how to grow certain vegetables, they compared the climate and environmental conditions in Cambodia with the conditions in their hometown. In art class, they used materials and techniques to develop the 3-D effect of the scale model garden.

- The math focus group expanded upon the scale-model house design and built three-dimensional houses to reflect their study of the typical architecture of Cambodian houses. They carried their house to and from the art room each day, adding structural and technical details, surface design, and texture to try to depict an authentic-looking Cambodian house. In art class, they compared U.S. houses to Cambodian houses and used images from the book *Material World: A Global Family Portrait* by Peter Menzel, Charles Mann, and Paul Kennedy[12] to consider the implications of consumerism in the United States.

- The social studies focus group decided to write and perform vignettes to demonstrate various refugee experiences throughout the world. Some students took on the role of the United Nations. Others took on the role of the Red Cross and the Red Crescent, while some wrote and performed the parts of the refugees and some took on the role of military guards in refugee camps. In art class, they worked on

scenery, props, and costumes informed by their research projects and news media images.

Demonstration Day At the end of the focus group week, Team C students and teachers hosted Demonstration Day to illustrate their knowledge, understandings, and questions about Cambodia and the Cambodian American experience. All families, friends, and school personnel were invited. On a rotating schedule, visitors could enter each classroom to get a sense of what the students had learned. The science focus group set up their garden model in the art room, and the math focus group placed their houses in the garden to create a scale model of a Cambodian village. The students welcomed visitors and held discussions about contrasting and comparing the environments and houses in Cambodia to those of the New England valley where they lived. The English focus group performed mini-plays inspired by the Cambodian folktales but adapted by the seventh graders as "fractured fairytales" to reflect the intersection of U.S. popular culture, ancient stories, middle school humor, and symbolism of the Cambodian tales. The social studies focus group also performed their vignettes to "pull" their audience into the experiences of refugees. After each vignette, the group held a question-and-answer session with the audience, drawing upon their research findings.

The seventh grade students of Team C completed Demonstration Day with a feeling of fulfillment and accomplishment. Each student participated fully in the work of the intensive unit and individually evaluated their work. Each seventh grader engaged in self-directed participation within a collective group goal in their focus group. The students increased their skills in every academic content area, yet the teachers and students realized that there was still much to learn. Team C teachers asked the students to evaluate the learning experiences. Students wrote many statements about their challenges, accomplishments, and achievements. One Cambodian student, Prasour, wrote, "I liked this part of school when we studied my own culture. I thought it was awesome. The kids who aren't Cambodian thought it was awesome. It just makes you feel awesome to be Cambodian."

Curricular Adaptation 2: Transforming Pedagogy by Detracking Math

As established in Chapter 9, the structural and organizational issues in schools greatly influence student learning. Educational researcher Jeannie Oakes has consistently reported evidence that the practice of tracking negatively influences most students. Her research findings regarding tracking, especially how tracking in schools stratifies students by race and social class, have been confirmed by many others. This example of a curricular adaptation demonstrates the challenge of taking up the tracking issue in a middle school math department by following the work of a school principal and some determined teachers to transform the groupings of students for math classes.[13]

Belief systems

When considering the sociopolitical context of multicultural education to create change, we need to go beyond the classroom to confront the school's policies and practices as well as the societal ideologies that support them. The perspective that some kids can "handle" more abstract thinking and that others must be relegated to "skill and drill" is undergirded by a long-held math-instruc-

tion belief that students cannot learn about one concept until they master the "previous" concept. This belief system reinforces roadblocks to a fully integrated math curriculum for heterogeneous groups of students.

In U.S. schools, it is well documented that in kindergarten and first grade, most of the math material that students are learning is new information.[14] Yet, from kindergarten through seventh grade, there is a gradual but steady decline in new information that is introduced. By seventh grade, the larger piece of the math "pie" is review work, while a tiny percentage is new material. This remains the case until a student takes eighth grade algebra, when, rather suddenly, the abstract thinking and symbol manipulation introduced is almost entirely new. This, in turn, creates an even wider chasm if some students have greater access and opportunity to enroll in the algebra course, while others remain in "regular" math, consisting mostly of reviewing old concepts and revisiting skills.

The process of change

Changing this middle school math department's practices was a long process. To create effective change, it was necessary for the principal and the teachers to be critically cognizant of the belief system on which the old practices had been built. The former practice at the school in the seventh and eighth program segregated students by so-called ability. Students could sign up for "accelerated" math or "regular" math in seventh grade, which would feed into the eighth grade programs of algebra for the "accelerated" students and regular math for the "regular" students.

The principal of the school, who was a former math teacher, initially created structural change within the seventh grade math curriculum. As one step in the gradual process, the administration changed the way in which students would enter their seventh grade math classes. Instead of entering the seventh grade as either an "accelerated" math student or a "regular" math student (which was based on test scores and recommendations from sixth grade teachers), the students would enter seventh grade math curriculum in fully integrated, heterogeneous groups. At the end of the first quarter, after nine weeks of curriculum study and some testing, they would be re-grouped, dividing them into accelerated and regular classes for the second quarter. This was a strategic step in an attempt to meet students' needs in a more equitable way, but there were several pitfalls with the practice.

During the first quarter, the math teachers presented an equally challenging curriculum to all students. They also frequently offered "extensions" or an extra challenge as a choice for various assignments. During the first quarter, the seventh grade math teachers noted that most students took up the challenge and tried to solve the extensions with spirited enthusiasm. However, they witnessed a marked difference during the second quarter, after the classes had been designated "accelerated" or "regular." It comes as no surprise that most of the students in the "regular" math class stopped engaging in the extension lessons, while the students in the accelerated classes regularly pursued the extensions. For many students in the regular math class, it took less than one day's time to shift their perceptions about their possible math achievements from feeling capable of accomplishing the extensions to feeling incapable of meeting the challenge.

The practice of entering seventh grade as an integrated group and then shifting to accelerated and regular classes went on for a few years as the math department continued to struggle with how to make the curriculum more equitable while maintaining a rigorous academic program.

It's not only what we teach; it's how we teach

An eighth grade teacher, Mr. Mike Hayes, who at the time worked in the math department at the middle school, took note of the inequities. He witnessed that the accelerated curriculum engaged students in more abstract work and problem solving and the regular math curriculum offered more work on developing concrete skills at a lower level. Mr. Hayes critiqued the practice by noting, "This practice said that we believed kids needed different things to achieve in mathematics. The structures in place sent the message '*You* ["advanced" math students] should get an interesting, rich problem to work on and *you* ["regular" math students] should do fractions.' It said a lot about what we were com-

municating to students, parents, and guardians. It's not only what we teach; it's how we teach".

Mr. Hayes was inspired by the work of Robert Moses and Charles Cobb documented in the book: *Radical Equations: Civil Rights from Mississippi to the Algebra Project*.[15] In that text and in Moses' continuing work in public schools, he asserts, "The ongoing struggle for citizenship and equality for minority people is now linked to an issue of math and science literacy." Moses argues that in the 21st century, the unfinished work of the Civil Rights Movement is economic access. Moreover, economic access is critically dependent on science and math literacy. Mr. Hayes found that reading the work of Moses and Cobb transformed his teaching. He reported, "Reading that book gave my life's work a new sense of meaning." In addition to inspiration, the book gave theoretical substance and practical application to the questions about the pedagogy of the math department that Mr. Hayes had been asking and trying to solve.

While the adjustments were evolving in the seventh grade structure, Mr. Hayes was teaching eighth grade math. Building on the momentum of his principal's vision to detrack the math curriculum, he launched an effort to try to create more access to algebraic ideas for more eighth graders. He teamed up with fellow math teacher Alan Dallmann.[16] The two teachers piloted an approach they called *conceptual algebra*. This approach, which was directly inspired by the work of Robert Moses, strived to bridge the gap for students who were not enrolled in algebra. It offered students in the regular eighth grade math program the opportunity to participate in abstract symbol manipulation while continuing to develop their computation and arithmetic skills. In part, this teaching strategy built the challenges of more concrete math problems into more abstract-thinking challenges. This approach helped construct a scaffold of success for students who had not previously engaged in algebra. As a teaching strategy, this method also helped Mr. Hayes and Mr. Dallman assess their own teaching and get a sense of where the students were in terms of abstract thinking. The success of the conceptual algebra curriculum convinced these teachers that all students would benefit from engaging in algebraic thinking, regardless of their computational and technical skills. While a responsible curriculum would need to ensure that basic skills were constantly developed, such skill development would no longer be an impediment to participating in more theoretical ideas. These teachers believed and witnessed that students can learn about abstract concepts even when they are struggling with fractions.

This curricular change in the eighth grade math curriculum was one step to opening doors for more students to engage in higher level thinking. While the formal algebra class was still exclusive to about one-fourth of the students, the conceptual algebra approach in the regular math classes shifted practices throughout the math department. The teaching of conceptual algebra in eighth grade took hold throughout the math department as a structural change.

Beyond Math Class   While these math teachers were posing problems about the traditional structure of their department, other teachers in the school, outside the math departments, were raising questions about it as well. Teachers in the art, English, science, and social studies departments all noticed that the team of students was grouped by specific classes that reflected the enrollment in the accelerated math class. For example, even though there were no ability groups or "tiered" classes by achievement level in science and English departments, the science and English classes were populated in ways that accommodated the accelerated math schedule. Therefore, the practice of one department was influencing the learning and the administrative structure of all the content-area classes, resulting in what were, for all intents and purposes, tracked classes.

The English and science teachers brought questions to the school governing board called the *Leadership Council*, where issues were discussed and debated. The teachers asked, "Why do we have accelerated math classes in our school? Does the practice of accelerated math match the mission of our school?" Within this wider school discussion, the math department proposed that it was time to detrack the seventh grade math classes.

At the same time, another school structure was undergoing change. The school was adopting the policy of teams of teachers "looping" with students so that one team of students and teachers would remain together as a consistent learning community throughout seventh and eighth grade. Mr. Hayes

would be teaching seventh grade the following year and remaining with that team of kids for their eighth-grade year. Envisioning an opportunity, he proposed to the principal that he pilot a completely heterogeneous, untracked seventh grade math program only for his team of students. Mr. Hayes emphasized that rather than eliminating accelerated math curriculum, the fully integrated program would offer every student an opportunity to participate in accelerated math.

Support for All Students   Mr. Hayes realized he and his students would need support to make his plan work. He was determined to increase the skill level of students who would have been left out of the traditional accelerated program and to challenge the students who were already demonstrating strengths. The special education teacher, Blanca Zelaya, co-taught the math classes with Mr. Hayes.[17] They partnered on teaching strategies and techniques. The students viewed Mr. Hayes and Ms. Zelaya as co-teachers rather than perceiving each as the teacher of a certain group. By sharing the classroom and curriculum, they offered a richer curriculum to every student.

The following year, the school followed Mr. Hayes's pilot model and embarked on the practice of every seventh grade student's participating in the full math curriculum. The accelerated component was offered in completely heterogeneous groupings for all students.

The math teachers and administrators realized the importance of the community's support to create sustainable change. Before launching the new seventh grade math approach, they held meetings to discuss every aspect of the change. They knew that each component of the community would need to be included in the dialogue. They met with math teachers from the elementary schools and high school to clarify the goals of the changes within the broader scope of the math curriculum in the school district. At their middle school, they held a faculty meeting that engaged every teacher in the school in a dialogue about the implications of the structural change within the math department, that is, how the change would affect the whole school. The math teachers and administrators also held meetings for the parents and guardians.

The decision to detrack the math curriculum did not reflect a unanimous community vision. Within each of these community groups, there was some support for the new model and some dissent. The most common concern of detractors was that heterogeneous groupings might "water down" the curriculum. This common concern often leads to amplification of voices representing high-achieving students and muting of the concerns of students who have traditionally been marginalized. The public meetings emphasized that by offering accelerated math curriculum to all students, the children who have consistently achieved would continue to engage in robust, creative problem solving and skill development. Simultaneously, the children who had previously been relegated to regular math would be able to participate in higher level thinking and skill development. Moreover, students who need additional support to meet the highest challenge would also be buttressed by a team teaching approach to the curriculum. While disagreements continued, it became evident that most people were eager to get on board when they realized that all children would be more challenged within the new structure.

With every seventh grade math class adopting a heterogeneous approach, the special education teachers co-taught lessons with the math teachers. For students needing to hone certain competencies, the school provided extra support for sharpening skills in a program called math tune-up. The math tune-up class was not a special education program. A teacher of regular math taught the tune-up class during slots in the students' schedules that did not "pull out" the students from their regular math classes. The entire school schedule was examined creatively to create these possibilities.

More Work Ahead The detracking of one seventh grade math curriculum is an ongoing process. The teachers described several promising developments, as well as pitfalls in their department's effort, that generated school-wide implications. The positive aspects were many: Students from all backgrounds, regardless of previous accomplishments, engaged in rigorous math curriculum that pushed the edges of student potential. Academic achievement increased for many students. Perceptions on who gets to be included were expanded by school discourses about "smartness", "intelligence", "good students," and "talent". The teachers reported feeling invigorated by the continual challenge to creatively present material to make it more engaging, understandable, and achievable to a wide range of learners. The limits of the change became clearer as students moved from seventh grade to eighth grade and then from eighth grade to the high school. When the seventh grade students moved to eighth grade, they were grouped into algebra groups or regular math groups. The eighth grade curriculum had changed significantly to offer more abstract thinking and symbol manipulation to the regular math groups, but the course offerings were separate, with little "wiggle room" to move from one course to the other during the eighth grade year.

Additionally, in an effort to create more access to a rigorous curriculum for a wider range of learners, the structure of the high school math department had shifted in configuration. Yet, while the high school math curriculum offered a wide range of courses for math credit, the classes that held more academic sway, such as honors and AP credit, continued to be "gated" by the eighth grade algebra requirements, thus perpetuating implicit messages about who belongs where. Even within a math department and school district committed to making serious structural change to achieve multicultural goals, external forces choke off much of the progress toward equitable change. Teachers who are supported by principals and curriculum directors are still pressured by *perceptions* of what a rigorous math curriculum should look like. College entrance requirements and state and national testing policies shape a great deal of high school math curricula. This middle school math department made significant change within the structures of the school and the wider school district. Yet the struggle to create a more inclusive math curriculum that asserts academic challenge remains contained mostly within the seventh grade program. The forces at play within the broader math department in this school district mirror the struggles of most math departments in U.S. schools concerning math ability and achievement.

The perimeters of social change at the macro level, that is, U.S. public schools, did not prevent Mr. Hayes and his colleagues from pursuing social justice at the micro level, that is, within his department. They looked at the structural limitations of their K–12 program and made changes specifically

---

Resources for Teaching and Detracking Math

Gutstein, Eric, *Reading and Writing the World with Mathematics: Toward a Pedagogy for Social Justice* (New York: RoutledgeFalmer, 2005).

Gutstein, Eric, and Bob Peterson, *Rethinking Mathematics: Teaching Social Justice by the Numbers* (Milwaukee: Rethinking Schools, 2005).

Moses, Robert, and Charles Cobb, *Radical Equations: Civil Rights from Mississippi to the Algebra Project* (Boston: Beacon Press, 2002).

Nasir, Na'ilah Suad, and Paul Cobb, eds., *Improving Access to Mathematics: Diversity and Equity in the Classroom* (New York: Teachers College Press, 2006).

Oakes, Jeannie, *Keeping Track: How Schools Structure Inequality,* 2nd ed. (New Haven, CT: Yale University Press, 2005).

Sinclair, Nathalie, *Mathematics and Beauty: Aesthetic Approaches to Teaching Children* (New York: Teachers College Press, 2006).

Stavy, Ruth, and Dina Tirosh, *How Students (Mis)Understand Science and Mathematics: Intuitive Rules* (New York: Teachers College Press, 2000).

Webb, Norman L., and Thomas A. Romberg, eds., *Reforming Mathematics Education in America's Cities: The Urban Mathematics Collaborative Project* (New York: Teachers College Press, 1994).

---

within their spheres of influence: the grades they taught at the middle school. The determination and achievements of these students and teachers demonstrate the qualities of social justice education. The ongoing efforts of the math department provided all students with the *material resources* necessary to learn to their full potential. The changes in the seventh grade math curriculum also provided students with *emotional resources* by demonstrating a belief in students' ability and worth; maintaining high expectations of them; imposing rigorous academic standards; and providing essential social and cultural capital to negotiate the world. By transforming the way in which students perceive themselves and their peers as mathematical thinkers, this case also exhibits a social-justice learning environment that promotes critical thinking and agency for social change.

Curricular Adaptation 3: Expanding Definitions of Family

Another approach to transforming a curriculum is the strategy of examining a particular theme from a variety of perspectives. In the case study that follows, we offer a glimpse into a study of *family* as the theme. The concept of family has always been both deeply political and intimately personal. The political framework for defining family has become a contentious issue in recent years because of the lesbian, gay, bisexual, transgender (LGBT) community's struggle to gain legal marital status. The voices of political parties and special interest lobbying groups that claim ownership of the definition of *family values* have punctuated the controversy.

This case is divided into descriptions of three approaches to curricular adaptation. The first two examine the topic of family in two settings: first grade and middle school. These two approaches set the stage for an innovative approach to curricular adaptation in a third setting: a high school English literature course.

Why the topic of family?

The topic of family is an attractive theme for teachers because it offers many promising possibilities. The promise lies in the idea that every student from preschool through high school may be able to tell a story about family and relate to ideas about family change. Such stories and ideas provide ways for teachers and students to collaborate and involve every student in the curriculum. Yet, if these attributes are not approached with a problem-posing multicultural perspective, a curriculum about family can prove to be problematic—and even damaging to students. What is often thought to be a "universal" theme requires acknowledgement of multiple experiences and perspectives, with specific attention to deep-seated myopic views of the definition of *family* that may work to support institutional oppression of some people.

Who is included?

For example, families who are headed by lesbian, gay, bisexual, and transgender people have been the specific target of recent oppressive political campaigns, and they are frequently ignored or deliberately silenced in school curricula. Also, families who are headed by adults who are not married, whether homosexual or heterosexual, are excluded from traditional definitions of family, and the children of these families may be questioned about the validity of their family structure. Families headed by single parents are still not affirmed in many curricula. Students who have family members who are incarcerated rarely see a welcome opportunity to share their story, and they are silenced by some teachers if they attempt to raise the topic. Families caring for members with mental illness may be reluctant to participate in a classroom invitation to share stories from home. The perspective of children of adoption is frequently omitted in classroom discussions about heredity and family trees. There are as many pitfalls

in approaching family as a theme as there are families in our schools, so how does a teacher develop a curriculum about family that embraces the potential to draw from the strength of one of the most elemental human experiences and simultaneously lead students to fight oppression, develop critical thinking skills, and affirm all community members?

When teachers embark on the study of family with clarity about the long-term goals of the unit, it helps students tap into the shared understanding of human experience. Long-term goal setting may help avoid activities that exclude some students from the classroom community. In its most effective form, a curriculum rooted in big ideas or enduring understandings will lead students to actively pursue human rights for all families.

Avoiding pitfalls

A common activity in curriculum about family includes students' researching the history of their names. While this can be a powerful community-building activity, it is also rife with difficulties, especially when it is not grounded by an overarching long-term goal. Many students may know the family story of their name or may have easy access to it by asking family members who are eager to share the story. However, many children may not. Children of adoption and children in foster care may not know the origin of their name and may feel that such an assignment will lower their status as a classroom community member. Other students may have painful associations with the history of their name, such as one student we met who reported that he was named after a family member who had been incarcerated for abusing him.

Rather than discard the assignment about researching one's name and relegate such potentially robust activities to the "untouchable" category, teachers may develop a menu of various assignments from which students can choose. For example, if the big idea of the assignment is to *engage in research skills related to naming and personal history*, the menu of activities might include:

- Research the name of the street on which you live (or the name of the building, housing community, neighborhood, the name of the building in which your faith community, or the land on which your tribal community lives). Find out when it was named and why. Tell us something about its history, and if you choose the place where you live (building, street, housing community, or tribal community land), find out when your family moved there or started living there. Some "family moves" are exciting and celebratory. Other "family moves" may be a response to family and community difficulties such as economic strife, natural disasters, or political oppression. Tell us only what you and your family would like to share.

- Research the name of our school and compare it to the name of another school in our district that you have never attended. Tell us something about the history of the school between the time it was named and the time you began attending the school.

- Research the name of an important person in your family, your religious community, your tribal community, or your cultural community. Tell us something about what the name means. Tell us something about the history of the person between the time she or he was named and the time you were born.

- Research your name and its origins. Find out who chose your name and why. Tell us something about what your name means. Tell us something about the history of your family between the time you were named and the time you began attending this school.

A culminating activity may involve each student's creating an artistic representation of his or her own name to display as a heading for his or her research presentations. The artistic representations may provide another way for students to demonstrate knowledge while simultaneously bringing a unifying activity to a classroom where students have been engaged in an assortment of research projects.

The pitfalls and promises of the history-of-your-name activity are examples of why it is critical to begin a curriculum with big ideas or enduring understandings rather than simply planning activities. This curricular activity also exemplifies the delicate balance inherent in a teacher's role. Even the most thorough multicultural curriculum cannot solve personal crises that some children face. When students reveal painful memories or dangerous situations, it is critical that teachers tap into the resources in the school and community through guidance counselors and social workers to keep their students healthy and safe.

What follows are examples of curriculum for three different grade levels: one created by first grade teachers and students, another created by a middle school team of teachers, and the last developed by a high school English teacher.

First grade curriculum based on big ideas

The first grade curriculum about family stems from the following four big ideas—or enduring understandings and essential questions:

1. There are all kinds of families.
   - What is a family?
   - How do we know a group of people make up a family?

2. Families have "wants & needs":
   - What do families need? (Food, water, clothing, shelter, love).
   - What is the difference between a need and a want?
   - What are some things that you must have to survive?
   - Is money a want or a need? Are some things "in between"? Do all families need a way to exchange goods?

3. Responsibilities
   - What are the responsibilities that parents and guardians attend to while kids are at school?
   - What are the responsibilities of each child in the family?

4. Experiencing *change* is common to all families. (Examples of change: marriage, divorce, getting older, moving, illness, getting well, death, birth.)
   - Does change happen in all families?
   - Why do we like or dislike change?
   - Can we prepare for change in families?

With these enduring understandings in mind, the first grade teachers start each school year with the integrated social studies unit on family and spend approximately six weeks incorporating these big ideas into all aspects of the curriculum. Additionally, as the year unfolds, they study other units in specific content areas that reinforce and revisit many of the enduring understandings that were established during the unit on family. The other units in the social studies and science curricula throughout the year are anchored in the big ideas concerning the family unit.

All Kinds of Families The teachers deliberately take an anti-bias approach throughout the six-week unit on family as well as through the school year, by teaching first graders that there are all kinds of families. Through children's literature, the daily calendar, math problems, and other activities of classroom life, the students consistently see images of, and learn about, family diversity. Specific attention is given to affirming the particular families of the children in the classroom while simultaneously expanding the students' views of what family can be. Some of the many examples of "all kinds of families" include families headed by gay dads and lesbian moms, families experiencing divorce, families created or expanded through adoption, single-parent families, families struggling with financial resources, multiracial families, foster families, families experiencing illness or death, families in which the grandparents are raising the children, families with stepparents and step siblings, families from a wide range of different racial, ethnic, and religious backgrounds as well as those that may be defined as *nuclear* or *traditional families*.

Families in the Classroom In many schools, the practice of bringing family members from all walks of life into the classroom as helpers and experts has had more support in recent years. In a unit about family, this is certainly a dynamic component. Teachers can develop many creative means for parents, guardians, and extended family members to be present. However, making *all* families "visible," and the diversity of their life experiences honored, is a challenging endeavor. To explore the big idea about families and responsibilities, one teacher developed an activity that rises to the challenge.

At the beginning of this activity, the classroom community discusses the idea of responsibilities. The students complete a series of assignments to explore and document the responsibilities of adults and children in the family. The assignments are designed to raise awareness of responsibilities but also to make every child's family visible in the classroom. The students in the class make a list of responsibilities that they have in school or "jobs" they need to accomplish. This simple task expands the notion of what it means to have a "job" beyond a place of work where one gets paid money. Especially for children in families struggling with unemployment, this wide view of jobs and responsibilities affirms the work of all family members. The class also makes a list of jobs that kids do at home such as making their beds, walking the dog, carrying their plates to the sink, helping to carry groceries, folding towels, etc.

After developing their understandings of responsibilities, each first grader conducts a family survey by interviewing the adults in the family, asking questions such as: What responsibilities do you have while I am at school? What jobs do you do, either at home or away from home? These interview questions allow for a range of replies to be respected, as opposed to the more narrow question that children frequently hear: "Where do your parents work?" The first graders learn more about what their caregivers are doing and about the assortment of possibilities of adult responsibilities, and the teacher gains an intimate view into the complex workings of each student's family. The assignment results in adult replies such as caring for younger children or elders, searching for employment, cleaning or fixing up the home, taking care of the yard, volunteer work, going to school, resting to go to the night shift at work, and much more. The students hear about a variety of places that people call *work:* the office, the school, the fire station, the bakery, the construction site, the chemistry lab, the home, the sandwich shop, the hospital, grandma's house, the cafeteria, the hotel, and more.

Part of the interview requires the students to ask the adults what they have to be "good at" to accomplish their responsibilities. This kind of questioning affirms the multiple intelligences required for everyday life. Children hear about skills such as talking to people, knowing when the baby is hungry, using special tools, keeping things organized, being a good listener, making food taste good, knowing different kinds of plants, figuring out when a burning building might fall down (in the case of a parent who is a firefighter), etc. The assignment continues with students' researching the jobs for which all the children in their home have responsibility. Eventually, they investigate what the adults in their families imagined they would be when they grew up and how this compares to the adult responsibilities they now have.

Finally, the students spend time drawing, writing, and presenting their investigations, culminating in imagining several kinds of responsibilities they would like to have when they grow up.

The work of multicultural education is not only to affirm students about who they are, but also to challenge them about who they may become. This variation on a common early childhood activity of "What do you want to be?" is designed to provide multiple models, unleash imaginations, and expand the possibilities these first graders imagine for themselves. All the while, every family "comes to life" in the class, even if the adults in the family could not enter the classroom door.

Children's Literature The first grade teachers use children's literature to emphasize that there is not one "normal" way to experience family, but rather that diversity is normal. While reading lively and engaging children's literature such as *1,2,3: A Family Counting Book* by Bobbie Combs and illustrated by Dannamarie Hosler, students see paintings that depict families headed by gays and lesbians, including two dads reading a bedtime story to their kids, two moms sharing popsicles with their kids on the porch, and several families gathered in community activities.[18] Using children's literature that includes encounters with families with same-sex parents deliberately combats heterosexism in early childhood and provides opportunities to teach explicitly about human rights for all families. When students learn accurate, respectful language and vocabulary regarding the LGBT community, they may ask questions that uncover anti-LGBT perspectives.

While the selection of children's literature that depicts families headed by LGBT people is still limited, it has grown significantly in breadth and depth since 1989, when Leslea Newman wrote and self-published *Heather Has Two Mommies*.[19] With the 20th anniversary of that book approaching, Newman and many other authors and publishers have expanded children's literature selections with texts that affirm families headed by gay and lesbian couples, single people, and LGBT parents who have separated. Some recent titles for early childhood literacy activities that include a more inclusive defi-

nition of family and affirm families headed by lesbian, gay, bisexual, and transgender people are listed on the GLSEN website.[20]

There is a growing list of titles in children's literature that affirm LGBT identity. Early childhood teachers and students who are engaging in the "dangerous discourse" we discussed in our assertion of multicultural education as education for social justice in Chapter 8, use these books and other similar resources.[21] Dangerous discourse becomes common practice and unthreatening when these books are integrated into daily literacy activities that develop reading and listening skills, motivate class discussion, and make interdisciplinary connections. Along with books that depict many other kinds of families, a rich children's literature collection affirms diverse family structures and questions those who exclude families headed by gay, lesbian, bisexual, and transgender parents from fully participating in a democracy.

Early childhood is an essential phase of development in which to address heterosexism by integrating this literature. Children are on the cusp of what Louise Derman-Sparks calls *pre-prejudice*. They are asking questions that may be naive about society's oppressions or they may be ventriloquating social epithets without understanding the meaning behind the words. First grade is an educational stage ripe with opportunity to expand a child's world.[22]

Problem-posing teachers realize that developing a children's literature collection is an ongoing, organic process. We are not suggesting that a first grade book shelf or a unit about family diversity should focus only on families headed by lesbian, gay, bisexual, and transgender people. Such an approach would obviously not affirm the families of all students in the class. However, given the sociopolitical context of the human rights struggles of the LGBT community, a critical component of a multicultural curriculum confronts the negative ways that LGBT people are depicted by the popular media. An expanding children's literature collection may act as a counter-narrative to oppressive acts and highlight the positive role of LGBT-headed families in the classroom. These books broaden the scope of a curriculum that also includes quality literature depicting families with diverse ethnic and racial identities, religious practices, socioeconomic situations, disabilities/abilities, languages, and so forth, as well as the myriad ways that families are shaped through birth, adoption, foster care, extended families, and more.

Daily Calendar and Family Concepts   Every day in these first grade classrooms starts with a morning meeting and calendar activity. Using a model created by teacher Val Penniman and parent Debbie Shumway, the teachers introduce alphabet skills, vocabulary, math patterns, and concepts about the current unit through the calendar activity.[23] For the family unit, the teachers designed daily calendar pieces (using clip art) to delve into concepts and vocabulary with which the children are familiar but which they may not always have the opportunity to use to develop academic knowledge.

For example, on calendar day number 4, the alphabet letter is D and the vocabulary words are *difference, dad, divorce, deaf*. By including words such as *divorce, difference,* and *deaf* along with words that may be more typical of a family unit such as *dad,* the classroom curriculum is normalizing experiences so children may engage in academic skill development while some who are usually marginalized are being affirmed in their family experiences. Simultaneously, other children are challenged to expand their perspective of families. Integrating vocabulary words such as *divorce* and *deaf* provides a means for students to ask questions and share stories in an emotionally safe and academically rigorous environment. Abilities, disabilities, and family change are studied through stories and studying vocabulary.

All Kinds of Family Portraits   Artistic expression is honored in these classrooms as a form of sharing knowledge. Every student creates a family portrait. By studying various examples of family portraits from contemporary and historical artists, the first graders gain a panoramic view of the multitude of ways that the concept of family can be expressed. A curriculum that expands the definition of family also expands the notion of what is included in a family portrait. The book *Honoring Our Ancestors: Stories and Pictures by Fourteen Artists,* edited by Harriet Rohmer, is illustrated with lively paintings by various artists who depict "ancestors" in poetic and metaphorical ways.[24] The paintings in this book represent family memories, spiritual stories, family quotes, and even a room with nobody in it to re-

Calendar piece from Gina Simm's and Susie Seco's first grade class. Design inspired by Val Penniman's and Debbie *Shimway's Calendar Connections.* www.calendar-connections.com

mind the viewer of the loss of a loved one. Each painting is accompanied by an artist's narrative in very "kid-friendly" language, which leads first graders through robust literacy activities that integrate the visual image with the written word.

In another strategy to connect visual imagery and text, teachers and students study the books created by *Family Diversity Projects,* in which many different kinds of families are portrayed in captivating photographs with accompanying interviews of family members. Resources that use photography and interview text to depict the true stories of real families are powerful tools for developing critical thinking. In addition to using the books as curriculum resources, many teachers and schools display the touring photo-text exhibits, which can be rented from the Family Diversity Projects collection. Currently there are four traveling exhibits:[25]

- *In Our Family: Portraits of All Kinds of Families*
- *Love Makes a Family: Portraits of Lesbian, Gay, Bisexual and Transgender People and Their Families*
- *Nothing to Hide: Mental Illness in the Family*
- *Of Many Colors: Portraits of Multiracial Families*

I like to play sports with my family. I like when my dad plays baseball with me. I like it when my mom tucks me in bed.

Michael Warren, in Gina Simm's class. *Family portrait.* Mixed media, 2005.

Throughout the study of family, first graders see images and hear stories of families that remind them of their own. These images and stories serve the concurrent purpose of stretching their understanding of what other families are like. The work of multicultural education for social justice begins in the earliest grades with the most elemental of human experience to help students imagine a fair world for "all kinds of families."

Middle school integrated curriculum

The exhibits and books of the Family Diversity Projects also serve as an anchor for the integrated middle school curriculum about family. The middle school teachers developed big ideas to expand skills and inquiry across all content areas. The enduring understanding is that *oppression and resistance are experienced and acted upon in diverse ways by families in our society,* the essential questions are:

• How do we create an inclusive definition of family?

• What is family?
• Where do I belong?

Bearing in mind the difficulties that some students may encounter with a curriculum about families, the teachers did not ask students to bring in family photographs. They knew that many children would not have family photos and that some children would feel uncomfortably exposed by a requirement to share family photos. Instead, the team focused on the materials in the Family Diversity Projects phototext exhibit *In Our Family* and on books as points of departure for research, as well as the discussions about the teachers and staff members' families. Thus, all teachers brought their own family photos to share with the students at the beginning of the unit. These family photos provided opportunities to discuss the various ways of defining family and to share with the middle school students some aspects of the teachers' lives beyond the classroom walls.[26]

Diversity Within Groups At first glance, it would appear that the team of teachers who undertook this unit was a group of middle class White people. This is true, but it is not the whole story. The teachers were critically aware of the dominance of their identities and asserted that their students deserved to see many different kinds of families modeled in class discussions. So the team presented their family photos to the students, and the classroom community discussions pointed out the many ways in which the teachers' families were different.

In this case, one female teacher was married to a man who had children from a previous union, so she had stepchildren. One male teacher was married to a woman and had no children. One female teacher had three sons: one from her first marriage, one from her second marriage in which she was still partnered, and one foster son who was different racially from her other family members. One female teacher lived with her lesbian partner and was adopting a child of a different race. One White male teacher was married to a White woman and they had two biological children—the only "nuclear" or "traditional" family among the teaching team.

These differences opened up opportunities for considering other kinds of diversity. Teachers invited other school faculty and staff members to visit their classrooms and bring some of their family photos. The faculty and staff visitors included a Jewish woman who told the story of her parents' surviving the Holocaust and the loss of her husband to cancer, as well as the triumph of her niece over cancer; an African American man who is married to a woman and raising their grandson; and a biracial gay man who had been adopted by a white family.

These conversations about the families in which the adults live provided models for students' consideration of the topic of family as an academic subject, rich with research possibilities. The students saw the teachers as full participants in the unit of study rather than simply as "deliverers" of information. The unintended consequence of this activity was that students witnessed different adults sharing their family experiences at varying levels of disclosure with distinct styles of storytelling. It gave students a range of models from which to embark on their academic work.

Studying Our Own Assumptions   The social studies teacher launched the study by bringing each class to the Family Diversity Projects photo exhibit before the accompanying text was installed in the display. (A similar activity could be designed by looking at books and photocopies of pictures of families.) The students examined each photograph and wrote responses to prompts such as:

- Find a family with whom you think you have something in common.
- Find a family with whom you think you have nothing in common.
- Pick a photo that makes you curious; write your questions.
- Pick a photo that makes you smile; tell us why.
- Pick a photo that makes you sad; tell us why.

The social studies students compared each other's responses to the photos. They began to look critically at assumptions they were making on the basis of a photograph. Then the teachers added the companion text to each photograph, and the students revisited the exhibit, with plenty of time to read the text.

The reading and analysis of the text pointed to the sociological objectives of the unit. Students uncovered ways in which they made assumptions about some families and how those assumptions may stem from, or lead to, stereotypes. Students also learned ways in which they made accurate guesses about some of the families. For example, Jeffrey pointed out a family of four—comprised of a mom, a dad, and two sons who were both wearing baseball caps—as one that was similar to his own family. The family structure and the love of baseball were similar traits to those of Jeffrey's family. Upon reading the text, Jeffrey learned that all four people in the photo are deaf and communicate in American Sign Language, which is different from Jeffrey's family's hearing and language abilities.

Group Membership and Responsibility   These activities eventually led to a study of how people group themselves and how society groups people. The students started with examining their membership roles in family and then expanded to examining their membership in other groups such as basketball teams, lunch-table groups, after-school clubs, religious communities, racial groups, ability groups, and so forth. This examination included analyzing group behavior and social influences on groups. When juxtaposed with the histories of various groups, these analyses helped to flesh out stories of historical oppression and resistance in the minds of these middle school students. Rather than demonizing one group or romanticizing another, students began to see the links of social power, social position, and group power. Ultimately, the students critically analyzed their own group membership and their social responsibilities within groups. They worked cooperatively to develop strategies to take responsibility when these groups dominate other groups in the microcosm of the middle school as well as in the larger society.

Reading, Writing, Researching, and Reflecting

The language arts curriculum explored the experiences of diverse families through a range of literature. The middle school students selected books from an array of titles. Like photo-text exhibits, literature offers students an opportunity to engage in other families' experiences, some that may resonate with their own and some that may open new worldviews to their early adolescent minds.

Poetry was a central vehicle for expression and questioning in the English class. Building on the curriculum advanced by Linda Christensen in *Reading, Writing and Rising Up,* each student composed a poem called "I am From" to articulate the multiple dimensions of identity within family.[27]

While the work of poetry writing and literature circles was evolving in the English classroom, the students embarked on homework research projects to investigate their family histories. Again, if such a project is undertaken, it is advisable to provide a menu of assignments from which every student may choose to find meaningful, affirming work that also expands their academic skills. For example, a common project may be to assign students to research and report on when their family immigrated to this country. But when a teacher approaches the curriculum with the big idea in mind (*Oppression and resistance are experienced and acted upon in diverse ways by families in our society*), the exclusion of Native American children in an assignment about immigration becomes more obvious. Approaching the big ideas with critical pedagogy, the classroom considers multiple views of what immigration means to various families. This array of perspectives may include the forced migration and extermination of Native Nations, the forced immigration of enslaved people, immigration to escape war and political oppression, refugee experiences, the circular migration/immigration families in U.S. territories (called

colonies by some) such as Puerto Rico, and the on-going political oppression and resistance of families caught in the crossfire of U.S. immigration restrictions. When research findings based on each student's own family's perspective are integrated in a critical classroom context, voice is given to stories that have been silenced, encouraging students to question narratives that exclude some family experiences.

Measuring, Reflecting, and Representing   In math class, the middle students spent a two-week period that the math teacher called *A Day in the Life,* carefully measuring how their time was spent. They created circle graphs ("pie charts") and bar graphs to analyze the percentage of time spent with family, comparing this percentage to time spent on homework, extracurricular events, friends, and other details such as grooming. (Grooming was a substantial piece of most middle school students' pie charts and graphs!) Students learned critical time-management skills as well as gained an understanding of the diverse ways that their peers' families spend time.

Genetics, Probability, and Critical Pedagogy Starting with two essential questions—*What is family?* and *Where do I belong?*—the science curriculum was integrated with math to study probability equations related to genetics and human traits such as eye color. By studying the science of genetic structure and the mathematical strategies to predict human traits, students of all family backgrounds and configurations are affirmed. Rather than starting with what each student knows about their heritage, teachers can start with what they *do not* know and what they are curious about to form hypotheses about their ancestor's genetic composition. Science teachers can pose a variety of examples from which students may choose to develop their equations and predictions. This activity is more welcoming to children of adoption and others who may have no information about their biological heredity. The students learn academic skills for analyzing data and pursuing deeply personal questions.

Old Arguments, New Knowledge, and Social Justice   A scientifically grounded study of genetics also provides well-informed arguments against racism and ethnic oppression. A critical pedagogy examines misinformation about intelligence and ability and replaces it with methodologically rigorous academic knowledge. With race-based and ethnic-based hate crimes and genocides across the globe, from the United States to Rawanda, Darfur, and Iraq, students can develop accurate, rational, and scientifically sound refutations to historically and ethnically rooted oppressions. By integrating their sociological research findings on group behavior and group membership with scientific and mathematical skills, middle school students can make assertive choices about human rights issues that affect their own families. They can become activists about global concerns.

Research Questions The development of students as activist scholars was woven throughout each subject, and social studies objectives were evident in all content areas. In one of the final social studies assignments, students chose a research question to pursue through a variety of methods. For example, one student's question was "What gets families through hard times?" She practiced social science research methodologies such as reading the photo-text exhibit, interviewing her own family members, and interviewing friends and neighbors. She contrasted these real-life families' experiences with those of families she saw on TV. Many students were compelled to compare their research data with the representation of families in the media. Students learned how to organize their data by themes and write essays with a critical eye toward the media's representation of family.

Visual Art and Visual Culture To address the many visual and verbal messages regarding what families look like in visual culture, the interdisciplinary art curriculum was integrated with the social studies skills the students had developed. By examining images of families in film, web media, print media, and various expressions of popular culture, students can develop skills in critical and visual literacy. Within this dialogue, the middle school students consciously drew a self-portrait in the context of a family portrait. By developing confidence in art-making skills, this lesson encouraged student expressions about diverse families while expanding concepts about art and the powerful role of visual culture.

Identity and Beauty Critical understanding of facial features and value systems was underscored in the context of a visual arts drawing lesson stemming from the big idea of the unit. The art teacher and social studies teacher integrated concepts surrounding physical anthropology that also drew upon the math and science research in genetics. They studied skin color and other various human traits. They asked why certain groups in specific geographic locations developed unique adaptations that we see today in the diversity of the human form, which is most obvious in facial features, hair texture, and skin color. Exploring these concepts in the process of self-portrait drawing deepened students' critical perceptions. The class discussion sharpened analytical questions about who gets to define *beauty* and how judgments about physical appearances in U.S. society may be shaped by commercially driven aims and conformist values. The culminating works of art created by the students communicated many messages that stemmed from their understanding of oppression and resistance based on discussions throughout the unit. Students used layers of collage, glue, papers, paint, and oil pastel to express academic research, scientific and mathematical skills, poetic insights, and socially active engagement with their multiple and inclusive definitions of family.

A Family Celebration As a culminating event, a celebration of the students' accomplishments and a demonstration of their knowledge was held, and every student on the team invited their families to school for the event. A huge art and text display was mounted wherein each student exhibited a collaged frame of three items: a self-portrait, a family portrait, and an "I am From" poem. Every social studies essay, mathematical graph, and scientific research project was on display. Parents, grandparents, caregivers, guardians, and siblings listened intently as students read poetry and excerpts of essays. Many family members who had never before entered the school building attended the event. Students grabbed the hands of loved ones to escort them to each exhibit. The teachers noticed how students proudly "showed off" their work to their visitors, but on a surprising note, many students were eager to point out the work of their classmates as well. Teachers overheard students telling the stories of their peers' families and how they related to the research assignments.

The most popular display was the dessert table; every family had contributed a favorite family dessert! Excited students urged peers and teachers to taste the snacks such as Jalissa's grandmother's flan or Ari's uncle's favorite chocolate-chip concoction. After the families and children went home and the last paper plates were cleaned up, teachers reported a feeling of transformation precipitated by the Family Dessert and Demonstration Day that closed the unit. Teachers described knowing their students more deeply and intimately.

Students wrote self-assessments of their work and told of making connections with teachers and peers in unexpected ways, "wanting to work [their] hardest," and feeling that the project was "awesome". The sense of accomplishment and community bond among the team of teachers and students continued to grow throughout the school year. Teachers talked about their growing knowledge about oppression and resistance as well as their expanding definitions of family, and students and teachers cultivated an enduring sense of belonging.

Curricular change in high school literature

This portion of the case presents another example for multicultural changes in the curriculum. The deliberate anti-bias work that we saw in the first grade and middle school unit on family paves the way for students to engage in inclusive high school curriculum. The following example is the curriculum for a high school English literature course called *Gay and Lesbian Literature*.[28]

The course was conceived and designed by an English teacher, Ms. Sara Barber-Just. Initially, it was Ms. Barber-Just's research, creativity, and commitment to education for social justice—backed by a supportive department chair, principal, and superintendent—that brought the curriculum to the classroom. Eventually the English department at the high school and the school board approved this course as an integral part of the school curriculum.

Imagining Possibilities   Ms. Barber-Just was teaching in the English department of a high school that offered a range of familiar high school litera-

ture courses such as Foundations of American Literature, Masterpieces of Ancient and Medieval Worlds, and Masterpieces of the Renaissance and Modern Worlds as well as more assertively multicultural courses such as Women in Literature and African American Literature. Teachers in the department had developed these courses over the years and they had become integrated into the school's course offerings. Ms. Barber-Just imagined that the models in place for the African American Literature and Women in Literature courses could be applied to a course called *Gay and Lesbian Literature*. Both of the former courses dealt with identity issues, and the African American Literature course was organized chronologically by historical time periods.

Ms. Barber-Just developed a proposal for a course combining a wealth of research from her graduate studies and her experiences with the department's curriculum. Her research portfolio reflected an extensive review of gay and lesbian literature with a theoretical grounding in social justice education. In planning the Gay and Lesbian Literature course, she used a course structure that paralleled those of the two courses that were already offered, focusing on group-specific content from a social justice perspective. Her course mirrored the high academic standards within the department, with expectations for students to read thoroughly and critically, write expressively and analytically, and discuss the work passionately and fairly. The following is an excerpt from the proposal she wrote, which became part of the course description:

> Students in public schools have been reading literary classics by gay, lesbian, and bisexual authors for more than a century; however, gay authors' lives are often concealed rather than rightfully explored. This course closely examines the struggles and triumphs of these artists—as well as the historical periods during which they wrote—allowing readers to more deeply analyze their diverse literary contributions. *Gay and Lesbian Literature* is split into five major sections, moving in chronological order from the early 1900s to the 1990s. Class readings include works written by gay and lesbian authors during eras of severe legal and social oppression; conformity and self-loathing; anger, activism, and radicalism; and, finally, pride and acceptance. The course

Snapshot

Eugene Crocket

Usually I think of my family as an adoptive family more than a gay family.

Eugene Crocket,[1] a soft-spoken Irish American ninth grader, carries himself in a poised manner that commands respect. He has a slight build and longish brown hair that falls into his eyes, which become animated and sparkle as he speaks. Eugene grew up in the rural New England community of Hilton and attends a regional high school in nearby Howardstown, with students from a variety of backgrounds. Eugene spoke at length about his best friend, a Tibetan student, and described how they are both active in an after-school club, Students for a Free Tibet.[2] In this snapshot, Eugene focuses on his experience of being adopted and raised by two gay dads.

There are six people in my family. I have three brothers and two dads. [Both dads are European American]. One of my dads, Tom, lives in Puerto Rico right now and sells real estate. My other dad, Ted, cleans houses. I call Tom *Dad* and Ted *Poppy,* like *Pop* but *Poppy.*

I am the youngest in the family. My oldest brother Ronnie is 21. Then there's Michael. He's 19. Mark, he's 17, and I'm 15. Ronnie lives in Howardstown and has his own apartment. Michael is getting his own apartment soon. Mark is going away to college, so pretty soon it's going to be just me at home. Ronnie and Mark are more into sports, but me and Michael like to play video games more.

Most people, if they look at my family, they might think it's weird or something. They might think it's odd because it's not the so-called ordinary family. Personally, I don't see being in my family as too much different, because it's my family and I've known them my whole life. It's just regular to me, being in my family.

All four of my brothers are biological brothers. My dads adopted all of us at the same time. I was six months old, and the others were three years old, four, and six. Ronnie probably remembers it most. Basically, our parents were getting into drugs, and not able to take care of us. My oldest brother Ronnie was pretty much, like, he would feed me the bottle and change my diaper and stuff. My parents just weren't able to take care of us. I'm not really sure if they sought the adoption agency, or if they were reported by a neighbor or something. We were foster kids and then we got adopted. There was a whole controversial thing in the community, because my dads were in the newspaper a lot. They had to argue for being two gay men to get us. I guess they got threatened sometimes. I know they were in the newspaper a lot. This was in the early 1990s.

These days, I'm pretty comfortable talking about it. Not too many people ask, but my close friends pretty much already know about my two dads. I've told them why we were adopted. If I make friends with someone, and they get to know my family, then they might ask questions.

When I was around the age of 11 or 12, I would notice people looking at us. They could probably put together what our family is, like, "Huh, look at that." I felt different, and I didn't like it. Now if that happens, I don't really care.

(continued)

Usually I think of my family as an adoptive family more than a gay family. In Hilton, there were three adoptive families in my grade, including me. I did feel different, because the three of us were adopted, but I was the only one that had two dads. I didn't really mind that people knew I was adopted and stuff. But sometimes it was a little awkward telling them about my parents. So I felt different, and I didn't like having both my parents come to school. I wasn't ashamed, but more embarrassed. I don't know, I didn't want people to think of me as different. Now, my dad Tom, he lives in Puerto Rico, and Ted, he's not really involved with school or the PTA or whatever. Usually Ted is the one who goes to parent night. I know one other kid at my school now who has two moms, and I know this other girl who was adopted who also has lesbian moms.

At home everything is normal, like everyone else's family. Going out in public is a little more different. I was going to have a class get-together one time, in seventh grade. I wanted to have a bunch of friends over, but I was, like, "How about not at my house, guys," just because I didn't want them to see pictures or something. The sense of stress was only for that moment, so I just kept it to myself. If we're ever talking about family, I usually just say "my dad," rather than "my dads." Usually I try to get to know people well before I tell them that I have two dads, so I already know what their opinions are, and stuff. I have to be pretty sure I can trust them before I can tell them. I did have one friend who was Christian. I used to be better friends with him, but now I'm not as good friends with him. I made sure not to tell him, because of the Bible and all that. I don't know what he would have done, so I thought it best not to tell him.

At my high school, there's lots of using the word *gay* and the f-a-g word, like, "That's so gay." They don't actually mean it, but it's become like an insult or something. So homophobia isn't that bad in our school. It doesn't make me too uncomfortable, but it bothers me a little bit, though. If I know the person saying it, I might say something. It matters who says it.

At our school, we have a gay and lesbian literature class. We also have a Gay-Straight Alliance.[3] I think it's a good idea. I know some people in it. People might assume you were gay or lesbian if you joined it. I don't really know what the GSA does. It has maybe ten people in it, maybe more.

One time in Spanish class, we were doing the family words. My teacher was asking everyone about their mother and their father, and I didn't want to get called on. I didn't want her to be, like, "Oh, what does your mom do?" "I don't have a mom, I don't know." I didn't get called on; I lucked out. I probably would have just said, "I don't have a mom." Another time in high school, we had to do a family tree. The teacher said we didn't have to do our parents, we could do our grandparents and our aunts and stuff. I only put in one of my parents. But in fourth grade, when we had to do a family tree, I did put in both my dads. I always felt more comfortable in elementary school. We were doing the family tree on our heritage, and I did it based on my adoptive parents, because they're the parents that I know.

Being in this family, I have learned to, if I see someone who is different, to not think of them as odd or weird, but to accept people for who they are. I try not to make stereotypes, like not ask people about their mom's name and their dad's name, because I know that not everyone has a mom and a dad. Stuff like that. If I have to fill out a form at school and it says "mother's name," I just cross that out and write "father's name." I haven't ever seen a teacher react to that.

My sixth grade teacher, Ms. Kamp, she really helped me a lot. She made me more comfortable. I was really shy and she made me a lot more comfortable speaking to groups. Academically, I got better. If we had a topic like this, she would ask me if I felt comfortable with it, like if we talked about gay/lesbian stuff. She would ask me in private—like when people were talking, she would come over and whisper it to me. She was also my neighbor.

Commentary

Eugene's snapshot raises the issue of how children of gay and lesbian parents must negotiate "outing" themselves—and their parents—as members of families headed by gay parents. Even in liberal Howardstown, with its GSA and gay and lesbian literature class, issues of homophobia and limited understanding of what makes a family arise in school, causing students like Eugene to feel uncomfortable, if not unsafe. At the same time, Eugene reported feeling particularly supported by one teacher, Ms. Kamp, who perhaps knew him better than most, since she was also his neighbor in their small town.

As one of four brothers who were all adopted as a sibling group, Eugene benefited from built-in emotional support at home. Other adopted children may feel more isolated, particularly if they are the only adopted child in their family. Even with his family support and his relatively tolerant school environment, Eugene's anecdotes about offensive put-downs and questions from insensitive teachers and classmates sharpens the discussion of homophobia in schools. Teachers can do a better job of monitoring the school environment for offensive language that sets students apart. They can take care to incorporate flexibility, openness, and inclusivity in their approaches to both the pedagogy and curriculum.

Finally, Eugene's participation in the Tibetan club underscores the importance of choice. Whereas, concerned adults might assume that students like Eugene would be better served by joining the Gay-Straight Alliance or even a group specifically for children of gay/lesbian parents,[4] in this case, Eugene took comfort in his close friendship with a Tibetan student and preferred to join Students for a Free Tibet as one of only two white students in the group. Perhaps as he progresses through high school, Eugene may be drawn to GSA or another student group. The important note for school officials is making certain that schools provide a variety of outlets that address diverse student interests and various comfort levels.

Notes

1. We appreciate the work of our friend and colleague Dr. John Raible, who interviewed Eugene and developed the introduction and commentary for the snapshot.
2. Students for a Free Tibet is an international organization on college and high school campuses committed to nonviolent direct action in solidarity with the Tibetan people. For more information go to www.studentsforafreetibet.org/

(continued)

3. The Gay-Straight Alliance Network provides resources and information on how to start a Gay-Straight Alliance in your school or community group at www.gsanetwork.org/index.html
4. One such group for children of gay/lesbian parents is GLSEN (Gay, Lesbian, Straight Education Network).

focuses on renowned modern and contemporary American authors such as Willa Cather, James Baldwin, Rita Mae Brown, and Michael Cunningham, and concludes with an examination of Sri Lankan author Shyam Selvadurai and a study of short stories from around the world. Each unit includes a combination of critical essays, poetry, short story, and/or film, providing a rich cultural and historical context for the featured literature.[29]

Sara Barber-Just explained that for purposes of this course, she would base the definition of *gay and lesbian literature* on two criteria: (1) literature written by LBGT people and (2) literature including gay themes in the content. (A list of some texts, films, and websites from the course is included in the resource section at the end of this chapter section.)

With several caveats, the curriculum director and the principal quietly agreed to offer this course during the pilot model. It would be offered for independent study credit only. Students could sign up for the course if their schedules allowed and they would acquire credit for it, but the credit would not count toward the English credits required to graduate. To teach the course, Ms. Barber-Just would need to fit it into her free period and continue to carry a regular English teacher's course load. She would not earn any additional pay. That is how the course was offered during its first term. As a matter of fact, Ms. Barber-Just dropped her teaching contract down to less than fulltime to make space for the Gay and Lesbian Literature course in her schedule. She was teaching the same amount of courses and numbers of students for less pay.

Student Requests and Requirements Word spread like wildfire among the student body about the new Gay and Lesbian Literature course, and the class quickly filled up, with a waiting list of students eager to take the course. During the first term that the course was offered, the students were excited and engaged in the work. They began to question why they were not gaining English department credit for the rigorous academic work. By the second term that the course was offered, the students urged Ms. Barber-Just to appeal for English credit on their behalf. It did not seem fair to them that they were reading five major novels, producing high-level writing, attending all the classes, and yet not being awarded department credit. After reviewing the syllabus and the impressive academic accomplishments of the students in the class, the English department voted unanimously to award English department credit for the course.

A vote by the school board was needed to add a new class to the program of studies. Ms. Barber-Just compiled portfolios of student work to be reviewed by the school board. The student portfolios included analytical and reflective writing about the five major units of study and the accompanying five books, short stories, poetry, essays, films, and course discussions. The board approved the addition of the course to the official English department's study program.

Student Voices The literary products in the student portfolios were superior by many standards. The knowledge of historical events, social influences on literature, and writing techniques that they reflected were remarkable. But the most compelling facet of the students' work was the consistency with which they mentioned the power of giving voice to unspoken realities. Students wrote about their own biases and their own sexual orientations: gay, straight, and bisexual. They reflected on the importance of this course to support LGBT and questioning youth and build understanding among heterosexual teens. They spoke of lack of

Resources for Teaching about Expanding Definitions of Family

These resources are divided into three categories: early childhood, middle school, and high school.

Children's Literature Resources for Early Childhood*

Combs, Bobbie, *ABC: A Family Alphabet Book* (Ridley Park, PA: Two Lives, 2001).

de Haan, Lisa, *King and King* (Berkeley, CA: Tricycle Press, 2002).

Elwin, Rosamund, and Michele Plause, *Asha's Mums* (London, England: Women's Press, 2000).

Garden, Nancy, *Molly's Family* (New York: Farrar, Straus and Giroux, 2004).

Hoffman, Eric, *Best Colors/Los Mejores Colores* (St. Paul, MN: Redleaf Press, 1999).

Newman, Leslea, *Felicia's Favorite Story* (Ridley Park, PA: Two Lives, 2002).

Newman, Leslea, and Diana Souza, *Heather Has Two Mommies* (Boston: Alyson Publications, 2000).

Parr, Todd, *The Family Book* (New York: Little, Brown Young Readers, 2003).

Richardson, Justin, and Peter Parnell, *And Tango Makes Three* (New York: Simon & Schuster, 2005).

Setterington, Ken, *Mom and Mum Are Getting Married* (Toronto, Canada: Second Story Press, 2004).

Simon, Norma, *All Families Are Special* (Morton Grove, IL: Albert Whitman, 2003).

Skutch, Robert, *Who's in a Family?* (Berkeley, CA: Tricycle Press, 1997).

Valentine, Johnny, *The Duke Who Outlawed Jelly Beans and Other Stories* (Boston: Alyson Publication, 2004).

Wickens, Elaine, *Anna Day and the O-Ring* (Boston: Alyson Publications, 1994).

*Special thanks to Nancy Alach from Cambridge Friends School in Cambridge, MA, for this suggested bibliography of children's literature.

Resources Used in the Middle School Curriculum

Beard, Jean J., Peggy Gillespie, Kay Redfield Jamison, Kenneth, Duckworth, and Gigi Kaeser, *Nothing to Hide: Mental Illness in the Family* (New York: New Press, 2002).

Gillespie, Peggy, and Gigi Kaeser, *Of Many Colors: Portraits of Multiracial Families* (Amherst: University of Massachusetts Press, 1997).

Kaeser, Gigi, and Peggy Gillespie, *Love Makes a Family: Portraits of Lesbian, Gay, Bisexual and Transgender Parents and Their Families* (Amherst: University of Massachusetts Press, 1999).

Kaeser, Gigi, and Peggy Gillespie, *In Our Family: Portraits of all Kinds of Families* (with Curriculum Guide). (Amherst, MA: Family Diversity Projects, 2003).

Rohmer, Harriet, ed., *Honoring Our Ancestors: Stories and Pictures by Fourteen Artists* (San Francisco: Children's Book Press, 1999).

Rohmer, Harriet, ed., *Just Like Me: Stories and Self-Portraits by Fourteen Artists* (San Francisco: Children's Book Press, 1997).

(continued)

Film and Literature Resources Used in the High School Gay and Lesbian Literature Course

Baldwin, James, *Giovanni's Room* (New York: Dial, 1956).

Brown, Rita Mae, *Rubyfruit Jungle* (Plainfield, VT: Daughters Inc., 1973).

Cather, Willa, *A Lost Lady* (New York: Alfred A. Knopf, 1923).

Cunningham, Michael, *The Hours* (New York: Farrar, Straus and Giroux, 1998).

Far from Heaven, Dir. Todd Haynes, 2002.

Forster, E. M., *Maurice* (New York: Norton, 1971).

Ma Vie en Rose, Dir. Alain Berliner, 1997.

Shyam Selvadurai, *Funny Boy* (Harvest Books, 1997).

The Celluloid Closet, Dir. Rob Epstein and Jeffrey Friedman, 1995.

The Trial of Oscar Wilde, Dir. Ken Hughes, 1960.

Woolf, Virginia, *Mrs. Dalloway* (Richmond, England: Hogarth Press, 1925).

information about the LGBT community and critiqued the misinformation of the mass media. Consistently, student reflections mentioned the safety of their classroom community and their commitment to be engaged in social justice. In some of the most moving pieces, students wrote their reflections in the form of letters to their parents.

Evolution of curriculum

Multicultural curriculum is a process, as we described in Chapter 8; it grows organically along with the needs and struggles of the community. This is true of the Gay and Lesbian Literature course launched by Ms. Barber-Just. In response to student demands, the school added an extra section of the course each year. Moreover, advanced placement recognition (AP credit) may now be achieved through the Gay and Lesbian Literature course. What started out as an independent study offering became socially sanctioned knowledge—a school course—as English department credit, and optional AP credit, through the determination of high school students and the courage of a teacher.

One teacher and her students could not have made these changes in isolation, however. As Christine Sleeter points out, "While teachers have varying degrees of agency to construct multicultural curriculum, teachers also work in systems that institutionalize particular concepts of curriculum, learning, teaching and relationships."[30] While maintaining

high academic standards, a stalwart department chair, a supportive principal, and ultimately a visionary school board recognized the needs of a community and acted with resolve to reshape the school curriculum, which continues to become more just and inclusive.

The Gay and Lesbian Literature course reflects the needs and identities of students and families in the immediate community of the school, including LGBT and their straight allies. Perhaps more significantly, the curriculum is responding to the urgency of nation-wide social change. Melinda Miceli's statement affirms this reality: "Today, LGBT and straight ally students are in a position to imagine the possibilities of change that they can accomplish by capitalizing on the progress made by the gay rights movement."[31] The "imagined possibilities of change" accomplished by Sara Barber-Just with so many students, families, colleagues, administrators, and school board members provides a model of fierce hopefulness in the ongoing process of making school curriculum—and society—more changeable.

To Think About

1. What is the difference between discussing the facts and descriptions of current events in the classroom and cultivating a critical perspective on the power structures that surround current events? Consider these two approaches in

the context of a current event in the news this week.

2. When you hear a student use the word *gay* as a put down (or pejorative term sometimes invoked to insult LGBT identity), what is your response? What does that student learn from your response? What do other students learn from your response? How can you make it a teachable moment about vocabulary, human rights, and courage?

3. Many school structures that divide students by so-called ability appear to be impenetrable to a single teacher's efforts. If such structures are in place in your school, how can you adapt your curriculum to challenge those structures? Do you have to do it alone? What will be the long-term effects of the changes you make to your approach, your classroom, and your curriculum?

4. When students name racism that they see in society, mass media, curricular materials, or the school hallways, how do you respond? How can you affirm and make student voices audible while cultivating a classroom discussion around social justice in which all students feel welcome to participate?

5. Do you call on families to participate in the curriculum? When does it happen? Is it around holiday celebrations? Heritage festivals? How can you expand the role of families in your classroom while including and honoring the families who may not be able to participate in school activities?

Activities for Personal, School, and Community Change

1. Study the demographics of your classroom, your grade level, your team, or your school. Think about students' heritages and cultural backgrounds. Take note of a specific group about which you may have little knowledge or experience and commit to implementing some curriculum about it. How might you create a unit of study to deepen the understanding of this group's experience? How can you do this in such a way that does not "exoticize" the group or create greater isolation for the members of that group? The teachers of the unit

about Cambodia started by educating themselves; they also realized that they would learn more by diving in, researching, and teaching with their students. Where will you begin in your own classroom? Draw in colleagues for support, co-teaching, content integration, and expansion of this idea.

2. Many teachers are challenged by the notion of implementing multicultural curriculum in the current standards-based climate. Start a teacher book-discussion group based on Christine Sleeter's book *Un-Standardizing Curriculum: Multicultural Teaching in the Standards-Based Classroom* (see note 18). Ask your principal, superintendent, curriculum director or PTO to purchase the books. Meet at least once a month throughout the school year with the end goal of each teacher designing a new unit, or redesigning a former curriculum unit with their fresh ideas inspired by Sleeter's practical, yet revolutionary approach.

3. LGBT identity continues to be a target of institutional and personal oppression. Collaborate with colleagues to make your school a "safe zone" for LGBT students and their families. Collect resources from GLSEN and PFLAG (see appendix) and create an action plan in your school for students to feel affirmed and protected. Educate yourself, colleagues, students, and administrators. Plan curriculum and community events to welcome, affirm and express solidarity with LGBT students, family and communities members.

Companion Website

For access to additional case studies, weblinks, concept cards, and other material related to this chapter, visit the text's companion website at **www.ablongman.com/nieto5e.**

Notes to Chapter 13

1. We would like to thank the teachers of Amherst Regional Middle School, Amherst, Massachusetts: Margarita Bonifaz, Sarah Lange Hayes, Gale Kuhn, Lynn Podesek, Sokhen P. Mao, Paul Plummer, and Maura Neverson, whose work and dedication made this unit of study about

Cambodia a success for all of their students. Patty also worked on this curriculum team as the art teacher.

2. Ronnie J. Booxbaum, PhD, and Sokhen P. Mao, MEd, developed this staff development course and wrote a handbook to accompany it.

3. Loung Ung, *First They Killed My Father* (New York: HarperCollins, 2000).

4. See Luong Ung, *Lucky Child: A Daughter of Cambodia Reunites with the Sister She Left Behind* (New York: HarperCollins, 2000) and Molyda Szymusiak, Jane Hamilton-Merritt (translator), and Linda Coverdale, *The Stones Cry Out: A Cambodian Childhood*, 1975–1980 (Bloomington: Indiana University Press, 1999).

5. Grant Wiggins and Jay McTighe, *Understanding by Design*, 2nd ed. (Alexandria, VA: Association for Supervision and Curriculum Development (ASCD), 2005).

6. Bill Bigelow, Brenda Harvey, Stan Karp, and Larry Miller, eds., *Rethinking Our Classrooms: Teaching for Equity and Justice*, vol. 2 (Milwaukee, WI: Rethinking Schools, 2001).

7. The Cambodian Masters Program supports revival of the traditional art forms of Cambodia and inspires contemporary artistic expression. They have visiting artists, lecturers, and performances. Available at: www.cambodianmasters.org/masters/index.htm

8. The Angkor Dance Troupe helps Cambodian young people navigate the balance between contemporary youth culture and their cultural heritage. See www.angkordance.org

9. *Monkey Dance* is a documentary film by Julie Mallozzi about three teens coming of age in Lowell, Massachusetts. See www.monkey-dance.com/ and www.juliemallozzi.com/monkey.html

10. The Peace Pagoda Nipponzan Myohoji Sangha Buddhist temple was created as a collaborative effort by Vietnam Veterans Against the War and the Cambodian American Community. See www.peacepagoda.org

11. See the Resources for Teaching About Cambodia at the end of this case study, which includes many of the folktales that Margarita Bonifaz used in this unit.

12. Peter Menzel, Charles C. Mann, and Paul Kennedy, *Material World: A Global Family Portrait* (San Francisco: Sierra Club Books, 1995).

13. We are grateful to Michael Hayes for being so generous with his time to help us create this case study. Michael recently left the classroom and became a co-principal at Amherst Regional Middle School, Amherst, Massachusetts.

14. See National Council of Teachers of Mathematics (NCTM) at www.nctm.org. Also see Jeannie Oakes, *Keeping Track: How Schools Structure Inequality*, 2nd ed. (New Haven, CT: Yale University Press, 2005).

15. Robert Moses and Charles Cobb, *Radical Equations: Civil Rights from Mississippi to the Algebra Project* (Boston: Beacon Press, 2002).

16. We are grateful for Alan Dallmann's role in the transformation of this curriculum and in this case study.

17. We are grateful to Blanca Zelaya for her critical role in the math curriculum and the development of this case study.

18. Bobbie Combs and Dannamarie Hosler, illus., *1,2,3: A Family Counting Book* (Ridley Park, PA: Two Lives, 2001).

19. Leslea Newman and Diana Souza, Illustrator, *Heather Has Two Mommies* (Boston: Alyson, 2000).

20. GLSEN (Gay, Lesbian, Straight Education Network) is a national organization working to end anti-gay biases in schools. The group is striving to assure that each member of every school community is valued and respected regardless of sexual orientation or gender idetity/expression. GLSEN's website (www.glsen.org) has innumerable resources for teachers of students of all ages.

21. Ellen Bigler, *American Conversations: Puerto Ricans, White Ethnics and Multicultural Education* (Philadelphia: Temple University Press, 1999).

22. Louise Derman-Sparks, *Teaching/Learning Anti-Racism: A Developmental Approach* (New York: Teachers College Press, 1997).

23. Val Penniman and Debbie Shumway's "Calendar-Connections," which helps teach critical thinking in a classroom curriculum, may be found at www.calendar-connections.com

24. Harriet Rohmer, ed., *Honoring Our Ancestors: Stories and Pictures by Fourteen Artists* (San Francisco: Children's Book Press, 1999).

25. Family Diversity Projects is a nonprofit organization co-founded by Peggy Gillespie and Gigi Kaeser. It produces and circulates photo-text ex-

hibits to educate people about the many facets of diversity. The exhibits tour nationally and internationally. See www.familydiv.org

26. We are grateful to the teachers who developed this curriculum and gave it their heartfelt attentions for three years at Amherst Regional Middle School. They are Beth Adel Wohlleb, social studies teacher; Phil Covelli and Gale Kuhn, science teachers; Mari Hall, health teacher; Esther Haskell, English teacher; and Robert Lord, math teacher. Dr. John Raible worked as a consultant on the curriculum. Patty worked as an art teacher with the team. Also, Kristen French provided feedback with a critical multicultural perspective for the unit.

27. Linda Christensen, *Reading, Writing and Rising Up* (Milwaukee: Rethinking Schools, 2000).

28. We are grateful to Sara Barber-Just for her inspiring contributions to the field of high school English language arts teaching, and for the time she spent helping us to develop this case study.

29. Sara Barber-Just, "Curriculum Proposal for Amherst Regional High School" 2001.

30. Sleeter, *Un-Standardizing Curriculum: Multicultural Teaching in the Standards-Based Classroom,* 179.

31. Melinda Miceli, *Standing Out, Standing Together: The Social and Political Impact of Gay-Straight Alliances* (New York: Routledge, 2005): 12.

CHAPTER 14

Pluralism in Schools: The Promise of Multicultural Education

> 66 Learning to read was, for slaves, not an immediate passport to freedom but rather a way of gaining access to one of the powerful instruments of their oppressors: the book. 99

Alberto Manguel (1948–)

Learning and schooling are critical for every person in any society. The future of our diverse society will depend on how schools educate the coming generations, and pluralism must be a significant factor in that education. During an interview for a college administrative position, an African American candidate asked about his views on diversity responded, "First, let me say that I'm a pluralist. After all, we had a diverse society when we had slaves." This is an important distinction. Many people refer to *diversity* and *pluralism* as if the two terms were synonymous, but **diversity** simply describes the existence of many different groups of people within a society, whereas **pluralism** describes a society in which diversity is accepted and supported. A pluralistic society is one in which diverse groups function together effectively with mutual respect. In a society that is diverse but not pluralistic, schools tend to teach principally about the dominant group—its influence on the evolution of society, and its literature, art, and music. In a diverse society committed to pluralism, schools would teach about all groups within the society, from most ancient to most recent.

Misunderstanding of terms occurs when we fail to clarify meanings and intentions. No study of human differences is complete without special terms, and precise communication exists only when everyone involved is clear about their meaning. So we must begin by clarifying our definition of multicultural education and explaining our vision of its importance for the future of our diverse society.

Defining Multicultural Education

Multicultural education is based on a commitment to pluralism; its guiding purpose is to prepare students to be active participants in a diverse, democratic society. There is confusion and considerable debate about multicultural education, even among educators who advocate for it. Some people regard multicultural education simply as the process of integrating issues and information about race and ethnicity into school curricula, but that describes what Banks (2006) defines as **multiethnic education.** In a study cited by Gayle-Evans and Michael (2006), some teachers regarded multicultural education as a curriculum for teaching about cultures around the world, but that is usually called **global (or international) education.** Others say multicultural education includes recognition of women, gays and lesbians, people with disabilities, and other minority groups; opponents to this idea argue that such groups do not constitute distinct cultures and therefore should not be included. This confusion raises many questions that must be answered before we can understand what multicultural education is and recognize schools that are engaged in an authentic form of this educational approach.

In addition to conflicting opinions about the definition of the term *multicultural education* and about who should be included, there are numerous perceptions about who benefits from it. Americans seem to agree that students of color benefit from multicultural education, especially in urban multiracial and multiethnic classrooms; yet many educators and parents in suburban or rural school districts consisting predominantly or exclusively of white students appear to believe that multicultural education provides no benefits. Gayle-Evans and Michael (2006) review several studies reporting that many teachers were uncomfortable incorporating multicultural issues into their content because they felt that the topics were "too sensitive"; educators also said they did not feel that their teacher education programs adequately prepared them to implement multicultural education practices. Some educators in elementary and secondary schools with predominantly white students have included the contributions of a few people of color into their curriculum, but such an addition does not represent an education that is genuinely multicultural.

What does it mean for education to be called *multicultural*?

As early as 1974, Hilliard wrote that **multicultural** refers to a society "made up of a number of cultural groups based upon race, ethnicity, religion, language, nationality, income, etc." (p. 41). Because income level is not usually regarded as representing a different culture—rich or poor, we're all Americans—Hilliard's comment is assumed to mean that the term *multicultural* includes other subordinate groups that he did not specifically identify, such as women, gays and lesbians, and people with disabilities.

As for the term *education,* we must distinguish between *education* and *training.* Some dictionaries suggest that education and training are synonyms,

but people take classes to train them in a particular skill. A person can be trained to drive or cook, or even be trained to train a dog. Education is a broader concept. Partridge (1983) explained that *educate* derives from the Latin word *ducere,* which means to lead; "educere" means to lead out or bring forth (p. 169). By extrapolation, *education* means to bring forth the potential of an individual. In addition to developing cognitive skill and affective sensitivity, education entails developing an understanding of previous achievements in subjects such as history, literature, and science as a basis for making individual and societal choices in the future. Carse (1986) distinguished education from training:

> Education discovers an increasing richness in the past because it sees what is unfinished there. Training regards the past as finished and the future to be finished. Education leads toward a continuing self-discovery; training leads toward a final self-definition. (p. 23)

Multicultural education integrates information about past issues with achievements of diverse groups to describe how they have influenced our society. Children and youth from all groups are thereby provided with a sense of belonging to our society by understanding how their group has helped to shape what it is and by appreciating the potential they have for influencing what it will become.

What is an appropriate definition for multicultural education?

Multicultural education is a journey that leads students to self-discovery and to a sense of personal efficacy. Nieto (2008) provides a comprehensive definition and description of multicultural education that includes the components to be addressed in this chapter:

> **Multicultural education** is a process of comprehensive school reform and basic education for all students. It challenges and rejects racism and other forms of discrimination in schools and society and accepts and affirms the pluralism (ethnic, racial, linguistic, religious, economic, and gender, among others) that students, their communities, and teachers reflect. Multicultural education permeates the

FIGURE 14.1 Frank and Ernest

Frank and Ernest

© 1998 Thaves / Reprinted with permission. Newspaper dist. by NEA, Inc.

schools' curriculum and instructional strategies, as well as the interactions among teachers, students, and families, and the very way that schools conceptualize the nature of teaching and learning. Because it uses critical pedagogy as its underlying philosophy . . . multicultural education promotes democratic principles of social justice. (p. 44)

Nieto's definition and description of multicultural education emphasizes that it is not a "business-as-usual" approach to schooling. It requires changes in teaching methods and perspectives on learning because of critical philosophical differences between traditional education and multicultural education.

Traditional Assumptions in American Education

The development of American schools has been based on a conservative philosophy that was eventually labeled *essentialism,* and essentialist assumptions are still in place. The term stems from the belief that an essential body of knowledge and essential human values that have stood the test of time can be identified and transmitted to students. Essentialists describe the purpose of schools as the transmission of the most significant accumulated knowledge and values from previous generations to the coming generation.

What body of knowledge have essentialists identified?

Essentialist scholars maintain that knowledge from four disciplines is essential: social studies, science, mathematics, and English language and literature; therefore these four subjects are emphasized in elementary, middle, and high school. Graduation requirements for high school students usually include a minimum of two years of course work, often three or even four, in social studies, science, mathematics, and English. To essentialists, subjects such as art, music, and physical education are accepted principally to make school more enjoyable, but they are regarded as additional rather than essential. When administrators consider budget reductions, programs in art, music, and physical education are scrutinized and are most likely to be reduced or eliminated. Similar assumptions continue into college, where general education programs often require students to choose among a selection of courses in social studies, science, math, and English literature and composition.

What essential human values do schools teach?

As indicated in Chapter 1, Myrdal (1944) identified core American values embraced by most citizens and taught in most schools. In addition, Americans presume that certain values represent the American middle class: promptness, honesty, hard work, competitiveness, and efficiency. Teachers implement traditional approaches to teaching values (see Chapter 1) to convince children and youth that the core values are worthwhile and should be adopted. Students may say they believe in these values because it's expected of them, even though their behavior often does not suggest that they have a genuine commitment to them.

How do essentialists define or describe learning?

Essentialists define learning as the acquisition of essential knowledge and values. Metaphors used by essentialists to describe learning portray knowledge as water and students as empty vessels to be filled or as sponges ready to absorb. To assess learning, essentialists favor objective tests with questions about factual information to ascertain if students absorbed

> Teachers open the door, but you must enter by yourself.
>
> **Chinese Proverb**

the information. (If not, teachers may review the information and test students again.) In extreme cases, students may repeat a grade to have a second chance to learn material in the hope that the teacher, perhaps a different teacher, will be more successful helping them acquire the information. Maturity and readiness are considered secondary in this process.

What is the role of the essentialist teacher in helping students learn?

An essentialist teacher is supposed to be a skillful transmitter of information and an advocate for American values. Teachers are expected to be role models for our society's values—both inside and outside the classroom. As transmitters of information, teachers are expected to use technology to make information interesting and thereby promote

acquisition of knowledge. Although teachers may select from a variety of pedagogical techniques, the goal is to motivate students to remember information provided in textbooks, lectures, and media. The problem is that few students can demonstrate that they are learning what teachers are teaching.

Why are students not learning in essentialist schools?

The first problem has to do with what has been considered essential. During the past several decades, research in various fields, especially the sciences, has generated what scholars have called a *knowledge explosion*. Given so much new knowledge, how is one to determine which facts are most important? Feminists and scholars of color have developed alternative interpretations of historical events that challenge conventional views; they believe their perspectives should be included in school curricula. Whereas women and writers of color were minimally represented in previous literature anthologies, advocates are increasingly demanding that their voices and ideas be acknowledged. Curriculum reformers suggest that most students regard traditional essentialist curriculum as inaccurate, irrelevant, and not at all motivational.

Another problem is that we know students learn at different rates. If teachers transmit information at the same rate, some students learn all of it, some learn most of it, and some retain very little of it; yet teachers often must proceed as if all students learned equally. The solution essentialists have developed to address incomplete learning is to group students according to ability, which is known as *tracking*. Studies of tracking have found that excellent students learn just as well in heterogeneous groups as in homogeneous groups where they are grouped by ability, but that the achievement of moderate and slow learners improves significantly when they are in mixed groups rather than when they are grouped according to academic ability (Kershaw, 1992; Oakes, 2005; Oakes & Wells, 1996; Oakes et al., 2000). Despite these consistent research conclusions, essentialist schools tend to continue to group students according to ability.

Perhaps the most significant obstacle to learning in essentialist schools is the problem of retention and transfer. **Retention** refers to student recall of knowledge; **transfer** is the ability of students to apply that knowledge both inside and outside the classroom. Students have long complained about cramming before taking exams that require them to memorize material. Studies have consistently found that when tested for retention of information, students tend to recall no more than 20% of what they had supposedly learned the first time they took the exam.

Assumptions of Multicultural Education

To resolve problems related to student learning, as parents or educators, we must change our assumptions about curriculum content, learning, teaching, and the purpose of schools. As described by Nieto (2008), Banks (2008), Sleeter (1996), and others, multicultural education challenges us to change those assumptions.

What assumptions do multicultural educators make about curriculum?

Nieto's widely accepted definition of multicultural education includes an affirmation of diversity that must permeate the curriculum to provide honest representations of diversity in American society. At present, textbooks continue to be dominated by the art, music, history, literature, perspectives, and images of white Americans. Sleeter and Grant (2003) reviewed forty-seven textbooks in social studies, reading, language arts, science, and mathematics for elementary and middle-level students. They reported that whites were featured predominantly in all of them. Although some improvements have been found in more recent textbooks, when people of color are included, the textbooks typically have provided:

> A sketchy account of Black history and little sense of contemporary Black life. Asian Americans appear mainly as figures on the landscape with virtually no history or contemporary ethnic experience. . . . Native Americans appear mainly as historical figures. (p. 22)

American elementary, middle, and secondary textbooks also tend to omit or provide only minimal representation of other groups: women, gays and lesbians, people with disabilities, and low-income families. School textbooks not only represent a problem for minority children but also are apt to teach white children a dishonest perspective of their society. As Baker (1994) explained, "Non-minority children are led to believe that their behavior, the ways they are taught to respond, are the only accepted ways of behaving" (p. 8). To present a realistic understanding of our multicultural society and the influence of diverse groups on our society, advocates support a multicultural curriculum for all students, not just for students of color.

A multicultural curriculum examines the influences of diverse groups on historical events, literary developments, musical styles, artistic expression, athletic achievements, and other facets of American society—but the goal is not simply to memorize facts. Appleton (1983) described multicultural curriculum as "a conceptual approach that provides a framework for understanding the experience and

> It is probably never really wise, or even necessary, or anything better than harmful, to educate a human being toward a good end by telling him lies.
>
> **James Agee (1910–1955)**

perspectives of all the groups" (p. 211). The need for a conceptual approach is another assumption about curriculum by multicultural educators.

Why is it necessary to take a conceptual approach to curriculum?

Because of the knowledge explosion, it is impractical to emphasize memorization. It is not possible for us to remember all available information in every subject; we also know that much information soon will be obsolete or supplanted by new knowledge. In a multicultural curriculum, understanding broad concepts is preferable to memorizing facts. Gay (1977) described a multicultural curriculum design based on a thematic approach and a conceptual framework. In the thematic approach, students employ information from different disciplines to explore universal themes such as the search for identity, communication and conflict resolution, human interdependence, economics and exploitation, or the struggle for a just society.

Curriculum based on a conceptual framework also requires an interdisciplinary approach. Beginning with a concept such as power, alienation, or socialization, students could collect data from various sources addressing the concept, leading them to the identification and exploration of related concepts. Gay (1977) argued that both curriculum designs must be interdisciplinary because they require "the use of knowledge, concepts, and principles from many different disciplines" (p. 101). In either a thematic or a conceptual framework approach, students examine past and present experiences to develop an integrated understanding of principles and relationships between concepts.

Because multicultural curriculum is based on concepts rather than on specific content, students are involved in an ongoing and dynamic search for knowledge that is never finished, whereas the monocultural curriculum traditionally presented in schools is a finished product. As Nieto (2008) wrote,

> When reality is presented in schools as static, finished, and flat, the underlying tensions, controversies, passions and problems faced by people throughout history and today disappear. (p. 55)

Identifying concepts for students to analyze and discuss to clarify their understanding is the foundation of multicultural curriculum; to be effective, it is critical that the curriculum not be sabotaged by the hidden curriculum in school.

What is the hidden curriculum?

Pai and Adler (1997) define **hidden curriculum** as the indirect means by which schools teach students "the norms and values of their society" (p. 148). They describe the hidden curriculum as subtle messages learned from pictures displayed on bulletin boards or from school policies such as tardy slips and tracking. Messages may be intentional or unintentional; still, they have an impact on learners. Through the hidden curriculum, schools can promote such values as punctuality, assertiveness, or competitiveness. Pai and Adler suggest that the hidden curriculum may vary according to socioeconomic status, with upper-class children being

taught leadership skills and having opportunities for creativity and problem solving in contrast to low-income students being taught to respect authority and receiving rewards for compliance and conformity.

Everyday situations reveal a hidden curriculum in school policies and practices, and subtle messages can even be found in formal curriculum. An education professor entered a Los Angeles high school English classroom, where 80% of the students were Hispanic; she noticed that only white authors were featured on wall posters. An unmarried high school student was expelled from the local chapter of the National Honor Society because she was pregnant. A student teacher in a fourth-grade classroom of predominantly white students wanted to make a "Black History Month" bulletin board for February, but her supervising teacher rejected the idea because she believed that the students were "too young" for that (Koppelman, 2001).

Teaching that Columbus discovered America tells children that Native Americans were irrelevant and can be ignored; perhaps it is no coincidence that the white majority ignores Native Americans who protest Indian mascots for school sports teams. Brigham Young took his followers to Mexican territory because of the oppression and violence Mormons had encountered in the United States. Teaching that Mormons settled in Utah instead of Mexican territory implies that religious groups have always been able to practice their beliefs freely in the United States and ignores the difficulty America has experienced living up to the principle of religious freedom. Teaching that Old World art refers only to ancient Greek and Roman cultures denies the artistic heritage of many—especially non-Western—countries. Nieto (2008) argued that present-

> The wise person can see a question from all sides without bias. The foolish person is biased and can see a question only from one side.
>
> **Confucius (551–479 BCE)**

ing history only from the perspective of the dominant group teaches a skewed version of the truth. Educators implementing multicultural curricula must be especially sensitive to subtle messages provided by the hidden curriculum.

Why have schools implemented multicultural curriculum?

Many schools across the United States, especially in urban areas, have developed their own multicultural materials to supplement inadequate textbooks. Banks (2008) categorized the efforts into four approaches, two of which also satisfy Nieto's definition of multicultural education: the transformation approach and the social action approach (see Figure 14.2).

A *transformation* approach to multicultural curriculum design emphasizes concepts and themes. Students are presented with multiple perspectives on issues, and the goal is not to identify a "right perspective," but to understand how each perspective contributes to a richer understanding of issues. Critical thinking skills are emphasized as students

develop their own insights and conclusions and logically justify them.

A *social action* approach to multicultural curriculum design encourages students to take action based on their ideas and conclusions. Students—individually or collectively—pursue projects at school and in their community to address problems they identify and study. The goal of a social action approach is to empower students and to demonstrate that learning is not a game of *Trivial Pursuit*. Knowledge can lead to social action and create positive change. By encouraging critical thinking and active learning, multicultural educators combine theory and practice about conditions necessary to promote effective learning.

How do multicultural educators describe learning?

Advocates for multicultural education rely on cognitive development theory to describe how people

FIGURE 14.2 Approaches to Multicultural Curriculum Reform

Source: From *Multicultural Education: Issues and Perspectives*, 9/e by James A. Banks and Cherry A. McGee Banks. Copyright © 2004. Reprinted with permission of John Wiley & Sons, Ltd.

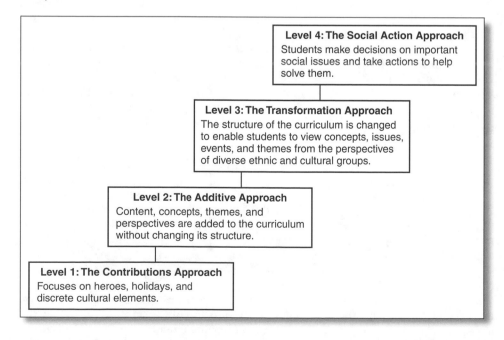

learn. In essence, learning is a process of meaning making. Learners organize ideas, information, and experiences they encounter to make sense of them. They may categorize, seek relationships, and simplify complex issues to achieve understanding. According to Sleeter and Grant (2003), "Learning is a process of constructing knowledge through the interaction of mind and experience" (p. 196). Piaget (1974) observed that children learn by interacting physically and intellectually with their environment. If students are provided information through lecture, they may attempt to extract relevant meaning from it, but if they perceive no relevance in the information, they are not likely to make the effort.

Learning results from the interaction learners encounter when they are required to be active. Learning also requires meaningfulness. Information regarded as meaningless will not be learned. Being an active learner promotes the development of competence and confidence, the basis for Dewey's insistence that children "learn by doing." Feeling competent and gaining self-confidence leads to a sense of power. As Hilliard (1974) wrote, "Learning is related to a sense of power over some of the forces which impinge upon our lives" (p. 47). If students feel powerless, they have little motivation to learn; when students are active, they develop skills and demonstrate abilities that reinforce self-confi-

> In every child who is born, under no matter what circumstances, and of no matter what parents, the potentiality of the human race is born again; and in (that child) . . . and in each of us, our terrific responsibility towards human life; toward the utmost idea of goodness.
>
> **James Agee (1910–1955)**

dence and give a sense of personal competence, and they acquire an enthusiasm for learning.

With regard to skill development, learning must not be limited to basic academic skills—reading, writing, computing—but must include a multitude of skills related to critical thinking, creativity, decision making, problem solving, information accessing, in-

terpersonal and cross-cultural communication, conflict resolution, visual literacy, and self-analysis. Gay (1977) argued that an education that "does not include the development of skills that will increase and enhance student's capabilities to live and function in a culturally pluralistic setting is incomplete" (p. 98). Although students may develop skills, an obstacle to facilitating skill development is that students have multiple ways of learning; therefore a single teaching strategy may be inadequate. Teachers committed to multicultural education must believe that all children can learn—if learning activities are designed to accommodate each child.

In what different ways do individuals learn?

Considerable research has been conducted to identify and explain styles of learning, but the result has been to categorize learning as a complex assortment of more than a dozen different learning styles. In more recent years, multicultural educators have been attracted to the work of Gardner (1993), whose theory of multiple intelligences is regarded by many as one of the best explanations of the diversity in learning. Gardner defines intelligence as the ability to process information and to generate solutions or products of value within a particular context.

Gardner originally identified seven distinct ways that people demonstrate intelligence (Gardner, 1993), but since then he has added an eighth category of intelligence (Gardner, 1999). According to Gardner, each person has the potential to engage in all eight means of processing information, although an individual is likely to be more competent in certain dimensions based on personal idiosyncrasies or the influence of his or her culture. (See Table 14.1.) The theory rejects the educational practice of recognizing and rewarding primarily two intelligences: logical-mathematical and linguistic. Gardner's theory describes a more complete means of understanding intelligence and identifying intellectual abilities. The challenge for teachers is to create instructional strategies and assessment procedures that accommodate more than one kind of intelligence. If teachers can meet this challenge, more students will have successful learning experiences, which will promote self-confidence.

TABLE 14.1 Descriptions of Multiple Intelligences

1. *Logical-Mathematical:* Ability to understand and solve logical problems, especially involving the use and manipulation of numbers.

2. *Linguistic:* Ability to understand nuances of meanings and multiple meanings of words, including a special appreciation for the sounds and rhythms of language.

3. *Bodily-Kinesthetic:* Ability to learn and master physical tasks involving motion and balance, and including manual manipulation of objects.

4. *Musical:* Ability to understand, reproduce, and appreciate musical sounds and rhythms in a range of musical expressions.

5. *Spatial:* Ability to understand spatial relationships in the environment and to cognitively modify those relationships for particular purposes.

6. *Interpersonal:* Sensitivity to nonverbal expressions of feelings and desires of other people and the ability to respond appropriately to them.

7. *Intrapersonal:* Ability for self-analysis, to understand clearly one's own feelings and desires and to apply that knowledge in one's choices and behaviors.

8. *Naturalist:* Ability to discern similarities and differences in plants and animals that leads to an enhanced understanding of established classifications.

Source: Gardner (1999).

Why is self-confidence necessary for learning?

Attitudes affect learning. It is generally understood that if students think they cannot learn something, they aren't likely to learn it. Combs (1979) claimed, "People behave in terms of what they believe about themselves. Whether we feel adequate or inadequate greatly affects how we approach a task" (p. 108). Research studies have confirmed that attitudes of teachers (and others) can positively or negatively affect student self-confidence. Research cited by Baker (1994) concluded, "There appears to be a high correlation between achievement in school and students' self-concept of academic ability as determined by the expectations and evaluations of significant others" (p. 9). By "significant others" Baker meant teachers and other school personnel. Although expectations should not be unrealistic, teachers must express high expectations for students to facilitate learning.

What must teachers do to implement a multicultural education approach?

Educators must determine which multicultural education approach they will implement. Sleeter and Grant (2003) identified five distinct approaches, two of which also satisfy the criteria included in Nieto's description: multicultural education and education that is multicultural *and* social reconstructionist (see Table 14.2). For purposes of clarity, the latter is referred to here as the *social reconstructionist approach.*

Principles underlying a multicultural education approach are reflected in a statement entitled "No One Model American" issued by the Commission on Multicultural Education (Hunter, 1974):

Multicultural education values cultural pluralism. Multicultural education rejects the view that schools should seek to melt away cultural differences or the view that schools should merely

TABLE 14.2 Approaches to Multicultural Education

Teaching the Exceptional and the Culturally Different

GOALS: To help low-achieving students succeed within traditional education by building bridges between them and the curriculum, and providing special assistance.

CURRICULUM: Based on the traditional curriculum but incorporates students' experiences (especially those who are culturally different). Uses classroom materials that include meaningful contexts for the students.

INSTRUCTION: Implements English as a Second Language or transitional bilingual education for language minority students and culturally relevant teaching for culturally different students; provides remedial classes including special education placement for temporary but intensive remediation; displays images relevant to students on wall posters and bulletin boards.

Human Relations

GOALS: To maintain traditional educational assumptions but with an emphasis on reducing prejudice, developing positive student self-concepts, and promoting acceptance of individual diversity.

CURRICULUM: Based on the traditional curriculum but including content on prejudice and stereotypes, similarities and differences among groups and individuals, and societal contributions from members of diverse groups in society, especially those groups represented by the students in the school.

INSTRUCTION: Uses strategies that build student-student relationships such as conflict mediation, role playing, simulations that address interpersonal relationships, and cooperative learning; displays student work on walls and bulletin boards.

Single Group Studies

GOALS: To provide knowledge about a particular group (Women's Studies, Chicano Studies, etc.) including an examination of structural inequalities affecting members of this group and encouraging students to work for social change.

CURRICULUM: Provides information (for a unit or course) about cultural characteristics and historical experiences of a group with emphasis on perspectives of group members and how this group has been and still is oppressed.

INSTRUCTION: Responds to learning style differences of the group with accommodations for individual learning styles; incorporates media, music, performances, and guest speakers to address aspects of the culture or issues related to the group; wall displays and bulletin boards emphasize societal contributions from individual members of the group.

Multicultural Education

GOALS: To promote cultural pluralism by emphasizing respect for human differences, including individual lifestyles, equal opportunity for all in school and society, and the need for power equity among diverse groups in society.

CURRICULUM: Provides content on diverse groups and their contributions to society with emphasis on perspectives from members of each group; incorporates student experiences to enhance curriculum relevance, and emphasizes the need to be aware of and understand alternative

(continues)

TABLE 14.2 (*Continued*)

perspectives on issues; addresses "hidden curriculum" by including diversity in special events, holidays, school menus, etc.

INSTRUCTION: Responds to student learning styles and skill levels with emphasis on an analysis of curriculum content and critical thinking activities; promotes respect for and use of other languages and dialects while learning standard English; displays wall posters and bulletin boards that reflect human diversity represented by race, ethnicity, gender, disability, religion, and other diverse groups, as well as issues reflecting individual student interests.

Education That Is Multicultural and Social Reconstructionist

GOALS: To promote cultural pluralism and structural equality for diverse groups in our society, to prepare students to be active participants in our democratic society by understanding structural inequalities and promoting equal opportunity.

CURRICULUM: Provides content on current social issues of oppression and structural inequalities for diverse groups using perspectives of members of those groups including the perspectives of students and community members; emphasizes historic and contemporary life experiences for self-reflection, for analyzing oppression, and for understanding alternative perspectives; addresses "hidden curriculum" by including diversity in special events, holidays, school menus, etc.

INSTRUCTION: Responds to student learning styles and skill levels with emphasis on active student involvement in democratic decision making in the school; engages students in critical thinking and in problem solving to promote the development of social action skills that empower students; employs cooperative learning and group projects, especially those involving the community; avoids testing and tracking procedures that represent narrow views of student learning that label some students as failures; displays wall posters and bulletin boards that reflect cultural diversity, social action themes, and student interests.

Source: Sleeter and Grant (2003).

tolerate cultural pluralism. Instead, multicultural education affirms that schools should be oriented toward the cultural enrichment of all children and youth through programs rooted to the preservation and extension of cultural diversity as a fact of life in American society. (p. 21)

A *multicultural education approach* insists that a diverse society can achieve unity through diversity; it need not eliminate cultural differences. Although some advocates of this approach focus on racial and ethnic groups, most promote an inclusive view of diversity by incorporating information on women, gays and lesbians, low-income families, and people with disabilities.

Multicultural education advocates support integration, inclusion, and "de-tracking" to create heterogeneous classrooms emphasizing skill development to gain knowledge and a better understanding of diverse groups in American society. Further, a multicultural education approach calls for curricular reform to correct omissions and distortions in textbooks concerning diverse groups, and provides multiple perspectives on important historical or contemporary events. Advocates have criticized visual images in textbooks for not representing diversity in

American society adequately and for continuing to depict certain groups in stereotypical ways. They urge teachers to use bulletin boards and media to provide accurate representations of diverse groups.

Advocates for the multicultural education approach challenge teachers to be sensitive to language that is derogatory toward any group and to model use of inclusive language. Teachers must study and understand diverse ways of learning and design or modify lessons to accommodate differences. In addition to having high expectations for students, multicultural teachers encourage cooperation between students in the classroom through group activities. Teachers need not strive to treat students equally—treating all students the same— but to address students equitably with responses based on the diverse needs of individual students.

A *social reconstructionist approach* shares many principles and practices of a multicultural education approach. Four major differences include: (1) attention to structural inequalities in America; (2) emphasis on democratic decision making in the classroom; (3) development of social action skills to empower students; and (4) use of an activist curriculum with student projects addressing problems in schools and communities.

Social reconstructionism has roots in the Progressive Education movement and in Dewey's 1920 book, *Reconstruction in Philosophy* that inspired the term. In the early 1930s, Counts and Rugg, leaders of a group called "Frontier Thinkers," were concerned about inequities in American society and urged that schools play a more active role in creating a more equitable society (Kneller, 1971). In his 1956 book, *Toward a Reconstructed Philosophy of Education,* Brameld became an influential advocate for reconstructionism, suggesting that schools create a new social order by fostering democratic principles and demanding more citizen control over major institutions and resources.

A social reconstructionist approach to multicultural education focuses less on awareness of cultural diversity and more on the ongoing struggles of diverse groups against oppression. The curriculum includes examples of successful resistance to oppression by subordinate groups and actions against injustice by individuals from the dominant group. This approach emphasizes democratic classroom practices to develop student decision-making skills and to encourage social action projects.

What does it mean to implement democratic practices in schools?

In describing schools employing democratic practices, Apple and Beane (1995) noted that all people in these schools must participate in governance issues and policymaking. In classrooms, students and teachers must work together to create learning environments responsive to student questions, interests, issues, and aspirations; however, as stated in Sleeter and Grant (2003), "Democratizing power relationships in the classroom does not mean turning all power over to the students" (p. 197). Teachers still represent adult authority and, like the state or federal government, they must take action if a majority of students makes decisions creating inequity or injustice in the classroom. In the history of the United States there have been numerous occasions when the majority was wrong, and as Griffin said, "Rule by majority is a great idea, but the majority has no right to rule wrong based on prejudice" (Terkel, 1980, p. 311). According to Michelli (2005), one major goal of a democratic classroom is to help students defend their beliefs while they also learn to be open to contrasting ideas and recognize when more effective arguments are being expressed.

In addition to emphasizing democratic practices, a social reconstructionist approach encourages students to analyze their own lives, reflecting Dewey's insistence that education take account of students' life experiences. Analyzing their own lives can lead students to a better understanding of their experiences with injustice, and provide a basis for developing constructive responses for future encounters. Self-analysis leading to action not only strengthens a student's self-concept, but also develops social action and interaction skills when coalitions are necessary to address issues. Social action projects can be as simple as examining the nutritional value of various fast foods or as complex as examining factors influencing a pattern of lower scores on standardized tests for females or students of color. By making curriculum personal, it becomes relevant; by emphasizing social action, it becomes empowering. Students are encouraged to regard citizenship in a democracy as active participation by individuals and groups to resolve personal and social dilemmas.

Engaging in democratic practices has enormous implications for a teacher's choice of instructional approaches. Before describing teaching strategies, it is important to recall an important point from Hilliard (1974), that teachers implementing multicultural education must believe "a multicultural orientation is beneficial to them personally" (p. 49). Howard (2006) argued that teachers have no choice about dealing with diversity; their only choice is how they will respond to diversity. If teachers implement strategies for multicultural education merely to *help* students, especially students of color, they are not likely to be effective.

What specific instructional strategies are recommended for teachers?

Sleeter (1996) insisted that implementing multicultural education effectively requires that teaching not be regarded as experimenting with a variety of classroom strategies; instead she described the importance of "listening to oppressed people, including scholars, with the aim of learning to hear and understand what is being said" (p. 134). By listening to students and their parents, teachers will develop appreciation for and understanding of their students, and will genuinely project high regard and high expectations for all students. As Nieto (2008) described it, "Becoming a multicultural teacher . . . means first becoming a multicultural person" (p. 424). Becoming a multicultural person means knowing about human differences and desiring to learn more; examining attitudes for biases, stereotypes, and prejudices; and understanding the need to look at issues from more than one perspective.

Advocates for either of the two multicultural education approaches just described agree that for a multicultural curriculum, teachers must employ **critical pedagogy.** Nieto (2008) describes critical pedagogy as a liberating experience that "encourages students to take risks, to be curious, and to question. Rather than expecting students to repeat teachers' words, it expects them to seek their own answers" (p. 56). Critical pedagogy is also illustrated by Sleeter's (1996) description of *Why? Papers:* In this activity students are assigned the task of asking a question about some issue involving race, social class, or gender. In doing research and writing their responses to the questions, students are asked to take the perspective of the oppressed group identified in the question. Examples of "Why?" questions include:

- Why are Mexican American children frequently absent from school?
- Why do Native American students drop out of school?
- Why are many African American males in prison? (p. 120)

According to Sleeter, taking the minority perspective has been effective because students talk with members of oppressed groups as they search for answers; this provides them with unique insights on the group's past experiences and their perspectives on problems addressed. Multiple insights and perspectives influence the analysis and conclusions students present in their papers:

> They framed concrete observations of inequality in terms of institutional discrimination and uncovered strategies oppressed groups use to cope with or attempt to advance from a minority position. (p. 123)

Appleton (1983) recommended process-oriented teaching strategies such as role playing, simulation games, using students as discussion leaders, and assigning individual or group projects based on student interests. Using the community to create learning experiences is essential for social action activities, but communities also have human resources—such as students' parents—who can be invited to the classroom to discuss the impact of past or current issues on the community. For students who struggle with nonstructured tasks, teachers might provide a mastery learning activity in which learning is partitioned into a series of sequential tasks and students can periodically evaluate themselves to determine when they achieve mastery. Effective multicultural teaching must allow for the flexibility to modify learning activities so that students will have the opportunity to be successful learners.

Maintaining such flexibility illustrates the point that the goal of multicultural teachers is not to think "I am fair because I treat all students equally." Cymrot (2002) argues that "equally" in this context usually means "the same," but each student is a unique person, in part because of lessons learned from his or her culture. Diller and Moule (2005) emphasize the need for teachers to be culturally competent. Although the dominant culture in the United States emphasizes individual achievement, other cultures place more value on the collective needs of the group. A teacher should avoid making assumptions about a student's behavior based on the norms of the teacher's culture. For example, it is easy to misinterpret the behavior of a child whose culture has taught him that possessions are to be shared and not used exclusively by one person. Having many different cultures represented in classrooms should not be viewed as a challenge but as a learning opportunity for teachers as well as students. In culturally diverse classrooms, Cymrot (2002) argues, "good teaching is about an exchange of cultures" (p. 17).

Because tracking practices have tended to diminish diversity in classrooms as well as academic achievement, multicultural educators deplore tracking and encourage the use of learning centers or cooperative groups as effective strategies in heterogeneous classrooms. Tiedt and Tiedt (2002) describe a learning center as a part of the classroom set aside for the study of a specific topic or for the purpose of developing a specific set of skills; it may be devoted to studying the issue of prejudice or filled with exercises requiring critical thinking. Before using a learning center, students are given directions concerning the center's activities and instructions for using equipment or materials. Students involved in learning center activities can proceed as individuals learning at their own pace or they can be organized into teams.

Cooperative learning strategies are especially attractive to advocates of multicultural education because they involve students of mixed abilities in learning tasks that have clearly defined responsibilities for each group member. Each person must complete his or her task in order for the group to complete the project. According to Sleeter and Grant (2003), research findings suggest that this strategy works well with children from diverse racial and ethnic groups, not only in terms of academic achievement but also in terms of developing positive interpersonal relationships. In reviewing research on cooperative learning, Kagan (2006) cites studies documenting that young children in schools with diverse student populations initially interact with others and choose their friends without regard to race, but by the end of their second grade year, self-segregation by race has begun and is dramatically apparent by the end of elementary school. Yet, research studies have also found that in classrooms that have implemented cooperative learning strategies, self-segregation was virtually eliminated. Based on his review of four decades of research, Kagan concluded: "Cooperative learning, when it includes heterogeneous teams and team-building, is the single most powerful tool this nation has for improving race relations" (2006, p. 53).

How can multicultural education help to reduce student prejudice?

Reducing prejudice and developing conflict resolution skills are important objectives in multicultural education. Referring to a review of prejudice reduction programs, Nieto (2008) reported that activities designed to reduce prejudice were more effective if students viewed cognitive learning as the primary objective. When prejudice reduction was the primary objective of an activity, students tended to feel as if they were being manipulated to "say the right thing," and they became defensive or resentful. The success of indirect approaches emphasizing cognitive tasks for reducing student prejudice may explain why studies have found cooperative learning strategies to be effective in this area.

Prejudice is not simply a black and white issue. Sheets (2005) cited a study of a school with diverse students in which African American children expressed negative attitudes toward children who were Asian American or Hispanic American, and there have been numerous incidents of interracial conflict between youth from diverse groups in schools and in communities. Based on the results of several studies, Stephan (1999) concluded that teaching conflict resolution skills can reduce the influence of prejudice on intergroup relations in schools. One study reported that helping students develop conflict resolution skills "improved students' abilities to manage conflicts, increased their social support from other students, and decreased

> Prejudices, it is well known, are most difficult to eradicate from the heart whose soil has never been loosened or fertilized by education; they grow there, firm as weeds among stones.
>
> **Charlotte Bronte (1816–1855)**

victimization by others" (p. 70). Stephan added that teaching conflict resolution skills to students had a positive effect on decreasing student anxiety, increasing self-esteem, and improving intergroup relations. Engaging students in prejudice reduction activities and developing their skills in conflict resolution to improve intergroup relationships is a persuasive rationale for all educators. In addition, teachers are increasingly being challenged to teach in ways that take into account the diverse cultures from which their students come. This approach has been called "culturally responsive teaching."

Multicultural Education as a Context for Culturally Responsive Teaching

Multicultural education incorporates the idea that all students—regardless of their gender, social class, ethnic, racial, or cultural differences—should have an equal opportunity to learn in school (Banks & Banks, 2003). However, the public school system in the United States is plagued with vast inequalities, and on virtually every measure, students of color and students from lower economic classes achieve below the level of their white and middle-class counterparts. This disparity in outcomes is called "the achievement gap." Mainstream explanations tend to blame the achievement gap on uninformed assumptions about families and communities (i.e., "they just don't value education"), but advocates for multicultural education have examined the ways schools are structured, and they report that institutional characteristics of schools systematically deny some groups of students equal educational opportunities (Banks & Banks, 2003). For example, in the early grades, the academic achievement of students of color is nearly the same as that of white middle-class students, but the longer students of color stay in school, the more the achievement gap widens (Banks, 2004). Students in high poverty, high minority schools are routinely provided fewer resources, fewer qualified teachers, fewer advanced level courses, and higher levels of policing in their schools than their more affluent white peers. As a result, they experience lower academic achievement, lower rates of high school graduation, and

more interaction with the criminal justice system (Orfield, Losen, Wald, & Swanson, 2004). Thus, a major goal of multicultural education is to improve the academic achievement of students who are traditionally marginalized in school by considering several interconnected aspects of schooling itself. Many multicultural educators advocate culturally responsive teaching as a key strategy to achieve some of their major goals.

How does culturally responsive teaching address multicultural education goals?

Culturally responsive teaching addresses the goal of changing school practices that marginalize nontraditional students. Culturally responsive teaching is grounded in the perception of schooling as linked to social forces in the broader society. Schooling is a primary site of socialization, and, as such, schools play a key role in sorting students into predetermined places within a society that is hierarchical and socially stratified: Schools prepare students to occupy roles in society that have unequal value, for example, vocational training versus college preparation or special education versus honors courses (Anyon, 2003; Oakes, Wells, Jones, & Datnow, 1997). Because schools are such a powerful site of social reproduction, all aspects of schools are inherently political. Knowledge is never neutral; it is infused with the implicit cultural assumptions, frames of reference, biases, and interests of those who hold the power to determine which aspects of knowledge are valid and how they will be measured. Yet schools present the cultural norms, styles, and perspectives of dominant social groups as objective and reward those who fit these norms and penalize those who don't.

Other aspects of schooling that contribute to the achievement gap include standardized testing, culturally biased curriculum, ability tracking, unequal funding between urban and suburban schools, low expectations for students of color, and zero tolerance policies that criminalize minority students and channel them from school into the prison system (Clark, 2007). As defined and promoted by multicultural education advocates, culturally responsive teaching seeks to interrupt these inequitable aspects of schooling (Banks & Banks, 2003; Ladson-Billings, 1995; Nieto, 1999). While challenging these structural inequities will take time and society-wide effort, multicultural education advocates argue that individual teachers can make an immediate difference in their classrooms by infusing culturally responsive teaching.

Gay (2000) defines culturally responsive teaching as using the cultural knowledge, prior experiences, and performance styles of diverse students to make learning more appropriate and effective for them. Rather than viewing these students as deficient, culturally responsive pedagogy teaches to their specific strengths. According to Gay (2000), culturally responsive teaching has the following characteristics:

- It acknowledges the legitimacy of the cultural heritages of different ethnic groups, both as legacies that affect students' dispositions, attitudes, and approaches to learning and as worthy content to be taught in the formal curriculum.
- It builds bridges of meaningfulness between home and school experiences as well as between academic abstractions and lived sociocultural realities.
- It uses a wide variety of instructional strategies that are connected to different learning styles.
- It teaches students to know and praise their own and each others' cultural heritages.
- It incorporates multicultural information, resources, and materials in all the subjects and skills routinely taught in schools (p. 29).

Culturally responsive teaching is an all-encompassing and ever-present "lens" through which teachers view their practice; at its core is the expectation that all students can experience academic success while developing the critical consciousness to challenge the inequity of the status quo.

What are some current issues that make culturally responsive teaching difficult?

Despite the common belief that racial segregation is a practice of the past, our schools are more segregated than ever before (Kozol, 2005; Villegas & Lucas, 2002). Most students of color and lower income students are concentrated in urban areas, whereas most middle class and white students attend suburban schools in which they have very little authentic interaction with students who are different from them. In addition, the teaching force is getting *more*, not less, homogeneous. Trends continue to indicate that the teaching force is becoming increasingly white and middle class (Gordon, 2005), while at the same time, the student population is getting more diverse (National Center for Education Statistics, 2005). Over one third of U.S. public school students are children of color, whereas fewer than 16% of teachers are educators of color (Kearney, 2008; Stevens, Hamman, & Olivarez, 2007). The vast majority of teachers are white, and they also tend to come from segregated suburban schools and neighborhoods. In addition, they are challenged in their understanding of children from backgrounds different from their own. Howard (2003) states that "Teachers need to understand that racially diverse students frequently bring cultural capital to the classroom that is oftentimes drastically different from mainstream norms and worldviews" (p. 197). Because teachers and students often come from dissimilar backgrounds, teachers must "construct pedagogical practices in ways that are culturally relevant, racially affirming, and socially meaningful for their students" (p. 187).

Although urban schools may indeed be located in cities and be composed predominantly of low-income students and students of color, "urban" does not necessarily indicate location. In more affluent cities such as Seattle, San Francisco and Boston, schools located inside the city limits that are primarily white are not labeled "urban"; the term *urban* is used as the dominant culture's code for indicating the existence of a percentage of students of color that is "too high" for white families to feel comfortable with. Johnson and Shapiro (2003) found that perceptions of white parents regarding "good schools" were often based on the racial demographics of the school; the whiter the student body, the better the school was perceived to be. They concluded that race may be not just a factor in school choice for white families, but rather *the primary factor*. Schools that are not perceived as "good" because of the presence of a percentage of students of color are labeled "urban" (or "inner-city"). In turn, these schools are abandoned by white families and have unequal funding and resources, which perpetuates the cycle (Kozol, 1991; Kozol, 2005).

Although these factors complicate the efforts of teachers to engage in culturally responsive teaching, they also provide reasons for engaging in such practices to help students.

What students benefit from culturally responsive teaching?

Because race appears to be a key issue in decisions white people make when choosing schools and neighborhoods, one could easily argue that *all* students and *all* teachers could benefit from culturally responsive teaching, regardless of the overall racial demographics of their schools or neighborhoods. White children attending segregated schools need to be prepared, perhaps more so than any other group, to interact in a culturally diverse society (DiAngelo, 2006). Culturally responsive teaching builds a foundation for all students to engage in the critical tasks of empathetic and equitable engagement with the diversity that is so often lacking in their immediate world because of pervasive segregation in our schools and neighborhoods (Derman Sparks & Ramsey, 2004). The bigger question is not who benefits from culturally responsive teaching, but what is required for an individual teacher to successfully implement culturally responsive teaching.

What characteristics are necessary to be a culturally responsive teacher?

The following characteristics of culturally responsive teachers are adapted from Villegas and Lucas (2002) and Gay (2000). Culturally responsive teachers are those who:

- Understand teaching as a contextual and situational process in which students' prior experiences, community settings, cultural backgrounds, and ethnic identities are acknowledged and infused into the curriculum.
- Are familiar with their students' prior knowledge and beliefs, derived from both personal and cultural experiences and well-designed instruction that builds on what students already know while stretching them beyond the familiar.

- Have sociocultural consciousness; they recognize that the ways people perceive the world, interact with one another, and approach learning are deeply influenced by such factors as race/ethnicity, social class, and language.
- Are aware that they also are sociocultural beings, with a particular and limited cultural viewpoint: They know that no human is objective and they consistently engage in self-reflection and self-examination of their beliefs, values, and assumptions about those who are different from them.
- Have a positive perspective on students and families who are from diverse backgrounds, seeing resources for learning in all students rather than viewing differences as deficiencies, or problems to be solved.
- Communicate high expectations for all children.
- Have a sense that they are capable of and responsible for bringing about educational change that will make schooling more responsive to students from diverse backgrounds.

The characteristics outlined above involve ongoing education and self-awareness, particularly for those who have not grown up in environments that offered consistent and sustained opportunities to build relationships with people different from themselves in key social areas, such as race and class. Because culturally responsive teaching challenges our conventional worldviews and our sense of self in relation to others, it develops over a lifetime and is not achieved in the short term. At the same time, educators can't grow into culturally responsive teachers without practice, trial and error, and risk-taking. Although a school-wide commitment is necessary for authentic transformation in education (Villegas & Lucas, 2002), individual teachers may infuse culturally responsive teaching into their classroom practice without waiting for support or encouragement from outside of their classroom.

What actual classroom experiences illustrate culturally responsive teaching?

A social studies teacher with the non-Western first name of Özlem begins her class by explaining how her name is written and pronounced, and what it means in her first language, Turkish. She has students practice writing and saying her name. She explains how in North America the "dots" are often absent from the "O," and then tells her name's "story." She talks about the script change from Turkish to English and wonders aloud how the change in the spelling of her name affects her cultural identity. She shares why the Turkish spelling of her name is significant to her as someone whose family immigrated to Canada from Turkey. After this brief discussion, she invites each student to teach the class how to pronounce and spell his or her name and to "tell us the story of your name." If needed, she provides prompts such as "Who named you? What does your name mean? Do you have a nickname you prefer to be called? If so, how did you get it? Do you know the roots of your name?" She doesn't move on to the next student until the last student to share his or her name is satisfied that everyone has learned to pronounce it correctly. This exercise builds community by affirming cultural diversity as represented by the names of students in her class, allowing students to claim their names and tell their stories, and providing a culturally relevant framework for issues that will be discussed in the class, such as the following.

- *The cultural dimensions of names and the connections between religion and culture.* Students will find that many names are influenced by religion; for example, the middle names "Kaur" (for girls) and "Singh" (for boys) indicate Sikh heritage, just as Paul and John have religious significance for families of Christian heritage.
- *The cultural connections that have been lost by institutional practices that shortened or "corrected" immigrants' names.* Upon their arrival in the United States an immigrant with a name such as *Yih-Shue* could be changed to *Sherry*. The inability to make or represent certain sounds in different languages; the power relations imbedded in whose names are adapted or modified upon immigration; and the politics of who decides how that will be done are some of the issues students could discuss.
- *The impact of marriage on names, and the norms for patriarchal versus matriarchal societies.* Students could discuss who changes their surname when they get married, and why? Further, how are

naming norms changing over time, with gender roles evolving and the legalization of same-sex marriages in some states in the United States and Canada?

This activity also illustrates a key tenet in multicultural education: recognition of the individual *as well as* the society in which the individual is embedded. Following this exercise, students make decorative nameplates for their desks. As new students join the class, the sharing of names is repeated to include the newcomers (adapted from Sensoy, 2009).

Another teacher, Ms. Walker, infuses culturally responsive teaching into a history lesson on heroes. Instead of asking students to stand outside of their own lives and write in the third person about people chosen for them by their textbooks, she asks her students to choose a "hero" from their community who works for social justice and interview that person. If a student is having trouble identifying a hero, Ms. Walker offers a range of possibilities based on her knowledge of leaders in the child's community and the interests of the child. The students generate questions that might include: What accomplishments are you proud of? What challenges did you face in achieving your goals? What methods did you use to affect change? What do you regret? What advice do you have for others? The students' community heroes are then invited to be guest speakers in the class so that all students may meet and learn from them. If students' heroes are not available for interviews, the students write essays as if they were the hero reflecting on the same questions at the end of his or her life. This lesson humanizes heroes, and rather than presenting overwhelmingly white and male figures from the dominant culture with the same few sanitized exceptions of Susan B. Anthony, Martin Luther King, Jr., and Rosa Parks, it affirms the range of communities from which the students come. The students' communities are brought directly into the classroom and utilized as a resource for everyone, and mainstream definitions of what makes a hero are challenged.

As Jana Dean (2007) has shown, even a math teacher can incorporate culturally responsive teaching in a lesson by using typical wages in her students' community to build a bridge between her students' lives and algebra; the mathematics in this lesson are clearly culturally relevant. Her students calculate and graph daily and monthly incomes in service sector jobs, using a day's wages and a month's wages for four full-time service industry occupations that many in their community hold—for example, a retail clerk at Wal-Mart, a security guard, a fast food restaurant cook, and a home nursing aide. Her students graph four linear relationships on the same coordinate grid and write equations for each. Along the way, they discuss questions such as: What is a minimum wage and who gets to set it? She says, "Following an example that I had prepared in advance, students worked together to draw an *x*- and *y*-axis on 11 by 17-inch graph paper. I told them that they would be graphing one day's wages, or eight hours, and that the size of one's paycheck depends on the number of hours worked; therefore, money—the dependent variable—belongs on the *y*-axis. The independent variable, however, will be the same for everyone: You are all going to work an eight-hour day."

After students complete the graphs, she introduces the variables *x* and *y*. In this case, *y* represents the paycheck and *x* stands for the number of hours worked. Ms. Dean also challenges her students to write an equation for each line that would show the relationship between time and earnings, and they arrive at equations to represent the lines on their graphs. She then asks her students to respond in writing to the following prompt: "How does the rate of pay affect the shape and steepness of the lines on your coordinate grid? Describe the shape of a graph for the wage of a job at $20 per hour. Describe the shape of a graph for the wage of a job at the federal minimum of $5.15 per hour." The prompt leads students to observe that the steeper the line, the higher the wage, and that each of the situations produces a straight line. Both observations pave the way for introducing the term "slope," meaning the rate of increase, and "linear," meaning a relationship that graphs as a straight line. This prompt also serves to identify the coefficient of *x* or the number that multiplies *x* as the value that determines the steepness of the line. Once students recognize linear relationships, Ms. Dean introduces the concept of *y*-intercept by having students make a table showing pay minus expenses for the first ten hours of work. This gives students a real-world context for operating with negative numbers. Other dimensions of her "living algebra" lesson include calculating the cost of housing and other expenses,

comparing state and national minimum wages, and learning about the activism and organizing effort behind her state's highest-in-the-nation minimum wage (adapted from Dean, 2007).

What other strategies for culturally responsible teaching have been advocated?

Some strategies can be quite simple as long as the teacher understands the goal of the strategy. As Nieto (1999) explains, whether it's an informal chat as the parent brings the child to school, or through phone calls, home visits, and newsletters sent home in the first language of the families, teachers can begin a genuine dialogue that results in learning about each of the families represented in their classroom community. At Brown University, a consortium of educators called the Education Alliance is committed to enhancing the ability of teachers to work effectively and equitably with English Language learners. They have identified numerous culturally responsive teaching strategies, and some examples are provided below (2006):

1. **Learn about students' cultures**
   - Have students share artifacts from home that reflect their culture
   - Have students write about traditions shared by their families
   - Have students research different aspects of their culture
   - Have members of the community speak to students on various subjects
   - Ask members of the community to teach a lesson or give a demonstration (in their field of expertise) to the students
2. **Promote positive perspectives on parents and families**
   - Conduct home visits in which parents are able to speak freely about their expectations and concerns for their children
   - Send weekly/monthly newsletters (in the home language) informing parents of school activities
   - Host family nights at school to introduce parents to concepts and ideas children are learning in their classes and to share interactive journals

- Research the cultural background of students' families
- Visit local community centers to find out about cultural activities and beliefs of the students

3. **Bridge cultural differences through effective communication**
   - Teach and talk to students about differences between individuals
   - Show how differences among the students make for better learning
   - Attend community events important to the students and discuss the events with the students
   - See your classroom as a community of learners, rather than as individuals learning separately from one another
   - Use cooperative learning strategies

4. **Promote student engagement**
   - Have students generate lists of topics they wish to study and/or research
   - Allow students to select their own reading material
   - Share responsibility of instruction with students and community members
   - Have students lead discussion groups or reteach concepts
   - Create classroom projects that involve the community

5. **Provide culturally mediated instruction using diverse teaching strategies**
   - Use role-playing strategies
   - Assign students research projects that focus on issues that apply to their own community or cultural group
   - Ask educators who come from the same cultural background as the students about effective ways to teach them
   - Allow the use of the student's first language to enhance learning
   - Use classroom management techniques that are culturally familiar to students

6. **Reshape the curriculum**
   - Use resources other than textbooks for study
   - Have students research aspects of a topic within their community

- Encourage students to interview members of their community who have knowledge of the topic they are studying
- Provide information to the students on alternative viewpoints or beliefs about a topic
- Allow students to set their own goals for a project

Although culturally responsive teaching requires extra effort and may even seem daunting, it is no more difficult than any strategy promoting successful classroom practices that are effective with diverse students. Good teaching is never easy, but in the history of education, including our current era, there have always been numerous teachers who have been effective in the classroom, so we know it's not impossible. This should be the response to the complaints from some critics who feel that culturally responsive teaching in particular and multicultural education in general are too idealistic to work in the "real world" of challenges inherent in the everyday task of classroom teaching.

Is multicultural education too idealistic?

The purpose of multicultural education is to prepare children and youth to be active, positive participants in a diverse, democratic society. Although this chapter can only provide an overview of multicultural education, the intent is to provide a framework that describes schools committed to multicultural education and teachers who have implemented multicultural education in their classrooms. Educators may not achieve the ideals of multicultural education, but they can have a significant impact on students by engaging in efforts consistent with the purpose of multicultural education. If teachers address that purpose with students now and in the future, this diverse nation we live

> Ideals are like stars: you will not succeed in touching them with your hands, but like the seafarer . . . you choose them as your guides and following them you reach your destiny.
>
> **Carl Schurz (1829–1906)**

in will make progress toward achieving two related goals: more effective schools for all students and a more accepting society.

Elementary, middle level, and secondary educators committed to principles of multicultural education have implemented strategies and activities

> The role of the teacher remains the highest calling of a free people. To the teacher, America entrusts her most precious resource, her children; and asks that they be prepared, in all their glorious diversity, to face the rigors of individual participation in a democratic society.
>
> **Shirley Hufstedler (1925–)**

described in this chapter. The National Education Association (NEA) has promoted multicultural education since the 1960s, and the National Council for Accreditation of Teacher Education (NCATE) requires teacher education programs to address diversity issues and to include principles and practices of multicultural education to receive accreditation for the preparation of teachers. Professional organizations advocate pluralism not just as a response to diversity but to meet our needs as a democratic society. Pai and Adler (1997) succinctly state the relationship between democracy, diversity, and multicultural education:

> In a truly democratic society, no single group rules over others because of the implicit faith in the human capacity for intelligent behavior. Democracy requires a method of resolving conflicts by inquiry, discussion, and persuasion rather than by violence. Hence, the kind of education that cultivates reflective thinking and conflict resolution through discussion and persuasion is essential. (p. 110)

AFTERWORD

Diversity is not just an issue for K–12 schools; most universities and colleges mandate diversity courses in their general education programs, and corporations implement policies promoting diversity and

provide diversity training for managers and employees. Churches, community organizations, and civic groups already articulate pluralistic mission statements about the value of diversity in our society. Idealistic or not, multicultural education is likely to become increasingly influential in American schools in the twenty-first century. Fortunately, we have many excellent resources that describe teaching strategies based on principles of multicultural education (Derman-Sparks & Ramsey, 2004; Ladson-Billings, 2001; Pasternak, 1986; Sapon-Shevin, 1999; Shade, Kelly, & Oberg, 1997; Sleeter & Grant, 2009; Tiedt & Tiedt, 2002).

The challenge confronting us today is how to become multicultural individuals. In the teaching profession, that question will be answered primarily by white middle-class people—primarily women. As our schools increasingly consist of students from subordinate groups—students of color, students from low-income families, children and youth who are not Christian, gay and lesbian youth, learners with disabilities—teachers continue to enter the profession from our dominant societal group. Cochran-Smith (2003) cites demographers analyzing 2000 census data and reporting that 86% of all teachers are white; students of color constitute almost 40% of the school population (p. 4); although the percentage of white teachers is predicted to re-

TABLE 14.3 U.S. Public School Teachers

Category	Percentage
Gender	
Female	79
Male	21
Race	
White	84.3
Black	7.6
Hispanic	5.6
Highest Degree	
Bachelor's	61.9
Master's	23.1
Years of Experience	
Less than 10	41.7
10–20	28.5
More than 20	29.8

Source: U.S. Department of Education. (2006). National Center for Education Statistics.

main stable, the percentage of students of color is predicted to be 57% by 2035 (see Table 14.3).

Pang (2005) has urged white teachers to engage in self-analysis to understand how being white has shaped their identity, and how oppression has affected and shaped the identities of members of subordinate groups in our society. Self-analysis is part of the journey toward becoming a multicultural teacher; it may often feel uncomfortable, but if pursued, it can also be liberating. In the end, white teachers can develop a profound appreciation for both diversity and democracy—and the need to be pluralistic to promote and sustain both in our schools and in our society.

myeducationlab

Now go to Topics #11, 12, 13: **Curriculum, Strategies,** and **School-wide Diversity Issues** in the MyEducationLab (www.myeducationlab.com) for your course, where you can:

- Find learning outcomes for these topics along with the national standards that connect to these outcomes.
- Complete Assignments and Activities that can help you more deeply understand the chapter content by viewing classroom video and ABC News footage.
- Apply and practice your understanding of the core teaching skills identified in the chapter with the Building Teaching Skills and Dispositions learning units.

TERMS AND DEFINITIONS

Critical pedagogy   Providing opportunities for students to analyze perspectives and use their analysis to understand and act on perceived inconsistencies

Diversity   The presence of human beings with perceived or actual differences based on a variety of human characteristics

Global (International) education   Teaching about the cultures of nations around the world

Hidden curriculum   Indirect means by which schools teach the norms and values of a society

Multicultural   Any society composed of a number of subordinate groups based on race, ethnicity, religion, language, nationality, income, gender, sexual orientation, and degree of physical, mental, or emotional ability

Multicultural education   A process of comprehensive school reform that rejects discrimination in schools and society and accepts and affirms pluralism

Multiethnic education   Integrating issues and information about race and ethnicity into school curricula

Pluralism   The equal coexistence of diverse cultures, institutions, and/or individuals within a mutually supportive relationship within the boundaries of one nation

Retention   The ability of students to recall knowledge they have been taught

Transfer   The ability of students to apply retained knowledge to situations occurring inside and outside the classroom

DISCUSSION EXERCISES

Exercise #1 The Hidden Curriculum: American Indians

Directions: Might children and youth be learning lessons that we aren't aware they are being taught? Through misunderstanding or lack of adequate knowledge of facts, curriculums may be teaching American children to be biased or to stereotype others. The statements below were originally developed as an elementary punctuation exercise [which is why they have no punctuation marks at the end of each statement].

Explain in what way each phrase or sentence is biased. Underline the word or words that you judge need replacement.

Other than learning correct punctuation, what else might children completing this exercise have learned that wasn't intended?

1. Indians lived in our country many years before the white man
2. Have you ever seen an Indian
3. Indians belong to the red race
4. Their skin is of a copper color
5. Most of the men are called warriors
6. The women are called squaws
7. Do they live in wigwams and tepees
8. The red man's name for corn was maize
9. Were bows and arrows used for hunting by the Indians
10. A group of Indians living together is called a "tribe"
11. Do little Indian girls and boys play games
12. The squaws carried their babies on their backs
13. What does each Indian tribe call its "leader"
14. The leader of each tribe is called a "chief"
15. A few Indian tribes still live in the western part of our country

Exercise #2 Whom would you hire? Selecting Elementary Teachers

Introduction: Being fair to schoolchildren and youth involves providing the best teachers to help them.

Imagine that you are a committee member with responsibility for hiring new teachers. You have four positions open in grades 1 to 3 and eight applicants from whom to choose. You have interviewed all eight, and each has impressed you favorably.

Directions: Read the brief descriptions below and select the four you would hire.

Candidate 1: Forty-year-old woman, single, lives alone with eighteen years outstanding experience; highly successful with typically unsuccessful children. Possibly in a lesbian relationship.

Candidate 2: Twenty-four-year-old man, single, two years experience in a ghetto school. A near genius, he brings outstanding recommendations. Leader of local black power group; his students use African names and openly reject "slave" names.

Candidate 3: Thirty-five-year-old man, married, father of six. Community minded, interested in Cub Scouts. Known for having very well-organized planned lessons and classes. Ten years of experience. Native American heritage.

Candidate 4: Forty-year-old man, single, living with elderly parents. The candidate has extensive experience from being a local business entrepreneur before returning to college for credentials. Just completed requirements and received a $20,000 grant to work with junior high school students in distributive education. Native of India; practicing Catholic.

Candidate 5: Twenty-six-year-old woman, divorced, supports self and three small children. Highly creative; three years of experience; outstanding recommendations on professional capability. Native of Puerto Rico.

Candidate 6: Fifty-eight-year-old man, highly respected former Episcopal minister who left pulpit to work full time with children. Has just completed teaching credentials.

Candidate 7: Forty-eight-year-old woman, widowed. Twenty-five years of experience, including three years in the Infants School of England. Wants to incorporate Infant School concepts here. Independently wealthy through both her own and her spouse's families.

Candidate 8: Twenty-two-year-old woman, single, a year of experience, excellent recommendations. Voluntarily tutored all four years in college, including full time in summers. Living openly in the community with a man of another race.

Follow-up: Discuss the selections of each committee member. When your group has selected four teacher candidates for the jobs, post your selections and compare your choices with those of other groups.

REFERENCES

Anyon, J. (2003). Inner cities, affluent suburbs, and unequal educational opportunity (pp. 85–102). In J.A. Banks, & C.M. Banks, (Eds.), *Multicultural education: Issues & perspectives* (4th ed.). New York: John Wiley & Sons.

Presents statistical data and curriculum examples to address the disparities in education children receive based on the economic status of their families and communities.

Apple, M.W., & Beane, J.A. (Eds.). (1995). *Democratic schools.* Alexandria, VA: Association for Supervision and Curriculum Development.

Includes narratives written by those involved in reform efforts in four schools and describes how educators and students established democratic policies and practices.

Appleton, N. (1983). *Cultural pluralism in education: Theoretical foundations.* New York, NY: Longman.

Examines how the United States has become pluralistic, how American education has responded to pluralism, and what our pluralistic society might look like in the future.

Baker, G.C. (1994). *Planning and organizing for multicultural instruction.* Reading, MA: Addison Wesley.

Presents a conceptual approach to multicultural education and practical suggestions for implementing multicultural education in curriculum and instruction.

Banks, J.A. (2008). *An introduction to multicultural education* (4th ed.). Boston, MA: Pearson Allyn & Bacon.

Explains major concepts, principles, theories, and practices in multicultural education.

Banks, J.A. (2006). *Cultural diversity and education: Foundations, curriculum and teaching* (5th ed.). Boston, MA: Allyn & Bacon.

Discusses the evolution of multiethnic, pluralistic education and analyzes curricular issues and teaching strategies for implementing multiethnic content.

Banks, J.A. (2004). Multicultural education: Characteristics and goals (pp. 3–27). In J.A. Banks, & C.M. Banks, (Eds.), *Multicultural education: Issues & perspectives* (5th ed.). New York: John Wiley & Sons.

Updates text by including emergent issues post 9/11 and new chapters on diversity in religion, socio-economic class, and recruiting gifted students from unrepresented racial and ethnic groups.

Banks, J.A. (2003). Multicultural education: Characteristics and goals (pp. 3–30). In J.A. Banks, & C.M. Banks, (Eds.), *Multicultural education: Issues & perspectives* (4th ed.). New York: John Wiley & Sons.

Provides an overview of multicultural education in general, and discusses specific issues pertaining to various culturally diverse groups.

Bazron, B., Osher, D., & Fleischman, S. (2005). Creating culturally responsive schools. *Educational Leadership, 63*(1), 83–84.

Discusses how a culturally responsive approach to education can make classroom instruction more congruent with the cultural value system of a diverse student population.

Brameld, T.B.H. (1956). *Toward a reconstructed philosophy of education.* New York, NY: Dryden Press.

Advocates for school reform promoting a more democratic society.

Carlisle, L.R., Jackson, B.W., & George, A. (2006). Principles of social justice education: The Social Justice Education in Schools project. *Equity & Excellence in Education, 39,* 55–64.

Argues for an approach to multicultural urban education based on social justice principles to increase equity and student achievement.

Carse, J. (1986). *Finite and infinite games: A vision of life as play and possibility.* New York, NY: Free Press.

Describes two philosophical orientations toward life, one collaborative and the other competitive, and explains their divergent responses to life experiences.

Clark, C. (2007). *Understanding neoliberalism and its impact on education.* NAME Conference, Baltimore, November 2007.

Explains how educational standardization undermines ideals of democratic engagement and critical thinking and creates a "school to prison pipeline" for minority students.

Cochran-Smith, M. (2003). Standing at the cross-roads: Multicultural teacher education at the beginning of the 21st century. *Multicultural Perspectives, 5*(3), 3–11.

Describes three issues of critical interest to U.S. educators: teacher/student demographic data and trends, competing school reform agendas, and criticisms of educational research.

Combs, A.W. (1979). *Myths in education: Beliefs that hinder progress and their alternatives.* Boston, MA: Allyn & Bacon.

Analyzes many myths about values, human nature, and education that influence educators and students and interfere with students learning and being successful in school.

Cymrot, T.Z. (2002). What is diversity? In L. Darling-Hammond, J. French, & S.P. Garcia Lopez (Eds.), *Learning to teach for social justice* (pp. 13–17). New York, NY: Teachers College Press.

Examines the concept of diversity and teachers' reluctance to acknowledge differences.

Darling-Hammond, G. (2002). Learning to teach for social justice. In L. Darling-Hammond, J. French, & S.P. Garcia Lopez (Eds.), *Learning to teach for social justice* (pp. 1–7). New York, NY: Teachers College Press.

Explains how Stanford Teacher Education Program faculty assist teacher preparation students to become educators teaching for social change.

Darling-Hammond, L., French, J., & Garcia-Lopez, S.P. (2002). *Learning to teach for social justice.* New York, NY: Teachers College Press.

Examination of experiences and concerns of student teachers committed to teaching about social justice.

Dean, J. (2007). Living algebra, living wage. *Rethinking Schools* Vol. 21 #4, pp. 31–35.

Describes in detail a lesson plan for incorporating students' lived experiences related to work, pay, costs of living, and budgeting into an algebra lesson.

Derman Sparks, L., & Ramsey, P. (2004). *What if all the kids are white?: Anti-bias multicultural education with young children and families.* New York, NY: Teachers College Press.

Provides strategies for teachers to engage young children in anti-racist learning; Chapter 4 provides a rationale for culturally responsive teaching and explains how teachers can implement this approach in primarily white and suburban schools.

DiAngelo, R. (2006). "I'm leaving!": White fragility in racial dialogue. In B. McMahon & D. Armstrong (Eds.), *Inclusion in urban educational environments: Addressing issues of diversity, equity, and social justice* (pp. 213–240). Centre for Leadership and Diversity. Ontario Institute for Studies in Education of the University of Toronto.

An analysis of the impact of racial segregation on white students' ability to withstand the discomfort of talking about race with students of color.

Diller, J.V., & Moule, J. (2005). *Cultural competence: A primer for educators.* Belmont, CA: Wadsworth.

Describes cross-cultural teaching using numerous classroom examples.

The Education Alliance Brown University (2006). Principles for culturally responsive teaching. Retrieved May 6th, 2009, from http://www.alliance.brown.edu/tdl/tl-strategies/crt-principles.shtml.

Promoting educational change and advocating for populations whose access to excellent education has been limited or denied, this website is filled with practical resources, including curriculum guides, publications, and access to diversity consultants.

Gardner, H. (1999). *Intelligence reframed: Multiple intelligences for the 21st century.* New York, NY: Basic Books.

Explains the theory of multiple intelligences, examines three possible additions to the theory, addresses myths and realities concerning the theory and its practical applications.

Gardner, H. (1993). *Multiple intelligences: The theory in practice.* New York, NY: Basic Books.

Reviews earlier theories of intelligence and discusses the evidence in support of the existence of a number of intelligences and the implications of this theory for educators.

Gay, G. (2000). *Culturally responsive teaching: Theory, research, & practice.* New York, NY: Teachers College Press.

Provides insights from theory, research and classroom practice to show that the performance of underachieving minority pupils is improved when teaching is filtered through their cultural experiences and frames of references.

Gay, G. (1977). Curriculum design for multicultural education. In C.A. Grant (Ed.), *Multicultural education: Commitments, issues, and applications* (pp. 94–104). Washington, DC: Association for Supervision and Curriculum Development.

Describes a philosophy of multicultural education as a basis for developing specific objectives and organizational principles for designing a multicultural curriculum.

Gayle-Evans, G., & Michael, D. (2006). A study of pre-service teachers' awareness of multicultural issues. *Multicultural Perspectives, 8*(1), 44–50.

Reviews research on teacher awareness of multicultural issues and presents results of their study on the awareness of preservice teachers to these issues.

Gordon, J.A. (2005). In search of educators of color: If we make school a more positive experience for students of color, they'll be more likely to continue with their education, and perhaps select teaching as a profession. *Leadership, 35*(2), 30–36.

Argues that culturally responsive teaching can make school a more positive experience for students of color and motivate more students of color to enter the teaching profession.

Hilliard, A. (1974). Restructuring teacher education for multicultural imperatives. In W.A. Hunter (Ed.), *Multicultural education through competency-based teacher education* (pp. 40–55). Washington, DC: American Association of Colleges for Teacher Education.

Provides definitions, rationale, general aims, methods, and content for a multicultural preparation of teacher education students.

Howard, G.R. (2006). *We can't teach what we don't know: White teachers, multiracial schools* (2nd ed.). New York, NY: Teachers College Press.

Discusses issues such as social dominance and racial identity development in relation to helping teachers, especially white teachers, become effective multicultural educators.

Howard, T. (2003). Culturally relevant pedagogy: ingredients for critical teacher reflection. *Theory into Practice 42*(3), 195–202.

Outlines theoretical and practical considerations for culturally relevant teaching and argues that the development of culturally relevant teaching strategies is dependent upon the ability of teachers and students to reflect critically on their race and culture.

Hunter, W.A. (1974). Antecedents to development of and emphasis on multicultural education. In W.A. Hunter (Ed.), *Multicultural education through competency-based teacher education* (pp. 11–31). Washington, DC: American Association of Colleges for Teacher Education.

Provides a historical overview of intergroup relations in the United States, the rise of cultural pluralism, and the need and support for multicultural education.

Johnson, H.B., & Shapiro, T.M. (2003). Good neighborhoods, good schools: Race and the "good choices" of white families. In A.W. Doane & E. Bonilla-Silva (Eds.), *White out: The continuing significance of race*. New York: Routledge.

Presents racist beliefs of white parents in a study in which these parents identified race as the primary factor in choosing schools for their children.

Kagan, S. (2006, Fall). The power to transform race relations. *Teaching Tolerance, 30*, 53.

Provides a brief review of research on the influence of cooperative learning on race relations.

Kearney, J.E. (2008). Factors affecting satisfaction and retention of African American and European American teachers in an urban school district: Implications for building and maintaining teachers employed in school districts across the nation. *Education and Urban Society, 40*(5), 613–627.

Describes how an urban school district recruited and retained minority teachers and examines data on factors that increase or decrease minority teacher satisfaction.

Kershaw, T. (1992). The effects of educational tracking on the social mobility of African Americans. *Journal of Black Studies, 23*(1), 152–170.

Analyzes criteria used to determine student placement in tracking systems; explains how black students are discriminated against and the negative consequences of such decisions.

Kneller, G.F. (1971). *Introduction to the philosophy of education* (2nd ed.). New York, NY: Macmillan.

Examines the intellectual foundations for five contemporary educational philosophies.

Koppelman, K. (2001). Like a whale. In *Values in the key of life: Making harmony in the human community* (pp. 57–63). Amityville, NY: Baywood.

Examines the difficulty that Americans have accepting human diversity.

Kozol, J. (2005). *The shame of the nation: The restoration of apartheid schooling in America*. New York, NY: Crown.

Examines evidence of race and class segregation and the inadequacy of facilities for low income students in urban schools.

Kozol, J. (1991). *Savage inequalities: Children in America's schools*. New York, NY: HarperPerennial, 1991.

Discusses documented disparities in education between schools of different classes and races and includes observations of various classrooms in urban public school systems.

Ladson-Billings, G. (2001). *Crossing over to Canaan: The journey of new teachers in diverse classrooms.* San Francisco, CA: Jossey-Bass.

Describes the experiences of eight teachers starting their careers in urban elementary schools and their use of student cultures to enhance academic achievement.

Ladson-Billings, G. (1995). Toward a theory of culturally relevant pedagogy. *American Educational Research Journal, 32* 3, 465–491.

Describes the teaching practices of eight exemplary teachers of African American students and offers a way to define and recognize culturally relevant pedagogy.

Laosa, L. (1974). Toward a research model of multicultural competency-based education. In W. Hunter (Ed.), *Multicultural education through competency-based education.* Washington, DC: American Association of Colleges for Teacher Education.

Discusses the value of cultural diversity and the need for competency-based programs to prepare teachers for working with culturally diverse students.

Michelli, N.M. (2005). Education for democracy: What can it be? In N.M. Michelli & D.L. Keiser (Eds.). *Teacher education for democracy and social justice* (pp. 3–30). New York, NY: Routledge.

Examines limitations often imposed on the concept of citizenship, the barriers to an appropriate education for citizens of a democracy, and hopeful signs for the future.

Myrdal, G. (1944). *An American dilemma: The Negro problem and modern democracy.* New York, NY: Harper & Row.

Describes values and contradictions in American culture and how they relate to the pervasive prejudice in American society.

National Center for Education Statistics. (2005). The nation's report card: Mathematics 2005 (No. NCES 2006453). Washington, DC: U.S. Government Printing Office.

Presents results of the National Assessment of Educational Progress (NAEP) 2005 in fourth- and eighth-grade mathematics assessments for U.S. students showing that math scores have increased overall.

Nieto, S. (2008). *Affirming diversity: The sociopolitical context of multicultural education* (5th ed.). Boston, MA: Pearson Allyn & Bacon.

Provides a comprehensive analysis of how schools are failing to meet the needs of students of color and suggests strategies for more effective teaching based on research and practice.

Nieto, S. (1999). *The light in their eyes.* New York, NY: Teachers College Press

Describes teaching and learning as a social as well as an academic pursuit and provides many examples of teachers practicing multicultural education.

Oakes, J. (2005). *Keeping track: How schools structure inequality.* (2nd ed.). New Haven, CT: Yale University Press.

Documents how tracking practices have perpetuated racial and social class inequalities.

Oakes, J., & Wells, A.S. (1996). *Beyond the technicalities of school reform: Policy lessons from detracking schools.* Los Angeles, CA: UCLA Graduate School of Education and Information Studies.

Describes problems affecting students in tracked classes and strategies for detracking schools.

Oakes, J., Selvin, M., Karoly, L., & Guiton, G. (1992). *Educational matchmaking: Academic and vocational tracking in comprehensive high schools.* Santa Monica, CA: RAND.

Examines tracking practices in five high schools in terms of curriculum, consequences, and participation by race and gender.

Oakes, J., Quartz, K.H., Ryan, S., & Lipton, M. (2000). *Becoming good American schools: The struggle for civic virtue in school reform.* San Francisco, CA: Jossey-Bass.

Describes the effort of sixteen schools in five states to move away from tracked classes and implement other reforms to improve the education of all students.

Orfield, G., Losen, D., Wald, J., & Swanson, C. (2004). *Losing our future: How minority youth are being left behind by the graduation rate crisis.* Cambridge, MA: The Civil Rights Project at Harvard University. Contributors: Advocates for Children of New York, The Civil Society Institute.

Explores the increasing drop in high school graduation rates for students of color and challenges policymakers to address this as an urgent educational and civil rights crisis.

Oakes, J., Wells, A.S., Jones, M., & Datnow, A. (1997). Detracking: The social construction of ability, cultural politics, and resistance to reform. *Teachers College Record, 95* (3), 482–510.

Presents results from a 3-year longitudinal study of 10 racially and socio-economically mixed secondary schools participating in detracking reform; explores how broadly held conceptions of intelligence intervene in efforts to detrack schools.

Pai, Y., & Adler, S. (1997). *Cultural foundations of education* (2nd ed.). Upper Saddle River, NJ: Merrill Prentice Hall.

Examines education as a cultural phenomenon, the implications for schooling, and provides information about curriculum and pedagogy as a foundation for multicultural education.

Pang, V.O. (2005). *Multicultural education: A caring-centered, reflective approach.* (2nd ed.). Boston, MA: McGraw-Hill.

Presents stories and classroom examples to illustrate concepts of culture, discrimination, and social justice, explaining how teachers can effectively address these concepts. Uses actual experiences to illustrate major concepts in multicultural education and explains how these concepts can be incorporated into school classrooms.

Partridge, E. (1983). *Origins: A short etymological dictionary of modern English* (p. 92). New York, NY: Greenwich.

Citation notes that the Latin *ducere* means to lead and is the basis for Duke, p. 169.

Pasternak, M.G. (1986). *Helping kids learn multicultural concepts: A handbook of strategies.* Champaign, IL: Research Press.

Describes activities developed for an urban school system to create a multicultural environment for a multiethnic student population.

Piaget, J. (1974). *The language and thought of the child* (Rev. ed.). New York, NY: New American Library.

Includes a collection of preliminary studies on the exchange of thought between children, their verbal understanding, and how social conditions affect the development of thought.

Sapon-Shevin, M. (1999). *Because we can change the world: A practical guide to building cooperative, inclusive classroom communities.* Boston, MA: Allyn & Bacon.

Provides strategies and activities that reflect principles of multicultural education, although it is primarily intended for creating cohesive classrooms in elementary schools.

Sensoy, Ö. (in press, 2009). It's all in your name: Seeing ourselves in historical and cultural context. In E. Heilman, R. Fruja, & M. Missias (Eds.), *Social studies and diversity teacher education: What we do and why.* New York, NY: Routledge.

Describes in detail a culturally responsive lesson using student names, and provides an in-depth analysis and rationale for the lesson.

Shade, B.J., Kelly, C., & Oberg, M. (1997). *Creating culturally responsive classrooms.* Washington, DC: American Psychological Association.

Examines the impact of culture on learning and suggests strategies to motivate students from diverse cultural groups in the United States.

Sheets, R.H. (2005). *Diversity pedagogy: Examining the role of culture in the teaching-learning process.* Boston, MA: Pearson Education.

Discusses the significance of culture for student learning and explains how teachers can engage in classroom practices to take advantage of cultural differences.

Sleeter, C.E. (1996). *Multicultural education as social activism.* Albany: State University of New York Press.

Explores the value of multicultural education for white people and the impact of the connections between race, gender, and class in the struggle for social justice.

Sleeter, C.E., & Grant, C.A. (2003). *Making choices for multicultural education: Five approaches to race, class, and gender* (4th ed.). New York, NY: John Wiley.

Examines how concepts of race, class, and gender are presented to students and how students are asked to respond in five different approaches to multicultural education.

Sleeter, C.E., & Grant, C.A. (2009). *Turning on learning: Five approaches for multicultural teaching plans for race, class, gender, and disability* (5th ed.). Hoboken, NJ: Wiley.

Provides lesson plans consistent with each of the five approaches to multicultural education the authors identified in previous research.

Stephan, W. (1999). *Reducing prejudice and stereotyping in schools.* New York, NY: Teachers College Press.

Reviews theories of prejudice and stereotyping, examines conditions to promote changes in negative attitudes and describes techniques for improving race relations in schools.

Stevens, T., Hamman, D., & Olivarez, A. (2007). Hispanic students' perception of white teachers' mastery goal orientation influences sense of school belonging, *Journal of Latinos and Education, 6*(1), 55–70.

Presents a study finding that Hispanic students were more likely to feel a sense of belonging in school when white teachers held high expectations for them.

Terkel, S. (1980). *American dreams: Lost and found.* New York, NY: Ballantine.

Includes interviews with diverse people about their perceptions of America, including the author of *Black Like Me*, John Howard Griffin.

Tiedt, P.L., & Tiedt, I.M. (2002). *Multicultural teaching: A handbook of activities, information, and resources* (6th ed.). Boston, MA: Allyn & Bacon.

Provides strategies for thematic studies and learning modules with specific multicultural lessons in various disciplines for teachers in elementary and middle level classrooms.

Tobin, K., & Roth, W-M. (2005). Implementing co-teaching and cogenerative dialoguing in urban science education. *School Science and Mathematics, 105,* 313–322.

Describes the preparation of science educators to teach in urban schools by decreasing teacher isolation, mitigating turnover and retention, and addressing contradictions that may arise from the cultural and ethnic diversity of students and teachers.

Villegas, A., & Lucas, T. (2002). *Educating culturally responsive teachers: A coherent approach*. New York: State University of New York Press.

Offers a conceptual framework and practical strategies for preparing teachers for culturally responsive teaching in schools with increasingly diverse racial and ethnic student populations.

CHAPTER 15

Pluralism in Society: Creating Unity in a Diverse America

66 How many goodly creatures are there here!
How beauteous mankind is!
O brave new world,
That has such people in't. *99*

William Shakespeare (1564–1616)

All around us, a brave new world is indeed taking shape in America. Despite a wealth of **diversity,** America has not yet become a pluralistic society. **Pluralism** entails perceiving human differences as enriching, and valuing that diversity in our society. Yet Americans are still wary of one another, and fearful when conflicts occur between groups. Nevertheless, changes are taking place that encourage us to become more accepting of others and more pluralistic. It is obvious that students in K–12 schools and colleges today will shape our society in the future; yet many Americans don't realize that almost 40% of all K–12 children and youth are students of color. According to 2000 census data, students of color in California and Texas comprise 50% of the K–12 population. Immigrants constitute 12% of the American workforce, and 20% of all K–12 students are foreign-born or have foreign-born parents (Cochran-Smith, 2003; Pipher, 2002). U.S. trade agreements guarantee that these figures will increase.

The diversity and location of racial and ethnic groups have changed dramatically: for example, more than 600 Somali refugees live in Owatonna, Minnesota. And although our media still tend to present U.S. diversity as principally African American, Hispanic Americans have become the largest ethnic minority group. As these societal changes occur, they are reflected in organizations such as the American military: More than 1,400 Muslims and 1,240 Buddhists serve in the U.S. Armed Forces. One out of every five soldiers recruited by the army is a woman, and half are African American (Katzenstein & Reppy, 1999; Matthews, 1999).

To capitalize on these unprecedented demographic changes, Americans must realize the need for new approaches to living and working together and must create new partnerships with people in their communities. In Billings, Montana, a Jewish family decorated their home for Hanukkah and placed a menorah by their front window. After a vandal threw a cinder block through their window, thousands of Christian families put pictures of menorahs in their windows so vandals could not identify for certain which homes in their community had Jewish families (Eck, 2001).

America is the most diverse society in our diverse world: The global presence of major U.S. corporations requires sensitivity to diverse global issues and cultures. Americans come from almost every country on the planet; our diversity is represented by differences not only in geographical origins (ethnicity) but also in religion, social class, disabilities, gender, sexual orientation, age, region, and dialect, as well as individuals in multiple categories.

Psychologist Howard Gardner (2006) identified five categories of mental abilities that will be increasingly necessary in the future, not just in the United States but globally, and he argues that schools and professional training programs need to be cultivating these skills now. He calls one of these categories "The Respectful Mind," and it is characterized by a person's ability to encounter others without being threatened by their individual or cultural differences, but rather to respond to them with acceptance and respect. Gardner believes this mental ability can be taught, especially when teachers successfully model this behavior, but the lessons cannot come from teachers alone: "Messages of respect or disrespect, tolerance or intolerance, are signaled throughout a society" (p. 111). Gardner insists that simply tolerating differences is an inadequate response to the human diversity that is increasing in societies around the world; he rejects the idea of ignoring differences such as pretending to be "color-blind," but advocates for fostering pluralistic attitudes that enable people to interact and collaborate more effectively with the diverse individuals they will inevitably encounter

> For each age is a dream that is dying. Or one that is coming to birth.
>
> **Arthur O'Shaughnessy (1844–1881)**

in schools, while shopping, at recreational activities, at work, and even in neighborhoods as intolerance and old patterns of racial segregation finally begin to break down.

Forces at work in all areas of society increasingly recognize pluralism as a preferred alternative to the Anglo conformity demanded in the past. Although the transformation from America's preference for conformity to an unequivocal acceptance of human differences will not be resolved for decades to come, we must be aware of recent changes and prepare for future challenges. This chapter reports on five major societal areas—the federal government, higher education, business, mass media, and the military—and how each is making conscious and deliberate efforts to respond positively to diversity in the United States. The information provided is based on these three questions:

How do advocates promote pluralism?
How do detractors oppose pluralism?
What changes illustrate progress toward pluralism?

Regardless of the profession chosen, most individuals starting their careers are likely to encounter some form of the challenges and changes described in this chapter.

Federal Government

President John F. Kennedy first used the phrase **affirmative action** when he issued Executive Order 10025 mandating that the federal government aggressively recruit and hire African Americans (Painter, 2005). Title VII of the 1964 Civil Rights Act expanded this concept to include people of color and women being employed by private companies contracted to do work for the federal government. Companies had to file affirmative action plans with hiring goals and timetables for those goals. By mandating affirmative action, the federal government began a major initiative to promote pluralism by reducing acts of discrimination and providing opportunity for women and people of color. Title VII stated that if a court rules a finding of discrimination is justified, the court might order an employer "to take such affirmative action as may be appropriate." A 1972 Title VII amendment added "or any other equitable relief as the courts deem appropriate" (Greene, 1989, p. 15). Title VII has been controversial from the moment the Civil Rights Act became law, consistently keeping the issue of equal opportunity for all Americans in the public eye.

According to the Civil Rights Act, affirmative action plans represent voluntary programs unless a court orders that an affirmative action plan be designed and implemented. Determining the need for an affirmative action plan begins by analyzing the diversity of employees at a business or agency, or the student population at a university. If population variation is similar to that of available applicants, there is said to be no equity problem. If disparities exist, however, each phase of the application and selection process is evaluated for bias that may advantage some applicants and disadvantage others.

The Affirmative Action Debate

Debate concerning affirmative action has resonated from the public square to the U.S. Supreme Court.

The crux of the debate concerns whether affirmative action was intended only to redress victims of intentional discrimination or if it mandates that programs create a more just distribution of women and minorities in the workforce and in higher education. In the business community, the principal emphasis has been on compensating victims of discrimination; institutions of higher education have implemented admissions policies designed to increase the numbers of women and minorities admitted.

Affirmative action advocates argue that aggressive action is required to address inequities in hiring and college admissions. Proponents insist our society must guarantee equal opportunity to every citizen, and they argue that ample evidence demonstrates our failure to achieve this goal. Because a college education is required to become qualified for certain jobs, policies and practices of college admission are scrutinized, just as businesses and corporations are monitored to ensure that women and minorities have the same opportunity as white men to work and to receive promotions. Affirmative action advocates explain that monitoring is not intended as punitive, but rather that it meets a broader goal of strengthening our society by creating racial, gender, and ethnic unity. Greene (1989) argued that if white men "continue to hold positions of power and prestige to the exclusion of other groups . . . divisions will continue to exist" (p. 10).

Affirmative action opponents counter that equal opportunity programs have created greater American disunity. They denounce affirmative action plans as racist when race is emphasized to create quotas, establishing what they term "preferential treatment." Opponents also claim that businesses and schools have often been forced to accept women and minorities who are less qualified than the rejected white men. They say it is ironic that affirmative action with a goal of reducing discrimination is engaging in "reverse discrimination"— decreasing opportunity for qualified white men. Eastland (2000) expressed gratitude for reverse discrimination lawsuits because they remind us of the principle "that no one in America should be discriminated against on account of race" (p. 175). Opponents also suggest that affirmative action plans have an adverse effect on society because quality and competence are being compromised, making the "solution" worse than the problem.

Judicial Limitations on Affirmative Action

Quality and competence were the focus of the *Griggs v. Duke Power* case heard by the U.S. Supreme Court in 1971. Job applicants at the Duke Power Company were required to have a high school diploma or passing scores on a specific standardized test. Lawyers argued that the requirement excluded a higher percentage of blacks than whites because unequal educational opportunities and other inequities prevented more black than white youth from earning high school diplomas. The U.S. Supreme Court ruled that any hiring practice that was intended to select the most qualified candidates was legitimate. Companies could not be held accountable for past discrimination that adversely affected individuals in the present. As long as job requirements were related to work performance, they could not be labeled discriminatory, even if they did advantage some job applicants.

Based on the same concept, the U.S. Supreme Court also upheld the *seniority system* to determine layoffs during economic downturns. Because of past discrimination against women and minorities, adhering to **seniority system** priorities required employers to lay off people with least seniority: "last hired is the first fired." Although the procedure seemed race neutral, lawyers provided evidence that the majority of women and minority employees had low seniority and were most likely to be dismissed. Supreme Court justices acknowledged the problem but consistently have found the seniority system constitutional because it does not represent intentional discrimination. The Court has ruled with the same consistency on cases where the affirmative action plan appears to include a racial quota, that is, a specific number of people hired or accepted based on race.

Affirmative Action and Quotas

Whenever **racial quotas** have been employed, the U.S. Supreme Court has always ruled against them, declaring that Title VII never mandated racial (or other) quotas. Indeed, the justices are correct. There is no mention of quotas in Title VII, nor anything to suggest that employers must hire unqualified applicants; as Greene (1989) noted, section 703 (j) of Title VII states:

Nothing contained in this title shall be interpreted to require any employer, employment agency, labor organization, or joint labor-management committee subject to this title to grant preferential treatment to any individual or group. (p. 60)

One of the clearest judgments against racial quotas was the Supreme Court's ruling in the case of *Regents of California v. Bakke*. In 1970, 80% of the 800 students of color attending medical school in the United States were enrolled in programs at two historically black universities. Because minorities were never more than 3% of students at the University of California–Davis Medical School, the university decided to reserve eight of their admissions places (16%) for minority applicants. For two consecutive

> One who gains strength by overcoming obstacles possesses the only strength which can overcome adversity.
>
> **Albert Schweitzer (1875–1965)**

years, Alan Bakke was rejected by UC–Davis despite having a grade-point average and Medical College Admissions Test scores higher than those of several minority applicants admitted. Ball (2000) explained the strategy of Bakke's lawyers in arguing relentlessly against the concept of racial quotas while UC–Davis lawyers argued that the university only accepted academically qualified applicants to their medical school and that preferential treatment of minorities was necessary to increase the numbers of minorities in professions "from which minorities were long excluded because of generations of pervasive racial discrimination" (p. 92).

The final decision on *Bakke* in 1978 fragmented the Court. Four justices approved UC–Davis affirmative action procedures, and four justices rejected them, arguing that race should play no role whatsoever on admission decisions. Justice Powell cast the deciding vote. In his written opinion, Powell declared that racial quotas were an unconstitutional strategy for achieving affirmative action goals, but that race could be used as one factor among others in considerations of college applicants.

Affirmative Action for Minority-Owned Businesses

Another affirmative action strategy rejected by the courts was the practice of setting aside a certain percentage of tax-funded projects for minority-owned businesses. In 1983, the city of Richmond, Virginia, was 50% African American, but in the previous five years, less than 1% of funds spent on city projects had been paid to minority-owned businesses. The Richmond city council approved an affirmative action plan to require recipients of city construction projects to subcontract at least 30% of the dollar value of these projects to minority-owned businesses. When J.A. Croson Company insisted it could not find any suitable minority-owned businesses and asked for a waiver of the subcontracting requirement, the city refused and informed the company that it would resubmit their part of the project for new bids. The company brought the case to federal court, and the Supreme Court ruled on the case in 1989.

Writing for the majority in the *City of Richmond v. J.A. Croson Co.*, Sandra Day O'Connor criticized Richmond's **set-aside program** for its apparently arbitrary determination of the 30% figure and for not providing evidence demonstrating that previous major contractors had intentionally discriminated against minority-owned businesses. O'Connor said the Richmond City Council could have implemented effective, race-neutral strategies rather than establishing set-aside quotas. The court affirmed the right to remedy past discrimination, but again rejected racial quotas as a legitimate constitutional strategy (Crosby & VanDeVeer, 2000).

The Future of Affirmative Action

In 1995, the National Employment Lawyers Association issued a position paper citing a number of studies in support of affirmative action to substantiate their contention that affirmative action had "significantly reduced job discrimination and improved occupational status and mobility for minorities and women" (2000, p. 711). Yet because of ongoing criticism of affirmative action, during that same year, President Clinton appointed a task force to review all federal affirmative action programs. Although some changes were recommended, the task force concluded that programs reviewed did not include quotas, did not mandate preferences for unqualified individuals, and did not engage in reverse discrimination. Instead, the programs were designed to remedy past discrimination and "lead the nation toward the goal of equal opportunity" (Ball, 2000, p. 163).

California voters did not agree. In 1996, they voted to approve **Proposition 209,** prohibiting preferential treatment to individuals or groups in hiring, awarding public contracts, and college admissions. According to Ball (2000), African American admissions to California law schools dropped 72% the year after the proposition was approved, and admission of all students of color to UC–Berkeley dropped 50%. The following year, UCLA and Berkeley reported continuing decreases in numbers of students of color. In response to complaints of increased segregation on state university campuses, California legislators voted to guarantee admission to any California university campus to all high school students graduating in the top 4% of their class. Critics said the vote represented a cynical recognition of racial segregation in California high schools. Although other states such as Oregon have

passed propositions similar to Proposition 209, advocates argued that eliminating affirmative action was premature, and most would agree with the perspective expressed by Clayton and Crosby (2000):

> When the goals of true equality have been reached . . . affirmative action will be unnecessary. We have not yet reached such a happy state of being. Sexism and racism are still strong forces in American society, and both hostility toward and stereotypes about women and people of color influence decisions. (p. 88)

Higher Education

Since the 1960s, colleges and universities have implemented affirmative action plans to increase the numbers of students of color on their campuses. Although many administrators initially viewed affirmative action as unnecessary interference, in recent years administrators have displayed a pluralistic attitude, arguing that diversity of all kinds benefits

FIGURE 15.1

Source: Courtesy of *The Daily Cardinal,* University of Wisconsin.

the entire student population. Administrators, faculty, and student leaders on college campuses have consistently supported setting diversity goals. Musil (1996) summarized their perspective:

> To invite that diversity onto campus is not simply an act of charity. It is an act of raw self-interest. . . . it will make higher education better than it is. It expands our notion of learning. It widens what we study and how we study it. It improves our pedagogy. It adds to our resources in human capital. (p. 225)

Criticism of Diversity Goals in Higher Education

Affirmative action plans in higher education and the increased diversity they have helped produce have been the subject of much criticism. Even some people of color say affirmative action has stigmatized students of color, as white students question their academic ability and believe they are admitted through lower standards. Some faculty blame affirmative action for a perceived decline in academic standards and for promoting a multicultural curriculum that has caused a decline in the rigor of traditional college education.

Critics persist in denouncing changes in traditional curriculum, accusing faculty who are creating a more inclusive curriculum of having a "political agenda" rather than purely academic objectives. However, it would seem equally appropriate to accuse advocates for the preservation of a curriculum emphasizing white people as having a political agenda as well. One persistent criticism is that there has been widespread elimination of traditional Western civilization courses by universities in response to pressure from "multiculturalists." According to a 1999 survey, almost 60% of college faculty believed that Western civilization courses are the foundation of undergraduate education, and more than half of all U.S. colleges still require Western civilization courses (Yamane, 2001).

The critics are correct in insisting that feminists and people of color are challenging the lack of relevance and inclusiveness in college curricula. Duncan (2002) noted that women and students of color in college courses encounter minimal information written by or about their groups, and often the information provided misrepresents or distorts the group being described. Even worse, Duncan claimed that students of color find "both explicit and subtle racist themes in what they . . . study" (p. 45). What is included in college curricula is a critical issue, as Groff and Cain explained: "Curriculum is a microcosm of the culture: its inclusions and exclusions are an index of what the culture deems important" (Yamane, 2001, p. 6).

Diversity in College Faculty and Course Content

In addition to the omission of people of color in curriculum, few faculty of color are represented at most universities. Tusmith and Reddy (2002) reported that people of color constitute less than 15% of higher education faculty, and that the majority were nontenured lecturers or instructors. Browne-Miller (1996) quoted an Asian American student observing that the teaching styles of her white professors were "geared to white middle-class males, overlooking the fact that this may not be the most effective . . . with non-white students and women" (p. 90). Courses taught by faculty of color would benefit all students, including white students, by presenting perspectives they are not likely to have encountered. Reddy (2002) noted,

> Students—especially but not exclusively white students—arrive in our college classrooms with predictable baggage. Prepared by virtually every element of the society in which we live, they come ready to accept white authority, intelligence and rightness while discounting the views and experiences of people of color. (p. 54)

Because of Reddy's "predictable baggage," it is not inevitable that positive outcomes will occur if white students and students of color are brought together on a college campus; they may or may not enjoy each other or learn from each other. (See Figure 15.1.) Almost a century ago, journalist John Reed observed that participating in a diverse community may bring "pain, isolation of separateness, [or] intellectual exhilaration, greater self-knowledge and . . . human reconciliation" (Lowe, 1999, p. 22). To ensure productive interactions between members of diverse groups, colleges sponsor frequent diversity workshops and seminars, require all students to take at least one course on diversity, encourage relevant academic departments to include at least one course with significant content on diversity issues in their majors and minors, and encourage all faculty to integrate content about diversity issues into the courses they teach.

Since the 1960s, professors in numerous institutions of higher education have created scholarly courses focusing on one or more diverse groups. As these professors have grappled with diversity issues, their efforts have been learning experiences for themselves as well as their students. To struggle with diversity issues is to engage in an evolutionary process of change. According to Musil (1996), colleges cannot assume that they can "simply add diversity and stir and think the recipe will not be fundamentally altered" (p. 224). To illustrate, Musil went on to describe the limitations of initial courses developed to examine diversity issues, and what professors and students involved in those courses learned:

> Black studies were typically about only men. Women's studies were typically only about white women. Gay and lesbian studies had no practicing Christians or Jews. And none of the three paid much attention to those in the group who were old, working class or disabled. Today it is largely commonplace in the most influential texts . . . in these kinds of courses to recognize the reality of our multiple identities. (p. 228)

Unfortunately, enrollment figures indicate that only a few white students take ethnic studies courses, and there have been few men enrolled in women's studies courses. Duncan (2002) believes that most white students, especially white males, are so accustomed to white experience being the focus of curriculum that they feel strange, defensive, and uncomfortable as they struggle to understand information that focuses on experiences of women or people of color. Despite these difficulties, colleges and universities continue to promote the goal of students gaining knowledge about diverse groups. Although designed to heighten student acceptance of diverse populations, courses on diversity have tended to be an addition to rather than a replacement for traditional curriculum. Kolodny (1998) addressed the importance of adding diversity content to the traditional curriculum:

> We are expanding our students' repertoire of reading and interpretive strategies, teaching them to comprehend and appreciate the aesthetic rules and cultural practices governing the Zuni story of emergence as well as those governing the composition of a Shakespeare play. (p. 49)

In 1989, the University of Wisconsin System—consisting of 13 four-year and 12 two-year institutions of higher education—implemented a **Design for Diversity** plan mandating changes in policies and practices on all campuses to make them more welcoming places for students of color. Across America, universities have instituted changes to create positive environments for the increasingly diverse college student population. Humphreys (2000) presented results of a survey finding that 63% of colleges and universities either have at least one diversity course as a graduation requirement or they are developing such a course; 42% require more than one course; 25% have had such a requirement for more than ten years.

Results and Possibilities

Diversity courses not only provide greater understanding of diverse groups, but they also help students appreciate the benefits of diversity. In Browne-Miller (1996), one student learned "More diversity allows for more possibilities, be it knowledge, friends, understanding between people" (p. 83). In a society as diverse and democratic as the United States, colleges and universities must actively facilitate understanding between diverse groups. Ball (2000) commented, "For democracy to flourish, college students have to be able to interact with other students who are different from them" (p. 13). In a series of diversity reports, the American Association of Colleges and Universities (AACU) argued that diversity challenges democratic commitments: "instead of creating fragmentation and alienation . . . [AACU] asserts that only through diversity can we achieve a deeper and lasting national unity" (Musil, 1996, p. 226).

Diversity does not only refer to obvious differences of race, ethnicity, gender, or disabilities. Diversity includes other changes taking place in students attending college today: Almost 50% of all college students are over twenty-four years old, more than 50% are the first in their family to attend college, and students with learning disabilities are the fastest growing category of disabled students on our campuses. Individuals accepted today may re-

> Democracy is a way of life . . . a vibrant, living sweep of hope and progress which constantly strives for the fulfillment of its objective in life—the search for truth, justice, and human dignity.
>
> **Saul Alinsky (1909–1972)**

quire modifications of and accommodations within traditional policies and practices governing campuses. Yet as demographic developments and affirmative action plans change the face of our campuses, opponents struggle to maintain the status quo. White students filed suit against both graduate and undergraduate admissions programs at the University of Michigan for including race in their admissions procedures. In 2003, the Supreme Court's ruling on this case maintained its consistent position of allowing race to be used as a factor in admissions procedures while rejecting approaches that appear to establish racial quotas. Although there are likely to be further cases, this ruling affirmed the university's argument that having a diverse student body benefited all students at the University of Michigan; in addition, the justices provided further clarification concerning how universities can include race as a factor in admissions procedures.

Corporate and Small Business

It surprised some opponents of affirmative action to discover that several Fortune 500 corporations filed amicus briefs in support of Michigan's program; for the past two decades, the private sector has been in support of affirmative action. In the early 1980s, many corporations opposed the Reagan administration's efforts to reduce the demand for contractor compliance on federal projects. According to responses from Corporate Executive Officers (CEOs) reported by Reskin (2000), 122 of 128 major corpo-

rations would "retain their affirmative action plans [even] if the Federal government ended [required] affirmative action" (p. 111). On surveys, CEOs tend to agree that affirmative action has improved hiring, marketing, and productivity. According to Harvard business professor David Thomas, a diverse workforce is an "inescapable reality" for any corporation with over 100 employees no matter where it is located (Hymowitz, 2005).

In recent years, American business has become more attentive to diversity. They have to be. White men represent only 35% of the workforce today, and by 2010 people of color will constitute 40% of those entering the workforce (Daft, 2003). In a 2005 article for the *Wall Street Journal,* Hymowitz stated, "If companies are going to sell products and services globally, they will need a rich mix of employees with varied perspectives and experiences" (p. R1). Business leaders understand that responding positively to diversity by implementing pluralistic policies and practices is necessary because not only is the work force becoming more diverse, but so are the customers. Mor-Barak (2005) rejects the old workplace model requiring workers to conform to established organizational values and norms reflecting the dominant culture; instead, she argues for promoting a respect for "all cultural perspectives represented among its employees" (p. 8).

The numbers of women and people of color in the workforce mirror the percentage they represent as consumers, one certain to increase. In 2000, Secretary of Commerce Norman Mineta predicted, "America's population will increase 50% over the next 50 years, with almost 90% of that increase in the minority community" (Williams, 2003, p. 442). When people have money to spend, they command attention from American business. Williams claimed that people of color represent almost $800 billion of purchasing power, and 134 million American women have $1.1 trillion of purchasing power (see Table 15.1). One corporate president has insisted that more women must be appointed to corporate boards of directors primarily because "Women either control or influence nearly all consumer purchases" (Jones & George, 2003, p. 118).

Corporate Litigation

American demographic changes represent compelling reasons for corporate America to value di-

TABLE 15.1 Diversity and Purchasing Power Among U.S. Consumers

Group	Population Numbers	Purchasing Power
Gays and lesbians	20 million	$608 billion
People with disabilities	51 million	$220 billion
African Americans	34 million	$646 billion
Asian Americans	10 million	$296 billion
Hispanic Americans	35 million	$580 billion
Women	144 million	$1.1 trillion

Source: Census Bureau (2006) at www.census.gov and Cultural Access Group (2006) at www.accesscay.com

versity. Discrimination litigation has also provided motivation. In the 1980s and early 1990s, Denny's Restaurants were the sites for several alleged racist incidents such as one involving 21 secret service agents en route to Annapolis to make security preparations for a presidential visit. When they stopped at a Denny's restaurant to eat supper, the white agents were given what they ordered, but the black secret service agents were never served any food. Despite being one of the largest restaurant chains in the United States, Denny's hired few minority employees, and none of its major suppliers was a minority-owned firm. At the time of its purchase by Advantica Corporation, Denny's had just paid $54 million out of court to settle discrimination claims. According to Williams (2003), Advantica's CEO said the lawsuits had turned Denny's into "a poster child for racism" (p. 467).

Advantica took aggressive action to change the Denny image. As the twenty-first century began, 42% of Denny's employees were minorities, as were 33% of its managers. Nearly 20% of its suppliers were minority-owned firms, and 35% of its franchises were minority owned. Denny's commitment to diversity was recognized by *Fortune* magazine, which identified it as one of the top ten companies in its support of minorities. (see Table 15.2.)

In 1998, Arab American workers and managers alleged discrimination in decisions on promotions and pay raises in a class action lawsuit filed against Detroit Edison, the largest electric utility in Michigan. Detroit Edison representatives began negotiations immediately and promised changes. They kept their promises. They recruited and hired an Arab American widely known throughout the state to serve as vice president, and their contracts with suppliers included an increased number of businesses owned by people of Middle Eastern descent. In response, the Arab American community commended Detroit Edison, and its CEO accepted an invitation to serve on the advisory board of the Michigan chapter's Arab-American Anti-Discrimination committee (Millman, 2005).

Denny's and Detroit Edison's experiences are not isolated incidents. Shoney's Restaurants paid $132.8 million to settle a claim of racial discrimination in hiring; Edison International paid $11 million for the same offense. Bell Atlantic Telephone paid $500 million for discrimination against blacks in employee promotions. After making significant changes in policies and practices, all three companies are now listed among *Fortune* magazine's top 50 companies for their support of minorities (Williams, 2003). Global corporations such as Nike have also changed their policies and practices in response to accusations of discrimination or exploition (see the box on page 431).

Workplace Diversity

Most businesses do not address diversity issues in response to legal action, but rather because they recognize the advantages of promoting workplace diversity. In areas with significant Hispanic populations, Sears and Target Stores have profited by accommodating Hispanic consumers, as have Darden's Restaurants by providing Spanish menus (Jones & George, 2003). Furthermore, having diverse managers and employees increases the likelihood of appropriate responses to customer needs. To recruit a more diverse workforce, businesses use tactics such as (1) providing college scholarships and workplace mentors, (2) disseminating information on available jobs to local churches and Spanish-

> This country will not be a good place for any of us to live in unless we make it a good place for all of us to live in.
>
> **Theodore Roosevelt (1858–1919)**

language radio and television stations, (3) sponsoring seminars on diversity for managers, (4) establishing a full-time position as diversity coordinator, or (5) sponsoring community events such as Cinco de Mayo or a Gay Pride march (Hymowitz, 2005).

Having a positive work environment to accommodate diversity improves productivity and reduces turnover costs. The Employment Management Association estimates the average costs for hiring a new employee is $10,000 (Jones & George, 2003). According to Griffin (2002), one pharmaceutical corporation saved $50,000 by lowering its turnover rate among women and minorities. The creation of positive work environments for diverse employees may be one reason why 62% of job seekers said they would prefer to work for organizations

demonstrating a commitment to diversity (Daft, 2003).

Creating a positive work environment is not a simple task, but it must be done. In discussing current issues, Griffin (2002) stated that a fundamental trend in business "is that virtually all organizations . . . are becoming more diverse" (p. 169). Businesses define diversity as not only the obvious differences of race and gender, but also less obvious differences including status as single parents or dual-career couples. To accommodate diversity, some U.S. companies have created day care centers at their work sites or have instituted flexible working hours. Benefits packages have been structured to address the diverse needs of employees. Being flexible does not have to be expensive, even when providing accommodations for people with disabilities. According to Williams (2003), the average cost of accommodating workers with disabilities was $250; 20% of accommodations involved no direct cost.

Diversity Training Programs

Diversity training programs are not new, but older programs have been considered largely ineffective because they tended to use one of two approaches: sensitivity training, which appeared to have little practical value, or a confrontational approach that antagonized white men. Current diversity training covers a broader range of topics, focuses on a pragmatic business rationale for promoting diversity,

TABLE 15.2 America's Best Companies for Minorities

Company	Board of Directors	Officials and Managers	Total Workforce
McDonald's, Oak Brook, IL	2 of 16	36%	53%
Fannie Mae, Washington, D.C.	5 of 17	33%	44%
Denny's, Spartanburg, SC	3 of 9	29%	47%
Union Bank of CA, San Francisco, CA	3 of 12	39%	55%
Sempra Energy, San Diego, CA	4 of 12	29%	48%
Southern Cal Edison, Rosemead, CA	2 of 11	28.5%	44%
SBC Communications, San Antonio, TX	3 of 21	21.7%	38%

Source: *Fortune*, June 24, 2003

From Exploitation to Exemplary Practice

Critics of America's involvement in the global economy have expressed concerns not just about outsourcing jobs to other countries but also about the exploitation of workers of color in those countries. When Nike Corporation was founded in the 1960s, executives wanted to experiment with the idea of focusing on marketing shoes, but not manufacturing them. The shoes were designed in the United States, but the final product was purchased from independent contractors in Asian or Southeast Asian countries where wages were low. This innovative approach became so profitable that it soon became the norm for American corporations.

Beginning in the 1990s, national and local media published news reports about inhumane labor conditions at Nike's overseas factories. When consumers expressed outrage, Nike executives insisted that they only purchased the shoes, and it was not their responsibility to tell the Asian or Southeast Asian factory owners how to run their businesses. News coverage continued to reveal disturbing allegations, especially concerning child labor abuses, and Nike's stock value dropped. Eventually Nike executives recognized that they had to take action to counter the bad press, so they implemented programs to ensure better monitoring of labor conditions at the factories making Nike products.

Today, Nike pre-screens factories before signing contracts with a supplier, and the company has become a role model for other corporations because of its careful monitoring of worksite conditions. Nike publishes the names and addresses of all factories producing its products and publicly discloses its workplace monitoring activities. Nike has now become such a leader in this area that its web site (www.nikebiz.com) has been acknowledged as an excellent resource on international labor standards (Frank, 2008).

---

and develops specific skills in communication and management. Many businesses are implementing intensive diversity training programs not only to improve work relations between diverse employees and managers, but also to ensure that employees will interact effectively with diverse customers. At the conclusion of diversity training, some businesses engage in evaluations of how employees and managers respond to diversity (Egodigwe, 2005). A quarterly survey of Allstate Insurance employees included a "diversity index" for evaluating managers on diversity issues: 25% of a manager's bonus pay was determined by that score (Daft, 2003).

To promote a positive environment for diversity at the worksite, some U.S. companies have instituted **diversity training** programs for managers and employees. Training programs may include **diversity pairing,** where people from diverse backgrounds are paired to provide them with opportunities to interact and become better acquainted. Such pairs may be combined with mentoring as when a white male manager is paired with an employee of color or a woman. Many businesses create multicultural teams for more effective problem solving; these terms also provide an opportunity for workers to learn more about their colleagues. (See Figure 15.2.)

Jones and George (2003) described the diversity training program at United Parcel Service (UPS) that requires upper-level managers to participate in community programs for a full month. Approximately 40 managers per year work in organizations such as homeless shelters, Head Start centers, migrant farm worker assistance groups, and detention centers. Since 1968, over 800 managers have been involved in the program, and UPS believes it has had a positive impact on the abilities of its managers to respond more effectively to diversity issues.

Some U.S. corporations have been especially aggressive in their commitment to diversity. In 1995, the CEO at International Business Machines (IBM) was concerned that his senior executive team had minimal diversity, despite IBM's affirmative action efforts. He implemented a new diversity initiative, which over a ten-year period resulted in an increase of five times the number of female senior executives and tripled the number of those who were U.S.-born minorities. In 2000, IBM had no women as country managers for its overseas operations, but by 2005, the company had hired nine women general managers for such countries as France, Spain, Thailand, New Zealand, and Peru. IBM also increased its activities with women and minority-owned businesses with revenues rising from $10 million in 1998 to $40 million in 2001 (Hymowitz, 2005). IBM's efforts illustrate a comment from a CEO of another multinational corporation: "Affirmative action brings people in the door, and the inclusion piece brings people to the table. You really need both to be successful" (Egodigwe, 2005, p. R4).

Lingering Problems

Diversity problems still arise in the business community. Jones and George report that women and minorities continue to be disadvantaged because of the way they are regarded by white colleagues, especially at work sites where they are a numerical minority. Daft (2003) cited two studies; one reported that 59% of minority managers believed there was a "racially motivated double standard in the delegation of assignments" (p. 443). Another study found that employees of color believed they had to work longer hours and make extra efforts to be given the same respect as white co-workers. Salary data documents that women and minorities still earn substantially less money than white men and that minorities are still underrepresented in

management. Although African Americans and Hispanics constitute 26% of the U.S. population, they represent only 13% of managers—8% and 5%, respectively (Daft, 2003).

Women hold 49.5% of managerial positions and appear to be fairly represented, but the **glass ceiling** prevents them from rising as high as their abilities should permit. Jones and George (2003) reported on evidence of women's managerial ability, with one study concluding that female executives outperformed males on listening, motivating others, communicating effectively, and producing high-quality work. Another study of 425 top executives assessed 52 skills and found that women received higher ratings than men on 42 of them; yet women remain underrepresented in top executive positions. Williams (2003) reported that 90% of women executives said the glass ceiling had restricted their career growth; 80% indicated that they left their last job because the glass ceiling hurt their chances for promotion. Studies show that women are increasingly leaving organizations to start their own businesses because of their perception of a glass ceiling at work.

Corporate leaders know that problems arising from human differences must be resolved if U.S. businesses are to remain competitive in the global economy. Multinational corporations with headquarters in nations other than the United States have openly promoted diversity and implemented policies to assure that diverse workers receive fair treatment in the workplace. As Mor-Barak (2005) has written: "The second half of the twentieth century witnessed an unprecedented global trend in antidiscrimination and equal opportunity legislation" (p. 17). To match the efforts of their global counterparts, corporate leaders in the United States are likely to continue to publicly promote diversity, hire job seekers who appreciate corporate commitments to diversity, and provide diversity training to create a positive work environment for diverse employees. As Williams (2003) stated,

> The general purpose of diversity programs is to create a positive work environment where no one is advantaged or disadvantaged, where "we" is everyone, where everyone can do their best work, where differences are respected and not ignored, where everyone feels comfortable. (pp. 438–439)

FIGURE 15.2

The cartoon illustrates why many corporations and businesses believe it is necessary to engage in diversity training for employees.

Mass Media

Ellmore (1991) defines **mass media** as "The various vehicles used for sending information to a mass audience: radio, television, CATV, newspapers, magazines, books, discs" (p. 351). The best evidence of mass media promoting pluralism is the increasing involvement of women and minorities. Because it is a visible medium, increased presence of people of color on television has been noticeable. In the 1950s and 1960s, few television programs cast minority characters; of those who were featured, most appeared in stereotypical roles. Stereotypes in television remain, but Americans also see people of color as news reporters, as anchors on local and network news programs, and as actors on television and in films. In 2002, Oscars for best performances by an actor and actress were both awarded to African Americans. Media spokespersons explain that diversity is promoted and appreciated in media

because the industry understands the economic advantages of rewarding talent, regardless of gender, race, or ethnicity.

Actually, a weakness of the media industry argument is suggested in the representation of human diversity in media: People of color constitute 28% of the population, yet Popper (2000) found that people of color occupied 11.6% of the positions on newspaper staffs. And although diversity is represented on television and theater screens, the vast majority of jobs in television are behind the camera—writers, producers, camera operators, and technicians. According to Larson (1999), a study of U.S. news stations reported that in the top 25 markets, 81% of the news staff was white. Of the 19% minority staff, 9% was African American, 7% was Latino, 3% was Asian American, and 1% was Native American. In the 26–50 top markets, 91% of the news staff was white; in the 51–100 top markets—which included cities like Las Vegas, Nevada, and Jackson, Mississippi—94% of the staff was white. Popper (2000) responded to the question of future changes: "Most industry people expect on-air staff to remain diverse, since that's what the audience sees. What happens behind the scenes is less clear" (p. 67).

In entertainment programming, Johnson (2000) identified 55 African Americans among 839 writers for prime time shows—6.6% of the total—with 45 of the 55 writing for black-themed shows. Only one black writer was employed by a white-themed show, a seemingly blatant form of segregation suggesting that black writers can't write scripts for white actors even though white writers have written for black actors for years. In reference to segregation, the majority of black-themed shows are on the cable networks.

Increasing Media Representation of Human Diversity

According to data from the 2000 census, 12.5% of Americans are Latino, blacks constitute 12.3% of the population, Asian Americans are 3.6%, and American Indians are 0.9%. Yet fewer than 2% of reporters for network news are Hispanic Americans compared to 17% for African Americans, 3% for Asian Americans, and 2% for Native Americans (Ramos, 2002). Representation of diversity on television programs continues to be inadequate, and the NAACP, as well as Children Now, an advocacy group, are lobbying the entertainment industry to increase diversity on television programs. The Latino community includes 35 million potential television viewers, but Ramos cites a study conducted by Children Now that identified about 2% of the characters in prime-time shows as Hispanic: 47 of 2,251 characters examined.

Because of underrepresentation of people of color among television employees, the Federal Communications Commission (FCC) disseminated ambitious requirements for affirmative action plans to be submitted by communications corporations, but in 1998, a federal appeals court overturned the FCC requirements. Affirmative action advocates were encouraged, however, when the fifteen largest broadcast networks agreed to follow FCC requirements as guidelines in developing their affirmative action plans (Childs, 1998).

Media Presentation and Language

Another area of concern is how American media report diversity issues such as affirmative action. Reviewing media coverage of affirmative action controversies, Gabriel (1998) found a tendency to reinforce misperceptions such as "affirmative action = quotas = lowering standards = discrimination against white males = racism" (p. 87). Gabriel also reported that media coverage typically stated or implied that affirmative action benefited people of color at the expense of white men, yet only peripherally recognized that white women have been major beneficiaries of affirmative action programs.

Jackson (2000) referred to a study that revealed the media's tendency to portray poor people in the United States as African American. Although black people constitute about a third of Americans living in poverty, they accounted for 65% of the images of poor people presented on network news. African Americans were also featured in 62% of the pictures of Americans living in poverty published in major news magazines such as *Time, Newsweek,* and *U.S. News and World Report.* Similarly, Ferguson (1998) discussed a study of television news programming in twenty-nine North American cities that reported a tendency for newscasts to engage in both positive and negative stereotypes by covering successful black athletes and entertainers and providing frequent images of blacks as criminals, welfare mothers, and others representing a range of antisocial behaviors.

Bacon (2003) found a double standard in news coverage of black public figures. Although social activist Jesse Jackson ran two credible campaigns for the president of the United States, reporters and columnists frequently describe him as a "publicity hound" and "a race hustler." Betraying a total lack of understanding and respect for African American oral traditions, one Boston columnist chided Jackson because he "regularly substitutes rhyme for reason" (p. 27). Although professor Cornel West has consistently engaged in social justice issues, newspaper articles have referred to him as "a con man" and a "clownish minstrel." Some reporters have excerpted difficult passages from West's scholarly writing to illustrate their contention that West is impossible to understand. By creating such distractions, reporters have avoided addressing substantive issues being raised by Jackson and West. In Bacon's conclusion, she asks,

Why do mainstream media approach progressive African American leaders with such evident contempt? . . . Why are they so reluctant to engage in arguments, preferring instead to ridicule and misrepresent them? (p. 29)

Perhaps part of the answer stems from white dominance of mainstream media. To grow up white in America is to believe in a world defined by white perspectives that are reinforced in schools and in media. As Ferguson (1998) stated, "Whiteness, and the power that goes with it, have been represented as so utterly normal that any other possibility seems like an aberration" (pp. 180–181). Gabriel (1998) cites June Jordan's reflection on media use of language to frame issues and images in stereotypes familiar to their white audience:

I came to recognize media constructions such as "The Heartland" or "Politically Correct" or "The Welfare Queen" or "Illegal Alien" or "Terrorist" . . . for what they were: Multiplying scattershots intended . . . to establish and preserve white supremacy. (p. 11)

Media has the power to provide positive images of people and promote social change. In 1984, Levi Jeans aired the first advertisement providing a positive portrayal of a person with a disability. The energetic wheelchair user "popped a wheelie" to demonstrate his enthusiasm for Levi Jeans. The positive response to this advertisement caused a few more businesses to use people with disabilities in their advertisements. Although their presence remains minimal, people with disabilities were no longer completely absent from television. In the six years following that Levi Jeans commercial, more than 200 businesses produced over 2,600 advertisements with closed captions for hard-of-hearing people (Riley, 2005). Such changes are not simply altruistic. According to Corkery (2005), people with disabilities have $220 billion of purchasing power, and their inclusion in corporate advertising may influence not only their consumer choices but also the choices of their families and friends.

Representation of Diversity in Media: Present and Future

The creation of positive or negative images is not restricted to news reporting or television. Films have portrayed women and people of color in both positive and negative ways. Although American films have featured female characters overcoming obstacles, filmmakers have long been criticized for consistently producing films that link sex and violence. Similarly, although people of color have been portrayed as admirable and heroic individuals, we are still offered more negative images of people of color as drug dealers, thieves, and violent criminals.

When filmmakers depict oppression, the result often seems self-serving. Gabriel (1998) observed that films like *To Kill a Mockingbird* (1962) and *A Time to Kill* (1996) are part of a pattern of films that denounce racism but present blacks as powerless, requiring white people to save them. *Mississippi Burning* (1988) incensed people who knew that many black men, women, and children in Mississippi had courageously defied racist authorities and been jailed—some were killed—while the FBI did

> We are now at the point where we must decide whether we are to honor the concept of a plural society which gains strength through diversity or whether we are to have bitter fragmentation that will result in perpetual tension and strife.
>
> **Justice Earl Warren (1891–1974)**

little to help them, instead tapping Martin Luther King, Jr.'s telephone to gather evidence that might prove a communist connection. For the film to portray white FBI agents as heroes saving frightened blacks was an outrageously racist revision of historical truth.

Media critics suggest that increasing the diversity of people writing and producing mass media in the United States will be the best way to reduce bias and stereotypes. Data show that women and people of color are entering media professions in increasing numbers. McQueen (2002) reported that 61% of journalism and mass communication students were female and that 27% were students of color. Mc-Queen also noted that only 35% of journalism and mass communication faculty was female and 15% were faculty of color. By 2035, experts predict that 40% of students in journalism and mass communication will be students of color. In mission statements, media organizations often claim to reflect the diversity of their community. That does not describe the reality, but it should be the goal.

Military Services

Diversity in the armed forces of the United States is not a new issue; it is only the nature of the diversity that has changed. Although the military kept no records in its earliest years, there is anecdotal evidence that ethnic diversity in society was reflected in its military, and we know of at least one woman—Deborah Sampson—who disguised herself as a man and engaged in combat during the Revolutionary War (Craft-Fairchild, 1997).

Starting in 1856, records exist showing a significant percentage of ethnic immigrants serving in the army—a shortcut to being granted citizenship—but they also reveal problems. During the Mexican-American War, many Irish Catholic soldiers were reluctant to kill Mexican Catholics, and a number of them deserted to avoid doing so (Johnson, 1999). Nevertheless, diversity continued to exist in the U.S. Army. According to Buckley (2001), at the end of the Civil War there were 140 black regiments with over 100,000 soldiers, and the army continued to recruit blacks and immigrants. Johnson (1999) cited an 1896 army report documenting that 7% of that year's recruits were black and 33% were ethnic immigrants.

Significant differences concerning diversity in the military today include racial desegregation, inclusion of women, and exclusive reliance on volunteers. Each difference has created unique problems for military leadership to address, parallel to similar problems stemming from race and gender in the larger society. Dansby, Stewart, and Webb (2001) wrote, "In many ways the military has always been a mirror of American society, reflecting back the scars and blemishes as well as the face of the nation" (p. xvii). Although diversity problems have

FIGURE 15.3

This Coast Guard rescue swimmer saved a drowning fisherman 35 miles at sea.

(Her boyfriend just stopped by to bring her lunch.)

not yet been resolved, the U.S. military has made substantial progress, even more than society in general has made, according to sociologists Moskos and Butler (1996).

Military Desegregation

Desegregation in the military began with a research project during World War II. Black army platoons were integrated into white infantry companies and the social experiment was carefully monitored. The research team found that no unusual problems occurred and that all soldiers functioned effectively. Despite positive results, military leaders continued to oppose racial desegregation, even after President Truman issued an executive order mandating military racial desegregation. Because of racist attitudes among military leaders, the executive order was not fulfilled until the Korean War when desegregation became necessary for the sake of efficiency.

Dansby, Stewart, and Webb (2001) described problems with desegregation that came to the forefront during the Vietnam War. African Americans protesting against unequal treatment rioted at Fort Dix, Fort Bragg, on two aircraft carriers, and at Travis Air Force base. As the Vietnam War was ending in the early 1970s, General Creighton Abrams testified that poor race relations had had a negative impact on combat effectiveness. Complicating matters further, in 1973, Congress ended the draft and established an all-volunteer army. Recruiting and retaining quality soldiers would be affected by how the army addressed issues of race relations.

The army's response was to create a Defense Race Relations Institute charged with the responsibility of creating a race relations training program. The initial program lasted for six weeks; it was later expanded to include sexual harassment and discrimination, and now has become one of the army's most ambitious programs. Dansby and Landis (2001) report that the current training program lasts 16 weeks and, according to the American Council on Education, is equivalent to 23 undergraduate semester college credits. A major objective is "To create an environment that values diversity and fosters mutual respect and cooperation" (p. 9).

Integration Problems

Johnson (2001) evaluated the Defense Race Relations program and concluded that the training had an immediate positive effect on participant attitudes and improved subsequent work performance. Even so, problems with race relations in the U.S. military persist. Katzenstein and Reppy (1999) referred to a 1996 task force that found evidence of racism at 4 of 19 military facilities evaluated. Individual soldiers have been involved in incidents of racial violence; some continue to be members of extremist groups promoting racism or white supremacy, even though military policy prohibits active participation in such groups. Waldman (1996) explained the reason for that policy: "The nature of the military means that anything that gets in the way of mission accomplishment is unacceptable. Racism gets in the way" (p. 27).

Sexism gets in the way as well. Prior to the establishment of the all-volunteer army, fewer than 2% of recruits were women, with 90% of them receiving medical or administrative assignments (Katzen-

stein & Reppy, 1999); to maintain recruitment standards, however, the pool of candidates was expanded (see Figure 15.3.). According to Peterson (1999), female recruits have tended to be better educated, to have higher scores on aptitude tests, and to be less likely to cause disciplinary problems. According to Katzenstein and Reppy (1999), women represent approximately 14% of enlisted personnel, 14% of officers, and 20% of those in basic training. Peterson (1999) concluded, "The Army fields the highest quality force in its history owing to the gains brought about by the all-volunteer force" (p. 100).

Increasing the role of minorities and women in the military has challenged male recruits because of cultural messages some men have internalized about masculinity. Katzenstein and Reppy (1999) explain, "Cultural ideas of masculinity encourage recruits to prove their fitness for military life by flaunting their masculine prowess in bigoted and sexist behavior" (p. 2). Military leaders did not understand this cultural influence at first. Defense di-

> Injustice anywhere is a threat to justice everywhere. We are caught in an inescapable network of mutuality, tied in a single garment of destiny. Whatever affects one directly affects all indirectly.
>
> **Martin Luther King, Jr. (1929–1968)**

rectives about **sexual harassment** had been in place for many years before the 1991 Tailhook incident, in which drunken navy pilots forced female officers to walk through a gauntlet while they were groped and verbally humiliated. The chief of naval operations said later, "Until Tailhook we dealt too often with sexual harassment . . . one case at a time, rather than understanding it as a cultural issue" (Katzenstein & Reppy, 1999, p. 2). The problem was intensified five years later when rape charges were brought against drill sergeants at the Aberdeen Army base. In 2002, cadet women of the Air Force Academy reported allegations of sexual assault, indicating the ongoing challenge for the U.S. military to address male concepts of power and gender superiority.

Diversity Policy and Gender

As military leaders study the gender problem, they realize that rules are not always being observed. Kier (1999) reported that no action was taken for 56% of all sexual harassment complaints. Women had reported sexual harassment for years but had been ignored or encouraged to drop their complaint; some encountered hostile reactions from their male superiors. Katzenstein and Reppy (1999) conclude, "It was not a failure to have rules; [these] are problems emerging out of a culture at odds with [military] institutional policy" (p. 3). The 2002 and 2003 allegations of sexual harassment and even sexual assault at the Air Force Academy (AFA) demonstrated that more must be done to resolve these problems. Almost half of female AFA cadets reported that they had personally experienced sexual harassment, 64% heard derogatory remarks based on gender, and 66% reported being discriminated against because of their gender. Despite this evidence, AFA leaders denied that there were any serious gender issues at the Academy, causing the authors of the 2003 report to conclude that gender problems at the AFA were a consequence of "a lack of leadership at the Academy and at the highest levels of the Air Force itself" (Zeigler & Gunderson, 2005, p. 121).

Some people opposed to women in the military argue that sexual harassment is a reaction to double standards that allow women to perform at lower levels of competence. The army's response is that levels are adjusted to take account of physiological differences for men as well as for women. Roush (1999) pointed out that for soldiers of the same height, men are allowed to weigh 30 pounds more than women before being required to enter weight control programs. In areas where no weight adjustment is necessary, women and men compete on an equal basis. Women soldiers have demonstrated excellent marksmanship by winning the army's highest awards, and have participated on marksmanship teams at the Olympics (Carter, 2002). Shooting skills are only part of women's impressive record of achievement that has opened doors to new responsibilities.

During the 1970s and 1980s, the U.S. Army employed a **risk rule** that measured how close certain roles would bring a participant to battle and did not assign women to roles that would bring them into combat. Carter (2002) observed that the 1989 Panama invasion altered the rules when women soldiers engaged in battle while working in support units that were fired on. Women driving convoy trucks and flying helicopters to transport wounded men to safety were fired on and women in military police units assisted with cordoning off neighborhoods in search of guerrillas. Some women would have earned medals if their assignments had officially listed them as combatants.

In 1991, Desert Storm provided another opportunity for women to prove their combat readiness. Despite predictions of critics, mixed-gender units displayed as much cohesiveness as single-gender units. Because of their performance in the Gulf War, women are now assigned to command military police companies, pilot helicopters, and serve in artillery units. The 2003 Iraq war placed thousands of women in battle zones, and actual combat assignments no longer seem unthinkable. Perhaps the performance of women soldiers under fire is one reason why a survey of Reserve Officer Training Corps (ROTC) cadets conducted by Zeigler and Gunderson (2005) found that almost 60% of ROTC cadets said that women should be allowed to volunteer for combat and should be assigned to combat roles just as men are.

In a survey of civilians, 53% agreed that women should be permitted to serve in combat, but a survey of military leaders revealed that 62% of them did not favor using women in diverse combat roles (Zeigler & Gunderson, 2005). Guenther-Schlesinger (2001) reported that 70% of women want to be assigned to combat roles because major promotions are more likely to be given to those who prove themselves on the battlefield. Kier (1999) believes women will never be treated as equals in the military culture as long as their names are "missing from the rostrum of heroes, stories, and myths" arising from combat (p. 49).

Having studied demographic predictions, military leaders expect the percentage of women and minorities in the armed forces to increase; they are prepared to do much more recruiting from the growing pool of Hispanic American and Asian American candidates. Although there will be twice as many African Americans in the candidate pool by 2050, half of the U.S. population growth from 2000 to 2050 will occur among Latinos, with a smaller yet significant growth of Southeast Asians. Recruiters are encouraged by 1997 data showing that more Hispanics joined the military than any other ethnic group, but a major concern is the high dropout rate: Army policy requires that 90% of all recruits must have high school diplomas. According to a 1996 study by the National Center for Educational Statistics, 30% to 35% of Hispanic students drop out of high school, the highest rate of all groups included in their study (Diaz, 1999).

Religion and Sexual Orientation

Racial, ethnic, and gender diversity is only the beginning. The American military now has procedures for accommodating religious differences. And although the issue of lesbians and gays in the military is still debated, there is a growing sentiment that openly gay men and lesbians should be allowed to serve their country: "To be denied the right to serve is to have one's citizenship denied, and to be restricted in one's form of military service is to have one's citizenship restricted" (Segal, Segal, & Booth, 1999, p. 225).

Gay Americans have always fought in this country's wars, but their sexual orientation was not an issue until World War I, when military regulations excluded openly gay men from military service. Even so, there were gay men in uniform when World War II began, including gay sergeants responsible for training the massive numbers of new soldiers enlisted after the attack on Pearl Harbor (Estes, 2007). The formation of the Women's Army Corps (WACs), the Women Accepted for Volunteer Emergency Service (WAVES), and the admission of women into the Marines in 1943 brought lesbians as well as straight women into military service. The presence of lesbians was well known to military leaders, who waited until the war was over before purging lesbians from the ranks by giving them dishonorable discharges. As for gay men, although psychiatrists involved in screening procedures rejected slightly less than 5,000 recruits perceived as gay, it is estimated that as many as 650,000 of the 16 million American troops were gay men (Estes, 2007). From an interview with one of those soldiers, Estes quotes the veteran: "We were not about to be deprived of the privilege of serving our country in a time of great national emergency by virtue of some stupid regulation about being gay" (p. 5).

Although military leaders continue to express opposition to gay and lesbian soldiers, Matthews

(1999) reported results of a survey of 270 male soldiers, finding only 36% strongly opposed to serving with gay soldiers; twice as many women soldiers said they would serve with lesbians as those who said they would not. Opponents to gays and lesbians serving in the military say the army is not the place for social experiments, but Katzenstein and Reppy (1999) note that the army and other units of America's armed forces have always been affected by societal changes: "The American military has at different times trailed, led or simply mirrored efforts to combat prejudice, but it has never been isolated from those prejudices" (p. 10).

Military Leadership

As military recruiters make contact with an increasingly diverse pool of candidates, they must offer evidence that advancement is possible. According to Stewart and Firestone (2001), minorities are under-

> One of the most successful institutions in American society in dealing with racial integration has been the United States Army. At the other extreme . . . (public) schools are among the most segregated associations in the country.
>
> **Eugene Y. Lowe, Jr. (Contemporary)**

represented at the general officer level. Jones (1999) recommended that military services immediately identify and attract more minority officer candidates to function as a "source of inspiration" for minority soldiers. Sayles (1999) discussed the importance of women and minority role models at all levels in the military organizational structure to provide women and minorities proof of genuine opportunity for advancement in the military—rather than a glass ceiling. All branches of the service have been asked to address the need for minority officers in their affirmative action plans; as an example, the navy goal is to commission at least 7% black and 4% Hispanic officers each year. Jones (1999) stated, "Commitment to diversity and equal opportunity is the keystone to our entire value structure" (p. 62).

AFTERWORD

In his discussion of diversity issues in the military, Jones (1999) commented, "Americans tend to be ignorant about other societies and even about subcultures within their own society" (p. 62). His comment echoes a concern multicultural education advocates have expressed for several years: that too many K–12 schools do not address diversity issues adequately. This book was written to address diversity issues with college students, but the issues need to be addressed in K–12 classrooms as well. Schools in rural or suburban areas with predominantly white students tend to offer too little information about diversity. White teachers are often uncomfortable with controversies related to diverse groups, some insisting that they don't need to address diversity because there are no—or few—students of color in their schools!

If white students rarely encounter people of color, it is even more important for teachers to provide accurate cognitive information about history, contributions, and issues affecting diverse populations in this country both historically and today. Further, this is not just a need for white students: Jones's comment referred to American recruits from diverse groups. African American students may know little about cultures or experiences of Native Americans; Native American students may only know about the "model minority" and have little knowledge of the past oppression, achievements, and current barriers of Asian Americans. Latino students may not understand why Somali students are in their school, and Somali students may have learned negative stereotypes about Latinos. Middle-class students need to understand the realities for low-income families; nondisabled students must confront misperceptions about people with disabilities; heterosexual students can unlearn myths they have been taught about gays and lesbians. In a diverse society, everyone needs to learn more about the diverse groups of people calling themselves Americans.

This book has offered an array of information about diverse groups of people and intergroup relations, but does acquiring new information change a person's beliefs and attitudes? For those who are interested in exploring their own attitudes about diversity, go to the MyEducationLab web site (www.myeducationlab.com) and respond to the selected statements in the Attitude Inventory. Your responses to these statements should clarify your beliefs or attitudes about the diverse issues being addressed, and for those who responded to the Attitude Inventory previously, consider how and why your current answers may be different from your earlier responses.

During the debate over ratifying the U.S. Constitution, some state leaders focused on the many differences dividing the states and argued that they could never be melded into a single union but should remain independent states. Alexander Hamilton rejected the argument, insisting that a unified nation encompassing those diverse cultures had already formed, and the Constitution would simply reflect the shared values and vision of that union (Chernow, 2004).

Today, people living in our fifty states are not defined as much by the state where they live as by their membership in social groups determined by race, gender, disability, social class, and sexual orientation; yet we are all Americans. We live in a nation that adopted the motto "E Pluribus Unum" in 1782, originally meaning: "from many states, one nation." The motto has also been a metaphor for the people in a nation built on foundations established by Native Americans, profiting from import of Africans, and exploiting the labor of immigrants and women: Each group has struggled to find its place in the kaleidoscope of changing images and altered realities. Their achievements were based on an American dream of a good life for themselves and their families, of a nation where they had freedom to work, worship, and live as they pleased among diverse people who were also guaranteed equal rights and equal opportunities.

That American dream has always been an ideal. Some groups were granted this ideal more readily than others, but all have sought it. America's history is a history of that struggle. We are farther along than ever today, yet we still have much to do to bring the dream closer to reality for all Americans. Pluralism represents a vehicle to move us forward. Committing ourselves to being pluralistic represents a commitment to the American dream, a

> When we dream alone, we are merely dreaming; but when we dream together, that's the beginning of reality.
>
> **Brazilian Proverb**

commitment to make our nation's motto—"out of the many, one"—a description of the nation we are becoming. That is a dream worth dreaming.

TERMS AND DEFINITIONS

Affirmative action   A written plan required of businesses and institutions of higher education to reduce discrimination in hiring, public contracting, and college admissions

Design for Diversity   A Wisconsin program that mandates changes in policies and practices on all thirteen UW System campuses to make them more welcoming places for diverse students

Diversity   The presence of human beings with perceived or actual differences based on a variety of human characteristics

Diversity pairing   A diversity training strategy where two people from diverse backgrounds are paired to provide them with opportunities to interact and become better acquainted

Diversity training   Programs designed by businesses to promote a positive environment for diverse employees and managers at the worksite

Glass ceiling   An informal upper limit that keeps women and minorities from being promoted to positions of greatest responsibility in work organizations

Mass media   The various vehicles employed to provide information to a mass audience: radio, television, cable TV, newspapers, magazines, books, CDs, and so on

Pluralism   The equal coexistence of diverse cultures in a mutually supportive relationship within the boundaries of one nation

Proposition 209   A California statute prohibiting preferential treatment to individuals or groups in hiring, awarding public contracts, and college admissions

Racial quota   Designation of a specific number of applicants to be hired or admitted based on their race

Risk rule   An army practice of measuring how close certain roles would bring a participant to combat and not assigning women to any role that would bring them too close

Seniority system   Requires employees with least seniority to be laid off work if the employer needs to release a certain number of employees

Set-aside program   Requiring contractors to hire a certain percentage of minority subcontractors if they are awarded a project funded by tax dollars

Sexual harassment   Deliberate and repeated behavior that has a sexual basis and is not welcomed, requested, or returned

DISCUSSION EXERCISES

Exercise #1 Enhancing Unity in America Discussion: What Should We Do Next?

Directions: America today demonstrates its diversity in our military, marketplace, and manufacturing, in our media, and in federal, state, and local governments. The following questions ask for your speculation to resolve current issues for our future well-being.

1. Should our federal government eliminate, or modify, the current affirmative action program?
   - If you believe it should be eliminated, explain why.
   - If you believe it should be modified, explain how and why.
2. Do you agree that increased diversity among students on a college campus strengthens the education of all students?
   - How many—or what type—of diversity-related courses should all students be required to take?
   - What should be the outcome of any study of American cultural, racial, and societal human differences?
3. Assume that you have majored and matriculated in some aspect of business; following graduation you receive two job offers: one with a company that has a good reputation for having a positive environment for diversity; the other offers a higher salary with better benefits but with little or no record of attention to attracting a diverse workforce.
   - Which one would you choose, and why?
   - How can a diverse workforce create unity in America?
4. Now that women are approximately half of all managers, why are women still being excluded from a proportional share of top management positions?
   - What will it take to eliminate this glass ceiling?
   - How might business and industry change if women were adequately represented in leadership roles?

5. If the predictions are correct and twenty years from now print and broadcast media employ significantly greater numbers of women and people of color, how will it make a difference in the following areas:
   - What news stories are covered by print and broadcast journalists
   - How new stories are covered
   - What stories are presented by news programs (e.g., *20/20* and *Dateline*)
   - Which images and text are presented in advertisements
   - What content and diversity of characters is available in prime-time programming
6. Simply requiring that American societal institutions establish policies against sexual harassment has not been effective.
   - What must the military services do to eliminate the problem of sexual harassment?
   - Business and manufacturing?
   - Nonprofit and religious institutions?

Exercise #2 A Personal Post-Test Self Check: What Will You Be?

Directions: Respond to each of the items below with brief remarks; be sure to explain your responses *and* to hear and comment on the responses from your partners.

A Personal Post-Test Self Check

1. List what you believe personally are three of the most important human differences.
2. Explain one instance where you have witnessed racism as the belief that some human population groups are inherently superior or inferior to others. Tell your personal suggestion of how that situation could have been avoided.
3. Give an example of a situation that illustrates cultural blindness. Explain how it could be remedied.
4. Describe a real or imagined situation in which you might confront "ethnocentrism."

5. List three terms that you think are acceptable replacements for "handicapped" or "disabled."
6. Describe your current ability at cultural communication.
7. List four recommendations for how one might better recognize cultural and ethnic heritage when communicating.
8. Suggest two or more ways that you could be an active advocate for diversity.
9. Name several ways that current American culture—workplace and personal—affects women, disabled, or any other minority groups.
10. Tell what one practice you have resolved to adopt to be an active pluralist within our diverse America.

Adopted from Evelyn Harden. *Rural Health Care: Cultural Competency Training Workbook.* National Rural Health Association, 2002

REFERENCES

Bacon, J. (2003). Disrespect, distortion and double binds: Media treatment of progressive black leaders. *Extra, 16*(2), 27–29.

Analyzes media treatment of three black social activists and describes a pattern of remarks reflecting personal attacks without responding to the issues they raise.

Ball, H. (2000). *The Bakke case: Race, education, and affirmative action.* Lawrence: University Press of Kansas.

Examines law and politics providing a context for the Bakke case, presents key arguments from both sides, and reviews more recent events stemming from the Bakke decision.

Browne-Miller, A. (1996). *Shameful admissions: The losing battle to serve everyone in our universities.* San Francisco, CA: Jossey-Bass.

Discusses college admissions policies and practices and how they help or hinder fair access to equal opportunity for all applicants and what happens after a person is accepted to college.

Buckley, G. (2001). *American patriots: The story of blacks in the military from the Revolution to Desert Storm.* New York, NY: Random House.

Includes statistics and stories about African Americans who fought in America's wars.

Carter, P. (2002). War dames. *The Washington Monthly, 34*(12), 32–37.

Reviews recent history of women in the military and how their role has evolved from serving only in support units to having responsibilities that bring them into combat.

Chernow, R. (2004). *Alexander Hamilton.* New York, NY: Penguin.

Describes Hamilton's life with emphasis on his activities as one of the leading intellects shaping the new nation of the United States.

Childs, K. (1998). Media affirmative action pact. *Editor & Publisher, 131*(32), 11.

Describes the reaction of broadcast networks to a federal court's ruling against affirmative action requirements established by the Federal Communications Commission.

Clayton, S.D., & Crosby, F.J. (2000). Justice, gender, and affirmative action. In F.J. Crosby & C. VanDeVeer (Eds.), *Sex, race, and merit: Debating affirmative action in education and employment* (pp. 81–88). Ann Arbor: University of Michigan Press.

Explains the purpose of affirmative action, examines the denial of discrimination by victims of discrimination, and discusses the future of affirmative action.

Cochran-Smith, M. (2003). Standing at the crossroads: Multicultural teacher education at the beginning of the 21st century. *Multicultural Perspectives, 5*(3), 3–11.

Describes three issues of critical interest to U.S. educators: teacher/student demographic data and trends, competing school reform agendas, and criticisms of educational research.

Corkery, M. (2005, November 14). A special effort. *Wall Street Journal* (p. R8).

Describes Starbucks Corporation's commitment to hiring employees with disabilities and making the workplace welcoming to customers with disabilities.

Craft-Fairchild, C. (1997, Fall). Women warriors in the 18th century. *St. Thomas,* 32–35.

Describes eighteenth-century women who dressed as men in Great Britain or the United States, in some cases becoming soldiers, to have the advantages of men.

Crosby, F.J., & VanDeVeer, C. (Eds.). (2000). *City of Richmond* v. *J.A. Croson Co.* In *Sex, race, and merit: Debating affirmative action in education and employment* (pp. 280–293). Ann Arbor: University of Michigan Press.

Contains a brief introduction by the editors and presents an abridged version of Sandra Day O'Connor's text explaining the court's decision with comments from other justices.

Daft, R.L. (2003). Managing diverse employees. In *Management* (4th ed., pp. 436–468). Versailles, KY: Thompson Southwestern.

Discusses the current status of affirmative action, various dimensions of diversity in the workforce, and how corporate culture is changing to accommodate diversity.

Dansby, M.R., & Landis, D. (2001). Intercultural training in the United States military. In M.R. Dansby, J.B. Stewart, & S.C. Webb (Eds.), *Managing diversity in the military: Research perspectives from the defense equal opportunity management institute* (pp. 9–28). New Brunswick, NJ: Transaction.

Describes the background, philosophy, and status of intercultural training in the military.

Dansby, M.R., Stewart, J.B., & Webb, S.C. (Eds.). (2001). Overview. In *Managing diversity in the military: Research perspectives from the defense equal opportunity management institute* (pp. xvii–xxxii). New Brunswick, NJ: Transaction.

Summarizes the role of women and minorities in military history as a context for the essays in this book and explains the organization of the book.

Diaz, R.F. (1999). The Hispanic market: An overview. In L.J. Matthews & T. Pavri (Eds.), *Population diversity and the U.S. Army* (pp. 87–98). Carlisle, PA: Strategic Studies Institute.

Describes the current location and predicted growth of Hispanics and strategies for effectively recruiting Hispanics at the present time and in the future.

Duncan, P. (2002). Decentering whiteness: Resisting racism in the women's studies classroom. *Race in the college classroom: Pedagogy and politics.* In B. Tusmith & M.T. Reddy (Eds.), *Race in the college classroom: Pedagogy and politics* (pp. 40–50). New Brunswick, NJ: Rutgers University Press.

Describes conflicting racial perspectives between white students and students of color in college and how professors often behave as if white students are of primary concern.

Eastland, T. (2000). Ending affirmative action: The case for colorblind justice. In F.J. Crosby & C. VanDeVeer (Eds.), *Sex, race, and merit: Debating affirmative action in education and employment* (pp. 174–175). Ann Arbor: University of Michigan Press.

Argues that affirmative action has failed by harming those it was intended to help.

Eck, D.L. (2001). *A new religious America: How a "Christian country" has become the world's most religiously diverse nation.* New York, NY: HarperCollins.

Examines the growth of diverse religions in the United States, especially with regard to immigration patterns since 1965, and describes its impact and its potential.

Egodigwe, L. (2005, November 14). Back to class. *Wall Street Journal*, p. R4.

Describes how corporate diversity training programs have changed along with the rationale for implementing them.

Ellmore, R.T. (1991). *NTC's mass media dictionary.* Lincolnwood, IL: National Textbook.

Includes definitions of numerous terms related to mass media.

Estes, S. (2007). *Ask & tell: Gay and lesbian veterans speak out.* Chapel Hill, NC: The University of North Carolina Press.

Interviews gay and lesbian veterans of diverse races and ethnicities who participated in World War II or in wars since then.

Ferguson, R. (1998). *Representing "race": Ideology, identity and the media.* London, England: Arnold.

Reviews research to discuss relationships between racism and media representations of reality, and analyzes the ideology employed in maintaining racial hierarchies.

Frank, T. A. (2008, April). Confessions of a sweatshop inspector. *The Washington Monthly 40*(4), 34–37.

Explains the difficulties involved in monitoring workplaces in overseas factories to detect and address abuses of sweatshop workers.

Gabriel, J. (1998). *Whitewash: Racialized politics and the media.* London, England: Routledge.

Focuses on case studies to analyze media dissemination of language that normalizes white privilege and creates a racialized discourse influencing political and economic change.

Gardner, H. (2006). *Five minds for the future.* Boston, MA: Harvard Business School Press.

Describes five mental abilities increasingly necessary for the future: a disciplined mind, a synthesizing mind, a creating mind, a respectful mind, and an ethical mind.

Greene, K.W. (1989). *Affirmative action and principles of justice.* New York, NY: Greenwood.

Analyzes the philosophical and legal issues related to affirmative action and responds to the emotional reactions created by the affirmative action debate.

Griffin, R. (2002). The cultural and multicultural environment. In *Management* (7th ed., pp. 162–191). Boston, MA: Houghton Mifflin.

Discusses how trends in diversity affect the corporate environment, advantages of diversity, and suggests strategies for effective management of diversity.

Guenther-Schlesinger, S. (2001). Persistence of sexual harassment: The impact of military culture on policy implementation. In M.F. Katzenstein & J. Reppy (Eds.), *Beyond zero tolerance: Discrimination in military culture* (pp. 195–212). Lanham, MD: Rowman & Littlefield.

Reviews the history of sexual harassment in the military and identifies unique aspects of military culture that enable sexual harassment to persist.

Humphreys, D. (Ed.). (2000, Fall). National survey finds diversity requirements common around the country. *Diversity Digest*, pp. 1–2.

Presents results from a survey of 543 colleges and universities from every region of the country and representing an array of types of institutions.

Hymowitz, C. (2005, November 14). The new diversity. *Wall Street Journal*, pp. R1, R3.

Discusses how the global economy is influencing attitudes in American corporations about diversity and provides efforts of specific corporations to be more inclusive.

Jackson, D.Z. (2000). Lazy lies about welfare. In J. Birnbaum & C. Taylor (Eds.), *Civil Rights since 1787: A reader on the black struggle* (pp. 803–804). New York, NY: New York University Press.

Describes the role of media in promoting stereotypes of African Americans living in poverty and collecting welfare.

Johnson, D. (1999). The U.S. Army and ethnic diversity: A historical overview. In L.J. Matthews & T. Pavri (Eds.), *Population diversity and the U.S. Army* (pp. 45–56). Carlisle, PA: Strategic Studies Institute.

Describes the ethnic composition of the U.S. army in the past, reasons why ethnic groups joined the army, and issues related to the historic diversity of the American army.

Johnson, J.L. (2001). Local effects and global impact of Defense Equal Opportunity Management Institute Training. In M.R. Dansby, J.B. Stewart, & S.C. Webb (Eds.), *Managing diversity in the military: Research perspectives from the defense equal opportunity management institute* (pp. 178–188). New Brunswick, NJ: Transaction.

Evaluates effectiveness of DEOMI training in terms of local effects (mastery of content, development of skills and attitudes) and global impact (subsequent work performance).

Johnson, S.D. (2000, June). Keep the pressure on. *Essence, 1*(2), 184.

Discusses the participation of African American writers in prime-time television shows.

Jones, G.R., & George, J.M. (2003). Managing diverse employees in a diverse environment. *Contemporary Management* (3rd ed., pp. 112–149). New York, NY: McGraw-Hill.

Describes increasing diversity among consumers and in the workforce and provides strategies for managers to work effectively with diverse employees.

Jones, J.C. (1999). Diversity in the 21st century: Leadership issues. In L.J. Matthews & T. Pavri (Eds.), *Population diversity and the U.S. Army* (pp. 57–68). Carlisle, PA: Strategic Studies Institute.

Analyzes predicted demographic trends for implications on future recruitment and the importance of having more women and minority officers to enhance recruitment.

Katzenstein, M.F., & Reppy, J. (Eds.). (1999). Introduction: Rethinking military culture. In *Beyond zero tolerance: Discrimination in military culture* (pp. 1–21). Lanham, MD: Rowman & Littlefield.

Describes American military culture, how it has functioned as a social laboratory, and why it needs to change because of the increasing numbers of women and minorities.

Kier, E. (1999). Discrimination and military cohesion: An organizational perspective. In M.F. Katzenstein & J. Reppy (Eds.), *Beyond zero tolerance: Discrimination in military culture* (pp. 25–32). Lanham, MD: Rowman & Littlefield.

Uses knowledge from organizational theory to discuss the military's organizational culture and how that culture must change to end discrimination against women, gays, and lesbians.

Kolodny, A. (1998). *Failing the future: A dean looks at higher education in the twenty-first century.* Durham, NC: Duke University Press.

Describes issues in higher education, especially in a public research university, from perspectives of students, teachers, and administrators, and recommends changes.

Larson, M. (1999, November). News hues. *Brandweek, 40*(43), 4043.

Discusses participation of racial minorities in news stations at various market levels.

Lowe, E.Y., Jr. (Ed.). (1999). Promise and dilemma: Incorporating racial diversity in selective higher education. *Promise and dilemma: Perspectives on racial diversity and higher education* (pp. 3–43). Princeton, NJ: Princeton University Press.

Examines the history of societal efforts to accommodate racial diversity and identifies recurring phenomena that have helped or hindered these efforts.

Matthews, L. (1999). Introduction: Primer on future recruitment of diversity. In L.J. Matthews & T. Pavri (Eds.), *Population diversity and the U.S. Army* (p. 116). Carlisle, PA: Strategic Studies Institute.

Discusses issues affecting future recruitment, such as accepting gay and lesbian soldiers, increasing religious diversity in the army, and women engaging in combat.

McQueen, M. (2002, July/August). What about diverse faculty? *Quill, 90*(6), 19–22.

Discusses the presence of women and minorities as students and faculty in journalism/mass communication departments in higher education.

Millman, J. (2005, November 14). Delayed recognition. *The Wall Street Journal*, p. R8.

Describes the response of Detroit Edison to resolve a discrimination lawsuit brought by Arab Americans.

Mor-Barak, M.E. (2005). *Managing diversity: Toward a globally inclusive workplace*. Thousand Oaks, CA: Sage Publications.

Explains the benefits of implementing inclusive practices in the workplace and refers to case studies from businesses both within and outside of the United States.

Moskos, C.C., & Butler, J.S. (1996). *All that we can be: Black leadership and racial integration in the army*. New York, NY: Basic Books.

Provides evidence and arguments in support of their thesis that racial integration has been successfully achieved in the U.S. Army.

Musil, C.M. (1996 November/December). The maturing diversity initiatives on American campuses. *American Behavioral Scientist, 40*(2), 222–232.

Describes the increasing value for diversity expressed in corporate culture and in higher education and how the two mutually reinforce each other.

National Employment Lawyers Association. (2000). Position paper on affirmative action. In J. Birnbaum & C. Taylor (Eds.), *Civil Rights since 1787: A reader on the black struggle* (pp. 708–713). New York, NY: New York University Press.

Presents information and arguments in support of affirmative action.

Painter, N.I. (2005). *Creating Black Americans: African-American history and its meaning, 1619 to the present*. Oxford, England: Oxford University Press.

Describes historical and aesthetic developments, using artwork by blacks, to explain how certain people and events shaped black Americans.

Peterson, M.J. (1999). Women in the U.S. military. In L.J. Matthews & T. Pavri (Eds.), *Population diversity and the U.S. Army* (pp. 99–106). Carlisle, PA: Strategic Studies Institute.

Describes characteristics of women in the military, issues affecting them, and how their presence has enhanced the quality of the army.

Pipher, M. (2002). *The middle of everywhere: The world's refugees come to our town*. New York, NY: Harcourt.

Presents stories about a variety of recent immigrants, the conditions that forced them to immigrate, and the difficulties they encounter trying to adjust to American culture.

Popper, B. (2000). Minority hiring may be facing retrenchment. *USA Today Magazine, 128*(2658), 66–67.

Discusses the participation of racial minorities in newspapers and television news.

Ramos, J. (2002). *The other face of America*. New York, NY: Rayo.

Provides statistics and describes studies focusing on the contributions of Latinos and the implications of Latino immigration to the United States.

Reddy, M.T. (2002). Smashing the rules of racial standing. In B. Tusmith & M.T. Reddy (Eds.), *Race in the college classroom: Pedagogy and politics* (pp. 51–61). New Brunswick, NJ: Rutgers University Press.

Examines strategies—and describes the mixed outcomes—for dealing with presumptions of authority based on whiteness and for decentering whiteness in the classroom.

Reskin, B.F. (2000). The realities of affirmative action in employment. In F.J. Crosby & C. VanDeVeer (Eds.), *Sex, race, and merit: Debating affirmative action in education and employment* (pp. 103–113). Ann Arbor: University of Michigan Press.

Compares employers with and without affirmative action plans, and examines how affirmative action affects the workplace and the people it was designed to help.

Riley, C.A. II. (2005). *Disability and the media: Prescriptions for change.* Lebanon, NH: University Press of New England.

Provides examples to critique the media's presentation of people with disabilities and disability issues and gives suggestions for improvement.

Roush, P.E. (1999). A tangled Webb the navy can't afford. In M.F. Katzenstein & J. Reppy (Eds.), *Beyond zero tolerance: Discrimination in military culture* (pp. 81–100). Lanham, MD: Rowman & Littlefield.

Responds to James Webb's arguments against women being in the military.

Sayles, A.H. (1999). Person to person: The diversity challenge for the Army after next. In L.J. Matthews & T. Pavri (Eds.), *Population diversity and the U.S. Army* (pp. 107–124). Carlisle, PA: Strategic Studies Institute.

Discusses the benefits of diversity in the military and describes a program called Consideration of Others that is designed to enhance appreciation for diversity.

Segal, D.R., Segal, M.W., & Booth, B. (1999). Gender and sexual orientation diversity in modern military forces: Cross-national patterns. In M.F. Katzenstein & J. Reppy (Eds.), *Beyond zero tolerance: Discrimination in military culture* (pp. 225–250). Lanham, MD: Rowman & Littlefield.

Discusses issues affecting the acceptance of women, gay men, and lesbians in the military and the role of the "citizenship revolution" in promoting change in the military culture.

Stewart, J.B., & Firestone, J.M. (2001). Looking for a few good men: Predicting patterns of retention, promotion, and accession of minority and women officers. In M.R. Dansby, J.B. Stewart, & S.C. Webb (Eds.), *Managing diversity in the military: Research perspectives from the defense equal opportunity management institute* (pp. 231–256). New Brunswick, NJ: Transaction.

Reviews the literature on officer promotion, explains the issue of white male dominance, and makes recommendations to increase the numbers of women and minority officers.

Tusmith, B., & Reddy, M.T. (2002). Introduction: Race in the college classroom. In B. Tusmith & M.T. Reddy (Eds.), *Race in the college classroom: Pedagogy and politics* (pp. 1–3). New Brunswick, NJ: Rutgers University Press.

Defines affirmative action, summarizes the main arguments in the debate over affirmative action, and describes the organization of the book.

Waldman, A. (1996, November). GIs: Not your average Joes: What the military can teach us about race, class, and citizenship. *The Washington Monthly,* pp. 26–33.

Discusses the military's historic role in assimilating immigrants for future success in society and how the military has now achieved the same result for people of color.

Williams, C. (2003). Managing individuals and a diverse work force. In *Management* (2nd ed., pp. 434–471). Versailles, KY: Thompson Southwestern.

Explains why diversity is being promoted in the corporate world, the benefits of diversity, and principles for being an effective manager of diverse employees.

Yamane, D. (2001). *Student movements for multiculturalism: Challenging the curricular color line in higher education.* Baltimore, MD: Johns Hopkins University Press.

Addresses the problem of the color line in higher education curriculum and the process by which students have challenged this color line by demanding multicultural courses.

Zeigler, S.L., & Gunderson, G.G. (2005). *Moving beyond G. I. Jane: Women and the U.S. military.* Lanham, MD: University Press of America.

Summarizes and analyzes issues affecting women in the military, especially sexual harassment and assigning women to combat roles.

Index